NEW BOOK OF FESTIVALS
AND COMMEMORATIONS

NEW BOOK OF FESTIVALS AND COMMEMORATIONS

A Proposed Common Calendar of Saints

PHILIP H. PFATTEICHER

FORTRESS PRESS
MINNEAPOLIS

NEW BOOK OF FESTIVALS AND COMMEMORATIONS
A Proposed Common Calendar of Saints

Contents—including the calendar listings, propers, and prayers provided herein—represent the opinions and proposals of the author. Readers should consult the resources of their denominations—for example, *Book of Common Prayer* and *Lesser Feasts and Fasts* for the Episcopal Church, and *Evangelical Lutheran Worship* for the Evangelical Lutheran Church in America and the Evangelical Lutheran Church in Canada—for the calendar listings, propers, and prayers currently authorized or commended for use in their churches.

Cover images: St. Paul Preaching to the Jews in the Synagogue at Damascus. Byzantine mosaic, twelfth century, Duomo, Monreale, Italy. Photo © Giraudon / Art Resource, NY. Used by permission. Engraving of Martin Luther posting Ninety-five Theses on the castle church door at Wittenberg. Photo © Foto Marburg / Art Resource, NY. Used by permission.
Detail of The Holy Family with Saint Theresa of Avila, Alessandro Tiarini (1577-1688), Italian. Photo © Christie's Images / SuperStock. Used by permission. Martin Luther King Jr., May, 1956. Photo © Michael Ochs Archives / Corbis. Used by permission. Statue of Dietrich Bonhoeffer. Photo © Dean and Chapter of Westminster. Used by permission.
Cover design: Laurie Ingram
Book design: Ivy Palmer Skrade

This book was typeset using Minion and Metron.

Library of Congress Cataloging-in-Publication Data
Pfatteicher, Philip H.
New book of festivals and commemorations :
a proposed common calendar of saints / Philip H. Pfatteicher.
p. cm.
Includes bibliographical references and indexes.
ISBN 978-0-8006-2128-5 (alk. paper)
1. Devotional calendars. 2. Church year meditations. 3. Church history.
4. Christian biography. I. Title.
BV4811.P43 2008
263'.98—dc22   2007044772

The paper used in this publication meets the minimum requirements of American National Standard for Information Sciences—Permanence of Paper for Printed Library Materials, ANSI Z329.48-1984.

Manufactured in the U.S.A.

12   11   10   09   08   1   2   3   4   5   6   7   8   9   10

For Lois
as always

and

For Allan Bevier Warren III
exemplary
priest and pastor

and for
Mary Wilder Warren
in memoriam

CONTENTS

Abbreviations

AM	The Anglican Missal
BCP	*The Book of Common Prayer . . . according to the Use of the Episcopal Church*. New York: Church Hymnal Corporation, 1979.
CB	*Church Book for the Use of Evangelical Lutheran Congregations*. Philadelphia: General Council Publication Board, 1892. [1st ed. 1868]
CMG	Charles Mortimer Guilbert
CSB	*Common Service Book of the Lutheran Church Authorized by the United Lutheran Church in America*. Philadelphia: Board of Publication of the United Lutheran Church in America, 1917, 1918.
CSI	Church of South India
DvD	Dirk van Dissel
ELW	*Evangelical Lutheran Worship*. Minneapolis: Augsburg Fortress, 2006.
H30	*The Hymnal . . . of the Protestant Episcopal Church in the United States of America* 1916, rev. 1930. New York: Church Pension Fund, 1933.
H40	*The Hymnal of the Protestant Episcopal Church in the United States of America 1940*. New York: Church Pension Fund: 1940, 1943.
H82	*The Hymnal 1982 according to the Use of the Episcopal Church*. New York: Church Hymnal Corporation, 1985.
JWP	Joseph W. Poole
LBW	*Lutheran Book of Worship prepared by the Churches participating in the Inter-Lutheran Commission on Worship*. Minneapolis: Augsburg Publishing House, and Philadelphia: Board of Publication, Lutheran Church in America, 1978.
LFF	*Lesser Feasts and Fasts 2006*. New York: Church Publishing, 2006. [previous editions: 1963; rev. ed. 1973; 3d ed. 1980; 1997, 2000, 2003] The texts of these prayers are from *Lesser Feast and Fasts 2006*, copyright © 2006 by the Church Pension Fund. All rights reserved. Used by permission.
LSB	*Lutheran Service Book*. St. Louis: Concordia, 2006.
PHP	Philip H. Pfatteicher
RC	Roman Catholic
RS	*The [Roman] Sacramentary*. Collegeville: Liturgical, 1985. [Roman Missal 1970, 2nd ed. 1975] The texts of these prayers, except where otherwise noted, are from the English translation of the Roman Missal © 1973, International Committee on English in the Liturgy, Inc. All rights reserved.
SBH	*Service Book and Hymnal authorized by the Lutheran Churches cooperating in the Commission on the Liturgy and Hymnal*. Minneapolis: Augsburg Publishing House, and Philadelphia: Board of Publication, Lutheran Church in America, 1958.
TLH	*The Lutheran Hymnal authorized by the Synods constituting the Evangelical Lutheran Synodical Conference of North America*. St. Louis: Concordia, 1941.

Preface

During the latter twentieth century, many denominations examined the Roman Catholic revision of the traditional lectionary, accepted its principles, and made their own adaptations of it. Since the work of many denominations was moving along similar lines, a Common Lectionary was seen as desirable, and the resulting Revised Common Lectionary enjoys widespread use throughout North America. In the light of such converging agreement on the lectionary, it seems appropriate to suggest another area in which ecumenical cooperation and progress seems promising: a common calendar of commemorations.

At the time of the Reformation, the Lutheran and the Anglican churches retained a limited number of saints' days on their calendars (even if these days often went unobserved in many parishes). These included the days of the four evangelists; the twelve apostles and St. Paul; St. Stephen, the first of martyrs; and the general celebration of All Saints. In the latter twentieth century, in both churches, a desire to expand the calendar judiciously was making itself known. In the Episcopal Church, *The Calendar and the Collects, Epistles and Gospels for the Lesser Feasts and Fasts and for Special Occasions* (1963) and the preparatory drafts of the *Book of Common Prayer* (1973 and 1976), and in the Lutheran Church, *The Calendar: Church Year and Lectionary* [Contemporary Worship 3] (1973), opened up the sanctoral calendar to a great many additional commemorations. The Lutheran calendar was more inclusively ecumenical and more venturesome, including some popes (John XXIII, for example), some who were once perceived as enemies (John Calvin), some far out of the Catholic and liturgical tradition (George Fox), some at the fringes of Christianity (Dag Hammarskjöld). The Lutheran calendar was further expanded with the publication of the Spanish-language service book *Libro Liturgia y Cántico* (1998) and to a lesser degree *This Far by Faith: An African American Resource for Worship* (1999). The publication of *Evangelical Lutheran Worship* (2006) by the Evangelical Lutheran Church in America and the *Lutheran Service Book* (2006) by the Lutheran Church—Missouri Synod continues the expansion of the calendar among Lutherans. The calendar in the *Book of Common Prayer* has been increasingly enriched with the continuing publication of successive editions of *Lesser Feasts and Fasts* (1963, 1973, 1980, 1997, 2000, 2003, 2006) and in addition has in the 1997 edition created guidelines for further additions to (and deletions from) the calendar. Moreover, the Order of St. Luke has published a calendar of commemorations with explanatory material called *For All the Saints: A Calendar of Commemorations for United Methodists* (1995). From time to time individual Presbyterians have expressed an interest in the sanctoral cycle. As a result of the Second Vatican Council, the Roman Catholic Church has simplified its calendar, defining a General Roman Calendar for the whole church and allowing a variety of national additions to it.

With such developing interest, expansion, and enrichment of the calendar, the time has perhaps come for an examination of the possibilities of a common calendar of festivals and commemorations along the pattern of the Roman Catholic revision. There could be a general calendar to be shared by cooperating bodies and, in addition to that, denominational adaptations and additions to the general calendar. Such a common calendar can serve as a further means of binding Christians closer to one another in the communion of saints by enhancing the memory of the rich history of the church.

This book, a complete recasting and rewriting of my earlier book, *Festivals and Commemorations: Handbook to the Calendar in Lutheran Book of Worship* (1980), seeks, in a modest way, to provide a draft of such a common calendar, reflecting the present Lutheran and Episcopal calendars but also moving beyond them, proposing not merely a conflation but rather a creative adaptation as an encouragement to the churches to consider the value of a broad and ecumenical calendar of holy days and holy people.

The work of the Very Reverend Canon Dirk van Dissel of the Anglican Church in Australia, particularly his *St. Francis Daily Missal* (1987), as well as the successive editions of *Lesser Feasts and Fasts* of the Episcopal Church, have been of particular importance in the preparation of this book.

Introduction

Why have saints? It is a useful question to ask occasionally, for the answer takes us to the rich core of the Christian gospel.

Christ's triumphant passage from death to life is the heart and center of Christian faith and life. He recapitulates the experience of his ancestors in their deliverance from Egypt and the passage through the Red Sea from slavery to freedom. But Christ's paschal victory, by opening the gates of everlasting life, also anticipates the victory in which his followers participate. Through Holy Baptism each Christian is given a share in that passage from death to life and the transforming grace of God, and Christ's resurrection becomes theirs. The saints are not like the heroes of the world who achieved fame through their own strength and courage and perseverance. The saints of Christianity are those in whom the paschal victory of Christ is clearly manifest. They are people in whom the holy and life-giving Spirit of God is clearly at work.

In the Byzantine Churches the commemoration of all the saints is kept not on November 1 as it is in the West, but it is observed in close proximity to Easter, on the Sunday following Pentecost. That is to say, as soon as the great Fifty Days are concluded, the next Sunday is the Feast of All Saints. Thus the calendar teaches that the saints are to be understood as an extension of the paschal victory of Christ.

There are several places in the New Testament in which all believers are called "saints" (Rom. 12:13, 16:2; 1 Cor. 6:1, 16:1; Eph. 2:19, 5:3; 1 Tim. 5:20, for example.) The New Testament understanding, however, is much richer than the simple assertion one often hears, especially in Protestant circles, "We are all saints." St. Paul declares that believers are "called to be saints" (Rom. 1:17; 1 Cor. 1:2): sanctity for him is not a present possession but a goal toward which we are to move. Martin Luther expounds such an understanding: "This life, therefore, is not righteousness, but growth in righteousness; not health, but healing; not being, but becoming; not rest but exercise. We are not yet what we shall be, but we are growing toward it."[1]

In the world of the New Testament church, Christians were a small number of people who were tested and purified by opposition and hostility, and that entire brave band of believers could truly be called saints. But as the church grew and became more diverse, some of the faithful stood out from the rest because of their exemplary witness, and such people came to be regarded as worthy of special honor. In the modern world vast numbers of people call themselves Christians but have little concern for actually practicing "the faith that was once for all entrusted to the saints" (Jude 3). In such a setting it makes little sense and is in fact dangerous to say of merely nominal Christians, "We are all saints." That title now properly belongs to those in whom the grace of God is clearly revealed and who have earned the distinction by taking the faith seriously and acting upon their baptismal adoption into God's family and who are worthy of emulation.

To some, familiar with the secular custom of celebrating the birthdays of its heroes (such as those of George Washington, Abraham Lincoln, and Martin Luther King Jr.), it is surprising and disconcerting that church calendars list the commemoration of certain departed Christians on the day of their death. But the church is wise in its practice, for it understands the truth about death. Death does not silence those whom it claims, and the dead can speak with a powerful and commanding voice. The writer to the Hebrews remarked, "Abel . . . died, but through his faith he is still speaking" (Heb. 11:4). In *Little Gidding*, T. S. Eliot observes more explicitly,

> And what the dead had no speech for, when living,
> They can tell you, being dead: the communication
> Of the dead is tongued with fire beyond the language of the living.

The dead, whose lives in this world have been completed, speak with a force that those who are still living here, with potential and possibility before them, cannot achieve. Of the dead we know (from an earthly perspective) a whole story, the beginning and the ending. The story of the living, however, is as yet inconclusive. The church therefore remembers its dead and listens to their testimony, for departed believers, especially those whose witness to the goodness of God has been exemplary, can by the wholeness of their lives and examples instruct and encourage those members of the church whose work is not yet done.

Therefore, it is significant that the church remembers the departed saints on the day of their death, which is their "heavenly birthday," the day of their birth from this world of death into the next world of life. One the day of their death, by the grace of God, they pass through the gate of everlasting life, and then, as Luther teaches in his magnificent essay "The Holy and Blessed Sacrament of Baptism" (1519), baptism is completed, and the saint is lifted out of the water into life that has no end. Thus, because of the resurrection, it is not morbid but entirely appropriate to remember the saints on the day of their death, the day on which they share fully in the triumph of their Lord.

The renewed interest in saints that emerged in many churches during the latter part of the twentieth century is directly traceable to the renewed attention paid to Holy Baptism. Celebrating the saints dramatizes the meaning of baptism as the foundation of the Christian life, expressed with its many biblical and traditional metaphors—new birth, dying and rising, adoption into a new family, the opening of a new life of possibility, a call to sacrifice and service.

Baptism as a radically new beginning suggests an understanding of the sacrament not as a long-past event in an individual's life, but as an entrance upon a new and continuing way of life. The baptismal rite itself is not an isolated "moment" but rather a complex of actions that together constitute the sacrament of initiation into the community of faith: presentation of the candidate, thanksgiving over the water, renunciation of evil and profession of faith in Christ, washing in water, laying on of hands and signation with the cross, welcome and incorporation into the congregation. Moreover, the event of baptism breaks out beyond the boundaries of the liturgical rite to embrace and involve the whole future life of each one who is baptized.

Baptism therefore does not stand alone. It is the beginning of a pilgrimage for those who would be "of the Way" (Acts 9:2) and who seek to follow him who is himself the Way. Baptism is expected to make a change in a person's life and to set that person on the pilgrim's road. Thus, the work of baptism continues throughout life. Flannery O'Connor has written that "in us the good is something under construction."[2] Baptism, properly understood as initiation, the radical beginning of a life-long process, stands as an invitation to sanctification; it summons those who have been made new in its waters to "the practice of the presence of God"; it is an encouragement to an ever-deeper holiness, a calling to sanctity.

Those who come from the water of baptism are to present themselves as "living sacrifices" (see Rom. 12:1) offered to God for whatever God wills for them. The call may not be restful or pleasant; it will probably involve some sort of suffering. But for those who have been baptized, "There is only one misery, and that is—not to be saints."[3]

In a calendar of saints, therefore, a community beholds representative men and women who took their baptism seriously and let God's grace given in the mystical washing change their lives. The calendar of saints instructs those who have been baptized, "Go and do likewise."

Saints help to preserve and foster a sense of history. Christian history is intimately intertwined with secular history, and the study of one enhances the study of the other. On the fiftieth anniversary of the end of the Second World War, many took the occasion to remember the events that caused the war and those that eventually led to the liberation of Europe from the grip of Nazism. Over these commemorations echoes the cry carved in stone at the Bergen-Belsen concentration camp: "Earth, conceal not the blood shed on thee."

Like the secular world, the church, too, has often neglected its own history or forgotten the richness of its long and varied development, attempting to understand the present situation of the church without benefit of memory. In the Reformers' rejection of the fantastic legends and the extremes of the invocation and worship of the saints, the wholesome examples of the saints were often lost, and the knowledge of the church and its history shriveled. Many Christians conceive of the church only in terms of a narrow and often quite recent experience. A calendar of saints representing all times and all places of the Christian story can keep memory alive and encourage historical investigation and analysis as a way of understanding the present. Saints help us to remember who we are.

At the Easter Vigil, following the baptisms, it is customary in many places to sing the Litany of the Saints as, one by one, many of the great saints are implored to "pray for us." This litany is sung not simply to cover the action of moving from the font to the altar but more importantly to instruct the baptized in their family history. These holy people named in the litany are now the ancestors of those who have been baptized.

The calendar of commemorations is a kind of genealogical exploration of one's spiritual ancestors. It is a way of encouraging people to examine the personal stories of certain representative women and men to learn of the richness and the potential of human life lived by the grace of God in Jesus Christ. A study of the calendar is thus at once a course in theology, spirituality, prayer, church history, and sometimes secular history as well.

A calendar of commemorations can convey something of the breadth of Christian history and provide a richly assorted variety of the young and old, learned and untutored, people of action and contemplatives, whose common denominator is simply that the grace of God worked mightily within them. In certain remarkable and particular ways, they have shown the world something of the greatness of God revealed in Jesus Christ and in human lives as well, and for that they are remembered with thanksgiving.

Within the body of Christ there are various gifts and functions, callings and responsibilities. The baptismal life of sanctification is not the same for all, and there are many byways along the Way. Calendars of saints ought to be correspondingly rich and varied. The calendar must provide a variety of models and examples so that within the body of Christ one may find one's vocation and take one's place in the grand pilgrimage procession until at last, joined to the choir of heaven that forever sings the Easter Alleluia, we shall together praise the One who has called us to be saints and who has supported us by his grace.

Remembering the saints should encourage each of us to become all that we are capable of being. Sometimes, unfortunately, Christians have presented saints as elevated far above ordinary mortals, as if they shine with a bright light and shame the meanness and ordinariness of the lives of others. In such a view there are two classes of people, saints and sinners, the aristocracy and the common people, and the saints appear almost as a different race. It was against such an exaltation of saints above the common lot of humanity that the Reformers protested. They rediscovered that in the New Testament all believers were called saints, those who had been made holy by being baptized into the body of Christ and filled with the holy, life-giving, and sanctifying Spirit. In addition, the Reformers' emphasis on sin underscored the unworthiness of all believers. We are saints because we believe and are baptized, and we believe and are baptized because we need the deliverance that comes from Christ alone. It is not just a Protestant emphasis. In the Counter-Reformation, also, people like Philip Neri rejected the elevation of saints far above ordinary life and understood that saints often come from the common folk.

The remarkably astute painter Caravaggio (1571–1610) reflects this tradition. In his altarpiece for the Contarelli Chapel in the Church of San Luigi dei Francesci in Rome, "The Inspiration of St. Matthew," Caravaggio deliberately associated the evangelist with the lowest elements of the social order. The saint sits, bare legs crossed, an unshod and unwashed foot projecting toward the spectator, an angel guiding his hand as one does to teach a child to write.

Caravaggio's "Madonna de Loreto" (the Madonna of the Pilgrims) in the Calivetti Chapel of Sant'Agostino shows two working-class pilgrims kneeling before the virgin and child who stand in the doorway. The feet of one of the pilgrims, projecting toward the viewer, are noticeably dirty. He is a pilgrim, and so the dirt is an emblem of his journey to the virgin's shrine; but the dirt on his feet also betokens the humility (the word is derived from *humus*, "earth") required of those who approach the incarnate Lord.

A third painting by Caravaggio, "The Death of the Virgin," caused considerable controversy when it was first displayed. It shows the Blessed Virgin very dead indeed, lying with her belly swollen and bare feet projecting in the viewer's direction. The mother of God is one of the common folk. Again and again, Caravaggio effectively makes the point that the people are for the church and that the church is for the people. The saints as Caravaggio portrayed them are not idealized but are close to ordinary experience. Caravaggio, himself a proud and quarrelsome thug with a prison record, possessed a remarkable insight into holiness. He understood that the grace of God was present in ordinary people and that even in the lowest classes of society the light of revelation may be discerned by those who have eyes to see.

There is, therefore, a sense in which the people commemorated gratefully by the church are a consolation to us. In their holiness they do not forsake their humanity. They are people not unlike us, who made it successfully through this life and its trouble, disappointments, frustration, pettiness.

The existence of saints is also discomforting, for they are constant reminders that we must never be content with this world but must press on toward the kingdom. They are a living judgment upon our small and satisfied lives. And because they are, after all, not so different from us, they urge us to follow their path.

The saints, then, are not characterized by a negative goodness of abstinence, deprivation, and rejection, but rather by a drive toward wholeness, a total personal integrity that is rooted in a more than human achievement. Theirs has been a life of prayer and love and sacrifice, of charity perfected in suffering.

The holiness of wholeness has been expressed in astonishingly varied ways and forms. The Christian calendar ought to represent a most diverse collection of women and men, for as John the Scot (*ca.* 810–*ca.* 877) observed, "There are as many unveilings of God [theophanies] as there are saintly souls." Rigid doctrinal tests are therefore not helpful and perhaps not even possible if a calendar is to suggest something of this richness and diversity of the revelation of God through the lives of the people of God. We are thus urged by the calendar to listen to new voices that we are unaccustomed to hearing, with their insistent challenges that impel us to grow in our faith and knowledge of the nature of the church and God's ways with the world. In the evangelical tradition, the saints are remembered not so that they may hear us but that we may once again hear them.

A calendar of commemorations ought to expand our understanding of the size and extent of the church. For the church is larger than the individual congregation, larger than the denomination, larger even than the whole church on earth. It includes also all those who have gone before us in faith and whom we recall by remembering selected examples of that vast throng. Such remembering and rejoicing in the support of the cloud of witnesses who surround us is an important element of Christian life and testimony.

The phrase in the Apostles' Creed, *sanctorum communio*, translated "the communion of saints," Robert Wilken has suggested is best translated "fellowship with the saints" or "communion with the saints."[5] The phrase is an affirmation that the church is a community that enjoys fellowship with the saints through prayer, pilgrimage to their shrines, telling their stories, and imitating their holy lives. It is an understanding admirably expressed in the collect of All Saints' Day written by Archbishop Thomas Cranmer for the 1549 Book of Common Prayer and used by the Lutherans since 1868: "Almighty God, you have knit together your elect in one communion and fellowship in the mystical body of your Son Christ our Lord: Give us grace so to follow your blessed saints in all virtuous and godly living, that we may come to those ineffable joys that you have prepared for those who truly love you."

The calendar suggested in this book—limited, as is traditional, to the festivals appointed on specific dates and excluding moveable days and feasts (Ash Wednesday, Easter, Ascension Day, Pentecost, Trinity Sunday)—seeks to present a balanced reflection of the richness of Christian history. It follows the tradition of the Western church and does not include for specific commemoration the holy men and women of the Old Testament. This exclusion is not universal, however. The Eastern Orthodox Churches include certain Old Testament figures on their calendar. (The Holy Prophet Malachi is remembered on January 3; Job the Longsuffering on May 6, for example.) Wilhelm Löhe, the nineteenth-century Lutheran liturgist, included many Old Testament figures on his eclectic calendar (see Appendix 2); his innovation has been resurrected by the *Lutheran Service Book*. Local Anglican calendars sometimes remember collectively the Holy Men and Women of the Old Testament, often on the octave day of All Saints, November 8.

The men and women selected for commemoration on this calendar are not only ecclesiastics and those who have served the church organization. Also included are some who, within the Christian church, in various ways by their service to society, by their creations, by their discoveries sought to open humanity's eyes to the beauty and manifold grace of God.

According to the long-standing tradition of the church, the date chosen for a commemoration is normally that of a person's death, the "heavenly birthday." The calendar in the *Lutheran Book of Worship* followed that practice even when it meant doubling up otherwise unrelated commemorations (Polycarp and Ziegenbalg on February 23; Perpetua and Thomas Aquinas on March 7; Mary, Martha, and Lazarus of Bethany and also Olaf on July 29; Francis and Fliedner on October 4). In actual practice, however, such a doubling proved not helpful, and this calendar almost always separates such commemorations and moves one, usually the more recent one, to the next open date.

On certain days, however, related figures are gathered for a joint commemoration, such as the companions of St. Paul on January 26 and on January 27 three women who ministered with the apostles. This practice also allows for certain emphases, such as artists (Dürer, Michelangelo, Grünewald, and Cranach on April 6), church musicians (Bach, Schütz, and Handel on July 28), or teachers of science (Copernicus, Euler, and Kepler on May 24).

In a few cases (Thomas Aquinas on January 28, Basil on June 14, Ambrose on December 7), the commemoration is not on the date of the person's death but is on a date that has the support of tradition and the revisions of the calendar in the Roman Catholic and Episcopal Churches and represents a significant event in the person's life.

A calendar of commemorations is notable not only for who is included but also for who is omitted. There are, of course, many additional people who might appropriately be included, but, keeping in mind the unhappy condition of the calendar at the time of the Reformation, the aim is an inclusive and representative calendar that avoids being overburdened and overwhelming in the number of people listed. It has, frankly, been a continuing dilemma for the church, intensifying in the twenty-first century, that advocates of particular causes insist on the addition of representatives of their particular interests to the calendar.

The following pages present a brief biography of each person commemorated on the calendar. To each, a brief bibliography is appended to guide further investigation. The biographies of people whose commemoration is peculiar to the Episcopal calendar are given only in brief form so as not to trespass on another's territory; readers are referred to the current edition of *Lesser Feasts and Fasts* for fuller details about those people.

It is an ancient custom, when remembering worthy people of the past, that those commemorated should speak on their feast days. They can often address us through a reading of something they have written. If they have been hymnwriters, they can address us through one or more of their hymns. In those cases where no appropriate reading is available for the reading, a selection from another writer is provided. The reading is often further instruction in the life and work of the one commemorated and can serve as a supplement to the biography. The reading can be used following the reading of the scriptural lessons (especially in Morning and

Evening Prayer) as an additional lesson. It may sometimes serve as a brief homily for the day. It may also be used as a devotional reading in private prayer.

The Hymn of the Day (as the hymn after the sermon, the principal hymn of the liturgy, is called in Lutheran circles) is a hymn by the person commemorated when such a hymn is available. When it is not, a hymn appropriate to the nation where that person's contribution was made or a hymn appropriate to the work of the person is suggested. Sometimes the name of a hymn tune is related to the person being commemorated.

Suggestions for intercessions are made to guide those who are responsible for composing prayers for a service. The suggestions are intended to make the calendar of commemorations relevant to a variety of concerns. They are not to be understood as exhaustive. Other additional prayers may be locally appropriate.

The inclusion of optional days on this calendar indicates that users of the calendar are not necessarily expected to observe all the days that are listed here. Indeed, a continuing concern is that recent enrichments of the calendar in many quarters may tend to return the church to the medieval situation in which the sanctoral calendar obscured and nearly overwhelmed the basic structure of the church's seasons and the yearly reliving of the life and work of Christ.

The commemoration of exemplars of the faith always finds its proper focus in Christ, who works through his holy people and whose Spirit lives in them. Although many ancient calendars began with November 30, St. Andrew's Day, the feast closest to the beginning of Advent, it is fitting that this book and the year begin with the Holy Name of JESUS.

The days included in the calendar proposed in this book comprise five classes.

1. The most important days of the church's year are classified as Solemnities in Roman Catholic terminology, as Principal Festivals in the *Book of Common Prayer*, and as Greater Festivals in the *Lutheran Book of Worship* tradition. These days are indicated by being printed in ALL CAPITAL LETTERS in the calendar, and marked with this symbol where they appear in the main text (see fig. 1).

2. The days that are classified as Feasts in the Roman Catholic Church, as Holy Days in the *Book of Common Prayer*, and as Lesser Festivals in Lutheran use are printed in the calendar in SMALL CAPITAL LETTERS and marked with this symbol where they appear in the main text (see fig. 2).

3. Some days are not necessarily intended to be celebrated with a full liturgy of their own. Such days are called in Roman Catholic use Memorials, in the *Book of Common Prayer* Days of Optional Observance, and in Lutheran practice Commemorations. The days are indicated in the calendar by being printed in Roman type and marked with the symbol (fig. 3) where they appear in the main text. To observe such a Memorial, one adds the appropriate prayer (collect) after the Prayer (Collect) of the Day.

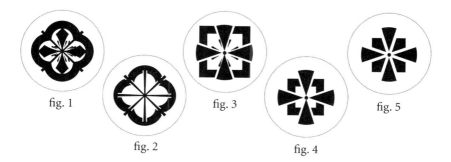

fig. 1   fig. 3   fig. 5

fig. 2   fig. 4

4.   The Roman Catholic calendar has a category of Optional Memorials, which may be observed as seems locally appropriate. It seems a useful classification, and such days, not all of them from the Roman Catholic calendar, are indicated by being printed in the calendar in *Italics* and marked with this symbol (fig. 4) where they appear in the main text.

5.   Finally, a number of post-Reformation days on the calendar proposed in this book are of interest largely to a particular denomination. Bartholomäus Ziegenbalg, the first missionary sent out by the Lutheran Church, and Jackson Kemper, the first Episcopal Missionary Bishop in the United States, are examples. These days are indicated by being printed *[in Italics within square brackets]* and those given major entreaties are marked with this symbol (fig. 5) where they appear in the main text.

1. "An Argument in Defense of All the Articles of Dr. Martin Luther Wrongly Condemned in the Roman Bull" (1521), trans. Charles M. Jacobs, in *Works of Martin Luther*, vol. 3 (Philadelphia: Muhlenberg Press, 1930), 31. The translation was revised and weakened in *Luther's Works*, vol. 32 (Philadelphia: Fortress Press, 1958), 24.

2. Flannery O'Connor, "An Introduction to a Memoir of Mary Ann," in *Mystery and Manners,* ed. Sally and Robert Fitzgerald (New York: Farrar, Straus & Giroux, 1969), 26.

3. Leon Bloy, *The Woman Who Was Poor* (New York: Sheed and Ward, 1947), 356.

4. John the Scot [Eriugena *or* Erigena], *De divisione naturae* I, 8. See John the Scot, *Periphyseon: On the Division of Nature,* ed. and trans. Myra L. Uhlfelder (Indianapolis: Bobbs-Merrill, 1976), 10.

5. Robert Wilken, "Sanctorum Communio: For Evangelicals and Catholics Together," *Pro Ecclesia* 11, no. 2 (Spring 2002): 159–66.

A Common Calendar

The following Common Calendar, as explained in the introduction above, is not an exhaustive listing of all the names, feasts, and memorials described in the main text of this volume, but represents my contribution toward a proposed common calendar for the major Western Christian traditions. For a complete alphabetical listing of all the names that appear in the body of this book, please turn to the names and days index, beginning on page 682. For an explanation of the typographical scheme used in this calendar, and of the accompanying icons that appear throughout this book, see above, pages xxvi–xxvii.

Key to the typographical scheme:
SOLEMNITIES/PRINCIPAL FEASTS/GREATER FESTIVALS
FEASTS/HOLY DAYS/LESSER FESTIVALS
Memorials/Days of Optional Observance/Commemorations
Optional Memorials
[Days of primarily denominational interest]

January

1   THE HOLY NAME OF JESUS
2   *Johann Konrad Wilhelm Löhe, Pastor, 1872*
3   *[Charles Porterfield Krauth, Teacher, 1883]*
4
5   Kaj Munk, Martyr, 1944
6   THE EPIPHANY OF OUR LORD
7
8
9   *[Julia Chester Emery, Mission Supporter, 1922]*
10 *[William Laud, Archbishop of Canterbury, 1645]*
11
12 *Aelred, Abbot of Rievaulx, 1167*
13 Hilary, Bishop of Poitiers, 367
14 *Eivind Josef Berggrav, Bishop of Oslo, 1959*
15
16 George Fox, Renewer of Society, 1691
17 Antony, Abbot in Egypt, 356; Pachomius, Abbot, 346
18 THE CONFESSION OF ST. PETER; The Week of Prayer for Christian Unity Begins

19 Henry, Bishop of Uppsala, Missionary to Finland, Martyr, 1156
    Wulfstan, Bishop of Worcester, 1095
20 Fabian, Bishop of Rome, Martyr, 250
21 Agnes, Martyr at Rome, 304
22 Vincent, Deacon of Saragossa, Martyr, 304
23 *Phillips Brooks, Bishop of Massachusetts, 1893*
24 Francis de Sales, Bishop of Geneva, 1622
    [Ordination of Florence Li Tim-Oi, First Woman Priest in the Anglican Communion, 1944]
25 THE CONVERSION OF ST. PAUL; The Week of Prayer for Christian Unity Ends
26 Timothy, Titus, and Silas; Companions of St. Paul
27 Lydia, Dorcas, and Phoebe; Helpers of the Apostles
28 Thomas Aquinas, Teacher, 1274
29
30
31

February

1	*Brigid (Bride), Abbess 523*	16	
2	THE PRESENTATION OF OUR LORD	17	*[Janani Luwum, Archbishop of Uganda and Martyr, 1977]*
3	Ansgar, Archbishop of Hamburg, Missionary to Denmark and Sweden, 865	18	Martin Luther, Renewer of the Church, 1546
4	*Cornelius the Centurion*	19	
5	Paul Miki and His Companions, Martyrs of Japan, 1597	20	*[Rasmus Jensen, First Lutheran Pastor in North America, 1620]*
6	*[Philipp Jakob Spener, Renewer of the Church, 1705]*	21	
7		22	
8		23	Polycarp, Bishop of Smyrna, Martyr, 156
9		24	ST. MATTHIAS, APOSTLE
10		25	*[Elizabeth Fedde, 1921; Emma Francis, 1945; Deaconesses]*
11		26	*[Bartholomäus Ziegenbalg, Missionary to India, 1719]*
12		27	
13	*[Absalom Jones, Priest, 1818]*	28	
14	Cyril, Monk, 865; Methodius, Bishop, 885; Missionaries to the Slavs		
15	*[Thomas Bray, Priest and Missionary, 1730]*		

March

1	George Herbert, Priest, 1633 *David, Bishop of Menevia, Wales,* ca. *544*	19	ST. JOSEPH, HUSBAND OF MARY AND GUARDIAN OF OUR LORD
2	John Wesley, 1791; Charles Wesley, 1788; Renewers of the Church *Chad, Bishop of Lichfield, 672*	20	*Cuthbert, Bishop of Lindisfarne, 687*
		21	*Thomas Ken, Bishop of Bath and Wells, 1711*
3		22	Jonathan Edwards, Teacher, Missionary to the Native Americans, 1758 *[James DeKoven, Priest, 1879]*
4			
5			
6		23	Gregory the Illuminator, Bishop of and Missionary to Armenia, *ca.* 332
7	Perpetua and Her Companions, Martyrs at Carthage, 202	24	Óscar Arnulfo Romero, Archbishop of San Salvador, Martyr, 1980
8		25	THE ANNUNCIATION OF OUR LORD
9		26	
10		27	*[Charles Henry Brent, Bishop of the Philippines and of Western New York, 1929]*
11			
12	Gregory the Great, Bishop of Rome, 604		
13		28	
14		29	*John Keble, Priest, 1866* *[Hans Nielsen Hauge, Renewer of the Church, 1824]*
15			
16		30	
17	Patrick, Bishop, Missionary to Ireland, 461	31	John Donne, Priest, 1631
18	Cyril, Bishop of Jerusalem, 386		

April

1   Amalie Wilhelmina Sieveking, Renewer
    of Society, 1859
    Frederick Dennison Maurice, Priest,
    1872
2   *[James Lloyd Breck, Priest, 1876]*
3   Richard, Bishop of Chichester, 1253
4   Martin Luther King, Jr, Renewer of
    Society, 1968
    Benedict the African, Friar, 1589
5
6   *Albrecht Dürer, Painter, 1528; Lucas*
    Cranach the Elder, Painter, 1553;
    Matthäus Grünewald, Painter, 1528;
    Michelangelo Buonarotti, Artist, 1564
7
8   *William Augustus Muhlenberg, Priest,*
    1877
9   Dietrich Bonhoeffer, Teacher, Martyr,
    1945
10 *Mikael Agricola, Bishop of Turku,*
    Renewer of the Church, 1557;
    William Law, Priest, 1761
11 *[George Augustus Selwyn, Bishop of New*
    Zealand and of Lichfield, 1878]
12
13
14
15
16
17
18
19 *Alphege, Archbishop of Canterbury,*
    Martyr, 1012
    Olavus Petri, Priest, 1552; Laurentius
    Petri, Archbishop of Uppsala, 1573;
    Renewers of the Church
20
21 Anselm, Archbishop of Canterbury,
    Teacher, 1109
22
23 Toyohiko Kagawa, Renewer of Society,
    1960
24
25 ST. MARK, EVANGELIST
26
27
28
29 Catherine of Siena, Teacher, 1380
30

* Remembrance of the Holocaust on or near
the date of the Jewish Yom HaShoah (April/
May)

May

1   ST. PHILIP AND ST. JAMES, APOSTLES
2   Athanasius, Bishop of Alexandria, 373
3
4
5
6
7
8   Dame Julian of Norwich,
    Anchoress, *ca.* 1417
9   *Nicolaus Ludwig, Count von Zinzendorf,*
    Renewer of the Church, 1760
10
11
12
13
14
15
16
17
18 *Erik, King of Sweden, Martyr, 1160*
19 Dunstan, Archbishop of Canterbury,
    988
20 Alcuin, Deacon, Abbot of Tours, 804
21 John Eliot, Missionary to the Native
    Americans, 1690
22 *Helena, Mother of Constantine, ca. 330*
23 *[Ludwig Ingwer Nommensen,*
    Missionary to Sumatra, 1918]
24 *Nicolaus Copernicus, 1543; Johannes*
    Kepler, 1630; Leonhard Euler, 1783;
    Teachers
    [Jackson Kemper, First Episcopal Mission-
    ary Bishop to the United States, 1870]
25 Bede the Venerable, Priest, Monk of
    Jarrow, 735
26 Augustine, First Archbishop of Canter-
    bury, Missionary, 605
27 John Calvin, Renewer of the Church,
    1564
28
29 *[Juraj Tranovsky, Hymnwriter, 1637]*
30
31 THE VISITATION

June

1   Justin, Martyr at Rome, *ca.* 165
2   Blandina and Her Companions, Martyrs at Lyons, 177
3   *The Martyrs of Uganda, 1886*
4   John XXIII, Bishop of Rome, Renewer of the Church, 1963
5   Boniface, Archbishop of Mainz, Missionary to Germany, Martyr, 754
6   [*William Alfred Passavant, Renewer of Society, 1894*]
7   Sealth (Seattle), Chief of the Duwamish Confederacy, 1866
8
9   Columba, Abbot of Iona, 597; Aidan, Bishop of Lindisfarne, 651
10 Ephrem of Edessa, Deacon, 373
11 ST. BARNABAS, APOSTLE
12
13
14 Macrina, Monastic, Teacher, 379; Basil the Great, Bishop of Caesarea, 379; Gregory of Nazianzus, Bishop of Constantinople, *ca.* 389; Gregory, Bishop of Nyssa, *ca.* 385

15 Evelyn Underhill, Teacher, 1941
16 [*Joseph Butler, Bishop of Durham, 1752*]
17
18 [*Bernard Mizeki, Catechist and Martyr in Rhodesia, 1896*]
19
20
21 [*Onesimos Nesib, Translator, Evangelist, 1931*]
22 *Alban, the First Martyr in Britain, ca. 304*
23
24 THE NATIVITY OF ST. JOHN THE BAPTIST
25 *The Presentation of the Augsburg Confession, 1530*
    Philipp Melanchthon, Renewer of the Church, 1560
26
27 *Cyril of Alexandria, Bishop, Teacher, 444*
28 *Irenaeus, Bishop of Lyons, ca. 202*
29 ST. PETER AND ST. PAUL, APOSTLES
30 [*Johann Olof Wallin, Archbishop of Uppsala, Hymnwriter, 1839*]

July

1   John Mason Neale, 1866; Catherine Winkworth, 1878; Hymnwriters
2
3
4
5
6   Jan Hus, Martyr, 1415
7
8
9
10
11 Benedict of Nursia, Abbot of Monte Cassino, *ca.* 547; Scholastica, Monastic, *ca.* 547
12 Nathan Söderblom, Archbishop of Uppsala, 1931
13 [*Johannes Flierl, Missionary to Australia and Papua New Guinea, 1947*]
14
15 Olga, Princess of Kiev, Confessor, 969; Vladimir, First Christian Ruler of Russia, 1015
16
17 Bartolomé de Las Casas, Missionary to the Indies, 1566
    [*William White, Bishop of Pennsylvania, 1816*]

18
19
20 *Elizabeth Cady Stanton, 1902; Amelia Jenks Bloomer, 1894; Sojourner Truth, 1883; Harriet Ross Tubman, 1912; Renewers of Society*
21
22 ST. MARY MAGDALENE
23 Birgitta of Sweden, Renewer of the Church, 1373
24 *Thomas à Kempis, Priest, 1471*
25 ST. JAMES THE ELDER, APOSTLE
26 The Parents of the Blessed Virgin Mary
27 [*William Reed Huntington, Priest, 1919*]
28 Johann Sebastian Bach, 1750; Heinrich Schütz, 1672; George Frederick Handel, 1759; Musicians
29 Mary, Martha, and Lazarus of Bethany
    Olaf, King of Norway, Martyr, 1030
30 *William Wilberforce, Renewer of Society, 1833*
31 Ignatius of Loyola, Priest, Monastic, and Founder of the Society of Jesus, 1556

August

1 *Joseph of Arimathea*
2
3
4
5
6 THE TRANSFIGURATION OF OUR LORD
7
8 Dominic, Priest and Friar, 1221
9
10 Lawrence, Deacon and Martyr at Rome, 258
11 Clare, Abbess at Assisi, 1253
12
13 Florence Nightingale, 1910; Clara Maass, 1901; Renewers of Society
Jeremy Taylor, Bishop of Down, Connor, and Dromore, 1667
14 *Maximilian Mary Kolbe, Priest, Martyr, 1941*
[Jonathan Myrick Daniels, Civil Rights Witness, 1965]
15 ST. MARY THE VIRGIN, MOTHER OF OUR LORD

16 Stephen, King of Hungary, 1038
17
18 *[William Porcher DuBose, Priest, 1918]*
19
20 Bernard, Abbot of Clairvaux, 1153
21
22
23
24 ST. BARTHOLOMEW, APOSTLE
25 Louis, King of France, 1270
26
27 Monica, Mother of Augustine, 387
[Thomas Gallaudet, 1902, with Henry Winter Syle, 1890]
28 Augustine, Bishop of Hippo, Teacher, 430
Moses the Black, Monk and Martyr, ca. 400
29 The Beheading of St. John the Baptist
30
31 John Bunyan, Teacher, 1688

September

1 *[David Pendleton Oakerhater, Deacon and Missionary, 1931]*
2 *Nikolai Frederik Severin Grundtvig, Bishop and Renewer of the Church, 1872*
[The Martyrs of Papua New Guinea, 1942]
3
4 Albert Schweitzer, Missionary to Africa, 1965
[Paul Jones, Bishop, 1941]
5 Mother Teresa of Calcutta, Renewer of Society, 1997
6
7
8 The Nativity of the Blessed Virgin Mary
9 Peter Claver, Priest, Missionary to Colombia, 1654
[Constance, Nun, and Her Companions, 1878]
10 *[Alexander Crummell, Priest, 1898]*
11
12 *[John Henry Hobart, Bishop of New York, 1830]*
13 John Chrysostom, Bishop of Constantinople, 407

14 HOLY CROSS DAY
15
16 *Cyprian, Bishop and Martyr at Carthage, 258*
Ninian, Bishop, Missionary to Scotland, ca. 430
17 Hildegard, Abbess of Bingen, Renewer of the Church, 1179
18 Dag Hammarskjöld, Peacemaker, 1961
[Edward Bouverie Pusey, Priest, 1882]
19 *Theodore of Tarsus, Archbishop of Canterbury, 690*
20 *[John Coleridge Patteson, Bishop of Melanesia, and His Companions, Martyrs, 1871]*
21 ST. MATTHEW, APOSTLE, EVANGELIST
22 *[Justus Falckner, First Lutheran Pastor Ordained in North America, 1723]*
[Philander Chase, Bishop of Ohio and of Illinois, 1852]
23
24
25 Sergius of Radonezh, Abbot of Holy Trinity, Moscow, 1392
26 *Lancelot Andrewes, Bishop of Winchester, 1626*

September (continued)

27   Vincent de Paul, Priest, Renewer of
     Church and Society, 1660
28   *[Jehu Jones Jr., Pastor, 1852]*
29   ST. MICHAEL AND ALL ANGELS
30   Jerome, Translator and Teacher, Priest
     and Monk of Bethlehem, 420

October

1   *Remigius, Bishop of Rheims, ca. 533*
2
3
4   Francis of Assisi, Friar, Renewer of the
     Church, 1226
5   *Frederike Fliedner, 1842; Theodor
     Fliedner, 1864; Karolin Fliedner, 1892;
     Renewers of Society*
6   William Tyndale, Priest, Translator,
     Martyr, 1536
7   *[Henry Melchior Muhlenberg, Mission-
     ary to America, 1787]*
8
9   *Robert Grosseteste, Bishop of Lincoln,
     1253*
10
11   *Philip, Deacon and Evangelist*
12
13   *Elizabeth Fry, Renewer of Society, 1845*
14   *[Samuel Isaac Joseph Schereschewsky,
     Bishop of Shanghai, 1906]*
15   Teresa of Avila, Renewer of the Church,
     1582
16   Thomas Cranmer, Archbishop of
     Canterbury, 1556
     *[Hugh Latimer and Nicholas Ridley,
     Bishops, 1555]*

17   Ignatius, Bishop of Antioch, Martyr, *ca.*
     115
18   ST. LUKE, EVANGELIST
19   *[Henry Martyn, Priest and Missionary
     to India and Persia, 1812]*
20
21
22
23   ST. JAMES OF JERUSALEM, BROTHER OF
     OUR LORD JESUS CHRIST, MARTYR, *ca.* 62
24
25
26   Philipp Nicolai, 1608; Johann Heer-
     mann, 1647; Paul Gerhardt, 1676;
     Hymnwriters
     *Alfred the Great, King of the West Sax-
     ons, 899*
27
28   ST. SIMON AND ST. JUDE, APOSTLES
29   *[James Hannington, and His Compan-
     ions, Martyrs, 1885]*
30
31   Reformation Day

November

1   ALL SAINTS' DAY
2   Commemoration of the Faithful De-
     parted
3   *Martin de Porres, Renewer of Society,
     1639*
     [Richard Hooker, Priest, 1600]
4
5   Elizabeth and Zechariah, Parents of St.
     John the Baptist
6   *William Temple, Archbishop of Canter-
     bury, 1944*
7   *Willibrord, Archbishop of Utrecht, Mis-
     sionary to Frisia, 739*

8   *[John Christian Frederick Heyer, Mis-
     sionary to India, 1873]*
9
10   Leo the Great, Bishop of Rome, 461
11   Martin, Bishop of Tours, 397
12   *Søren Aabye Kierkegaard, Theologian,
     1855*
     [Charles Simeon, Priest, 1836]
13
14   *[Consecration of Samuel Seabury, First
     American Episcopal Bishop, 1784]*
15
16   Margaret, Queen of Scotland, 1093

November (continued)

17 Elizabeth of Thuringia, Princess of
    Hungary, 1231
    Hugh, Bishop of Lincoln, 1200.
18 Hilda, Abbess of Whitby, 680
19 Mechtild of Magdeburg, 1282;
    Mechtild of Hackeborn, 1298; Ger-
    trude the Great, 1302; Renewers of the
    Church
20 *Edmund, King of East Anglia, Martyr,
    870*
21
22 Clive Staples Lewis, Apologist and
    Spiritual Writer, 1963

23 Clement, Bishop of Rome, *ca.* 100
24 Miguel Agustin Pro, Priest, Martyr,
    1927
25 Isaac Watts, Hymnwriter, 1748
    *[James Otis Sargent Hannington, Priest
    and Monk, 1935]*
26
27
28 *[Kamehameha, 1864, and Emma, 1885,
    King and Queen of Hawaii]*
29
30 ST. ANDREW, APOSTLE

December

1   *Nicholas Ferrar, Deacon, 1637*
2   *[Channing Moore Williams, Missionary
    Bishop to China and Japan, 1910]*
3   Francis Xavier, Missionary to Asia,
    1552
4   John of Damascus, Priest, *ca.* 760
5   *Clement of Alexandria, Priest, ca. 210*
6   Nicholas, Bishop of Myra, *ca.* 342
7   Ambrose, Bishop of Milan, 397
8
9
10
11 *[Lars Olsen Skrefsrud, Missionary to
    India, 1910]*
12
13 *Lucy, Martyr at Syracuse,* ca. 304
14 John of the Cross, Renewer of the
    Church, 1591

15
16
17 *O Sapientia*
18
19
20 *Katharina von Bora Luther, 1552*
21 ST. THOMAS, APOSTLE
22
23 *Thorlak, Bishop of Skalholt, 1193*
24
25 THE NATIVITY OF OUR LORD
26 ST. STEPHEN, DEACON, MARTYR
27 ST. JOHN, APOSTLE, EVANGELIST
28 THE HOLY INNOCENTS, MARTYRS
29 *Thomas Becket, Archbishop of Canter-
    bury, Martyr, 1170*
30
31

The Festivals and Commemorations

January 1

The Holy Name of Jesus

From the sixth century of the Christian era, March 25, the Annunciation, was understood as the beginning of the Incarnation and the inauguration of the new age (see Dante, *Paradiso* 16:34-39) and was accepted throughout much of Christendom as the beginning of the year. In Germany, however, the year began with Christmas; in France and the Low Countries it began with Easter; the Orthodox Church, reflecting Jewish practice as it frequently does, begins the new church year on September 1.

The names of the months September, October, November, and December (seventh, eighth, ninth, tenth) preserve the prehistoric Roman practice of observing March 1 as New Year's Day; September is the seventh month counting from the first month of March. March 1 was also the beginning of the year among the Franks until the eighth century, and also among the Turks and the Russians.

There was, nonetheless, an old and persistent tradition that recognized January 1 as New Year's Day. In 153 B.C.E. the Roman consuls entered office on January 1, the beginning of the month immediately following the winter solstice, indicating that that date was being accepted by the Roman Empire as the beginning of the year. When Julius Caesar reorganized the Roman calendar in 46 B.C.E., the beginning of the year was set on January 1, and it was celebrated by the "saturnalia."

The observance of January 1 as New Year's Day was increasingly frequent from the thirteenth century under the influence of Roman law and later humanism, in France in 1563, in Scotland in 1600, in Russia in 1700. In 1582 Gregory XIII reformed the calendar and set the beginning of the year on January 1. The adoption of the Gregorian date spread slowly. It was not accepted in England and the American colonies until 1752.

In the pagan world New Year's Day was a celebration in honor of Janus, the god who faces two directions, and the celebration was a time of widespread revelry and license. For some centuries, therefore, the Christian church gave no liturgical notice to the day whatever. "I see you have come here," St. Augustine is reported to have said to the crowds in church on January 1, "as if we had a feast today." When the church noted the day at all, it was kept as a day of fasting and penitence. Several early missals provided a mass for use on January 1 against idolatrous practices. "During these days when they revel," Augustine declared, "we observe a fast in order to pray for them," church attendance being seen as an antidote to participation in pagan revels. In a sermon for this day (no. 198), Augustine said, "Let them get drunk; you should fast. Let them rush to the theater; you should rush to church." (Watch Night services on New Year's Eve, popular especially among Methodists, are a modern equivalent.) The Second Council of Tours (567) prescribed penitential devotions modeled on the Lenten fast for the first three days of January in an effort to eliminate pagan practice. In the year 633, the Fourth Council of Toledo in Spain prescribed a strict fast and abstinence for January 1, and it became a day of such solemnity that "Alleluia" was omitted from the liturgy as it was during Lent. Throughout the church in these centuries there were repeated prohibitions against participation by Christians in the revels of the new year. The continued repetition of the prohibitions indicates that although the church opposed the celebration, the people continued their revels.

In the seventh century, however, probably under Pope Boniface IX (615), January 1 was made a church holiday, called simply "the Octave of the Lord," the title in the Gelasian and the Gregorian sacramentaries, in imitation of the eighth day of Easter and of the Epiphany. Since the celebration of the new year could not be suppressed, the church did as it has often done and transformed the pagan holiday into a church festival. The appointed place (the "station") of the pope's mass that day was the church of St. Mary beyond the Tiber, the oldest church dedicated to the mother of the Lord; and so the day became connected with Mary, and the old Roman calendars call the day "The Feast of St. Mary." It is in a sense, therefore, the oldest feast of Mary in the Western Church, celebrated on the eighth day after the birth of her Son. The Roman Catholic calendar echoes this ancient name and calls the day "Octave of Christmas: the Solemnity of Mary, the Mother of God."

The celebration of Jesus' circumcision on the eighth day after his birth began about the middle of the sixth century particularly in Gaul but also in Spain. The celebration is not mentioned in the Eastern Church before the eighth century; it became established in Rome after the ninth century. This newer commemoration soon overshadowed the Octave of Christmas and came to be combined with the Octave in the title of the day: "The Circumcision of Our Lord and the Octave of the Nativity." In the middle ages, the day also came to be associated with devotion to the Holy Name of Jesus, since the one-verse Gospel for the eighth day of Christmas, Luke 2:21, reported both the circumcision and the giving of the divinely chosen Name. In the fifteenth century John of Capistrano, Bernardine of Siena, and the Franciscans worked to spread the cult of the Holy Name of Jesus. In 1530 the Franciscan Order received permission to celebrate the Name of Jesus as a separate festival on January 14. The observance spread, and in 1721 Pope Innocent XIII fixed the Feast of the Holy Name on the Second Sunday after the Epiphany; in 1913 Pius X assigned the festival to the Sunday between January 1 and 6, or on January 2 if no Sunday occurred. That practice is now suppressed in the Roman Church, and propers are provided for a votive mass of the Holy Name which may be celebrated whenever convenient. Certain Eastern rites kept the celebration of the Holy Name on January 1.

In late medieval practice in England, shown in the later forms of the Sarum rite, the feast of the Holy Name was observed on August 7, a day that still appears on

certain Anglican calendars as "St. Saviour" (that is, the holy Savior), because in Hebrew the name Jesus means "savior," as the angel explained to Joseph (Matt. 1:21).

In previous Anglican Prayer Books January 1 is called simply "The Circumcision of Christ"; in the 1979 Prayer Book the day is given a new designation, "The
Holy Name of Our Lord Jesus Christ." There had been objection in some quarters to the former title and particularly to the former collect, which, reflecting St.
Paul's teaching in Romans 2:29, asked for "the true circumcision of the Spirit,"
since the focus seemed to be on circumcision itself rather than circumcision as
an event in the life of Christ. (See F. E. Brightman, quoted in Massey Shepherd,
Oxford American Prayer Book Commentary, [Oxford, 1950], 105–06.) In Christian
devotion, circumcision as a rite of purification is taken to be a symbol of baptism,
and the first blood shed by Christ for the cleansing of his people. (In the church
in Ethiopia, circumcision is performed between the third and the eighth day after
birth, before the child is baptized.)

Lutheran calendars retained the medieval association of the Circumcision
and the Name of Jesus because of their biblical basis, and so the title reads in most
Lutheran service books (for instance, *The Church Book* of 1868, *The Common
Service Book* of 1918, *The Lutheran Hymnal* of 1941, the *Service Book and Hymnal*
of 1958, the *Lutheran Service Book* of 2006). The *Lutheran Book of Worship* (1978),
followed by *Evangelical Lutheran Worship* (2006), borrowed the name of the day
in the American the *Book of Common Prayer* (the Holy Name of Jesus) and gives
it in a simplified form: "The Name of Jesus."

The office hymns for the Feast of the Holy Name derive from a long poem
ascribed to Bernard of Clairvaux, *Jesu dulcis memoria*, and are still sung in English
as "Jesus, the very thought of thee," "O Jesus, king most wonderful," and "Jesus,
thou joy of loving hearts." The fifteenth-century hymn *Gloriosi salvatoris,* translated by John Mason Neale and others as "To the Name of our salvation," sung to
the stirring tune *Oriel*, makes clear that devotion to the holy Name is devotion to
Jesus, the Name being a synonym for Jesus himself, who for long generations lay
hidden in God's foreknowledge but now has been revealed to the world. The long-
held secret, now made public, in our time can be boldly sung aloud. (The splendid
hymn is an explication of Ephesians 3.)

READING

From *Worship* by Evelyn Underhill

Eastern Catholicism . . . has . . . a technique . . . of a simple and beautiful kind, for
the production and deepening of that simple, inclusive, and continuous act of
communion with God, that humble prayer of the heart, which is the substance
of its mystical worship. This technique, so simple that it is within the compass
of the humblest worshipper, yet so penetrating that it can introduce those who
use it faithfully to the deepest mysteries of the contemplative life, consists in the

unremitting inward repetition of the Holy Name of God; usually in the form of the so-called "Jesus prayer"—"Lord Jesus Christ, Son of God, have mercy upon me!" This prayer has a unique place in the spiritual life of Orthodoxy. All monastic rules of devotion, and spiritual direction given by monks to the pious laity, aim at its development. It carries the simple and childlike appeal of the devout peasant, and the continuous self-acting aspiration of the great contemplative.

It can, when needful, replace the Divine Office and all other prayers; for it is of universal validity. The power of this prayer does not reside in its content, which is simple and clear (it is the prayer of the publican) but in the holy Name of Jesus. The ascetics testify that in this Name there resides the power of the Presence of God. Not only is God invoked in it, but He is already present in the invocation . . . thus the Name of Jesus present in the human heart communicates to it the power of that deification which the Redeemer has bestowed on us. . . . The light of the Name of Jesus pours through the heart, to irradiate the universe, a foretaste of that final transfiguration in which God shall be all in all.

Excerpts from *Worship* by Evelyn Underhill, copyright, 1936 by Harper & Brothers. Reprinted by permission of HarperCollins Publishers and Hodder & Stoughton.

PROPERS

Eternal Father, you gave to your incarnate Son the holy Name of Jesus to be a sign of our salvation: Plant in every heart, we pray, the love of him who is the Savior of the world, our Lord Jesus Christ, who lives and reigns with you and the Holy Spirit, one God, in glory everlasting.

Cambridge Bede Book, 1936; rev. 1979, BCP; rev. in LBW, ELW.

Readings:	Numbers 6:22-27 [RCL] *or* Exodus 34:1-8
	Psalm 8
	Galatians 4:4-7 [RCL] *or* Philippians 2:9-13
	Luke 2:15-21
Hymn of the Day:	
	"To the Name of our salvation" (H82 248, 249; CSB 36)
	"O Jesus, joy of loving hearts" (LBW 356, ELW 658)
Prayers:	For a deeper devotion to our Lord and a greater reliance on his saving power
	For the cleansing of God's people from sin
	For reverence for the holy name of Jesus
	For God's blessing on the new year
Preface:	Christmas/Incarnation
Color:	White

ALSO ON JANUARY 1

New Year's Day as such has no liturgical significance, but the church's continuing struggle to keep the celebration of the secular new year out of its own distinctive year, the first day of which is the First Sunday in Advent, has proved to be futile.

In Germany after the Reformation the new year was given a certain liturgical recognition (see Bach's *Christmas Oratorio*). In North America the 1868 Lutheran *Church Book* provided a collect for the New Year translated from the 1695 Ober-Lausitz Agenda, which itself derived from the Austrian order of 1571:

> Almighty and everlasting God, from whom cometh down every good and perfect gift: We give thanks for all thy benefits, temporal and spiritual, bestowed upon us in the year past, and we beseech thee of thy goodness, grant us a favorable and joyful year, defend us from all dangers and adversities, and send upon us the fullness of thy blessing; through thy Son Jesus Christ our Lord, who liveth and reigneth with thee and the Holy Ghost, one God, world without end.

The collect was continued in the 1918 *Common Service Book*, the 1941 *Lutheran Hymnal*, and the 1958 *Service Book and Hymnal*.

The 1928 Proposed English *Book of Common Prayer* provided a similar collect for the new year. The present *Roman Sacramentary* provides for a mass At the Beginning of the New Year. The *Lutheran Book of Worship* (1978), the *Lutheran Service Book* (2006), and *Evangelical Lutheran Worship* (2006) all provide propers for New Year's Eve, but these are not listed under the church year but rather under "Occasions."

January 2

Johann Konrad Wilhelm Löhe, Pastor, 1872

Wilhelm Löhe (Loehe), the epitome of a faithful pastor, was a remarkable advocate of confessional, liturgical, devotional, mission-minded Lutheranism. He was born at Fürth, Bavaria, February 21, 1808. His father died in 1816, and the boy seems to have led a lonely childhood. He attended C. L. Roth's Gymnasium in Nuremberg and in 1826 entered Erlangen University to study theology. There he came under the influence of Christian Krafft, a Reformed professor and preacher, who encouraged him to read deeply in dogmatic theology, and there he also discovered the Lutheran Confessions. Following his work at Erlangen, Löhe went to Berlin for further study. He was ordained July 25, 1831, in Ansbach. From 1831 to 1837 Löhe served as vicar and administrator (*Pfarrerweser*) in a number of places, and in 1837 he became pastor in Neuendettelsau, an insignificant village in Bavaria. His efforts to obtain a city parish failed, and he remained for the rest of his ministry in Neuendettelsau, raising the village to international prominence and giving it lasting fame. Although Löhe was born and reared in the city, he seems to have adapted well to rural life, and, although he never left Germany, he was able from this little parish to influence church life on five continents. In his company, it was observed, "one was impressed as though he was always praying, and even when he spoke of small, outward things, it was as the breath of the Spirit of the kingdom of God."

Löhe was an ideal parish pastor, who got on well with all classes of people and who in the parish was able to make practical application of his studies, particularly those of the Confessions and of the liturgy. He developed an understanding of the Holy Communion as the center of the life of the congregation from which flowed liturgical renewal and social service. He combined a high view of the ministry, which he viewed as not dependent on the congregation's call but as transmitted from Christ himself through ordination, with an emphasis on the importance of the role of the laity in worship and in missionary activity at home and abroad.

Löhe's missionary interest is seen in his pastoral concern, beginning in 1841, for Lutherans who emigrated to North America. He solicited funds through periodicals, and he sent books and other necessary commodities to Lutheran communities. He was instrumental in sending "emergency pastors" to North America to serve the settlers and to convert the native peoples. Löhe's emissaries assisted in the founding of the Synod of Ohio (although he withdrew support in 1845 because of the synod's differences over theology and the use of English.) With congregations established by C. F. W. Walther, Löhe's pastors formed the Missouri Synod at Fort Wayne, Indiana, in 1846. Löhe wrote the spiritual and secular regulations for a series of German colonies that were being established in Michigan—Frankenmuth, Frankenlust, Frankentrost, Frankenhilf. In 1853 Löhe's pastors moved into Iowa and in the following year, joined by others from Neuendettelsau, established the Evangelical Lutheran Synod of Iowa and Other States. Moreover, his Neuendettelsau Foreign Mission Society sent pastors not only to North America but also to Brazil, the Ukraine, Australia, and New Guinea.

Löhe's interest was not only in missions. In 1849 he founded the deaconess motherhouse in Neudettelsau, which became the center of social and educational service in schools, hospitals, and allied agencies. He also struggled with the territorial church in Bavaria to give it a clear confessional basis. His relations with the church were strained for several years between 1848 and 1852, but at length the conflict was resolved. He died January 2, 1872, at the age of sixty-three. The chapel at Wartburg Seminary in Dubuque, Iowa, is dedicated to his memory.

FOR FURTHER READING

Deinzer, J. *Wilhelm Löhes Leben: Aus seinem schriftlichen Nachlass zusammengestellt* 3 vols. Gütersloh: C. Bertelsmann, 1929. The standard biography.

Hauch, Albert. "Johann Konrad Wilhelm Loehe." In *New Schaff-Herzog Encyclopedia of Religious Knowledge*. 13 vols. VII: 9-10. Grand Rapids: Baker, 1951–1955.

Schaaf, James Lewis. *W. Löhe's Relation to the American Church*. 1962. Includes a portrait of Löhe, p. 199; a portrait may also be found online at http://www.nicoly.de/frankenmuth/loehe.htm (accessed Aug. 31, 2007).

———, trans. *Three Books about the Church by Wilhelm Löhe*. Philadelphia: Fortress Press, 1969.

READING

From a statement by Wilhelm Löhe

What do I want? I want to serve. Whom do I want to serve? The Lord in the person of his poor suffering children. And what is my reward? I serve neither for reward nor thanks, but out of gratitude and love; my reward is that I am permitted to serve. And if I perish in doing so? If I perish, I perish, said Esther, who, after all, did not know him who for love of me perished and who will not let me perish. And if I grow old in his service? Then my heart shall flourish like the palm tree, and the Lord will satisfy me with grace and mercy. Therefore, without anxiety I walk in peace.

Wilhelm Löhe, quoted in *Minister's Prayer Book,* ed. John W. Doberstein (Philadelphia: Fortress Press, 1986), 218; rev. PHP.

PROPERS

Everlasting, gracious heavenly Father, you have given to your church the holy ministry of Word and Sacrament: Grant that the pastors of your church, following the example of Wilhelm Löhe, may fearlessly proclaim your word against every error, false doctrine, and abuse; and may so minister your divine mysteries in all their purity and fullness, that your people may be strengthened to serve those in need wherever they may be, for the sake of your Son, Jesus Christ our Lord; who lives and reigns with you and the Holy Spirit, one God, now and forever.

PHP, adapted from a prayer by Löhe

Readings:	Jeremiah 1:4-10
	Psalm 46
	1 Corinthians 3:11-23
	Mark 10:35-45
Hymn of the Day:	
	"Lord, whose love through humble service" (LBW 423, LSB 848, ELW 712, H82 610)
	or "O Son of God, in co-eternal might" (CSB 529), by Löhe, trans. Harriet Reynolds Krauth Spaeth with a tune by her husband, Adolph Spaeth
	or "Wide open stand the gates" (LSB 639), by Löhe
Prayers:	For truth
	For doctrinal purity and clarity
	For missionary concern at home and abroad
	For a deeper understanding of the Holy Communion
	For parish pastors
Preface:	Christmas/Incarnation
Color:	White

January 3

Charles Porterfield Krauth, Teacher, 1883

Charles Porterfield Krauth, the most accomplished American Lutheran scholar and theologian of the nineteenth century, was born in Martinsburg, Virginia (now West Virginia), March 17, 1823. He was graduated from Pennsylvania (later called Gettysburg) College, of which his father, Charles Philip Krauth, was the first president, and from Gettysburg Lutheran Seminary (1841), where his father was a professor. After being licensed to preach by the Maryland Synod in 1841 he served a mission in Canton, Baltimore (1841–1842). He was ordained in 1842 and served Second English Lutheran Church in Baltimore on Lombard Street (1842–1847), Shepherdstown and Martinsburg, [West] Virginia (1847–1848), Winchester, Virginia (1848–1855), First English Lutheran Church in Pittsburgh (1855–1859), and St. Mark's Church in Philadelphia (1859–1861). In 1844 he married Susan Reynolds. Because of her ill health, they wintered in Santa Cruz, West Indies, 1852–1853; she died in 1853. They had three children, one of whom died in infancy. In 1861 Krauth became editor of *The Lutheran and Missionary*, a merger of Philadelphia's *The Lutheran* and William Passavant's *The Missionary*, an influential organ for conservative Lutheran thought.

When the Lutheran Theological Seminary at Philadelphia was founded in 1864 he was named Norton Professor of Dogmatic Theology. Four years later, in addition to his work at the seminary, he became Professor of Mental and Moral Philosophy at the University of Pennsylvania, and in 1873 he became vice-provost of the university. In 1880, authorized by the Ministerium of Pennsylvania, he traveled to Europe to research a life of Luther, which he was not able to begin, and, in addition to his other duties, in 1881 he was named Professor of History at the University of Pennsylvania.

In 1855 Samuel Simon Schmucker of Gettysburg Seminary published his *Definite Platform . . . An American Recension of the Augsburg Confession* in which he charged the basic Lutheran confession of 1530 with five errors, among which were, he said, baptismal regeneration and the real presence of Christ in the sacrament; moreover, he made radical changes to twelve of the twenty-one doctrinal articles of the confession. An opposition conservative party emerged, and one of its principal leaders was Krauth, strongly supported by his Pittsburgh parish. In his inaugural editorial in *The Lutheran and Missionary* (1861), Krauth wrote, "We are 'American Lutherans.' . . . [Our church] must not be afraid to trust herself on this wild current of the quick life of America. She must not cloister herself, but show in her freedom, and in her wise use of the opportunity of the present, that she knows how robust is her spiritual life, and how secure are her principles, however novel or trying the tests to which they are subjected. . . . And yet we are not

American Lutherans, if to be such means that we are to have a new faith, a mutilated confession, a life which abruptly breaks with all our history, a spirit alien to that of the genuine Lutheranism of the past."

The controversy in the Lutheran Church between those who sought accommodation with the prevailing American Protestantism and those who sought to form Lutheran identity as a distinct voice among the American churches led to a division in 1866 and the formation of the General Council out of the leftward-moving General Synod in 1867. Dr. Krauth (he had been awarded the D.D. degree by Pennsylvania College in 1856) was the leading theologian of the General Council, serving for ten years as its president (1870–1880), and contributing mightily to the creation of its liturgical compendium, *The Church Book* (1868). His thorough scholarship was widely recognized outside the Lutheran Church. His great work was *The Conservative Reformation and Its Theology* (1871). In addition to many books and essays in the fields of theology and philosophy, he wrote poems, translated hymns from Latin and German, and was a frequent contributor to religious periodicals. His daughter, Harriet Reynolds Krauth, became the wife of the eminent Lutheran pastor, Adolph Spaeth, and also herself translated hymns from German and the Scandinavian languages and was music editor for *The Church Book with Music* (1893) and the complement to the *Church Book,* the *Sunday School Book.*

Krauth died in Philadelphia January 2, 1883, not yet sixty years old.

FOR FURTHER READING

Krauth, Charles Porterfield. *The Conservative Reformation and its Theology*. St. Louis: Concordia, 2007. Reprint.

Spaeth, Adolph. *Charles Porterfield Krauth, D.D., LL.D.* Vol. I, 1823–1859. New York: Christian Literature Company, 1898. Vol. II, 1859–1883. Philadelphia: General Council Publication House, 1909. The standard and authoritative biography, by Krauth's son-in-law.

READING

From *The Conservative Reformation and Its Theology* by Charles Porterfield Krauth

Well might Luther write upon the table at Marburg: "This is My body;" simple words, framed by infinite wisdom so as to resist the violence and all the ingenuity of men. Rationalism in vain essays to remove them with its cunning, its learning, and its philosophy. Fanaticism gnashes its teeth at them in vain. They are an immovable foundation for faith in the Sacramental mystery, and the gates of hell cannot shake the faith of the Church, that our Lord Jesus Christ with the true body and true blood which He gave for our redemption on the Cross, is truly present in the Holy Supper, to *apply* the redemption through the very organs by which it was *wrought out*. The sacrifice was made once for all—its application goes on to the end of time. The offense of the Master's Cross now rests upon His table, and thither the triumph of the Cross shall follow it. On the Cross and at the table the saints discern the body of the Lord, and in simple faith are determined to know in both nothing but Jesus Christ and Him crucified.

. . . [I]f it be granted that the presence of the body and blood of Christ in the Supper is one which is fixed, absolute, and unchanging, then it must be substantial, and not imaginary; not a thing of our minds, but of His wonderful person; not ideal, but true; faith does not make it, but finds it, unto life; unbelief does not unmake it, but, to its own condemnation, fails to discern it. The sacramental presence is fathomless, like the Incarnation; like it, also, it is in the sphere of supernatural reality, to which the natural is as the shadow. The presence of the communicant at the Supper belongs to a lower sphere of actuality than the presence of the undivided Christ in it; and the outward taking and eating is the divinely appointed means whereby the ineffable mystery of the communion of Christ's body and blood is consummated, a communion heavenly and spiritual in its manner over against all that is earthly and fleshly; but in its essence more true than all earthly truth, more real than all earthly reality, more substantial than all earthly substance. The body and blood of Christ are more truly present in the Supper than are the bread and wine, because their sphere of presence is divine; the bread and wine are but the gifts of the hand of God, the body and blood of Christ are inseparable constituents of God's incarnate person.

Charles Porterfield Krauth, *The Conservative Reformation and Its Theology* (Philadelphia: Lippincott, 1871; Philadelphia: General Council Publication Board, 1899), 619, 647–48.

PROPERS

Almighty God, source of knowledge, wisdom, and faith: We praise you for the gifts you richly bestowed on your servant Charles Porterfield Krauth; and we pray that, by his teaching and example, we may honor the tradition that has been entrusted to us, cherish it, and hand it on in its fullness to generations after us; through your Son Jesus Christ our Lord, who lives and reigns with you and the Holy Spirit, one God, now and forever.

PHP

Readings: Proverbs 3:1-7
              Psalm 119:89-104
              1 Corinthians 2:6-10, 13-16
              Matthew 13:47-52
Hymn of the Day:
              "The bells of Christmas chime once more" (LBW 62, ELW 268), trans. C. P. Krauth
                  [original: "The happy Christmas comes once more" (SBH 28, CSB 23)]
              or "Wide open are your hands" (LBW 489), trans. C. P. Krauth

Prayers: For a renewed appreciation of the tradition of the church
              For a deepened concern for truth and doctrine
              For scholars, teachers, professors, and administrators
              For charity and understanding in times of quarrel and dissent
Preface: Christmas/Incarnation
Color: White

January 5

Kaj Munk, Martyr, 1944

Kaj Harald Leininger Petersen (his given name is pronounced KYE to rhyme with "sky") was born January 13, 1898, in Maribo, on the island of Lolland, Denmark. His father was a tanner and shopkeeper. After his father died, his mother attempted to continue the business but soon died of tuberculosis. The boy, not yet six, was adopted by the Munk family, his distant cousins, in Opanger, and he took their name as his own. He has left a tender tribute to his adoptive mother upon the occasion of her death, in his sermon for the Sixth Sunday after Easter, collected in his volume of collected sermons, *By the Rivers of Babylon*. The pietistic home left a deep impression on the boy and influenced his decision to become a priest. He was tutored privately by Oscar Geismar, a poet and literary critic and supporter of Nikolai Grundtvig's ideas (see September 2), who encouraged him to read the *Iliad* and the *Odyssey* and Scandinavian mythology. Although his family was poor, they were able to send him to Nykøping Cathedral School and at the University of Copenhagen, where he took a degree in theology in 1924. While he was there he came under the influence of Søren Kierkegaard, from whom he learned that the truths of Christianity can only be realized in action.

Munk was ordained priest in 1924 and became pastor at Vedersø in western Jutland, one of the smallest parishes in Denmark. It was his only parish. He married his housekeeper, and they had four children and adopted one child. He was influenced by the two strands of Danish devotion, Grundtvigianism and the evangelical fervor of Indre [Inner] Mission. Munk was respected and loved by his people, and when he suggested that he ought to resign his parish to devote himself to his writing, the parishioners urged him to stay and called an assistant to help with the pastoral work. For a time in the 1930s Munk had admired Hitler and Mussolini, as he had admired Napoleon, but after the occupation of Denmark by Nazi forces in 1940, his powerful sermons drew masses to the resistance, and his own opposition became so outspoken that his plays were banned.

He wrote his first play, *Pilatus* (published in 1938), when he was only nineteen. It revealed his fascination with powerful leaders who triumph over all obstacles.

Munk, an exponent of religious drama with a strong sense of theater, revived heroic Shakespearean and Schillerian drama with writing of a passionate intensity.
His three best plays are *En Idealist*, 1928 (in English translation, *Herod the King*,
1955), which was panned by the critics when it was first staged in Copenhagen;
Ordet, 1932 (English translation, *The Word*, 1955), a miracle play set among the
peasants of Jutland; and *Han Sidder ved Smeltedigeln*, 1938 (English translation,
He Sits at the Melting Pot, 1944), a drama of Hitler's Germany, attacking the persecution of the Jews and presenting a weak man as a hero.

Because of his outspoken resistance, Munk was arrested in the fall of 1943
but was released at Christmas. On the night of January 4, 1944, Munk was taken
from his vicarage by the Gestapo. His body was found the next day in a ditch near
Hørbylunde on the main road to Silkeborg. He had been shot through the head.
His Bible was found some twenty meters from his body, as if it had been taken
away from him before he was killed. More than four thousand people defied Nazi
orders and attended his funeral at Vedersø. A marble cross now marks the place
of his execution.

Kaj Munk is commemorated not only for his own bold witness to the faith
but also as a symbol of the many thousands who bravely but with less attention
resisted Nazi tyranny. A popular telling of the stories of the heroes is found in John
Oram Thomas, *The Giant Killers: The Story of the Danish Resistance Movement
1940–1945* (London: Michael Joseph, 1975). Munk's *Five Plays*, with a preface and
English translations was published in 1953. His sermons have appeared in English
as *Four Sermons* and *By the Rivers of Babylon*. A brief biography is appended to
each volume. *Kaj Munk Playwright, Priest, and Patriot*, ed. R. P. Keigwin, appeared
in 1944. *Kaj Munk* by Sven Stolpe was published in 1944. He is included in the
Encyclopedia of World Literature in the Twentieth Century (vol. 3, 1999). There is a
portrait of Munk in the *Encyclopedia of the Lutheran Church*.

READING

From a sermon for New Year's Day by Kaj Munk

Do not trust too much in the preachers. As a rule they are poorly paid. They are
brought up as humanists. They have forgotten—or never learned—what Christianity is. They have imbibed lo-o-o-ve with the bottle milk in the cradle. In a world
of men they too often plead the cause of the effeminate. They "abstain from politics." They preach peace at any price for the uplift of the devil, who rejoices to see
evil develop in peace. The Scriptures do not say: When your neighbor is smitten
on one cheek it is your duty to hold him so that he may be smitten on the other
cheek also. Do not trust the preachers until they wake up and remember that they
are servants of the whole gospel, and of the Prince of Peace who came not to bring
peace but a sword; of Him who forgave Peter and permitted Judas to hang himself;

JANUARY

of Him who was meek and humble of heart and yet drove the sacrilegists from the temple courts.

And do not trust the majority, which likes to take things easy and therefore is easy to please. . . . Do not trust the great neglected masses. I believe that the heart of the nation is strong, but it has become encased in fat. . . .

This is what our old nation needs; a rejuvenating power, God's rejuvenating strength, that a new people may come forth, which is yet the old, worthy sons of the fathers. The gospel will have to teach the Danish nation to think as a great people; to choose honor rather than profit, freedom rather than a well paid guardianship; to believe in the victory of the spirit of sacrifice; to believe that life comes out of death, and that the future comes out of giving oneself;—in short, faith in Christ. What would it profit a people if it gained all the advantages of the world, but lost its soul?

The cross in our flag—it is long since we realized that it stands for something, and we have forgotten that now. And yet it is the cross that characterizes the flags of the North.—We have come to church—the few of us who go to church, and we have heard about the cross, about Christ's example of suffering, and Christ's words about self-denial and struggle. We have thought that this was all to be taken in a spiritual sense, and that it did not pertain to our time. We thought we were Christians when we sat in Church and sang Amen. But No, No! We are Christians only when we go out into the world and say No to the devil, renounce all his works and all his ways, and say Yes to the Holy Spirit.

Lead us, thou cross in our flag, lead us into that Nordic struggle where shackled Norway and bleeding Finland fight against an idea which is directly opposed all to our ideas. Lead old Denmark forth to its new spirit. Not by the grace of others, or by their promises, shall Danneborg again become a free banner. For freedom only God can give; and he gives it only to those who accept its responsibilities. Lead us, cross in our flag, forward toward unity with other flags of the cross. With honor and liberty regained, the old Denmark in the young North—that vision looms before us this New Year's Day. We who have the vision will give ourselves to its realization. We promise we will. May God hear our vow and add his Amen!

Kaj Munk, *Four Sermons*, trans. J. M. Jensen (Blair: Lutheran Publishing House, 1944), 27, 30–32.

PROPERS

Gracious Lord, in every age you have sent men and women who have given their lives for the message of your love: Inspire us with the example of your servant Kaj Munk, whose faithfulness led him in the way of the cross, and give us courage to bear full witness with our lives to the victory over sin and death won by Jesus Christ our Lord; who lives and reigns with you and the Holy Spirit, one God now and forever.

LBW, ELW Common of Martyrs, rev. PHP

Readings: Ezekiel 20:40-42
                 Psalm 5
                 Revelation 6:9-11
                 Mark 8:34-38
Hymn of the Day:
                 "Thy strong word did cleave the darkness" (LBW 233, LSB 578, ELW 511)
Prayers: For strength to follow Christ into the world
                 For those under persecution
                 For all who resist tyranny
                 For courage to proclaim the whole gospel
                 For the theater: writers, actors, audiences, and all who produce and perform
                 drama
Preface: Christmas/Incarnation
Color: Red

January 6

The Epiphany of Our Lord

A Christian observance of January 6 is found as early as the end of the second century in Egypt, as attested by the writings of Clement of Alexandria. After Easter and Pentecost, the Epiphany is therefore the oldest festival in the church year.

Easter and Pentecost both have Jewish antecedents. The Epiphany also has ancient sources, but the origins of the feast are disputed. Older studies suggested that both Christmas and Epiphany are related to pagan solstice festivals. Epiphanius (*ca.* 315–403) notes that in Egypt there was a night festival on the 11th of Tybi (January 5–6) celebrating the birth of the god Aion, god of time and eternity and protector of Alexandria, from a virgin, Kore. The waters of the Nile, it was thought, acquired miraculous powers and turned to wine that night, and the celebration involved a ritual drawing of water from the Nile at the beginning of the year. A festival in honor of Dionysus on January 5, Pater Liber, is mentioned by Pliny the Younger. The Christian celebration focused on the Baptism of Jesus because the Egyptian Church at the beginning of the year began the reading of the Gospel according to St. Mark, which begins with Jesus' baptism. There came into existence, at least in the East, a Christian festival that echoed the ancient solstice celebration and which was called "the Holy Day of Lights" or "the Day of Holy Lights," commemorating the manifestation of God in the birth and baptism of Jesus.

Such is what has been called the "history of religions hypothesis." Careful study of the sources, however, fails to establish a close relationship between any pagan festivals and the Epiphany, and in the later twentieth century another hypothesis was developed based on the relationship between the date of Jesus' death and conception and birth. In Asia Minor Christians celebrated their paschal festival at the same time as the Jewish Passover. Passover is celebrated on the 14th day of Nisan, the first month of spring in the Jewish lunar calendar. The Christians followed a solar calendar and set their paschal feast on the 14th day of Artemesios, the first month of spring in the solar calendar. When that Asian date was replaced with the Roman version of the Julian calendar, the result was April 6. Because Christian devotion understood Jesus' perfect life to have begun and ended on the same date, the beginning of the Incarnation, his conception, was thought to have taken place on what was also to be date of his crucifixion, April 6. His birth therefore would have been exactly nine months later, January 6.

The oldest name for this feast, still used by the Orthodox Churches, seems to have been "Theophany," suggesting the origin of the day as a commemoration of the incarnation as the revelation of God. The name *Epiphany* derives from a Greek word meaning "appearing" or "manifestation." In the Graeco-Roman world, a state visit of a king or emperor to a city of his realm, especially when he showed himself publicly to the people, was called an epiphany. In the East the Epiphany of Christ has always had a more theological and less historical or commemorative character, so the baptism rather than the birth of Christ was selected as the event to illustrate the doctrine of the manifestation of God to the world in Jesus Christ. The generous use of incense on this day is especially appropriate to honor God whose revelation is celebrated.

The Church in Alexandria emphasized the baptism of Jesus as a principal component of the Epiphany festival as a manifestation of who Jesus is. Mark's Gospel, traditionally associated with Alexandria, begins directly with the account of the baptism of Jesus by John. By the fourth century, especially in Gaul and northern Italy, Jesus' first miracle and revelation of his divine power, turning water into wine at the wedding at Cana, had became a part of the thematic richness of the feast of the Epiphany. Very early in the celebration of this feast, three mysteries of the manifestation of the divinity of Christ were combined: the visit of the Magi, the baptism of Christ, and Jesus' first miracle at the wedding feast at Cana. These several themes are gathered and interwoven in a splendid antiphon to the Benedictus at Lauds (Morning Praise) for the Epiphany:

> Today the Bridegroom claims his bride, the Church,
> > since Christ has washed away her sins in the waters of the Jordan;
> the Magi hasten to the royal wedding;
> and the wedding guests rejoice, for Christ has changed water into wine, alleluia.

In the East, therefore, January 6 was observed as a feast of the baptism of Jesus and of his first miracle at Cana; in the West, the observance of December 25 was a celebration of Jesus' birth and the visit of the Magi. In the second half of the fourth century an exchange of feasts took place, and both feasts came to be celebrated by the vast majority of Christians in both East and West.

With the spread of Christmas as the celebration of Christ's birth, the Epiphany was, in the West, coming to be associated with the visit of the Magi, in part, perhaps, because of the transfer of the relics of the Magi from Constantinople in the fifth century. The *Excerpta et Collecteana* associated with the Venerable Bede gives the number of the Magi as three and supplies their names as well as a fanciful description of each and a symbolic interpretation of the gift each brought.

> The Magi were the ones who gave gifts to the Lord. The first is said to have been Melchior, an old man with white hair and a long beard . . . who offered gold to the Lord as king. The second, named Gaspar [Caspar], young and beardless and ruddy-complexioned . . . honored him as God by his gift of incense, and offering worthy of divinity. The third, black-skinned and heavily bearded, called Balthasar . . . by his gift of myrrh testified to the Son of Man who was to die.

This description has influenced the portrayal of the Magi ever since.

Matthew's note that the Magi entered "the house" to offer their gifts to the Christ Child encouraged the development of the practice in many parts of Europe of blessing homes on this feast. As a sign of the blessing, three initials representing the traditional names the Magi (K [Kaspar, sometimes Caspar or Gaspar], M [Melchior], and B [Balthasar]), were marked in chalk over the doors of houses, each initial preceded by a cross signifying "holy or "saint." Thus for the year 2008: 20 ✚ K ✚ M ✚ B 08. The letters have also been understood to stand for *Christus mansionem benedicat*, Christ bless this house. The Roman Catholic *Book of Blessings* still has a form for blessing of chalk for this use; there is an order for such blessing of houses in the Episcopal *Book of Occasional Services.*

A useful Epiphany custom is a procession to the crib with children dressed and crowned as kings, bearing symbolic gifts for the Christ child: gold (money), incense (perhaps just a stick of incense to be burned in his honor), and a cross or other sign of his death. The three gifts have been understood to proclaim three mysteries: gold for a king, incense for a God, and myrrh for his burial. A star on a staff may replace the processional cross on this day.

Before people had ready access to calendars, it became a custom at the Epiphany to announce the dates of the feasts that would occur later in the year: Septuagesima (pre-Lent), Ash Wednesday, Easter Day, the Ascension, Pentecost, and the First Sunday in Advent. A modern form of the announcement is this, for the year 2008.

> Dear brothers and sisters, the glory of the Lord has shone upon us, and shall ever be manifest among us until the day of his return. Through the rhythms and times and seasons, let us celebrate the mystery of salvation. Let us recall the year's culmination, the Easter Triduum of the Lord: his Last Supper, his crucifixion, his burial, and his resurrection celebrated between the evening of the 20th of March and the evening of the 23rd of March. Each Easter, as on each Sunday, the holy Church makes present the great and saving deed by which Christ has for ever conquered sin and death. From Easter are reckoned all the days we keep holy. Ash Wednesday, the beginning of Lent, will occur on the 6th of February. The Ascension of Our Lord will be commemorated on the 1st of May, and the joyful conclusion of Easter, the Day of Pentecost, will be

celebrated on the 11th of May. Likewise the pilgrim Church proclaims the Passover of Christ in the feasts of the holy mother of God, in the feasts of the apostles, martyrs, and saints, and in the commemoration of the faithful departed.

To Jesus Christ, who was, who is, and who is to come, the Lord of time and history, be endless praise, forever and ever.

The tradition of the announcement of the church year has been preserved in some places and revived in many others because it teaches that the celebration of the Nativity is only the beginning of the liturgical celebration of Christ's life and that it has its culmination in the Paschal Mystery, the center of the liturgical year. Moreover, the announcement on the feast of the Epiphany, the manifestation of Christ to the Gentiles, is an anticipation of the parousia, when Christ will come again in all his glory to gather the nations under his gentle rule.

FOR FURTHER READING

Adam, Adolf. *The Liturgical Year*. New York: Pueblo, 1981.

Alexander, J. Neil. *Waiting for the Coming: The Liturgical Meaning of Advent, Christmas, Epiphany*. Washington: Pastoral, 1993.

Brown, Raymond E. *The Birth of the Messiah*. Garden City: Doubleday, 1977.

Nocent, Adrian. *The Liturgical Year,* vol. 1 Advent, Christmas, Epiphany. Collegeville: Liturgical, 1977.

Talley, Thomas J. *The Origins of the Liturgical Year: Second Emended Edition*. Collegeville: Liturgical, 1991.

READING

From a sermon by Ernst P. Pfatteicher

The testimony of the Magi is the testimony of the learned men of their day; the testimony of heathen lands, a testimony that Christ had come to "lighten the Gentiles."

The final testimony . . . follows a preliminary testimony which demands a trial of their faith. In the case of the shepherds the message "unto you is born this day in the city of David a Savior" calls forth faith as the shepherds say, one to another, "let us now go even unto Bethlehem, and see this thing which is come to pass, which the Lord made known unto us." In the case of Simeon and Anna, life has been a long-continued assertion of faith. Their constant attendance upon temple services and ministrations was the resultant of their faith, a faith that was to find its full fruition in the coming of the Messiah. Was the faith of the Magi a lesser thing as it impelled them to seek the fruition of their hopes in subjecting themselves to a long and tedious caravan journey? The New Testament is thus born in an atmosphere of faith. As Abraham's faith was tested many centuries before when he was told to count the stars and thus count his seed, the New Testament points to but one star, it may be, but lends to it a significance which is supreme. . . .

To the Magi the study of the heavenly bodies . . . was their program of life. They sought thus to interpret life. Fortunately they did not spend all their time in star gazing. They endeavored to apply the lessons which star gazing taught them. Why did they leave home? Was it to obtain a better vantage point from which to observe the peculiar constellation which had swung into their ken? Was it to consult with others eminent as star gazers? You know very well from the statement with which they greeted Herod what their purpose was in setting forth upon their journey. "Where is He that is born King of the Jews? For we have seen His star in its rising, and are come to worship Him." The star had not appeared to them the day before. They had had abundant opportunity to be cured of any superstitious emotions, moods of frenzy or fanatical zeal on their journey, and perhaps for some time before they started, for when Herod later carried his terrible decree concerning the Innocents into execution, he ordered that all children two years of age and under must be put to death "according to the time which he had diligently enquired of the wise men." The remarkable thing about this story is its very deliberateness. Not that they might advance their studies, but that they might worship the King of the Jews did the Magi set forth upon their pilgrimage. The constellation was not the goal of their journey. They lost sight of that, and they expressed manifest surprise when it reappeared as they were leaving Jerusalem. Nor did they look upon an interview with Herod as their goal. They followed their star from the holy city to the little town of Bethlehem and there lost sight of it, not necessarily because the constellation was no longer visible, for we are clearly told that it stood over the house where the young child was, but because they needed no planetary constellation after having approached the Light of the World. . . .

Herod's thoughts centered solely in the preservation of his throne. He ignored personal and national righteousness. The appearance of the Star of the Christ signifies the ultimate destruction of the sort of power, the sort of reign he represented. The door of entrance into the spiritual kingdom of the King of the Jews was open to Herod and his court. He might have accompanied the Magi in their onward march. He would have sacrificed nothing by so doing. The star of Herod was not the star of the Christ, however. The gloom and misery and darkness in Rama were caused by a conflict between these stars. The powers of darkness will ever continue to endeavor to obscure the true star. Herod will ever try to outwit the Magi. . . .

The Magi are representatives of the Gentile world and would tell us ere the story of the Nativity must give way to other stories of the Christ that the good tidings are, without doubt, intended for all people who will arise and accompany them to Bethlehem.

From Ernst P. Pfatteicher, *Sermons on the Gospels: Advent to Trinity* (Philadelphia: General Council Publication House, 1918), 80–86.

PROPERS

O God, by the leading of a star you manifested your only Son to the peoples of the earth: Lead us, who know you now by faith, to your presence, where we may see your glory face to face; through Jesus Christ our Lord, who lives and reigns with you and the Holy Spirit, one God, now and forever.

Gregorian sacramentary, trans. (BCP)

Readings: Isaiah 60:1-6 (9)
                Psalm 72
                Ephesians 3:(1) 2-12
                Matthew 2:1-12
Hymn of the Day:
                "Earth has many a noble city" (H82 127, LBW 81)
Prayers: For the nations of the earth
                For seekers of wisdom
                For the spirit of humility and reverence
                For those who bring offerings to God
                For churches named for the mystery of the Epiphany, for which this day is their
                        feast of title
Preface: Epiphany
Color: White

January 9

The Episcopal *Lesser Feasts and Fasts 1997* introduced on this date the commemoration of **Julia Chester Emery**, who was for forty years Secretary of the Woman's Auxiliary of the Board of Missions of the Episcopal Church. She traveled widely throughout the United States and the world, visiting and encouraging missions and mission support. She died in 1922.

January 10

William Laud was born in 1573 and became Archbishop of Canterbury in 1633. Because of his opposition to the Puritans and his advocacy of pre-Reformation practices he was widely disliked. He was beheaded January 10, 1645, honored by some as a martyr and condemned by others as intolerant. His deep piety and loving concern for the Church is evident in his prayer,

> Gracious Father, we pray for thy holy Catholic Church. Fill it with all truth, in all truth with all peace. Where it is corrupt, purify it; where it is in error direct it; where in

anything it is amiss, reform it. Where it is right, strengthen it; where it is want, provide for it; where it is divided, reunite it, for the sake of Jesus Christ, thy Son our Savior. [BCP p. 816, no. 7; SBH p. 218, no. 4; LBW p. 45, no. 189; ELW p. 73.]

January 12

Aelred, Abbot of Rievaulx, 1167

Aelred [or Ailred; his name, variously spelled, is a contraction of Aethelred], a singularly attractive figure of particular interest to English Christians, was born in 1109, the son and grandson of Saxon priests. At an early age he was taken into the service of King David of Scotland. When he was twenty-four, after an inward struggle, he entered the Cistercian Order at the abbey of Rievaulx (pronounced ree-VOH) in 1133 and soon became a major figure in English church life, earning a reputation as "the English St. Bernard" [of Clairvaux]. He founded a new abbey at Revesby in 1143, and in 1147 returned to Rievaulx as its abbot. He died at his monastery in 1167. Since at the time of Aelred's death the papacy had not yet centralized the process of canonization, there was no formal ratification by the Roman See of Aelred's sanctity.

Aelred was distinguished for his energy and his sympathetic gentleness, particularly associated with friendship both human and divine. His major work was *Spiritual Friendship*, a kind of counterpart to Cicero's *On Friendship*, and one of the most beautiful works of the Middle Ages, defining spiritual friendship as perfect mutuality in charity, attaining on earth a first realization and foreshadowing of the joy of heaven. Aelred's biography was written by his pupil Walter Daniel (*The Life of Ailred of Rievaulx by Walter Daniel*, English trans. with notes, 1950).

Aelred was introduced to the Episcopal calendar in *Lesser Feasts and Fasts 1997*; he is not on the General Roman nor on the Lutheran calendar.

FOR FURTHER READING

Dutton, Marsha L., ed. *Aelred of Rieveaulx. The Historical Works*. Trans. Jane Patricia Freeland. Collegeville: Cistercian, 2005.

Harvey, T. Edmund. *St. Aelred of Rievaulx*. London: H. R. Allenson, 1932.

Powicke, F. M., trans. *The Life of Aelred of Rievaulx by Walter Daniel*. Washington: Cistercian, 1994.

Sommerfeldt, John R. *Aelred of Rievaulx: Pursuing Perfect Happiness*. Mahwah: Paulist, 2005.

Squire, Aelred. *Aelred of Rievaulx: A Study*. London: SPCK, 1981.

READING

From *Spiritual Friendship* by Aelred of Rievaulx

[A] friend praying to Christ on behalf of his friend, and for his friend's sake desiring to be heard by Christ, directs his attention with love and longing to Christ;
then it sometimes happens that quickly and imperceptibly the one love passes
over into the other, and coming, as it were, into close contact with the sweetness of Christ himself, the friend begins to taste his sweetness and to experience
his charm. Thus ascending from that holy love with which he embraces a friend
to that with which he embraces Christ, he will joyfully partake in abundance of
the spiritual fruit of friendship, awaiting the fullness of all things in the life to
come. Then, with the dispelling of all anxiety by reason of which we now fear
and are solicitous for one another, with the removal of all adversity which it now
behooves us to bear for one another, and, above all, with the destruction of the
sting of death together with death itself, whose pangs now often trouble us and
force us to grieve for one another, with salvation secured, we shall rejoice in the
eternal possession of Supreme Goodness; and this friendship, to which here we
admit but few, will be outpoured upon all and by all outpoured upon God, and
God shall be all in all.

Aelred of Rievaulx, *Spiritual Friendship* III.133-134, trans. Mary Eugenia Laker (Washington:
Cistercian, Consortium, 1974), 131–32.

PROPERS

Pour into our hearts, O God, the Holy Spirit's gift of love, that we, clasping each
the other's hand, may share the joy of friendship, human and divine, and with
your servant Aelred draw many to your community of love; through Jesus Christ
the Righteous, who lives and reigns with you and the Holy Spirit, one God, now
and forever.

LFF

Readings:	Psalm 36:5-10 *or* 145:8-13*
	Philippians 2:1-4
	John 15:9-17 *or* Mark 12:28-34a
	(* "Because the Psalm assigned to a given Proper can sometimes occur at Morn-ing or Evening Prayer on the same day, alternative Psalmody is always pro-vided . . . drawn from a small corpus of selected psalms." LFF, p. 85.)
Hymn of the Day:	
	"What a friend we have in Jesus" (LBW 439, LSB 770, ELW 742, H40 422)
Prayers:	For our friends
	For the gift of gentleness and understanding
	For increased love for our neighbors
	For greater love for God
Preface:	A Saint (2) (BCP)
Color:	White

January 13

Hilary, Bishop of Poitiers, 367

Hilary (his name derives from *hilaris*, "cheerful"), praised by Augustine as "the illustrious doctor [that is, teacher] of all the churches," was born in Poitiers, Gaul, about 315 to a wealthy and powerful pagan family. He was baptized when he was about thirty years of age, and in 350, although he was married and a layman, he was made bishop of Poitiers by popular acclamation and insistence. His tenure was troubled by controversy with the Arians, who denied the divinity of Christ. In 356 the Emperor Constantinus, because Hilary did not accede to his demand that all Western bishops adhere to a compromised Nicene faith, banished him to Phrygia in Asia Minor. He remained there for three years, writing scriptural commentaries and his great work *On the Trinity*. He was allowed to return to Poitiers in 360, to the great joy of his people, and from that time on his teaching gained general acceptance in Gaul. He became the most respected Latin theologian of his age, and because of his time in Asia Minor he was able to introduce some of the insights of the Eastern theologians into the Western Church.

St. Jerome says that Hilary wrote the first Latin hymns. During his exile Hilary was profoundly impressed with the singing of Greek hymns, and he says that when he returned to the West he brought some of these hymns with him. Most of Hilary's hymns have perished, but a few, notably *Lucis largitor splendide*, are with some reliability attributed to him. These hymns, in the judgment of John Julian's *Dictionary of Hymnology*, "are not without a certain rugged grandeur, well befitting the liturgical purposes they were intended to serve." These hymns introduced "the first germs of Latin rhythms" which were to flourish in later Latin hymnody. But Hilary's efforts at introducing hymns into the Church in Gaul were unsuccessful, and he complained that the Gauls were unteachable in sacred song. Success in introducing hymn singing in the West came with Ambrose.

An inveterate and vigorous controversialist and a tireless defender and teacher of Orthodoxy, Hilary was nonetheless a compassionate and loving pastor. Among his disciples was Martin, later Bishop of Tours (see November 11). Hilary died in Poitiers on this date in 367.

READING

From Book 1 of *On the Trinity* by Hilary

Almighty God and Father, I regard it as the chief duty of my life to make my every thought and word speak of you. The gift of speech which you gave me cannot have a more noble use than to serve you by making you known as the Father of the only-begotten Son of God, and preaching this to the world that does not know you and to the heretics who refuse to believe in you.

That is what I desire to do. But I need to pray for your help and mercy, so that, when I spread the sails of our faith you will fill them with the breath of your Spirit to drive us onward. I need not be afraid. We have the promise, and he who made the promise is trustworthy, "Ask and it will be given you; search, and you will find; knock, and the door will be opened for you" [Matt. 7:7].

In our need we will ask for what we lack. We will study the writings of your prophets and apostles with unflagging attention and knock on the doors where meaning is kept. But it is for you, Lord, to give when asked, to be present when we seek you, and to open when we knock.

Our nature is sluggish, and in our attempt to penetrate your truth the weakness of our minds holds us in the prison of ignorance. Nonetheless, we are able to comprehend divine ideas by earnest attention to your teaching and by obedience to the faith which carries us beyond the natural range of our minds.

Help us therefore as we begin this ambitious venture, and bless it with good results. Give us a share in the spirit of your prophets and apostles so that we may understand precisely what they meant to say and express their meaning in appropriate terms. Our subject will be the mystery of which they spoke: you, the eternal God, the Father of the eternal, only-begotten God; you, the unbegotten God and the one Lord Jesus Christ, born of you from all eternity. He is not another god, as though different from you in nature, but he is himself true God, born of you who are the true God and Father.

Impart to us, then, the meaning of the words of Scripture and the light to understand it, honoring the doctrine and confident of its truth.

Trans. PHP, based on that of *A Short Breviary* by St. John's Abbey and the International Committee on English in the Liturgy.

PROPERS

Almighty God, your servant Hilary defended the divinity of Jesus Christ your Son: Give us, we pray, a deeper understanding of this mystery and help us profess it in all truth, that we may rejoice in having you for our Father, and may abide in your Son, in the fellowship of the Holy Spirit; who live and reign, one God, now and forever.

PHP, Proper of Poitiers, RS, ✝ LFF

Readings:	Psalm 37:3-6, 32-33 *or* 119:97-104
	1 John 2:18-25
	Luke 12:8-12 *or* John 15:9-17
Hymn of the Day:	
	"Father, most holy" (LBW 169, LSB 504, ELW 415)
	see "Hail this joyful day's return" (H82 223, 224), a hymn for Pentecost attributed to Hilary

Prayers:	For teachers of theology facing opposition because of the adherence to the apostolic faith
	For bishops that they defend and maintain the catholic faith
	For closer relations between the Eastern and the Western Churches
Preface:	Trinity Sunday
Color:	White

January 14

Eivind Josef Berggrav, Bishop of Oslo, 1959

E ivind Berggrav was born October 25, 1884 in the port city of Stavanger, in the southwestern part of Norway. He was the son of the bishop of Hamar, Otto Jensen. The name Berggrav, taken by the son, is thought to mean "mountain diggers," for his ancestors, like Luther's, were miners in Thuringia. They were invited to Norway in 1624 to work the Konigsberg silver mines. Eivind Berggrav first planned a career in engineering, but he was drawn to the ministry and received his master's degree in theology in 1908. Nonetheless, for ten years following his graduation he served as editor of *Kirke og Kultur*, studying the psychology of religion and wrestling with his own vocation. He also served as a teacher in a folk school in Eidsvoll, 1909–1914, and as headmaster of Holmestrand Teachers' College, 1914–1915. He studied at Oxford and Cambridge Universities in 1914 and in Berlin in 1916. Finally, in 1919 he was ordained by the Church of Norway and became the pastor of a rural parish, Hurdal, near Oslo. In 1925 he became a prison chaplain in Oslo, and while there he earned his doctorate from the University of Oslo for his work *The Threshold of Religion*.

In 1928 he was elected bishop of Tromsø in the extreme north of Norway, a diocese of fishermen, fur trappers, and seamen, which reached to the land of the Lapps. In 1937 he was made Bishop of Oslo and Primate of Norway.

He was elected president of the World Alliance for Promoting International Friendship through the Churches in 1938 and in the following year on the outbreak of war called a conference of Scandinavian Church leaders. In May 1940, a month after the Nazis invaded the country, Berggrav was named one of the negotiators to determine the intentions of the Nazi occupation. He withdrew from the commission after two days, refusing to offer a compromise to the Germans. With the six other bishops of Norway he led the opposition to the Nazi edicts and insisted on the right of clerical confidence, noninterference in the spiritual province of the Church, and the rights of the Jews. With the other bishops he resigned February 24, 1941, "what the state has committed to my charge," at the same time declaring, "the spiritual calling which has been ordained to me at the altar of God remains mine by God and by right." Berggrav consolidated a united front against the Nazis and wrote declarations and confessional documents in the *Kirchenkampf* (church struggle).

On February 1, 1942, Vidkun Quisling was appointed head of the Nazi-controlled government. Bishop Berggrav, deprived by Quisling of the title of bishop and designated "an ordinary private person," was put under house arrest on Maundy Thursday, April 2. In protest, all the bishops and 797 of the 861 priests of the Church of Norway resigned their offices at Easter. Berggrav was then imprisoned on the charge of instigating rebellion and then placed again under house arrest as a solitary prisoner in a log cabin on the outskirts of Oslo, reportedly at the direction of Adolf Hitler because of reports of widespread public unrest. An underground church was formed to continue religious life independent of the Quisling regime. Berggrav in disguise was able to meet with the church. In April 1945 he escaped and remained in hiding in Oslo until the liberation of Norway shortly afterward.

After the war, in the reorganization of the Church, he recommended a more active participation by lay people in the affairs of the Church. He was a leader in the World Council of Churches from its founding in 1948 and in the Lutheran World Federation. Ill health forced him to resign his bishopric in 1950. He died on this date in 1959.

Berggrav published many books in the area of the psychology of religion: *Soldier Life and Religion* (1915), *The Threshold of Religion* (1925), *Religious Feelings* (1928), *The Prisoner's Soul* (1928), *Body and Soul* (1933). His *Biblical History* and his edition of Luther's *Small Catechism* have been widely used in schools in Norway. He also published *With God in the Darkness* (1943) and *When the Fight Came* (1945) about his war experiences, *Church Order in Norway* about the reorganization of the Church, and *Man and State*, a study of basic ethical questions. He translated into English a hymn by Peter Dass, "Mighty God, to thy dear Name be given," which was included as hymn number 357 in the *Service Book and Hymnal* (1958).

FOR FURTHER READING

Godal, Odd. *Eivind Berggrav. Leader of the Christian Resistance.* London: SCM, 1949.

Johnson, Alex. *Eivind Berggrav: God's Man of Suspense.* Trans. K. Jordhelm with H. Overholt. Minneapolis: Augsburg, 1960.

READING

From Eivind Berggrav, *Man and State*, written secretly
while under house arrest by the Nazis

It cannot be denied that revolt is Christian. Nor is it enough to say that one must
only turn in cases of necessity to revolt with arms or without. When men are
mutiny-minded they can insist that a case of necessity exists every time something
opposes their own wishes. That is why it is a good thing that revolt or mutiny
always involves great outward risk. For one who is subject to an authoritative conscience, however, there is an even greater risk of the judgment of God.

Christianity has always maintained that a willingness to suffer is a practical test
of whether we are rightly related to God. Christianity has therefore designated as
absolutely sinful any mutiny based solely on personal desire. At this point the Christian Church must preach uncompromising obedience. Here Paul and the Epistle to
the Romans are in complete agreement with the popular Lutheran interpretation.
The Christian must even be willing to suffer considerable injustice against himself.
If opposition to those in power is necessary it should be on the ground that others
have suffered unduly and on the presupposition that such action would bring still
more suffering to oneself. Thomas Aquinas says, "To bear with patience the evil
which is committed against one is a sign of perfection. To be patient, however, with
the evil which is done to others, is a sign of imperfection yea, it is a sin."

It must be remembered, however, that suffering can be a dangerous test if one
takes as one's starting point the natural desire to want to get off cheap. In that case
the possibility of suffering would restrain one from undertaking anything. That
is why it is equally important to make the Christian's burning challenge to withstand all unrighteousness the criterion. Where God's orders are trodden underfoot and the right of one's fellow man to live is threatened at the very outset, there
the Christian must be willing to go the way of sacrifice, even if it involves revolt
against illegal authority. Keeping in touch with the conscience of one's fellows,
i.e., with the corporate conscience, will constitute the greatest controlling factor.
At a time of decision Cromwell said to his followers, "I charge you, Christians, to
search your hearts and to consider whether you may not have erred."

But if conscience is rooted in God then a social matter is *also* God's concern.
It is inappropriate for a Christian to say that the freedom of the Church or of
God's Word is not yet directly threatened and we ought to take suffering and strife
upon ourselves just for the sake of "secular matters." There are no such things
as "secular matters" for a Christian conscience. The moment that God calls on
him to assume them they are God's concern as far as he is concerned. This is the
explanation of that fact that the two expressions "to suffer for Jesus' sake" and "to
suffer for righteousness' sake" stand side by side in the Sermon on the Mount. The
moment conscience has received its orders and is willing to accept suffering and
sacrifice, the thing becomes more than social. It then signifies covenant relationship with God.

The words on John Knox's tombstone are a challenging note about the strongest radical guaranty in this life: "Here lies the man who never feared the face of any man."

Eivind Josef Berggrav, *Man and State,* trans. George Aus (Philadelphia: Muhlenberg, 1951), 282–84.

PROPERS

Mighty God, you gave your servant Eivind Berggrav, together with the bishops and faithful priests of Norway, strength and courage to resist tyranny, to defend your ancient people the Jews, and to uphold the rights of your church: So strengthen our faith by their witness, we pray, that we in our generation may serve you faithfully and confess your Name before the world; through your Son, Jesus Christ our Lord, who lives and reigns with you and the Holy Spirit, one God, now and forever.

PHP

Readings:	Ezekiel 34: 11-16
	Psalm 84
	1 Peter 5:1-4
	John 21:15-17
Hymn of the Day:	
	"Bow down your ear, almighty Lord" (LBW 286)
	or "Mighty God, to thy dear Name be given" (SBH 357; see LBW 244, ELW 730)
Prayers:	For those under persecution
	For those who resist tyranny
	For those in prison
	For those who explore relationships between religion and culture
	For colleges and schools
Preface:	Epiphany
Color:	White

January 15 [see April 4]

This day, ***Martin Luther King Jr.'s*** birthday, may be observed as his commemoration as the calendars in the *Lutheran Book of Worship* and *Evangelical Lutheran Worship* provide in recognition of the civil holiday in the United States. The observance of the civil holiday, however, takes place not on January 15 but on the third Monday in January. It is more liturgically appropriate for the commemoration to be kept on the day of his death, April 4 (unless the day conflicts with Holy Week or Easter Week), as the Episcopal *Lesser Feasts and Fasts* and the Methodist *For All the Saints* provide. Information about Dr. King therefore may be found at April 4.

January 16

George Fox, Renewer of Society, 1691
(transferred from January 13)
   with William Penn, 1644
   Robert Barclay, 1690
   John Woolman, 1772

George Fox, a weaver's son, was born in July 1624 in the village of Drayton-in-the-Clay (now Fenny Drayton), Leicestershire, England. He was apprenticed for a time to a shoemaker; he may also have been a shepherd. There is little evidence that he had any formal education, yet he read extensively.

His religious background seems to have been Puritan, but he found this not entirely satisfying. At the age of eighteen, he left home on a religious quest. During his search he experienced several "openings" as he called them in his *Journal,* which he thought corrected traditional concepts of faith and life in English religion. He went beyond the Puritan reaction to the forms of the established Church, and after long and intense struggle, he arrived at the central belief of his life, that God speaks inwardly and directly to a person's heart. Finding no comfort in the Church and receiving no help from its ministers, he became a wandering preacher, proclaiming the God-given inward light as the real source of authority above creeds and even above Scripture itself.

He traveled on foot, preaching in the Midlands and then in the northern counties of England. Local congregations were established by Fox and by other itinerant men and women preachers who called themselves "Publishers of the Truth." Fox had most success first in Westmoreland and later in Lancashire, Yorkshire, and London. His radical views and his peculiar habits (wearing a leather suit, sitting in hollow trees, refusing to take his hat off to anyone) provoked derision and hostility. He was beaten, stoned, put in the stocks, imprisoned. Between 1649 and 1673 he was jailed eight times. Altogether in his lifetime he spent seven years in jail, often in filthy conditions, which he sought to reform. Nevertheless, he persisted and gained a considerable following, not only among the poor and uncultured but also among people of wealth and distinction such as William Penn, who left an important summary of Fox's character. A man of enormous yet attractive self-confidence, Fox covered England with his influence and generated a new sense of morality. Shopkeepers of this persuasion were universally respected for their integrity.

His followers were persecuted because they refused to take oaths or to pay tithes. The restoration of the monarchy in 1660 led to special legislation and action against the "Quakers" as they were derisively nicknamed. Fox encouraged the local groups of his followers to organize into regular monthly and quarterly business meetings, and this became the permanent pattern of church government for the "Religious Society of Friends." Not until the Toleration Act of 1689 were the Quakers legally accepted.

In 1669, after his return from a missionary trip to Ireland, Fox married Margaret Fell, one of his early converts. She was the widow of Judge Thomas Fell of Swarthmore Hall, Ulverston, Lancashire. It was in this house that Fox lived from time to time in the years following. From 1671 to 1673 he visited the British colonies in the Caribbean and North America, especially Maryland and Rhode Island, strengthening communities of Friends there. He also saw firsthand the horrors of the slave trade, and upon his return to England, he founded the abolitionist movement. In 1677 and 1684 he journeyed to Holland and northern Europe.

Fox died on the thirteenth of January (or as the Friends style it, First Month), 1691 and was buried in the Friends' burial ground near Bunhill Fields. He is commemorated on this date, January 13, on the calendar in the *Lutheran Book of Worship,* the Methodist *For All the Saints,* the German Lutheran Calendar of Names by Frieder Schulz and others (1962), and the *Christian Year* calendar (1997) of the Church of England. George Fox contributed to the renewal of the church by calling into question its pride and self-satisfaction. But perhaps his greatest contribution is to the renewal of society in two principal ways: complete religious toleration and the equality of everyone before the law.

FOR FURTHER READING

Elwood, Thomas, ed. *The Journal of George Fox.* Introduction by William Penn. 1694.

Ingle, H. Larry. *First Among Friends: George Fox and the Creation of Quakerism.* New York: Oxford University Press, 1994.

Jones, Rufus M. *George Fox: Seeker and Friend.* New York: Harper, 1930.

Nickalls, John L., ed. *The Journal of George Fox.* Cambridge: Cambridge University Press, 1952.

Noble, Vernon. *The Man in Leather Breeches.* New York: Philosophical Library, 1953.

Wildes, Harry Emerson. *The Voice of the Lord.* Philadelphia: University of Pennsylvania Press, 1965.

Together with George Fox, three others of the Society of Friends might fittingly be remembered. **William Penn** was born in 1644, the son of a Cromwellian admiral who had become rich and powerful. He was a quiet, introspective child, naturally drawn to the teachings of George Fox, perhaps the first person of means, learning, and high social standing to join the Society of Friends. He took the teaching of George Fox and combined it with the work of a French theologian Moise

Amyraut, who had argued that God's laws live in the hearts of people and that one learns by listening to the voice of conscience, and popularized it through tracts and pamphlets, printed secretly and disseminated widely. Penn, like others in the movement, was often imprisoned. He obtained the forty-five-thousand square miles of Pennsylvania from Charles II in 1682 and regarded his colony there as a "holy experiment." Steadfastly committed to democratic principles, he established free public education in his commonwealth as well as chartering a public school (in current American usage a private school) in Philadelphia that now bears his name, the William Penn Charter School, worked for better food and housing, regarded women as the equals of men, and established religious freedom. He suffered two strokes and lived out his last years in England in frail health. He died there July 30, 1718. Penn is included on the German Evangelical Calender of Names (1966) on July 30.

Robert Barclay was the foremost theologian of the Society of Friends and, with William Penn, the movement's most influential writer. He was born December 23, 1648, and was educated at the Roman Catholic Scottish College in Paris. He joined the Society of Friends in 1667. His humanitarian and his pacifist precepts are still followed, but his most important writing was *An Apology for the True Christian Divinity: Being an Explanation and Vindication of the People Called Quakers* (Latin 1676, English 1678). This became the standard statement of Quaker doctrine and set forth fifteen propositions against both the Roman Catholic and the Protestant positions, affirming that neither church nor Scripture could claim ultimate authority, but that both church and Scripture are secondary to the work of the Holy Spirit. Barclay was often imprisoned for his beliefs. He traveled through Germany and Holland advancing his views, and upon his return home he won the friendship of the Duke of York (later James II), who helped him obtain a patent to settle New Jersey. In 1683 Robert Barclay was himself governor of eastern New Jersey. He returned to his native Scotland, where he died at his estate in Aberdeen, October 3, 1690.

John Woolman, judged by Elton Trueblood to be "the most highly respected Quaker who ever lived," is a notable exemplar of ethical living. Born in 1720, he lived in Mount Holly, New Jersey, near Philadelphia, and worked as a tailor. He traveled widely as an itinerant preacher. He vigorously attacked slavery and roused the conscience of the Quakers against it and through them the whole Western world. He refused to pay taxes in support of the French and Indian War. He taught and practiced simple living both for individual and for social good, to the extent of giving up his store when business got too brisk and became an encumbrance. He sought to experience himself the hardships of slaves, seamen, and Indians so that he might have "a quick and lively feeling of the afflictions of my fellow creatures." John Woolman was one who radiated love and humility and who exemplified the sensitivity of the Quaker conscience and their steadfastness of purpose. His *Journal* (1774) is a classic of devotion and of literature; it begins with the sentence, "I have often felt a motion of love to leave some hints in writing of my experience of the goodness of God." John Woolman died of smallpox October 7, 1772. He is commemorated on October 6 on the Methodist calendar in *For All the Saints* of the Order of St. Luke.

FOR FURTHER READING

Cadbury, M. C. *Robert Barclay*. London, 1912.

Emerson, Wildes Harry. *William Penn*. New York: Macmillan, 1974.

Moulton, Phillips P., ed. *The Journal and Major Essays of John Woolman*. New York: Oxford University Press, 1971.

READING

From the *Journal* of George Fox

After I had received that opening from the Lord, that to be bred at Oxford or Cambridge, was not sufficient to fit a man to be a minister of Christ, I regarded the priests less, and looked more after the dissenting people. Among them I saw there was some tenderness; and many of them came afterwards to be convinced, for they had some openings. But as I had forsaken the priests, so I left the separate preachers also, and those called the most experienced people; for I saw there was none among them all that could speak to my condition. And when all my hopes in them and in all men were gone, so that I had nothing outwardly, to help me, nor could tell what to do; then, O then, I heard a voice which said, "There is one, even Christ Jesus, that can speak to thy condition." When I heard it, my heart did leap for joy. Then the Lord let me see why there was none upon earth that could speak to my condition, namely, that I might give him all the glory. For all are concluded under sin, and shut up in unbelief, as I had been, that Jesus Christ might have the pre-eminence, who enlightens, and gives grace, faith, and power. Thus when God doth work, who shall let [i.e., hinder] it? This I knew experimentally. My desires after the Lord grew stronger, and zeal in the pure knowledge of God, and of Christ alone, without the help of any man, book, or writing. For though I read the Scriptures that spake of Christ and of God, yet I knew him not by revelation, as he did who hath the key did open, and as the Father of life drew me to his Son by his Spirit. The Lord led me gently along, and let me see his love, which was endless and eternal, surpassing all the knowledge that men have in the natural state, or can get by history or books. . . .

Thus in the deepest miseries, in the greatest sorrows and temptations that beset me, the Lord in his mercy did keep me. I found two thirsts in me; the one after the creatures, to have got help and strength there; and the other after the Lord the

Creator, and his Son Jesus Christ; and I saw all the world could do me no good. If I had a king's diet, palace and attendance, all would have been as nothing; for nothing gave me comfort but the Lord by his power. I saw professors, priests, and people, were whole and at ease in that condition which was my misery, and they loved that which I would have been rid of. But the Lord did stay my desires upon himself, from whom my help came, and my care was cast upon him alone. Therefore, all wait patiently upon the Lord, whatsoever condition you be in; wait in the grace and truth that comes by Jesus; for if ye do so, there is a promise to you, and the Lord God will fulfill it in you. Blessed are all they indeed that do indeed hunger and thirst after righteousness, they shall be satisfied with it. I have found it so, praised the Lord who filleth with it, and satisfieth the desires of the hungry soul.

Passages from the Life and Writings of George Fox Taken from His Journal (Philadelphia: Friends Book Store, 1881), 18–20.

PROPERS

Holy and righteous God, you created us in your image: Illumine our hearts and our minds with your light that we may recognize injustice, and, strengthened by your might and encouraged by the example of George Fox, may contend fearlessly against oppression and bring justice and peace among peoples and nations; through your Son Jesus Christ our Lord, who lives and reigns with you and the Holy Spirit, one God, now and forever.

PHP

Readings:	1 Kings 19:9-13
	Psalm 94
	Romans 12:9-21
	Luke 6:20-36
Hymn of the Day:	
	"Dear Lord and Father of mankind" (H82 652, 653; LBW 506)
Prayers:	For seekers after truth
	For those in prison
	For the outcast and those out of step with society
	For equal justice for all
Preface:	Epiphany (BCP)
Color:	White

January 17

Antony, Abbot in Egypt, 356
with Pachomius, Abbot, 346

Antony (or Anthony), the founder of monasticism, was born near Memphis in Lower Egypt *ca.* 251. When he was a young man, he was so moved by hearing the command in the Gospel, "Go, sell your possessions, and give the money to the poor, and you will have treasure in heaven; then come, follow me" (Matt. 19:21), that he did just that with his considerable inheritance and went to live alone in the desert of Upper Egypt as an anchorite, a solitary ascetic, spending time in prayer and study, making baskets to earn a living.

He lived in complete solitude for twenty years and underwent severe spiritual and physical temptations, tormented by demons in various guises. He became aware of the dangers of solitude for those who are unprepared, and, as in time a number of disciples gathered around him, he organized them into loosely knit communities and exerted a certain authority over them. He initiated a formula of monastic rule where common life, prayer, and the rule of a superior and fraternal love proved more secure means of holiness of life than eremitic practices. His preference, however, was for solitude, so about the year 312 he withdrew further away and lived in a cave on Mount Colzim (or Kolzim) in the harsh mountainous landscape of the Eastern Desert, near the northwest corner of the Red Sea. He fell in love with the place at first sight and remained there for the rest of his life.

People of all kinds sought out Antony to get his advice or simply to see the man out of curiosity. He would occasionally visit his followers in their hermitages. At an advanced age he went to Alexandria to encourage opposition to Arianism, which denied the full divinity of Christ. Notably moderate in contrast to the more eccentric austerities of other solitaries, Antony was a man of spiritual wisdom, whose disciplined pursuit of holiness was always directed toward the better service of God.

He remained a layman all his life and was over one hundred when he died, in perfect health, in 356. The Monastery of St. Antony, which still exists, was built a few years after his death.

Antony is remembered on this date on the Eastern, Roman Catholic, Episcopal, Lutheran, and Methodist calendars.

Antony's younger contemporary, **Pachomius**, may appropriately be remembered with him. He was born *ca.* 290 near Esneh in Upper Egypt of pagan parents and was later conscripted into the imperial army. After his discharge in 313 he became a Christian and was baptized. He founded a monastery at Tabennisi near the Nile about 320 where his fame soon attracted large numbers of monks. Pachomius applied the administrative skills he learned in military service to the preparation of a rule and the organization of the communal life of monks, emphasizing life in community, work according to one's craft, and common prayer. To keep the monks from spiritual pride, he did not permit any to be ordained to the priesthood but had a priest come from outside the monastery to celebrate the Divine Liturgy. He set the example himself, it is said, by fleeing when the renowned Patriarch of Alexandria, Athanasius, sought to ordain him a priest. Pachomius is honored as the founder of Christian cenobitic (community) monasticism. At his death in 346 he was ruling as abbot-general over nine communities for men and two for women. Pachomius's feast day in the East is May 15, May 14 in the West, May 9 in the Coptic Church. He is not on the General Roman Calendar nor on the Episcopal calendar; he is, however, on the 1962 German Evangelical Calendar and among the "Witnesses to the Faith" in the Lutheran African American service book, *This Far By Faith* (1999) and, together with Antony, has been added to the calendar in *Evangelical Lutheran Worship* (2006).

FOR FURTHER READING

St. Athanasius. *The Life of St. Antony.* Ed. Walter J. Burghart. Mahwah: Paulist, 1978.

Cowan, James. *Journey to the Inner Mountain: In the Desert with St. Antony.* London: Hodder and Stoughton, 2002.

Knowles, David. *From Pachomius to Ignatius: A Study in the Constitutional History of the Religious Orders.* New York: Oxford University Press, 1966.

READING

From *The Life of St. Antony* by St. Athanasius

When Antony was about eighteen or twenty years old, his parents died, leaving him alone to care for a very young sister and to look after the family property.

Some six months later, on his way to church, he thought of how the apostles had left everything and followed the Savior, and also of how the Christians, recorded in the book of Acts, had sold their possessions and brought the money to the apostles for distribution to those in need. He reflected on the great hope stored up in heaven for such as these. All this was all in his mind when he entered the church just as the Gospel was being read, and he heard the Lord's words to the rich man, "If you wish to be perfect, go, sell your possessions, and give the money to the poor, and you will have treasure in heaven; then come, follow me." [Matt. 19:21]

It seemed to Antony that it was God who had brought the early saints to his mind and that the words of the Gospel had been spoken directly to him. Immediately he left the church and gave away to the villagers all the property he had inherited, about two hundred acres of very beautiful and fertile land, so that it would no longer distract his sister and himself. He sold all his other possessions as well, and gave the money to the poor, except for a small sum to care for his sister.

On another occasion when he went to church he heard the Lord say in the Gospel, "Do not worry about tomorrow." [Matt. 6:34] Without hesitation he went out and gave the poor all that he had left. He placed his sister in the care of some trustworthy nuns and arranged for her to be brought up in the convent. Then, not far from his home, he dedicated himself to the ascetic life, keeping a careful watch over himself and practicing great austerity. He worked with his hands because he had heard the words, "Anyone not willing to work should not eat." [2 Thess. 3:10] With the profit from this work he bought bread for himself and gave the rest to the poor.

Having learned that we should pray always, even when we are by ourselves, he prayed constantly. Indeed, he was so attentive when Scripture was read that nothing escaped him, and because he retained all that he heard, his memory became his library.

Seeing the kind of life he lived, the villagers and all the virtuous people in the neighborhood called him the friend of God, and they loved him as both son and brother.

Athanasius, *The Life of St. Antony,* chaps. 2–4. Trans. PHP, based on *A Short Breviary* by St. John's Abbey and the English translation of the Office of Readings from the Liturgy of the Hours.

PROPERS

O God, by your Holy Spirit you called Antony [and Pachomius] to renounce the world and to serve you in the solitude of the desert, withstanding the temptations of the world, the flesh, and the devil: Grant us grace to learn by his [their] example to deny ourselves, to love you above all things, and, with pure hearts and minds, to follow you, the only God; through Jesus Christ our Lord, who lives and reigns with you and the Holy Spirit, one God, forever and ever.

PHP, RS ✚ LFF

Readings:	1 Peter 5:6-10
	Psalm 91:9-16 *or* Psalm 1
	Mark 10:17-21 *or* Matthew 19:16-26 (RC)
Hymn of the Day:	
	"Fight the good fight with all thy might" (H82 552, 553; LSB 664, LBW 461)
Prayers:	For all whom God is calling to the Religious Life
	For all monks and nuns and for all communities in which men and women seek a deeper faith and a fuller life
	For an appreciation of the virtues of poverty, chastity, and obedience
	For deliverance from acquisitiveness and from attachment to the things of this world
Preface:	A Saint (2) (BCP)
Color:	White

January 18

The Confession of St. Peter

The Week of Prayer for Christian Unity Begins

Since the fourth century there has been a festival of Peter, called "the Chair of Peter," which honors both Peter as the head of the Roman Church and also his *cathedra*, his chair of episcopal authority as the focus of Church unity founded on the leader of the twelve apostles. The Roman Catholic Church now observes this feast on February 22, the older date, but because it often falls in Lent many churches had moved the celebration to February 18.

The Episcopal Church in the 1979 *Book of Common Prayer* took the feast of the Chair of Peter with its gospel of Peter's confession that Jesus is "the Christ, the Son of the living God," renamed it the Confession of St. Peter, and set it at the beginning of the Week of Prayer for Christian Unity. The calendar in the *Lutheran Book of Worship* followed that precedent and gave the week of prayer a standing in the calendar that is unequalled in any other church.

The martyr deaths of Peter and Paul are commemorated jointly on June 29. St. Paul has a festival of his own marking his conversion (January 25), which is the conclusion of the Week of Prayer for Christian Unity. It therefore seemed logical to the drafters of the *Book of Common Prayer* and the *Lutheran Book of Worship* to introduce a festival of St. Peter and to set it at the beginning of that week, thus including the week in the calendar of the church. The Week of Prayer for Christian Unity is therefore set between the two great apostles of Christianity, Peter and Paul. Moreover, the two represent in a way the two faces of biblical tradition: Peter, the apostle to the Jews, represents the Mosaic tradition of law; and Paul, the apostle of the Gentiles, represents the Abrahamic tradition of faith.

When Peter with characteristic boldness confessed, "You are the Christ and the Son of the living God," Jesus responded, "You are Peter, and on this rock I will build my church." The exact referent of "rock" is much disputed, some claiming that it is Peter himself, some claiming that it is Peter's confession. The one who made the great and central confession of the Christian faith was himself a fisherman, impetuous, often stumbling, intense, who at the arrest of Jesus denied knowing him. After the resurrection. however, he strengthened the church and was its acknowledged leader, courageously preaching the news about Jesus, and eventually laying down his life for his Lord.

Peter's traditional symbol in Christian iconography is two crossed keys, representing the power to bind and to loose, bestowed on him by Jesus (Matt. 16:9, today's Gospel).

Prayers for the unity of the divided church date at least from the time of the Reformation. (See Archbishop Laud's well-known prayer for the Church given above at January 10.) The first Lambeth Conference of Anglican bishops in 1867, in the Preamble to its Resolutions, emphasized prayer for unity. In 1894 Pope Leo XIII encouraged the practice of a Prayer Octave for Unity in the context of Pentecost. Paul Wattson, an Anglican priest who later became a Roman Catholic, initiated a Church Unity Octave in January 1908. In 1926 the Faith and Order Movement began the publication of "suggestions for an Octave of Prayer for Christian Unity." Abbé Paul Courtier in 1935 in France advocated a Universal Week of Prayer for Christian Unity on the basis of prayer "for the unity Christ wills by the means he wills." In 1964 the Second Vatican Council in its Decree on Ecumenism (II.7) emphasized that prayer is "the soul of the whole ecumenical movement" and encouraged prayer for Christian unity.

James Keefer has suggested a helpful plan for comprehensive prayer for Christian unity:
> January 18: Eastern Orthodox, Coptic, and other Eastern Churches
> January 19: Roman Catholic and Uniate Churches
> January 20: Anglican, Old Catholic, and allied churches
> January 21: Lutheran, Moravian, and Methodist Churches
> January 22: Congregational, Presbyterian, and Reformed Churches
> January 23: Baptist, Amish, Mennonite, Hutterite, and Christian (Disciples of Christ) Churches
> January 24: Pentecostal and charismatic churches
> January 25: Nonmainstream communities; theologians and councils seeking to promote Christian unity while preserving Christian truth.

http://hillsdale.edu/Sept/Phil&Rel/Biography (accessed March 21, 2008)

FOR FURTHER READING

Brown, Raymond E., Karl P. Donfried, and John Reumann, eds. *Peter in the New Testament.* Minneapolis and New York: Augsburg and Paulist, 1973.

Clément, Olivier. *You Are Peter: An Orthodox Reflection on the Exercise of Papal Primacy.* Hyde Park: New City, 2003.

Cullmann, Oscar. *Peter: Disciple, Apostle, Martyr.* Trans. Floyd V. Filson. 2d rev. ed. Philadelphia: Westminster, 1953.

Goodspeed, E. J. *The Twelve.* New York: Holt, Rinehart, Winston, 1957.

Grant, Michael. *Saint Peter.* New York: Scribner's, 1995.

Kelly, J. N. D. *The Oxford Dictionary of Popes.* New York: Oxford University Press, 1986.

Lowe, John. *St. Peter.* New York: Oxford University Press, 1956.

O'Connor, Daniel William. *Peter in Rome: The Literary, Liturgical, and Archaeological Evidence.* New York: Columbia University Press, 1969.

Perkins, Pheme. *Peter: Apostle for the Whole Church.* Minneapolis: Fortress Press, 2000.

Tronzo, William. *St. Peter's in the Vatican.* Cambridge: Cambridge University Press, 2004.

Walsh, Michael. *An Illustrated History of the Popes: Saint Peter to John Paul II.* New York: St. Martin's, 1980.

READING

From *Peter: Disciple, Apostle, Martyr* by Oscar Cullmann

[D]uring the lifetime of Jesus Peter did not show himself a "rock" at all; on the contrary, his human weakness was very striking. The scene at the Sea of Genessaret gives a concrete illustration of Peter's character. He is impulsive and enthusiastic; in the first burst of enthusiasm, he does not hesitate to throw himself into the sea when Jesus calls him, but his courage soon fades and fear grips him. So, too, he is the first to confess loudly his loyalty to his Master, but he is the first one who will deny him in the hour of danger. And yet, so one assumes, precisely this character, with its notable contradictions, makes Peter appear as the disciple with special psychological fitness to be the "rock" among the other disciples. The exuberant enthusiasm, the fiery zeal of this disciple are said to be in fact the human qualities that are necessary to deserve such a title of honor. His instability and weakness are said to be only the dark side of these qualities.

Nevertheless, it is hardly possible to give a psychological basis for the unique position of Peter and for the giving to him of this name. Indeed, we should not ask at all why Jesus singled him out as "rock" instead of choosing another disciple. According to our sources, we can only confirm the fact of this distinction. Probably, however, it is also a mistake to say that the representative position of the disciple Peter and the qualities mentioned were derived only from the giving of the name. We can hardly say that only by this act did he become conscious that in his person he represented, so to speak, the totality of the disciples, even during thee earthly life of Jesus. Again we can only state the fact: Peter lets us see clearly everything that the call to discipleship involves in human weakness and privilege.

Oscar Cullmann, *Peter: Disciple, Apostle, Martyr,* trans. Floyd V. Filson, 2d rev. ed (Philadelphia: Westminster, 1962), 31–32.

PROPERS

Almighty God, who inspired Simon Peter, first among the apostles, to confess Jesus as Messiah and Son of the living God: Keep your Church steadfast upon the rock of this faith, so that in unity and peace we may proclaim one truth and follow the one Lord, our Savior Jesus Christ; who lives and reigns with you and the Holy Spirit, one God, now and forever.

BCP, based on RS February 22

Readings:	Acts 4:8-13
	Psalm 23
	1 Peter 5:1-4
	Matthew 16:13-19
Hymn of the Day:	
	"How sweet the Name of Jesus sounds" (H82 644, LBW 345, LSB 524, ELW 620)
	[tune: *St. Peter*])
	or "You are the Christ" (H82 254)
Prayers:	For the unity of the church
	For clarity and boldness in the church's preaching
	For reconciliation between the Roman and the non-Roman churches
Preface:	Apostles
Color:	White

JANUARY

January 19

Henry, Bishop of Uppsala, Missionary to Finland, Martyr, 1156

Henry, or Henrik as he is called throughout Scandinavia, was born in England early in the twelfth century. While living in Rome, he was chosen to accompany the papal legate, Cardinal Breakspear (later Pope Hadrian [Adrian] IV) to Scandinavia in 1151. In the following year the cardinal consecrated him bishop of Uppsala in Sweden, and he is, therefore, generally known as St. Henry of Uppsala. In the first dated event in the history of Christianity in Finland, Henry accompanied St. Erik, the king of Sweden (who is commemorated May 18), on a expedition to the Finns in 1155 which was intended both to Christianize the people and to bring them under firmer control of the Swedish crown. After the king returned, Bishop Henry remained and began the organization of the Church. In January of the following winter (1156), Bishop Henry was slain with an axe on frozen Lake Köyliö by a Finnish farmer named Lalli (Lawrence). The generally accepted version of St. Henry's death is that Lalli was a murderer who had been censured by the bishop and disciplined by the Church. There is also a Finnish folk ballad which tells the story that Lalli slew Henry out of resentment for his wife's selling provisions to the bishop and that he was punished by God for his act.

Henry was not the first to preach the gospel among the Finns, but the missionary bishop and martyr was the effective founder of the Church in Finland, although full outward Christianization of Finland was not completed until the appointment of a Finn, Magnus, as bishop of Åbo (Turku) in 1291. Henry's body was buried in Nousainen, north of Turku, and within a few years St. Henry was commemorated on the date of his death. On a small artificial island at the place where St. Henry was killed a memorial chapel was built, apparently in the fourteenth century, and this became a popular place of pilgrimage in the Middle Ages. All that remains of the chapel now are scattered stones. The first document in which Bishop Henry is referred to as a saint is a letter of Pope Boniface VIII from the year 1296.

At the beginning of the thirteenth century, the first bishop of Finland, Thomas (d. 1248), also English-born, transferred the see from Nousainen to Koroinen, an old trading center close to Turku. A little later the see was transferred again to the new Turku, where a cathedral, the most impressive building in medieval Finland, was built before the end of the thirteenth century, and on June 18, 1300, St. Henry's earthly remains were transferred from Nousainen to the new cathedral at Turku. The church was closely related to the cult of St. Henry, who by then had come to be regarded as the patron of Finland. In 1720 his relics were stolen from Turku by Russian troops and, except for a treasured arm bone, disappeared.

St. Henry is listed on the calendar in the *Lutheran Book of Worship* but is not on the Episcopal or the general Roman Catholic calendar.

FOR FURTHER READING

Borenius, T. "St. Henry of Finland: An Anglo-Scandinavian Saint." *Archaeological Journal* 87 (1930): 340–56.

Hunter, L. S., ed. *Scandinavian Churches.* 68–75. London: Faber & Faber, 1965.

Sinnemäki, Maunu. *The Church in Finland.* Helsinki: Otava, 1973.

READING

From *The Imitation of Christ* by Thomas à Kempis

What do you seek here, since this world is not your resting place? Your true home is in Heaven; therefore remember that all the things of this world are transitory. All things are passing, and yourself with them. See that you do not cling to them, lest you become entangled and perish with them. Let all your thoughts be with the Most High, and direct your humble prayers unceasingly to Christ. If you cannot contemplate high and heavenly things, take refuge in the Passion of Christ, and love to dwell within His Sacred Wounds. For if you devoutly seek the Wounds of Jesus and the precious marks of His Passion, you will find great strength in all troubles. And if men despise you, you will care little, having small regard for the words of your detractors.

Christ himself was despised by men, and in His direst need was abandoned by his friends and acquaintances to the insults of His enemies. Christ was willing to suffer and to be despised; and do you presume to complain? Christ had enemies and slanderers; and do you expect all men to be your friends and benefactors? How will your patience be crowned, if you are not willing to endure hardship? Suffer with Christ, and for Christ, if you wish to reign with Christ.

Had you but once entered perfectly into the Heart of Jesus and tasted something of his burning love, you would care nothing for your own gain or loss; for the love of Jesus causes a man to regard himself very humbly. The true, inward lover of Jesus and the Truth, who is free from inordinate desires, can turn freely to God, rise above self, and joyfully rest in God.

Thomas à Kempis, *The Imitation of Christ*, trans. Leo Sherley-Price (Baltimore: Penguin, 1952), 68–69, 88–89, 83, 206–206, 72. Introduction and Translation copyright 1952 by Leo Sherley-Price. Reprinted by permission of Penguin Books Ltd.

PROPERS

Almighty God, your servant Henry of Uppsala brought the light of the gospel to the people of Finland and confirmed his preaching by martyrdom: Shine, we pray, in our hearts, that we, also, in our generation may show forth your praise, who called us our of darkness into your marvelous light; through Jesus Christ our Lord, who lives and reigns with you and the Holy Spirit, one God, now and forever.

PHP ✚ BCP, Of a Missionary

Readings:	Isaiah 49:1-6
	Psalm 98
	Acts 17:22-31
	Matthew 28:16-20
Hymn of the Day:	
	"Lost in the night do the people yet languish" (LBW 394, ELW 243)
Prayers:	For the Church of Finland
	For faithfulness
	For zeal in preaching the gospel
	For the unity of the church
Preface:	Epiphany
Color:	Red

ALSO ON JANUARY 19

Wulfstan, Bishop of Worcester, 1095

Wulfstan (Wulstan), a Benedictine monk, who was bishop of Worcester 1062–1095, passed his entire career in Worcester. The first English bishop to have systematically visited his parishes, he encouraged the building of churches and made Worcester a center of learning. After the Norman Conquest he supported King William I and was, therefore, allowed to retain his diocese. He assisted in the abolition of the practice of selling English as slaves in Ireland, and he enforced the discipline of priestly celibacy. The most respected prelate of the Anglo-Saxon Church, Wulfstan died January 18, 1095.

Wulfstan is on the calendar in the *Book of Common Prayer* but not on the General Roman nor the Lutheran calendar.

READING

From *The Life of St. Wulfstan* by William of Malmsbury

Wulfstan heard at least two Masses daily; and at each he made his oblation: and sang a third Mass himself. When he was traveling he would begin the psalter as he mounted his beast and paused not till the end. To this he added Litanies with many Collects; and Vigils and Vespers of the dead. If the journey was still prolonged, he repeated the psalms of the hours. His clerks and monks rode with him ready to take up the alternate verses, or to help his memory if he seemed to stumble. Thus he bade them do that they might avoid idle talking which so easily comes in the way of men on a journey. For then many things take the eye, and there is the more to talk of. His chamberlain rode by him, bearing a purse which was the common treasury of all needy folk. For no man who asked for alms of Wulstan ever had to complain of denial. When the day's journey was done, and they came to their lodging, he would never, as I have said, enter his chamber till he had saluted the Church with his prayers. He bade a priest purge all the rooms of the lodging with holy water and the sign of the Cross. So, he said, should hostile powers be driven away, and friendly powers brought in.

William of Malmsbury, "The Life of St. Wulfstan," *Vita Wulfstani* III, 5, trans. J. H. F. Peile (New York: Oxford University Press, 1934), 74.

PROPERS

Almighty God, who through days of change and turmoil kept your holy bishop Wulfstan strong in his simplicity, his compassion, and his faith: Multiply in your church leaders of his quality, faithful to themselves, to your people, and to you; through Jesus Christ our Lord, who lives and reigns with you and the Holy Spirit, one God, forever and ever.

JWP, DvD, PHP

Readings:	Exodus 3:1-12
	Psalm 146:4-9 *or* 84:7-12
	John 15:5-8, 14-16
Hymn of the Day:	
	"Rise up, ye saints of God! Have done with lesser things" (H82 551, SBH 541)
Prayers:	For all bishops
	For all who work to improve the social conditions of their society
	For all regular communicants and especially those who attend daily worship
Preface:	Baptism (BCP)
Color:	White

January 20

Fabian, Bishop of Rome, Martyr, 250

Fabian (Fabianus) was a Roman layman who, according to the historian Eusebius (*Church History* VI, 29), came into the city from his farm one day as the clergy and people were preparing to elect a new bishop. While the names of several noble and illustrious candidates were being considered, Eusebius reports, a dove flew in and settled on the head of Fabian, whereupon, although he was a stranger, not a candidate, and a layman, he was elected unanimously. The *Liber Pontificalis* says that he made many administrative reforms, dividing the city into seven districts each supervised by a deacon for practical and charitable purposes, developed the parochial structure of the Church in Rome, and established the custom of venerating martyrs at their tombs in the catacombs. He led the church for fourteen years and died a martyr's death during the persecution of Decius in 250, one of the first to die in that persecution. Cyprian, the Bishop of Carthage, wrote to Fabian's successor Cornelius that Fabian was an "incomparable man" whose glory in death befitted the purity and holiness of his life. In the Catacombs of St. Callixtus (Callistus), the burial place of the early bishops of Rome, a stone that covered Fabian's grave may still be seen, broken into four pieces, bearing the Greek words, "Fabian," "bishop," "martyr." The Roman Catholic calendar also commemorates on this date Sebastian (257?–288?) about whom nothing is known historically except that he was a Roman martyr and was venerated in Milan even in the time of St. Ambrose, who said that Sebastian was born in Milan and that he was buried on the Appian Way. He is mentioned on several martyrologies as early as 350. The pious legend that he was a soldier who was condemned to be killed by archers for protecting martyrs became a popular subject for Renaissance painters.

Fabian is on the General Roman Calendar and the calendar in the *Book of Common Prayer* and is included in the Methodist *For All the Saints*.

READING

From a letter by Cyprian of Carthage about the death of Fabian

When he was informed of the death of Pope Fabian, Saint Cyprian sent this letter to the priests and deacons of Rome: "My dear brothers, while the news of the death of my good colleague was still uncertain, and opinions were divided, I received your letter delivered through the subdeacon Clementius, in which I learned the full details of Fabian's glorious death. I was quite happy that his virtuous death crowned the integrity of his administration. I also congratulate you that you honor his memory with such a splendid and praiseworthy testimony. We can see quite clearly what an honor for you is the glorious heritage of one who was your leader, and what an example of faith and courage it offers us. For just as the defection of a leader can have a harmful effect on those who follow him, so the constancy of a bishop's faith offers an healthful and profitable example to his brothers."

Before Cyprian received this letter, the Church of Rome had given the community at Carthage testimony of its loyalty in time of persecution in the following letter. "Our church stands unshaken in the faith, although some have lapsed because they fear the loss of their high positions or other personal sufferings. Although these have left us, we have not abandoned them. We have urged them and now we continue to encourage them to repent, in the hope that they may receive pardon from the One who can give it. If they were abandoned by us, their situation might become worse.

"And so you see, brothers, you should act in the same manner. Perhaps in this way those who have lapsed, having been converted through your encouragement, and, if they are arrested again, might confess their faith and so might make up for their previous failure. You have other responsibilities as well. If any of those who have defected should become ill and, after repenting, should desire to receive communion, they should certainly be assisted. Widows, the destitute who cannot support themselves, and those who are in prison or who have been evicted from their homes should surely have assistance; likewise catechumens who are ill ought not to be disappointed in their hope of receiving help.

"Your brothers who are in prison send you their greetings, and also the priests, the whole Church which lies awake in great anxiety to pray for all those who call on the Name of the Lord. And we ask you in turn to remember us."

Letters 9 and 8. Trans. PHP, based on *A Short Breviary* by the monks of St. John's Abbey and the International Committee on English in the Liturgy.

PROPERS

O God, in your providence you singled out the holy martyr Fabian as worthy to be chief pastor of your people, and guided him so to strengthen your church that it stood fast in the day of persecution: Grant that the example of your martyr Fabian may help us to imitate his faith and offer you our loving service; through Jesus Christ our Lord, who lives and reigns with you and the Holy Spirit, one God, now and forever.

PHP; CMG + LFF + RS

Readings: 2 Esdras 2:42-48
Psalm 110:1-4 *or* 126
Matthew 10:16-22

Hymn of the Day:
"Hearken to the anthem glorious" (H82 240, 241)
or "God, whose giving knows no ending" (LBW 408, ELW 678)
Prayers: For all who today are facing persecution, suffering, and death for their faith
For all who are engaged in church administration
For the lapsed
For the fearful
For parishes throughout the world, particularly those in great cities
For the unity of the church
Preface: A Saint (3) (BCP)
Color: Red

ALSO ON JANUARY 20

The *Lutheran Service Book* (2006) of the Lutheran Church–Missouri Synod, following the practice of the Eastern Church, a practice introduced in the West by the calendar of Wilhelm Löhe (see January 2), commemorates certain people from the Hebrew Bible. On January 20 the *Lutheran Service Book* remembers **Sarah**; she is listed on January 19 on Löhe's calendar.

January 21

Agnes, Martyr at Rome, 304

Agnes, a young Roman woman, executed in 304 at the age of twelve or thirteen, is one of the most famous of Roman martyrs, even though little is known about her life. She was martyred in Rome under the persecution of the Emperor Diocletian and was buried in the cemetery on the Via Nomentana, where the daughter or granddaughter of Constantine built a church in her honor *ca.* 350. Her name and the date of her feast day occur on the calendar of martyrs drawn up in 354.

Her story seems to be that at age twelve or thirteen she refused to consider marriage and consecrated her virginity to God. When persecution broke out, she left home and offered herself for martyrdom, resisted threats, and was executed by being stabbed in the throat, a common Roman form of execution. Her willingness to offer herself as a sacrifice made a deep impression on the Church because it contrasted sharply with the massive defections that were ravaging the Roman community at this time. In Rome, because of the similarity of her name to *Agnus*, lamb, two lambs are presented and blessed on this day at her altar in the church of St. Agnese fuori le Mura and then are cared for by nuns of Santa Cecelia in Trastavere. Their wool is used for the white cloth of the pallium the pope confers to archbishops as a sign of respect and affection.

Agnes is commemorated on this date in both East and West and is found on
the General Roman Calendar, the calendar in the *Book of Common Prayer,* the
Methodist *For All the Saints,* the 1997 Church of England calendar the *Christian
Year,* and *Evangelical Lutheran Worship* (2006).

READING

From a treatise on Virgins by St. Ambrose

Today is the birthday of a virgin; let us imitate her purity. It is the birthday of a
martyr; let us offer ourselves in sacrifice. It is the heavenly birthday of Saint Agnes,
who is said to have suffered martyrdom at the age of twelve. The cruelty that did
not spare her youth shows all the more clearly the faith that found a witness in
one so young.

There was little room in that small body for a wound. Although she was
scarcely large enough to be struck, she was great enough to overcome it. Girls her
age cannot bear even their parents' frowns and think the jab of a needle a serious
wound. But Agnes showed no fear of the blood-stained hands of her executioners.
She did not cringe at the harsh sound of heavy chains. She offered her whole body
to be put to the sword by fierce soldiers; she was too young to know of death, yet
was ready to face it. Dragged to the altar, she stretched out her hands to the Lord
in the midst of the flames, making the triumphant sign of Christ the victor on
the altars of sacrilege. She put her neck and hands in iron chains, but they were
too large for her tiny limbs. A new kind of martyrdom! She was too young to be
punished, yet old enough for a martyr's crown; she was unfitted for the contest,
yet effortless in victory. She showed herself an exemplar in valor despite her youth.
Were she a bride she would not hasten to her husband with the same joy that she
showed on her way to punishment, crowned not with flowers but with holiness of
life, adorned not with braided hair but with Christ himself.

In the midst of tears, she shed no tears herself. The crowds marveled at her
recklessness in throwing away a life untasted, as if she had already lived life to the
full. All were amazed that one not yet of legal age could give her testimony to God.
So she succeeded in convincing others of her testimony about God, though her
testimony in human affairs could not yet be accepted. What is beyond the power
of nature, must come from its creator.

What menaces there were from the executioner, to frighten her; what promises made, to win her over; what influential people desired her in marriage! She
answered: "To hope that any other will please me does wrong to my Spouse. I will
be his who first chose me for himself. Executioner, why do you delay? If eyes that
I do not want can desire this body, then let it perish." She stood still, she prayed,
she offered her neck.

You could see fear in the eyes of the executioner, as if he were the one condemned; his right hand trembled, his face grew pale as he saw the girl's peril, while

she had no fear for herself. One victim, but a twin martyrdom, to modesty and to religion; Agnes preserved her virginity, and gained a martyr's crown.

Book 1, trans. PHP, based on *A Short Breviary* by the monks of St. John's Abbey and the International Committee on English in the Liturgy.

PROPERS

Almighty and everlasting God, you choose those whom the world deems powerless to put the powerful to shame: Grant us so to cherish the memory of your youthful martyr Agnes, that we may share her pure and steadfast faith in you; through Jesus Christ our Lord, who lives and reigns with you and the Holy Spirit, one God, forever and ever.

1952 Roman Missal, RS, trans. LFF

Readings:	Song of Solomon 2:10-13
	Psalm 45:11-16 or 116:1-8
	Matthew 18:1-6
Hymn of the Day:	
	"Blessed feasts of blessed martyrs" (H82 238, 239)
	or "Lord, take my hand and lead me" (LBW 333, LSB 722, ELW 767)
Prayers:	For all Christian children and teenagers, especially those enduring ridicule for their faith and life
	For church schools and Christian youth groups
	For those who teach and work with young people
	For a willingness to learn from children
	For the unity of the church
Preface:	A Saint (3) (BCP)
Color:	Red

January 22

Vincent, Deacon of Saragossa, Martyr, 304

Vincent, the most celebrated of Spanish martyrs, is for the Church in Spain what Stephen was for Jerusalem and Lawrence was for Rome. He was deacon of the Church in Saragossa and was executed in the persecution under Diocletian at Valencia in 304. Further trustworthy details are lacking. He is said to have regularly preached and taught on behalf of his bishop Valerius, who suffered from a severe stammer. The governor sent them both to prison for their firm adherence to the Christian faith, and while Valerius was exiled, Vincent was sentenced to torture and death. Prudentius wrote a hymn in his praise telling of a martyr who underwent imprisonment, semi-starvation, being clamped in stocks, racked, grilled (like Lawrence). Such imaginative pictures of his stoic endurance of torture spread his fame rapidly and far, as St. Augustine testifies. Several churches in England were dedicated to his honor in the Middle Ages.

Vincent is on the General Roman Calendar, the calendar in the *Book of Common Prayer,* and in the Methodist *For All the Saints.* He was on Löhe's calendar (1868) and the 1962 German Calendar of Names.

READING

From a sermon by St. Augustine

"He has granted you the privilege not only of believing in Christ, but of suffering for him as well." [Phil. 1:29]

Vincent received both these gifts and preserved them both. For how could he have them if he had not received them? And he showed his faith in what he said, his endurance in what he suffered.

No one ought to rely on one's own feelings when speaking out, nor be confident in personal strength when undergoing temptation. For whenever we speak as wisely as we should, our wisdom must come from God, and whenever we endure evils courageously, our patience must come from him.

Remember how Christ our Lord in the Gospel exhorted his disciples. He is the king of martyrs equipping his troops with spiritual armament, telling them of battles ahead, offering them support, and promising them their reward. He said to his disciples, "In the world you face persecution. But take courage; I have conquered the world!"

There is no need to wonder then, dearly beloved, that Vincent conquered in him who conquered the world. He said, "In the world you will face persecution," but to face persecution is not to be overcome, and to be attacked is not to be conquered. Against Christ's army the world arrays a twofold battle line. It offers temptation to lead us astray; it strikes terror into us to break our spirit. Do not cling to your own pleasures, and do not fear the cruelty of others; then the world is conquered. At both of these approaches Christ rushes to our aid, and the Christian is not conquered. If you were to consider in Vincent's martyrdom only human endurance, then his act is unbelievable from the outset. But recognize that power is from God, and then Vincent ceases to be a source of wonder.

Such savagery was being vented upon the martyr's body while such serenity issued from his lips; such harsh cruelties were being inflicted on his limbs while such assurance rang out in his words, that we should think that, by some miracle, as Vincent suffered, one person was speaking while another was being tortured. And this was in fact true; another person was speaking. Christ in the Gospel promised this to those who were to be his witnesses, to those whom he was preparing for contests of this kind. For he said, "Do not worry about what you are to say; for it is not you who speak, but the Spirit of your Father speaking through you." [Matt. 10:19-20] Thus it was Vincent's body that suffered, but the Spirit who spoke. And at his voice, impiety was not only vanquished but human frailty was given consolation.

Augustine, Sermon 276, 1-2, trans. PHP, based on *A Short Breviary* by the monks of St. John's Abbey and the International Committee on English in the Liturgy.

PROPERS

Eternal God, you gave your deacon Vincent the courage to endure torture and death for the gospel: Fill us with your Spirit to endure all adversity with invincible and steadfast faith, and strengthen us in your love; through Jesus Christ our Lord, who lives and reigns with you and the Holy Spirit, one God, forever and ever.

PHP, RS ✚ LFF

Readings:	Psalm 31:1-5 *or* 116:10-17
	Revelation 7:13-17
	Luke 12:4-12
Hymn of the Day:	
	"Lord Christ, when first you came to earth" (H82 598, LBW 421, ELW 727)
Prayers:	For the Church in Spain, its bishops, clergy, and people
	For all deacons and deaconesses
	For freedom from fear
	For a will to embrace our calling to serve the world
	For the unity of the church
Preface:	A Saint (3) (BCP)
Color:	Red

January 23

Phillips Brooks, Bishop of Massachusetts, 1893

One of the great preachers of the nineteenth century, Phillips Brooks was born in Boston December 13, 1835, descended from a number of Pilgrim families of the Massachusetts Bay Colony. He grew up in a musical home, where singing and reciting hymns was such a regular part of devotion that by the time he went to Harvard, he is said to have memorized some two hundred hymns. After graduation in 1854, he taught briefly at Boston Latin School, from which he had graduated but was said to be "a conspicuous failure." After graduating from Virginia Seminary, he served as rector of the Church of the Advent in Philadelphia

(1859–1862) and as rector of Holy Trinity on Rittenhouse Square, Philadelphia, from 1862 to 1869. When Abraham Lincoln's coffin lay in state in Independence Hall on its way to Springfield for burial, Phillips Brooks delivered the eulogy for the martyred president. Later that year he was given a leave of absence from the Church of the Holy Trinity to tour Europe and the Middle East. He timed his tour so that he would be in Bethlehem for Christmas, 1865. He wrote home, "Before dark we rode out of town to the field where they say the shepherds saw the star. Somewhere in those fields we rode through, the shepherds must have been. As we passed, the shepherds were still 'keeping watch over their flocks' or 'leading them home to fold.'" Back home he wrote the lovely carol, "O little town of Bethlehem" for the children of the parish to sing at the Christmas service in 1868; the tune, *St. Louis*, was composed by the organist and superintendent of the church school, Lewis H. Redner (1831–1908).

In 1869 Brooks returned to Boston as rector of Trinity Church, which three years before had been destroyed in the Boston fire. Despite worshiping in temporary quarters, the congregation under Brooks's leadership grew and flourished and four years later was able to dedicate a magnificent architectural achievement, Henry Hobson Richardson's Trinity Church, which continues to grace Copley Square. At Trinity Church Brooks gave the evangelical faith a new standing in cultured, increasingly Unitarian Boston. Beside the splendid church stands a celebrated statue by Augustus Saint-Gaudens of the six-foot four-inch preacher behind whom stands Christ with his cross, Brooks's constant theme, with his hand resting on the preacher's shoulder.

Phillips Brooks was a kind and caring pastor, an inspiring leader, a careful teacher of preaching. In 1891 he was elected Bishop of Massachusetts. He owed his influence to his impressive stature and personality, his wide sympathies, and his passionate sincerity. As a humanitarian and as a preacher he was famous throughout the land and abroad.

Brooks never married, but he had a special affection for children and wrote many delightful letters to his brother's children and to the children of his parish. When he died at the age of fifty-seven (January 23, 1893), the mother of a girl of five, who had been one of his special favorites, entered the room where her daughter was playing and announced through her tears, "Bishop Brooks has gone to heaven." "O Mamma," the child replied, "how happy the angels will be!" Phillips Brooks House at Harvard was built by his alma mater as a memorial to him.

Phillips Brooks was added to the Episcopal calendar in the 1979 *Book of Common Prayer*.

FOR FURTHER READING

Allen, Alexander V. G. *Life and Letters of Phillips Brooks*. 5 vols. New York: E. P. Dutton, 1901.

Woolverton, John F. *The Education of Phillips Brooks.* Chicago: University of Illinois Press, 1995.

READING

From a sermon for Palm Sunday by Phillips Brooks

So Jesus came into Jerusalem. He came at once as an Intruder and a King. There were men along the streets who owed to Him the straightness of their limbs, the sight of their eyes, the clear, sane reason of their brains. They made the old streets ring with shouts of welcome. There were other men whom he had disappointed and defeated. He had trampled on their traditions, contradicted their doctrines, spoiled their trade. With muttered curses they saw him go by in His triumph. What a confusion! The city was divided against itself. But through it all Jesus held on His way, claiming the town for His town because it was His Father's. Whether it owned His claim or spurned it, whether it welcomed Him or cursed Him, through the mixed tumult of its welcome and its curses He went on His way, claiming it all for His own. And so He claims our hearts. An Intruder and a King at once He seems to those hearts as He stands there on their threshold. There is something in every one of them that says to Him, "Come in, come in!" There is something, too, in every one of them that rises up at His coming and says, "Begone, begone! We will not have this Man to rule over us." But through their tumult, their struggle, Christ, whether He be King or Intruder, whether He be welcomed or rejected, goes on His way, pressing on into each heart's most secret places, claiming always that He and He alone is the heart's King. And the struggle in any heart cannot keep on evenly balanced forever. Every heart has to decide. Jerusalem had to decide. Before the week was over she had decided. On Friday she crucified Christ. Still even round the cross there was love and faith and lamentation. But they were crushed and only heard in sobs. The hatred had triumphed, and Jerusalem had crucified her King. And so must every Jerusalem decide. So must your heart say finally to Jesus, "Come" or "Go." He never will go until you obstinately bid Him. He cannot come into the inmost temple until you welcome Him.

Phillips Brooks, *Sermons for the Principal Festivals and Fasts of the Church Year,* 1895.

PROPERS

O everlasting God, you revealed your truth to your servant Phillips Brooks and so formed and molded his mind and heart that he was able to mediate that truth with grace and power: Grant, we pray, that all whom you call to preach the gospel may steep themselves in your Word, and conform their lives to your will; through Jesus Christ our Lord, who lives and reigns with you and the Holy Spirit, one God, forever and ever.

LFF

Readings: Psalm 84:7-12 *or* 33:1-5, 20-21
                Ephesians 3:14-21
                Matthew 24:24-27
Hymn of the Day:
                "O little town of Bethlehem" (H82 78, 79 [note especially the frequently-omitted
                    Stanza 4], LBW 41, LSB 361, ELW 279)
Prayers: For all who preach the gospel
                For a lively sense of social justice
                For a burning desire to bring the world to Christ
                For the unity of the church
Preface: A Saint (1) (BCP)
Color: White

January 24

Francis de Sales, Bishop of Geneva, 1622

Francis was born in the Château de Sales in the Savoy district of France in 1567 and educated at Annecy, Paris, and Padua. In 1593, despite some opposition from his father, he was ordained priest in the Diocese of Geneva. He served there for twenty-nine years, first as priest to the people of his native Chablais country, who had become Calvinists. He approached them in the spirit of love (he said, "Whoever preaches with love preaches effectively"), surviving attacks by assassins, and by the end of four years most of the people had returned to the Roman Catholic Church.

In 1602 Francis was appointed bishop of Geneva. With characteristic gentle persuasion, he began the reform and reorganization of a most difficult diocese. He gave away his private money and lived very simply, resisting all efforts by the French king to have him move to Paris. He governed his diocese with love and gentleness. Children adored him and he himself taught them when they came to the cathedral for instruction. He devoted himself especially to guiding the laity in the spiritual life, something that was previously regarded as the preserve of the religious. He is responsible for what became a spiritual classic, *Introduction to the Devout Life*, based on notes he originally wrote for one of his penitents, showing how it is possible to live a spiritual life while living in the world. Perhaps his greatest book is *The Love of God*. His works have been published in twenty-six volumes.

With Jane de Chantal (1552–1641; feast day August 21) he founded the Order of the Visitation in 1610 for the religious education of young girls. Francis died of a stroke in Lyons in 1622 at the age of fifty-five. A Calvinist minister said of him, in a much-quoted remark, "If we honored any man as a saint, I know no one since the days of the apostles more worthy of it than this man."

Francis de Sales was introduced to the Lutheran calendar by Wilhelm Löhe (1868) and is on the 1997 calendar of the Church of England, the *Christian Year*.

FOR FURTHER READING

Henry-Couannier, Maurice. *Francis de Sales and His Friends*. Trans. Veronica Morrow. New York: Alba, 1964.

Sanders, E. K. *St Francois de Sales, 1567–1622*. London: SPCK, 1928.

READING

From *Introduction to the Devout Life* by Francis de Sales, Part 1, chapter 3

When God the Creator made all things, he commanded the plants to bring forth fruit each according to its own kind; he has likewise commanded Christians, who are the living plants of his Church, to bring forth the fruits of devotion, each in accord with one's individual character, station, and calling.

I say that devotion must be practiced in different ways by the noble and by the worker, by the servant and by the master, by the widow, by the unmarried girl, and by the married woman. But even this distinction is not sufficient; for the practice of devotion must be adapted to the strength, to the occupation, and to the duties of each individual person.

Do you think, my dear Philothea, that it is proper for a bishop to want to lead a solitary life like a Carthusian; or for married people to be no more concerned than a Capuchin about increasing their income; or for a worker to spend the whole day in church like a religious; or on the other hand for a religious to be, like a bishop, constantly meeting the needs of our neighbor? Is not this sort of devotion ridiculous, unorganized, and intolerable? Yet this absurd error occurs very frequently. True devotion, however, does not destroy anything at all. Instead, it perfects and fulfills all things. Devotion that contradicts anyone's legitimate station and calling is certainly false devotion.

The bee collects honey from flowers in such a way as to do the least damage or destruction to them, and it leaves them whole, undamaged and fresh, just as it found them. True devotion does still better. Not only does it not injure any sort of calling or occupation, it even embellishes and enhances it.

Moreover, just as every sort of gem, cast in honey, becomes brighter and more sparkling, each according to its color, so each person becomes more acceptable and fitting in personal vocation by setting vocation in the context of devotion. Through devotion your family cares become more peaceful, mutual love between husband and wife becomes more sincere, the service we owe to the master becomes more faithful, and our work, no matter what it is, becomes more pleasant and agreeable.

It is therefore an error and even a heresy to wish to exclude the exercise of devotion from the military life, the workshop, the court, or the family. I acknowledge, my dear Philothea, that the type of devotion which is purely contemplative, monastic, and religious surely cannot be exercised in those occupations, but there are many other kinds of devotion suitable for perfecting those who live in secular life.

Therefore, in whatever situations we happen to be, we can and we must aspire to spiritual perfection.

Trans. PHP, based on *A Short Breviary* by the monks of St. John's Abbey and the English translation of the Office of Readings from the Liturgy of the Hours by the International Committee on English in the Liturgy.

PROPERS

O God, you gave your blessed bishop Francis de Sales the spirit of compassion to befriend all on the way of salvation: By his example, lead us to show to the world the tenderness of your own love in the service of others; through your Son Jesus Christ our Lord, who lives and reigns with you and the Holy Spirit, one God, now and forever.

RS, trans. PHP

Readings:	Ephesians 4:1-7, 11-13
	Psalm 94:1-14
	John 15:9-17
Hymn of the Day:	
	"Faith of our fathers, living still" (H82 558, SBH 516; LBW 500, ELW 812) [Stanza 3 describes Francis de Sales's way of love; the meaning, however, has unfortunately been undermined in the LBW and ELW alteration of the original text.]
Prayers:	For devotion to Christ in our daily lives, whatever our circumstances
	For faithful stewardship of possessions
	For men and women in their everyday life
	For writers and journalists
	For the unity of the church
Preface:	A Saint (1) (BCP)
Color:	White

ALSO ON JANUARY 24

Florence Li Tim-Oi (1907–1992), the first female priest in the Anglican Communion, was ordained by the bishop of Hong Kong, Ronald Hall, on January 25, 1944, because of difficulties in obtaining the service of priests occasioned by the Japanese occupation of China. In 1946, to diffuse controversy, she chose to refrain from exercising her priestly duties, after which she lived through extraordinarily difficult times in China. In 1983 she emigrated to Canada and in the following year was reinstated as a priest. She died in Toronto on February 26, 1992. She was added to the calendar of the Episcopal Church in *Lesser Feasts and Fasts 2003*.

January 25

The Conversion of St. Paul

The Week of Prayer for Christian Unity Ends

This feast celebrates a momentous event: the sudden, dramatic, and radical change in Saul, the fanatical persecutor of the young church, who became Paul, the "fool for Christ" (2 Cor. 11:16-17), the apostle to the nations. He who had set out to destroy the Church spent his life building and extending it. This great triumph of the risen Christ over a dedicated enemy was of such decisive importance for the young church that the story of his conversion is told three times in Acts (9:1-22; 22:3-21; 26:9-20), and Paul himself makes mention of this experience three times in his letters (Gal. 1:11-16; 1 Cor. 9:1-12; 15:3-11).

The origin of the observance of the Conversion of St. Paul is obscure. The commemoration seems to have begun in Gaul, as contrasted with the Festival of Saints Peter and Paul, which began in Rome. In the fourth-century martyrology of St. Jerome, the day is called the "translation" of St. Paul, which suggests that the day may have begun as a celebration of the anniversary of the moving of the relics of Paul to his basilica outside Rome. The day does not seem to have been generally observed until about the twelfth century. The festival was especially popular in northern Europe, and this, in addition to its biblical basis, perhaps accounts for the retention of the day on both Lutheran and Anglican calendars. The day was traditionally of lower rank than the feasts of the apostles, however, and in England it was retained on the calendar only with some difficulty.

The day marks the conclusion of the Week of Prayer for Christian Unity.

The feast is not celebrated in the East.

FOR FURTHER READING

Dunn. James D. G. *The Cambridge Companion to St. Paul.* Cambridge: Cambridge
    University Press, 2004.
———. *The Theology of Paul the Apostle.* Grand Rapids: Eerdmans, 1998.
Hooker, Morna. *Paul: A Short Introduction.* Oxford: Oneworld, 2004.
Jewett, Robert. *A Chronology of Paul's Life.* Philadelphia: Fortress Press, 1978.
Käsemann, Ernst. *Perspectives on Paul.* Philadelphia: Fortress Press, 1979.
Roetzel, Calvin. *Paul: The Man and the Myth.* Minneapolis: Fortress Press, 1999.
Sandmel, Samuel. *The Genius of Paul.* Philadelphia: Fortress Press, 1979.
Schnelle, Udo. *Apostle Paul: His Life and Theology.* Trans. Eugene Boring. Grand
    Rapids: Baker Academic, 2006.
Stendahl, Krister. *Paul Among Jews and Gentiles.* Philadelphia: Fortress Press,
    1975.

READING

From *The Word of God and the Word of Man* by Karl Barth

We all know the curiosity that comes over us when from a window we see the people in the street suddenly stop and look up—shade their eyes with their hands and look straight up into the sky toward something which is hidden from us by the roof. Our curiosity is superfluous, for what they see is doubtless an aeroplane. But as to the sudden stopping, looking up, and tense attention characteristic of the people of the Bible, our wonder will not be so lightly dismissed. To me personally it came first with Paul: this man evidently sees and hears something which is above everything, which is absolutely beyond the range of my observation and the measure of my thought. Let me place myself as I will to this coming something that in enigmatical words he insists he sees and hears, I am still taken by the fact that he, Paul, or whoever it was who wrote the Epistle to the Ephesians, for example, is eye and ear in a state which expressions such as inspiration, alarm, or stirring or overwhelming emotion, do not satisfactorily describe. I seem to see within so transparent a piece of literature a personality who is actually thrown out of his course by seeing and hearing what I for my part do not see and hear who is, so to speak, captured, in order to be dragged as a prisoner from land to land for strange, intense, uncertain, and yet mysteriously well-planned service.

And if ever I come to fear lest mine is a case of self-hallucination, one glance at the secular events of those times, one glance at the widening circle of ripples in the pool of history, tells me of a certainty that a stone of unusual weight must have been dropped into deep water somewhere tells me that, among all the hundreds of peripatetic preachers and miracle-workers from the Near East who in that day must have done along the same Appian Way into imperial Rome, it was this one Paul, seeing and hearing what he did, who was the cause, if not of all, yet of the most important developments in that city's future.

Karl Barth, *The Word of God and the Word of Man,* trans. Douglas Horton (Boston: Pilgrim, 1928), 62–63.

PROPERS

O God, by the preaching of your apostle Paul you have caused the light of the Gospel to shine throughout the world: Grant, we pray, that we, having his wonderful conversion in remembrance, may show ourselves thankful to you by following his holy teaching; through Jesus Christ our Lord, who lives and reigns with you and the Holy Spirit, one God, now and forever.

Gregorian sacramentary, RS, trans. BCP

Readings: Acts 22:3-16 (RC)/Acts 9:1-22 (LBW, ELW, LSB)/Acts 26:9-21 (BCP)
              Psalm 117 (RC)/Psalm 67 (BCP, LBW, ELW)
              Galatians 1:11-24 (BCP, LBW, ELW, LSB)
              Mark 16:15-18 (RC)/Luke 21:10-19 (LBW, ELW)/Matthew 10:16-22 (BCP)/
              Matthew 19:27-30 (LSB)
Hymn of the Day:
              "We sing the glorious conquest before Damascus' gate" (H82 255)
              or "O Spirit of the living God" (H82 531, LBW 388)
Prayers: For the unity of the church
              For renewal of faith
              For preachers of the gospel
              For opening our eyes to see beyond this world
Preface: Apostles
Color: White

January 26

Timothy, Titus, Silas; Companions of St. Paul

Three young companions of St. Paul are commemorated together on the day after the festival of Paul's conversion. Thus the church is reminded that not age but love of Christ and faithful care of the church are the important qualities for Christian witness in the world. Two of these three disciples who are remembered together today, Silvanus (Silas) and Timothy, are linked with St. Paul in the address of 1 Thessalonians 1:1.

Timothy, who accompanied Paul on his second missionary journey, is described by Paul as a "brother" (1 Thess. 3:2) and was apparently converted by Paul when Paul first visited Lystra in Asia Minor (1 Cor. 4:17; 1 Tim. 2:2, 18; 2 Tim. 1:2). Timothy's father was a Greek; his mother, Eunice (according to Acts 16:1-3, a Jew), was the daughter of a Christian, Lois (2 Tim. 1:5). Paul had Timothy circumcised so that he would be acceptable to the Jews as well as the Gentiles. Timothy first appears in the New Testament as a young associate of Paul and Silas at Corinth. He went with Paul to Philippi and then to Beroea, where he remained for a time, rejoining Paul again in Athens. Paul then sent Timothy back to the Thessalonian church to strengthen their faith during a time of persecution. Timothy returned to Paul at Corinth with a report of their steadfastness (1 Thess. 1:6-9). Timothy was apparently the bearer of Paul's letter to Corinth, and 1 Corinthians 16:10-11 urges the Corinthians to put the emissary at ease, as if he were somewhat shy. While at Corinth, Timothy preached the same message as had Paul and Silas (1:19), but the problems of that church remained. Because his father was a Gentile, Timothy was sent to strengthen Gentile churches, for he seemed to have their confidence (Phil. 2:20-22). Paul seems to have sent his young companion ahead to prepare for Paul's visit to Macedonia and Achaia and later to Jerusalem. According to Hebrews 13:23 he was imprisoned for a time.

John of Damascus says that Timothy, the first bishop of Ephesus, witnessed Mary's assumption. According to tradition, Timothy was beaten and stoned to death in 97 C.E. under Nerva because he opposed heathen worship, and in 356 his supposed remains were moved to Constantinople by Constantine. His feast day in the Greek and Syrian Churches is January 22; his feast day in the West had been January 24 (where it continues to be in the calendar in the *Lutheran Service Book*), but the calendars in the *Book of Common Prayer* and in the *Lutheran Book of Worship* and *Evangelical Lutheran Worship* have followed the lead of the Roman Catholic Church and commemorate Timothy with Titus on January 26, remembering those two companions of Paul immediately after the celebration of Paul's conversion.

Timothy had delivered First Corinthians. The bearer of Second Corinthians is Titus, who seems to be Paul's new deputy. He plays an important role in the Corinthian correspondence from this point on. Titus is not mentioned in Acts, but he is frequently referred to in Paul's letters. He was born of Gentile parents (Gal. 2:3) and was perhaps a native of Antioch, since he was in the delegation from Antioch to Jerusalem (Acts 15:2; Gal. 2:1-3), and he may have been converted by Paul (Titus 1:4). He and a companion were sent to Corinth after 1 Corinthians had been delivered there, because of reports Paul had received about that troublesome church. The mission was a delicate one. Paul had expected to meet Titus at Troas (2 Cor. 2:12-13), but instead Titus met him in Macedonia with good news (7:6, 13-14), and he returned to Corinth with Second Corinthians (8:6, 13, 23). The epistle to Titus gives the information that Titus had been left on Crete to oversee the organization of the churches there. Titus's mission to Dalmatia is alluded to in 2 Timothy 4:10. Tradition says that Titus lived in Crete as the first bishop of Gortyna and died there at the age of 93. His head was later transferred from Gortyna to St. Mark's in Venice after the invasion of the Saracens in 823. Ancient sources provide no further information. In the writings of Paul Titus is pictured as vigorous, resourceful, decisive, efficient, zealous; yet with it all of a kindly disposition. In the Pastoral Letters a rather different picture is drawn. Titus there needs to be reminded to exercise his authority (Titus 2:15). This clear difference in characterization is a primary reason why many think that the Pastoral Letters are pseudonymous.

Titus's feast day in the Greek and Syrian Churches is August 25. In the West it had been observed on January 4, but it was transferred to February 6 by Pius IX to avoid a conflict with what was then (January 4) the octave of the Holy Innocents. On the present Roman Catholic calendar and on the Episcopal, Lutheran, and Methodist calendars, Titus is remembered with Timothy on January 26.

Silas (as he is called in Acts; in the epistles to the Thessalonians he is called Silvanus, his Latin and Hellenistic name, which resembles his Armenian name, Saul)

was a leader in the church at Jerusalem (Acts 15:22) who was sent with Paul to tell the Christians of Antioch of the decision of the Jerusalem Council concerning Gentile Christians. Paul chose Silas to replace John Mark on the second missionary journey when Mark and Barnabas left, and so Silas was one of the first Christian missionaries on the continent of Europe (Acts 15:22-40). Paul and Silas were imprisoned together at Philippi (Acts 16:19-40), and Silas was with Paul during the riot at Thessalonica. He was then sent away to Beroea and remained there when Paul went on to Athens. He rejoined Paul at Corinth. When Paul left Corinth, Silas remained, and this seems to be the end of the relationship between the two. Silas is not mentioned again. Silas-Silvanus was probably the Silvanus who delivered First Peter (5:12); some say he was the author of 1 Peter or at least the amanuensis. Legend says that he was bishop of Corinth and that he died in Macedonia. His traditional feast day in the West has been July 13. The Lutheran calendar joins his commemoration with that of Timothy and Titus on January 26.

READING

From an essay by Wilhelm Löhe

Among the means which the Church uses to save souls, preaching stands first. It is the means by which those are called who stand afar off, and those who have been called are rendered steadfast in their calling and election. In preaching, the Church does not aim to support the holy Word by human art, but the chief matter is not to hinder its power and operation and not to impose upon the Word any kind or manner of operation which does not befit it.

The preacher proclaims salvation in Christ Jesus with the consciousness that it is not what he does, but the noble contents of the Word itself that must separate souls from the world and bring them near to God. Of course the preacher believes and therefore speaks, and it is a detestable contradiction to preach and yet not believe; but a true preacher will not try to recommend the truth by imparting his faith and experience; rather he seeks to bring his people to say with the Samaritans: "Now we believe, not because of your saying; for we have heard him ourselves, and know that this is indeed the Christ, the Savior of the world."

An upright preacher does not purposely withdraw himself, nor does he purposely make himself prominent, but he comes with the Word and the Word comes with him; he is a simple, faithful witness of the Word, and the Word witnesses to him; he and his Word appear like one thing. All his preaching is based upon holy peace. Even when he rebukes, and zeal for God's house eats him up, it is not the wrath of the restless world, but the wrath of the unapproachable God of peace, that burns within him. It is not he that speaks, but the Lord speaks in him and through him, and his execution of his office is worthy of the Lord.

Wilhelm Löhe, *Three Books Concerning the Church,* trans. Edward T. Horn (Reading: Pilger, 1908), 181f., rev. PHP.

PROPERS

Almighty God, you called your saints Timothy and Titus [and Silas] to the work of evangelists and teachers, and made them strong to endure hardship and joyful in prison: Strengthen us to stand firm in adversity and to live lives that are self-controlled, upright, and godly in this present time, that with sure confidence we may wait for the blessed hope and the manifestation of the glory of our great God and Savior Jesus Christ, who gave himself for us and who now lives and reigns with you and the Holy Spirit, one God, now and forever.

Titus 2:12-13, LFF, rev. PHP

Readings:	Isaiah 62:1-7
	Psalm 112:1-9 *or* 23
	2 Timothy 1:1-8 *or* Titus 1:1-5 *or* Titus 2:11-15
	John 10:1-10
Hymn of the Day:	
	"Spread, O spread, thou mighty Word" (H82 530, LBW 379, LSB 830, ELW 663)
Prayers:	For the hesitant
	For reconciliation
	For mixed marriages
	For Christians in Turkey
	For the Greek Orthodox Church in Greece and Crete
Preface:	Epiphany (or Pentecost, BCP)
Color:	White

January 27

Lydia, Dorcas, and Phoebe; Helpers of the Apostles

On the day following the commemoration of Timothy, Titus, and Silas, the *Lutheran Book of Worship* introduced a commemoration of three women who were helpers of the apostles.

Lydia was Paul's first convert in Europe. He met her, a woman from Thyatira in Asia Minor (it was a Lydian city; her name may originally have been an adjective), at Philippi. She is described in Acts 16:11-40. St. Paul does not refer to her in his writings. She sold purple-dyed goods, an occupation that required considerable capital; she was therefore probably well-to-do. (Both Philippi and Thyatira were famous for their dyeing.) After her baptism she invited Paul and his companions to stay in her house, which relieved Paul of the necessity of earning his support, as was his custom elsewhere. St. Paul had a special love for the church at Philippi as shown in his letter to that church; Lydia's help was doubtless a cause of this special relationship.

Dorcas or Tabitha (the name means "gazelle" and was a favorite name among both Greeks and Jews) was a Christian woman from Joppa, a friend and helper of the poor. When she died, Peter restored her to life (Acts 9:36-43), the first such miracle by an apostle. The miracle won many believers for the church. Dorcas is called a "disciple" in a feminine form of the word that in the New Testament is applied only to her. The Dorcas Societies of churchwomen devoted to good works are named for her.

Phoebe (her name means "bright" or "radiant") was a deaconess at the church in Cenchreae, the east seaport of Corinth. The word translated "deaconess" might perhaps be better translated "patron" or "helper," for Paul (2 Cor. 11:23; Col. 1:23, 25) does not mean that he is a *deacon* when he applies a similar word to himself. Nonetheless, Phoebe, by her work and her service, became the inspiration for the more regular order of deaconesses that was to emerge in the Church in the third and fourth centuries. In Romans 16:1-2 Paul commends her to the Roman Church upon her move there, and this fact that she was free to travel suggests that she was perhaps a widow. Her specific service that earned her the title of "helper" or "deaconess" was perhaps her willingness to stand by foreigners in their uncertainties.

The Eastern Church commemorates Blessed Tabitha on October 25, and the *Lutheran Service Book* (2006) remembers these three women on that date.

READING

From *Light of Christ* by Evelyn Underhill

There are two sides to every vocation: unconditional giving of self to the call of God—"Here I am, send me!"—and the gift of power which rewards the total gift of self to God. In Christ's life we see these two movements in perfect balance. How humbly he submitted to the Will of the Father, totally absorbed in His business, and to the tests, pressure, suffering that came through circumstances; and yet how, though never in His own interest and never apart from His love and pity for man, there is always the Power to intervene, save, mould, defeat opposition, transform even the humble accidents of life. In all men and women of prayer deeply united to God that double state exists too. That handing of self over and the mysterious power that somehow acts through self in consequence—the right word said, the right prayer prayed. But only in proportion to the self-effacement. The power of course is God's, not ours. One hears people say, "He (or she) is simply wonderful!" Not at all! He or she is the self-emptied channel of the only Wonderful—the Mighty God, the Everlasting Father. When we give ourselves to Him without reserve we become points of insertion for the rescuing spirit of Love. We are woven into the Redeeming Body so that we may provide more and more channels for God.

Evelyn Underhill, *The Light of Christ* (London: Longmans, 1945), 74–75, 91–92, 64, 27–28, 28–29, 82–83. Reprinted by permission of Wipf and Stock Publishers.

PROPERS

Almighty God, you inspired your servants Lydia, Dorcas, and Phoebe to support and sustain your church by their deeds of generous love: Open our hearts to hear you, conform our will to love you, and strengthen our hands to serve you; for the sake of your Son Jesus Christ our Lord, who lives and reigns with you and the Holy Spirit, one God, now and forever.

PHP, after James E. Kiefer

Readings:	Ecclesiasticus 2:7-11
	Psalm 1
	1 Corinthians 1:26-31
	Matthew 25:1-13
Hymn of the Day:	
	"Lord, speak to us that we may speak" (LBW 403, ELW 676)
Prayers:	For the poor
	For foreigners in a strange land
	For deaconesses
	For all who assist in the proclamation of the word of God
Preface:	All Saints
Color:	White

January 28

Thomas Aquinas, Teacher, 1274

Next to Augustine, Thomas is perhaps the greatest theologian in the history of the Western Church. His insistence that the Christian scholar must be prepared to meet other scholars on their own ground, to become familiar with their viewpoints, to argue from their premises, has been a permanent and valuable contribution to Christian thought. During the thirteenth century, the works of Aristotle began to be available again in the West through Eastern European sources and through Islamic Arab sources in Africa and Spain. Some began to embrace Aristotle as an alternative to Christianity; some denounced him as an enemy of the Christian faith; some tried to hold both Aristotelian and Christian ideas side by side. Thomas, immersing himself in the ideas of Aristotle, undertook to explain Christianity in a language that would make sense to followers of Aristotle. It was at the time a radical and dangerous idea.

Surprisingly little is known with certainty about the life of this enormously influential theologian. Thomas, one of nine children, was born of a noble family at Roccasecca, near Aquino in southern Italy, *ca.* 1225. In 1231, at the age of five or six, he was given to the nearby Benedictine monastery of Monte Cassino, of which an uncle had been abbot; his parents had planned that he follow in the footsteps of his successful relative. As a monk he was sent to complete his education at the University of Naples from 1239 to 1244. While there he was introduced to the writings of Aristotle.

The young monk was drawn to the new Dominican Order of Preachers when he was nineteen, and toward the end of April 1244, he received the mendicant habit at the Priory of San Domenico in Naples. His family strongly opposed his entrance into this new order of begging monks and brought him home by force. They were, however, unable to change his mind, and by the summer of 1245 he returned to Naples to rejoin the monastery there. In 1245 or 1246 Thomas went to Paris, then to Cologne, where he studied under Albert the Great. As a student he was large in stature and shy by nature. His fellow students dubbed him the Dumb Ox.) At Paris a conflict between the mendicant and the secular clergy became so intense that when Thomas finally gave his inaugural lecture as a master, he and his audience had to be protected by soldiers. The university refused to recognize his status, despite papal intervention on his behalf. Thomas and his exact contemporary Bonaventure were finally admitted to full magistral privileges August 12, 1257, with the bishop and most of the secular masters conspicuously absent.

Paris in the 1250s enjoyed the presence of a remarkable trio of saints. The king was St. Louis IX (see August 25), St. Thomas occupied the chair of theology assigned to his order, and the head of the school, another Italian theologian, was a Franciscan, St. Bonaventure. All three were friends. Bonaventure, born in 1221 at Bagnoregio near Viterbo, is known for his deep mystical piety as well as his profound theological and philosophical learning. Like Thomas, Bonaventure knew Aristotle well but regarded him as inferior to Plato. In 1265 he rejected the pope's invitation to become Archbishop of York, but in 1273 he acceded to the pope's insistence that he become cardinal and Bishop of Albano. He died at the Council of Lyons, July 15, 1274; his traditional feast day is July 15. (See Christopher M. Cullen, *Bonaventure* [New York: Oxford University Press, 2006].)

Thomas returned to Italy in 1259. His exact movements are unclear, but he was in Orvieto when, according to Bartholomew of Lucca, Thomas composed the Corpus Christi office, which was introduced in 1264. His authorship of the texts has been disputed, but now it is increasingly accepted. His hymns continue to be sung in many contexts: *Adoro te devote*, "Humbly I adore thee, verity unseen"; *Lauda Sion*, "Zion, praise thy Savior singing"; *Pange, lingua, gloriosi corporis mysterium*, "Now, my tongue, the mystery telling"; *Salutaris hostia*, "O saving victim, opening wide the gate of heaven"; *Tantum ergo*, "Therefore we before him bending."

In 1265 Thomas was in charge of a studium in Rome in the priory of Santa Sabina and spent much of his time writing. (One skill that Thomas never learned was good handwriting. His manuscripts are notorious for their illegibility.)

Thomas returned to Paris by 1269. The old controversy broke out again, this time concerning the traditional Augustinian theology versus the newly discovered Aristotle, as well as the old hostility against the mendicants. The hostility of the traditionalists against Aristotle led by the bishop of Paris on December 10, 1270, to condemn eighteen errors in the teaching of what was an exaggerated Aristotelianism.

The atmosphere at Paris was clearly uncongenial to scholarship, so Thomas left for Florence in 1272 to attend a general meeting of his order, and then went to Naples where he taught for the remaining two years of his life. On December 6, 1273, at the conclusion of the St. Nicholas Mass he departed from his usual custom of spending the rest of the day after mass writing or teaching, and never again wrote or dictated anything. For whatever reason—stroke, mystical experience, mental breakdown—his productive life was over. Questioned by his companion Reginald, he is said to have replied, "I cannot go on. . . . All that I have written seems to me like so much straw compared to what I have seen and what has been revealed to me."

In poor health he was summoned to the Council of Lyons, where reconciliation of the Eastern and Western Churches was planned. He fell sick on the journey and was taken to the Cistercian Abbey of Fossa Nuova near Maenza where he died March 7, 1274, not yet fifty years old. He was canonized in 1323 and since 1567 has been known by the title "the Angelic Doctor."

Thomas's work is one of the great expressions of the relationship between the experienced facts of everyday life and the teaching of Catholic theology. His boldly innovative system attempted to make sense of life without destroying its mystery, and it saved Christian theology from the corroding effects of non-Christian Aristotelian and Arabic philosophy. Finally, Thomas for all his intellectual gifts, was a man of humility and deep piety.

On the calendar in the *Lutheran Book of Worship* Thomas is commemorated on the date of his death, March 7, but this date is also the commemoration of Perpetua and her companions. It is more convenient therefore to remember him on January 28, the date of the removal of his relics to Toulouse in 1369; this is the date of his commemoration on the Roman Catholic, Episcopal, Methodist, and *Evangelical Lutheran Worship* calendars.

FOR FURTHER READING

Davies, Brian. *The Thought of Thomas Aquinas.* New York: Oxford University Press, 1992.

Foster, Kenelm. *The Life of St. Thomas Aquinas: Biographical Documents.* London: Longmans, Green, & Co.; Baltimore: Helicon, 1959.

Gilson, Etienne. *The Christian Philosophy of St. Thomas Aquinas.* New York: Random House, 1956; Notre Dame: Notre Dame University Press, 1994.

Kretzmann, Norman, and Eleanore Stump, eds. *The Cambridge Companion to Aquinas.* Cambridge: Cambridge University Press, 1993.

Maurer, Armand, et al., eds. *St. Thomas Aquinas, 1274–1994: Comparative Studies.* 2 vols. Toronto: Pontifical Institute of Medieval Studies, 1974.

Nichols, Aidan. *Discovering Aquinas: An Introduction to His Life, Work, and Influence.* Grand Rapids: Eerdmans, 2003.

Walz, Angelus. *Saint Thomas Aquinas: A Biographical Study.* Trans. S. Bullough. Westminster: Newman, 1951.

Weisheipl, James A. *Friar Thomas D'Aquino. His Life, Thought, and Works.* Oxford: Blackwell, 1975.

READING

From *Summa Contra Gentiles* by Thomas Aquinas

The pursuit of wisdom is more perfect than all human pursuits, more noble, more useful, more full of joy.

It is more perfect because as one gives oneself to the pursuit of wisdom one even now shares in true beatitude. Therefore a wise man has said, "Happy are those who fix their thoughts on wisdom." [Ecclesiasticus 14:20]

The pursuit of wisdom is more noble because especially through this pursuit one approaches a likeness to God, who made all things by wisdom [Ps. 104:24]. And since likeness is the cause of love, the pursuit of wisdom joins humanity to God in friendship. That is why it is said of wisdom, "She is an inexhaustible treasure for humanity, and those who profit by it become God's friends." [Wisd. 7:14]

The pursuit of wisdom is more useful because through wisdom we arrive at the everlasting kingdom: "Honor wisdom so that you may reign for ever." [Wisd. 6:21]

The pursuit of wisdom is more full of joy because "there is no bitterness in her company, no pain in life with her, only gladness and joy." [Wisd. 8:16]

And so, in the name of the divine Mercy, I have the confidence to embark upon the work of wisdom, even though this may surpass my powers; and I have set myself the task of making known, so far as my limited powers will permit, the truth that the Catholic* faith professes, and of setting aside the errors that are opposed to it. In the words of Hilary, "I am aware that I owe this to God as the chief duty of my life, that every word and sense may speak of him."

Trans. PHP, based on the translation of Anton C. Pegis.

*In this passage, "Catholic" means, of course, the same as it does in the Creeds: whole, entire, complete in all its parts. The opposite of Catholic is heretic: a person, faith, or church, which accepts only selected parts of the received teaching.

PROPERS

Almighty God, you have enriched your church with the singular learning and holiness of your servant Thomas Aquinas: Enable us, we pray, to grow in wisdom by his teaching and deepen our devotion by the example of his faith and holy life; through Jesus Christ our Lord, who lives and reigns with you and the Holy Spirit, one God, now and forever.

PHP, RS ✚ LFF

Readings: Wisdom 7:7-14
               Psalm 37:3-6, 32-33 *or* 119:97-104
               1 Corinthians 3:5-11
               Matthew 13:47-52
Hymn of the Day:
               "Now, my tongue, the mystery telling" (H82 329, LBW 120, LSB 630)
               or "Humbly I adore thee, verity unseen" (H82 314; LBW 199, LSB 640, ELW 476)
Prayers: For the spirit of inquiry
               For the gift of wisdom
               For grace to perceive the mystery of God's presence
               For teachers of theology
               For the grounding of theology always in prayer and in the life and worship of the
                  church
Preface: Trinity Sunday
Color: White

February 1

Bride (Brigid), Abbess, 523

In Ireland, St. Brigid (or Brigit), "the Mary of the Gael," is honored nearly as much as Patrick. In England her name became St. Bride. Little is known about her life. Stories of miracles abound, and despite many being far-fetched and more than a little tinged with folklore, they portray a strong, happy, compassionate woman abounding in charity toward her needy neighbors. She founded a community of women at Kildare, and is honored as the founder and abbess of the first women's community in Ireland. She died in Kildare *ca.* 523 and was buried there, but during the Danish invasions her remains were taken to Downpatrick to be reburied with those of St. Patrick. Her cult spread widely. In England and Scotland churches were dedicated in her honor as St. Bride, the most famous being St. Bride's, London, near Fleet Street. Rebuilt between 1671 and 1675 by Sir

Christopher Wren, St. Bride's has the tallest of Wren's steeples, a magnificent spire that has inspired the popular tiered shape of wedding cakes.

Bride was added to the Episcopal calendar in *Lesser Feasts and Fasts 1997.* She is not on the General Roman Calendar but is on the calendar of the Eastern Church as Brigid of Ireland and the Church of England's 1995 calendar, the *Christian Year,* as Brigid, Abbess of Kildare.

FOR FURTHER READING

O'Brian, Felim. *St. Brigid, Her Legend, History and Cult.* London, 1938.
Curtayne, Alice. *St. Brigid of Ireland.* Dublin: Browne and Nolan, 1934; rep. 1954.

READING

From Evelyn Underhill, *Worship*

Christian worship in its fullness should include and harmonize all the various phases of our human experience. It has room for the extremes of awestruck adoration and penitent love, humble demand and inward assurance. All levels of life and action are relevant to it; for they are covered and sanctified by the principle of incarnation. It can therefore weave every detail of the daily routine into the devotional life. It is thoroughly sacramental; and shows its true quality, not by increasing abstraction and other-worldliness, but by an ever-deepening recognition of the sacredness and inexhaustible meaning of homely things. Especially a deep realism as regards human imperfection and sin, and also human suffering and struggle, is at the very heart of the Christian response to God; which if it is to tally with the Christian revelation of disinterested love as summed up in the Cross, must include the element of hardness, cost, and willing pain. It is this sacrificial suffering, this deliberate endurance of hardship for the sake of the Unseen, which gives nobility and depth to worship. The costly renunciations and total self-stripping of the consecrated life contribute something to the Church's oblation, without which her reasonable and holy sacrifice would not be complete.

Christian worship is never a solitary undertaking. Both on its visible and invisible sides, it has a thoroughly social and organic character. The worshipper, however lonely in appearance, comes before God as a member of a great family; part of the Communion of Saints, living and dead . . . immersed in that life, nourished by its traditions, taught, humbled, and upheld by its saints.

[The] personal life of worship, unable for long to maintain itself alone, has behind it two thousand years of spiritual culture, and around it the self-offerings of all devoted souls. Further, . . . public worship, and commonly . . . secret devotion too, are steeped in history and tradition; and apart from them, cannot be understood. There are few things more remarkable in Christian history than the continuity through many vicissitudes and under many disguises of the dominant strands in Christian worship. On the other hand the whole value of this personal life of worship abides in the completeness with which it is purified from all taint of egotism, and the selflessness and simplicity with which it is added to the common store. Here the individual must lose his life to find it; the longing for personal expression, personal experience, safety, joy, must more and more be swallowed up in Charity. For the goal alike of Christian sanctification and Christian worship is the ceaseless self-offering of the Church, in and with Christ her head, to the increase of the glory of God.

Excerpts from *Worship* by Evelyn Underhill, copyright 1936 by Harper & Brothers. Reprinted by permission of HarperCollins Publishers and Hodder & Stoughton.

PROPERS

Everliving God, we rejoice today in the fellowship of your blessed servant Brigid, and we give you thanks for her life of devoted service. Inspire us with life and light, and give us perseverance to serve you all our days; through Jesus Christ our Lord, who lives and reigns with you and the Holy Spirit, one God, forever and ever.
LFF

Readings:	1 Corinthians 1:26-31
	Psalm 138 *or* Psalm 1
	Matthew 6:25-33
Hymn of the Day:	
	"Be thou my vision, O Lord of my heart" (H82 488, ELW 793)
Prayers:	For the gift of joyful compassion
	For all who lead lives of prayer
	For communities of women
	For brides
Preface:	A Saint (2) (BCP)
Color:	White

February 2

The Presentation of Our Lord

This feast brings the celebration of Christmas to an end, and by the Gospel's prophecy that a sword will pierce the soul of the Mother of Jesus, the day also looks ahead to the crucifixion. It is therefore a bridge between the Nativity and the Passion.

The Gospels do not permit a bland and sentimental interpretation of the arrival of Christ. Simeon, with the infant Messiah in his arms and filled with the prophetic spirit, acknowledges not only the light to the nations but also the shadows that this light must necessarily cast. The long-awaited Messiah will achieve no easy triumph. He will be the center of storm and controversy that will reveal the secret disposition of many hearts and will bring piercing grief to his own mother. The Messiah, who comes to lead Israel to glory, must go by the path of suffering, and his people must go with him along that same path.

A central figure in the lovely drama that is at the heart of this festival is the venerable Simeon, who, representing the expectant nation of Israel, at last, after years of patient and faithful waiting, held the infant Savior in his arms. This meeting is the occasion of his song, the consolation of Israel and the nations. The child was being presented to God by his parents, but in this child God was coming to meet his people, so that he who is the light of the world might make his people lamps shining in a dark world that others might see the right path.

In origin, the Presentation of Jesus in the Temple by his parents is a festival of the Lord (called by the Armenians "The Coming of the Son of God into the Temple"), but it is also the occasion of the Purification of the Virgin Mary, the day on which the Old Testament law released the Virgin Mary from what was considered to be the impurity of childbirth and demanded a sacrifice of turtledoves from Joseph in exchange for the life of his firstborn son.

In the Eastern Churches, where the feast originated, the day is called *Hypapante*, "the Meeting" (of Christ with Simeon, and, by extension, of Israel with the Messiah, of God with his people). The day was observed in Jerusalem at the end of the fourth century and was introduced in Constantinople by the Emperor Justinian in 542. In the West, the day seems first to appear in the sacramentaries of Gelasius (seventh century) and of Gregory (eighth century), where it is called the Purification of Mary. Pope Sergius (d. 701) seems to have introduced the practice of a procession with lighted candles on this date (as well as the other Marian feasts), and the procession, somewhat incongruously, was in its origins a penitential rite; down to modern times violet vestments have been worn for this part of the ceremonies of the day.

In the Gospel, Simeon sings that the infant Christ is "a light to lighten the Gentiles," and so the procession shows the entrance of the true light into the world and the gradual illumination of the world by him. St. Sophronius (died *ca.* 638) in a sermon for the Presentation exhorts his congregation:

> . . . Everyone should be eager to join the procession and to carry a light.
>
> Our lighted candles are a sign of the divine splendor of the one who comes to expel the dark shadows of evil and to make the whole universe radiant with the brilliance of his eternal light.
>
> Our candles also show how bright our souls should be when we go to meet Christ.
>
> . . . So let us all hasten together to meet our God.*

*Oratio de Hypapante 6, 7. From the English translation of the Office of Readings © 1974 by the International Commission on English in the Liturgy, Inc. All rights reserved.

Sometime after the introduction of the procession, the custom arose of blessing all the candles to be used during the year on this festival of light, therefore called "Candlemas" in England, to remind participants of Christ "the light for revelation to the Gentiles." The day is the appropriate time for candlelight services marking the conclusion of the forty days of Christmas.

A seventeenth-century English carol for Candlemas Day (1661) laments,

> Christmas hath made an end,
> Welladay, welladay;
> Which was my dearest friend,
> More is the pity:
> For with an heavy heart
> Must I from thee depart
> To follow plough and cart
> All the year after.
>
> Lent is fast coming on . . .
> All our good cheer is gone . . .
>
> It grieves me to the heart,
> Welladay, welladay,
> From my friend to depart,
> More is the pity:
> Christmas, I mean 'tis thee
> That thus forsaketh me;
> Yet till one hour I see
> Will I be merry.

Because the Presentation is the conclusion of the celebration of Christmas, the Preface appointed in the *Lutheran Book of Worship* and *Evangelical Lutheran Worship* is the Preface of Christmas, which easily can be related to the Gospel for the day, although the Preface of the Epiphany with its reference to light is also appropriate and is appointed in the *Book of Common Prayer*.

Even before the coming of Christ to enlighten the nations, February 2 was kept as a holy day by the pagan peoples of northern Europe. Among the Celts, the day was the feast of *Imbolg,* one the four "cross-quarter" days that fall between the spring and autumn equinoxes and the winter and summer solstices. The day was sacred to the goddess Brigantia, who presided over the birth of the spring lambs, preparations for spring sowing, and the refurbishing of boats in order to begin the fishing season. In Christian times the Celtic saint Brigid was said to give her blessings on this day to flocks and fields and to the harvest of the sea. Sacred fires in fields and in homes celebrated the return of the sun and looked forward to the coming of spring. The ancient Germans preserved the belief that the weather today would either promise an early harvest or warn of hunger in days to come, a belief that came from Germany to America as "Groundhog Day."

READING

From *The Light of the World* by Jaroslav Pelikan

The cleansing power of the light has penetrated the darkness in the coming of Christ. Those who had received it and had been cleansed by it no longer lived in darkness, but had become "children of light." . . . They knew what Christ was because they experienced what Christ did in them and to them. The illumination in which they now lived showed that the radiance had shone in them. And the radiance, in turn, pointed beyond itself to the light with which it was one. As the Church contemplated what the light had brought and as it worshipped the source of its own being, its illumination reflected his light. The Church viewed itself and its world differently because the illumination had come in Christ. It viewed God differently too, because his personal radiance had brought the illumination that transformed and healed every human vision. The gift of this salvation, accomplished by God the light in Christ the radiance, Athanasius found represented in the image of light, as confessed by the psalmist: "In thy light do we see light."

Over the darkling world the demonic powers had drawn a veil, to keep men from realizing that this was still God's world. But God had pierced the veil by coming in Christ, who was "light from light" and the very radiance of the Father. By him God had saved and illumined the darkling world, "to give light to those who sit in darkness and in the shadow of death."

Jaroslav Pelikan, *The Light of the World: A Basic Image in Early Christian Thought* (New York: Harper, 1962), 91–92, 110.

PROPERS

Almighty and everliving God, we humbly pray that, as your only-begotten Son was this day presented in the temple, so may we be presented to you with pure and clean hearts by Jesus Christ our Lord; who lives and reigns with you and the Holy Spirit, one God, now and forever.

Gregorian sacramentary, RS, trans. BCP

Readings: Malachi 3:1-4
               Psalm 24:7-10 *or* 84:1-6
               Hebrews 2:14-18
               Luke 2:22-40
Hymn of the Day:
               "Hail to the Lord who comes" (H82 259)
               or "In his temple now behold him" (LBW 184, LSB 519, ELW 417)

Prayers:	For the illumination of the darkness of the world
	For the aged
	For those who wait patiently for salvation
	For those who have become mothers
Preface:	Presentation (RC), Christmas (Lutheran), Epiphany (Episcopal)
Color:	White

February 3

Ansgar, Archbishop of Hamburg, Missionary to Denmark and Sweden, 865

The Commemoration of Ansgar (or Anskar) encourages a long and patient view of Christian history. The immediate result of his devoted and perilous missionary work was slight: two churches established on the border of Denmark and one priest settled in Sweden. The rich harvest of conversion would not be gathered for three generations.

The Frankish missionary to Scandinavia, often called "the Apostle of the North," was born in 801 near Amiens. He became a monk of the Benedictine monastery of Corbie nearby and later transferred to the monastery of New Corbie on the Weser River. He was a man of great personal piety, and he combined an eager desire to explore new lands with an unusual organizing ability.

At the beginning of the ninth century the Church was just starting its efforts to spread the gospel to Scandinavia, and the founding of the bishopric of Hamburg in 804 was one of the first important steps in this direction. The first actual missionary venture was in 826 and was connected with the attempt of the newly converted King Harald of Denmark to regain his throne. Harald was unsuccessful in his political aim, and Ansgar, who went along with him as a missionary, also met with little success, although he established contact with merchants and travelers from Scandinavia.

In the summer of 829, a group of merchants from the trading town of Birka in Sweden asked the emperor, Louis the Pious, to send a Christian mission, and again Ansgar was chosen. During the long trip northward, Ansgar and his companions were attacked by Viking pirates and robbed, arriving in Birka almost penniless. King Bjorn and the local authorities gave permission to preach the new faith and to establish a church. Most of the Christians there seem to have been slaves who had brought their faith with them, but a few Swedes were converted and baptized. Among them was the king's bailiff in Birka, who at his own expense built a church, the first Christian church in all of Scandinavia. After a year and a half of work, Ansgar returned home.

In 831 Ansgar was appointed Abbot of Corbie and Archbishop of Hamburg, with the idea that this would be the base for missionary operations in Scandinavia as opportunities arose. For the next thirteen years Ansgar preached and organized missions in northern Germany and Scandinavia. He participated in the consecration of Gotbert, the first bishop for Sweden. In 845, however, the Vikings destroyed the city of Hamburg by fire, and Sweden and Denmark relapsed into paganism. In 848 Ansgar was made archbishop of the combined sees of Bremen and Hamburg, and he began the restoration of his missions in Denmark. His patient work led to small success, but after his death on February 3, 865, in Bremen, practically all that he had accomplished in Scandinavia was lost, and three centuries passed before Christianization really resumed.

St. Ansgar was a prophetic figure, and the church in Scandinavia honors his memory. He is often portrayed with a fur collar on his bishop's vestments, holding a church in his hand. He is respected by Scandinavian Lutherans, especially the Danes, and numerous churches, societies, and educational institutions are dedicated to his memory. There are about a dozen Lutheran churches in North America named for him.

FOR FURTHER READING

Adam of Bremen. *History of the Archbishops of Hamburg-Bremen.* Trans. F. J. Tschan. New York: Columbia University Press, 1959.

Hunter, L. S., ed. *Scandinavian Churches: A Picture of the Development and Life of the Churches of Denmark, Finland, Iceland, Norway, and Sweden.* London: Faber and Faber, 1965.

Rimbert. *Anskar, The Apostle of the North, 801–865.* Trans. from the Vita Anskarii by Charles H. Robinson. London: SPCK, 1921.

READING

From *The Imitation of Christ* by Thomas à Kempis

When God bestows spiritual comfort, receive it with a grateful heart; but remember that it comes from God's free gift, and not your own merit. Do not be proud, nor over joyful, nor foolishly presumptuous; rather, be the more for this gift, more cautious, and more prudent in all your doings, for this hour will pass, and temptation will follow it. When comfort is withdrawn, do not immediately despair, but humbly and patiently await the will of Heaven; for God is able to restore to you a consolation even richer than before. This is nothing new or strange to those who know the ways of God, for the great Saints and Prophets of old often experienced these changes.

I have never found anyone, however religious and devout, who did not sometimes experience a withdrawal of grace, or feel a lessening of devotion. And no

Saint ever lived, however highly rapt and enlightened, who did not suffer temptation sooner or later. For he is not worthy of high contemplation who has not
suffered some trials for God's sake. Indeed, the temptation that precedes is often
a sign of comfort to follow. For heavenly comfort is promised to those who have
been tried and tempted. "To him who overcomes," says God, "I will give to eat of
the Tree of Life."

Thomas à Kempis, *The Imitation of Christ*, trans. Leo Sherley-Price (Baltimore: Penguin, 1952),
68–69, 88–89, 83, 206–206, 72. Introduction and Translation copyright 1952 by Leo Sherley-Price.
Reprinted by permission of Penguin Books Ltd.

PROPERS

Almighty and everlasting God, you sent your servant Anskar as an apostle to the
people of Scandinavia, and enabled him to lay a firm foundation for their conversion, though he did not see the results of his labors: Keep your Church from
discouragement in the day of small things, knowing that when you have begun a
good work you will bring it to a fruitful conclusion; through Jesus Christ our Lord,
who lives and reigns with you and the Holy Spirit, one God, forever and ever.

CMG, LFF

Readings:	Isaiah 62:1-7
	Psalm 96:1-7 *or* 98:1-4
	Acts 1:1-9
	Mark 6:7-13
Hymn of the Day:	
	"O Christ our light, O Radiance true" (LBW 380, LSB 839, ELW 675)
Prayers:	For courage and resolution in the face of defeat
	For the church in Sweden
	For the church in Denmark
Preface:	Epiphany (LBW, ELW), Apostles (BCP)
Color:	White

ALSO ON FEBRUARY 3

In addition to Ansgar, the Roman Catholic General Calendar also commemorates
on this date **St. Blaise (Blasius)**, who according to a late and historically dubious
legend was bishop of Sebaste in Armenia, where he was martyred early in the
fourth century. Because of the story that he miraculously saved a young child
who was choking on a fish-bone, he became extraordinarily popular, especially in
Germany, and his feast day was observed with the blessing of throats. The blessing
is still done, especially in many Roman Catholic churches.

The Eastern Church on this day following the Presentation of Our Lord in the Temple commemorates **Righteous Simeon** and **Anna the Prophetess**. All we know of them is given in Luke 2:33-38.

February 4

Cornelius the Centurion

Cornelius was the first Gentile converted to the Christian faith. What is known about Cornelius is given in chapters 10 and 11 of the Acts of the Apostles. A centurion was commander of a company of one hundred men in the Roman army; he was a Roman citizen, a well-paid career military officer.

The book of Acts reports that the conversion of Cornelius occurred as a result of divine intervention and revelation and as a response to the preaching of St. Peter, and his conversion, together with that of his household, was regarded as a new Pentecost and an anticipation of the later decision to admit Gentiles as full and equal members of the Church.

According to tradition, Cornelius was the second bishop of Caesarea, the metropolitan see of Palestine. He was included on the Episcopal calendar in 1979 *Book of Common Prayer* and in the Methodist *For All the Saints*, but he is not on the General Roman Catholic calendar. Cornelius is commemorated by the Eastern Churches on September 13.

READING

From a sermon by Theodore P. Ferris

Christianity grew up in much the same way as an individual grows up, and growing up is never easy. One of the most difficult problems in growing up is the problem of leaving home. One cannot nestle in the shelter of home forever, nor can one ignore the fact that sheltering there would have been no life at all. A man must break away from home as a bird leaves the nest, and yet he must not forget the fact that he owes his life to his home.

Christianity was born in a Jewish home. It can never repay its debt of gratitude to that home. There it learned about the moral majesty of God. In that home it learned that religion and morality should go hand in hand in an inseparable union. But like all offspring, it had to leave home. The world-wide implications of Christianity could not be confined within the walls of Judaism. Judaism was the religion of a nation; Christianity was the religion of all nations. The swaddling clothes had to be stripped away; the exclusiveness of Judaism had to be overridden; its provincialism had to be displaced by universalism. The break had to be made; and it was made.

The process of growing up is usually punctuated by specific events. An adolescent leaps from stage to stage and each stage is begun by a specific event: the first trip away from home; the first love affair; a failure in school; the loss of a friend; the first money ever earned. In much the same way Christianity grew up. It was a succession of events, no one of which by and in itself might seem to be of any great significance, but each of which marked a new stage in the growth of the Jewish child. The story of Peter and Cornelius is such an event. It is the story about the first time a Gentile was publicly and officially welcomed into the Christian fellowship without conforming to the requirements of the Jewish law.

. . . When Peter and Cornelius finally met, it was as though a great wall was once and for all removed. Here were a Jew and Gentile standing face to face with nothing between them. Peter proceeded to tell the story which he had already told many times, the story of how Jesus went about doing good, how God was with him, how he was killed and God raised him on the third day, how he is now the judge of all people everywhere. That was all Cornelius needed to know. Without any more ado, without any ceremony whatsoever, Cornelius and all his family and friends were filled with the Holy Spirit, and on the basis of that they were baptized.

Theodore P. Ferris, "Exposition of the Acts of the Apostles," in *The Interpreter's Bible* (New York and Nashville: Abingdon, 1954), 9:132–33, 136.

PROPERS

O God, by your Spirit you called Cornelius the Centurion to be the first Christian among the Gentiles: Grant to your Church such a ready will to go where you send and to do what you command, that under your guidance it may welcome all who turn to you in love and faith, and proclaim the Gospel to all nations; through Jesus Christ our Lord, who lives and reigns with you and the Holy Spirit, one God, forever and ever.

LFF

Readings:	Psalm 67 *or* 33:1-5, 20-21
	Acts 11:1-18
	Luke 13:22-29
Hymn of the Day:	
	"Soldiers of Christ, arise" (H82 548, SBH 564)
	or "Lead on, O King eternal" (H82 555, LBW 495, ELW 805)
Prayers:	For those in military service
	For converts to the faith
	For an inclusive church
Preface:	Pentecost (BCP)
Color:	White

February 5

Paul Miki and His Companions, Martyrs of Japan, 1597

Christianity was brought to Japan by Francis Xavier (see December 3), and the faith spread with remarkable success. The rapid advance, however, led to resentment and opposition on the part of the native Buddhists and Shintoists. There was suspicion of the methods of the missionaries, which involved mass conversions, and there was rivalry between the several religious orders. These suspicions, coupled with a fear of foreign invaders, resulted in increased persecution of Christians. On February 5, 1597, twenty-six Christians—six European Franciscan missionaries, three Japanese Jesuits, and seventeen Japanese laymen, three of whom were young boys—were killed by a kind of crucifixion at Nagasaki. They were raised on crosses and then stabbed with spears. (The Franciscans may have been singled out for persecution because of the careless remarks of a Spanish captain, wrecked off the Japanese coast, that led the Japanese to believe that the increasingly active Franciscans, based in the Spanish-held Philippines, were preparing the way for the conquest of Japan by Spain.) Within a year, more than 130 churches were burned. After a time the persecution subsided, but in 1613 it broke out again, and by 1630 what was left of Christianity in Japan had been driven underground. Nonetheless, the faith was preserved, although the church in Japan was without clergy until the missionaries returned at the end of the nineteenth century.

The first victims of the persecution, the twenty-six martyrs of 1597, were canonized by the Roman Catholic Church in 1862. Paul Miki, a Japanese Jesuit priest, is the most celebrated of the martyrs. The Franciscan missionaries were led by a Spanish priest, Peter Baptist. One of the laymen was a Korean, Leo Karasuma.

The Nippon Sei Ko Kai (the Holy Catholic Church of Japan), which is affiliated with the Anglican Communion, adopted this commemoration on its calendar of 1959 as an inclusive festival of all those who have given their lives for the Christian faith in Japan. The 1979 American *Book of Common Prayer,* the *Lutheran Book of Worship, Evangelical Lutheran Worship,* and the *Christian Year* include the observance.

FOR FURTHER READING

Boxer, C. R. *The Christian Century in Japan, 1549–1650.* Berkeley: University of California Press, 1951.

Carey, Otis. *A History of Christianity in Japan.* 2 vols. New York: Revell, 1909.

Drummond, Richard H. *A History of Christianity in Japan.* Grand Rapids: Eerdmans, 1971.

READING

From *The Imitation of Christ* by Thomas à Kempis

Be assured of this, that you must live a dying life. And the more completely one dies to self, the more one begins to live for God. No one is fit to understand heavenly things unless he is resigned to bear hardships for Christ's sake. Nothing is more acceptable to God, and nothing more salutary to yourself, than to suffer gladly for Christ's sake. And if it lies in your choice, you should choose rather to suffer hardships for Christ's sake, than to be refreshed by many consolations; for thus you will more closely resemble Christ and all His Saints. For our merit and spiritual progress does not consist in enjoying such sweetness and consolation, but rather in the bearing of great burdens and troubles.

Had there been a better way, more profitable to the salvation of mankind than suffering, then Christ would have revealed it in His word and life. But He clearly urges both His own disciples and all who wish to follow Him to carry the cross, saying, "If any will come after me, let him deny himself, and take up his cross and follow Me." Therefore, when we have read and studied all things, let this be our final resolve: "that through much tribulation we must enter the Kingdom of God" (Acts 14:22).

Thomas à Kempis, *The Imitation of Christ*, trans. Leo Sherley-Price (Baltimore: Penguin, 1952), 68–69, 88–89, 83, 206–206, 72. Introduction and Translation copyright 1952 by Leo Sherley-Price. Reprinted by permission of Penguin Books Ltd.

PROPERS

God our Father, source of strength to all your saints, you brought the holy martyrs of Japan through the suffering of the cross to the joys of eternal life: Grant that we, encouraged by their example, may hold fast the faith we profess, even to death itself; through Jesus Christ our Lord, who lives and reigns with you and the Holy Spirit, one God now and forever.

Leonine, rev. 1970 Roman Missal, trans. LFF

Readings:	Ezekiel 20:40-42
	Psalm 116:1-8 or 16:5-11
	Galatians 2:19-20
	Matthew 28:16-20 (RC) *or* Mark 8:34-38 (LFF)
Hymn of the Day:	
	"Hearken to the anthem glorious" (H82 240, 241)
	or "Have no fear, little flock" (LBW 476, LSB 735, ELW 764)
Prayers:	For the church in Japan
	For boldness to confess Christ
	For the spirit of Christ to forgive our enemies
Preface:	Holy Week (BCP)
Color:	Red

ALSO ON FEBRUARY 5

The *Lutheran Service Book* on the date commemorates the patriarch **Jacob** (Israel).

February 6

Philipp Jakob Spener, Renewer of the Church, 1705

Philipp Jakob Spener, the founder of German Pietism, was born of devout parents in Alsace in 1635, during the Thirty Years' War. He was profoundly influenced by *Wahres Christenthum* ("True Christianity") by the Lutheran Johann Arndt (1555–1621). Spener studied history and philosophy at the University of Strassbourg from 1651 to 1653. On a visit to Switzerland, he came under the influence of Jean de Labadie (1610–1674), a Jesuit who had converted to the Reformed Church, and his piety took on a personal and interior character. After serving as pastor in Strassbourg, Spener in his parish in Frankfort, ravaged by thirty years of war, introduced *Collegia Pietatis* ("piety groups," from which came the name "Pietism"), twice-weekly devotional meetings in his house; and published his *Pia Desideria* ("Devout Desires," 1675) with six major proposals for reform and revitalization of the church. He also developed a new type of catechization for adults as well as children, which led in may places to a recovery of the practice of confirmation and instituted strict discipline. His independent spirit and his efforts to give the laity a role in the church earned him the hostility of many of the clergy, and in 1686 he gladly moved to Dresden in Saxony as chaplain to the Elector and court preacher. After coming into conflict with the theological faculty at Leipzig, Spener in 1691 moved to Berlin to become rector of the Nikolaikirche. By this time his movement had become known as Pietism and made rapid progress. In 1694 the University of Halle was founded, largely under his influence, and became a powerful center of the Pietistic movement. An orphans' home with associated schools was opened, a publication house established, a hospital founded. The first Lutheran missionaries to India, Ziegenbalg and Plütschau (see February 23) and, later, Christian Frederick Schwartz, were sent out from Halle, as was Henry Melchior Muhlenberg, the patriarch of the Lutheran Church in America (see October 7). Although Lutheran orthodoxy opposed him, he won many ardent supporters, and the movement spread throughout Saxony and elsewhere in Germany and into Denmark, Norway, Sweden, Finland, and Iceland. In 1698 Spener withdrew from the continuing struggle and devoted his last years to pastoral work. Spener died on this date in 1705.

His effort to establish a deeper Christian life and reform of the Lutheran Church was not a separatist movement, and his insistence on "vital godliness," the inner religious life of the individual, helped renew the Church from the doctrinal rigidity, spiritual aridity, and moral laxity that followed the Thirty Years' War. Pastors were made to recognize the importance of personal character and belief as essential for their ministry. They were taught a new type of biblical interpretation and effective preaching, less polemical and more edifying. Bible reading, prayer, and personal devotion were promoted. The privilege and responsibility of the laity to witness to the truth by the quality of their lives were stressed; leadership in the congregation passed to the laity, often to laywomen. Missionary effort was given a new emphasis.

Pietism, however, produced an unbalanced type of Christianity that came to overemphasize individual, personal experience and promoted an asceticism, not unlike that of the Middle Ages, in its opposition to card playing, dancing, the opera, and theater, and its stress upon moderation in dress, food, and drink. The private assemblies, composed largely of laity, led to an undervaluation of the church's liturgy, sacraments, and clergy. The emphasis on individual piety and purity led to complacency and condemnation of the "unawakened" and "unconverted" and "unworthy." Spener's later followers moved further from the liturgical and theological tradition, and the damage had to be repaired in the nineteenth and twentieth centuries.

Spener is included on the German Evangelical Calendar of Names compiled by Frieder Schulz and others (1962) and on the Methodist calendar in *For All the Saints*.

FOR FURTHER READING

Erb, Peter C., ed. *Pietists: Selected Writings.* New York: Paulist, 1983.
Spener, Philipp Jakob. *Pia Desideria.* Ed. and trans. Theodore G. Tappert. Philadelphia: Fortress Press, 1964.

READING

From *Pia Desideria* by Philipp Jakob Spener

Every Christian is bound to offer himself and what he has, his prayer, thanksgiving, good works, alms, etc., but also industriously to study the Word of the Lord, with the grace that is given him to teach others, especially those under his own roof, to chastise, exhort, convert, and edify them, to observe their life, pray for all, and insofar as possible be concerned about their salvation. If this is first pointed out to the people, they will take better care of themselves and apply themselves to whatever pertains to their own edification and that of their fellow men. On the other hand, all complacence and sloth derives from the fact that this teaching is not known and practiced. Nobody thinks this has anything to do with him. Everybody imagines that just as he was himself called to his office, business, or trade and the minister was neither called to such an occupation nor works in it, so the minister alone is called to perform spiritual acts, occupy himself with the Word of God, pray, study, teach, admonish, comfort, chastise, etc., while others should not trouble themselves with such things and, in fact, would be meddling in the minister's business if they had anything to do with them. This is not even to mention that people ought to pay attention to the minister, admonish him fraternally when he neglects something, and in general support him in all his efforts.

No damage will be done to the ministry by the proper use of this priesthood. In fact, one of the principal reasons why the ministry cannot accomplish all that it ought is that it is too weak without the help of the universal priesthood. One man is incapable of doing all that is necessary for the edification of the many persons who are generally entrusted to his pastoral care. However, if the priests do their duty, the minister, as director and oldest brother, has splendid assistance in the performance of his duties and his public and private acts, and thus his burden will not be too heavy.

Philipp Jacob Spener, *Pia Desideria,* part 3, section 2, trans. Theodore G. Tappert (Philadelphia: Fortress Press, 1964), 94–95.

PROPERS

Almighty God, from whom every good prayer comes, you pour out on all who desire it the spirit of grace and supplication: By your Spirit and by the example of your servant Philipp Jakob Spener, deliver us, when we draw near to you, from coldness of heart and wanderings of mind, that with steadfast thoughts and kindled affections we may worship you in spirit and in truth; through Jesus Christ our Lord, who lives and reigns with you and the Holy Spirit, one God, now and forever.

Zech. 12:10, John 4:23; William Bright, BCP, SBH, alt. PHP

Readings:	Jeremiah 1:4-10
	Psalm 46
	1 Corinthians 3:11-23
	Mark 10:35-45
Hymn of the Day:	
	"Thee will I love, my strength, my tower" (LBW 502, LSB 694)
Prayers:	For a living faith
	For the work of Christian laity
	For lay leaders in the church
	For a holy life
Preface:	Lent (1) (BCP)
Color:	White

February 13

The Episcopal Church remembers today *Absalom Jones*, the first man of African descent to be ordained an Episcopal priest (1804). He was an earnest preacher, an example of persistent faith. He died in 1818. Those of an ecumenical inclination may choose to observe this day in conjunction with the commemoration of the first African American Lutheran pastor, Jehu Jones (see September 28).

The Eastern Church on this date commemorates *Aquila and Priscilla* (Prisca), early Christian converts. Aquila, a tentmaker, and his wife Priscilla were prominent members of the early church; see Acts 18. The calendar in the *Lutheran Service Book* (2006) lists on this date Priscilla and Aquila together with *Apollos*, a learned Jew who completed his Christian education under Priscilla and Aquila.

February 14

Cyril, Monk, 865; Methodius, Bishop, 885; Missionaries to the Slavs

These brothers, known as "the apostles to the Slavs," were two of seven children of a wealthy and scrupulously orthodox family in Thessalonika, Greece.

Methodius, the older of the two, was born about 825 and attained high rank in his province of Macedonia before he withdrew to a monastic life. Cyril, as he is known, was born in 827 and was given the name Constantine. He was educated at Constantinople and became a noted professor of philosophy there about 850. After a time, he withdrew to the monastic life in Bithynia, not far from Methodius. In 862 the king of Moravia, to counteract the expanding power in his lands of the German bishops, asked for missionaries who would teach the people in their native language, Slavonic. The Patriarch of Constantinople chose the two brothers to lead the mission.

In Moravia Cyril took an interest in the vernacular language and invented an alphabet, Glagolitic, in order to translate the Gospels and the liturgy into Slavonic. The Cyrillic alphabet (modern Russian), from Greek capital letters, is based on this work. His interest in the vernacular was opposed by the Western clergy in Moravia who recognized only the three languages of Pilate's sign above the cross of Jesus: Hebrew, Latin, and Greek. Cyril journeyed to Rome and was there received by Pope Hadrian II in 887, and the pope confirmed Cyril's Slavonic translations. Cyril had been in poor health for some time, and at Rome, February 14, 869, fifty days after taking the monastic habit and the name Cyril by which he is known, died at the age of forty-two. He had given the pope the supposed relics of St. Clement and so was buried in the basilica of San Clemente. Until the revision of the Roman calendar after Vatican II, his feast day in the West had been July 7. In the East his commemoration is May 11.

After Cyril's death, Pope Adrian (Hadrian) made Methodius Metropolitan of Sirmium, and Methodius returned to the Slavic mission field for sixteen more years. He encountered violent opposition from the German bishops and even from his own suffragan, despite reconfirmation of his liturgy by Pope John VIII in 879. Methodius died in his cathedral church April 6, which was Tuesday in Holy Week, 885. Opposition to the work of the two brothers continued even after their deaths, and their followers scattered, spreading with them the spiritual, liturgical, and cultural work of the brothers.

The Slovaks, Czechs, Croats, Serbs, and Bulgars all revere the memory of Cyril and Methodius as founders of their alphabet, translators of their liturgy, and builders of the foundation of their literature, as well as heralds of the gospel in their land.

FEBRUARY

FOR FURTHER READING

Dittrich, Z. R. *Christianity in Greater Moravia.* Groningen, 1962.
Dvornik, Francis. *The Slavs: The Early History and Civilization.* Boston: American
    Academy of Arts and Sciences, 1956.

READING

From a letter by Martin Luther to Philipp Melanchthon

Now let me deal with the "prophets."

In order to explore their individual spirit, too, you should inquire whether they have experienced spiritual distress, and the divine birth, death, and hell. If you should hear that all [their experiences] are pleasant, quiet, and devout (as they say), and spiritual, then don't approve of them, even if they should say that they were caught up into the third heaven. The sign of the Son of Man is then missing, which is the only touchstone of Christians and a certain differentiator between the spirits. Do you want to know the place, time, and manner of [true] conversations with God? Listen: "Like a lion he has broken all my bones"; "I am cast out from before your eyes"; "My soul is filled with grief, and my life has approached hell." The [Divine] Majesty (as they call it) does not speak in such a direct way to man that man could [actually] see it; but rather, "Man shall not see me and live." [Our] nature cannot bear even a small glimmer of God's [direct] speaking. As a result God speaks through men [indirectly], because not all can endure his speaking. The angel frightened even the Virgin, and also Daniel. And Jeremiah pleads, "Correct me [O Lord] but in just measure," and, "Be not a terror to me." Why should I say more? As if the [Divine] Majesty could speak familiarly with the Old Adam without first killing him and drying him out so that his horrible stench would not be so foul, since God is a consuming fire! The dreams and visions of the saints are horrifying too, at least after they are understood. Therefore examine [them] and do not even listen if they speak of the glorified Jesus, unless you have first heard of the crucified Jesus.

Luther's Works 48, *Letters I*, trans. Gottfried G. Krotel (Philadelphia: Fortress Press, 1963), 365, 366–67.

PROPERS

Almighty and everlasting God, by the power of the Holy Spirit you moved your servant Cyril and his brother Methodius to bring the light of the Gospel to a hostile and divided people: Overcome all bitterness and strife among us by the love of Christ, and make us one united family under the banner of the Prince of Peace; who lives and reigns with you and the Holy Spirit, one God, now and forever.
RS, rev. LFF

> *or*

O Lord our God, through the ministry of your servants Cyril and Methodius you brought the gospel to the Slavic nations: Protect your faithful people, make them known for their unity and their faith, guide them by your word and teaching, and ever protect them under the shadow of your wings; through your Son Jesus Christ our Lord, who lives and reigns with you and the Holy Spirit, one God, now and forever.
PHP, adapted from the last prayer of Cyril, given in the Old Slavonic Life of Cyril.

Readings:	Psalm 96:1-7 *or* 98:1-4
	Ephesians 3:1-7
	Mark 16:15-20
Hymn of the Day:	
	"God, my Lord, my strength" (LBW 484, ELW 795)
Prayers:	For those under persecution and attack
	For the Slavic churches
	For linguists and translators
	For respect for the past and openness to the future
Preface:	Epiphany (LBW/ELW), Apostles (BCP)
Color:	White

ALSO ON FEBRUARY 14

The *Lutheran Service Book,* with its penchant for the old Roman calendar, commemorates **Valentine** on this date. There were apparently two Valentines who were martyrs: a third-century Roman priest who was killed on the Flaminian Way under the Emperor Claudius (*ca.* 269) and a Bishop of Terni (Interamna) who was taken to Rome and martyred there and whose remains were later taken back to Terni. The surviving legends obscure whatever the historical facts may be; possibly the two Valentines are the same person. John Donne has a poem that begins, "Hail, Bishop Valentine, whose day this is."

February 15

Thomas Bray (1656–1730), an Anglican priest and missionary, is remembered on this date on the Episcopal calendar. As representative of the Bishop of London, Bray visited the colony of Maryland and for the rest of his life showed his concern for the Church in America. His interest in extending Anglicanism abroad is seen in his founding of the Society for Promoting Christian Knowledge and the Society for the Propagation of the Gospel, both of which continue to this day.

The Eastern Church on this date (and also November 22) commemorates **Apostle Onesimus** (of the Seventy). The calendar in the *Lutheran Service Book* (2006), following Löhe's calendar (February 16), lists **Philemon** and his slave Onesimus on February 15; their story is given in the New Testament book Philemon.

February 16

The *Lutheran Service Book*, departing from the church's tradition of celebrating only three earthly birthdays (Jesus, John the Baptist, and the Virgin Mary) commemorates today the **birth of Philipp Melanchthon**. See June 25.

February 17

The 1995 calendar of the Church of England and *Lesser Feasts and Fasts 2003* of the Episcopal Church introduced the commemoration on this date of the murder of **Janani Luwum** (1922–1977), Archbishop of Uganda and Martyr, by the regime of the military dictator of Uganda, Idi Amin.

February 18

Martin Luther, Renewer of the Church, 1546

Martin Luther was born November 10, 1483, in Eisleben, Saxony. He was baptized the following day, St. Martin's feast day, and was given the name of that saint. His intellectual abilities were evident early, and his father, who was a miner, planned a career for him in law. After attending schools in Mansfeld,

Magdeburg, and Eisenach, Luther at the age of eighteen entered the University of Erfurt, where he completed his master's examination in 1505 and began the study of law. His real interest, however, lay elsewhere, and on July 17, 1505, he entered the local Augustinian friary. He was ordained priest April 3, 1507, and a month later celebrated his first mass in the presence of friends and his father, who had disapproved of his son's entrance into the friary.

Luther had seen his first Latin Bible in the school at Magdeburg, and at the monastery, with the encouragement of his superiors, he continued his study of the Scriptures. He helped with the instruction of novices in the order and served as a teaching assistant in moral philosophy at the new University of Wittenberg. In 1510 he made a trip to Rome for the Augustinian order. There, like St. Francis and others before him, he was shocked by the laxity and worldliness of many of the clergy.

In October 1512 Luther received his doctorate in theology, and shortly afterward, he was installed as a professor of biblical studies at the University of Wittenberg. His lectures on the Bible were popular, and within a few years, he had made the university a center of biblical humanism. (When Luther died, Wittenberg was the largest university in Germany.) As a result of his theological and biblical studies he called into question the practice of selling indulgences (remissions of the punishment to be undergone in purgatory). On the eve of All Saints' Day, October 31, 1517, he posted on the door of the Castle Church in Wittenberg, as was the custom, the notice of an academic debate on indulgences, listing ninety-five theses for discussion. Luther's theses spread rapidly throughout Germany and other parts of Europe. As the effects of the theses became evident, the pope called upon the Augustinian order to discipline their member. After a series of meetings, political maneuvers, and attempts at reconciliation, Luther, at a meeting with the papal legate in 1518, refused to recant, and in debate with John Eck, he was forced to admit that some of his views were not in accord with the official doctrines of the Church.

Up to this time Luther had attempted to reform the Church from within, but it was now clear that a break was inevitable, and on June 15, 1520, the pope issued a bull that gave Luther sixty days to recant. Many schools burned Luther's books, and he retaliated by burning a copy of the papal bull and books of canon law. He was excommunicated on January 3, 1521, and Emperor Charles V summoned him to the meeting of the Imperial Diet at Worms. There Luther resisted all efforts to make him recant, insisting that he had to be proved in error on the basis of Scripture. The Diet was divided in its judgment, but it finally passed an edict calling for the arrest of Luther. Luther's own prince, the Elector Frederick of Saxony, had him spirited away and placed for safekeeping in his castle, the Wartburg.

Here Luther translated the New Testament into German and began the translation of the Old Testament. In March 1522 Luther returned to Wittenberg against the wishes of the prince in order to settle the disturbed situation of the churches there, which were under the disruptive leadership of Andreas von Karlstadt. Luther preached a series of eight famous sermons in which he restored order to the community and set the lines of the Reformation.

He then turned his attention to the organization of worship and education. He introduced the congregational singing of hymns, composing many himself, and he issued model orders of worship in Latin (*Formula Missae* 1523) and, for more general use, in German (*Deutsche Messe* 1526). In 1529 he published his large and small catechisms for instruction in the faith and also a series of sermons. During the years from 1522 to his death, Luther wrote a prodigious quantity of books, letters, sermons, and pamphlets. The American Edition of his works is fifty-five large volumes, and that does not include everything extant that he wrote.

On June 13, 1525, when he was forty-two, Luther married Katherine von Bora, one of a number of nuns rescued from the cloister of Nimbschen in 1523 because of their evangelical persuasion (see December 20). The couple had six children.

In 1546 Luther was called to Eisleben to mediate a family quarrel among the princes of Mansfeld, and after resolving the quarrel, Luther died there in the town of his birth on February 18. Thousands of people came to the service for the great reformer, and his body was interred in the Castle Church in Wittenberg on February 22.

Lutherans have named many churches, colleges, and societies after Luther. There are monuments to Luther in many cities; the most famous is the one at Worms in which Luther rests his hand on the Bible and is surrounded by likenesses of earlier reformers and his protectors and friends.

Events in Luther's life have been commemorated on various dates. The anniversary of the posting of the ninety-five theses has become on Lutheran calendars the Festival of the Reformation, and it is also observed by other Christian churches. Many Lutheran communities have remembered Luther on the day of his death; on the centennial in 1646 the day was observed particularly in Wittenberg and Erfurt, and later the observance became more widespread.

The commemoration of Martin Luther is included on the calendar in the Methodist *For All the Saints* (1995) and was added to the Episcopal calendar in *Lesser Feasts and Fasts 1997*. He is remembered on the 1997 calendar of the Church of England, the *Christian Year,* on October 31.

FOR FURTHER READING

Althaus, Paul. *The Theology of Martin Luther.* Philadelphia: Fortress Press, 1966.

Bainton, Roland. *Here I Stand: A Life of Martin Luther.* New York and Nashville: Abingdon, 1950.

Brecht, Martin. *Martin Luther.* Trans. James L. Schaaf. 3 vols. Minneapolis: Fortress Press, 1990–1993.

Ebeling, Gerhard. *Luther: An Introduction to His Thought.* Philadelphia: Fortress Press, 1970.

Kittelson, James M. *Luther the Reformer: The Story of the Man and His Career.* Minneapolis: Fortress Press, 2003.

Lohse, Bernhard. *Martin Luther: An Introduction to His Life and Work.* Minneapolis: Fortress Press, 1986.

Marty, Martin. *Martin Luther.* New York: Lipper/Viking, 2004.

Schwiebert, E. G. *Luther and His Times.* St. Louis: Concordia, 1950.

Swihart, Altmann K. *Luther and the Lutheran Church 1483–1960.* New York: Philosophical Library, 1960.

READING

From Luther's *Preface to the Complete Edition of Luther's Latin Writings* (Wittenberg, 1545)

I had indeed been captivated with an extraordinary ardor for understanding Paul in the Epistle to the Romans. But up till then it was not the cold blood about the heart, but a single word in chapter 1 [:17], "In it the righteousness of God is revealed," that had stood in my way. For I hated that word "righteousness of God," which, according to the use and custom of all the teachers, I had been taught to understand philosophically regarding the formal or active righteousness, as they called it, with which God is righteous and punished the unrighteous sinner.

Though I lived as a monk without reproach, I felt I was a sinner before God with an extremely disturbed conscience. I could not believe that he was placated by my satisfaction. I did not love, I hated the righteousness of God who punishes sinners, and secretly, if not blasphemously, certainly muttering greatly, I was angry with God and said, "As if, indeed, it is not enough that miserable sinners, eternally lost through original sin, are crushed by every kind of calamity by the law of the decalogue, without having God add pain to pain by the gospel and also by the gospel threatening us with his righteousness and wrath!" Thus I raged with a fierce and troubled conscience. Nevertheless, I beat importunately upon Paul at that place, most ardently desiring to know what St. Paul wanted.

At last, by the mercy of God, meditating day and night, I gave heed to the context of the words, namely, "In it the righteousness of God is revealed, as it is written, 'He who through faith is righteous shall live.'" There I began to understand that the righteousness of God is that by which the righteous lives by a gift of God, namely, by faith. And this is the meaning: the righteousness of God is revealed by the gospel, namely, the passive righteousness with which merciful God justifies us by faith, as it is written, "He who through faith is righteous shall live." Here I felt that I was altogether born again and had entered paradise itself through open gates. There a totally other face of the entire Scripture showed itself to me.

Thereupon I ran through the Scriptures from memory. I also found in other terms an analogy, as, the work of God, that is, what God does in us, the power of God, with which he makes us strong, the wisdom of God, with which he makes us wise, the strength of God, the salvation of God, the glory of God.

And I extolled my sweet word with a love as great as the hatred with which I had before hated the word "righteousness of God." Thus that place in Paul was for me truly that gate to Paradise.

Luther's Works 34, *Career of the Reformer IV,* ed. Lewis W. Spitz, trans. Lewis W. Spitz Sr. (Philadelphia: Fortress Press, 1960), 336–37.

PROPERS

Almighty God, through the preaching of your servants, the blessed Reformers, you have caused the light of the Gospel to shine forth: Grant, we pray, that, knowing its saving power, we may faithfully guard and defend it against all enemies, and joyfully proclaim it, to the salvation of souls and the glory of your holy Name; through your Son Jesus Christ our Lord, who lives and reigns with you and the Holy Spirit, one God, now and forever.

CSB, SBH, Reformation Day

> *or*

God, our refuge and our strength: You raised up your servant Martin Luther to reform and renew your Church in the light of your Word. Defend and purify the Church in our own day and grant that, through faith, we may boldly proclaim the riches of your grace which you have made known in Jesus Christ our Savior, who with you and the Holy Spirit, lives and reigns, one God, now and forever.

LFF

Readings:	Isaiah 55:6-11
	Psalm 16 *or* 46
	Revelation 14:6-7 *or* Galatians 2:16-21
	John 2:13-17 *or* 15:1-11
Hymn of the Day:	
	"Lord, keep us steadfast in your Word" (LBW 230, LSB 655, ELW 517)
Prayers:	For the continual cleansing of the church
	For an ever-new discovery of the good news of God
	For the unity of the church
Preface:	Trinity Sunday (BCP)
Color:	White

FEBRUARY

February 20

Rasmus Jensen, First Lutheran Pastor in North America, 1620

In the spring of 1619, King Christian IV of Norway and Denmark sent an expedition consisting of two ships, the *Unicorn* and the *Lamprey* and sixty-four men to North America to search for the Northwest Passage to India. The chaplain of the expedition was Rasmus Jensen, who became the first Lutheran pastor in the New World. Little is known of his life; he may perhaps have been from the parish of Aarhus. The expedition was under the leadership of the most traveled and experienced officer in the Danish navy, Jens Munk (Munck), who was born June 3, 1579, and who died June 23, 1628. The ships left Denmark on May 9, touched the coast of Greenland, reached the North American shore on July 8, crossed Hudson Bay (where the explorers named the area Nova Dania [New Denmark]), and landed at the mouth of a river on the western shore of Hudson Bay at what is now Churchill, Manitoba. Locked in ice for the long winter, the explorers made the first settlement of Lutherans in the New World. The captain wrote in his journal:

> On the 24th of December, which was Christmas Eve, I gave the men wine and strong beer, which they had to boil afresh, for it was frozen at the bottom; so they had quite as much as they could stand, and were very jolly, but no one offended another with as much as a word.
>
> The Holy Christmas Day we all celebrated and observed solemnly, as a Christian's duty is. We had a sermon and Mass; and, after the sermon, we gave the priest an offertory, according to ancient custom, each in proportion to his means. There was not much money among the men, but they gave what they had; some of them gave white fox-skins, so that the priest got enough wherewith to line a coat. However, sufficiently long life to wear it was not granted to him.
>
> During all the Holy Days, the weather was rather mild; and, in order that the time might not hang on hand, the men practiced all kinds of games; and whoever could imagine the most amusement was the most popular. The crew, most of whom were, at that time, in good health, consequently had all sorts of larks and pastimes; and thus we spent the Holy Days with the merriment that was got up.

The foreboding that shadows Munk's narrative was fulfilled, and soon most of the members of the crew, attacked by scurvy, died.

> On the 23rd of January, died one of my two mates, Hans Brock by name, who had been ill, in and out of bed, for nearly five months. On the same day, it was fine weather and beautiful sunshine; and the priest sat up in his berth and gave the people a sermon, which sermon was the last he delivered in this world. . . .
>
> On the 20th of February, in the evening, died the priest, Mr. Rasmus Jensen aforesaid, who had been ill and had kept his bed a long time. . . .
>
> On the 14th of April, there was a sharp frost. On that day, only four, besides myself, had strength enough to sit up in the berth and listen to the homily for Good Friday.

> The 16th of April was Easter Day. Then died Anders Oroust and Jens, the cooper, who had been ill and in bed a long time; and, as the weather was fairly mild, I got their bodies buried. On the same day, I promoted my captain of the hold to be skipper, although he was ill, in order that he might assist me somewhat, as far as his strength allowed, because I was myself then quite miserable and abandoned by all the world, as everybody may imagine.

Munk himself had become deathly sick, but eventually recovered. With the last two remaining sailors he set sail in July in the smaller of the two vessels, the *Lamprey,* and reached Norway in September and arrived in Copenhagen on Christmas Day 1620. He published a diary of his voyage in Danish in 1624. An English translation appeared in 1897. It is a moving and melancholy account of hardship, death, and bravery.

A memorial to the expedition has been erected at Port Churchill. An island in the Canadian Northwest Territories at the head of the Foxe Basin, northwest of Baffin Island, is named Munk Island in honor of the explorer.

After this disheartening experience in Canada, Danish missionary activity was concentrated in India and in the Virgin Islands. By 1656 a Lutheran pastor, the second in the New World, Magister Lauritz Anderson Rhodius, was ministering to the tobacco-producing islands of the West Indies; and Kjeld Jensen Slagelse on January 8, 1665, became pastor at St. Thomas in the Virgin Islands, where a strong Lutheran tradition has been maintained. He died in June 1672. In 1917 the Danish Virgin Islands passed into the control of the United States.

FOR FURTHER READING

Cronmiller, Carl A. *A History of the Lutheran Church in Canada.* Kitchener, Ont.: Evangelical Lutheran Synod of Canada, 1961.

Gosch, C. C. A., ed. *Danish Arctic Expeditions 1605-1620. Book II—The Expedition of Captain Jens Munk.* N.P.: The Hakluyt Society, 1897.

Hansen, Thorkild. *The Way to Hudson Bay: The Life and Times of Jens Munk.* Trans. James McFarlane and John Lynch. New York: Harcourt, Brace, World, 1965.

Andersen, R. "The First Lutheran Pastor in America." *Lutheran Church Review* 17 (1898): 55–63. Includes a contemporary drawing of Munk's winter quarters at Hudson Bay.

READING

From *The Cost of Discipleship* by Dietrich Bonhoeffer

Happy are they who have reached the end of the road we seek to tread, who are astonished to discover the by no means self-evident truth that grace is costly just because it is the grace of God in Jesus Christ. Happy are the simple followers of Jesus Christ who have been overcome by his grace, and are able to sing the praises of the all-sufficient grace of Christ with humbleness of heart. Happy are they who, knowing that grace, can live in the world without being of it, who, by following Jesus Christ, are so assured of their heavenly citizenship that they are truly free to live their lives in this world. Happy are they who know that discipleship simply means the life which springs from grace, and that grace simply means discipleship. Happy are they who have become Christians in this sense of the word. For them the word of grace has proved a fount of mercy.

Dietrich Bonhoeffer, *The Cost of Discipleship,* rev. ed., trans. R. H. Fuller and Imgard Booth (New York: Macmillan, 1963), 60.

PROPERS

Most gracious God, your servant Rasmus Jensen, faithful through desolation and peril, accompanied an expedition to distant and forbidding places as their chaplain to keep the explorers close to your word and sacrament: Strengthen us by his example to share the hardships of others in the name of him who came to share ours, your Son Jesus Christ our Lord; who lives and reigns with you and the Holy Spirit, one God, now and forever.

PHP

Readings:	Ezekiel 34:11-16
	Psalm 23
	1 Peter 5:1-4
	John 21:15-17
Hymn of the Day:	
	"Unto the hills around do I lift up my longing eyes" (LBW 445) [a favorite hymn in Canada]
Prayers:	For the church in Canada
	For faithful pastors and chaplains
	Of thanksgiving for those who planted the church on these shores
Preface:	All Saints
Color:	White

February 23

Polycarp, Bishop of Smyrna, Martyr, 156

Polycarp, a principal connecting link between the apostolic age of the church and Christian life of the second century, was born about the year 70. Irenaeus, who had known him in his youth, says that Polycarp was a disciple of St. John the Apostle and that "Apostle in Asia" appointed him bishop of Smyrna (modern

Izmir, Turkey). He was a close friend of Ignatius of Antioch (see October 17), and it was probably at Polycarp's request that Ignatius wrote his famous epistles to various churches in Asia Minor and to Polycarp himself.

Only one work by Polycarp has survived, his *Epistle to the Philippians*, which many believe is actually composed of two letters, one written *ca.* 115 enclosing Ignatius's epistles and the other written about 135 to warn the Philippian church against the spreading Marcionite heresy, a dualistic faith that rejected the Old Testament and distorted orthodox doctrines. Polycarp's *Epistle* was still read in the churches in the time of St. Jerome, but it was not included in the canon of the New Testament.

During much of his life, Polycarp was in many ways the leading figure of Christianity in Asia Minor, and he was referred to with great respect and affection by Irenaeus and Ignatius. As a very old man Polycarp went to Rome to discuss the problem of the dating of Easter, a vexing problem for the early church. After his return to Smyrna, he died a martyr's death in 155 or 156 at the age of eighty-six. The commemoration of his death is the first saint's day whose observance is attested in the history of the church; a reliable account of his martyrdom is given in the eyewitness report, the *Martyrdom of Polycarp*. The report testifies to the assembly of the faithful at the old bishop's grave "as occasion allows" to celebrate "the day of his martyrdom as a birthday." As early as the mid-second century, commemorations of martyrs at their graves on the anniversary of their deaths was a Christian practice.

After some Christians had been thrown to the lions, Polycarp was called before the proconsul, and, when he refused to give divine honors to the emperor and confessed himself a Christian, he was condemned to death. Since the games were over he could not be thrown to the lions, as he fully expected, but was instead burned alive. The *Martyrdom of Polycarp* places his death on February 23, and the Eastern Churches have commemorated him on this date. From the eighth century the Western Church observed his day on January 26, but the present Roman calendar (1969) moved his commemoration to February 23, and the Episcopal Church and the Lutheran Church and the Methodist *For All the Saints* followed that precedent.

READING

From *The Martyrdom of Polycarp*

There was a great commotion when it was learned that Polycarp had been arrested. Therefore, when he was brought before him, the proconsul asked him if he were Polycarp. And when he confessed that he was, the proconsul tried to persuade him to deny the faith, saying, "Have respect to your age," and such other things as, "Swear by the fortune of Caesar; change your mind; say 'Away with the atheists!'"

Polycarp looked with earnest face at the whole lawless crowd in the arena, and gesturing to them with his hand, groaning, and looking up to heaven, he said, "Away with the atheists!"

The proconsul was insistent and said, "Take the oath, and I shall release you. Curse Christ."

Polycarp said, "Eighty-six years I have served him, and he never did me any wrong. How can I blaspheme my King who saved me?"

The proconsul persisted. "Swear by the fortune of Caesar." Polycarp answered, "If you vainly suppose that I shall swear by the fortune of Caesar, as you say, and pretend that you do not know who I am, listen carefully: I am a Christian. If you desire to learn the teaching of Christianity, appoint a day and give me a hearing."

The proconsul said, "Try to persuade the people."

But Polycarp said, "You, I should deem worthy of an account; for we have been taught to render fitting honor to rulers and authorities appointed by God so long as it does us no harm; but as for these, I do not consider them worthy that I should make a defense to them."

The proconsul said, "I have wild beasts. I shall throw you to them, if you do not change your mind."

Polycarp said, "Call them. Repentance from the better to the worse is not permitted us; but it is noble to change from what is evil to what is righteous."

Again the proconsul said to him, "If you do not fear the wild beasts, I shall have you consumed with fire, unless you change your mind."

Polycarp replied, "The fire you threaten burns but an hour and is quenched after a short time; but what you do not know is the fire of the coming judgment and everlasting punishment that is laid up for the impious. Why do you delay? Come, do what you will."

When he had said these things and more, he was inspired with courage and joy, and his face was full of grace, so that it did not fall with dismay at the things said of him, but quite the opposite. The proconsul was astonished, and he sent his own herald into the midst of the arena to proclaim three times, "Polycarp has confessed himself to be a Christian."

Quickly then they surrounded him with the material for the pyre. When they were about to nail him also, he said, "Leave me as I am. For the One who gives me strength to endure the fire will enable me also to remain steadfast on the pyre, without the nails."

So they did not nail him, but only tied him to the pyre.

He looked up to heaven and prayed, "Lord, almighty God, . . . I bless you for judging me worthy of this day and this hour, that in the company of martyrs I may share the cup of Christ. . . . Let me be received among the martyrs in your presence today as a rich and pleasing sacrifice."

When he had said the Amen and finished his prayer, those attending to the fire lighted it. When the flame leapt up, we who were permitted to see it saw a wonderful thing, and we have been spared in order to tell others what happened. The fire made a shape like a ship's sail filled by the wind, and made a wall around the body of the martyr. He was in the midst, not as burning flesh, but as bread baking or as gold and silver refined in a furnace. We smelled a sweet fragrance like the breath of incense or some other precious spice.

Finally, when the lawless officers saw that his body could not be consumed by the fire, they commanded an executioner to go to him and stab him with a dagger. When he did this, a great quantity of blood came forth, so that the fire was quenched and the whole crowd marveled that there should be such a difference between the unbelievers and the elect.

Later we took up his bones, more precious than costly jewels and more valuable than gold, and laid them away in a suitable place. There the Lord will permit us, so far as possible, to gather together in joy and gladness to celebrate the day of his martyrdom as a birthday, in memory of those athletes who have gone before us, and to train and make ready those who are to come hereafter.

The Martyrdom of Polycarp, chaps. 9.2–12.1; 13.3–14.2; 15.1–16.1; 18.2-3, trans. PHP.

PROPERS

O God, the maker of heaven and earth, you gave your venerable servant, the holy and gentle Polycarp, boldness to confess Jesus Christ as King and Savior, and steadfastness to die for his faith: Give us grace, following his example, to share the cup of Christ and rise to eternal life; through Jesus Christ our Lord, who lives and reigns with you and the Holy Spirit, one God, now and forever.

1970 Roman Missal, trans. LFF

Readings:	Psalm 116:10-17 (before Ash Wed)
	Psalm 34:1-8 (after Ash Wed.)
	Revelation 2:8-11
	Matthew 20:20-23
Hymn of the Day:	
	"How firm a foundation, O saints of the Lord" (H82 636, 637; LBW 507, LSB 728, ELW 796)
Prayers:	For a life of devotion
	For boldness to witness to the faith
	For courage to follow Christ, even to death
	For faithfulness to the apostolic tradition
Preface:	A Saint (3) (BCP), All Saints (LBW), Saints (ELW)
Color:	Red

February 24

St. Matthias, Apostle

Matthias was a late addition to the apostolic company to replace Judas and to restore the apostolic college to its full complement of twelve, representing the twelve tribes of Israel and the fullness of God's praise. The feast day itself was a late addition to the calendar.

Nothing is known for certain of the life of Matthias except for the account of his selection to replace Judas Iscariot, as recorded in the second reading, Acts 1:25-26. After Jesus' ascension, when about 120 of the followers of Jesus met in the upper room, Peter asked the group to choose a replacement for Judas, the betrayer of the Lord. Two witnesses of the resurrection were suggested, a certain Joseph Barsabbas, also known as Justus, and Matthias. The report of the choice of Matthias includes a condemnation of Judas, demonstrating the twofold authority of the church: speaking confidently the word of commendation as also with equal confidence the word of judgment.

Tradition has included both Joseph-Justus and Matthias among the seventy disciples sent out by Jesus, but neither is mentioned elsewhere than in Acts 1. After a prayer, the choice was left to the casting of lots, and Matthias became the twelfth apostle. St. Paul (1 Cor. 15:5-6) refers to a resurrection appearance of Jesus to "the Twelve"; Origen thought that this number included Matthias.

There has been some confusion in the apocryphal literature between Matthias and Matthew. Clement quotes a second-century Gospel of Matthias, now lost. A sixth-century "Acts of Andrew and Matthias (Matthew)" relates that the land of the cannibals fell to Matthias as the sphere of his missionary activity; an Old English poem, *Andreas,* tells the tale. There are stories of Matthias preaching in Judea and in Ethiopia, and one tradition asserts that he met his death in Colchis, near modern Georgia in the Caucasus. All the traditions at least agree that he was a martyr for the faith. His symbol, reflecting one of the traditions, sometimes appears as a double-headed axe resting on a Bible. His feast day was one of the last of the apostles' days to be added to the calendar, not dating back before the eleventh century. One reason for the late establishment of his feast day is that St. Paul was long thought to have been the one chosen to replace Judas and to restore the complement of twelve.

The reason for the traditional date of February 24 is not known. In the present Roman calendar, St. Matthias's day is moved to May 14 to avoid conflict with Lent and to place the commemoration in the Easter season, emphasizing Matthias's role as a witness to the resurrection; *Evangelical Lutheran Worship* has done the same. Other Lutheran churches and Anglicans retain the traditional Western date. In the Eastern Churches St. Matthias's Day is celebrated on August 9.

READING

From Luther's *Lectures on Galatians (1519)*

. . . Christ wanted no one to be made an apostle by men or the will of men but as the result to a call from Him alone. For this reason the apostles did not dare elect Matthias; they gained his appointment from heaven in answer to their prayer. And it was from heaven that God called Paul himself and made him an apostle, in particular through the voice of the Holy Spirit. "Set apart for Me," He says, "Paul and Barnabas for the work to which I have called them." Thus Paul boasts in Rom. 1:1f. that he was set apart for the Gospel of God, inasmuch as he himself, together with Barnabas, was set apart for the uncircumcised and the Gentiles, while the rest of the apostles were sent to those who were circumcised.

Note also that Paul makes the name "apostle" so emphatically expressive of an office and of dignity that he uses it as a participle and says "an apostle, not from men," which means "sent, not from men". . . . All these facts aim to make you see with what care Christ has established and fortified His church, lest anyone rashly presume to teach without being sent by Him or by those whom He has sent. For just as the Word of God is the church's first and greatest benefit, so, on the other hand, there is no greater harm by which the church is destroyed than the word of man and the traditions of this world. God alone is true, and every man a liar. Finally, just as David once left behind all the means by which Solomon was to build the temple, so Christ has left behind the Gospel and other writings, in order that the church might be built by means of them, not by human decrees.

"Lectures on Galatians," in *Luther's Works Vol. 27* © 1964, 1992 Concordia Publishing House. Used with permission.

PROPERS

Almighty God, who in the place of Judas chose your faithful servant Matthias to be numbered among the Twelve: Grant that your Church, being delivered from false apostles, may always be guided by faithful and true pastors; through Jesus Christ our Lord, who lives and reigns with you and the Holy Spirit, one God, now and forever.

BCP (1549); alt. in LBW, ELW

Readings: Acts 1:15-26
              Psalm 15
              Philippians 3:13-21
              John 15:1, 6-16
Hymn of the Day:
              "O Zion, haste, your mission high fulfilling" (H82 539, LBW 397, ELW 668)

Prayers:	For those who give testimony to the resurrection
	For a renewed life
	For faithfulness to Christ
	For those who are passed over in selection processes
Preface:	Apostles
Color:	Red

February 25

Elizabeth Fedde, Deaconess, 1921

with Emma Hermina Francesca Francis, Deaconess, 1945

E lizabeth Fedde was born on Christmas Day, 1850, at Feda, near Flekkefjord, Norway. At age nineteen, after the death of both her parents, she entered deaconess training at Lovisenberg Deaconess House under the supervision of Mother Katinka Guldberg, who had been trained at Fliedner's Motherhouse at Kaiserswerth, Germany. Following her training she began work in the state hospital blazing a path for trained, professional nursing sisters. During a typhoid epidemic in 1877 she nursed a young typhoid victim back to health. In the following year she founded a hospital in a remote area of northern Norway. A serious illness forced her to recuperate at the home of relatives. There, on her thirty-second birthday, Christmas Day, 1882, Sister Elizabeth received a letter asking her to come to New York and take up a ministry to the Norwegian seamen in port and on the ships in the harbor. "You can come immediately if you dare, can, and will take on this work." The letter was written by Gabriel Fedde, then the secretary to the Norwegian seamen's pastor, Mr. Mortensen. Sister Elizabeth, with no knowledge of the English language, accepted the challenge and left Christiana on March 25, 1883, and arrived in New York on April 9.

The work of the Norwegian deaconesses was officially established in America at a meeting held in Pastor Mortensen's home April 19, 1883, under the name of the Norwegian Relief Society. That work had its beginning in three small rooms (rented at $9 per month) at 109 Williams Street, next to the Seamen's Church and was marked by a service in that church June 11, 1883. Sister Elizabeth established a six-bed hospital that was to become a large medical center in Brooklyn. In 1885 the Deaconess House in Brooklyn was opened. The condition of the Norwegian immigrants to whom she ministered was indescribable; physical and mental illness, financial and spiritual poverty, abounded. In addition to her work with Norwegian seamen, she visited Ward Island Immigrant Hospital, founded homes for widows and orphans, collected and distributed food and clothing to the poor, made burial arrangements, taught Sunday school, solicited funds for ship fares for the disillusioned who wanted to return home. Sister Elizabeth also established the Lutheran Deaconess Home and Hospital of the Lutheran Free Church in Minneapolis in 1889.

Sister Elizabeth, plagued by ill health, returned to Norway in November 1895. There she married, and lived for nearly twenty-five years. She died at her home, Slettebo, Egersund, on February 25, 1921.

FOR FURTHER READING

Rolfsrud, Erling Nicolai. *The Borrowed Sister: The Story of Elizabeth Fedde.* Minneapolis: Augsburg, 1953.

It is appropriate to remember with Sister Elizabeth another deaconess, one who devoted her entire life to the diaconate and who shows its wide-ranging influence. **Emma Hermina Francesca Francis**, of African ancestry, was born in the British West Indies in 1875 and was educated in Antigua and in Germany. In 1908 she opened an orphanage, the Ebenezer Home for Girls, in Frederiksted on the island of St. Croix in the Virgin Islands. When the Virgin Islands passed from Danish control to the United States in 1917, she became associated with the Philadelphia Motherhouse of Deaconesses, and in 1922, at the age of forty-seven, she was consecrated a deaconess by the Philadelphia Motherhouse. As a canvasser for the West Indies Mission Board, Sister Emma helped found the Lutheran Church of the Transfiguration on 126th Street in New York City where she served as a parish worker for five years. In 1926 Sister Edith Prince, the second deaconess of African descent, joined the staff. In 1927 Sister Emma returned to Frederiksted, and at the Queen Louise Home resumed her work with children. So effective was her work and so great was the people's love for her that the attendance at her funeral in April 1945 was one of the largest on record in the Virgin Islands. The relationship between the Lutheran Virgin Islanders and parishes in New York City remains strong.

READING

From *Light of Christ* by Evelyn Underhill

The Triumphant Church is not a collection of pious people with robes washed white—it is the whole of life's energy running right, sublimated and woven into the loving self-expression of God—it is the Kingdom of Heaven. Its frontiers must stretch till they embrace the whole Universe in its power, mystery and beauty and bring it under the rule of Christ, the intellectual radiance full of love. For the work of the Incarnation, as St. Paul saw it, is not finished till the whole of the created order is filled with God and, at the heart of the universe, ruling it in its most majestic sweep and its homeliest detail, we find His uttered Word, His love. . . .

FEBRUARY

And you and I are committed as baptized Christians, to what has been given His deep and touching earthly revelation, to the steady loyal effort, in our own small place and way, towards bringing that mounting vision a little nearer completeness, bringing a little more of that Kingdom in. Each faithful upward glance, each movement of trust, each act of selfless love, helps it on. A time such as we have had here is only justified if it brings that mounting vision into focus again; reminds us of what it means to be Inheritors of Heaven. The Hallowing of the whole Universe, physical, mental, and spiritual in all its grades, the infinitely great and the infinitely small, giving our lives at whatever cost to the helping of the fulfillment of their sacramental promise—we must take sides in some way for that, because we are the Children of God.

Evelyn Underhill, *The Light of Christ* (London: Longmans, 1945), 74–75, 91–92, 64, 27–28, 28–29, 82–83. Reprinted by permission of Wipf and Stock Publishers.

PROPERS

Lord God, your Son came among us to serve and not to be served, and to give his life for the world: By his love, reflected in the sacrifice of your servants Elizabeth Fedde and Emma Francis, encourage us to serve those to whom the world offers no comfort and little help, giving hope to the hopeless, love to the unloved, peace to the troubled, and rest to the weary; through the same Jesus Christ our Lord, who lives and reigns with you and the Holy Spirit one God, now and forever.

LBW Common of Renewers of Society, rev. PHP

Readings:	Hosea 2:18-23
	Psalm 94:1-14
	Romans 12:9-21
	Luke 6:20-36
Hymn of the Day:	
	"Lord of glory, you have bought us" (LBW 424, LSB 851, ELW 707)
Prayers:	For the spirit of selfless service
	For sailors and mariners
	For the sick, the needy, the forgotten
	For those who minister to those in need
	For the liberation of women and men everywhere from bondage to stereotypes
Preface:	Baptism (BCP, LBW)
Color:	White

February 26

Bartolomäus Ziegenbalg, Missionary to India, 1719

with Christian Frederick Schwartz, Missionary to India, 1798
Hans Egede, Missionary to Greenland, 1758
Thomas von Westen, Missionary to Lapland, 1727

B*artholomäus Ziegenbalg* (Bar-tol-oh-MAY-us TZEE-gen-balg) was born in Pulsnitz, a little town in Saxony, June 10, 1682, the son of poor, devout parents. As a child he showed great ability in schoolwork and music. He studied at the University of Halle, then the center of the Pietistic movement in the Lutheran Church under the influence of August Hermann Francke. In 1705 Ziegenbalg responded to the call of King Frederik IV of Denmark to take the gospel to India. On July 9, 1706, Ziegenbalg and his associate Heinrich Plütschau (1676–1752) arrived in Tranquebar on the southeast coast of India, the first Protestant missionaries to that country.

Despite the hostility of the local Danish authorities as well as the Hindu religious leaders, Ziegenbalg and Plütschau carried on their work, baptizing their first converts on May 12, 1707. In 1712 a printing press was set up, and Ziegenbalg published important studies on the Tamil language and wrote voluminously on Indian religion and culture. Several of his manuscripts, including *The Genealogy of the Malabar Gods,* were sent to Halle, but they were never printed. His translation of the New Testament into Tamil (1715) was revised by a successor, Johann Fabricius, and is still in use. The Church of the New Jerusalem, built and dedicated by Ziegenbalg and his associates in 1718, is still used today.

During his brief lifetime (he died when he was thirty-six), Ziegenbalg had to endure poor health, lack of support from the Church, opposition of the civil authorities, and many misfortunes. Plütschau returned to Germany in 1714. The Copenhagen Mission Society, with the admirable goal of not making the new church a transplanted form of European Christianity, wanted its missionaries simply to preach the gospel and not to involve themselves in other matters. Ziegenbalg insisted, however, that the care of souls also implies a concern for the physical and mental welfare of the people and that such service is implicit in the preaching of the gospel.

The low point of Ziegenbalg's life was a period of four months between 1708 and 1709, spent in a stifling prison cell on the charge that by converting the Indians he was stirring up rebellion. The last three years of his life, however, were full of joy: his marriage in 1716, the arrival of a new and friendly governor, the publication of his New Testament, and the founding of a seminary to train native clergy. His cooperation with the Anglican Society for the Propagation of Christian Knowledge (see Thomas Bray, February 15) was one of the first ecumenical ventures. Ziegenbalg died in Madras on February 23, 1719, leaving as his monument a Tamil dictionary and grammar, a Tamil translation of the New Testament and the Old Testament as far as Ruth, some thirty-two tracts on Christian doctrine and duties, two church buildings, the seminary, and a community of 250 baptized Christians.

The work of the Ziegenbalg mission later declined and was in part taken over by Anglican missionaries, but it was the inspiration for missionary efforts elsewhere in the world, and it led indirectly to the flourishing Tamil-speaking Lutheran churches of India today. Dr. Rajah B. Manikam, the first Indian bishop of the Tamil Evangelical Lutheran Church, was consecrated in Tranquebar in 1956 during the year of celebration of the 250th anniversary of Ziegenbalg's arrival in India.

Ziegenbalg was included on the German Evangelical Calendar of Names (1962, 1965) and on the calendar in the *Lutheran Book of Worship*. An alternative date for the commemoration of Ziegenbalg is the date of his arrival in India, July 9, or the date of his first baptisms, May 12. *Evangelical Lutheran Worship* remembers Ziegenbalg on November 7 together with Father Heyer and Ludwig Nommensen.

FOR FURTHER READING

Bayreuther, E. *Bartholomäus Ziegenbalg.* Madras, 1955.

Firth, C. B. *An Introduction to Indian Church History.* Madras, 1961.

Lehmann, Arno. *Tranquebar: The Story of the Tranquebar Mission and the Beginnings of Protestant Christianity in India.* Trans. M. J. Lutz. Madras: Christian Literature Society, 1956.

Lehmann, E. A. *It Began at Tranquebar.* Madras, 1955.

Neill, Stephen. *A History of Christianity in India: Beginnings to A.D. 1707.* Cambridge: Cambridge University Press, 1984.

———. *A History of Christianity in India, 1707—1858.* Cambridge: Cambridge University Press, 1985.

Singh, Brijaj. *The First Protestant Missionary in India: Bartholomaeus Ziegenbalg (1687–1719).* New Delhi: Oxford University Press, 1999.

Swartley, C. H., ed. *The Lutheran Enterprise in India.* Madras: Diocesan, 1952.

Christian Frederick Schwartz (1726–1798), probably the most influential worker in the Tranquebar mission after Ziegenbalg, might also be remembered on this day. He involved himself in the political affairs of his people and was extraordinarily influential, respected for his integrity, and loved for his saintliness. He spent forty-eight years in India. His work was notably ecumenical (the English made him a chaplain at Trichinopoly), yet he remained a faithful Lutheran. He died on

February 12, 1798. He is commemorated on the German *Evangelical Calendar of Names* (1962, 1965) on February 13.

Another important early Lutheran missionary, also sponsored by the Copenhagen Mission Society, is **Hans Egede**, the Apostle of Greenland. He was born in 1686 in Norway. After studying theology in Denmark, he was a pastor for a time in his native country, but he was increasingly fascinated by the story of the Norse settlers of Greenland, from whom there had been no reports since the fifteenth century. After rebuffs by his bishop and by the King of Denmark, he raised money himself, bought a ship, and arrived in Greenland in 1721. He was disappointed to find only native people and not a trace of a Scandinavian settlement. With his wife, Gertrud Rask, he began missionary work there nonetheless. The mission made slow progress. It met competition with the arrival of Moravian missionaries in 1733 and suffered from an epidemic of smallpox. The selfless service of Gertrud Rask and her husband made a deep impression on the native peoples, however, and the work showed more promise. Rask died in 1735 and in the following year Egede returned to Denmark to train missionaries. His son Poul carried on the work in Greenland. Egede died November 5, 1758, and is commemorated on that day by the *Evangelical Calendar of Names.*

Yet another Lutheran missionary sent out by the Copenhagen Missionary Society was **Thomas von Westen**, the Apostle to the Lapps, remembered (April 10) on the German *Evangelical Calendar of Names* (1962, 1966). He died April 9, 1727.

FOR FURTHER READING

Aberly, John. "Christian Frederick Schwartz." *Lutheran Church Review* 3 (July 1926): 238ff.

READING

From the decree on the missionary activity of the Church by the Second Vatican Council

All followers of Christ are responsible in their own measure for the spread of the faith, but Christ the Lord is always calling from among his disciples those whom he wills, so that they may be with him and be sent by him to preach to the nations.

Those whom God calls must answer his call in such a way that, without regard for purely human counsel, they may devote themselves wholly to the work of the Gospel. This response cannot be given except with the inspiration and strength of the Holy Spirit.

Those who are sent enter into the life and mission of him who emptied himself, taking the nature of a slave. They must be ready, therefore, to be true to their vocation for life, to deny themselves, renouncing all that they had before, and to "become all things to all people." [1 Cor. 9:22]

In preaching the Gospel to the nations they must boldly proclaim the mystery of Christ, whose ambassador they are, so that in Christ they may have the courage to speak as they ought, and not be ashamed of the scandal of the cross. They must follow in the footsteps of the Master, who was gentle and humble of heart, and reveal to others that his yoke is easy and his burden light.

By a life that is truly according to the Gospel, by much endurance, by forbearance, by kindness and sincere love, they must bear witness to their Lord, even, if need be, by the shedding of their blood.

They will pray to God for strength and courage, so that they may come to see that for one who experiences great hardship and extreme poverty there can be abundant joy.

From the English translation of the Office of Readings from the Liturgy of the Hours by the International Committee on English in the Liturgy, rev. PHP. (In the Liturgy of the Hours, the reading is appointed for February 3, the commemoration of St. Ansgar.)

PROPERS

God of eternal and abounding love, you strengthened your servant Bartholomäus Ziegenbalg in his zeal for a true and living faith, upheld him through conflict and discouragement, and opened his mind to the culture of the Tamil people: Foster in your church such respect for those to whom the gospel is proclaimed, that with conviction, persistence, and love your saving word may be made real to all who do not know you; through Jesus Christ our Lord, who lives and reigns with you and the Holy Spirit, one God, now and forever.

PHP

Readings:	Isaiah 49:1-6
	Psalm 98
	Revelation 21:1-4
	Matthew 28:16-20
Hymn of the Day:	
	"Your kingdom come, O Father, to earth's remotest shore" (LBW 384)
	or "Praise God from whom all blessings flow. Praise him" (LBW 529), a Tamil hymn
Prayers:	For the church in India
	For schools and orphanages
	For those who seek to understand different cultures
	For those in frail health
	For a spirit of understanding, acceptance, and support for new work in the church
	For the church in Greenland
	For the church in Lapland
Preface:	A Saint (1) (BCP)
Color:	White

March 1

George Herbert, Priest, 1633

George Herbert, a model of the saintly parish priest, in his short life, made a lasting contribution to the Christian church and to English literature. He was born in Montgomery Castle April 3, 1593, the fifth son of an aristocratic and distinguished Welsh family. His father died in 1596, and the young son was raised by his mother, Magdalen Herbert, who was a friend of John Donne. Handsome, elegant, witty, Herbert excelled in classical scholarship, languages (Greek, Latin, Italian, Spanish, French), and music at Trinity College, Cambridge, and, as University Orator, (1620–1627), seemed destined for high political office.

He served as a member of Parliament for Montgomery from 1624 to 1625, but the death of his patron, James I, together with the influence of his friend Nicholas Ferrar (see December 1), whose religious community called Little Gidding he frequently visited, led him to decide upon the study of divinity, to which he had long been drawn. He was ordained a deacon sometime between 1624 and 1626 and was assigned to Leighton Bromswold in the diocese of Lincoln. Although he was still University Orator, he devoted himself to rebuilding the ruined church. He married Jane Danvers in 1629 after a courtship of three days; the marriage was apparently a happy one.

In April 1630, Herbert was instituted as rector of St. Peter's Fugglestone and St. Andrew, Bemerton (near Salisbury). He was ordained priest September 19, 1630. He served this tiny rural parish for but three years, exercising there unusual diligence in pastoral care and taking pains to instruct his largely unlettered parishioners in the significance of every part of the liturgy and in the meaning of the church year. Izaac Walton's biography (1670) of the man his parishioners with deep affection called "holy Mr. Herbert" reports that at the sound of the church bell announcing Morning and Evening Prayer, many of the parishioners "let their plough rest" that they might join their prayers with the morning and evening prayers of their beloved pastor.

Herbert, whose health had never been strong, died of consumption March 1, 1633, at the age of forty and was buried two days later beneath the high altar of his parish church in Bemerton.

His English poems were published shortly after his death by Nicholas Ferrar, to whom they had been left with the instruction that if Ferrar thought they might do good to "any dejected poor soul" he should have them published; otherwise, he should burn them. Two editions of the collection, *The Temple*, were published before the year was out; there were thirteen editions by 1679. The poems, called "the best collection of religious lyrics in English," breathe a gentle freshness and grace,

MARCH

not without earnest wrestling with worldly ambition and a continued struggle to submit to his vocation. Some of the poems are still sung as hymns: *The Elixir,* "Teach me my God and King"; *Antiphon,* "The king of love my shepherds is"; and "Let all the world in every corner sing." The graceful and moving poetry is a counterpart to the prose of Jeremy Taylor (see August 13), and it is W. H. Auden's judgment that "together they are the finest expression we have of Anglican piety at its best." Herbert's poetry is like John Bunyan's prose in that, although most carefully crafted, it leaves the impression of an unsophisticated mind, drawing its messages from ordinary life.

Herbert also wrote *A Priest to the Temple; or the Country Parson,* a simple and moving description of the parish pastor as well-read, temperate, given to prayer, devoted to his people: "Now love is his business and aim." In this book, Herbert might well have been describing himself.

George Herbert is commemorated in the calendar in the American *Book of Common Prayer* (1979) and on other Anglican calendars on February 27 to make room for the commemoration of St. David on March 1. The *Lutheran Book of Worship,* the Methodist *For All the Saints,* and *Evangelical Lutheran Worship* remember him on the date of his death, March 1.

FOR FURTHER READING

Charles, Amy M. *A Life of George Herbert.* Ithaca: Cornell University Press, 1978.

Hutchinson, F. E. *The Complete Works of George Herbert.* Oxford: Clarendon, 1941.

Summers, Joseph H. *George Herbert, His Religion and His Art.* Cambridge: Harvard University Press, 1954.

Tuve, Rosemond. *A Reading of George Herbert.* Chicago: University of Chicago Press, 1952.

Vendler, Helen. *The Poetry of George Herbert.* Cambridge: Harvard University Press, 1975.

Wall, John Nelson, ed. *George Herbert: The Country Parson and The Temple.* Mahwah: Paulist, 1981.

READING

From *A Priest to the Temple* by George Herbert

The country parson values catechizing highly: for there being three points of his duty, the one, to infuse a competent knowledge of salvation in every one of his flock; the other, to multiply and build up this knowledge to a spiritual Temple; the third, to inflame this knowledge, to press and drive it to practice, turning it to reformation of life, by pithy and lively exhortations; catechizing is the first point, and but by catechizing, the other cannot be attained. Besides, whereas in sermons there is a kind of state [stateliness], in catechizing there is an humbleness very suitable to Christian regeneration, which exceedingly delights him as by way of exercise upon himself, and by way of preaching to himself, for the advancing of his own mortification; for in preaching to others, he forgets not himself, but is first a sermon to himself, and then to others, growing with the growth of his parish. He useth and preferreth the ordinary Church-catechism, partly for obedience to authority, partly for uniformity sake, that the same common truths may be everywhere professed, especially since many remove from parish to parish, who like Christian soldiers are to give the word, and to satisfy the congregation by their catholic answers. He exacts of [from] all the doctrine of the catechism; of the younger sort, the very words; of the elder, the substance. Those he catechizeth publicly, these privately, giving age honour, according to the Apostle's rule 1 Tim. 5.1. He requires all to be present at catechizing: first, for the authority of the work; secondly, that parents and masters, as they hear the answers prove, may when they come home, either commend or reprove, either reward or punish. Thirdly, that those of the elder sort who are not well grounded may then by an honourable way take occasion to be better instructed. Fourthly, that those who are well grown in the knowledge of Religion may examine their grounds, renew their vows, and by occasion of both, enlarge their meditations. When once all have learned the words of the catechism, he thinks it the most useful way that a pastor can take, to go over the same, but in other words: for many say the catechism by rote, as parrots, without ever piercing into the sense of it. In this course the order of the catechism would be kept, but the rest varied: as thus, in the Creed: How came this world to be as it is? Was it made, or came it by chance? Who made it? Did you see God make it? Then there are some things to be believed that are not seen? Is this the nature of belief? Is not Christianity full of such things, as are not to be seen, but believed? You said, God made the world; Who is God? And so forward, requiring answers to all these, and helping and cherishing the answerer by making the question very plain with comparisons, and making much even of a word of truth from him. This order being used to one, would be a little varied to another. And this is an admirable way of teaching, wherein the catechized will at length find delight, and by which the catechizer, if he once get the skill of it, will draw out of ignorant and silly [uneducated] souls even the dark and deep points of Religion.

This is the practice which the parson so much commends to all his fellow-labourers; the secret of whose good consists in this, that at sermons and prayers, men may sleep or wander; but when one is asked a question, he must discover what he is.

George Herbert, "The Parson Catechizing," chap. 11 of *A Priest to the Temple,* in *George Herbert and Henry Vaughan,* ed. Louis L. Martz, The Oxford Authors (New York: Oxford University Press, 1986), 215–17.

MARCH

PROPERS

Our God and King, you called your servant George Herbert from the pursuit of worldly honors to be a pastor of souls, a poet, and a priest in your temple: Give us grace, we pray, joyfully to perform the tasks you give us to do, knowing that nothing is menial or common that is done for your sake; through Jesus Christ our Lord, who lives and reigns with you and the Holy Spirit, one God, forever and ever.
LFF

Readings:	Psalm 23 *or* Psalm 1
	1 Peter 5:1-4
	Matthew 5:1-10
Hymn of the Day:	
	"Come, my way, my truth, my life" (H82 487, LBW 513, ELW 816)
Prayers:	For poets and those who make language sing
	For humility
	For grace to find God in everyday life
	For devotion to prayer and dedication to service among clergy and laity
Preface:	A Saint (1) (BCP)
Color:	White

ALSO ON MARCH 1

David, Bishop of Menevia, Wales, *ca.* 544

David (the English approximation of the Welsh Dewi), the patron of Wales, is the best known and best loved of its many saints. Little is known of his life. He was born and ordained in Wales, and, after traveling and founding twelve monasteries, he settled at Menevia, where he founded the monastery since known as St. David's. These monasteries became centers for the spread of Christianity and bastions of learning, justice, and good order in a hostile environment. The monastic rule was very strict and the monks spent much time in prayer, worship, and good works. David is traditionally known as "the Waterman," perhaps because he insisted that his monks abstain from other drink or because he is said to have immersed himself daily in cold water in order to subdue the desires of the flesh. He is said to have made a pilgrimage to Jerusalem and was there consecrated bishop. At the Council of Brefi in Cardigan he was recognized as primate of Wales in place of Dubricius. Toward the end of his life he had several Irish saints as his pupils at the monastery. A life of St. David was written by Rhigyfarch *ca.* 1090, but its reliability is dubious.

David was included on the calendar in the 1979 *Book of Common Prayer.*

FOR FURTHER READING

Evans, D. Simon. *The Welsh Life of St. David.* Cardiff: Wales University Press, 1988.

Evans, J. Wyn, and Jonathan M. Wooding, eds. *St. David of Wales: Cult, Church, and Nation.* Woodbridge, Suffolk: Boydell and Brewer, 2007.

Wade-Evans, A. W., trans. *A Life of St. David.* London: SPCK, 1923.

READING

From *The Life of St. David* by Rhigyfarch

The father himself, overflowing with daily fountains of tears, and fragrant with a twofold flame of charity, consecrated with pure hands the due oblation of the Lord's Body. After matins, he proceeded alone to hold converse with the angels. . . . The whole of the day he spent, inflexibly and unweariedly, in teaching, praying, genuflecting, and in care for the brethren; also in feeding a multitude of orphans, wards, widows, needy, sick, feeble, and pilgrims: so he began; so he continued; so he ended. . . . To all men the holy bishop David was the supreme overseer, the supreme protector, the supreme preacher, from whom all received their standard and pattern of living virtuously. To all he was their regulator, he was their dedication, he was their benediction, he was their absolution, their reformation. To the studious, he was instruction; to the needy, life; to the orphans, upbringing; to widows, support; to fathers, a leader; to monks, he was their rule; to non-monastic clergy, the way of life; to all he was all things. . . . With what blaze of excellence did he shine!

D. A. Foster, *The Anglican Year* (London: Skeffington, 1953), 133.

PROPERS

Almighty God, you called your servant David to be a faithful and wise steward of your mysteries for the people of Wales: Mercifully grant that, following his purity of life and zeal for the whole Gospel of Christ, we may with him receive your heavenly reward; through Jesus Christ our Lord, who lives and reigns with you and the Holy Spirit, one God, forever and ever.

The Church in Wales, rev. DvD; LFF

Readings   Psalm 16:5-11 *or* 96:1-7
              1 Thessalonians 2:2b-12
              Mark 4:26-29
Hymn of the Day:
              "Guide me, O thou great Jehovah" (H82 690, LBW 344, LSB 918, ELW 618) (the only Welsh hymn in common use)

Prayers: For the church in Wales
             For the people and leaders of Wales
             For the spirit of simplicity and austerity
Preface: Apostles (BCP)
Color: White

March 2

John Wesley, 1791; Charles Wesley, 1788; Renewers of the Church

In the eighteenth century the Church of England was in serious decline. Worship was dull and formal, church buildings had been allowed to fall into decay, the poor were neglected, bishops were appointed for political reasons, many of the clergy were worldly and cynical. The Wesley brothers attempted the renewal of the English Church by taking seriously the obligations of the Christian life. Their religious movement began within the Church of England, but the Evangelical revival, as it came to be called, was not always welcome in the established Church and eventually moved outside it.

John (born June 17, 1703) was the fifteenth and Charles (born December 18, 1707) the eighteenth child of Susanna Wesley and her husband Samuel, the rector of Epworth in Lincolnshire, who was descended from an old Puritan family. Susanna was a demanding mother and imparted to her sons a sense of holiness and seriousness that remained with them to the end. The two brothers were both educated at Christ Church College, Oxford. John was ordained a priest in 1728, Charles in 1735. At Oxford, John became a member of the "Holy Society" founded by Charles. The group was composed of those who were dissatisfied with contemporary religious life and who sought mutual improvement. They emphasized frequent communion and fasting twice a week, and their service extended to social work as well. Their methodical program earned them the derogatory name "Methodists." John's powerful personality soon made him the leader of the group.

In 1735 the brothers went to Georgia, John sent by the Society for the Propagation of the Gospel and Charles as secretary to the governor, James Oglethorpe. The experience of both brothers was unhappy. John's purpose was to evangelize the colonists and the Indians, but his preaching against the slave trade and against gin alienated the colonists. He broke with the Calvinists and joined with the Moravians. The brothers returned to London in 1738 and frequented the Moravian chapel in Fetter Lane. Both experienced an inner conversion, Charles on May 21, 1738, and John three days later at a meeting in Aldersgate Street with a Moravian group. The eighteenth-century Evangelical revival was born.

John spent the rest of his long life in evangelistic work. He visited Count von Zinzendorf in Germany. The brothers were increasingly excluded from the established Church, though they continued to respect it, and they turned more and more to preaching in the fields. It is said that John traveled more than a quarter of a million miles on horseback all over England and preached more than forty thousand sermons, often several each day. On June 11, 1739, John wrote in his journal, "I look upon all the world as my parish; thus far I mean, that, in whatever part of it I am in, I judge it meet, right and my bounden duty, to declare unto all that are willing to hear, the glad tidings of salvation. This is the work which I know God has called me to; and sure I am that his blessing attends it."

In 1740 the brothers ended their connection with the Moravians and opened a "Methodist" chapel in Bristol. Both brothers wished to remain in the established Church but differed with each other concerning their right to ordain ministers if none were forthcoming from the Church of England.

Charles, the best of the hymn writers of the age, wrote, it is said, over six thousand hymns. He married in 1749, retired from itinerant preaching in 1756, and settled in Bristol. In 1771 he moved to London.

John, the greatest single force in the eighteenth-century revival, incurred hostility and violence at times. A ruthless antagonist, he was an able organizer and produced an enormous quantity of writing: a long journal, a Christian library of wide-ranging devotional works, hymn translations, two editions of George Herbert's poems. Much of his editing seems to have done while he was traveling on horseback. When there was an urgent and unfulfilled need for ministers, John, against the advice of Charles, in 1784 ordained Thomas Coke as superintendent or bishop and instructed him to ordain Francis Asbury in America as his colleague. John also ordained ministers for Scotland in 1785.

Charles died March 29, 1788, and was buried in the graveyard of Old Marylebone Church. John died on March 2, 1791, and was buried in the cemetery behind his chapel and house on City Road, London.

On the calendar in the *Book of Common Prayer* and on certain other Anglican calendars, John and Charles Wesley are remembered on March 3 to make room for the commemoration of Chad on March 2. The Methodist calendar in *For All the Saints* commemorates John Wesley on March 2, Charles Wesley on March 29, their father Samuel Wesley on April 24, and their remarkable mother Susanna Wesley on July 30.

FOR FURTHER READING

Ayling, Stanley. *John Wesley.* Cleveland: Collins, 1979.

Baker, Frank. *John Wesley and the Church of England.* London: Epworth, 1970.

Collins, Kenneth J. *John Wesley: A Theological Journey.* Nashville: Abingdon, 2003.

Hattersley, Roy. *A Brand from the Burning: A Life of John Wesley.* Boston: Little, Brown, 2002.

Hempton, David. *Methodism: Empire of the Spirit.* New Haven: Yale University Press, 2005.

The Hymn 39, no. 4 (October 1988). A series of articles on the Wesleys.

Outler, Albert C., ed. *John Wesley.* 2d ed. New York: Oxford University Press, 1970.

Rowe, Kenneth E., ed. *The Place of Wesley in the Christian Tradition.* Metuchen: Scarecrow, 1976.

Tyson, John R. *Assist Me to Proclaim: The Life and Hymns of John Wesley.* Grand Rapids: Eerdmans, 2008.

Wesley, Charles. *Journal.* Ed. T. Jackson. 2 vols. London, 1849.

Wesley, John. *Journal 1739–1791.* 4 vols. London, 1827. 8 vols., ed. N. Curnock, 1906–1916. Abridged ed., London: Everyman, 1902.

Whaling, Frank, ed. *John and Charles Wesley: Selected Writings and Hymns.* New York: Paulist, 1981.

Wiseman, F. L. *Charles Wesley: Evangelist and Poet.* New York: Abingdon, 1932.

READING

From the *Journal* of John Wesley, May 24, 1738

I think it was about five this morning that I opened my Testament on those words, "There are given unto us exceeding great and precious promises, even that ye should be partakers of the divine nature," Just as I went out, I opened it again on those words, "Thou art not far from the kingdom of God." In the afternoon I was asked to go to St. Paul's. The anthem was, "Out of the deep have I called unto thee, O Lord. O let thine ears consider well the voice of my complaint. If thou, Lord, wilt be extreme to mark what is done amiss, O Lord, who may abide it? For there is mercy with thee; therefore shalt thou be feared. O Israel, trust in the Lord; for with the Lord there is mercy, and with him is plenteous redemption. And he shall redeem Israel from all his sins."

In the evening I went very unwillingly to a society in Aldersgate Street, where one was reading Luther's preface to the Epistle to the Romans. About a quarter before nine, while he was describing the change which God works in the heart through faith in Christ, I felt my heart strangely warmed. I felt I did trust in Christ, Christ alone, for my salvation; and an assurance was given me that He had taken away my sins, even mine, and saved me from the law of sin and death.

I began to pray with all my might for those who had in a more especial manner despitefully used me and persecuted me. I then testified openly to all there what I now first felt in my heart. But it was not long before the enemy suggested, "This cannot be faith; for where is the joy?" Then was I taught that peace and victory over sin are essential to faith in the Captain of our salvation; but that, as to the transports of joy that usually attend the beginning of it, especially in those who have mourned deeply, God sometimes giveth, sometimes witholdeth them, according to the counsels of His own will.

The Heart of John Wesley's Journal, ed. Percy Livingston Parker (London: Revell, n.d.), 28–30.

PROPERS

Lord God, you inspired your servants John and Charles Wesley with burning zeal for the sanctification of souls, and endowed them with eloquence in speech and song: Kindle in your Church, we entreat you, such fervor, that those whose faith has cooled may be warmed, and those who have not known Christ may turn to him and be saved; who lives and reigns with you and the Holy Spirit, one God, now and forever.

CMG, LFF

Readings:	Isaiah 49:5-6
	Psalm 98:1-4 (5-10) *or* 103:1-4, 13-18
	Luke 9:2-6
Hymn of the Day:	
	"O for a thousand tongues to sing" (H82 493, LBW 559, LSB 528, ELW 886)
Prayers:	For a heart burning with love for God
	For a deepened spiritual life
	For a social conscience
	For the reconciliation of the Methodist and Anglican Churches
Preface:	Pentecost (BCP), or, if after Ash Wednesday, Lent
Color:	White

MARCH

ALSO ON MARCH 2

Chad, Bishop of Lichfield, 672

The Venerable Bede in his *Ecclesiastical History* draws a most attractive portrait of Chad. He was born in Northumbria early in the seventh century and trained in the Celtic tradition under Aidan at Lindisfarne (see June 9). In 664 he succeeded his brother Cedd as abbot of Lastingham and two years later was appointed Bishop of Northumbria with his see at York. In 669 Theodore, the new Archbishop of Canterbury who had arrived from Rome, judged Chad's consecration by British bishops to be irregular. Chad gladly resigned, "for I never thought myself worthy of it," and returned to his monastery. Theodore, however, impressed by Chad's humble character, reordained him and made him Bishop of Mercia and Northumbria with his seat at Lichfield where Chad served until his death from the plague three years later, in 672.

Chad is on the calendar in the *Book of Common Prayer* but is not on the General Roman Calendar.

READING

From *History of the English Church and People* by the Venerable Bede (Book III, chapter 3)

The most reverend bishop Chad always preferred to undertake his preaching missions on foot rather than on horseback; but Theodore (Archbishop of Canterbury) ordered him to ride whenever he undertook a long journey. He was most reluctant to forego this pious exercise which he loved, but the Archbishop, who recognized his outstanding holiness and considered it more proper for him to ride, himself insisted on helping him to mount his horse. So Chad received the Bishopric of the Mercians and the people of Lindsey, and administered his diocese in great holiness of life after the example of the early Fathers. . . .

Chad established his Episcopal seat in the town of Lichfield, where he also died and was buried, and where succeeding bishops of the province have their see to this day. There he built himself a house near the church, where he used to retire privately with seven or eight brethren in order to pray or study whenever his work and preaching permitted. In addition to his many virtues of continence, preaching, prayer and many others, he was filled with the fear of God and mindful of his last end in all he did.

Bede, *History of the English Church and People,* trans. with an introduction by Leo Sherley-Price, Revised by R. E. Latham (Penguin Classics 1955, Revised edition 1968), 207, 208. Copyright © Leo Sherley-Price, 1955, 1968. Reprinted by permission of Penguin Books Ltd.

PROPERS

Almighty God, for the peace of the Church your servant Chad relinquished cheerfully the honors that had been thrust upon him, only to be rewarded with equal responsibility: Keep us, we pray, from thinking of ourselves more highly than we ought to think, and make us ready at all times to step aside for others, that the cause of Christ may be advanced; through the same Jesus Christ our Lord, who lives and reigns with you and the Holy Spirit, one God, now and forever.

CMG, LFF, rev. DvD

Readings: Psalm 84:7-12 *or* Psalm 23
              Philippians 4:10-13
              Luke 14:1, 7-14
Hymn of the Day:
              "Father all loving, who rulest in majesty" (H82 568)
              or "Spirit of God, descend upon my heart" (LBW 486, ELW 800)
Prayers: For the cathedral and diocese of Lichfield

For deliverance from deception by dreams of worldly greatness
For the gift of holiness and true humility
For charity in all our actions

Preface: A Saint (2) (BCP), or, if after Ash Wednesday, Lent
Color: White

March 7

Perpetua and Her Companions, Martyrs at Carthage, 202

N o saints are more uniformly honored in all the early calendars and martyrologies than these African martyrs. In 202 the emperor Septimus Severus forbade conversions to Christianity, and harsh persecution ensued. Arrested in Carthage were Vibia Perpetua, a noblewoman from Thuburbo, twenty-two years old; her infant child; Felicity, a pregnant slave; Revocatus, a slave; Saturninus; Secundulus. All were catechumens. Later their catechist, Saturus, was arrested also. While under house arrest, they were baptized.

Perpetua's father urged her to renounce the faith, but she refused and was imprisoned. In prison she had a vision of a golden ladder guarded by a dragon and sharp weapons that prevented ascent, but nonetheless she walked over the dragon and reached a beautiful place. Her father repeated his plea in vain and repeated it again before the people in the arena.

The steadfast Christians were condemned to be given to wild beasts at a celebration in honor of Caesar Geta. Perpetua had another vision, this time of her seven-year-old brother Dinocrates, who had died of cancer, in heaven. Felicity was not to have been executed with the others since it was illegal to execute a pregnant woman, but three days before the spectacle Felicity gave birth prematurely to a girl, who was adopted by a Christian family, and she gladly joined the others in martyrdom. After being scourged, they were led to the amphitheater, and according to the apparently contemporary account of the martyrdom, they were mangled by the beasts, but survived to be beheaded with a sword.

The record of the *Passion of Perpetua and Felicity* is one of the most ancient reliable histories of the martyrs extant. Part of the *Passion* is said to have been written by Perpetua herself as a kind of diary record of her visions, and part by Saturus the catechist. The introduction and the conclusion are by an apparent eyewitness, said by some to have been the church father Tertullian. The *Passion*, which recalls the biblical book of Revelation, is an important document in understanding early Christian ideas of martyrdom, providing a vivid insight into the beliefs of the young and vigorous African church. It was enormously popular, and St. Augustine, who quotes it often, has to warn against it being put on the same level as Holy Scripture. Perpetua and her companions were very popular in Carthage, and a basilica was erected over their tomb.

In the *Passion,* four other martyrs are also mentioned: Jocundus, Saturninus, and Artaxius, all of whom had been burned, and Quintus, who died in prison.

In the Roman Church, the commemoration of Perpetua and Felicity had been moved to March 6 to make room for Thomas Aquinas on March 7, but the present Roman calendar, having moved Thomas to January 28, restores the commemoration of Perpetua and Felicity to March 7, and the Episcopal Church, the Lutheran Church, and the Methodist *For All the Saints* have followed that change.

FOR FURTHER READING

Dodds, E. R. *Pagan and Christian in an Age of Anxiety.* Cambridge: Cambridge University Press, 1965.

Musurillo, Herbert, ed. and trans. *The Acts of the Christian Martyrs.* New York: Oxford University Press, 1972.

Salisbury, Joyce E. *Perpetua's Passion: The Death and Memory of a Young Roman Woman.* New York: Routledge, 1997.

Shewring, W., ed. and trans. *The Passion of SS. Perpetua and Felicity, MM.* London: Sheed and Ward, 1931.

READING

From the *Martyrdom of Saints Perpetua and Felicitas*

The day of their victory dawned, and they marched from the prison to the amphitheatre joyfully as though they were going to heaven, with calm faces, trembling, if at all, with joy rather than fear. Perpetua went along with shining countenance and calm step, as the beloved of God, as a wife of Christ, putting down everyone's stare by her own intense gaze. With them also was Felicitas, glad that she had safely given birth so that now she could fight the beasts, going from one blood bath to another, from the midwife to the gladiator, ready to wash after the childbirth in a second baptism.

They were led up to the gates and the men were forced to put on the robes of priests of Saturn, the women the dress of the priestesses of Ceres. But the noble Perpetua strenuously resisted this to the end.

"We came to this of our own free will, that our freedom should not be violated. We agreed to pledge our lives provided that we would do no such thing. You agreed with us to do this."

Even injustice recognized injustice. The military tribune agreed. They were to be brought into the arena just as they were. Perpetua then began to sing a Psalm:

she was treading on the head of the Egyptian. Revocatus, Saturninus, and Saturus began to warn the onlooking mob. Then when they came within sight of Hilarianus, they suggested by their motions and gestures; "You have condemned us, but God will condemn you" was what they were saying.

At this the crowds became enraged and demanded that they be scourged before a line of gladiators. And they rejoiced at this that they had obtained a share in the Lord's sufferings.

First the heifer tossed Perpetua and she fell on her back. Then sitting up she pulled down the tunic that was ripped along the side so that it covered her thighs, thinking more of her modesty than of her pain. Next she asked for a pin to fasten her untidy hair; for it was not right that a martyr should die with her hair in disorder, lest she might seem to be mourning in her hour of triumph.

Then she got up. And seeing that Felicitas had been crushed to the ground, she went over to her, gave her her hand, and lifted her up. Then the two stood side by side.

. . . [B]ut the mob asked that their bodies be brought out into the open that their eyes might be the guilty witnesses of the sword that pierced their flesh. And so the martyrs got up and went to the spot of their own accord as the people wanted them to go, and kissing one another they sealed their martyrdom with the ritual kiss of peace. The others took the sword in silence without moving, especially Saturus, who being the first to climb the stairway, was the first to die. For once again he was waiting for Perpetua. Perpetua, however, had yet to taste more pain. She screamed as she was struck on the bone; then she took the trembling hand of the young gladiator and guided it to her throat. It was as though so great a woman, feared as she was by the unclean spirit, could not be dispatched unless she herself were willing.

Ah, most valiant and blessed martyrs! Truly are you called and chosen for the glory of Christ Jesus our Lord! And any man who exalts, honors, and worships his glory should read for the consolation of the Church these new deeds of heroism which are no less significant than the tales of old. For these new manifestations of virtue will bear witness to one and the same Spirit who still operates, and to God the Father almighty, to his Son Jesus Christ our Lord, to whom is splendor and immeasurable power for all the ages. Amen.

Martyrdom of Saints Perpetua and Felicitas, in The Acts of the Christian Martyrs, ed. and trans. Herbert Musurillo (1972), 129–31. Reprinted by permission of Oxford University Press.

PROPERS

O God, the King of saints, in whose strength your servants Perpetua and Felicitas and their companions made a good confession, staunchly resisting, for the cause of Christ, the claims of human affection, and encouraging one another in their time of trial: Grant that we who cherish their blessed memory may share their pure and steadfast faith, and win with them the palm of victory; through Jesus Christ our Lord, who lives and reigns with you and the Holy Spirit, one God, forever and ever.

LFF, rev. PHP

Readings: Psalm 34:1-8 *or* Psalm 124
              Hebrews 10:32-39
              Matthew 24:9-14
Hymn of the Day:
              "Jerusalem the golden" (H82 624, LBW 347, LSB 672)
Prayers: For faithfulness
              For confidence in God's care
              For courage to confess Christ
              For strength to support those who suffer
Preface: A Saint (3) (BCP), or, if after Ash Wednesday, Lent
Color: Red

March 10

On this day, *Evangelical Lutheran Worship* lists **Harriet Tubman** and **Sojourner Truth**. In this proposed common calendar, they have been moved to July 20 with Elizabeth Cady Stanton and Amelia Jenks Bloomer, renewers of society, as commemorated in *Lesser Feasts and Fasts* (1997).

March 12

Gregory the Great, Bishop of Rome, 604

Gregory I, called "the Great," was born in Rome *ca.* 540 to a distinguished Christian family of senatorial rank. His grandfather had been a pope after he had become a widower. Gregory as a young man had a palace and immense wealth. He was educated in the law and entered civil service. As Prefect of Rome, the chief administrative officer of the city, he presided over the Roman Senate, gathering knowledge of political and business affairs. Shortly after Gregory took office, his father died, and not long afterward Gregory became a monk.

About 575 he turned his family home into a monastery dedicated to St. Andrew, provided for the founding of six monasteries on his father's property in Sicily, and gave the surplus of his inheritance to the poor.

He reentered what he liked to call the turbulence of life in the world when he was ordained deacon by Benedict I. In 579 he was sent as the papal representative to the Byzantine court at Constantinople where he increased his knowledge of the political and religious problems disturbing the empire. (During his stay in Constantinople he lived with the monks who accompanied him and apparently never learned Greek.)

He was recalled to Rome *ca.* 586 to be a counselor to Pope Pelagius II. It was a troubled time for the city. A plague spread through Rome, killing many, including the pope, and Gregory was elected his successor by popular acclaim. His consecration as Bishop of Rome was delayed until the approval of the Byzantine emperor could be secured. Meanwhile, Gregory ministered to the sick and dying in the then-plague-ridden city and organized penitential processions.

In 592 the Lombards invaded Rome. In the absence of secular leadership, Gregory rallied the people to defend the city and agreed to pay a yearly tribute to save Rome. The Byzantine emperor had refused aid; civil government had failed. The people, therefore, saw the pope as their protector who had assumed responsibility when they had no other helper.

Gregory showed concern for the poor and for justice, insisted upon a high standard of spirituality in Church administrators and reformed the process of raising money from the papal patrimonies so that unjust amounts of money were not collected. He put his stamp on the liturgy by reviving the "station churches" to which the pope processed and celebrated Mass on certain days; writing some prayers of the Gregorian sacramentary; changing the second petition in the threefold Kyrie to "Christ have mercy"; ordering that Alleluia be sung throughout the year except on penitential days; fostering the development of music; emphasizing the importance of the sermon; and fixing the present order of the Our Father in the Mass.

MARCH

Gregory struggled with the Patriarch of Constantinople who claimed to be the "ecumenical patriarch," and in opposition to him Gregory claimed universal jurisdiction for the Bishop of Rome, not as lord but as "servant of the servants of God" (a title not original with Gregory but typical of his approach).

Gregory's use of monks as missionaries to the Anglo-Saxons was his single most influential act in determining the future of Christian culture and institutions. In 597 he sent Augustine of Canterbury (see May 26) and forty monks to evangelize Britain. The story told by Bede is that Gregory saw some fair-haired slaves in Rome and, being told that they were Angles, is said to have replied, "Not Angles but angels," and decided that they must be Christianized.

Gregory is remembered not for the brilliance of his writing or his thought, although his *Pastoral Care* is a classic work on the ministry, but rather as an austere and masterful statesman who managed the Church in a complex and changing world. And this was the work of a man who described himself as sickly and who constantly yearned to return to monastic seclusion. Called by some the greatest man of the sixth century, Gregory forms a bridge between the ancient and the medieval worlds, and his episcopate was a model for his successors.

Gregory died March 12, 604. His feast day in the Roman Catholic calendar is September 3, the date of his election as Bishop of Rome. This avoids celebrating his feast during Lent. The Episcopal and Lutheran Churches and the Methodist *For All the Saints* retain March 12 as the date of his commemoration.

FOR FURTHER READING

Battifol, Pierre. *St. Gregory the Great.* Trans. J. Stoddard. New York, 1929.

Dudden, Frederick Holmes. *Gregory the Great: His Place in History and Thought.* New York: Russell and Russell, 1967 [1905].

Gregory. *Pastoral Care.* Trans. H. Davis. London, 1950.

Markus, R. A. *Gregory the Great and His World.* Cambridge: Cambridge University Press, 1997.

Oden, Thomas C. *Care of Souls in the Classical Tradition.* Philadelphia: Fortress Press, 1984.

Straw, Carole. *Gregory the Great: Perfection in Imperfection.* Berkeley: University of California Press, 1988.

READING

From a sermon on Ezekiel by Gregory the Great

"Mortal, I have made you a sentinel for the house of Israel." [Ezekiel 3:17; 33:7] Note that one whom the Lord sends forth as a preacher is called a sentinel. A sentinel always stands on a height in order to see from afar what is coming. Anyone appointed to be a sentinel for the people must stand on a height throughout life to help them by such foresight.

How hard it is for me to say this, for by these very words I denounce myself. I cannot preach with any competence, and yet insofar as I do succeed, still I myself do not live my life according to my own preaching.

I do not deny my responsibility; I recognize that I am slothful and negligent, but perhaps the acknowledgement of my fault will win me pardon from my just judge. Indeed when I was in the monastery I could curb my idle talk and usually be absorbed in my prayers. Since I assumed the burden of pastoral care, my mind can no longer be collected; it is concerned with so many matters.

I am forced to consider the affairs of the Church and of the monasteries. I must weigh the lives and acts of individuals. I am responsible for the concerns of our citizens. I must worry about the invasions of roving bands of barbarians, and beware of the wolves who lie in wait for my flock. I must become an administrator lest the religious go in want. I must put up with certain robbers without losing patience and at times I must deal with them in all charity.

With my mind divided and torn to pieces by so many problems, how can I meditate or preach wholeheartedly without neglecting the ministry of proclaiming the Gospel? Moreover, in my position I must often communicate with worldly men. At times I let my tongue run, for if I am always severe in my judgments, the worldly avoid me, and I can never attack them as I would. As a result I often listen patiently to chatter. And because I am too weak, I find myself drawn little by little into idle conversation, and I begin to talk freely about matters which once I would have avoided. What once I found tedious I now enjoy.

So who am I to be a sentinel, for I do not stand on the mountain of action but lie down in the valley of weakness? Truly the all-powerful Creator and Redeemer of the human race can give me in spite of my weaknesses a higher life and effective speech; because I love him, I do not spare myself in speaking of him.

From the English translation of the Office of Readings from the Liturgy of the Hours by the International Committee on English in the Liturgy, Inc., rev. PHP.

PROPERS

Almighty and merciful God, guiding your people with kindness and governing us with love, you raised up Gregory of Rome to be a servant of the servants of God: Give the Spirit of wisdom to those whom you call to be the shepherds of your church and that your people, growing in holiness and fruitful in every good work, may receive the crown of glory that never fades away; through Jesus Christ our Lord, who lives and reigns with you and the Holy Spirit, one God, forever and ever.

PHP, after RS and LFF

MARCH

Readings:	1 Chronicles 25:1a, 6-8
	Psalm 57:6-11 *or* 33:1-5, 20-21
	Mark 10:42-45 *or* John 21:15-17
Hymn of the Day:	
	"O Christ, our king, creator, Lord" (by Gregory, LBW 101)
	or "Kind Maker of the world, O hear" (H82 152)
Prayers:	For the poor
	For social justice
	For renewed appreciation of the liturgy
	For a spirit of service
	For harried pastors and administrators, distracted by many concerns
Preface:	Apostles (BCP)
Color:	White

March 17

Patrick, Bishop, Missionary to Ireland, 461

Patrick (Patricius was his Latin name), the Apostle of Ireland, was born *ca*. 389 in Roman Britain, the grandson of a priest and the son of the alderman and later deacon Calpornius. The details of Patrick's life are uncertain. He admits in his brief *Confession* that he was not religious as a child and had little use for the Church. At the age of thirteen or fourteen, while staying at his father's country estate, he was seized by Irish raiders and sold as a slave in Ireland. There in hardship and isolation he began to pray every day. After six years as a shepherd he managed to escape, find a ship, and eventually reach home. His experience had been a spiritual conversion, and he now had a certain conviction of his vocation: he was to preach the faith to the Irish people. He studied for the priesthood on the continent. His superiors did not favor his mission to Ireland, apparently because of his deficient education, but upon the death in 431 of Bishop Palladius, who had been sent by Pope Celestine to the Irish, Patrick was named his successor and was consecrated bishop for Ireland.

Bishop Patrick's mission concentrated on the west and the north of Ireland where the gospel had not been preached before. He secured the protection of local kings and traveled extensively making many converts and founding monasteries. The clergy for the country were first brought from Gaul and Britain, but increasingly they were drawn from the native converts. The claim of Armagh to be Patrick's church, although not recorded before the seventh century, seems to be genuine.

Patrick was criticized by the British when he demanded the excommunication of the British Prince Coroticus, who, in a retaliatory raid on Ireland, killed some of Patrick's converts and sold others into slavery. Despite physical danger and harassment, his was a vigorously heroic life. The well-known hymn called "St. Patrick's Breastplate," although probably not by him, expresses his faith and zeal in a powerful and memorable way. The hymn belongs to the genre of *loricae*, an invocation of the Holy Trinity, angels, prophets, the powers of heaven and earth, and finally Christ himself against the powers of evil.

Patrick died at Saul in County Down in 461. He is remembered on the Roman Catholic, Episcopal, Lutheran, and Methodist calendars.

FOR FURTHER READING

Bieler, Ludwig. *The Life and Legend of St, Patrick.* Dublin, 1942.
———. *St. Patrick and the Coming of Christianity.* Dublin: M. H. Gill, 1967.
Carney, James. *The Problem of St. Patrick.* Dublin: Dublin Institute, 1961.

Hanson, R. P. C. *St. Patrick: His Origins and Career.* New York: Oxford University Press, 1968.

———. *The Life and Writings of the Historical St. Patrick.* New York: Seabury, 1983.

O'Donoghue, Noel. *Aristocracy of Soul: Patrick of Ireland.* New York: Michael Glazier, 1987.

READING

From the Confession of St. Patrick

I give unceasing thanks to my God, who kept me faithful in the day of my testing. Today I can confidently offer the living sacrifice of myself to Christ, who kept me safe through all my perils. I can say now: Who am I Lord and what is my calling that you worked through me with such divine power? You did all this so that today among the Gentiles I might constantly rejoice and glorify your Name wherever I may be, both in prosperity and in adversity. Whatever happens to me, I can with serenity accept good and evil equally, always giving thanks to God, who has shown me how to trust in him always, as one who is never to be doubted. He answered my prayer in such a way that in the last days, ignorant though I am, I might be bold enough to take up so holy and so wonderful a task, and imitate in some degree those whom the Lord had so long ago foretold as heralds of his Gospel, bearing witness to all nations.

Where did I get this wisdom, that was not mine before? I did not know the number of my days, or have knowledge of God. How did so great and salutary a gift come to me, the gift of knowing and loving God, though at the cost of homeland and family? I came to the Irish people to preach the Gospel and endure the taunts of unbelievers, putting up with reproaches about my earthly pilgrimage, suffering many persecutions, even imprisonment, and losing my birthright of freedom for the benefit of others.

If I am worthy, I am ready also to give up my life, without hesitation and most willingly, for his name. I want to spend my life here until death, if the Lord grant me this favor. I am deeply in his debt, for he gave me the great grace that through me many people should be reborn in God, and then made perfect by confirmation and everywhere among them clergy ordained for a people so recently coming to believe, one people gathered by the Lord from the ends of the earth. As God had prophesied of old through the prophets, "The nations shall come to you from the ends of the earth, and say, 'How false are the idols made by our fathers: they are useless.'" [see Tobit 13:11; Judith 5:7] In another prophecy he said, "I will give you as a light to the nations, that my salvation may reach to the ends of the earth." [Isa. 49:6]

It is among that people that I want to wait for the promise made by him, who assuredly never tells a lie. He makes this promise in his Gospel, "They shall come

MARCH

from the east and west, and sit down with Abraham, Isaac, and Jacob." [See Matt. 8:11] This is our faith: believers are to come from the whole world.

Chaps. 14–16, from the English translation of the Office of Readings from the Liturgy of the Hours by the International Committee on English in the Liturgy, Inc., rev. PHP.

PROPERS

Almighty God, who in your providence chose your servant Patrick to be the apostle of the Irish people, to bring those who were wandering in darkness and error to the true light and knowledge of you: Grant us so to walk in that light, that we may bring others to the peace and joy of your gospel and come at last with them to the light of everlasting life; through Jesus Christ our Lord, who lives and reigns with you and the Holy Spirit, one God, forever and ever.

PHP, LFF **+** RS

Readings: Isaiah 52:7-10
              Psalm 97:1-2, 7-12 *or* 96:1-7
              1 Thessalonians 2:2b-12
              Matthew 28:16-20
Hymn of the Day:
              "I bind unto myself today" (H82 370; LBW 188 and LSB 604 [abbreviated], ELW
              450 [less abbreviated])
Prayers: For the church and people of Ireland
              For an end to the many sufferings of the country and deliverance from terrorism
              and oppression
              For missionaries in physical danger and harassment
              For zeal in God's service
              For renewed respect for the natural world
Preface: Epiphany or Apostles (BCP)
Color: White

March 18

Cyril, Bishop of Jerusalem, 386

Cyril, one of the most attractive Christian leaders of the fourth century, was born near Jerusalem *ca.* 315. He was ordained priest about 345 and despite his youth was entrusted with the preparation of candidates for baptism, a task that bishops generally reserved for themselves. The *Catechetical Lectures* he delivered before Easter in 347 are justly famous and are the clearest surviving exposition of the early Church's teaching of adults who presented themselves for the rites of initiation. Cyril became Bishop of Jerusalem probably in 349 and held that office until his death on March 18, 386. He spent sixteen of those thirty-seven years in exile, having been deposed and subsequently reinstated three times during the stormy doctrinal controversies of the period.

Jerusalem was the principal focus for pilgrimage, and it is likely that Cyril organized the devotions and instituted the observances of Palm Sunday and Holy Week during the latter years of his episcopate in Jerusalem. As Christians returned home, they took with them the liturgies of Holy Week and so the observance of those holy days spread throughout the Church. The renewed rites of Holy Week in the several Christian churches derive in large measure from Cyril's understanding and work.

Cyril is included on the General Roman Calendar, the calendar in the *Book of Common Prayer,* and the Methodist *For All the Saints.* He is also on the 1962 German *Evangelical Calendar of Names.*

FOR FURTHER READING

Telfer, W., ed. *Cyril of Jerusalem and Nemesius of Emesa.* Library of Christian Classics 4. Philadelphia: Westminster, 1955.

READING

From the *Catechetical Lectures* of Cyril of Jerusalem, 3,1-3

"Let the heavens be glad, and let the earth rejoice." [Ps. 96:11] For these people who are about to be sprinkled with hyssop will be cleansed spiritually. His power will purify them, for during his passion the hyssop touched his lips. Let the heavenly angels rejoice. Let those who are about to be wedded to a spiritual spouse prepare themselves. "A voice cries out, 'In the wilderness prepare the way of the Lord.'" [Isa. 40:3] And so, children of righteousness, follow John's exhortation, "Make straight the way of the Lord." Remove all obstacles and stumbling blocks so that you will be able to travel straight along the road to eternal life. Through a sincere faith prepare yourselves to receive the Holy Spirit. Wash your garments through repentance, so that when you are summoned to the spouse's bedchamber, you will be found spotless.

Heralds proclaim the Bridegroom's invitation and summon all humanity to the wedding feast, for he is a generous lover. Once the crowd has assembled, the bridegroom marks out those who will enter the wedding feast. This is sacramentally effected through baptism.

Give your name at the gate and enter. I hope that none of you will later hear the words, "Friend, how did you get in here without a wedding robe?" [Matt. 22:11] Rather may all of you hear the words, "Well done, good and trustworthy slave; you have been trustworthy in a few things, I will put you in charge of many things; enter into the joy of your master." [Matt. 25:21]

Up to this point in the history of salvation you have stood outside the gate. Now I hope you will all hear the words, "The king has brought me into his chambers. My spirit rejoices in God my Savior. He has clothed me with the garments of salvation and in the cloak of joy. He has made me a bridegroom by placing a crown on my head. He has made me a bride by adorning me with jewels and golden ornaments." [Song of Sol. 1:4; Luke 1:46; Isa. 61:10]

. . . [T]his is a truly great occasion. Approach it with caution. You are standing in front of God and in the presence of the hosts of angels. The Holy Spirit is about to impress his seal on each of your souls. You are about to be pressed into the service of a great King.

And so prepare yourselves to receive the sacrament, not with the gleaming white garments you are about to put on, but rather with the devotion of a clean conscience.

Trans. PHP, based on *A Short Breviary* by the monks of St. John's Abbey and the English translation of the Office of Readings from the Liturgy of the Hours by the International Committee on English in the Liturgy.

PROPERS

O Lord our God, through Cyril of Jerusalem you led your church to a deeper understanding of the mysteries of salvation: Strengthen the bishops of your church in their calling to be teachers and ministers of the Sacraments, so that they may effectively instruct your people in Christian faith and practice; and that we, taught by them, may enter more fully into the celebration of the Paschal mystery; through Jesus Christ our Lord, who lives and reigns with you and the Holy Spirit, one God, now and forever.

PHP, RS ✛ LFF

Readings:	Psalm 122 *or* 34:1-8
	Ecclesiasticus 47:8-10
	Luke 24:44-48
Hymn of the Day:	
	"All who believe and are baptized" (H82 298, LBW 194, LSB 601, ELW 442)
	or "Baptized into your name most holy" (LBW 192, LSB 590)
Prayers:	For the Patriarch of Jerusalem
	For the peace of Jerusalem and for reconciliation between Arabs and Jews
	For all Christians in Jerusalem, that their unity may increase and that their witness to the love of Christ may be seen by all
Preface:	Dedication of a Church (BCP)
Color:	White

March 19

St. Joseph, Husband of Mary and Guardian of Our Lord

N o fully historical account of even a part of Joseph's life is possible, for he left only a faint imprint on the tradition. He is not mentioned in Mark's Gospel; John mentions only his name in the phrase "Jesus son of Joseph" (1:45; 6:42).

Genealogies of Matthew 1:2-16 and Luke 3:23-38, although different, both trace Joseph's ancestry through David and are concerned with showing that Joseph was Jesus' legal father. While Matthew and Luke agree that Joseph's historical connections were with Bethlehem, Matthew implies that Joseph was a resident of Bethlehem who settled in Nazareth to avoid living under Archelaus in Judea (2:22-23), while Luke says that he lived in Nazareth before the birth of Jesus and went to Bethlehem according to the requirement of the enrollment (2:1ff., 39).

Joseph is an accessory figure in the infancy narratives who was present at the birth of Jesus (Luke 2:16), the circumcision (2:21), the presentation (2:22), and the search for Jesus in the Temple (2:41-52). His trade was that of a carpenter (Matt. 13:55), although the Greek term could mean simply "artisan," as was Jesus also (Mark 6:3). Joseph is portrayed as a "just" man (Matt. 1:19), that is, a devout adherent to the Law; one who was kind and wise, like the patriarchs gladly responding to visionary dreams; a faithful and affectionate father to Jesus.

He was apparently alive when Jesus' ministry began (Matt. 13:55), but we do not hear of him again. Presumably he had died by the time of the crucifixion so that Jesus commended his mother to the care of the beloved disciple (John 19:26-27), a gesture that would have been unnecessary if Mary's husband had been alive. Yet the usual portrayal of Joseph as an old man is not explicitly supported by the Gospels; it begins rather in the second century in a Gospel attributed to James the Less. A fifth-century *History of Joseph the Carpenter* says that Joseph was widowed at eighty-nine years of age and that Mary became his ward when he was ninety-one.

The first known commemoration of Joseph occurs in an eighth-century calendar from northern France or Belgium, which for March 20 lists Joseph and calls him "spouse of Mary." The title remained, and on the present Roman calendar as well as the United Methodist calendar in *For All the Saints*, Joseph is identified as "husband of Mary." In the early ninth-century calendars, such as the Reichenau Martyrology of *ca*. 850, Joseph is commemorated on March 19; the reason for the change in date is not known. The Franciscans, especially Bernardine of Siena (d. 1444), promoted the feast of St. Joseph. The celebration was introduced in Rome about 1479 and, especially since the fifteenth century, its popularity has greatly increased. Joseph's cult spread rapidly after Teresa of Avila dedicated the motherhouse of her order to him. The late spread of the feast probably accounts for its omission on Lutheran and Anglican calendars at the time of the Reformation. In 1870 Pius IX declared Joseph to be the patron and guardian of the universal Church; the 1920 edition of the Missal introduced a special proper preface for the day, retained in the present Roman Sacramentary (1970); in 1962 John XXIII introduced Joseph's name into the canon of the Mass. In 1955 the Roman Catholic Church added May 1 as the feast of St. Joseph the worker as a response to the Socialist May Day in honor of labor and a symbol of the rights of workers. The Feast of the Holy Family on the Sunday within the octave of Christmas (or, if there is no Sunday within the octave, on December 30) also commemorates the parents of Jesus.

In the Eastern Churches, Joseph is grouped with the patriarchs of the Old Testament. He is the last of that line, which culminates in Jesus, the "pioneer and perfecter of our faith" (Heb. 12:2), and when Joseph flees to Egypt with his family, he recapitulates the pilgrimage of the patriarch Joseph as a preparation for the new exodus and the Christian Passover (Genesis 37; 50:22-26; Hos. 11:1; Matt. 2:13-23).

St. Joseph is regarded as a patron saint of Canada.

FOR FURTHER READING

Brown, Raymond E. *The Birth of the Messiah.* Garden City: Doubleday, 1977.
Bulbeck, R. "The Doubt of St. Joseph," *Catholic Biblical Quarterly* 10 (1948): 296–309.
Filas, F. L. *The Man Nearest to Christ: The Nature and Historic Development of Devotion to St. Joseph.* Milwaukee: Bruce, 1944.

READING

From a sermon by Bernardine of Siena

There is a general rule concerning all special graces granted to any human being. Whenever the divine favor chooses someone to receive a special grace, or to accept a lofty vocation, God adorns the person chosen with all the gifts of the Spirit needed to fulfill the task at hand.

This general rule is especially verified in the case of Saint Joseph, the foster-father of our Lord and the husband of the Queen of our world, enthroned above the angels. He was chosen by the eternal Father as the trustworthy guardian and protector of his greatest treasure, namely, his divine Son and Mary, Joseph's wife. He carried out this vocation with complete fidelity until at last God called him, saying, "Good and faithful servant, enter into the joy of your Lord." [Matt. 25:21]

What then is Joseph's position in the whole Church of Christ? Is he not a man chosen and set apart? Through him and, yes, under him, Christ was fittingly and honorably introduced into the world. Holy Church in its entirety is indebted to the Virgin Mother because through her it was judged worthy to receive Christ. But after her we undoubtedly owe special gratitude and reverence to Saint Joseph.

In him the Old Testament finds its fitting close. He brought the noble line of patriarchs and prophets to its promised fulfillment. What the divine goodness had offered as a promise to them, he held in his arms.

Sermon 2, from the English Translation of the Office of Readings from the Liturgy of the Hours, International Committee on English in the Liturgy, Inc.

PROPERS

O God, who from the family of your servant David raised up Joseph to be the guardian of your incarnate Son and the spouse of his virgin mother: Give us grace to imitate his uprightness of life and his obedience to your commands; through Jesus Christ our Lord, who lives and reigns with you and the Holy Spirit, one God, forever and ever.

BCP; rev. in ELW

Readings:	2 Samuel 7:4, 8-16
	Psalm 89:1-29 *or* 89:1-4, 26-29
	Romans 4:13-18
	Luke 2:41-52 *or* Matthew 1:18-24a
Hymn of the Day:	
	"Our Father, by whose name all fatherhood is known" (H82 587, LBW 357, LSB 863, ELW 640)
	or "Come now and praise the humble saint" (H82 260)
	or "By the Creator, Joseph was appointed" (H82 262)
Prayers:	For fathers and foster parents
	For quiet confidence
	For humble service
	For those who work with their hands: artisans and laborers
	In thanksgiving for the patriarchs and prophets
Preface:	Epiphany (BCP)
Color:	White

MARCH

March 20

Cuthbert, Bishop of Lindisfarne, 687

Cuthbert, the most popular saint of the preconquest Anglo-Saxon Church, was born about 625, probably in Northumbria. As a young man tending sheep one night, Bede reports, he had a vision of angels conducting a soul to heaven and later learned that St. Aidan had died that night. As a result of the vision, Cuthbert became a monk at Melrose and applied himself to prayer, study, and rigorous self-discipline.

In 661 he was appointed abbot of the monastery. It was a year of the plague, and Cuthbert made long journeys, bringing cheer to many, sacrificing himself for others, and impressing everyone he met with his gentleness and holiness of life.

He became prior of Lindisfarne in 664, but withdrew to live as a hermit at Farne for nine years. In 684 he reluctantly accepted the bishopric of Northumbria, and not long afterward, when he felt the approach of death, he withdrew to his hermitage on Farne. He died there on March 20, 687. His remains were removed from Lindisfarne after the Viking raids began and eventually were interred in Durham cathedral; his bones were discovered in 1827 beneath the site of his medieval shrine.

He was a keenly observant man, interested in the ways of the birds and beasts. The ample sources for his life and character show a man of extraordinary charm and practical ability; Bede calls him "the child of God."

Cuthbert is on the calendar in the *Book of Common Prayer*; he is not on the General Roman Calendar.

FOR FURTHER READING

Colgrave, Bertram, trans. and ed. *Two Lives of St. Cuthbert*. Cambridge: Cambridge University Press, 1940.

Colgrave, Hilda. *St. Cuthbert of Durham*. Gateshead on Tyne: Northumberland, 1955.

READING

From *Life of Cuthbert* by the Venerable Bede

On Boisil's death Cuthbert became prior, an office which he carried out for many years with holy zeal. Inside the monastery he counseled the monks on the religious life and set a high example of it himself, and outside, in the world, he strove to convert people for miles around from their foolish ways to a delight in the promised joys of heaven.

Many who had the faith had profaned it by their works. Even while the plague was raging some had forgotten the mystery conferred on them in baptism and had fled to idols, as though incantations or amulets or any other diabolical rubbish could possibly avail against a punishment sent by God the Creator. To bring back both kinds of sinners he often did the rounds of the villages, sometimes on horseback, more often on foot, preaching the way of truth to those who had gone astray. . . .

Such was his skill in teaching, such his power of driving his lessons home, and so gloriously did his angelic countenance shine forth, that none dared keep back from him even the closest secrets of their hearts. They confessed every sin openly—indeed they thought he would know if they held anything back—and made amends by "fruits worthy of repentance," as he commanded.

He made a point of searching out those steep rugged places in the hills which other preachers dreaded to visit because of their poverty and squalor. This, to him, was a labor of love. He was so keen to preach that sometimes he would be away for a whole week or a fortnight, or even a month, living with the rough hill folk, preaching and calling them heavenwards by his example.

Venerable Bede, *Life of Cuthbert*, chap. 9, trans. J. F. Webb, in *The Age of Bede* (Baltimore: Penguin, 1965), 54, 55.

PROPERS

Almighty God, you called Cuthbert from following the flock to be a shepherd of your people: Mercifully grant that, as he sought in dangerous and remote places those who had erred and strayed from your ways, so we may seek the indifferent and the lost, and lead them back to you; through Jesus Christ our Lord, who lives and reigns with you and the Holy Spirit, one God, forever and ever.

A. C. Fraser, W. H. Frere, LFF

Readings:	Psalm 23 *or* Psalm 1
	2 Corinthians 6:1-10
	Matthew 6:24-33
Hymn of the Day:	
	"The King of love my shepherd is" (H82 645, 646; LBW 456, LSB 709, ELW 502)
Prayers:	For the indifferent and those who no longer practice their religion
	For a deeper understanding of the importance of prayer, meditation, and study
	For the north of England, its church and people
	For the cathedral and diocese of Durham
Preface:	A Saint (2) (BCP)
Color:	White

March 21

Thomas Ken, Bishop of Bath and Wells, 1711

Thomas Ken, the son of a lawyer, was born in 1637. He lived in politically disturbed times but was fearless in defense of the truth and in the rebuke of wrongdoing. He was chaplain to King Charles II but would not allow the king's mistress to enter his house. The king took no offense and in the following year, 1684, made him Bishop of Bath and Wells.

In 1684 when Charles's successor, James II, a Roman Catholic, to whom Ken had sworn allegiance, tried to undermine the authority of the Church of England, Ken and six other bishops refused to read the king's declaration of toleration for Protestant nonconformists and Roman Catholics. The seven bishops were imprisoned in the Tower of London but were acquitted in the courts and became popular heroes. James was deposed in 1688 and replaced with William of Orange, but Ken, believing himself bound by the oath of allegiance he swore to James II, could not acknowledge William and Mary as the lawful monarchs. He was deprived of his bishopric.

"Saintly Bishop Ken" was one of the many learned, devout, and holy people who are the glory of the seventeenth-century Church of England. Justly commemorated for his quiet insistence on the importance of doing right, he is remembered most of all today for his morning hymn "Awake, my soul, and with the sun" and his evening hymn "All praise to thee, my God, this night"; both conclude with the doxology "Praise God from whom all blessings flow," familiar to every Protestant denomination.

Thomas Ken is included on the calendar in the *Book of Common Prayer*.

READING

From a sermon by Bishop Ken

For what is Lent, in its original institution, but a spiritual conflict to subdue the flesh to the spirit, to beat down our bodies, and to bring them into subjection? A devout soul, that is able duly to observe it, fastens himself to the cross on Ash Wednesday, and hangs crucified by contrition all the Lent long; that, having felt in his closet the burthen and the anguish, the nails and the thorns and tasted the gall of his own sins, he may by his own crucifixion be better disposed to be crucified with Christ on Good Friday, and most tenderly sympathize with all the dolors and pressures and anguish and torments and desertion, infinite, unknown and unspeakable, which God incarnate endured when he bled upon the cross for the sins of the world; that being purified by repentance and made conformable to Christ crucified, he may offer up a pure oblation at Easter and feel the power and the joys and the triumph of his Saviour's resurrection.

"Sermon Preached in the King's Chapel at Whitehall in 1685," in *Prose Works of the Right Reverend Thomas Ken*, ed. W. Benham (London: Griffith, Farran, Okeden, 1889), 85.

PROPERS

Almighty God, you gave your servant Thomas Ken grace and courage to bear witness to the truth before rulers and kings: Give us strength also that, following his example, we may constantly defend what is right, boldly reprove what is evil, and patiently suffer for the truth's sake; through Jesus Christ our Lord, who lives and reigns with you and the Holy Spirit, one God, forever and ever.

Oxford Centenary Supplementary Missal, LFF

Readings:	Psalm 34:108 *or* 145:8-13
	Philippians 4:4-9
	Luke 6:17-23
Hymn of the Day:	
	"Awake, my soul, and with the sun" (LBW 269, LSB 868, ELW 557) [in the morning]
	Or "All praise to thee, my God this night" (LBW 278, LSB 883, ELW 565, H82 43) [in the evening]
Prayers:	For integrity, the grace to know what is right, and the courage to do it
	For those who teach young people the faith
	For the Cathedral Church of Wells and the diocese of Bath and Wells
	For an increase of understanding among the branches of the Christian church
Preface:	A Saint (2) (BCP)
Color:	White

MARCH

ALSO ON MARCH 21

On this day, *Evangelical Lutheran Worship* lists **Thomas Cranmer.** In this proposed common calendar, he has been moved to October 16, as commemorated in the 1979 *Book of Common Prayer.*

March 22

Jonathan Edwards, Teacher, Missionary to the Native Americans, 1758

Jonathan Edwards, a man of exceptional intellect who influenced theology not only in America but in Britain as well, was born in East Windsor, Connecticut, October 5, 1703. He was the fifth of eleven children and the only son of his father, who was the pastor of the Congregational Church there. After a rigorous education at home, the son enrolled at Yale when he was thirteen and received the B.A. in 1720. He continued in the study of divinity there for a time before a short pastorate in New York, from August 1722 to May 1723. He returned to Yale for the M.A., which he received in 1723 and stayed on again as tutor until 1726, when he became assistant to his grandfather Samuel Stoddard at Northampton, the most important church in Massachusetts outside Boston. He was ordained February

22, 1727. Five months later he married the seventeen-year-old Sarah Pierrepont; they were to have eleven children. In 1729 he succeeded his grandfather as pastor of the Northampton church.

As a young man he had already shown remarkable powers of observation and analysis and a wide variety of interests. At the age of fourteen, before any other American thinker, he had discovered in Locke's *Essay Concerning Human Understanding* a new theory of knowledge and a psychology that he was able later to use in support of traditional Calvinist doctrines. He had passionately worked through intellectual objections to his theological heritage and in a conversion experience early in 1721 had discovered a "delightful conviction" of divine sovereignty. He joined his profound learning with mystical experience and remarkable gifts in logic.

Edwards became convinced that the ills of the time were attributable to Arminianism, a popular theological position that minimized original sin, stressed free will, and tended to make morality the essence of religion. He preached a series of sermons on justification by faith alone in November 1734, which resulted in a revival of religion in the Connecticut valley in 1734–1735. Edwards reported the events in *A Faithful Narrative of the Surprising Work of God* (1737) in which he examined the several kinds of conversion experience.

Shortly after this revival of religion, the preaching of George Whitefield, the English Methodist evangelist, and Gilbert Tennant, a New Jersey Presbyterian preacher, led to the Great Awakening of 1740–1742. This widespread revival was defended by Edwards, notably in *A Treatise Concerning Human Affections* (1746), in which he maintained that the essence of all religion lies in holy love that proves itself by practical results. He was thus able to bridge the eighteenth-century polarization of intellect and emotion.

Despite the increasing reputation of the pastor (and in some measure perhaps because of it), Edwards's relations with his congregation became strained. Edwards restricted admission to the Holy Communion to the converted and so opposed the more liberal policies of his grandfather who had accepted the "Halfway Covenant," which allowed those who were baptized but not clearly converted to share the Lord's Supper and have their children baptized. Edwards's position was more in keeping with the situation of the Congregational Church after disestablishment, and the position eventually triumphed. Edwards himself, however, was dismissed by his congregation. He preached a dignified and moving farewell sermon July 1, 1750, and went to the frontier of Stockbridge, Massachusetts, to be a missionary to the Native Americans. Despite difficulties with language, sickness, conflict with personal enemies, and Indian wars, he nonetheless was able to publish his *Freedom of the Will* (1754) and *The Great Christian Doctrine of Original Sin Defended* (1758).

Late in 1757 Edwards accepted the presidency of the College of New Jersey (later Princeton University) and took up his duties in January. Princeton was at the time suffering from an outbreak of smallpox. Edwards was inoculated but suffered from a secondary infection and died March 22, 1758, in his fifty-fifth year. His worn gravestone is still to be seen in the cemetery there.

Edwards is on the calendar in the *Lutheran Book of Worship, Evangelical Lutheran Worship,* and the Methodist *For All the Saints.*

FOR FURTHER READING

Aldridge, A. C. *Jonathan Edwards.* New York: Washington Square, 1966.

Brown, Robert E. *Jonathan Edwards and the Bible.* Bloomington: Indiana University Press, 2003.

Danaher, William J. *The Trinitarian Ethics of Jonathan Edwards.* Louisville: Westminster John Knox, 2004.

Faust, Clarence E., and Thomas H. Johnson, eds. *Jonathan Edwards: Representative Selections.* Rev. ed. New York: Hill and Wang, 1962.

Holifield, E. Brooks. *Theology in America: Christian Thought from the Age of the Puritans to the Civil War.* New Haven: Yale University Press, 2004.

Jenson, Robert W. *America's Theologian: A Recommendation of Jonathan Edwards.* New York: Oxford University Press, 1988.

Lesser, M. X. *Jonathan Edwards.* Boston: Twayne, 1988.

Marsden, George M. *Jonathan Edwards: A Life.* New Haven: Yale University Press, 2003.

Miller, Perry *Jonathan Edwards.* New York: Sloane, 1949.

Stein, Stephen J., ed. *The Cambridge Companion to Jonathan Edwards.* Cambridge: Cambridge University Press, 2006.

READING

From Jonathan Edwards's *Personal Narrative*

The sense I had of divine things would often of a sudden kindle up, as it were, a sweet burning in my heart; an ardor of soul, that I know not how to express.

Not long after I began to experience these things, I gave an account to my father of some things that had passed in my mind. I was pretty much affected by the discourse we had together; and when the discourse ended, I walked abroad alone, in a solitary place in my father's pasture for contemplation. And as I was walking there and looking up on the sky and clouds, there came into my mind so sweet a sense of the glorious *majesty* and *grace* of God, that I know not how to express. I seemed to see them both in a sweet conjunction; majesty and meekness joined together; it was a gentle, and holy majesty; and also a majestic meekness; a high, great, and holy gentleness.

After this my sense of divine things gradually increased, and became more and more lively, and had more of that inward sweetness. The appearance of everything was altered; there seemed to be, as it were, a calm, sweet cast, or appearance of divine glory, in almost every thing. God's excellency, his wisdom, his purity, and love, seemed to appear in every thing; in the sun, moon, and stars; in the clouds, and blue sky; in the grass, flowers, trees; in the water, and all nature; which used greatly to fix my mind. I often used to sit and view the moon for continuance; and in the day, spent much time in viewing the clouds and sky, to behold the sweet glory of God in these things; in the mean time, singing forth, with a low voice, my contemplations of the Creator and Redeemer. And scarce any thing, among all the works of nature, was so delightful to me as thunder and lightning; formerly, nothing had been so terrible to me. Before, I used to be uncommonly terrified with thunder, and to be struck with terror when I saw a thunderstorm rising; but now, on the contrary, it rejoiced me. I felt God, so to speak, at the first appearance of a thunder storm; and used to take the opportunity, at such times, to fix myself in order to view the clouds, and see the lightnings play, and hear the majestic and awful voice of God's thunder, which oftentimes was exceedingly entertaining, leading me to sweet contemplations of my great and glorious God. While thus engaged, it always seemed natural to me to sing, or chant for my meditations; or, to speak my thoughts in soliloquies with a singing voice.

The Works of President Edwards, ed. S. B. Dwight, vol. 1 (New York: Converse, 1829), 60–62.

PROPERS

Almighty God, you gave to your servant Jonathan Edwards great gifts to understand and to teach your majesty and your grace: Grant that by his teaching your church may know you in your gentle and holy majesty and serve you in love and gratitude; through Jesus Christ our Lord, who lives and reigns with you and the Holy Spirit, one God, now and forever.

PHP

Readings:	Isaiah 6:1-8
	Psalm 119:89-104
	1 Corinthians 2:6-10, 13-16
	John 17:6-10
Hymn of the Day:	
	"My God, how wonderful thou art" (H82 463, LBW 524, ELW 863)
	or "Majestic sweetness sits enthroned" (H40 353, SBH 570)
	or "Eternal God, whose power upholds" (SBH 322)
Prayers:	For a deepened sense of the majesty of God
	For the spirit of inquiry
	For an awakened conscience
Preface:	A Saint (1) (BCP)
Color:	White

ALSO ON MARCH 22

The *Book of Common Prayer* commemorates **James De Koven** (1831–1879), professor of ecclesiastical history at Nashotah House, the Episcopal seminary in Wisconsin associated with the principles of the Oxford Movement. He was a defender of the ritualist cause in the Episcopal Church, most notably affirming the real presence of Christ in the Sacrament of the Altar.

March 23

Gregory the Illuminator, Bishop of and Missionary to Armenia, *ca.* 332

MARCH

Gregory, who was born about 257, is called "the Illuminator" or "the Enlightener" because he brought the light of the gospel to the people of Armenia. Extravagant legend clouds the details of Gregory's life. He is said to have been the son of a Parthian who assassinated the Persian King Khrosrov I. The infant Gregory was taken for safety to Caesarea in Cappadocia, where he was baptized and brought up. He married and had two sons, returned to Armenia about 280, and converted King Tiridates (Tradt) III. Gregory, in about 300, was consecrated a bishop at Caesarea and spent the rest of his life preaching and organizing the church in Armenia. Shortly before his death, Gregory, having appointed his son Aristages to be chief bishop (*katholikos*) of the Armenian Church in his place, withdrew into solitude.

Armenia was the first country to become officially a Christian nation and thus set a precedent for the adoption of Christianity by the Roman Emperor Constantine.

Gregory is on the calendar in the *Book of Common Prayer* because the Anglican Communion has enjoyed a warm friendship with the Armenian Church for many years. He is not included in the General Roman Calendar.

READING

From *The Life of St. Gregory the Illuminator* by Agathangelos

Throughout the whole land of Armenia, from end to end, Gregory extended the labor of preaching the Gospel.

All the time of his life, summer and winter, day and night, intrepidly and without hesitation in his course of preaching the good word, before the king and princes of all the heathen without let or hindrance he bore the name of Jesus the Savior of all, and he furnished every soul with divine vesture and spiritual arms.

He afforded salvation to many prisoners and captives and people oppressed by tyrants, freeing them by the awesome power of Christ's glory. . . . And to many in mourning or disheartened, through his consoling teaching he gave the expectation of hope in the appearance of the glory of our great God and Savior of all, Jesus Christ. And he turned everyone to the state of true piety.

. . . He himself at frequent intervals went out to deserted mountains where he made himself an example. He took various of the pupils from each monastery and went to live in the mountains in solitude; in grottoes and caverns they made herbs their daily food.

Agathangelos, *History of the Armenians,* chap. 13, trans. R. W. Thomson (Albany: State University of New York Press, 1976), 377–85.

PROPERS

Almighty God whose will it is to be glorified in your saints, and who raised up your servant Gregory the Illuminator to be a light in the world and to preach the Gospel to the people of Armenia: Shine, we pray, in our hearts, that we also in our generation may show forth your praise, who calls us out of darkness into your marvelous light; through Jesus Christ our Lord, who lives and reigns with you and the Holy Spirit, one God, now and forever.

BCP, LFF

Readings:	Psalm 33:6-11 *or* 98:1-4
	Acts 17:22-31
	Matthew 5:11-16
Hymn of the Day:	
	"Lord of light, your name outshining" (LBW 405, ELW 688)
Prayers:	For the church and people of Armenia
	For all who preach the gospel in the face of opposition and hardship
	For the light of Christ to shine in the darkness of the world
Preface:	Apostles (BCP)
Color:	White

March 24

Óscar Arnulfo Romero, Archbishop of San Salvador, Martyr, 1980

Óscar Arnulfo Romero y Galdámez was born in 1917 in Ciudad Barrios, in the mountains of El Salvador near the border with Honduras. He left school at twelve and began an apprenticeship as a carpenter. He showed promise as a craftsman, but while still very young he went to seminary. He trained at San Miguel and San Salvador and completed his theological studies in Rome. He was ordained priest there in 1942, but because of the Second World War no member of his family was present. He returned to El Salvador in 1944 and served as a parish priest in the country before becoming rector of the interdiocesan seminary of San Salvador. In 1946 he became secretary of the Bishops' Conference of El Salvador and remained in this post for twenty-three years.

He was consecrated bishop in 1970 and served as assistant to the aging Archbishop of San Salvador. In 1974 he was made Bishop of Santiago de María and in 1977 Archbishop of San Salvador. There was growing unrest in the country because of social injustices and widespread poverty, and the country was in virtual civil war. He had barely begun his work as archbishop when two of his priests were murdered. Romero demanded an inquiry into the events and set up a permanent commission for the defense of human rights. Accusations and attacks continued, even from within the Church. He continued to condemn all forms of what he called "the mysticism of violence."

In the evening of March 24, 1980, he was celebrating Mass in the small chapel of the Hospital of Divine Providence, which had been his home since his enthronement as archbishop. As he was about to elevate the bread and wine at the Offertory, Óscar Arnulfo Romero was shot through the heart. Minutes before, he had said in his sermon, "Those who surrender to the service of the poor through love of Christ, will live like the grain of wheat that dies. It only apparently dies. If it were not to die, it would remain a solitary grain. The harvest comes because of the grain that dies. . . . We know that every effort to improve society, above all when society is so full of injustice and sin, is an effort that God blesses, that God wants, that God demands of us." Aware that his life was in danger, he had already announced, "You may say, if they succeed in killing me, that I pardon and bless those who do it. Would, indeed, they might be convinced not to waste their time. A bishop will die, but God's Church, which is the people, will never perish."

Óscar Romero was added to the calendar in the Spanish-language service book produced by the Evangelical Lutheran Church in America, *Libro de Liturgica y Cántico* (Minneapolis: Augsburg Fortress, 1998) and is on the calendar in *Evangelical Lutheran Worship.* He is on the 1997 Church of England calendar, the *Christian Year,* and is among those commemorated in new statues on the west front of Westminster Abbey. He was added to the Episcopal calendar in *Lesser Feasts and Fasts 2006.*

FOR FURTHER READING

Brockman, James R. *Romero: A Life.* Maryknoll: Orbis, 1989.

Pelton, Robert S. *Monsignor Romero: A Bishop for the Third Millennium.* Notre Dame: University of Notre Dame, 2004.

Romero, Óscar, and James R. Brockman, eds. *The Violence of Love.* San Francisco: HarperSanFrancisco, 1988.

READING

A Meditation Attributed to Archbishop Romero, "Prophets of a Future Not Our Own"

It helps, now and then, to step back and take the long view. The kingdom is not only beyond our efforts, it is beyond our vision.

We accomplish in our lifetime only a tiny fraction of the magnificent enterprise that is God's work. Nothing we do is complete, which is another way of saying that the kingdom always lies beyond us.

No statement says all that could be said. No prayer fully expresses our faith. No confession brings perfection. No pastoral visit brings wholeness. No program accomplishes the Church's mission. No set of goals and objectives includes everything.

This is what we are about: We plant seeds that one day will grow. We water seeds already planted, knowing that they hold future promise. We lay foundations that will need further development. We provide yeast that produces effects beyond our capabilities.

We cannot do everything, and there is a sense of liberation in realizing that. This enables us to do something, and to do it very well. It may be incomplete, but it is a beginning, a step along the way, an opportunity for God's grace to enter and do the rest.

We may never see the end results, but that is the difference between the master builder and the worker. We are workers not master builders, ministers not messiahs. We are prophets of a future not our own.

http://www.nextreformation.com/wp-admin/general/romero.htm (accessed October 10, 2007). The meditation was written by Ken Untener (1937–2004), later Bishop of Saginaw, for John Cardinal Dearden in November 1979 for a celebration of departed priests; it has been widely attributed to Archbishop Romero.

PROPERS

Eternal God of justice and love, you hold in your mind a vision of creation as you intend it to be: By the example of your servant Óscar Arnulfo Romero give us such a view of your work that we may commit the future to you, confident that what we do in your Name will, in your good time, grow and flourish to your glory; through your Son Jesus Christ our Lord, who lives and reigns with you and the Holy Spirit, one God, now and forever.
PHP

Readings:	Ezekiel 20:40-42
	Psalm 5
	Revelation 6:9-11
	Mark 8:34-38
Hymn of the Day:	
	"Son of God, eternal Savior" (LBW 364, LSB 842, ELW 655)
Prayers:	For compassion for all in need
	For social justice
	For the poor and the oppressed
	For an end to violence
Preface:	A Saint (3) (BCP)
Color:	Red

March 25

The Annunciation of Our Lord

E xactly nine months before Christmas, the church celebrates the first moment of the coming of God to his people. With the Savior's conception the new age had begun, and so even into the eighteenth century this day was, in many places, considered the beginning of the year. It was also regarded in some places as being the day on which the world was created, this joining the first creation and the new creation, creation and redemption, on one day.

The day is a festival of Christ. The heights of Mary's exaltation as most favored, chosen to be the birth-giver of God, are surpassed by the splendor of that event of which she was the chosen vessel: the entrance of God into the world.

The celebration of the angel's announcement to Mary that she was to become the mother of the Savior seems to have originated in the East in the fifth century, where it is called *evangelismos*, the good news. The festival was introduced in the West during the sixth and seventh centuries and was universally celebrated by the time of the Tenth Synod of Toledo in 656. The date of March 25, precisely nine months before Christmas, is practically universal, but some churches in Spain kept the commemoration during Advent, on December 18. In the eleventh century, Spain accepted the traditional date but retained the December date also so that the Annunciation was celebrated twice. In the eighteenth century, Rome made December 18 "The Expectation of the Blessed Virgin of the Birth" of Christ.

The observance of March 25 presents certain practical problems, for the feast usually falls during Lent, when joyful celebration seems out of place, and often occurs in Holy Week, when the celebration must be postponed until after Easter week. Periodically, therefore, the suggestion is made that the day be moved to some time in Advent, closer to Christmas, when the church is anticipating the birth of Christ, but the suggestion has not been accepted. The tradition of counting back nine months is strong. In the Eastern Churches the Feast of the Annunciation is of such importance that it takes precedence over a Sunday in Lent with which it may coincide.

The title for the Blessed Virgin Mary, first used apparently by Cyril of Jerusalem (d. 387), *Theotokos* (the birth-giver of God), which in popular Latin usage became *Mater Dei* (mother of God), was affirmed by the Council of Ephesus in 431. The day commemorates Mary's acceptance of her vocation, assenting to the message of the angel Gabriel, and opening the way for God to accomplish the salvation of the world. In the mid-second century, Justin described Mary as "the new Eve." As mother of the new Israel, Mary is thus the counterpart to Abraham, the father of God's chosen people.

In the Middle Ages it was thought that, following a mystical conjunction of events, March 25 was not only the day on which the Incarnation began but was also the day on which creation began and the day on which Christ was crucified; so the great doctrines of creation, incarnation, and redemption were brought together as one. The Annunciation was therefore observed as New Year's Day for much of Christian Europe from the sixth century down into the eighteenth century.

Although the festival is often associated with Mary (in England it is called Lady Day), in its origins the day is a festival of the Lord. The oldest titles for the day are "Annunciation of the Lord" and "the Conception of Christ."

The Moravian Church observes this date as the Festival of All the Choirs. That observance suggests the possibility of a celebration in honor of those who serve the church through music, which joins the songs of earth to the praises of the heavenly chorus.

READING

From Athanasius, *On the Incarnation of the Word*

The incorporeal and incorruptible and immaterial Word of God came into our world, even though he was not absent from it before. For no part of creation was without his presence; with his Father he was present everywhere. He came in loving-kindness to make himself known openly to us. Seeing the race of rational creatures passing away and death reigning over them, he could not stand aside. He did not want creation to perish and his Father's work in creating human beings to be in vain. He therefore took a body no different from ours, for he did not simply will to be in a body or merely to be seen. If he had wanted simply to appear, he could have accomplished that by some another and higher means. Instead he took a body no different from ours.

Within the womb of the pure and spotless virgin he built himself a temple, a body. He made it his very own instrument in which to dwell among us and make himself known. He therefore took a body like ours, and since all were subject to death, he delivered that body to death for all, with supreme love offering it to the

Father. He did so to destroy the law of death passed against all humanity, since in him all died. The law, which had spent its force on the body of the Lord, no longer had any power against his people. Moreover, in this way the Word restored the immortality we had lost and recalled us from death to life. He destroyed the power of death, as a fire consumes chaff, by means of the body he had taken and the grace of the resurrection.

This is why the Word took a mortal body, so that this body, sharing in the Word who is Lord of all things, might submit to death in place of all, and yet, because the Word dwelt in that body, it would remain incorruptible, and all would be freed for ever from corruption by the grace of the resurrection.

The body he assumed, therefore, he offered to death as a spotless victim and so banished death from all humanity. For the immortal Son of God, united with all humanity, gained immortality for all humanity through resurrection from the dead.

Chaps. 8–9, trans. PHP

PROPERS

Pour your grace into our hearts, O Lord, that we who have known the incarnation of your Son Jesus Christ, announced by an angel, may by his cross and passion be brought to the glory of his resurrection; who lives and reigns with you, in the unity of the Holy Spirit, one God, now and forever.

Gregorian sacramentary no. 143, BCP, LBW, ELW

Readings:	Isaiah 7:10-14
	Psalm 40:7-11 *or* Psalm 40:1-11 *or* 40:5-10 *or* Magnificat
	Hebrews 10:(4) 5-10
	Luke 1:26-38
Hymn of the Day:	
	"Ye who claim the faith of Jesus" (H82 269)
	or "Blest are the pure in heart" (H82 656, SBH 394)
	or "The advent of our God" (LBW 22; LSB 331 alt.)
Prayers:	For purity of heart
	For obedience to the word of God
	For joyful submission to the will of God
Preface:	Christmas (or Epiphany, BCP)
Color:	White

March 27

Charles Henry Brent (1862–1929) is commemorated on the date in the Episcopal *Lesser Feasts and Fasts* since its revised edition (1973). A Canadian, he came to the United States, was elected Missionary Bishop of the Philippines, served as senior chaplain in World War I, and in 1918 accepted election as Bishop of Western New York. The central focus of his life and ministry was Christian unity.

March 29

John Keble, Priest, 1866

John Keble (KEE-bul), the son of a country parson, was born in 1792 at Fairford in Gloucestershire. At the age of eighteen, he graduated with highest honors from Corpus Christi College, Oxford, and was elected Fellow of Oriel College. In 1816 he was ordained priest and in 1823 returned home to assist his father. During this time he published anonymously his collection of religious poetry, *The Christian Year;* it went through ninety-five editions. In 1832 he was elected Professor of Poetry at Oxford. Four years later he began a thirty-year pastorate at the village of Hursley near Winchester in 1836, where he proved himself to be a devoted parish priest.

The revival of interest in the religious life stirred by the Wesley brothers had by this time been replaced by another period of laxity. The sacraments were neglected, worship was perfunctory, church buildings were left to decay. On July 14, 1833, in Oxford before a distinguished group of judges assembled in the University Church of St. Mary the Virgin, Keble preached a startling sermon entitled "National Apostasy" in which he attacked state interference in Church affairs. This sermon is commonly regarded as the beginning of the Oxford Movement, also called the "Tractarian" Movement from the series of "Tracts for the Times" written by Keble and others from Oxford. These pamphlets sought to recall the Church of England to its ancient sacramental heritage and taught that through its apostolic ministry of bishops, priests, and deacons, it was truly part of the Holy Catholic and Apostolic Church founded by Christ. The Tractarians encouraged the pursuit of personal holiness and emphasized reverence and beauty in worship. Within a generation new life had been breathed into the Church of England and its effects continue to this day.

Although fiercely attacked by his opponents, Keble's loyalty to the Church never wavered, and he unfailingly displayed consideration and courtesy. His depth of character and his devotion to the Lord impressed all who came into contact with him. He died on March 29, 1866. In 1870 Keble College, Oxford, was founded in his memory.

John Keble is included on the calendar in the *Book of Common Prayer.*

FOR FURTHER READING

Griffin, John R. *John Keble: Saint of Anglicanism.* Macon: Mercer University Press, 1987.

Ingram, K. *John Keble.* London: Allen, 1933.

READING

From a sermon by John Keble

Let us be only true to our sacred trust: let us put everything else by for the sake of handing down the whole counsel of God, our good deposit, entire as we received it: and who knows but we may by God's mercy be made instrumental in saving the English Church from ruin not unlike that which has fallen on Ephesus, Smyrna, or Sardis? At any rate, the Church Catholic, in one country or another, we are sure, will survive and triumph. As of old she has stood before kings and governors, and it turned to her for a testimony, so now blessed are they who divine providence shall choose and enable worthily to support her cause against popular delusion and tyranny. We, indeed, as priests of the second order, are but under-labourers in that most holy cause. Yet the least and lowest among us may look for his share of the blessing, as he has undoubtedly his share of the burthen and of the peril. Is there not a hope, that by resolute self-denial and strict and calm fidelity to our ordination vows, we may not only aid in preserving that which remains, but also may help to revive in some measure, in this or some other portion of the Christian world, more of the system and spirit of the apostolical age? New truths, in the proper sense of the word, we neither can nor wish to arrive at. But the monuments of antiquity may disclose to our devout perusal much that will be to this age new, because it has been mislaid or forgotten; and we may attain to a light and clearness, which we now dream not of, in our comprehension of the faith and discipline of Christ. We may succeed beyond what humanly appears possible in rekindling a primitive zeal among those who shall be committed to our charge.

John Keble, "Primitive Tradition Recognised in Holy Scripture," in R. Nye, ed., *The English Sermon 1750–1850* (Manchester: Carcanet, 1976), 197.

PROPERS

Grant, O God, that in all time of our testing we may know your presence and obey your will; that, following the example of your servant John Keble, we may accomplish with integrity and courage what you give us to do, and endure what you give us to bear; through Jesus Christ our Lord, who lives and reigns with you and the Holy Spirit, one God, forever and ever.

LFF

Readings:	Psalm 26:1-8 *or* Psalm 15
	Romans 12:9-21
	Matthew 5:1-12
Hymn of the Day:	
	"New every morning is the love" (H82 10, SBH 201)
	or, in the evening, "Sun of my soul, thou Savior dear" (H40 166, SBH 226)
Prayers:	For the renewal of the church and its recovery of its heritage
	For all poets and writers in the Christian tradition
	For the spirit of love and gentleness in all discussions and controversies about religion
	For Keble College, Oxford
Preface:	A Saint (1) (BCP)
Color:	White

ALSO ON MARCH 29

Hans Nielsen Hauge, Renewer of the Church, 1824

Hans Nielsen Hauge was born April 3, 1771, on a farm in Rolfsøen in southeastern Norway, about fifty miles from Oslo. His father, Niels Mikkelsen, was a farmer, and the farm was known as "Hauge Gaard" from which Hans Nielsen took his surname. The family was deeply concerned with their Christian faith, having regular family prayers and daily Bible reading, and from time to time attending lay religious meetings in the village. As a young boy Hauge thought deeply about religious matters and was troubled with a fear that he would not go to heaven when he died. This fear intensified through several experiences that brought him face to face with death.

Hauge never had much formal education, but he became very skilled in practical tasks such as carpentry and the repair of mechanical devices. Acting as village handyman and helping on the family farm, Hauge also became experienced in business affairs, and all of his life he not only was able to support himself while engaging in religious work but also was able to assist others in their everyday affairs.

He worked for a time in Fredrikstad where the temptations he encountered made him aware of the conflict between God and the world. As a young man his first interest was religion. He read deeply in Lutheran catechetical and devotional literature and participated in the worship of the parish church and in private prayer meetings. He spoke to others so frequently about their faith that his companions nicknamed him "Holy."

His parents called him home to work on their farm, and it was while working there on April 5, 1796, that he had a mystical experience that set the course of his life. He felt suddenly at peace about his own salvation and felt sure of his call to preach. He launched a one-man preaching crusade, beginning in his own community and then traveling throughout Norway and visiting Denmark in 1800. He also wrote about his faith, eventually producing some thirty books, of which the best known is his *Reiser og Vigtigste Haendsler* ("Journeys and Important Events"). The central concept of his preaching and writing was what he called "the living faith," the personal commitment to the Lord that transforms the believer's life.

Hauge encountered stern opposition, for it was thought unprecedented that a farm boy should teach religion, an area traditionally reserved for the clergy. He was in violation of the Ordinance of 13th January 1741, which required that the local pastor be informed of the time and place of any religious meetings to be held within his parish. The pastor was obliged to attend and had authority to forbid such meetings. Only a few people were permitted to gather, the meetings had to be held during the day, men and women were to meet in separate places, and it was forbidden that laypeople travel about and preach. The church authorities were opposed to Hauge because some thought that he laid too much stress on good works; the civil authorities were opposed to him because some feared he would stir up a peasants' revolt. After repeated arrests, he was taken into custody in 1804 to be held for full investigation, and his imprisonment lasted ten years. In prison, in the absence of Christian fellowship, Hauge's faith weakened. In 1809 he was released from prison to work on a project to extract salt from seawater (war with England had cut off supplies of salt by ship). He was arrested again, although he was permitted more freedom than before. In 1811 he was permitted to move to a small farm just outside Christiana called Bakkehaugen. In December 1813 he was sentenced to two years at hard labor and the costs of the trial for breaking the Ordinance of 13th January 1741 and for "invectives" against the clergy.

On January 27, 1815, Hauge married Andrea Nyhus, the housekeeper at his farm. She died not long afterward, leaving an infant son, Andreas. In 1817 Hauge married Ingeborg Oldsdatter, who bore him three sons, all of whom died young. Hauge moved to another farm, Bredveldt, where he was visited by friends, among whom by now were some bishops. His health broken after his long ordeal, Hauge died at 4 A.M. on March 29, 1824. He is buried in the cemetery at Aker Church in Oslo, where his grave is marked:

> He lived in the Lord,
> He died in the Lord,
> And by the grace of Christ he partakes of salvation.

Since Hauge's influence in Norway was at its peak during the period of greatest Norwegian immigration to America, the Haugean spirit was one of the main streams of Norwegian-American Lutheranism. It was an important force in the growth of the church and in deepening its spiritual life, particularly that of the laity, and for this reason Hauge appears on the calendar in the *Lutheran Book of Worship* and *Evangelical Lutheran Worship*. The Haugean Lutheran Synod,

MARCH

established in 1846, merged in 1917 with other Norwegian Lutheran bodies. A few churches in North America are named for Hauge.

FOR FURTHER READING

Aarflot, Andreas. *Hans Nielsen Hauge: His Life and Message.* Minneapolis: Augsburg, 1979.

Arden, G. Everett. *Four Northern Lights: Men Who Shaped the Scandinavian Churches.* Minneapolis: Augsburg, 1964. The four lights are Ruotsalainen of Finland, Hauge of Norway, Grundtvig of Denmark, and Rosenius of Sweden.

Arntzen, M. *The Apostle of Norway, Hans Nielsen Hauge.* Minneapolis: Norwegian Free Church Pub. Co., 1933.

Nelson, E. Clifford, and Eugene L. Fevold. *The Lutheran Church among Norwegian-Americans.* 2 vols. Minneapolis: Augsburg, 1960.

Nodvedt, Magnus. *Rebirth of Norway's Peasantry: Folk Leader Hans Nielsen Hauge.* Tacoma: Pacific Lutheran University Press, 1965.

Shaw, Joseph. *Pulpit Under the Sky: A Life of Hans Nielsen Hauge.* Minneapolis: Augsburg, 1955.

READING

From Hauge's *Autobiography,* April 5, 1796

The desire to please God grew more and more. In prayer to Him, I would kneel in heartfelt unworthiness of the great goodness He had shown me, ashamed because I had not served the Lord as I ought. Sometimes I fell on my knees and prayed almighty God for the sake of His Son to establish me on the spiritual rock, Christ Jesus. For I believed that then even the gates of hell would be powerless against me. I called upon the God of my salvation to reveal his Son's love in me and grant me His Holy Spirit to expose my wretchedness and impotence and teach me the way I should walk in order to follow in the footsteps of Christ.

One day while I was working outside under the open sky, I sang from memory the hymn, "Jesus, I Long for Thy Blessed Communion." I had just sung the second verse:

> Mightily strengthen my spirit within me,
> That I may learn what Thy Spirit can do;
> Oh, take Thou captive each passion and win me,
> Lead Thou and guide me my whole journey through!
> All that I am and possess I surrender,
> If thou alone in my spirit mayest dwell,
> Everything yield Thee, O Savior most tender,
> Thou, only Thou, canst my sadness dispel.

At this point my mind became so exalted that I was not myself aware of, nor can I express, what took place in my soul. For I was beside myself. As soon as I came to my senses, I was filled with regret that I had not served this loving transcendentally good God. Now it seemed to me that nothing in this world was worthy of any regard. That my soul experienced something supernatural, divine, and blessed; that there was a glory that no tongue can utter—that I remember as clearly as it had happened only a few days ago. And it is now nearly twenty years since the love of God visited me so abundantly.

Nor can anyone argue this away from me. For I know all the good that followed in my spirit from that hour, especially a deep, burning love to God and my neighbor. I know that I received an entirely changed mind, a sorrow for sin and a desire that other people should become partakers with me of the same grace. I know that I was given a special desire to read the holy Scriptures, especially Jesus' own teachings. At the same time I received new light to understand the Word and to bring together the teachings of all men of God to one focal point; that Christ has come for our salvation, that we should by His Spirit be born again, repent, and be sanctified more and more in accord with God's attributes to serve the triune God alone, in order that our souls may be refined and prepared for eternal blessedness.

It was as if I saw the whole world submerged in evil. I grieved much over this and prayed God that He would withhold punishment so that some might repent. Now I wanted very much to serve God. I asked him to reveal to me what I should do. The answer echoed in my heart, "You shall confess My name before the people; exhort them to repent and seek Me while I may be found and call upon Me while I am near; and touch their hearts that they may turn from darkness to light."

Hans Nielsen Hauge, *Autobiographical Writings,* trans. Joel M. Njus (Minneapolis: Augsburg, 1954), 41–43.

PROPERS

Gracious and loving Father, when the zeal and love of your church grow cold, you stir the hearts of your people by sending them men and women to preach repentance and renewal: In your mercy, grant that your church, inspired by the example of your servant Hans Nielsen Hauge, may never be destitute of such proclamation of the reality of your kingdom; through Jesus Christ our Lord, who lives and reigns with you and the Holy Spirit, one God, now and forever.

PHP

Readings: Jeremiah 1:4-10
            Psalm 46
            1 Corinthians 3:11-23
            Mark 10:35-45
Hymn of the Day:
            "In heaven above, in heaven above" (LBW 330, ELW 630) (The tune *I himmelen, I himmelen* is called *Hauge* in the *Service Book and Hymnal.*)

Prayers:	For lay readers and preachers
	For those persecuted for the exercise of their faith
	For confidence and courage
	For deepened spiritual life
	For growth in grace
Preface:	A Saint (2) (BCP) or of the Season
Color:	White

March 31

John Donne, Priest, 1631

John Donne (his surname rhymes with "sun") was born in London in 1572, the son of a prosperous ironmonger of an old Roman Catholic family at a time when anti-Catholic feeling was at its height. His father died in 1576. From 1584 to 1594 Donne studied at Oxford, Cambridge, and the Inns of Court where barristers received their training, and before 1596 traveled in France, Spain, and Italy. During these years, his adherence to the Roman Catholic Church seems to have weakened, and he began to study the claims of the churches of the Reformation. He probably became an Anglican by the end of the century.

With Raleigh and Essex he took part in hit-and-run naval expeditions to Cadiz in 1596 and to the Azores in 1597. In 1598 he became secretary to Sir Thomas Egerton and seemingly was set for a career in public service. He entered Elizabeth's last Parliament in 1601. He secretly married the sixteen-year-old niece of Egerton, Anne More. Furious at this breach of convention, Anne's father had Donne dismissed and imprisoned on the charge of marrying a minor without parental consent. His career ruined and his money gone ("John Donne, Anne Donne, Undone," he wrote), they were forced to live on the generosity of friends. He studied canon and civil law and traveled on the continent again. Although his circle of influential friends grew, he was unable to secure state employment. It was a time of debt, illness, frustration, and inner conflict.

In 1610 Donne contributed to a controversy between the Church of England and the Jesuits, urging English Roman Catholics to take the oath of allegiance to the crown. Donne still had secular hopes and won the king's favor, but after another trip to the continent with Sir Robert and Lady Drury, his hopes of civil employment were again dashed. In 1614 Donne entered Parliament, but within two months the king dissolved Parliament. Donne made one more application for state employment, but the king refused the petition, indicating that he wanted Donne to enter the Church. Donne was ordained priest in 1615.

He was appointed royal chaplain and was entrusted with diplomatic correspondence on a mission to Germany. His fame as a preacher grew, for the pulpit seemed to release anew the creative energies that earlier had found expression in his poetry. In 1621 he was considered the most renowned preacher of the time and was appointed Dean of St. Paul's Cathedral in London.

A serious illness in 1623, from which he nearly died, was the occasion for the composition of his *Devotions Upon Emergent Occasions*. He was able to return to a strenuous life of preaching, administration, and pastoral care. But in 1630 he was sick again, and on the first Friday in Lent, 1631, he preached what he knew was to be his last sermon, his funeral sermon. In March he had an artist sketch him in his shroud for his contemplation in his last days and for a design for his funeral monument. He died March 31, 1631, and was buried in his church with a marble monument that survived the fire of 1666 and the bombing of 1941.

Donne's poetry is divided into the secular poems, with their passion and intellectual wit, an intensity and excitement unrivaled in English poetry; and his divine (that is, religious) poetry, much of which was composed before he took orders. In his poetry he is constantly preoccupied with the interrelationship of the spiritual and the physical, presenting amorous experience in religious terms and presenting devotional experiences in erotic terms. His religious prose, written after his ordination, shows the richness of his mind. In poetry and prose he revealed an ability forcefully to touch the truth of experience with directness and honesty and give to the dim intuition of his readers and his hearers a universal voice. He distinguished himself not so much as a theologian but as a preacher.

In 1963 Donne's name, which had not previously appeared on any calendar, was proposed for inclusion on the calendar of the Episcopal Church and is listed in the present American *Book of Common Prayer,* the Church of England *Christian Year* (1997), the *Lutheran Book of Worship, Evangelical Lutheran Worship,* and the Methodist calendar in *For All the Saints.*

MARCH

FOR FURTHER READING

Bald, R. C. *John Donne: A Life.* New York: Oxford University Press, 1970.

Booty, John E., ed. *John Donne: Selections from Divine Poems, Sermons, Devotions, and Prayers.* New York: Paulist, 1990.

Carey, John. *John Donne: Life, Mind, and Art.* New York: Oxford University Press, 1981. 2nd ed., London: Faber and Faber, 1990.

Donne, John. *Sermons.* Ed. E. M. Simpson and G. R. Potter. 10 vols. Berkeley: University of California Press, 1953–1962.

Jackson, Robert S. *John Donne's Christian Vocation.* Evanston: Northwestern University Press, 1970.

Stubbs, John. *John Donne: The Reformed Soul.* New York: Viking, 2006.

READING

From John Donne, *Devotions Upon Emergent Occasions*

Nunc lento sonitu dicunt,	Now, this bell tolling
Morieris.	softly for another, says
	to me, Thou must die.

Perchance he for whom this bell tolls may be so ill as that he knows not it tolls for him; and perchance I may think myself so much better than I am, as that they who are about me and see my state may have caused it to toll for me, and I know not that. The Church is Catholic, Universal, so are all her actions; all that she does, belongs to all. When she baptizes a child, that action concerns me; for that child is thereby connected to that Head which is my Head too, and engrafted into that body of which I am a member. And when she buries a man, that action concerns me: all mankind is of one author and is one volume; when one man dies, one chapter is not torn out of the book but translated into a better language; and every chapter must be so translated; God employs several translators; some pieces are translated by age, some by sickness, some by war, some by justice; but God's hand is in every translation; and his hand shall bind up all our scattered leaves again, for that library where every book shall lie open to one another: as therefore the bell that rings for a sermon calls not upon the preacher only, but upon the congregation to come; so this bell calls us all: but how much more me, who am brought so near the door by this sickness.

There was a contention as far as a suit (in which both piety and dignity, religion and estimation were mingled) which of the religious orders should ring to prayers first in the morning; and it was determined that they should ring first that rose earliest. If we understand aright the dignity of this bell that tolls for our evening prayer, we would be glad to make it ours, by rising early in that application that it might be ours as well as his, whose indeed it is. The bell doth toll for him who thinks it doth; and though it intermit again, yet from that minute that that occasion wrought upon him, he is united to God. Who casts not up his eye to the sun when it rises? But who takes off his eye from a comet when that breaks out? Who bends not his ear to any bell, which upon any occasion rings? But who can remove it from that bell which is passing a piece of himself out of this world?

No man is an island, entire of itself; every man is a piece of the continent, a part of the main; if a clod be washed away by the sea, Europe is the less, as well as if a promontory were, as if a manor of thy friends or of thine own were; any man's death diminishes me, because I am involved in mankind; and therefore never send to know for whom the bell tolls; it tolls for thee. Neither can we call this a begging of misery or a borrowing of misery, as though we were not miserable enough of ourselves but must fetch in more from the next house in taking upon us the misery of our neighbors. Truly it were an excusable covetousness if we did; for affliction is a treasure and scarce any man hath enough of it.

No man hath affliction enough that is not matured and ripened by it, and made fit for God by that affliction. If a man carry treasure in bullion or in a wedge of gold and have none coined into current monies, his treasure will not defray him as he travels. Tribulation is a treasure in the nature of it, but it is not current money in the use of it except we get nearer and nearer our home, heaven, by it. Another man may be sick too, and sick to death, and this affliction may lie in his bowels, as gold in a mine, and be of no use to him; but this bell that tells me of his affliction digs out and applies that gold to me; if by this consideration of another's danger I take my own into contemplation and so secure myself by making recourse to my God, who is our only security.

John Donne, *Devotions Upon Emergent Occasions* [1624], XVII Meditation.

PROPERS

O eternal and most gracious God, you permitted darkness to be before light in the creation, and yet in the making of light so multiplied it that it enlightened even the night: Grant that by your light we may see that no sickness, no temptation, no sin, no guilt can remove us from the determined and good purpose which you have revealed in your Son and sealed by your Holy Spirit; who live and reign with you, one God, forever and ever.

PHP, from prayers by Donne, *Devotions XIV* and *VII*

Readings:	Wisdom 7:24—8:1
	Psalm 27:5-11 *or* 16:5-11
	John 5:19-24
Hymn of the Day:	
	"Wilt thou forgive that sin where I begun" (H82 140, 141) (by John Donne)
	or "O Lord, send forth your Spirit" (LBW 392)
Prayers:	For those who preach the gospel
	For poets and writers
	For an awareness of the shortness of life
Preface:	Epiphany (BCP)
Color:	White

ALSO ON MARCH 31

The *Lutheran Service Book* lists **Joseph** the patriarch for commemoration on this date. The well-told story of his adventures is in Genesis 37–50.

MARCH

April 1

Amalie Wilhelmina Sieveking, Renewer of Society, 1859; Frederick Denison Maurice, Priest, 1872

Two nineteenth-century social reformers may be remembered together on this day.

Amalie (Amelia) Sieveking, an early and vigorous worker for the emancipation of women, was born July 25, 1794, in Hamburg, Germany, and was orphaned at an early age. Not long afterward, her brother, who had been her support, also died, and she found a home with relatives. She grew in her love of the Bible and in her desire to help the poor. Vincent de Paul (1576–1660) and the Sisters of Mercy he founded (see September 27) had attracted a good deal of interest among evangelical leaders for their devoted service and their organization. The sisters belonged to a mother-house but went out to serve in hospitals and prisons, among the poor and the sick, and wherever they were needed. Their service was given in response to a specific human need. At the age of eighteen, Amalie Sieveking tried to create an evangelical sisterhood to work with the poor and needy but could not find support for her idea. With a few associates she began a school for young women and taught the poor on Sunday afternoons. In 1830 a cholera epidemic broke out in Hamburg, and, in the absence of trained nurses and her invitation to other women to join her being rejected, by herself she began caring for the victims of the epidemic. On December 13, 1831, the first cholera patient was admitted to the hospital, and Sieveking entered the hospital with her and remained there until the epidemic was ended.

In this work she encountered the deep poverty of large parts of the population and, as a result, in 1832 organized in Hamburg the Society for the Care of the Poor and the Sick. This group of women volunteered their time for the work of social welfare and the organization became a model for similar groups in many cities of northern Germany. Pastor Theodor Fliedner twice attempted to enlist her service at his institutions, once as Mother Superior at Kaiserswerth and again for Bethany in Berlin, but she would not give up her work in Hamburg. Amalie Sieveking died April 1, 1859. She is commemorated on that date by the German *Evangelical Calendar of Names* (1962).

Frederick Denison Maurice, the son of a Unitarian minister, was born in 1805. He attended Cambridge University but as a nonconformist was excluded from receiving a degree. After several personal crises, he became an Anglican, went to Exeter College, Oxford, and was ordained in 1834. Two years later he became chaplain of Guy's Hospital in London where he lectured regularly on moral philosophy and wrote the first and best-known of his many books, *The Kingdom of Christ* (1838). In this book, as in his other writings, he sought to apply the

Christian faith to social and political life. His strong belief in the incarnation and the visible church led him to take up the cause of social reform. He and his friends were known as "Christian Socialists" and awakened the Church of England to concern for the material as well as the spiritual welfare of the working classes. In 1854 he founded and served as the first principal of the "Working Man's College." To the Church he preached richer fellowship; to the socialists he proclaimed the necessity of Christianity. The Christian Socialist Movement, he declared, "will commit us at once to the conflict we must engage in sooner or later with the unsocial Christians and the unchristian Socialists." He died at Cambridge April 1, 1872. He is on the calendar in the American *Book of Common Prayer*.

FOR FURTHER READING

McClain, Frank Mauldin. *Maurice: Man and Moralist*. London: SPCK, 1972.
Ramsey, Arthur Michael. *F. D. Maurice and the Conflict of Modern Theology*. Cambridge: Cambridge University Press, 1951.

READING

From *The Kingdom of Christ* by Frederick Denison Maurice

Our Lord came among men that he might bring them into a kingdom of righteousness, peace, and joy, a kingdom grounded upon fellowship with a righteous and perfect Being. . . .

For that men are not to gain a kingdom hereafter, but are put in possession of it now, and that through their chastisements and the oppositions of their evil nature they are to learn its character and enter into its privileges, is surely taught in every verse of St Peter; and that love has been manifested unto men, that they have been brought into fellowship with it, that by that fellowship they may rise to the fruition of it, and that this fellowship is for us as members of a family, so that he who loveth God must love his brother also, is affirmed again and again in express words of St John.

Frederick Denison Maurice, *The Kingdom of Christ*, vol. 2, ed. A. R. Vidler (London: SCM, 1958), 256–57.

PROPERS

Almighty God, you restored our human nature to heavenly glory through the perfect obedience of our Savior Jesus Christ: Keep alive in your Church, we pray, a passion for justice and truth; that, like your servant[s] Frederick Denison Maurice [and Amalie Sieveking], we may work and pray for the triumph of your Christ; who lives and reigns with you and the Holy Spirit, one God, now and forever.

LFF alt.

Readings: Psalm 72:11-17 *or* 145:8-13
               Ephesians 3:14-19
               John 18:33-37
Hymn of the Day:
               "Father eternal, Ruler of creation" (H82 573, LBW 413)
Prayers: For all who are working for the renewal and unity of the church
               For the gift to see Christ in other people
               For all who apply the message of the Bible to national and civic life
               For a renewed sense of compassion for the poor and infirm
               For those who teach the underprivileged the way of God
Preface: Baptism (BCP, LBW)
Color: White

April 2

The American *Book of Common Prayer* commemorates on this date *James Lloyd Breck* (1818–1876), one of the most important missionaries of the Episcopal Church in the nineteenth century, a founder of Nashotah House, and a missionary in Wisconsin, Minnesota, and California.

April 3

Richard, Bishop of Chichester, 1253

Richard of Wyche was born in Droitwich, England, in 1197. As a young man he postponed his studies to restore the family farm after poor management by a guardian. He studied at Oxford under Robert Grosseteste (see October 9) and earned a degree in civil law from Bologna; in 1235 he became chancellor of Oxford but was soon called to be chancellor of the diocese of Canterbury of which his friend Edmund Rich was archbishop. When King Henry III forced Edmund into exile, Richard went with him to France and after Edmund's death was ordained priest in France in 1243. He returned to England and soon afterwards, in 1244, was elected Bishop of Chichester. His election led to a battle of wills between Henry III, who had appointed his own candidate, and the Archbishop of Canterbury. Although Richard was confirmed and consecrated by the pope in 1245, it was two years until the king gave way under threat of excommunication by the pope and Richard was allowed to take full possession of the diocese (1246).

Richard was a reformer of the state of the Church, merciless toward simony and nepotism, a man of simple personal habits, generous in his charities, strict with his clergy, and comfortable among the humbler people of his diocese. He died at Dover April 3, 1253, the day after consecrating a new church there in honor of his teacher, St. Edmund.

The essence of St. Richard's life is revealed in the prayer attributed to him:

> Thanks be to thee, O Lord Jesus Christ,
> For all the benefits thou hast given me,
> For all the pains and insults thou hast borne for me:
> O most merciful Redeemer, Friend, and Brother,
> May I know thee more clearly,
> May I love thee more dearly,
> May I follow thee more nearly,
> Day by day.

Richard was canonized in 1262. His shrine in Chichester Cathedral was destroyed by order of Henry VIII in 1538. Richard is on the calendar in the *Book of Common Prayer;* he is not on the General Roman Calendar.

FOR FURTHER READING

Capes, Mary Reginald. *Richard of Wyche: Labourer, Bishop, Saint.* London: Sands, 1913.

Jacob, E. F. "St. Richard of Chichester." *Journal of Ecclesiastical History* 7 (1956): 174–88.

Jones, D., ed. *Saint Richard of Chichester: The Sources for His Life.* Sussex Record Society, 79 (1993).

READING

From *The Life of St. Richard* by Ralph Bocking

Now it once happened that a pregnant woman, who was indeed guilty and deserved her punishment, was being held captive in bonds and in custody in one of the bishop's manors. When this became known to the bishop, he found an opportunity and went to the place where the same woman was held in confinement. After the warden of the prison had been directed by him on purpose to other things, he approached nearer and asked the woman the reason for her imprisonment. He learnt that she was to be handed over for execution, and that her death was to be postponed only till she had given birth. Thereupon giving her such help and instruction as he could, he advised her to repent of her sins, and to take refuge in a church which was close at hand; and this she did. The news of this spread abroad, and came to the ears of the Chief Steward, who went worried and with a long face to the episcopal palace. When the bishop made enquiry for the reasons of his distress, he replied, "Small wonder; for because of the escape of a woman from prison, we shall have to pay out of our poverty a hundred shillings to the King." The bishop exclaimed, "What or how much are a hundred silver shillings to the freeing of one captive. Blessed be God who has set her free!"

Ralph Bocking, *The Life of St. Richard*, book 1, chap. 3, para. 37, *Acta Sanctorum*, April I (5 June 1986): 293, trans. Antony Snell, S.S.M.

PROPERS

We thank you, Lord God, for all the benefits you have given us in your Son Jesus Christ, our most merciful Redeemer, Friend, and Brother, and for all the pains and insults he has borne for us; and we pray that, following the example of your saintly bishop Richard of Chichester, we may see Christ more clearly, love him more dearly, and follow him more nearly; who lives and reigns with you and the Holy Spirit, one God, now and forever.

LFF

Readings:	Psalm 84:7-12 *or* Psalm 3
	Philippians 4:10-13
	Matthew 25:31-40
Hymn of the Day:	
	"Day by day, dear Lord, of thee three things I pray" (H82 654), by St. Richard *or* "Let us ever walk with Jesus" (LBW 487, LSB 685, ELW 802)
Prayers:	For the diocese of Chichester, its cathedral, bishop, clergy, and people
	For all bishops and church administrators
	For grace to know, love, and follow Christ
Preface:	A Saint (2) (BCP)
Color:	White

April 4

Martin Luther King Jr., Renewer of Society, Martyr, 1968

Martin Luther King Jr., who led the first mass civil rights movement in the United States, was born January 15, 1929, in Atlanta, Georgia. An exceptional student, he entered Morehouse college in Atlanta at the age of fifteen under a special program and earned his B.A. in 1948. His earlier interests in medicine and law gave way to a decision to enter the ministry. He entered Crozer Theological Seminary in Chester, Pennsylvania, where he studied Gandhi's philosophy of nonviolence. King was elected president of the student body and graduated from the seminary in 1951. He then went to Boston University where he met Coretta Scott, who was a student at the New England Conservatory of Music. They married in 1953. King received the Ph.D. from Boston University in 1955. He became pastor of Dexter Avenue Baptist Church in Montgomery, Alabama, and while he was there, a group decided to challenge racial segregation of public busses. On December 1, 1955, Mrs. Rosa Parks refused to give up her seat on a bus to a white passenger and was arrested for violating the city's segregation law. The Montgomery Improvement Association was formed, and King was named its leader. His home was dynamited and his family threatened, yet he held fast. In a year, desegregation was accomplished. To capitalize on the success in Montgomery, King in 1957 organized the Southern Christian Leadership Conference, which gave him a base of operation and a national platform.

In 1960 he moved to Atlanta to become co-pastor of Ebenezer Baptist Church with his father. In October 1960 he was arrested for protesting the segregation of the lunch counter in a department store in Atlanta. The years 1960 to1965 marked the height of his influence. Although not always successful, the principle of nonviolence aroused the interest of many blacks and whites. In the spring of 1963, he was arrested in a campaign to end the segregation of lunch counters in Birmingham, Alabama. The police had turned fire hoses and dogs on the demonstrators and thus brought the incident to national attention. Some of the clergy of the city had issued a statement urging the citizens not to participate in the demonstrations, and King responded eloquently in his *Letter from Birmingham Jail.*

On August 28, 1963, two hundred thousand people marched on Washington in a peaceful assembly at the Lincoln Memorial and heard King's emotional and prophetic speech known as "I have a dream." The Civil Rights Act, passed later that year, authorized the federal government to enforce the desegregation of public accommodations and outlawed discrimination in publicly owned facilities and in employment. Also in 1964 Martin Luther King Jr. was awarded the Nobel Prize for Peace for his application of the principle of nonviolent resistance in the struggle for racial equality.

APRIL

King broadened his concern to include not only justice between the races but justice between the nations as well. In January 1966 he condemned the war in Vietnam, and his attack was renewed on April 4, 1967, at Riverside Church in New York and on April 15 at a huge rally for peace.

King had planned a Poor People's March on Washington but interrupted his plans in the spring of 1968 to travel to Memphis, Tennessee, in support of striking sanitation workers. On April 4, while standing on the balcony of a motel where he was staying, he was shot and killed by a sniper.

By his eloquent and often prophetic preaching, Martin Luther King Jr. called the United States to a new commitment to the ideal of justice, while at the same time consistently resisting the temptation to violence, even when provoked. Struggling against two sides at once—the status quo on the one hand and racial revolution on the other—he taught by word and example the value of what he liked to call "redemptive suffering," bringing the crucifixion into relation to modern society. He spoke God's word to a complacent nation, moving it toward the realization of the kingdom of God.

The birthday of Martin Luther King Jr. has been made a civil holiday in the United States, and for that reason the *Lutheran Book of Worship* set his commemoration on January 15. Because the observance of that federal holiday was in 1986 set on the third Monday in January, the observance of the religious commemoration on April 4, the date of his death, as is customary with commemorations and as observed in the Episcopal *Lesser Feasts and Fasts 1997* and in the Methodist *For All the Saints*, seems perhaps preferable.

FOR FURTHER READING

Ansbro, John J. *Martin Luther King, Jr.: The Making of a Mind.* New York: Orbis, 1982.

Bass, S. Jonathan. *Blessed Are the Peacemakers: Martin Luther King, Jr., Eight White Religious Leaders, and the "Letter from Birmingham Jail."* Baton Rouge: Louisiana State University Press, 2001.

Branch, Taylor. *Parting the Waters: Martin Luther King and the Civil Rights Movement 1954–1963.* New York: Macmillan, 1989.

Burns, Stewart. *To the Mountaintop: Martin Luther King Jr.'s Sacred Mission to Save America, 1955–1968.* San Francisco: HarperSanFrancisco, 2004.

Dyson, Michael Eric. *I May Not Get There with You: The True Martin Luther King, Jr.* New York: Free, 2000.

Garrow, David J. *Bearing the Cross: Martin Luther King, Jr. and the Southern Christian Leadership Conference.* New York: Morrow, 1986.

Lewis, Daniel L. *Crusader Without Violence.* New York: Praeger, 1970.

Lincoln, C. Eric, ed. *Martin Luther King, Jr.* New York: Hill & Wang, 1970.

Oates, Stephen B. *Let the Trumpet Sound: The Life of Martin Luther King, Jr.* New York: Harper & Row, 1982.

Westin, Alan F., and Barry Mahoney. *The Trial of Martin Luther King.* New York: Crowell, 1975.

READING

From *Letter from Birmingham Jail* by Martin Luther King Jr., April 16, 1963

I, along with several members of my staff, am here because I was invited here. I am here because I have organizational ties here.

But more basically, I am in Birmingham because injustice is here. Just as the prophets of the eighth century B.C. left their villages and carried their "thus saith the Lord" far beyond the boundaries of their home towns, and just as the Apostle Paul left his village of Tarsus and carried the gospel of Jesus Christ to the far corners of the Graeco-Roman world, so am I compelled to carry the gospel of freedom beyond my home town. Like Paul, I must constantly respond to the Macedonian call for aid.

Moreover, I am cognizant of the interrelatedness of all communities and states. I cannot sit idly by in Atlanta and not be concerned about what happens in Birmingham. Injustice anywhere is a threat to justice everywhere. We are caught in an inescapable network of mutuality tied in a single garment of destiny. Whatever affects one directly, affects all indirectly. Never again can we afford to live with the narrow, provincial "outside agitator" idea. Anyone who lives inside the United States can never be considered an outsider anywhere within its bounds. . . .

My friends, I must say to you that we have not made a single gain in civil rights without determined legal and nonviolent pressure. Lamentably, it is an historic fact that privileged groups seldom give up their privileges voluntarily. Individuals may see the moral light and voluntarily give up their unjust posture; but, as Reinhold Niebuhr has reminded us, groups are more immoral than individuals.

We know through painful experience that freedom is never voluntarily given up by the oppressor; it must be demanded by the oppressed. Frankly, I have yet to engage in a direct-action campaign that was "well timed" in the view of those who have not suffered unduly from the disease of segregation. For years now I have heard the word "Wait!" It rings in the ear of every Negro with a piercing familiarity. This "Wait" has almost always meant "Never." We must come to see, with one of our distinguished jurists, that "justice too long delayed is justice denied."

We have waited for more than 340 years for our constitutional and God-given rights. The nations of Asia and Africa are moving with jetlike speed toward gaining political independence, but we still creep at horse-and-buggy pace toward the gaining of a cup of coffee at a lunch counter. Perhaps it is easy for those who have never felt the stinging darts of segregation to say, "Wait." But when you have seen vicious mobs lynch your mothers and fathers at will and drown your sisters and brothers at whim; when you have seen hate-filled policemen curse, kick and even kill your black brothers and sisters; when you see the vast majority of your twenty million Negro brothers smothering in an airtight cage of poverty in the midst of an affluent society; when you suddenly find your tongue twisted and your speech stammering as you seek to explain to your six-year old daughter why she can't go to the public amusement park that has just been advertised on television, and see tears welling up in her eyes when she is told that Funtown is closed to colored children, and see ominous clouds of inferiority beginning to form in her little mental sky, and see her beginning to distort her personality by developing an unconscious bitterness toward white people; when you have to concoct an answer for a five-year old son who is asking: "Daddy, why do white people treat colored people so mean?"; when you take a cross-country drive and find it necessary to sleep night after night in the uncomfortable corners of your automobile because no motel will accept you; when you are humiliated day in and day out by nagging signs reading "white" and "colored"; when your first name becomes "nigger" and your middle name becomes "boy" (however old you are) and your last name becomes "John," and your wife and mother are never given the respected title "Mrs."; when you are harried by day and haunted by night by

APRIL

the fact that you are a Negro, living constantly at tiptoe stance never quite knowing what to expect next, and plagued with inner fears and outer resentments; when you are forever fighting a degrading sense of "nobodiness"—then you will understand why we find it difficult to wait. There comes a time when the cup of endurance runs over, and men are no longer willing to be plunged into the abyss of despair. I hope, sirs, you can understand our legitimate and unavoidable impatience.

Martin Luther King Jr., "A letter from Birmingham Jail" in *Why We Can't Wait* is reprinted by arrangement with The Heirs to the Estate of Martin Luther King, Jr., c/o Writers House, Inc. as agent for the proprieter. Copyright © 1963 by Martin Luther Kint Jr., copyright renewed 1991 by Coretta Scott King.

PROPERS

Holy and righteous God, you created us in your image. Grant us grace to contend fearlessly against evil and to make no peace with oppression. Help us, like your servant Martin Luther King, to use our freedom to bring justice among people and nations, to the glory of your Name; through Jesus Christ our Lord, who lives and reigns with you and the Holy Spirit, one God, now and forever.

BCP, rev. LBW, ELW Common of Renewers of Society

Readings:	Exodus 3:7-12
	Psalm 77:11-20 *or* 98:1-4
	Romans 12:9-21
	Luke 6:27-36
Hymn of the Day:	
	"Judge eternal, throned in splendor" (LBW 418, H82 596)
	or "Lift every voice and sing" (LBW 562, LSB 964, ELW 841, H82 599) (the African American anthem)
Prayers:	For peace
	For social justice
	For grace to learn that voluntary suffering can be redemptive
	For a quickening of the national conscience
Preface:	Baptism (BCP, LBW)
Color:	Red

ALSO ON APRIL 4

Benedict the African, Friar, 1589

St. Benedict the Black (Benedict the Moor) is remembered on this date on the Roman Catholic calendar, and on the calendar in *Evangelical Lutheran Worship* as Benedict the African.

Benedict was born near Messina, Italy, in 1526, the son of slaves who had been taken to Italy and later became Christians. He worked as a field hand until he was eighteen, when he was given his liberty. For the next ten years he made his living as a day laborer, sharing his meager wages with the poor and devoting much of his leisure time to the care of the sick. Although his race and his parents' servitude made him the object of frequent ridicule, he bore the humiliation with impressive dignity. His gentle replies to his tormenters attracted the attention of Jerome Lanzi, a young man who had withdrawn from the world to imitate the life of Francis of Assisi. Benedict joined Jerome's group of hermits. After Jerome died, Benedict reluctantly became their superior. When Pius IV directed all independent groups of hermits to affiliate with established religious orders, Benedict became a Franciscan lay brother. He worked for a number of years as a cook at the Friary of St. Mary of Jesus in Palermo. Domestic duties gave him opportunity to perform small acts of charity, well suited to his retiring nature.

In 1578 the illiterate lay brother was appointed guardian of the Friary, and he proved to be an ideal superior. His reputation for sanctity spread, and he chose to travel at night or in the daytime with his face covered. His ability to expound Scripture was impressive and his intuitive understanding of theological questions astonished scholars. Toward the end of his life he asked to be relieved of his duties as superior in order to return to the kitchen. He died at Palermo April 4, 1589, and was buried in the friary church. In 1611 the Spanish king Philip II donated to the church a shrine where Benedict's remains continue to be venerated.

Benedict the Black may be commemorated in conjunction with Martin Luther King Jr., one set of propers serving for both. If a separate remembrance is desired, his commemoration may be transferred to the following day.

APRIL

April 6

Albrecht Dürer, Painter, 1528; Lucas Cranach the Elder, Painter, 1553; Matthias Grünewald. Painter, 1528; Michelangelo Buonarotti, Artist, 1564

Albrecht Dürer, a methodical explorer of the world and of humankind's place in it, was born in Nuremberg, May 21, 1471, the son of a goldsmith. His artistic talent was recognized early, and at age sixteen he was apprenticed to a local painter. After three years he left his apprenticeship to travel in the Netherlands, Alsace, and Switzerland. By the end of May 1494, he was back in Nuremberg. On the seventh of July he married Agnes Frey; they had no children. In the autumn of 1494, Dürer went to Italy, and this visit, which lasted until the following spring, was a great influence on his work: Dürer was the first northern European artist to immerse himself in the art of the Italian Renaissance. Upon his return to Nuremberg in 1495, Dürer renewed his association with his boyhood friend

Willibald Pirkheimer (1470–1530), the noted humanist. Like Leonardo, Dürer had an enormously inquisitive mind and was one of the most learned of Renaissance artists and the friend of many distinguished people of the time.

His painting style vacillated between Gothic and Italian Renaissance style until the end of the century when he moved toward the Renaissance spirit. In the fall of 1505 he made his second journey to Italy and spent most of his time in Venice. The visit lasted until the winter of 1507. He returned to Nuremberg in February 1507, and bought a house near the zoological garden. This "Dürer Haus" still stands.

For a time he worked for the Emperor Maxmillian I. In July 1520 he went to the Netherlands again. At the coronation of Charles V, the successor to Maxmillian, at Aachen, Dürer met Matthias Grünewald, who ranked second only to Dürer in German art of the time. In April 1521 Luther stood before the Diet at Worms, and the emperor Charles V had concluded that he would "proceed against him as a notorious heretic." On the seventeenth of May, in Antwerp, Dürer heard the news. He wrote in his diary, "O Lord, you desire before you come to judgment that as your Son Jesus Christ had to die at the hands of the priests and rise from the dead and ascend to heaven, even so should your disciple Martin Luther be made conformable to him." Not knowing of Luther's refuge in the Wartburg, Dürer wrote again in his diary,

> I know not whether he lives or is murdered, but in any case he has suffered for the Christian truth. . . . If we lose this man, who has written more clearly than any other in centuries, may God grant his spirit to another. . . . His books should be held in great honor, and not burned as the emperor commands, but rather the books of his enemies. O God, if Luther is dead, who will henceforth explain to us the gospel? What might he not have written for us in the next ten or twenty years?

Nonetheless, despite his admiration of Luther, it is uncertain to what degree Dürer supported the Reformation.

Dürer returned to Nuremberg July 12, 1521. His health declined, and he spent his time writing letters, poems, and treatises on fortification. The Nuremberg city council adopted the Lutheran Reformation in March 1525; in 1526 Dürer gave the city council his painting *Four Apostles,* which includes quotations from Luther's translation of the Bible. He died April 6, 1528, and was buried in the churchyard of the Johanneskirche in Nuremberg. Luther, learning of his death, wrote to Eoban Hesse, "Affection bids us mourn for one who was the best of men, yet you may well consider him happy that he has made so good an end, and that Christ has taken him from the midst of this time of trouble. . . . May he rest in peace with his fathers. Amen."

Deeply religious in spirit, Dürer was affected by the apocalyptic spirit of the time in the face of famine, plague, and social and religious upheaval. His paintings and woodcuts are a close examination of the splendor of creation: the human body, animals, grasses, and flowers. He was, unfortunately, never able to fulfill his desire to paint Luther "as a lasting memorial to the Christian man who has helped me out of great anxiety."

Dürer, who is listed on the German Lutheran *Evangelical Calendar of Names* (1962) is on the calendar in *Evangelical Lutheran Worship* and also the *Lutheran Service Book*; he was included, together with Michelangelo, on the calendar in the *Lutheran Book of Worship*.

FOR FURTHER READING

Bartrum, Giulia, ed. *Albrecht Dürer and His Legacy.* London: British Museum, 2003.

Canaday, John. "Albrecht Dürer," *Horizon* 6, no. 3 (Summer 1964): 16–31.

Panovsky, Edwin. *The Life and Art of Albrecht Dürer.* Princeton: Princeton University Press, 1955.

Price, David Hotchkiss. *Albrecht Dürer's Renaissance: Humanism, Reformation, and the Art of Faith.* Ann Arbor: University of Michigan Press, 2003.

Strauss, Walter L. *The Complete Drawings of Albrecht Dürer.* 6 vols. New York: Abaris, 1975.

Lucas Cranach the Elder (1472–1553), Dürer's near-contemporary, whose work is lighter and more joyful than that of Dürer, was able to be the portraitist of the Reformers. He was on the most intimate terms with Luther. When Luther went into hiding in 1521, Cranach was among the very few with whom he kept in touch; when Luther married, Cranach was the sole lay witness; and Luther stood as godfather for Cranach's daughter. Cranach the Elder was a prolific conveyor of the message of the Reformation and was highly regarded by the humanists of his day. A court painter, he was a student of nature, morals, and eroticism. An exhibit of his work at Basel in 1974 vindicated his reputation in the eyes of many critics. Beneath an apparent simplicity, there lies a serious and intense effort of the northern Renaissance, a search for balance between the spirit and the body, God and the flesh, good and evil, humanity and nature. Cranach is commemorated on the German *Evangelical Calendar of Names* on October 16.

FOR FURTHER READING

Koerner, Joseph Leo. *The Reformation of the Image.* Chicago: University of Chicago Press, 2004.

Tisdall, Caroline. "Between Two Worlds," *The Guardian*, August 31, 1974, 20.

The fascinating and enigmatic painter *Matthias Grünewald* was born, it seems, in Würzberg sometime between 1455 and 1480. The name by which he is known is a fabrication of a seventeenth-century biographer. His original surname was Gothardt, to which he sometimes added the surname of his wife, Neithardt. He spent most of his life in the upper Rhine area under the patronage of the Archbishop of Mainz and then of Albrecht of Brandenburg. Grünewald's limited influence and renown is in contrast to those of Dürer, yet his works are highly

APRIL

valued. He was fascinated by the crucifixion as a subject for painting, and his greatest work, inspired by the mystical *Revelations* of Birgitta of Sweden (see July 23), is the Isenheim altarpiece with its combination of horror and mystical elevation. Grünewald died at Halle in August 1528, at the time secretly siding with the Reformation.

FOR FURTHER READING

Burkard, Arthur. *Matthias Grünewald: Personality and Accomplishment.* Cambridge: Harvard University Press, 1936.
Mellinkoff, Ruth. *The Devil at Isenheim: Reflections of Popular Belief in Grünewald's Altarpiece.* Berkeley: University of California Press, 1989.
Pevsner, Nickolaus, and Michale Meier. *Grünewald.* London: Thames, 1958.

READING

From Thomas Traherne, *Centuries*

You never enjoy the world aright, till the Sea itself floweth in your veins, till you are clothed with the heavens, and crowned with the stars: and perceive yourself to be the sole heir of the whole world, and more than so, because men are in it who are every one sole heirs as well as you. Till you can sing and rejoice and delight in God, as misers do in gold, and Kings in scepters, you never enjoy the world.

Till your spirit filleth the whole world, and the stars are your jewels; till you are as familiar with the ways of God in all Ages as with your walk and table: till you are intimately acquainted with that shady nothing out of which the world was made: till you love men so as to desire their happiness, with a thirst equal to the zeal of your own; till you delight in God for being good to all: you never enjoy the world. Till you more feel it than your private estate, and are more present in the hemisphere, considering the glories and the beauties there, than in your own house: Till you remember how lately you were made, and how wonderful it was when you came into it: and more rejoice in the palace of your glory, than if it had been made but to-day morning. Yet further, you never enjoy the world aright, till you so love the beauty of enjoying it, that you are covetous and earnest to persuade others to enjoy it. And so perfectly hate the abominable corruption of men in despising it, that you had rather suffer the flames of Hell than willingly be guilty of their error. There is so much blindness and ingratitude and damned folly in it. The world is a mirror of infinite beauty, yet no man sees it. It is a Temple of Majesty, yet no man regards it. It is a region of Light and Peace, did not men disquiet it. It is the Paradise of God. It is more to man since he is fallen than it was before. It is the place of Angels and the Gate of Heaven. When Jacob waked out of his dream, he said "*God is here, and I wist it not. How dreadful is this place! This is none other than the House of God, and the Gate of Heaven.*"

Thomas Traherne, *Centuries* (1672), I:29, 30, 31, introduction by John Farrar (New York: Harper & Bros., 1960), 14–15.

Michelangelo Buonarotti, the famed creator of gigantic sculpture was himself an awe-inspiring figure who was accorded, even in his lifetime, the high respect usually reserved for the great religious teachers.

Michelangelo was born March 6, 1475, at Caprese, a small town near Florence. He was of aristocratic stock, his father claiming descent from the counts of Canossa, but the family fortunes had declined. Overcoming family objections to his becoming an artist, Michelangelo at age thirteen was apprenticed briefly to Ghirlandaio, the most successful Florentine painter of the period, and then under the sculptor Bertoldo. The young artist attracted the attention of Lorenzo de Medici and lived for a time in his palace, meeting many artists and writers there. Before the expulsion of Piero de Medici in 1494, Michelangelo went to Venice and then Bologna and read Dante and Petrarch.

Michelangelo arrived in Rome in the summer of 1496 and there carved the *Pieta* now in St. Peter's Basilica in which the Virgin Mother holds in her lap the dead body of her Son. The work is a marvelous feat of technical skill and shows the sculptor's consummate mastery of his craft. Indeed, the story is that when admirers of the work doubted that it could be the work of a twenty-one-year old, he went back to the sculpture and inscribed in bold letters on the sash across the Virgin's breast, "Michelangelo made it."

In 1501 he returned to Florence to carry out commissions that expressed the pride, vigor, and idealism of the Medicis. The *David* is the great figure of power and magnificence from this period.

In March 1505 Michelangelo was again summoned to Rome to design the tomb of Pope Julius II. For eight months Michelangelo was at Carrara supervising the quarrying of huge blocks of marble for what was to be the greatest tomb in Christendom. He was inaccessible in that awe-inspiring landscape, surrounded by stone. He made such sojourns to Carrara several times in his life, and these times, like religious retreats, were preludes to spells of his greatest activity. When he returned to Rome in the winter of 1506–1507, he was refused immediate access to Pope Julius and in April 1506, returned to Florence. Seven months later he returned to Rome and the papal presence. He went to Bologna to make a bronze statue of the pope for the door of San Petronio there; then he went back to Florence but was recalled to Rome and was given the task of painting the ceiling of the papal chapel, called the Sistine Chapel. His prodigious frescoes were unveiled October 31, 1512, and illustrated the progression from servitude of the body (The Drunkenness of Noah) to the liberation of the soul (The Creation).

From this point on, Michelangelo's mood became more grave and his confidence in physical beauty diminished. He became increasingly preoccupied with death. Leo X succeeded Julius, and Raphael became the favored artist. Michelangelo returned to Florence, which underwent a revolution in 1527, and he was put in charge of the fortifications of the city against the expelled Medici.

In 1534 Paul III called Michelangelo back to Rome to paint the *Last Judgment* in the Sistine Chapel, which he completed in 1541. He then turned his attention to

APRIL

designing the dome of St. Peter's. He spent his last years with poetry, architecture, and drawing, writing in a sonnet that "only in darkness can men fully be." He died in his eighty-ninth year.

Michelangelo believed that classical antiquity and Christianity could be served simultaneously by a devotion to the human figure, and the greatest accomplishment of this sculptor, architect, painter, poet, and draftsman was his exploration of the mystery of life locked in the human body, particularly apparent in his drawings of the nude male body in action. For him the human form was the expression of God's purpose.

In commemoration of the five hundredth anniversary of his birth, a *New York Times* editorial said : "The art of Michelangelo was fueled by a largeness of soul and a frighteningly powerful belief—a *terribilita*—that would not be possible today. Grandeur is a term applied to the creative spirit on rare occasions, and the world is changed by it forever. So that great spirit and its transforming impact upon the world is celebrated" (March 6, 1975).

FOR FURTHER READING

Bull, George. *Michelangelo: A Biography.* New York: Viking, 1995.

Clements, Robert J. *The Poetry of Michelangelo.* New York: New York University Press, 1965.

Hibbard, Howard. *Michelangelo.* New York: Harper & Row, 1974.

Nims, John Frederick, trans. *The Complete Poems of Michelangelo.* Chicago: University of Chicago Press, 1998.

Ramsden, E. H., trans. and ed. *The Letters of Michelangelo.* 2 vols. Stanford: Stanford University Press, 1963.

Symonds, J. A. *The Life of Michelangelo Buonarotti.* 1892.

Von Einem, Herbert. *Michelangelo.* Trans. Ronald Taylor. London: Methuen, 1973.

READING

Michelangelo, "On the Brink of Death"

> Now hath my life across a stormy sea
> Like a frail bark reached that wide port where all
> Are bidden, ere the final reckoning fall
> Of good and evil for eternity.
> Now know I well how that fond phantasy
> Which made my soul the worshipper and thrall
> Of earthly art, is vain; how criminal
> Is that which all men seek unwillingly.
> Those amorous thoughts which were so lightly dressed,
> What are they when the double death is nigh?

The one I know for sure, the other dread.
Painting nor sculpture now can lull to rest
My soul that turns to His great love on high,
Whose arms to clasp us on the cross were spread.

Trans. J. A. Symonds

PROPERS

We give thanks to you, O God, creator and fashioner of the universe, for the work
of your servants Albrecht Dürer, Lucas Cranach, Matthias Grünewald, and Michelangelo; and we pray that by the vigor and strength of their creations you would
open our eyes to the wonder of life, the glories of creation, and the exploration
of our place in the world; through your Son Jesus Christ our Lord, who lives and
reigns with you and the Holy Spirit, one God, now and forever.
PHP

Readings:	Isaiah 28:5-6
	Psalm 96
	Philippians 4:8-9
	Matthew 13:44-52
Hymn of the Day:	
	"How marvelous God's greatness" (LBW 515, ELW 830)
Prayers:	For painters, sculptors, architects
	For a renewed appreciation of beauty as an attribute of God
	For joy in the natural world
	For a receptive mind to explore the beauty of creation
Preface:	All Saints
Color:	White

APRIL

April 8

William Augustus Muhlenberg, Priest, 1877

William Augustus Muhlenberg, great-grandson of Henry Melchior Muhlenberg, the patriarch of the Lutheran Church in America (see October 7)
and son of Frederick Augustus Muhlenberg, the first Speaker of the U.S. House of
Representatives, was born in Philadelphia September 16, 1796. He and his sister
grew up in an English-speaking home, attended Sunday school at Christ Episcopal
Church near their home because of its use of English, and grew to love the service
and its music. He graduated from the University of Pennsylvania in 1814 and was

ordained an Episcopal priest in 1817. There had been a great deal of movement from the Lutheran Church, when it insisted on the use of German in worship, to the Episcopal Church on the part of those who preferred to use the English language not only in business but in worship also. In New York City the first entirely English Lutheran congregation organized in the United States, Zion (1796), lost its pastor and a considerable number of its members to the Episcopal Church in 1805 and the remainder of their members and their pastor in 1810. The New York Ministerium had even officially declared that the Protestant Episcopal Church was "the English Lutheran Church" to which all Lutherans preferring English to German should be directed.

William Muhlenberg served a parish in Lancaster, Pennsylvania, and there apparently suffered a severe disappointment in love. He never married, and he understood this state to free him for a variety of ministries. He served as head of a boys' school, in Flushing, Queens, New York, and the use of music (the first boys' choir in New York), flowers, color, and the emphasis on the church year there had a powerful influence on the boys and many influential churchmen came from the school. Unhappy with the metrical psalter that then served as the hymnal of the Episcopal Church, he wrote hymns, some of which are still sung, and edited hymnals for the church. In 1846 he became rector of the Church of the Holy Communion, founded by his sister, at Twentieth Street and Sixth Avenue in New York City where his social conscience and liturgical emphasis was evident. The pews were free, not rented; there was a parish school, an unemployment fund, visits by poor children to the country. Holy Communion was at the center of the life of the parish, as its name indicated, and in this church in 1852 Anne Ayres founded the Sisterhood of the Holy Communion, patterned after the Deaconess Community in Germany. She and her pastor founded St. Luke's Hospital in 1857, and Muhlenberg made his home there for the rest of his life. He died April 6, 1877.

His concern for worship and for evangelism, advanced for his time, nonetheless prepared the ground for later liturgical reform and ecumenical activity. He embodied both the Lutheran tradition and the Anglican tradition that would later be joined in the agreement between the Episcopal Church and the Evangelical Lutheran Church in America authorizing intercommunion and the mutual recognition of ministry. William Augustus Muhlenberg was added to the calendar in the American Prayer Book of 1979.

FOR FURTHER READING

Muhlenberg, William Augustus. *Evangelical and Catholic Papers: A Collection of Letters, Essays and Tractates from the Writings of Rev. William Augustus Muhlenberg, D.D.* New York, 1875.

Mullin, Robert Bruce. *Episcopal Vision/American Reality: High Church Theology and Social Thought in Evangelical America.* New Haven: Yale University Press, 1986.

Skardon, Alvin W. *Church Leader in the Cities: William Augustus Muhlenberg.* Philadelphia: University of Pennsylvania Press, 1971.

READING

From Theodore L. Cuyler, *Recollections of a Long Life*

He was one of the most apostolic men I have ever known. . . . His gray head all men knew in New York. He commanded attention everywhere by his genial face and hearty manner of speech. . . . When very near the end, the chaplain of the hospital prayed at his bedside for his recovery. "Let us have an understanding about this," said Muhlenberg. "You are asking God to restore me and I am asking God to take me home. There must not be any contradiction in our prayers, for it is evident that he cannot answer them both." This was characteristic of his bluff frankness as well as of his heavenly-mindedness—he would not live always.

Quoted in Edward S. Ninde, *The Story of the American Hymn* (New York and Cincinnati: Abingdon, 1921), 168. The concluding reference is to Muhlenberg's hymn "I would not live alway," included in the Lutheran *Church Book* as no. 542.

PROPERS

Do not let your Church close its eyes, O Lord, to the plight of the poor and neglected, the homeless and the destitute, the old and the sick, the lonely and those who have none to care for them. Give us the vision and compassion with which you so richly endowed your servant William Augustus Muhlenberg, that we may labor tirelessly to heal those who are broken in body or spirit, and to turn their sorrow into joy; through Jesus Christ our Lord, who lives and reigns with you and the Holy Spirit, one God, forever and ever.

LFF

APRIL

Readings:	Psalm 84:1-6 *or* Psalm 133
	Ephesians 4:11-16
	Matthew 21:12-26
Hymn of the Day:	
	"Thine arm, O Lord, in days of old" (H82 567, LBW 431)
	or "O holy city seen of John" (H82 583 , SBH 332)
	or "Saviour, who thy flock art feeding" (SBH 261, H30 343), by W. A. Muhlenberg
Prayers:	For the poor, the neglected, the unemployed, the sick and those who suffer
	For St. Luke's hospital in New York City
	For a deeper understanding of the Holy Communion as the spring of the Christian life
	For those who would improve the quality of hymns in the church
	For a broad and tolerant spirit throughout the church
Preface:	A Saint (1) (BCP)
Color:	White

April 9
Dietrich Bonhoeffer, Teacher, Martyr, 1945

D ietrich Bonhoeffer was born in Breslau February 4, 1906, and grew up in the
university circles of Berlin, where his father Karl was professor of psychia-
try and neurology. He studied at the universities of Berlin and Tübingen from
1923 to 1927; his doctoral thesis was published in 1930 as *Communio Sanctorum*
("The Communion of Saints"). From 1928 to 1933 he was the assistant pastor of a
German-speaking congregation in Barcelona. He then spent a year as an exchange
student at Union Seminary in New York City and returned to Germany in 1931 to
lecture in systematic theology at the University of Berlin.

From the first days of the Nazi accession to power in 1933, Bonhoeffer was
involved in protests against the regime, especially its anti-Semitism. From 1933
to 1935 he was the pastor of two small German congregations in London but
nonetheless was a leading spokesman for the Confessing Church, the center of
Protestant resistance to the Nazis. In 1935 Bonhoeffer was appointed to organize
and head a new seminary at Finkenwald, which continued in a disguised form
until 1940. He described the community in *Life Together* (1939; English translation 1954, 1997). Out of his struggle also came his best-known book, *The Cost of
Discipleship* (1948; English translation 1959, 2001), which attacked the notion of
"cheap grace," an unlimited offer of forgiveness that masked moral laxity.

The Bishop of Chichester, G. K. A. Bell, became interested in efforts to interpret the Church struggle (*Kirchenkampf*) and became a friend of Bonhoeffer.
Bonhoeffer's own involvement became increasingly political after 1939, when his
brother-in-law introduced him to the group seeking Hitler's overthrow. In 1939
Bonhoeffer considered refuge in the United States, but he returned to Germany
where he was able to continue his resistance as an employee of the Military Intelligence Department, which was a center of resistance. In May of 1942 he flew to
Sweden to meet Bishop Bell and convey through him to the British government
proposals for a negotiated peace. The Allies rejected the offer, who insisted upon
unconditional surrender.

Bonhoeffer was arrested April 5, 1943, and imprisoned in Berlin (he had just
announced his engagement to be married). After an attempt on Hitler's life failed
April 9, 1944, documents were discovered linking Bonhoeffer to the conspiracy.
He was taken to Buchenwald concentration camp, then to Schönberg prison.
On Sunday, April 8, 1945, just as he concluded a service in a school building in
Schönberg in the Bavarian forest, two men came in with the chilling summons,
"Prisoner Bonhoeffer, come with us." As he left, he said to Payne Best, an English
prisoner who described the event in *The Venlo Incident*, "This is the end. For me,

the beginning of life." Bonhoeffer was hanged the next day, April 9, 1945, at Flossenburg prison.

When Bonhoeffer was included on the calendar in the *Lutheran Book of Worship* he was not described as a martyr because of some hesitation both in Germany and in America, since he was killed not for his adherence to the Christian faith but for his political activities against the German government. In *Lesser Feasts and Fasts*, which now lists him, he is called "Pastor and Theologian" but not "Martyr." The reluctance to call him a martyr, however, has largely dissipated in the face of the recognition that his resistance was rooted clearly in his Christian commitment. (A Berlin court ruled in 1996 that Bonhoeffer was innocent of high treason.) The German *Evangelical Calendar of Names* lists him as "Martyr in the Church Struggle," and there is in Bonhoeffer's life a remarkable unity of faith, prayer, writing, and action. The pacifist theologian came to accept the guilt of plotting the death of Hitler because he was convinced that not to do so would be a greater evil. Discipleship was to be had only at great cost.

Bonhoeffer was included on the calendar in the *Lutheran Book of Worship* and was added to the Episcopal calendar in *Lesser Feasts and Fasts 1997,* and is on the calendar in the Methodist book *For All the Saints.*

In remembering key figures in important religious and social movements such as Bonhoeffer or Martin Luther King Jr., one needs to keep in mind that these people are representatives who both clarify and have been nourished by the struggle of countless more obscure people who were no less brave in their witness.

FOR FURTHER READING

Bethge, Eberhard. *Dietrich Bonhoeffer: A Biography.* Ed. Victoria J. Barnett. Minneapolis: Fortress Press, 2000.

Bethge, Eberhard, Renate Bethge, and Christian Gremmels. *Dietrich Bonhoeffer: A Life in Pictures.* Trans. John Bowden. London/Minneapolis: SCM/Fortress Press, 1987.

Dramm, Sabine. *Dietrich Bonhoeffer: An Introduction to His Thought.* Trans. Thomas Rice. Peabody: Hendrickson, 2007.

Rasmussen, Larry. *Dietrich Bonhoeffer: His Significance for North Americans.* Minneapolis: Fortress Press, 1990.

Scholder, Klaus. *The Churches and the Third Reich.* Trans. John Bowden. 2 vols. Minneapolis: Fortress Press, 1987–1988.

READING

From a letter by Dietrich Bonhoeffer

I often ask myself why a "Christian instinct" often draws me more to the religionless people than to the religious, by which I don't in the least mean with any evangelizing intention, but, I might almost say, "in brotherhood." While I'm often reluctant to mention God by name to religious people—because that name somehow seems to me here not to ring true, and I feel myself to be slightly dishonest (it's particularly bad when others start to talk in religious jargon; I then dry up almost completely and feel awkward and uncomfortable)—to people with no religion I can on occasion mention him by name quite calmly and as a matter of course. Religious people speak of God when human knowledge (perhaps simply because they are too lazy to think) has come to an end, or when human resources fail—in fact it is always the *deus ex machina* that they bring on the scene, either for the apparent solution of insoluble problems, or as strength in human failure—always, that is to say, exploiting human weakness or human boundaries. Of necessity, that can go on only till people can by their own strength push those boundaries somewhat further out, so that God becomes superfluous as a *deus ex machina*. I've come to be doubtful of talking about any human boundaries (is even death, which people now hardly fear, and is sin, which they now hardly understand, still a genuine boundary today?). It always seems to me that we are trying anxiously in this way to reserve some space for God; I should like to speak of God not on the boundaries but at the center, not in weakness but in strength; and therefore not in death and guilt but in man's life and goodness. As to the boundaries, it seems to me better to be silent and leave the insoluble unsolved. Belief in the resurrection is *not* the "solution" of the problem of death. God's "beyond" is not the beyond of our cognitive faculties. The transcendence of epistemological theory has nothing to do with the transcendence of God. God is beyond in the midst of our life. The church stands, not at the boundaries where human powers give out, but in the middle of the village. That is how it is in the Old Testament, and in this sense we still read the New Testament far too little in the light of the Old. How this religionless Christianity looks, what form it takes, is something that I'm thinking about a great deal, and I shall be writing to you again about it soon. It may be that on us in particular, midway between East and West, there will fall a heavy responsibility.

From a letter to Eberhard Bethge (30 April 1944) from Tegel prison, in *Letters and Papers from Prison*, enlarged ed., ed. Eberhard Bethge (New York: Macmillan, 1971), 281–82.

PROPERS

Gracious Lord, the Christian faith of your servant Dietrich Bonhoeffer impelled him to defy the forces of darkness, to protest the evil of anti-Semitism, and finally, fearing not death but rather the greater evil of tolerating oppression, to lay down his life in witness to your rule: Grant us the same Spirit of courage to resist tyranny in all its forms and the strength to follow Christ into unfamiliar places, knowing that, whether we live or die, we are with you; through your Son Jesus Christ our Lord, who lives and reigns with you and the Holy Spirit, one God, now and forever.

PHP

Readings: Proverbs 3:1-7
              Psalm 119:89-96
              Revelation 6:9-11
              Matthew 13:47-52
Hymn of the Day:
              "God of grace and God of glory" (H82 594, 595; LBW 415, LSB 850, ELW 705)
Prayers: For a deepened discipleship
              For courage to resist tyranny in all its forms
              For strength to pay the price of following Christ into places where we are beyond
                  familiar rules
              For those whose names are not remembered who with Bonhoeffer resisted tyr-
                  anny
Preface: A Saint (3) (BCP)
Color: Red

April 10

Mikael Agricola, Bishop of Turku, Renewer of the Church 1557

with Paavali (Paul) Juusten, Bishop of Viipuri, 1576

Paavo Henrik Ruotsalaien, Evangelist, 1852

Mikael Agricola (the accent is on the first syllable of his surname: *AH-gree-co-la*) was born in Uusimaa, Finland, which was then a province of Sweden, in 1512. He went to school in Viipuri and later moved to Turku, where he stayed for six or seven years. He did well in his studies, and he was one of the eight Finnish students whom the aged Martinus Skytte, Bishop of Turku (1528–1550), a former Dominican monk, sent to study under Luther and Melanchthon at the University of Wittenberg. He received his master's degree there in 1539 and, returning with Luther's special recommendation in a letter to the king, became rector of the cathedral school and, in 1548, assistant to the bishop.

In 1554, after the death of Bishop Skytte, he was consecrated Bishop of Turku by the Swedish hierarchy without submitting his name for papal approval. He carried out in Finland a thoroughgoing Lutheran reformation comparable to that of the Petri Brothers in Sweden (see April 19), retaining much of the historic doctrines and practices of the Church but eliminating unscriptural elements and encouraging greater participation of the laity.

Bishop Agricola realized the need for the Finns to read the Scripture and participate in the services of the Church in their own language. He therefore devised an orthography, which is the basis for modern Finnish spelling, and prepared an ABC book; a prayer book (1544), probably his most widely read book, which contained miscellaneous secular information in addition to prayers; a translation of the New Testament (1548); and a vernacular translation of the Mass (1549). He began a collection of Finnish hymns and translated others. For these and other writings he became recognized as the creator of the Finnish literary language.

Bishop Agricola was one of the members of a royal commission sent to Russia to negotiate peace after the Russian-Swedish hostilities of 1555–1557, and on his return from this strenuous trip he fell ill on Palm Sunday, April 9, 1557, and died that night. He had been bishop but three years and was not yet fifty years old.

He is remembered as a learned man, interested in mysticism and the ancient religion of his homeland, moderate and conciliatory in dealings with others, but anxious for the well-being of the Church and the Christian life of its members. In 1948, on the four hundredth anniversary of his death, he was widely commemorated and many new articles and books on his life and works were published. The Finnish Lutheran Church in Toronto is named for him.

With Agricola, **Paavali (Paul) Juusten** (1516–1576) might also be remembered. He, too, had been sent by Bishop Skytte to Wittenberg (1543–1546). He was rector of the cathedral school at Turku, and in 1554 he was consecrated the first bishop of the newly established diocese of Viipuri (Viborg), near the Russian border. He later became a successor of Agricola and served as Bishop of Turku for thirteen years. Juusten wrote a catechism and a manual for the clergy, was concerned for the spiritual and intellectual welfare of the clergy of Finland, and, together with Agricola, revived the spirituality of the Church in Finland.

Paavo Henrik Ruotsalainen was a lay evangelist who in the eighteenth century revitalized the springs of the religious tradition. He was born July 9, 1777, and spent most of his life in Nilsia. A poor peasant, without formal education, this "prophet of the wilderness" nonetheless became the outstanding layman in the Church of Finland. He was known as a sympathetic confessor and spiritual counselor, an effective preacher despite harassment by ecclesiastical and secular officials. He died January 27, 1852, and is commemorated on that date by the 1962 German *Evangelical Calendar of Names*.

FOR FURTHER READING

Arden, G. Everett. *Four Northern Lights: Men Who Shaped Scandinavian Churches.* Minneapolis: Augsburg, 1964. (For Ruotsalainen)

Sentzke, Geert. *Finland: Its Church and Its People.* Helsinki, 1963.

Sinnemäki, M. *The Church in Finland.* Helsinki, 1973.

READING

From *Orthodoxy* by G. K. Chesterton

Mysticism keeps man sane. As long as you have mystery you have health; when you destroy mystery you create morbidity. The ordinary man has always been sane because the ordinary man has always been a mystic. He has permitted the twilight. He has always had one foot in earth and the other in fairy land. He has always left himself free to doubt his gods; but (unlike the agnostic of today) free also to believe in them. He has always cared more for truth than for consistency. If he saw two truths that seemed to contradict each other, he would take the two truths and the contradiction along with them. His spiritual sight is stereoscopic, like his physical sight: he sees two different pictures at once and yet sees all the better for that. Thus he has always believed that there is such a thing as fate, but such a thing as free will also. Thus he believed that children were indeed the kingdom of heaven, but nevertheless ought to be obedient to the kingdom of earth. He admired youth because it was young and age because it was not.

It is exactly this balance of apparent contradictions that had been the whole buoyancy of the healthy man. The whole secret of mysticism is this: that man can understand everything by the help of what he does not understand. The morbid logician seeks to make everything lucid, and succeeds in making everything mysterious. The mystic allows one thing to be mysterious, and everything else becomes lucid. The determinist makes the theory of causation quite clear, and then finds that he cannot say "if you please" to the housemaid. The Christian permits free will to remain a sacred mystery; but because of this his relations with the household become of a sparkling and crystal clearness. He puts the seed of dogma in a central darkness; but it branches forth in all directions with abounding natural health. As we have taken the circle as the symbol of reason and madness, we may very well take the cross as the symbol at once of mystery and of health. Buddhism is centripetal, but Christianity is centrifugal: it breaks out. For the circle is perfect and infinite in its nature; but it is fixed for ever in its size; it can never be larger or smaller. But the cross, though it has at its heart a collision and a contradiction, can extend its four arms for ever without altering its shape. Because it has a paradox in its centre it can grow without changing. The circle returns upon itself and is bound. The cross opens its arms to the four winds; it is a signpost for free travellers.

G. K. Chesterton, *Orthodoxy* (New York and London: John Lane, 1908), 49–50.

PROPERS

Almighty God, by the ministry of your servants Mikael Agricola, Paavali Juusten, and Paavo Ruotsalainen, you revived the Church in Finland and renewed its life: Raise up in our own day teachers and prophets inspired by your Spirit, whose voices will give strength to your church and proclaim the reality of your kingdom; through your Son, Jesus Christ our Lord, who lives and reigns with you and the Holy Spirit, one God, now and forever.

✚ LBW, ELW Common of Renewers of the Church, rev. PHP

Readings: Jeremiah 1:4-10
               Psalm 46
               1 Corinthians 3:11-23
               Mark 10:35-45
Hymn of the Day:
               "Lord, as a pilgrim through life I go" (LBW 485)
Prayers: For the Church in Finland: its archbishop, bishops, priests, and people
               For increasingly intelligent participation in the worship of the church
               For compassion and a conciliatory spirit, especially in controversy
               For those who study language and culture
Preface: A Saint (1) (BCP) or All Saints
Color: White

ALSO ON APRIL 10

William Law, Priest, 1761

The son of a village grocer in Kings Cliffe, Northamptonshire, William Law was born in 1686 and educated at Emmanuel College, Cambridge, of which he became a fellow in 1711. Three years later, because he refused to abjure the Stuarts and take the oath of allegiance to George I, he was compelled to resign from his position and was deprived of the usual means of making a living as a clergyman of the Church of England. He became a "Nonjuror" and retired into private life.

He worked as tutor to the father of Edward Gibbon, the historian, from 1727 to 1737. He then, in 1740, returned to his native village, where with a Mrs. Hutcheson and Hester Gibbon he organized schools and almshouses, and led a life of great simplicity, devotion, and charity. He defended the Scriptures and sacraments against the attacks of the Deists and spoke out eloquently against the warfare of his day. He was a stalwart defender of the poor and shared his food with them every day, a practice that so offended the local vicar that he preached a sermon denouncing such indiscriminate charity.

William Law's book *A Serious Call to a Devout and Holy Life* (1728) is one of the great classics of Christian devotion. In it, he insists that the moral virtues of temperance, humility, and self-denial, all animated by the intention to glorify God, should be the basis of daily living. "If we are to follow Christ," he wrote, "it must be in our common way of spending every day." The book, inspired by such spiritual writers as Johannes Tauler, John Ruysbroek, and Thomas à Kempis, is written with humor, based on accurate observation of manners, couched in straightforward prose set out in brief paragraphs that are easy to digest, and interspersed with character sketches that give point to the summons to a devout life. The book had a profound influence on John Wesley and George Whitefield and laid the foundation for the evangelical revival of the eighteenth century, the Evangelical Movement in England, and the Great Awakening in America.

William Law died April 9, 1761. His commemoration in the calendar of the American *Book of Common Prayer*, April 9, has in *Lesser Feasts and Fasts 1997* been moved to the next day to make room for the commemoration of Dietrich Bonhoeffer on April 9. Churches that remember Mikael Agricola on this date might choose to transfer the commemoration of William Law to April 11. The Methodist calendar in *For All the Saints* remembers both Dietrich Bonhoeffer and William Law on April 9.

FOR FURTHER READING

Law, William. *A Serious Call to a Devout and Holy Life.* Ed. Paul Stanwood and Austin Warner. Mahwah: Paulist, 1978.

Overton, J. H. *William Law, Non-Juror and Mystic.* 1881.

Talon, Henri. *William Law: A Study in Literary Craftsmanship.* New York: Harper, 1948.

Walker, A. Keith. *William Law: His Life and Thought.* London: SPCK, 1973.

READING

From *A Serious Call to a Devout and Holy Life* by William Law

If contempt of the world and heavenly affection is a necessary temper of Christians, it is necessary that this temper appear in the whole course of their lives, in their manner of using the world, because it can have no place anywhere else. If self-denial be a condition of salvation, all that would be saved must make it a part of their ordinary life. If humility be a Christian duty, then the common life of a Christian is to be a constant course of humility in all its kinds. If poverty of spirit be necessary, it must be the spirit and temper of every day of our lives. If we are to relieve the naked, the sick, and the prisoner, it must be the common charity of our lives, as far as we can render ourselves able to perform it. If we are to love our enemies, we must make our common life a visible exercise and demonstration of that love. If content and thankfulness, if the patient bearing of evil be duties to God, they are the duties of every day, and in every circumstance of our life. If we are to be wise and holy as the new-born sons of God, we can not otherwise be so, but by renouncing every thing that is foolish and vain in every part of our common life. If we are to be in Christ new creatures, we must show that we are so, by having new ways of living in the world. If we are to follow Christ, it must be in our common way of spending every day. . . .

If our common life is not a common course of humility, self-denial, renunciation of the world, poverty of spirit, and heavenly affection, we do not live the lives of Christians.

William Law, *A Serious Call to a Devout and Holy Life* (1728), Everyman Ed. 1906, 1912, pp. 6, 7.

PROPERS

Almighty and everlasting God, you called William Law to a life of contemplation, and gave him, in visions of eternity, the assurance of your unalterable love: Grant us also, amid the transient occupations of our workaday world, glimpses of the King in his beauty, your Son Jesus Christ our Lord, who lives and reigns with you and the Holy Spirit, one God, now and forever.

Isa. 33:17; *Oxford Centenary Supplementary Missal,* rev. JWP

Readings: Psalm 1 *or* 103:1-4, 13-18
                Philippians 3:7-14
                Matthew 6:1-6, 16-21
Hymn of the Day:
                "O for a closer walk with God" (H82 683, 684; SBH 466)
Prayers: For all those who by their writing and example, help Christians to pray
                For the church's work among the poor and needy
                For the timid and those who suffer at the hands of oppressors
                For grace that our lives may reflect our prayers
Preface: A Saint (2) (BCP)
Color: White

April 11

The *Book of Common Prayer* commemorates on this date *George Augustus Selwyn* (1809–1878), one of the greatest Anglican missionaries. He was consecrated missionary Bishop of New Zealand in 1841 and laid the foundations of the Anglican Church in New Zealand and Melanesia. He showed himself to be a true father in God to both the original Maori inhabitants of the islands and the English colonists, who for ten years were locked in violent struggle. He returned to England in 1867 and in the next year was appointed to the see of Lichfield and held that office until his death on this date in 1878.

April 19

Alphege, Archbishop of Canterbury, Martyr, 1012

Alphege (Aelfheah) was born in 954. He became a Benedictine monk, then prior of an abbey at Bath, and finally Archbishop of Canterbury at a time when England was being overrun by the Danes. When they attacked and captured Canterbury, Alphege urged them to spare the town, but they made him watch while they slaughtered many of the inhabitants and burned the cathedral; then they imprisoned him.

The Danes demanded that the people of Canterbury pay a ransom for his release, but Alphege refused to let his poor and overburdened people pay it. In a drunken fury his captors set upon him, pelting him with stones. Although one of them, Thorkell the Tall, tried to save him, he was killed by a blow on the head with an axe, the first Archbishop of Canterbury to suffer martyrdom. He died praying for his murderers. His death took place April 19, 1012.

READING

From the account of the martyrdom of Alphege by Osbern

Then the devil's henchmen, foaming out cruelty with poisoned breath, and no longer able to bear the weight of the words of Alphege, leaped from their seats with the force of savage lions, felled him with axes, and then one after another pelted him with stones. Alphege was already at the gates of life, when, remembering Christ the Lord hanging on the Cross for the salvation of all and praying to his Father for his enemies, he touched his right knee and his left foot to the ground. The he offered this prayer for himself and for those who without ceasing were tormenting him. "Only-begotten Son of the most high Father, Lord Jesus, who came into the world through the womb of the pure virgin to save sinners, receive me in peace, and have mercy on these men." Falling to the ground once but getting up again, he prayed once more, "Good Shepherd, unequalled Shepherd, watch over the children of the Church, whom I commend to you as I die." Then a man, whom the archbishop had himself baptized, ran up and seeing the holy man struggling still at the very brink of death, was moved by a wrong sense of duty and plunged an axe into his head. Alphege, resting at once in eternal peace, directed his victorious spirit with triumph to heaven. Who, I ask, after those who were the first leaders of the Lord's flock, lived more innocently than this man or ended his life more tranquilly? Or whose merits were so similar as those of this warrior of ours and of Stephen the first martyr?

But the Danish chieftains, desiring to conceal both their own foul deed and Alphege's glory, gathered together and resolved that his body should be thrown into the river, thinking that the enormity of their crimes could be easily hidden and that his memory could be taken away. But what Christ had devised for disgrace for the Danes, was glory to Alphege.

Osbern, *Life of St. Alphege*, chap. 7, paras. 35–36, *Acta Sanctorum*, April II (5 June 1986): 640; trans. PHP, based on Antony Snell.

PROPERS

O loving God, your martyr bishop Alphege of Canterbury suffered a violent death when he refused to permit a ransom to be extorted from his people: Grant that all pastors of your flock may pattern themselves on the Good Shepherd, who laid down his life for the sheep; and who with you and the Holy Spirit lives and reigns, one God, forever and ever.

CMG, LFF

Readings:	Psalm 34 *or* 31:1-5
	Revelation 7:13-17
	Luke 12:4-12
Hymn of the Day:	
	"King of the martyrs' noble band" (H82 236)
Prayers:	For all gentle people facing persecution and the violence of the world
	For our own enemies
	For those who harm others
	For those who find it difficult to forgive
Preface:	A Saint (3) (BCP)
Color:	Red

ALSO ON APRIL 19

Olavus Petri, Priest, 1552; Laurentius Petri, Archbishop of Uppsala, 1573; Renewers of the Church

Olavus and Laurentius Petri were two brothers who led the Reformation in Sweden in the sixteenth century. Olavus, the elder brother, was born in 1493, Laurentius in 1499, both in Örebro, the chief town of Nerike (modern Närke), from which Laurentius is sometimes called Nericius. The boys were educated in the local monastery, Uppsala, Leipzig, and then at Wittenberg, where they were deeply influenced by Martin Luther. Olavus seems to have been in Wittenberg at the time of the posting of the Ninety-five Theses, for he received his bachelor's degree in 1516 and the master's degree in 1518.

When Olavus returned to Sweden, he became chancellor to Bishop Matthias of Strengnäs and a close friend of Laurentius Andreae, who was the archdeacon. Olavus was ordained deacon and spread the teachings of the reformers among clergy and laity of the Church. After his coronation at Strangnäs, King Gustavus Vasa, who liberated Sweden from Danish rule, took Laurentius Petri to Stockholm as his chancellor and Olavus as pastor of the city church there and secretary of the city council. Half the townspeople were German, and Olavis's study in Germany stood him in good stead.

The character of the Reformation in Sweden was determined to a great extent by the writings of Olavus. He understood that the reformation of the Church depended upon the education of the clergy and people, and his writing gave the intellectual and liturgical basis for such education. He prepared a Swedish translation of the New Testament based on the Latin Vulgate, but with some reference to Luther's translation from the Greek. In the same year, 1526, he published a book of catechetical instruction, *A Useful Teaching*. In 1531 he issued a Swedish version of the Latin mass, simplified along the lines of Luther's *Deutsche Messe*, and in 1530 he published a collection of hymns and canticles in Swedish. In 1540 he was condemned to death for violating royal dignity because of his opposition to the king's desire for complete ecclesiastical control. Later he was pardoned and wrote his *Swedish Chronicles*. He died April 19, 1552.

Laurentius returned from Wittenberg in 1527 and, in spite of his youth (he was 28), he was appointed to a professorship at the University of Uppsala. He was ordained to the priesthood and four years later was the king's choice to fill the vacant see of Uppsala. An assembly of the clergy from the whole realm was called, and they voted overwhelmingly in favor of the young priest-professor. He was consecrated on September 22, 1531, at Stockholm, the first evangelical archbishop of Sweden. Uppsala had first become the seat of an archbishop in 1164 with Stephen as its first incumbent; the eight hundredth anniversary of this event was celebrated in 1964. Laurentius succeeded (against Gustavus Vasa who thought of abolishing the episcopal office) in preserving the historic episcopate for Lutheranism. (*Evangelical Lutheran Worship* is in error in calling Laurentius Petri "Bishop of Uppsala." There is in fact another person who is the diocesan bishop and not the primate.)

In 1541 the complete Bible in Swedish, the joint work of the Petri brothers, appeared with full royal approval. In the same year a revised liturgy prepared by Laurentius was issued in which the reformer began the transformation of the solemn mass in Latin without congregational communion into a service of Holy Communion sung in Swedish by the people, with a sermon required after the Gospel.

In 1561, at the coronation of King Eric XIV, Archbishop Laurentius preached a sermon setting forth the principles of the Reformation and making clear the relation between the two autonomous instruments of God's rule, the secular and the religious. Laurentius died in 1573, and twenty years later, when the Augsburg Confession was officially endorsed, the Reformation in Sweden was complete. During the lifetime of the two Petri brothers, Sweden had passed from Danish rule, subject to Rome, to an independent nation with a firmly established evangelical church.

FOR FURTHER READING

Bergendoff, Conrad. *Olavus Petri and the Ecclesiastical Transformation in Sweden.* Philadelphia: Fortress Press, 1965 (1928).

Senn, Frank C. *Christian Liturgy: Catholic and Evangelical.* Chapter 12. Minneapolis: Fortress Press, 1997.

Yelverton, Eric. *An Archbishop of the Reformation: Laurentius Petri Nericius, Archbishop of Uppsala, 1531–1573.* London and Minneapolis: Augsburg, 1957.

———. *The Manual of Olavus Petri.* London: SPCK, 1953.

READING

From The Church Manual of Olavus Petri

Our death has now through Christ's death become a medicine unto life, so that when we begin to die, then for the first time we really begin to live, because the sin with which we were born is so deeply rooted in us that we can not be free from it as long as we live. And we are not fit for eternal life as long as we live. And we are not fit for eternal life as long as we are laden with sin, which is active in our mortal members; therefore it is necessary that death comes and strikes down man in whom sin reigns, so that the body is brought to naught. For this reason death is now become a remarkable medicine. And although this medicine is bitter to experience, it is nevertheless beneficial for us, and we can observe from this severe remedy how grievous is the sickness of sin with which we are afflicted. And we are poor and wretched folk as long as we remain in this miserable life. In this poor world there is no security, but from all sides we are troubled by sin. Therefore, let us earnestly fall down before our heavenly Father, and pray him for grace not to fear or dread death, since it is quite beneficial that we for a short time taste this physical death with Christ, in order that we may also be raised again with him to blessedness. And we should not mourn and grieve too much that our friends have departed, because they are now separated from this misery and danger in which we still remain, and they are now come into the peace of Christ, where they shall rest until the last judgment. Then we shall be reunited with them and thus remain with Christ forever. With this we should now comfort one another. May God Almighty grant us his holy grace, that we may so walk here in this life, among those things which are temporal, as not to lose that which is spiritual and eternal. Amen.

Excerpted in *For All the Saints,* ed. Frederick J. Schumacher and Dorothy Zelenko, vol. 3 (Delhi: American Lutheran Publicity Bureau, 1995), 77–78.

PROPERS

Almighty God, through the labors of your learned servants Olavus and Laurentius Petri you gave the people of Sweden the Scriptures and the services of the church in their own tongue: Mercifully grant that people everywhere may hear and understand the good news of salvation, and be drawn to the kingdom of your blessed Son Jesus Christ our Lord, who lives and reigns with you and the Holy Spirit, one God, now and forever.

PHP

Readings:	Jeremiah 1:4-10
	Psalm 46
	1 Corinthians 3:11-23
	Mark 10:35-45

Hymn of the Day:
    "Oh, sing jubilee to the Lord" (LBW 256)
Prayers: For the Church in Sweden: its archbishop, bishops, priests, and people
    For the gift of wisdom and learning for the clergy
    For a deepened appreciation of the long tradition of the church
Preface: A Saint (1) (BCP)
Color: White

April 20

On this date the *Lutheran Service Book* commemorates **Johannes Bugenhagen** (1485–1558), called "Pomeranius." He was pastor in Wittenberg from 1523 to his death and led the organization of the Lutheran Church in northern Germany and in Denmark, where by ordaining seven bishops he caused the Danish Church to lose the apostolic succession.

April 21

Anselm, Archbishop of Canterbury, Teacher, 1109

Anselm was born in 1033 of noble parents near Aosta in the region of Piedmont in what is now northwestern Italy and what was then the frontier of Lombardy and Burgundy. After the death of his mother and quarreling with his father, Anselm left home at the age of twenty-three for travel in Burgundy and France, furthering his education. He was attracted to the Benedictine monastery of Bec in Normandy, which had been founded in 1040. His father died and left him all his property, and Anselm debated whether he should return to Italy or become a monk. He entered Bec as a novice in 1060, attracted by the intellectual brilliance of the prior Lanfranc, a fellow Italian. (There were a number of Italian scholars who came to Normandy in the late tenth and eleventh centuries.) After three years, when Lanfranc left to become prior of a new monastery, Anselm was elected his successor as prior of Bec. In 1078 when the founding abbot of Bec, Herluin, died, Anselm was unanimously elected abbot of the monastery. His skill as a teacher and his scholarly work made Bec an even more influential school of philosophical and theological studies than it had been under Lanfranc, and it became the foremost intellectual center of Europe.

    Lanfranc had become Archbishop of Canterbury, and in 1078 Anselm visited him, making a favorable impression in England. Lanfranc died in 1089 and after

APRIL

a delay while King William Rufus kept the see vacant to secure as much of the revenues of Canterbury as possible, Anselm was chosen as Lanfranc's successor. After extended pressure from all sides to accept the appointment, Anselm was enthroned as Archbishop of Canterbury September 25, 1093, and was consecrated archbishop December 4.

The gentle and scholarly monk now began a protracted and intense struggle with the king over ultimate authority. William Rufus refused to recognize Pope Urban IV, and the bishops, fearing the king, sided with him against Anselm at the Council of Rockingham in March 1095. The intervention of the secular princes prevented his immediate removal, but the struggle continued, and Anselm, realizing that the situation was hopeless, on October 15, 1097, left England for Rome without the king's permission, and the king took possession of the see of Canterbury.

The pope received Anselm graciously, refused to accept his resignation, and gave him a place of honor at the Council of Bari in 1098, which sought reunion with the Greek Church. Anselm there defended the teaching that the Holy Spirit proceeds from the Father and the Son and also had the council's excommunication of the English king postponed.

Anselm stayed for a time with the archbishop of Lyons and there learned of the death of William Rufus, August 2, 1100. The king's successor, Henry I, immediately recalled Anselm to England, but the struggle over authority was renewed when Anselm in obedience to a decree of the Council of Bari refused the king's insistence on a oath of allegiance to the crown. When no solution seemed possible, the king asked Anselm to go to Rome. At length, in 1106, a compromise was effected, and Anselm returned to his see. The difficulties were not yet over, for York claimed the primacy in England that had always belonged to Canterbury.

Anselm was by this time in poor health. His biographer, Eadmer, tells of his approaching death:

> Palm Sunday dawned, and we were sitting beside him as usual. One of us therefore said to him: "My lord, and father, we cannot help knowing that you are going to leave the world to be at the Easter court of your Lord." He replied: "And indeed if his will is set on this, I shall gladly obey his will. However, if he would prefer me to remain among you, at least until I can settle a question about the origin of the soul, which I am turning over in my mind, I should welcome this with gratitude, for I do not know whether anyone will solve it when I am dead.

Anselm died on Wednesday in Holy Week, April 21, 1109.

Before Anselm, the study of theology consisted of collecting authoritative texts, lining up authorities to settle disputed questions. Anselm strove to demonstrate the truth of faith by going beyond faith to an insight into it. The aim of his teaching was to make his hearers and readers think, to stretch their minds. He devised an ingenious and durable argument for the existence of God "than whom nothing greater can be conceived," a provocative explanation of the atonement (the "satisfaction theory," as Gustav Aulén calls it), and emphasized the role of the maternal in Christianity by encouraging devotion to Mary, although he was opposed to the doctrine of her immaculate conception (the teaching that Mary was conceived without sin), and in a prayer addressed Jesus, "Are you not a mother too? . . . Indeed you are, and the mother of all mothers, who tasted death in your longing to bring forth children to life." Above all he understood the pursuit of theology as prayer.

Anselm is on the Roman Catholic, Episcopal, Lutheran, and Methodist calendars.

FOR FURTHER READING

Cowdrey, H. E. J. *Lanfranc: Scholar, Monk, and Archbishop.* New York: Oxford University Press, 2003.

Evans, G. R. *Anselm.* London: Cassel, 1989.

Southern, R. W. *The Life of St. Anselm by Eadmer.* London: Thomas Nelson, 1962.

———. *St. Anselm and His Biographer.* Cambridge: Cambridge University Press, 1963.

———. *St. Anselm: A Portrait in a Landscape.* Cambridge: Cambridge University Press, 1991.

READING

From *Proslogion* by Anselm

APRIL

. . . I have written the little work that follows . . . in the role of one who strives to raise his mind to the contemplation of God and who seeks to understand what he believes.

I acknowledge, Lord, and I give thanks that you have created your image in me, so that I may remember you, think of you, love you. But this image is so obliterated and worn away by wickedness, it is so obscured by the smoke of sins, that it cannot do what it was created to do, unless you renew and reform it. I am not attempting, O Lord, to penetrate your loftiness, for I cannot begin to match my understanding with it, but I desire in some measure to understand your truth, which my heart believes and loves. For I do not seek to understand in order to believe, but I believe in order to understand. For this too I believe, that "unless I believe, I shall not understand" (Isa. 7:9).

St. Anselm's Proslogion (Oxford: Clarendon, 1965), Preface, I, trans. PHP.

PROPERS

Almighty God, you raised up your servant Anselm to study and teach the sublime truths you have revealed: Let your gift of faith come to the aid of our understanding, and open our hearts to your truth; through your Son Jesus Christ our Lord, who lives and reigns with you and the Holy Spirit, one God, now and forever.

RS, trans. PHP

Readings: Psalm 139:1-9 *or* 37:3-6, 32-33
              Romans 5:1-11
              Matthew 11:25-30
Hymn of the Day:
              "O Love, how deep, how broad, how high" (H82 448, 449; LBW 88, LSB 544, ELW
              322)
Prayers: For a sense of the majesty of God
              For forgiveness for those who wrong us
              For a spirit of prayer and devotion
              For those who inquire into the mysteries of God and God's relation to the world
              For those who seek to be certain of the existence of God
Preface: Epiphany
Color: White

April 22

The Lutheran Spanish-language service book, *Libro de Liturgia y Cántico,* lists this as **Dia de la Creacion**. In English, the observance is called **Earth Day**, instituted April 22, 1970, by Senator Gaylord Nelson of Wisconsin to emphasize the stewardship of environmental resources. The traditional liturgical expression of concern for the natural world has been on the Rogation Days observed in the spring, often just before the Ascension. They are retained in the *Book of Common Prayer* (pp. 207–08, 258–59, particularly no. III), in the *Lutheran Book of Worship* as the Stewardship of Creation (pp. 40–41), and in *Evangelical Lutheran Worship* (p. 60).

April 23

Toyohiko Kagawa, Renewer of Society, 1960

Kagawa (kah-GAAH-wah) was born July 10, 1888, at Kobe, Japan, the son of a member of the Japanese Cabinet and a geisha girl. He was orphaned at the age of four and was raised by his father's wife in Awa. It was an unhappy situation. He left to live with an uncle and enrolled in a Bible class to learn English. At fifteen he became a Christian and consequently was disinherited. With the help of missionaries, he studied at Presbyterian College at Kobe from 1905 to 1908. After a near-death experience, he vowed to dedicate his life to serving "God's children in the slums." From 1910 to 1924, with his wife Haru, he spent all but two years in a six-by-six-foot hut in the slums of Kobe, called Shinkawa, the worst slums anywhere in the world. In 1912 he organized the first labor union in Japan among shipyard workers. From 1914 to 1916 at Princeton he studied social techniques to relieve poverty and misery. In 1918 he founded the Labor Federation, in 1921 the Farmers' Union. He was arrested during the rice riots of 1919 and the shipyard strikes of 1921. He worked successfully for universal male suffrage, which was achieved in 1925, and for the modification of laws against trade unions.

In 1923 he was asked to supervise relief and social work in Tokyo. He organized the Bureau of Social Welfare, and his writings drew the attention of the government to the appalling conditions in the slums. He insisted upon a reorganization of the economic structure of the world to realize the Christian ideal of social order. In 1928 he founded the Anti-War League. In 1930 he began the Kingdom of God movement to promote the conversion of Japan to Christianity. He established credit unions, schools, hospitals, churches, and visited the United States five times to gain support for his projects of social reform.

In 1940 he was arrested for apologizing to China for Japan's attack on that country. In 1941 he was one of a group that went to the United States to try to avert the coming war. He returned to Japan in September 1941. During the war his pacifism and his patriotism struggled against each other, and he became militantly nationalistic.

After the war, in poor health, he led the effort to adapt democratic institutions to Japan. He died in Tokyo April 23, 1960. He is commemorated on the German *Evangelical Calendar of Names* and the calendar in the *Lutheran Book of Worship* and *Evangelical Lutheran Worship*.

FOR FURTHER READING

Axling, William. *Kagawa.* 8th rev. ed. New York: Harpers, 1946.

Davey, Cyril J. *Kagawa of Japan.* New York: Abingdon, 1960.

Shildgren, Robert. *Toyohiko Kagawa: Apostle of Love and Justice.* Berkeley: Centenary, 1988.

Simon, Charlie May. *A Seed Shall Serve: The Study of Toyohiko Kagawa, Spiritual Leader of Modern Japan.* New York: Dutton, 1964.

Trout, J. M. *Kagawa, Japanese Prophet.* New York: Association, 1959.

READING

From *Love: The Law of Life* by Toyohiko Kagawa

My soul, whither wilt thou flee, and where wilt thou find an oasis in this parched, loveless waste? Where wilt thou find a spring of healing Love? Search thou not for the springs of Love in the deep valleys, nor yet may they be found in the bosom of another being. Thou art wrong to try to quench thy thirst for Love from another. Thou must seek Love in thine own breast. The spring of Love must well up in thine own heart.

Therefore I do not lose hope, nor do I fear when I see this drought in the land. I shall dig down deeper, still deeper into my own soul. I shall dig down to the God who is within me. Then, if I strike the underground stream that murmurs softly in the depths of my heart, I will tenderly cherish this oasis of the soul; and to it will I lead a few thirsting comrades.

My real experience of religion came when I entered the Kobe slums. Everything in the slums was ugly: the people, the houses, the clothes, the streets—everything was ugly and full of disease. If I had not carried God beside me, I should not have been able to stay. But because I believed in God, and in the Holy Spirit, I had a different view of life, and I assure you that I enjoyed living in the slums. With active love and the love-motive, every moment was full of joy. Because I felt that the Holy Spirit of the Heavenly Father was living inside me, I was not afraid of anything—not of the many repeated threats from pistols, swords, ruffians, not even from the infectious diseases which infested the slums. My job was to help these people. I had free access to their homes, and so knew even more about them than the doctors. For me prayer is very real. If you pray with selfishness it will never be answered, but prayer for the sake of God and for the love of your fellow men will surely be answered. A gambler, dying, said to me that he was going back to his Heavenly Father. Then for the first time, like a flash, I was convinced that any man, even the most depraved, is able to grasp the idea of Jesus Christ.

Toyohiko Kagawa, *Love: The Law of Life* (St. Paul: Macalester Park Pub. Co., 1951), 25, 13–14.

PROPERS

Lord God, you planted in your servant Toyohiko Kagawa a fervent desire to relieve the misery of the poor and to establish in the social order the justice, love, and peace of the kingdom of God: Give to your church, we pray, such selfless compassion that we may find joy in the service of others and bring the light of hope where there is resignation and despair; though your Son, Jesus Christ our Lord, who lives and reigns with you and the Holy Spirit, one God now and forever.

PHP

Readings: Hosea 2:18-23
             Psalm 94:1-14
             Romans 12:9-21
             Luke 6:20-36

Hymn of the Day:
    "Where restless crowds are thronging" (LBW 430)
Prayers: For a renewed spirit of love for all people
    For the poor, the outcast, the forgotten
    For peace
    For the reconciliation of peoples and nations
    For laborers
    For those who work among the poor, the diseased, the unemployed
Preface: Baptism (BCP, LBW)
Color: White

April 24

On this date the *Lutheran Service Book* commemorates **Johann Walter** (Walther), the distinguished Lutheran kantor, organist, and composer who laid the foundations upon which composers of later generations built the traditions of Lutheran church music. He was born in Germany in 1496 and died at Torgau, March 25, 1570.

April 25

St. Mark, Evangelist

The oldest Christian tradition associated with this day is the singing of the litany in procession through the countryside to keep mildew from affecting the wheat harvest. There was a relic of this agricultural concern in the Gospel previously appointed for this day (John 15:1-11), which told of the vine and the vinedresser. Later, the day became associated with St. Mark, the sometime companion of St. Paul and the "interpreter of Peter" and the author of the earliest Gospel, which bears his name.

St. Mark is usually identified with the John Mark of the Book of Acts, although Marcus was a very common Roman name. His mother Mary owned the house where the infant church gathered for prayer (Acts 12:12), and some have suggested that this was also the site of the Last Supper. John Mark accompanied his cousin Barnabas and St. Paul on the first missionary journey. He had a falling out with Paul for some reason (youthful impulsiveness, jealousy over Paul's assuming the leadership over Barnabas, anger at the change of itinerary have all been suggested), and Paul refused to take him on the second journey (Acts 15:36-40). Later, however, they were reconciled.

The attribution of the Gospel that bears his name, thought to be the earliest Gospel, goes back to a statement by Papias (*ca.* 140) that Mark "was the interpreter of Peter," from whom he got much of the material for the Gospel.

According to an unsupported tradition, Mark was the first bishop of Alexandria and was martyred there in 64 C.E. because of his attempt during the reign of the emperor Trajan to stop the worship of Serapis. In 829 Mark's supposed remains were removed from Alexandria to Venice and the famous cathedral there.

From the beginning of the seventh century until 1969, April 25 in the West was kept as a rogation day marked by a procession known as the Major or Greater Litanies, which replaced an old pagan procession, the *robigalia*, which took place on the same day and was designed to prevent wheat mildew, *robigo*. Perhaps because of the procession, the understanding arose that April 25 was the day when Peter entered Rome for the first time. Later, in the ninth century, the commemoration of St. Mark was assigned to the day. The commemoration is thought to have begun earlier than the eighth century in the East. The commemoration of Mark does not appear on Roman calendars until the twelfth century, doubtless because Mark was not martyred or buried there.

The celebration of the feast day of St. Mark is especially appropriate in Year B of the lectionary cycle, when the Gospel readings are drawn primarily from St. Mark. His traditional symbol is the lion, drawn from the vision of Ezekiel (1:10).

FOR FURTHER READING

Black, C. Clifton. *Mark: Images of an Apostolic Interpreter.* Minneapolis: Fortress Press, 2001.

Gardner, Helen. "The Poetry of St. Mark." In *The Business of Criticism.* pp. 101-126. London: Oxford, 1959.

Gundry, Robert H. *Mark: A Commentary on His Apology for the Cross.* Grand Rapids: Eerdmans, 1993.

Kermode, Frank. *The Genesis of Secrecy: On the Interpretation of Narrative.* Cambridge: Harvard University Press, 1979.

Taylor, Vincent. *The Gospel according to St. Mark.* 2d ed. London: Macmillan, 1966.

READING

From *Worship* by J-J. von Allmen

The mystery of writing and reading—which might almost be called paschal, a death and resurrection—is something that has become so common that we have ceased to be aware of it. . . . It is forgotten that the Gospel is enclosed in the letter of the Bible and must be freed, that to read scripture is to experience paschal joy; the Lord reappears, He who is the Word, to tell us of His love and His will, to teach us who He is and who we are, to summon us and give us life. But he does not reappear automatically. In deciphering scripture, we can also draw from it a corpse, a dead letter. Hence, the reading of the Bible in worship is traditionally preceded by an epiklesis, an invocation of the Holy Spirit, that the Word may really come alive for us so as to accomplish its work of salvation and judgment. If reading alone had been incapable of this spiritual miracle, if preaching had been necessary to achieve it, the apostles would have written nothing and would have trusted oral tradition alone. The very fact that they buried their witness to Jesus Christ in these hieroglyphic signs that are letters proves that they believed the Spirit-inspired interpretation of these hieroglyphics would be able to resurrect their witness and enable them themselves to remain alive in the Church. "In the reading of the apostolic word, then apostle of Jesus Christ himself appears, with his witness that is basic for the Church, *hic et nunc* [here and now] at the heart of the community, to feed it with that living Word" (P. Brunner).

J.-J. von Allmen, *Worship: Its Meaning and Practice* (New York: Oxford, 1965), 132–33.

PROPERS

Almighty God, by the hand of Mark the evangelist you have given to your Church the Gospel of Jesus Christ the Son of God: We thank you for this witness, and pray that we may be firmly grounded in its truth; through Jesus Christ our Lord, who lives and reigns with you and the Holy Spirit, one God, forever and ever.

Gregorian; 1549, 1662, 1979 BCP

APRIL

Readings:	Isaiah 52:7-10
	Psalm 2 *or* Psalm 57
	Ephesians 4:7-8, 11-16 *or* 2 Timothy 4:6-11, 18
	Mark 1:1-15 *or* 16:15-20
Hymn of the Day:	
	"O God of light, your Word, a lamp unfailing" (LBW 237, LSB 836, ELW 507)
	or "Come, sing, ye choirs exultant" (H82 235)
Prayers:	For a heart to hear the gospel
	For faith to acknowledge Jesus as the Son of God
	For a sense of the mystery of the resurrection
	For fruitful fields and good crops
Preface:	All Saints
Color:	Red

April 29

Catherine of Siena, Teacher, 1380
with Johannes "Meister" Eckhardt, Mystic, 1327
Johannes Tauler, Mystic, 1361, and the Friends
*   of God*
Blessed Henry Suso, Mystic, 1366
Blessed John Ruysbroek, 1381, and Geert
*   Groote, 1384, Founders, Brethren of the*
*   Common Life*

Catherine was born in Siena probably in 1347, the twenty-third and last child in the large, devout Benincasa family. At age six she began to have visions of Christ, and throughout her life she continued to have mystical experiences, including visions and prolonged trances. Near the beginning of Lent 1367, a vision convinced her that she was to be a bride of Christ, and she accepted his command to carry her love for him to the world, subsequently receiving the stigmata.

> I saw the crucified Lord, coming down to me in a great light. . . . Then from the marks of his most sacred wounds I saw five blood-red rays coming down upon me, which were directed toward the hands and feet and heart of my body. Perceiving the mystery, I exclaimed, "Ah, my Lord God, do not let the marks appear outwardly on the body." While I was speaking, before the rays reached me, they changed their blood-red color to splendor and like pure light they came to the five places in my body—the hands, feet, and heart. The pain that I feel in those five places, but especially in my heart, is so great that unless the Lord works a new miracle, it does not seem possible that the life of my body can endure such agony.*

She claimed to have encountered St. Dominic in a vision and thereafter was permitted to wear the habit of the Dominican Third Order of Penance. She stubbornly clung to the vow of celibacy she made while still a child, despite her family's persistent pleas for a suitable marriage. Eventually, at the age of sixteen, she won the reluctant permission of her parents to live in a special closed-off room in her family's house, fasting and praying, and leaving the room only to go to church.

After three years, she emerged from her seclusion to devote herself to good works, doing household chores for her family and ministering to the sick and unfortunate in hospitals and in their homes. From 1368 to 1374 she gathered about her in Siena a group of friends whom she called her "family." They were men and women, priests and laity, and all (though older than she) called her "mother." During this period, she fasted almost constantly and continued the intense devotion to the sacrament that she had begun earlier. At the same time, she is reported to have maintained her merry, unpretentious manner, and she had a powerful spiritual influence on many people. She dictated letters of spiritual instruction

* E. G. Gardner, *St. Catherine of Siena* (1907), 134, quoted in Rufus M. Jones, *Studies in Mystical Religion* (London: St. Martin's, 1909), 302 rev.

and also dealt with public affairs, urging a crusade against the Turks. Her outspoken advice brought her misunderstanding and opposition.

The Dominican Order, which had been guiding her spiritual life for some years, gave her official protection in late spring 1374. During the period 1374–1378 her influence in public affairs was at its height. She opposed the war of Florence and its allies against the papacy (1376–1378). She pressed for the renewal of the Church, which was clearly in need of reform. Her naïve but earnest holiness made an impression on Gregory XI, whom she met at Avignon in June 1376. She urged him to return from his residence in France to his see in Rome. In the following year he did return to Rome, and the "Babylonian captivity" of the Church was ended.

In November 1378 Catherine went to Rome, where she worked for the unity of the Church and engaged in writing and prayer. Although she had not learned to read and write until her teens, she carried on a voluminous correspondence with leaders of the Church and state. Many of her letters have been preserved. She also dictated to her secretaries a book called the *Dialogue or A Treatise on Divine Providence* in which she reported what she felt were God's words to her about the fundamentals of Christian faith and practice. The book is still read by many who find comfort and wisdom in the words of this unschooled woman.

At the age of thirty-three, after a period of almost complete paralysis, Catherine died in Rome, April 29, 1380, surrounded by her "family." She was buried in the Church Santa Maria sopra Minerva. A woman of boundless energy, single-mindedness, and devotion to her ideals, she was able to deal effectively with rulers, diplomats, and leaders of all kinds, and she was also loved by the common people for her mystical christocentric spirituality. She was a forerunner of those women of later centuries who were to find their fulfillment not in marriage but in a professional career of service. These words of hers are worth pondering, "Do you think that our Lord would be pleased with us if we left works of mercy undone because our neighbor is unthankful?"

Catherine has been widely commemorated in Christian churches. She was canonized by the Roman Catholic Church in 1461, and her feast day was set on April 30, but the present Roman calendar as well as the Episcopal, Lutheran, and Methodist calendars commemorate her on the day of her death, April 29. Her feast day was popular in northern Europe, and she was retained on a number of Lutheran calendars after the Reformation, among them the *Evangelical Calendar of Names* (1965).

FOR FURTHER READING

Catherine of Siena. *The Dialogue.* Trans. Suzanne Noffke. Mahwah: Paulist, 1980.
Curtayne, A. *Saint Catherine of Siena.* New York: Sheed and Ward, 1935.
Jones, Rufus M. *Studies in Mystical Religion.* London: Macmillan, 1909.

APRIL

Jorgensen, Johannes. *St. Catherine of Siena*. New York: Longman's, Green, 1938.

Levasti, A. *My Servant Catherine*. Trans. D. M. White. Westminster: Newman, 1954.

Raymond of Capua. *Leggenda Maior*. Trans. G. Lamb, "The Life of St. Catherine of Siena." New York: Kenedy, 1960.

With Catherine, it may be useful also to remember other influential mystics of the fourteenth century.

Johannes "Meister" Eckhart, the founder of German mysticism and the originator of German philosophical language, was born at Hochheim in Thuringia, Germany, about 1260. He became a member of the Dominican Order, studied at Paris, returned to Germany as Provincial-Prior of the Dominican Order for Saxony, and went back to Paris for further study. He then went to Strasbourg, the foremost religious center of Germany and there became known as a great preacher; he next lived in Cologne. Rufus Jones said of him (*Studies in Mystical Religion*, 217), "He is a remarkable example of the union of a profoundly speculative mind and a simple, childlike spirit. No mystic has ever dropped his plummet deeper into the mysteries of the Godhead, nor has there ever been a bolder interpreter of those mysteries in the language of the common people." He was allowed to teach unmolested until the end of his life, although his teaching seemed to many to verge on pantheism. In 1326 the Archbishop of Cologne brought charges against him and before the matter was settled, Eckhart died in 1327. Two years later certain of his writings were declared heretical by a papal bull which concluded, "He wished to know more than he should." Meister Eckhart is on the German *Evangelical Calendar of Names* on March 27.

The Friends of God (*Gottesfreunde*) was a lay movement centered in the Rhineland and Switzerland that sought to renew the languishing Church. In a time of earthquake, natural disaster, and black death, the movement drew upon the strong apocalyptic strain in the German visionaries of earlier centuries Hildegard (1098–1179; see September 17), Elizabeth of Schönau (d. 1164), and Mechtild of Magdeburg (see November 19). The movement was founded by Rulman Merswin (d. 1382), with whom were associated Margaret and Christina Ebner, Henry of Nördlingen, and the unknown author of the classic *Theologica Germanica*, praised by Luther as for him next in value to the Bible and the writings of St. Augustine.

Johannes Tauler, the "illuminated doctor," and one of the noblest leaders of the Friends of God, was born in Strasbourg near the end of the thirteenth century and was ordained a priest of the Dominican Order. In 1339 he settled in Basel, returned to Strasbourg in 1352, and died there in 1361. In his teaching he insisted on a religion of experience "entering in and dwelling in the Inner Kingdom of God, where pure truth and the sweetness of God are found." He is on the *Evangelical Calendar of Names*, June 16.

Blessed Henry Suso (originally Berg) was born *ca.* 1295 of a noble Swabian family. He, too, entered a Dominican monastery for five years of study. At the age of eighteen, he had a spiritual awakening, endured extreme ascetic penance, and at length found what he sought. He went through Swabia as an itinerant preacher, *ca.* 1335–1348 and then settled in Ulm. He died in 1366. He had all the characteristic marks of the Friends of God: spiritual visions, spiritual crises, austerities, ecstasies, consciousness of the immediate presence of God. His feast day is January 23.

In addition to these, another pre-Reformation movement toward renewal might also be remembered. Blessed John Ruysbroek, "the ecstatic Doctor," who joined the Friends of God with the Brethren of the Common Life, was born in 1293, probably of German parents in the village of Ruysbroek between Brussels and Hal. He was ordained a priest about 1317. After a long and diligent pastorate, he retired at the age of fifty to the a hermitage at Grönendaal near Brussels and gave himself to meditation and writing. He died in 1381. He had influenced Tauler and later helped found the Brethren of the Common Life. He was beatified by the Roman Catholic Church in 1908; his feast day is December 2, and he is listed on that date by the German *Evangelical Calendar of Names.*

Geert (Gerard) Groote, a Dutch reformer, was born at Deventer in the Netherlands in 1340. He excelled as a student, but after a spiritual experience, he went into retirement to prepare for a different life. In 1379 he was licensed as an itinerant lay preacher in the diocese of Brussels and was noted for the simplicity both of his dress and his message. He founded the Brethren of the Common Life, which emphasized reading the Bible and included both clerical and lay members, who cultivated a biblical piety, stressing the inner life and the practice of virtues. Their spirituality was known as the *devotio moderna* and was influential in both Catholic and Protestant traditions of prayer. Erasmus was one of their pupils. Groote died in 1384. He is remembered on the *Evangelical Calendar of Names* on August 21.

See also Thomas à Kempis (July 24).

APRIL

FOR FURTHER READING

Clark, Anne L., trans. *Elizabeth of Schönau: The Complete Works.* New York: Paulist, 2000.

Colledge, Edmund, and Bernard McGinn, trans. *Meister Eckhart. The Essential Sermons, Commentaries, Treatises, and Defense.* New York: Paulist, 1981.

Davies, Oliver, ed. *Meister Eckhart: Selected Writings.* New York: Penguin, 1995.

Hoffman, Bengt, trans. *The Theologica Germanica of Martin Luther.* New York: Paulist, 1980.

Jones, Rufus M. *The Flowering of Mysticism: The Friends of God in the Fourteenth Century.* New York, 1939.

McGinn, Bernard, et al., eds. *Meister Eckhart: Teacher and Preacher.* New York: Paulist, 1986.

Shrady, Maria, trans. *Johannes Tauler: Sermons.* New York: Paulist, 1985.

Tobin, Frank, trans. *Henry Suso: The Exemplar, with Two German Sermons.* Mahwah: Paulist, 1989.

Van Engen, John, trans. *Devotio Moderna: Basic Writings.* Mahwah: Paulist, 1988. (For Groote) Wiseman, James A., trans. *John Ruusbroec: The Spiritual Espousals, the Sparkling Stones, and Other Works* Mahwah: Paulist, 1986.

READING

From Catherine of Siena, *A Treatise on Divine Providence*

[God is speaking.] Dearest daughter, the willing desire to bear every pain and fatigue, even unto death, for the salvation of souls is very pleasing to me. The more the soul endures, the more she shows that she loves me; loving me, she comes to know more of my truth, and the more she knows, the more pain and intolerable grief she feels at the offenses committed against me. You asked me to sustain you and to punish the faults of others in you, and you did not recognize that you were really asking for love, light, and knowledge of the truth, since I have already told you that with the increase of love, grief and pain increase; for whoever grows in love grows in grief. Therefore I say to you all, ask, and it will be given to you, for I deny nothing to anyone who asks of me in truth. Remember that the love of divine charity is in the soul so closely joined with perfect patience, that neither can leave the soul without the other. Therefore, if the soul choose to love me, she should choose to endure pains for me in whatever way or circumstance I may send them to her. Patience cannot be proved in any other way than by suffering, and patience is one with love. Therefore bear yourselves with courage, for, unless you do, you will not prove yourselves to be spouses of my truth and faithful children nor part of the company of those who relish the taste of my honor and the salvation of souls.

Trans. PHP, based on the translation of Algar Thorold, *The Dialogue of the Seraphic Virgin, Catherine of Siena . . . ,* new and abridged from the 1896 London edition (Westminster, Md.: Newman, 1944); and reprinted in *Late Medieval Mysticism,* ed. Ray C. Petry, Library of Christian Classics 13 (Philadelphia: Westminster, n.d.), 277–78.

PROPERS

Everlasting God, you so kindled the flame of holy love in the heart of blessed Catherine of Siena, as she meditated on the passion of your Son our Savior, that she devoted her life to the poor and the sick, and to the peace and unity of the Church: Grant that we also may share in the mystery of Christ's death, and rejoice in the revelation of his glory; who lives and reigns with you and the Holy Spirit, one God, now and forever.

RS, rev. LFF

Readings:	Psalm 36:5-10 *or* 16:5-11
	1 John 1:5—2:2
	Luke 10:38-42 (RC) *or* Luke 12:22-24, 29-31
Hymn of the Day:	
	"Love divine, all loves excelling" (H82 657, LBW 315, LSB 700, ELW 631)
Prayers:	For a desire to imitate the love of Christ
	For all women in the church and for their ministry
	For regular and devout communicants
	For a willingness to endure suffering with Christ
	For social workers
	For peace and reconciliation within families, neighborhoods, the nations
Preface:	A Saint (2) (BCP)
Color:	White

Nisan 27 on the Jewish calendar

Late April or early May on the Gregorian calendar

APRIL

Yom Hashoah (or Yom HaShoah), the remembrance Day of the Holocaust, is observed by the Jews on the 27th of the lunar month Nisan, the anniversary of the uprising in the Warsaw Ghetto. The date, after the celebration of Passover but within the time of the Warsaw Uprising and also the anniversary of the liberation of the death camp at Buchenwald (27 Nisan 5705 = 10 April 1945), was set aside by the Israeli Knesset on April 12, 1951, as a day of mourning for the victims of the Holocaust. The *Lutheran Book of Worship* (p. 39) notes the desirability of the observance of the day by Christians as well as Jews. On the Gregorian calendar in common use, 27 Nisan falls in the latter part of April or early May. It may be necessary for Christians to move the observance to a later date when it falls during Easter Week. *Lesser Feasts and Fasts 2006* of the Episcopal Church has added, on April 24, Genocide Remembrance Day.

FOR FURTHER READING

Dawidowicz, Lucy. *The War against the Jews.* London: Weidenfeld and Nicholson, 1977.

Friedlander, Henry. *The Origins of Nazi Genocide: From Euthanasia to the Final Solution*. Chapel Hill: University of North Carolina Press, 1996.

Gilbert, Martin. *The Holocaust: A History of the Jews of Europe during the Second World War*. New York: Holt, Rinehart and Winston, 1986.

Hellman, Peter, text. *The Auschwitz Album: A Book Based on an Album Discovered by a Concentration Camp Survivor, Lili Meier*. New York: Random House, 1981.

Hilberg, Raul. *The Destruction of the European Jews*. Rev. and definitive ed. 3 vols. New York: Holmes and Meier, 1985.

Wyman, David S. *The Abandonment of the Jews: America and the Holocaust 1941–1945*. New York: Pantheon, 1984.

Yahail, Leni. *The Holocaust: The Fate of European Jewry, 19391945*. Trans. Ina Friedman and Haya Galai. New York: Oxford University Press, 1991.

READING

See the Holy Innocents (December 28)

PROPERS

Almighty God, in penitence we come before you, acknowledging the sin that is within us. We share the guilt of those who, bearing the name Christian, slay their fellow human beings because of race or faith or nation. Whether killing or standing silent while others kill, we crucify our Lord anew. Forgive us and change us by your love, that your Word of hope may be heard clearly throughout the world; through your Son, Jesus Christ our Lord.

LBW, ELW

Readings:	Nehemiah 1:4-11a
	Psalm 6
	1 John 1:5-2:2
	Luke 15:11-32
Hymn of the Day:	
	"When in the hour of deepest need" (LBW 303, LSB 615)
Prayers:	For a remembrance of the Holocaust so that it will never happen again
	For the Jewish people that they remain faithful to the ancient covenant
	For tolerance and understanding
	For an appreciation of the rich fabric of human society
Preface:	Lent (LBW/ELW) or Weekdays
Color:	Violet

May 1

St. Philip and St. James, Apostles

The Fourth Gospel provides what information we have about Philip. He was born in Bethsaida, the same fishing village on the shores of Galilee from which Peter and Andrew came. He was among the first disciples, who, after Jesus found him, found Nathanael (sometimes identified with Bartholomew; see August 24) and brought him to Jesus (John 1:43-51). Apart from his own calling, the story of Nathanael, and his inclusion in the lists of the apostles, the only other incidents of Philip's life recorded in the Gospels are the time Jesus asked Philip how they would be able to feed the crowds (John 6:5-7), the occasion when some Greeks came to him (Philip is a Greek name) to ask his help in arranging an interview with Jesus (John 12:20-22), and his role in one of Jesus' major discourses (John 14:8-9).

According to tradition, Philip, after Pentecost, went first to Scythia on the north coast of the Black Sea to preach the gospel, where he was remarkably successful, and then to Phrygia (in modern Turkey), where he remained until his death. He is said to have met his death in the town of Hierapolis in Phrygia, according to some accounts by crucifixion and stoning. Traditions also tell of Philip's two unmarried daughters who survived him, lived to an old age, and were also buried in Hierapolis.

Philip the Apostle is represented in iconography by a Latin or sometimes a Tau cross, an emblem of his crucifixion, and two loaves of bread, recalling the miracle of the feeding of the five thousand (John 6:5-6).

Philip the Apostle is not to be confused with the Philip who with Stephen was a deacon in the Jerusalem church (Acts 6:5) and who is sometimes called Philip the Evangelist (see October 11).

James the son of Alphaeus is usually called James the Less (meaning either "short" or "younger"; the title derives from Mark 15:40) to distinguish him from James the Elder, the brother of John, who is commemorated July 25, and from James of Jerusalem, the brother of the Lord, who is commemorated October 23. The only certain reference to James the Less in Scripture is the inclusion of his name in the apostolic lists. James the son of Alphaeus may be the James whose mother Mary was one of those present at the crucifixion (Matt. 27:55-56 and Mark 15:40) and who had a brother named Joseph or, in the Greek form of the name, Joses.

The iconographical symbol of James the Less is a saw with which he is said by some traditions to have been dismembered or a fullers club with which, according to other accounts, he was beaten to death.

May 1 has been kept as the feast day of St. Philip and St. James since *ca.* 560 when on May 1 the supposed remains of the two saints were interred in the new Church of the Holy Apostles in Rome. The church was rebuilt in the fifteenth, sixteenth, and eighteenth centuries; the main altarpiece, the largest picture in Rome, is the Martyrdom of Saints Philip and James by Domenico Muratori (1661–1744).

To acknowledge the twentieth-century dedication of May 1 to labor and the working classes, Pope Pius XII in 1955 made May 1 the Feast of St. Joseph the Worker, and shifted the feast of Philip and James to May 11; the present Roman calendar (1969) moved the commemoration of the two apostles to May 3, closer to the original date. Lutherans and Anglicans have retained the traditional date. In the Eastern Churches the two apostles are commemorated separately. St. Philip's Day is November 14, and St. James the son of Alphaeus is remembered on October 9.

READING

From *The Saints in Daily Christian Life* by Romano Guardini

If we were to probe a little further . . . we would be able to recognize the outlines of the figure of a new type of saint. It is no longer a man or woman who does exceptional things, but simply one who does what every man or woman who wishes to act well in a given situation will do. No more. No less.

To desire these things: that is true love. And in that love, let us repeat, there are limitless possibilities: that of a truth which is always to be more complete, of good always to be made more pure, of action always to be more resolute. To see in these beginnings the all of which our Lord speaks: all of the heart, all of the soul, all of the strength; to be able to see all in these humble beginnings: it is that in which sanctity consists. And this sanctity grows in the continuing struggles against oneself: in the necessary renunciations, in the challenging effort toward an ever purer sincerity of spirit and intention.

Sanctity nourished in this way is less and less an obvious thing. One could almost say that this is a deliberately hidden sanctity: one that hides its greatness, one that does things of lesser and lesser importance *rightly*; but by that fact they become of greater and greater significance.

The saint will no longer be characterized by extraordinary behavior (as the historian, say, understands it); he will no longer appear to the world as separated from his fellow men or above them. On the contrary, he will be doing the same thing as everyone else: what needs to be done, what is right and just. But he will join to his behavior a purity of intention more and more deeply united to a great love of God; more and more detached from selfishness and self-satisfaction.

Romano Guardini, *The Saints in Daily Christian Life* (Philadelphia and New York: Chilton, 1966), 56–58, 61, 67–68.

PROPERS

Almighty God, who gave to your apostles Philip and James grace and strength to bear witness to the truth: Grant that we, being mindful of their victory of faith, may glorify in life and death the Name of our Lord Jesus Christ; who lives and reigns with you and the Holy Spirit, one God, now and forever.

1979 BCP; rev. in ELW

Readings:	Isaiah 30:18-21
	Psalm 119:33-40
	2 Corinthians 4:1-6
	John 14:6-14
Hymn of the Day:	
	"You are the way; through you alone" (LBW 464, LSB 526, ELW 758, H82 457)
Prayers:	For strength to follow Christ the way
	For grace to know the truth in Christ
	For courage to live the life of Christ
	For all laborers and workers
Preface:	Apostles
Color:	Red

May 2

Athanasius, Bishop of Alexandria, 373

Athanasius, "the Father of Orthodoxy," was the principal champion of Christian orthodoxy against the Arians, who denied the full divinity of the Second Person of the Holy Trinity and who claimed that "there was a time when the Son was not." It is not an exaggeration to say that by his tireless defense of the phrase in the Nicene Creed, "of one Being (*homoousios*) with the Father," he preserved orthodoxy for the Church in the East.

Athanasius was born in Alexandria about 295. Nothing is known of his family. His parents were probably Egyptians, and more than one commentator remarks about the unusual darkness of Athanasius's skin. He received a good education in the classics and in the Christian Scriptures and theology. For a time he seems to have served Antony (see January 17), the founder of Christian monasticism, who had sought increasingly barren and remote places for his spiritual struggle.

About the year 312, Athanasius entered the Alexandrian clergy and was ordained a deacon about 319 by Bishop Alexander. Athanasius accompanied the bishop to the Council of Nicaea in 325 where Arius's views were condemned and the Nicene Creed was written. Alexander, before his death in 328, designated

Athanasius his successor, and the choice was confirmed by the Egyptian bishops. The new bishop made extensive pastoral visits to the entire Egyptian province, but he faced vicious attacks by the numerous schismatics who had opposed his selection as bishop.

Athanasius was summoned to the Council of Tyre in 335, which found him guilty of a number of charges, but since the council was composed almost entirely of his enemies, he appealed directly to the emperor Constantine, who had him exiled to northern Gaul. When Constantine died in 337, his son allowed Athanasius to resume his episcopal duties, but at the Synod of Antioch in 337 or 338 he was deposed. This time Athanasius appealed to Rome with the support of other victims of anti-Nicene reaction. Pope Julius I convened a synod that declared Athanasius innocent of the charges against him. Since the Eastern bishops refused to accept the verdict, Athanasius remained in the West, traveling through Italy and Gaul.

Eventually Athanasius was allowed to return to Alexandria. He arrived in October 346, welcomed by the ninety-year-old Antony, and enjoyed a decade of relative peace, writing and promoting monasticism. Upon the death of the emperor Constans in 350, however, the enemies of Athanasius renewed their attack upon him, concentrating this time on the West. They got the Council of Arles in 353 and the Council of Milan in 355 to condemn him. In February 356 a detachment of soldiers interrupted a vigil service with the intention of arresting Athanasius, but he managed to escape and for six years went into hiding in the Libyan desert, moving secretly from place to place, supported by loyal monks and clergy who enabled him to make several secret visits to Alexandria. He spent his time writing and keeping in touch with developments in the world.

In 361 a new emperor, Julian the Apostate, set the exiled bishops free. Athanasius returned to Alexandria in February 362 and convened a synod that anathematized Arianism, supported the Nicene Creed, and made room for reconciliation with his opponents. Julian, however, promoted a revival of paganism, and, not interested in a strong Christianity, had Athanasius exiled yet again in October 362. The emperor died the following June, and Athanasius returned to his see. In February 364, the co-emperor Valens resumed the persecution of those opposed to the Arian creed, and yet again Athanasius went into hiding for four months before he was permitted to return to Alexandria, where he remained until his death May 2, 373. During his forty-five-year episcopate he had been exiled five times and had spent altogether seventeen years away from his see.

After Athanasius, Basil the Great, Gregory of Nyssa, and Gregory Nazianzus completed the struggle and secured the final victory of Nicene orthodoxy at the Council of Constantinople in 381.

The writings of this small but dauntless man are mainly polemical but are nonetheless of considerable importance. His *Defense against the Arians* and *The History of the Arians* are the best sources of knowledge about Christianity in the period from 300 to 350. His brilliant pamphlet *On the Incarnation,* written in his youth, and his *Discourse against the Arians* remain among the clearest and most forceful explanations of the unity of the triune God and of the incarnation of Christ. His *Life of St. Antony* was immensely popular and had a wide influence in spreading monastic ideals. Since Alexandria was recognized as having the best astronomers, it was the duty of the Bishop of Alexandria to send soon after the Epiphany each year a Festal or Easter letter announcing the proper date for the beginning of Lent and the celebration of Easter day. In the Easter letter he sent in 367, his thirty-ninth, Athanasius produced the oldest surviving list of the twenty-seven books in the New Testament, although in a different order than in modern Bibles, and declared them to be "the springs of salvation."

In some Lutheran parishes, preserving medieval practice, the creed named after him although not written by him, the Athanasian Creed (*Quicunque vult*) is used on Trinity Sunday. The text of the creed, one of the three ecumenical creeds of Western Christianity, is included in the *Lutheran Book of Worship* and the *Lutheran Service Book* and had appeared previously in *The Lutheran Hymnal* (1941), following German use. The creed had also appeared in earlier editions of the *Book of Common Prayer.*

By his tireless defense of the faith, Athanasius is recognized as one of the four great Greek doctors (that is, teachers) of the church; the others are Basil the Great, John Chrysostom, and Gregory Nazianzus. His feast day in the East, on which he is remembered with Cyril of Alexandria, is January 18. He was added to the Episcopal calendar in the 1979 *Book of Common Prayer*, to the calendar in the *Lutheran Book of Worship*, and the Methodist calendar in *For All the Saints.*

FOR FURTHER READING

Anatolios, Khaled. *Athanasius: The Coherence of His Thought.* New York: Routledge, 1998.

Barnes, Timothy D. *Athanasius and Constantinus: Theology and Politics in the Constantinian Empire.* Cambridge: Harvard University Press, 2001.

Von Campenhausen, Hans. *The Fathers of the Greek Church.* 67–79. Trans. Stanley Godman (New York: Pantheon, 1959).

Cross, Frank L. *The Study of St. Athanasius.* Oxford, 1945.

Kelly, J. N. D. *Early Christian Creeds.* 3d ed. London: Longmans, 1972.

———. *The Athanasian Creed.* New York: Harper & Row, 1972.

Pelikan, Jaroslav. *The Light of the World.* New York: Harper & Row, 1962.

READING

From Athanasius *On the Incarnation* (6, 8, 54)

Death having gained upon us and corruption abiding upon us, the human race was perishing; the rational creature made in God's image was disappearing, and the handiwork of God was in process of dissolution. . . . So, since the rational

MAY

creatures were wasting into ruin, what was God in his goodness to do? Allow corruption to prevail against them and let death hold them fast? What then would be the point of making them in the first place? It would be far better had they not been made than, once made, be left to neglect and ruin. For neglect reveals weakness and not goodness on God's part should he allow his own work to be ruined—more so than if he had never made human beings at all. For had he not made them, no one could attribute weakness to him, but once he had made them, creating them out of nothing, it would be monstrous for that work to be ruined, especially before the eyes of the creator. It was then out of the question to abandon mortals to the current of corruption because this would be unseemly and unworthy of God's goodness.

Therefore the incorporeal and incorruptible and immaterial Word of God comes to our realm, even though he was not far from us before. For no part of creation is without him; he has filled everything everywhere, yet remains present with his Father. Nonetheless, in condescension he comes to show mercy to us and to visit us. And seeing the race of rational creatures on their way to perish and death reigning over them by corruption . . . he took pity on our race, had mercy on our weakness, condescended to our corruption, and . . . takes for himself a body—a body no different from ours. . . . And . . . he handed it over in death in the stead of all and in mercy offered it to the Father.

If one should wish to see God, who by his nature is invisible, one may know and apprehend him in his works. Likewise, those who fail to see Christ with their understanding can at least apprehend him by the works of his body and test whether they are human works or divine. If they are human, let them scoff; but if they are not human but divine, let them recognize it and not laugh at what is no scoffing matter but rather let them marvel that by so ordinary a means things divine have been manifested to us and that by death immortality has reached us all, and that by the Word becoming flesh the universal providence has been known and its giver and maker the very Word of God. For he was made human that we might be made God; and he manifested himself by a body that we might receive the idea of the unseen Father; and he endured the insolence of mortals that we might inherit immortality. . . . And wherever one turns one's glance, one may behold the divinity of the Word and be struck with exceedingly great awe.

Trans. PHP, based on the translation of Archibald Robertson in the Library of Christian Classics III, *Christology of the Later Fathers,* ed. Edward Rochie Hardy (Philadelphia: Westminster, n.d.), 60–62, 107–08.

PROPERS

O God of truth, you raised up your servant Athanasius to be a courageous defender of the truth of Christ's divinity: Strengthen us by his teaching to maintain and proclaim boldly the Catholic faith against all opposition, trusting solely in the grace of your eternal Word, who took upon himself our humanity that we might share his divinity; who lives and reigns with you and the Holy Spirit, one God, now and forever.

PHP, 1950 Ambrosian Missal, RS ✚ LFF

Readings:	Psalm 71:1-8 *or* 112:1-9
	1 John 5:1-5
	Matthew 10:22-32
Hymn of the Day:	
	"Father, most holy, merciful and tender" (LBW 169, LSB 504, ELW 415)
	or "Holy, holy, holy Lord God of hosts, eternal King" (H40 270, SBH 135) to the tune *St. Athanasius*
Prayers:	For a deeper knowledge of Jesus Christ as the Son of God
	For tireless pursuit of the truth, even when the majority opposes
	For single-minded devotion
	For reconciliation between quarreling parties in the church
	For those who do not believe in the divinity of Christ
Preface:	Christmas (because Athanasius taught of the incarnation) or the Epiphany (LFF)
Color:	White

May 4

Monica (Monnica) is remembered on this date in the *Book of Common Prayer*, in the *Lutheran Book of Worship*, and in *Evangelical Lutheran Worship*; see August 27.

The *Lutheran Service Book* has introduced on this date the commemoration of **Friedrich Conrad Dietrich Wyneken** (1810–1876), a pastor and missionary who with C. F. W. Walther and Wilhelm Sihler founded what was to become the Lutheran Church—Missouri Synod. Wyneken was born in Germany, studied at Göttingen and Halle, and came to America in 1838. Under the auspices of the Ministerium of Pennsylvania he, like Father Heyer (see November 7) served as a "traveling missionary" and was a pastor in Baltimore and then Fort Wayne, Indiana.

MAY

May 5

The *Lutheran Service Book* commemorates on this date **Frederick III, the Wise** (1463–1525), Elector of Saxony, who founded the University of Wittenberg in 1502, protected Luther in the Wartburg Castle in 1521, and supported Lutheran changes in Wittenberg.

May 6

The Eastern Church on this date commemorates *Job the Longsuffering*. The calendar in the *Lutheran Service Book* (2006) lists Job on May 9.

May 7

The *Lutheran Service Book*, following *Lutheran Worship* (1982), on this date commemorates *Carl Ferdinand Wilhelm Walther* (1811–1887). He graduated from the University of Leipzig and in 1839 sailed with the Saxon immigrants to America. He was a pastor in St. Louis and professor and president of Concordia Seminary there from 1850 until his death. He was president of the German Evangelical Lutheran Synod of Missouri, Ohio, and Other States (now the Lutheran Church—Missouri Synod) from its founding in 1847 until 1850; he was succeeded by Friedrich Wyneken (see May 4) for fourteen years, and again was president from 1864 to 1868. Walther died on this date in 1887.

May 8

Dame Julian of Norwich, Anchoress, *ca.* 1417

Very little is known about the woman called Julian of Norwich except what she tells us in her writings. The name by which she is known may have been adopted when she became an anchoress in a cell attached to St. Julian's Church in Norwich. An anchoress (a male is called an anchorite) is a religious recluse confined to an enclosure, which she vowed never to leave. At the time of such enclosing the burial service was read signifying that the person enclosed was dead to the world and that the enclosure corresponded to a grave. The purpose of such confinement was to pursue without distraction the contemplative life.

Fifteen of Julian's visions, which she calls "showings," direct experiences of God's goodness, occurred in a five-hour period on May 13, 1373 (a sixteenth vision occurred on the next day) when she was "thirty year old and a half." The book in which these revelations are recorded is preserved in a long and a short version. The short version was written soon after the visions; the longer version was a product of more than fifteen years of meditation on their meaning. The mystical experiences were never repeated, but through constant study and contemplation they acquired greater clarity, richness, and profundity. Julian's interpretations of the visions derive from orthodox theology of her time but are colored by her own individual experience. One of her favorite adjectives is "homely," signifying the easy intimacy and familiarity of being at home. The book reveals Julian's extensive knowledge of the Bible and familiarity with medieval religious writings in English and in Latin. She draws upon, among other things, the anonymous fourteenth-century work *Cloud of Unknowing* and the early thirteenth-century rule for anchoresses, *Ancren Riule.* Her book is set out in accomplished Middle English prose, remarkable for its brilliant transformations of images drawn from everyday experiences. Julian, Evelyn Underhill observes, is "the first English woman of letters."

Although a recluse, Dame Julian was sought out for spiritual counsel, notably by the noted mystic Margery Kempe (*ca.* 1373–1438), who describes the meeting in a memorable passage in her autobiography, *The Book of Margery Kempe.*

Dame Julian was introduced to a wider audience by phrases used by T. S. Eliot in section III of the last of his *Four Quartets,* "Little Gidding": "Sin is behovely [inevitable], but / All shall be well / And all manner of thing shall be well."

From "Little Gidding", in *Collected Poems 1909-1962* by T. S. Eliot, © 1963 by Harcourt, Inc., copyright © 1964, 1963 by T. S. Eliot, reprinted by permission of the publishers of Harcourt Inc. and Faber and Faber Ltd.

Julian, whose name is sometimes given as Juliana, died about the year 1417.

Her commemoration was added to the Episcopal calendar in the 1979 *Book of Common Prayer,* to the Lutheran calendar in *Evangelical Lutheran Worship,* and to the Methodist calendar in *For All the Saints.*

FOR FURTHER READING

Bynum, Caroline Walker. *Jesus as Mother: Studies in the Spirituality of the High Middle Ages.* Berkeley: University of California Press, 1984.

Chambers, P. Franklin. *Juliana of Norwich.* New York: Harper, 1955.

Hummel, Jennifer P. *"God Is Our Mother": Julian of Norwich and the Medieval Image of Feminine Divinity.* Salzburg: Institute for English and American Studies, 1982.

Julian of Norwich. *Showings.* Trans. Edmund Colledge and James Walsh. New York: Paulist, 1978.

———. *Revelations of Divine Love.* Trans. Clifton Wolters. New York: Penguin, 1980.

Molinari, Paul. *Julian of Norwich: The Teaching of a Fourteenth-century English Mystic.* New York: Longmans, 1958.

Pelphrey, Brant. *Christ Our Mother: Julian of Norwich.* Wilmington: Glazier, 1989.

———. *Love Was Its Meaning: The Theology and Mysticism of Julian of Norwich.* Salzburg: Institute for English and American Studies, 1982.

White, Hugh, ed. *Ancrene Wisse: Guide for Anchoresses.* New York: Penguin, 1994.

READING

From *Revelations of Divine Love* by Julian of Norwich

A mother's is the most intimate, willing, and dependable of all services, because it is the truest of all. None has been able to fulfill it properly but Christ, and he alone

MAY

can. We know that our own mother's bearing of us was a bearing to pain and death, but what does Jesus, our true Mother, do? Why, he, All-love, bears us to joy and eternal life! Blessings on him! Thus he carries us within himself in love. And he is in labour until the time has fully come for him to suffer the sharpest pangs and most appalling pain possible—and in the end he dies. And not even when this is over, and we ourselves have been born to eternal bliss, is his marvelous love completely satisfied. This he shows in that overwhelming word of love, 'If I could possibly have suffered more, indeed I would have done so.'

He might die no more, but that does not stop him working, for he needs to feed us . . . it is an obligation of his dear, motherly, love. The human mother will suckle her child with her own milk, but our beloved Mother, Jesus, feeds us with himself, and, with the most tender courtesy, does it by means of the Blessed Sacrament, the precious food of all true life. And he keeps us going through his mercy and grace by all the sacraments. This is what he meant when he said, 'It is I whom Holy Church preaches and teaches.' In other words, 'All the health and life of sacraments, all the virtue and grace of my word, all the goodness laid up for you in Holy Church—it is I.' The human mother may put her child tenderly to her breast, but our tender mother Jesus simply leads us into his blessed breast through his open side, and there gives us a glimpse of the Godhead and heavenly joy—the inner certainty of heavenly bliss.

Julian of Norwich, *Revelations of Divine Love,* chap. 60, trans. Clifton Wolters (Baltimore: Penguin, 1966), 169–70.

PROPERS

Lord God, in your compassion you granted to the Lady Julian many revelations of your nurturing and sustaining love: Move our hearts, like hers, to seek you above all things, for in giving us yourself you give us all; through Jesus Christ our Lord, who lives and reigns with you and the Holy Spirit, one God, forever and ever.

Dame Julian, *Chain of Prayer*, CMG; LFF

Readings:	Psalm 27:5-11 *or* 103:1-4, 13-18
	Hebrews 10:19-24
	John 4:23-26
Hymn of the Day:	
	"Take my life and let it be consecrated, Lord, to thee" (H82 707, LBW 406, LSB 783, 784, ELW 685)
Prayers:	For love
	For all who are leading a life of solitary communion with God
	For the continuing enrichment of the church by the presence and prayers of visionaries
	Of thanksgiving for all who by their teaching and example have witnessed to the centrality of prayer
Preface:	The Epiphany
Color:	White

May 9

Nicolaus Ludwig, Count von Zinzendorf, 1760

Nicolaus Ludwig, Count of Zinzendorf (1700–1760), bears a relationship to the Lutheran Church not unlike the relationship of the Wesleys to the Church of England. Moreover, because John Wesley's profound religious experience arose out of his contact with the Moravians, Zinzendorf may be commemorated in conjunction with the commemoration of the Wesleys, March 2.

Zinzendorf, founder of the Herrnhuter "Brüdergemeinde" or Moravian Brethren, was born at Dresden into a noble Austrian Lutheran family with Pietistic leanings and was trained at Halle, the center of Pietism, and at Wittenberg University. After his graduation, he traveled to the Netherlands and France, married Erdmuth Dorothea von Reuss, and assumed his duties in the court of King August the Strong of Saxony. His real interest, however, lay in evangelization. He opened his home to Protestant emigrants from Austria, many of whom were descended from the Bohemian Brethren. In 1727 he resigned his government post to care for the growing colony, called Herrnhut, "the Lord's watch." His intense piety and his work were not welcome in the Lutheran Church of the time, but his beliefs were examined and approved by Lutheran theologians in 1734. Two years later he was exiled from Saxony until he was permitted to return in 1747. During and after his exile, he founded communities in the Baltic provinces, the Netherlands, England, the West Indies, and North America.

In 1737 Zinzendorf was consecrated a bishop in the Church of the Czech Brethren, a continuation of the *Unitas Fratrum* (Unity of the Brethren) begun by the followers of John Hus three centuries before, and which, because so much of its early history centered in the province of Moravia, became known as the Moravian Church. Zinzendorf sent out more than two hundred missionaries, and their influence throughout the world was enormous. He was a hymnwriter, whose hymns are still sung in churches of many denominations. His piety was not only intensely personal; he also had a deep concern for social justice. Zinzendorf died at Herrnhut May 9, 1760. At the time of his death, there were active missions from one end of the earth to the other, from Greenland to South Africa.

MAY

FOR FURTHER READING

Freeman, Arthur J. *Nicholas Ludwig von Zinzendorf.* Bethlehem: Moravian Church in America, 1998.

Lewis, Arthur J. *Zinzendorf: The Ecumenical Pioneer.* Philadelphia: Westminster, 1962.

Weinlick, John R. *Count Zinzendorf.* New York and Nashville: Abingdon, 1956.

READING

From a confession of faith presented to the theological faculty of Tübingen University, December 18, 1734

I was but ten years old when I began to direct my companions to Jesus, as their Redeemer. My deficiency in knowledge was compensated by sincerity. Now I am thirty-four, and though I have made various experiences, yet in the main my mind has undergone no change. My zeal has not cooled. I reserve to myself liberty of conscience; it agrees with my internal call to the ministry. Yet, I am not a freethinker. I love and honor the [established] church, and shall frequently seek her counsels. I will continue as heretofore, to win souls for my precious Savior, to gather his sheep, bid guests, and hire servants for him. More especially I shall continue, if the Lord please, to devote myself to the service of that congregation whose servant I became in 1727. Agreeably to her orders, under her protection, enjoying her care, and influenced by her spirit, I shall go to distant nations, who are ignorant of Jesus and of redemption in his blood. I shall endeavor to imitate the labors of my brethren, who have the honor of being the first messengers to the heathen. I will prove all things by the only criterion of evangelical doctrine, the Holy Scriptures. Among the brethren at Herrnhut and elsewhere I shall endeavor to maintain their ancient church discipline. The love of Christ shall constrain me, and his cross refresh me. I will cheerfully be subject to the higher powers, and a sincere friend to my enemies. . . . I am poor and needy, yet the Lord thinketh upon me. He shall deliver the poor and needy.

From *Ancient and Modern History of the Brethren*, 237, quoted in John R. Weinlick, *Count Zinzendorf* (New York and Nashville: Abingdon, 1956), 119–20.

PROPERS

Lord Jesus Christ, your death for us and your own holiness will be our clothing when we stand before your dread judgment seat: In your mercy grant that we, taught by your servant Bishop Zinzendorf, may hold fast in faith to your saving sacrifice for us, and ever rejoice in your love for the world; for you live and reign with the Father and the Holy Spirit, one God, now and forever.

PHP

Readings: Jeremiah 4:1-10
             Psalm 46
             1 Corinthians 3:11-23
             Mark 10:35-45
Hymn of the Day:
             "Jesus, still lead on" (LBW 341, LSB 718, ELW 624)

Prayers:	For a deeper knowledge of Christ and his benefits
	For missionaries
	For the Moravian Church
Preface:	Baptism (BCP, LBW)
Color:	White

ALSO ON MAY 9

Gregory of Nazianzus is commemorated on this date in the *Book of Common Prayer*. See June 14.

May 18

Erik, King of Sweden, Martyr, 1160

Erik was a twelfth-century king known for his crusades to spread Christianity in Scandinavia. As Erik IX Jedvardsson, he ruled over a considerable part of Sweden from about 1150 until his death a decade later. According to the *Legend of St. Erik*, dating from *ca.* 1270, Erik made an expedition to conquer and Christianize Finland, probably in 1155, accompanied by Henry of Uppsala (later St. Henry, see January 19), who founded the Church in Finland. Erik was a man of great personal goodness, who instituted salutary laws, helped the poor, and showed concern for the sick and infirm.

There are many stories of his crusades and of his murder in the church of Old-Uppsala on May 18, 1160 or 1161, at the hands of a pagan Danish prince, reinforced by rebels against Erik's rule. It was the day after Ascension Day. During Mass, Erik was told that a Danish army was close by. He is said to have replied, "Let us at least finish the sacrifice; the rest of the feast I shall keep elsewhere." The conspirators rushed upon him as he left the church and beheaded him.

As early as the end of the twelfth century, a calendar from the diocese of Uppsala mentions Erik as a saint (there was no formal canonization). National pride and independence mingled with religious memories. Erik's son Cnut encouraged the honor of his father to help strengthen his own position. At the same time Sweden was struggling to establish a separate archbishopric, and in 1164 a Swedish archbishop had been installed in Old-Uppsala. Soon afterward, not to be outdone by Norway and its St. Olaf (see July 29), Sweden had its own patron saint. In 1273 Erik's body was placed in the cathedral at Uppsala, and during the turmoil of the Reformation his relics were not disturbed; the silver reliquary in which his remains still rest dates from the 1570s. Erik was honored as the ancestor of a line of Swedish kings and came to be recognized as the principal patron of Sweden. He

MAY

is honored not only in Sweden (where his image appears on coins) but in Finland, Denmark, and Norway as well. He was added to the calendar in the *Lutheran Book of Worship* (1978).

FOR FURTHER READING

Oakley, Steward. *A Short History of Sweden.* New York: Praeger, 1966.

READING

From *The Imitation of Christ* by Thomas à Kempis

Jesus has many who love his Kingdom in Heaven, but few who bear his Cross. He has many who desire comfort, but few who desire suffering. He finds many to share his feast, but few his fasting. All desire to rejoice with him, but few are willing to suffer for his sake. Many follow Jesus to the Breaking of Bread, but few to the drinking of the Cup of his Passion. Many admire his miracles, but few follow him in the humiliation of his Cross. Many love Jesus as long as no hardship touches them. Many praise and bless him, as long as they are receiving any comfort from him. But if Jesus withdraw himself, they fall to complaining and utter dejection.

They who love Jesus for his own sake, and not for the sake of comfort for themselves, bless him in every trial and anguish of heart, no less than in the greatest joy. And were he never willing to bestow comfort on them, they would still always praise him and give him thanks.

Thomas à Kempis, *The Imitation of Christ*, trans. Leo Sherley-Price (Baltimore: Penguin, 1952), 68–69, 88–89, 83, 206–206, 72. Introduction and Translation copyright 1952 by Leo Sherley-Price. Reprinted by permission of Penguin Books Ltd. .

PROPERS

Lord God, your servant King Erik of Sweden reflected your transforming gospel in his own character and in his concern for the poor, the sick, and the infirm: Give to the leaders of the nations, we pray, such reverence for you and such an awareness of their duty toward the least members of society, that they may ever work selflessly for justice and for the good of all people; through your Son, Jesus Christ our Lord, who lives and reigns with you and the Holy Spirit, one God, now and forever. PHP

Readings: Micah 6:6-8
           Psalm 9:1-10
           1 Corinthians 1:26-31
           Mark 8:34-38
Hymn of the Day:
           "At the name of Jesus" (LBW 179, LSB 512, ELW 416, H82 435; set to the sprightly Swedish tune *St. Erik*, SBH 430)

Prayers: For the land and government and people of Sweden
              For all who govern
              For a spirit of self-sacrificing service
              For a right relationship between church and state
              For those who struggle with national pride and religious loyalty
Preface: (All) Saints
Color: Red

May 19

Dunstan, Archbishop of Canterbury, 988

Dunstan was born into a West Saxon noble family with royal connections at Baltonborough, Somerset, near Glastonbury, *ca.* 909. He was educated by Irish clerics and joined the household of his uncle Athelm, the Archbishop of Canterbury, and the court of King Athelstan. In 936 he made a private monastic profession to Alphege, the Bishop of Winchester (see April 19), and was ordained. He lived as a hermit near Glastonbury, supporting himself by working as a scribe, embroiderer, and silversmith. In 943, King Edmund, after a narrow escape from death while on a stag hunt, installed Dunstan as abbot of Glastonbury and provided financial support for the abbey. Dunstan introduced the Benedictine Rule, enlarged the buildings, and added to the library.

In 956, having criticized King Edward's conduct, Dunstan was exiled to Mont Blandin in Ghent (modern Belgium), where he became acquainted with continental monasticism. He was recalled to England by King Edgar in 957, and was made Bishop of Worcester, then of London in 959, and in 960 Dunstan was made Archbishop of Canterbury. The collaboration between the king and the archbishop was regarded by later writers as a golden age.

The Church in England had suffered severely during the Viking raids of the previous century, and monasticism seems practically to have disappeared in England by the middle of the tenth century. Its restoration was largely Dunstan's work. Under the aegis of King Edgar, Dunstan, together with Ethelwold (d. 984), Abbot of Abingdon before he became Bishop of Winchester, and Oswald (d. 992), Bishop of Worcester and then Archbishop of York, reestablished monasticism in England along Benedictine lines. The three great leaders of the renewal were deeply influenced by continental reforms that sought independence from lay founders and landlords, better education and discipline among the clergy, a revival of monastic life for women, carefully ordered liturgical worship, and a strict adherence to the Rule of St. Benedict. During the flowering of monasticism, monks occupied several important sees, and the monasteries enjoyed royal protection. In the

MAY

south and the midlands, Dunstan himself seems to have reformed or refounded Malmsbury, Bath, Westminster, and perhaps introduced monks at Canterbury Cathedral. In addition, he built churches, corrected abuses such as the neglect of celibacy by the clergy, encouraged laypeople in their devotions, and deepened the concern for justice. He is said also to have been an expert in metalworking and to have cast bells and made organs. He was a man of wide-ranging interests from books to affairs of court, but his chief fame is the reform of the monasteries, which became centers of religion and culture and provided bishops for England and missionaries for Scandinavia.

He sang his last service on Ascension Day 988 and died two days later, May 19. He is buried near the high altar of his cathedral.

In art, Dunstan is often represented with a pair of tongs. There is a legend that one day, while Dunstan was working in metal making a chalice, the devil, in the guise of a beautiful maiden, came to torment him. Dunstan turned, recognized him, tweaked the devil's nose with tongs hot from the fire, and returned to his work.

FOR FURTHER READING

Dales, Douglas *Dunstan: Saint and Statesman.* Cambridge: Lutterworth, 1988.

Duckett, Eleanor Shipley. *Saint Dunstan of Canterbury.* New York: Macmillan, 1955.

Knowles, David. *The Monastic Order in England.* 2d ed. Cambridge: Cambridge University Press, 1963.

Ramsay, Nigel, Margaret Sparks, and Tim Tatton-Brown, eds. *St. Dunstan: His Life, Times, and Cult.* Rochester, N.Y.: Boydell and Brewer, 1992.

Robinson, J. Armitage. *The Times of St. Dunstan.* Oxford: Clarendon, 1969 [1923].

READING

From *The Silent Life* by Thomas Merton

Let us face the fact that the monastic vocation tends to present itself to the modern world as a problem and as a scandal.

In a basically religious culture, like that of India, or of Japan, the monk is more or less taken for granted. When all society is oriented beyond mere transient quest of business and pleasure, no one is surprised that men should devote their lives to an invisible God. In a materialistic culture, which is fundamentally irreligious, the monk is incomprehensible because he "produces nothing." His life appears to be completely useless. Not even Christians have been exempt from anxiety over this apparent "uselessness" of the monk, and we are familiar with the argument that the monastery is a kind of dynamo which, though it does not "produce" grace, procures this infinitely precious commodity for the world.

The first Fathers of monasticism were concerned with no such arguments, valid though they may be in their proper context. The Fathers did not feel that the search for God was something that needed to be defended. Or rather, they saw that if men did not realize in the first place that God was to be sought, no other defense of monasticism would avail with them.

Is God then to be sought?

The deepest law in man's being is his need for God, for life. God is Life. "In him was life, and the life was the light of men, and the light shineth in the darkness and the darkness comprehendeth it not" (John 1:5). The deepest need of our darkness is to comprehend the light which shines in the midst of it. Therefore God has given us, as His first commandment: "Thou shalt love the Lord thy God with thy whole heart, and with thy whole soul and with all thy strength." The monastic life is nothing but the life of those who have taken the first commandment in deadly earnest, and have, in the words of St. Benedict, "preferred nothing to the love of Christ."

But Who is God? Where is He? Is Christian monasticism a search for some pure intuition of the Absolute? A cult of the supreme Good? A worship of perfect and changeless Beauty? The very emptiness of such abstractions strikes the heart cold. The Holy One, the Invisible, the Almighty is infinitely greater and more real than any abstraction of man's devising. But He has said: "No one shall see me and live" (Exodus 33:20). Yet the monk persists in crying out with Moses: "Show me Thy face" (Exodus 33:13).

The monk, then, is one who is so intent upon the search for God that he is ready to die in order to see Him. That is why the monastic life is a "martyrdom" as well as a "paradise," a life that it at once "angelic" and "crucified."

St. Paul resolves the problem: "God, who commanded the light to shine out of darkness, hath shined in our hearts to give the light of the knowledge of the glory God, in the face of Christ Jesus" (2 Corinthians 4:6).

The monastic life is the rejection of all that obstructs the spiritual rays of this mysterious light. The monk is one who leaves behind the fictions and illusions of a merely human spirituality in order to plunge himself in the faith of Christ. Faith is the light which illumines him in mystery. Faith is the power which seizes upon the inner depths of his soul and delivers him up to the action of the divine Spirit, the Spirit of liberty, the Spirit of love. Faith takes him, as the power of God took the ancient prophets, and "stands him upon his feet" (Ezekiel 2:2) before the Lord. The monastic life is life in the Spirit of Christ, a life in which the Christian gives himself entirely to the love of God which transforms him in the light of Christ.

Excerpt from *The Silent Life* by Thomas Merton. Copyright © 1957 by the Abbey of Our Lady of Gethsemani. Copyright renewed 1985 by the Merton Legacy Trust. Reprinted by permission of Farrar, Straus and Giroux, LLC.

MAY

PROPERS

O God of truth and beauty, you richly endowed your bishop Dunstan with skill in music and the working of metals, and with gifts of administration and reforming zeal: Teach us, we pray, to see in you the source of all our talents, and move us to offer them for the adornment of worship and the advancement of true religion; through Jesus Christ our Lord, who lives and reigns with you and the Holy Spirit, one God, now and forever.

CMG, LFF

Readings:	Psalm 57:6-11 *or* 33:1-5, 20-21
	Sirach (Ecclesiasticus) 44:1-7
	Matthew 24:42-47
Hymn of the Day:	
	"From thee all skill and science flow" (H82, 566, SBH 216)
	or "Let the whole creation cry" (LBW 242, ELW 876)
	or "He who would valiant be" (H82 564, LBW 498); the tune is *St. Dunstan's*
Prayers:	For a deepened commitment to the Christian life
	For god-fearing and wise leaders in church and state
	For monasteries and those who serve God there
	For those who explore the relationship between religion and culture
	For musicians and artists
Preface:	All Saints (LBW, ELW) or the Dedication of a Church (LFF)
Color:	White

May 20

Alcuin, Deacon, Abbot of Tours, 804

Alcuin (AL-kwinn), monk, deacon, teacher, author, friend of Charlemagne, and founder of organized learning in France, was born in Northumberland, England *ca.* 735 and educated at the Cathedral School of York. He was ordained deacon in 770 and became head of the York school. Under Aelberht, Bishop and then Archbishop of York, he visited Rome and the Frankish court and helped create a library at the cathedral where he was librarian and Master of the Schools. In 781 Charlemagne persuaded him to join the court scholars at Aachen (Aix la Chapelle) with primary responsibility to revive education and learning in the Frankish dominions. Alcuin was in England in 786 and from 790 to 793, but he generally resided in France until his death in 804. He withdrew from court life in 796 to become abbot of St. Martin's at Tours. He died there May 19, 804, and was buried in the Church of St. Martin.

His writings include biblical exegesis; a major work on the Trinity; moral and philosophical essays; manuals of grammar, rhetoric, orthography, and mathematics; and poems on a wide variety of subjects. He revised the Roman lectionary and adapted the Gregorian sacramentary for use in Gaul by incorporating elements from the Gelasian sacramentary and composing a series of festal and votive masses.

Alcuin was never canonized by the Roman Catholic Church. He is commemorated on the German Lutheran *Evangelical Calendar of Names* (1962) on the date of his death, May 19, and was added to the Episcopal calendar in the 1979 American *Book of Common Prayer*.

The Alcuin Club, founded in 1897, promotes the study of Christian liturgy and has issued a series of valuable publications.

FOR FURTHER READING

Duckett, Eleanor Shipley. *Alcuin: Friend of Charlemagne.* New York: Macmillan, 1951.

Ellard, Gerald. *Master Alcuin, Liturgist.* Chicago: Loyola, 1956.

Waddell, Helen, ed. and trans. *Medieval Latin Lyrics.* 78–95, 304–06. New York: Norton, 1977.

————, ed. and trans. *More Latin Lyrics.* 146–203. New York: Norton, 1977.

READING

From Notker (Balbulus) of St. Gall, *The Deeds of Charlemagne [Gesta Caroli]*

I must not seem to forget or neglect Alcuin; and will therefore make this true statement about his energy and his deserts: all his pupils without exception distinguished themselves by becoming either holy abbots or bishops. My master Grimald studied the liberal arts under him, first in Gaul and then in Italy. But those who are learned in these matters may charge me with falsehood for saying "all his pupils without exception"; when the fact is that there were in his schools two young men, sons of a miller in the service of the monastery of Saint Columban, who did not seem fit and proper persons for promotion to the command of bishoprics or monasteries; but even these men were, by the influence probably of their teacher, advanced one after the other to the office of minister in the monastery of Bobbio, in which they displayed the greatest energy.

So the most glorious Charles saw the study of letters flourishing throughout his whole realm, but still he was grieved to find that it did not reach the ripeness of the earlier fathers; and so, after superhuman labours, he broke out one day with this expression of his sorrow: "Would that I had twelve clerks so learned in all wisdom and so perfectly trained as were Jerome and Augustine." Then the

MAY

learned Alcuin, feeling himself ignorant indeed in comparison with these great names, rose to a height of daring that no man else attained to in the presence of the terrible Charles, and said, with deep indignation in his mind but none in his countenance, "The Maker of heaven and earth has not many like to those men and do you expect to have twelve?"

The Early Lives of Charlemagne, trans. A. J. Grant (London: Chatto and Windus, 1922), given in Charles W. Jones, ed., *Medieval Literature in Translation* (New York: Longmans, Green and Co., 1950), 172–73.

PROPERS

Almighty God, in a rude and barbarous age you raised up your deacon Alcuin to rekindle the light of learning: Illumine our minds, we pray, that amid the uncertainties and confusions of our own time we may show forth your eternal truth; through Jesus Christ our Lord, who lives and reigns with you and the Holy Spirit, one God, forever and ever.

LFF

Readings:	Psalm 37:3-6, 32-33 *or* 112:1-9
	Ecclesiasticus 39:1-9
	Matthew 13:47-52
Hymn of the Day:	
	"Eternal light, shine in my heart" (H82 465, 466)
Prayers:	For scholars who preserve and pass on the heritage of learning
	For integrity of character in teachers and students
	For those who revise and improve the church's liturgy
Preface:	A Saint (3) (BCP)
Color:	White

May 21

John Eliot, Missionary to the Native Americans, 1690

John Eliot, the apostle to the Native Americans and one of the most remarkable men of seventeenth-century New England, was born in England July 31, 1604, the third of seven children, and was baptized in the parish of St. John the Baptist in Widford, Hertfordshire, August 5. His father owned considerable property. Eliot entered Jesus College, Cambridge, in 1619, and received the B.A. in 1622. He excelled as a student, especially in the classics. He taught for a time in the grammar school at Little Baddow in Essex, where he came under the influence of Thomas Hooker. His religious life began, and he determined to become a clergyman.

He left England aboard the *Lyon* with some Puritan friends and the Winthrop family, whom he served as minister. They reached Boston November 3, 1631. A year later, October 1632, Eliot married Ann (or Hannah) Mumford and was ordained as a "teacher" of the church in Roxbury. Friends from Essex came to Massachusetts and settled in Roxbury, and for sixty years Eliot served as their minister, for forty years their only pastor.

From a captured Long Island Native American Eliot learned of Indian customs and language. In 1646 he first preached to the Indians, in English, at Dorchester Mills and Newton (Noantun). He began regular biweekly preaching and catechization, using the Native language by the summer of 1647. In 1649, inspired by Eliot's work, the first genuine missionary society, "The Company for Propagating the Gospel in New England and Parts Adjacent in North America," was incorporated in England and was a source of financial support. Eliot published *A Primer or Catechism* in 1654, and by 1658 he had translated the Bible into Algonkian, the dialect of the Native people of Massachusetts. The New Testament was printed in Cambridge, Massachusetts, in 1661 and the Old Testament in 1663, the first Bible in any language to be printed in North America. A revised edition was published in 1685. A copy of the "Eliot Indian Bible" in Cambridge, England, is inscribed to his alma mater there, Jesus College.

Eliot established a small Indian college at Cambridge and had hopes of Christianizing all the Native Americans in New England, but recognizing their dislike of being too close to the Europeans, he planned an Indian town in what was then the wilderness in Natick. In 1651 the town was laid out, and several families of "praying Indians" settled there as a self-governing community, free to manage their own affairs under the general laws of Massachusetts. By 1674 there were fourteen such towns with several thousand inhabitants. Each village had a school where Indians learned English and handicrafts to support themselves. Eliot carefully trained Native Americans to be missionaries to their own people, and himself traveled all over New England, encountering some opposition. The first Native American minister, Daniel Takawambpait, was ordained at Natick in 1681. (He might also be remembered on this day.)

The outbreak of King Philip's War in 1675 scattered the praying communities. Ten were never restored, and the remaining four dwindled away.

In the summer of 1680, Jasper Danckaerts, a visiting Dutch Reformed minister, reported in his diary of a visit to Boston.

> July 7th. Sunday. We heard preaching in three churches, by persons who seemed to possess zeal, but no just knowledge of Christianity. The auditors were very worldly and inattentive. The best of the ministers whom we have yet heard is a very old man, named Mr. John Eliot, who has charge of the instruction of the Indians in the Christian religion. He has translated the Bible into their language. After we had

already made inquiries of the Booksellers for this Bible, and there was none to be obtained in Boston, and they told us if one was to be had, it would be from Mr. Eliot, we determined to go on Monday to the village where he resided, and was the minister, called Rocsberry....

July 8th. Monday. We went accordingly, about six o'clock in the morning, to Rocsberry, which is three-quarters of an hour from the city, in order that we might get home early ... and in order that Mr. Eliot might not be gone from home. On arriving at his house, he was not there, and we therefore went to look around the village and the vicinity. We found it justly called Rocsberry, for it was very rocky, and had hills entirely of rocks. Returning to his house, we spoke to him, and he received us politely. As he could speak neither Dutch nor French, and we spoke but little English, we were unable to converse very well; however, partly in Latin, partly in English, we managed to understand each other. He was seventy-seven years old, and had been forty-eight years in these parts. He had learned very well the language of the Indians, who lived about there.

... We enquired how it stood with the Indians, and whether any good fruit had followed his work.

Yes, much, he said, if we meant true conversion of the heart; for they had in various countries, instances of conversion, as they called it, and had seen it amount to nothing at all.... He could only thank God, he continued, and God be praised for it, there were Indians whom he knew, who were truly converted of heart, and whose profession, he believed, was sincere.*

Eliot, who, Perry Miller says, "incarnated the Puritan ideal of saintly piety," wrote prolifically. Among his works were *The Christian Commonwealth* (1659), *Up-Bookum Psalmes* (1663), *The Communion of Churches* (1665), *The Indian Primer* (1669), *The Harmony of the Gospels* (1678). He joined with Richard Mather and Thomas Wilder in the production of the *Bay Psalm Book,* a metrical psalter that was in use for a century.

John Eliot died May 21, 1690, at Roxbury, survived by two of his six children.

He is commemorated on May 21 in the *Lutheran Book of Worship* and on July 21 on the German Lutheran *Evangelical Calendar of Names* (1962). A stained-glass window was dedicated to John Eliot in the Washington National Cathedral and unveiled in April 1956.

FOR FURTHER READING

Beals, Carleton. *John Eliot.* New York: Messner, 1957. Beals gives the date of Eliot's death as May 20.

Miller, Perry, and Thomas H. Johnson, eds. *The Puritans.* Rev. ed. Vol. II, 404–08, 496–511. New York: Harper, 1963.

Russell, Francis. "Apostle to the Indians," *American Heritage* 9, no. 1 (December 1957): 49, 117–19.

Winslow, Ola E. *John Eliot: "Apostle to the Indians."* Boston: Houghton Mifflin, 1968.

* *Journal of Jasper Danckaerts 1679–1689,* trans. Henry C. Murphy (1867), ed. Bartlett Burleigh James and J. Franklin Jameson (New York: Scribner's, 1913).

READING

From *Magnalia Christi Americana* by Cotton Mather

It has been observed, that they who have spoke many considerable things in their *lives* usually speak few at their *deaths*. But it was otherwise with our Eliot, who after much speech of and for God in his lifetime, uttered some things little short of *oracles* on his death-bed, which 'tis a thousand pities they were not more exactly regarded and recorded. . . .

This was the peace in the end of this perfect and upright man; thus was there another star fetched away to be placed among the rest that the third heaven is now enriched with. He had once, I think, a pleasant fear that the old saints of his acquaintance, especially those two dearest neighbors of his, Cotton of Boston, and Mather of Dorchester, which were got safe to heaven before him, would suspect him to be gone the wrong way, because he staid so long behind them. But they are now together with a blessed Jesus, beholding his glory and celebrating the high praises of him that has called them into his marvelous light. Whether heaven was any more heaven to him because of his finding there so many saints, with whom he once had his desirable intimacies, yea, and so many saints which had been the seals of his own ministry in this lower world, I cannot say; but it would be heaven enough unto him, to go unto that Jesus, whom he had loved, preached, served, and in whom he had been long assured, there does all fullness dwell. In that heaven I now leave him. . . . Blessed will be the day, O blessed the day of our arrival to the glorious assembly of spirits, which this great saint is now rejoicing with! . . .

If the dust of dead saints could give us any protection, we are not without it; here is a spot of American soil that will afford a rich crop of it at the resurrection of the just. Poor New-England has been as Glastonbury of old was called, A Burying Place of Saints. But we cannot see a more terrible Prognostick, than tombs filling apace with such bones as those of the renowned Eliot's; the whole building of this country trembles at the fall of such a pillar.

Cotton Mather. *Magnalia Christi Americana,* Book III (London, 1702; reprint, New York: Russell and Russell, 1967), 1:577–79].

MAY

PROPERS

Almighty and everlasting God, we thank you for your devout and earnest servant John Eliot, whom you called to preach the Gospel to the native peoples of New England; and we pray that you would raise up in every land evangelists and heralds of your kingdom, that your Church may proclaim in the language understood by the people the unsearchable riches of our Savior Jesus Christ; who lives and reigns with you and the Holy Spirit, one God, now and forever.

BCP, LBW Common of Missionaries, rev. PHP

Readings: Deuteronomy 32:10-12
                 Psalm 48
                 Romans 10:11-17
                 Luke 24:44-53
Hymn of the Day:
                 "The God of Abraham praise" (LBW 544, LSB 798, ELW 831, H82 401)
Prayers: For justice for the Native Americans
                 For respect for Native American traditions and culture
                 For concern for their welfare
                 For the spirit of prayer
                 For those who teach the church to sing
Preface: The Epiphany
Color: White

May 22

Helena, Mother of Constantine, *ca.* 330

On May 21 *Evangelical Lutheran Worship* has restored an old feast of St. Helen (or Helena); the *Lutheran Service Book* of the Lutheran Church—Missouri Synod, following the Byzantine calendar, commemorates Helen together with her son the emperor Constantine. The feast, originally celebrated August 18, is not on the General Roman Calendar nor on the Episcopal calendar. The Church of England *Christian Year* calendar (1997) commemorates Helena as "Protector of the Holy Places." Wilhelm Löhe's 1868 calendar commemorated Helena on May 22; the German *Evangelical Calendar of Names* (1962) commemorated Constantine the Great on May 21, transferring the date from May 22.

Constantine is honored by the Eastern Church as a saint; his personal conduct, among other things his arranging the murder of his first son, has embarrassed the Western Church.

Flavia Iulia Helena, the mother of Constantine the Great, was born about 255 in Drepanum (changed in 327 in her honor to Helenopolis) on the Nicomedian Gulf in Asia Minor. Her parents were of humble station; Ambrose refers to her as an innkeeper (*stabularia*). She became the wife or concubine of Constantinus Chlorus; their son was born in 274 in Naissus in Upper Moesia. In 292 Constantinus, now co-regent of the West, for political reasons, repudiated her in order to marry the stepdaughter of Emperor Maximianus Herculius, his patron. He died in 308 and was succeeded by his son Constantine, who brought his mother into the imperial court and conferred upon her the title Augusta. Under the influence of her son she became a Christian.

The Roman Empire had a custom of the Imperial *adventus* (from which the church season takes its name), the ceremonial means by which the emperor or his plenipotentiaries made the imperial presence felt even to the most distant of subjects. Within this tradition, in later life the empress Helen made a lengthy visit to the Holy Land, where she expended large sums of money in relief of the poor and other works of mercy and helped found churches on sacred sites connected to the life of Jesus, the Mount of Olives and Bethlehem, and encouraged honoring the site of the crucifixion and burial of Jesus. Since the end of the fourth century her name has been associated by Ambrose and others with the discovery of the cross on which Christ died, which was buried close to the hill of Calvary. Constantine's sole contemporary biographer, Eusebius, is silent on the matter, and the story of Helen's finding the true cross (there had been a feast commemorating this discovery on May 3 on the Roman calendar) is generally regarded as a pious legend.

Her son was with her when she died, at the age of eighty, the historian Eusebius says, about the year 330. Her body was brought to Constantinople and buried in the imperial vault of the Church of the Apostles. It is reported that in 849 her remains were transferred to the Abbey of Hautvillers in the French archdiocese of Rheims, and from this time devotion to her spread.

FOR FURTHER READING

Drijvers, J. W. *Helen Augusta: The Mother of Constantine the Great and the Legend of Her Finding the True Cross.* Leiden: Brill, 1991.

Lenski, Noel, ed. *The Cambridge Companion to the Age of Constantine.* Cambridge: Cambridge University Press, 2005.

READING

From *Holy Week: A Short History* by J. Gordon Davies

. . . [I]t is necessary to have a clear picture of the several churches in Jerusalem which played such an important part in the observances [of the Great and Holy Week].

Most conspicuous among these buildings were those enshrining Golgotha and the tomb of Christ, which were erected on the directions of Constantine. His motive apparently was to make the Holy Land a center of pilgrimage and a means of fostering the unity of Christendom, menaced, as it was, by the Arian heresy. . . . .The principal buildings were set out axially in a long line running from east to west. A great entrance at the former extremity led from the street into an atrium, a forecourt surrounded by colonnades. Out of this opened a five-aisled basilica, later called the Martyrium; it was floored with marble slabs of various colors and had its paneled ceiling overlaid with gold. The sanctuary end of the Martyrium was somewhat unusual and probably consisted of a dome, borne on twelve columns, half of it projecting beyond the west wall and half of it inside. This marked the place where the empress Helena had discovered what was believed to be the true cross. Beyond this building, still moving in a direct line westward, was a second atrium, also surrounded by colonnades, which contained, a little to one side, a small hill, the site of the crucifixion. The space between the Martyrium and this elevation is called *post crucem* by [the Spanish pilgrim] Egeria, while the space between it and the final feature, the Anastasis, is termed *ante crucem*. The Anastasis, or church of the resurrection, contained the tomb; at first this may have been an enclosure open to the sky, but it soon took the form of a rotunda with a wooden dome. To these four elements—atrium, Martyrium, Golgotha, and Anastasis—must be added the baptistery, which in all probability was close to the Anastasis, on its south side, and comprised three chambers, the central one of which enclosed the font.

When these three buildings were dedicated in 335, the new bishop of Jerusalem, Maximus, who was then enthroned, moved his seat to the Martyrium from a previously existing church . . . on the supposed site of the house with the upper room where the Apostles gathered when the Spirit descended.

. . . [On the Mount of Olives] was the Eleona, founded by the empress Helena and the product of considerable engineering skill, having been built upon three levels. A flight of steps led to a great portico, with six columns across the width of the building. Out of this three doors led into the atrium, what had a large cistern in the center. Another flight of steps ascended to the basilica itself, which had three aisles, a projecting apse, and a crypt at the east end which contained a cave wherein Jesus was believed to have delivered his apocalyptic discourse (Mark 13) to His disciples.

J. Gordon Davies, *Holy Week: A Short History* (Richmond: John Knox, 1963), 25–28.

PROPERS

Most loving and faithful God, in honoring the sites of your incarnate Son's birth and Passion you permitted blessed Helen to enrich the memory of your church: In your mercy grant that by the ransom paid on the tree of the cross we may attain eternal life; through the same Jesus Christ our Lord, who lives and reigns with you and the Holy Spirit, one God, now and forever.

PHP, after the Anglican Missal

Readings:	1 Timothy 3:14-16
	Psalm 111
	Luke 23:50-55
Hymn of the Day:	
	"In the cross of Christ I glory" (LBW 104, LSB 427, ELW 324; H82 441,442)
Prayers:	For women abandoned by their husbands
	For Christian families
	For the rulers of the nations

For peace in the Holy Land
For a deeper memory of the history of the faith
Preface: Dedication of a church
Color: White

May 23

Ludwig Ingwer Nommensen, Missionary to Sumatra, 1918

Ludwig Ingwer Nommensen, the apostle to the Bataks, was born February 6, 1834, on the island of Nordstrand in Schleswig-Holstein, which was at that time under the Danish crown. He was a man of deep faith, courage, prophetic vision, and indomitable resolution. He worked for a time as a hired hand and then as an assistant teacher. In 1857 he enrolled in the Barmen missionary school of the Rhenish Missionary Society. On October 4, 1861, he was ordained in the church at Barmen as a missionary to the Batak, and, after a two-month period of language training in Holland, he left on December 24, 1861, for Sumatra to join two German missionaries who had begun work there that year. On June 25, 1862, Nommensen landed at Barus, on the northwest coast and spent the rest of his life on the island. He moved inland, where he labored among the Bataks, a large tribal group then untouched by either Islam or Christianity.

In 1866 he was joined by P. H. Johannsen, a teacher, writer, and linguist. After initial troubles stemming partly from the difficulty of reconciling clan responsibilities and Christian faith, the mission began to succeed, first with the conversion of a number of chiefs and then thousands of their followers. By 1876 the membership reached two thousand. In 1885, to counter the advance of Islam, Nommensen moved northward to the Lake Toba plain. It proved to be a difficult time. His wife and four children died. In 1892 he married again, moved farther north in 1903, but his second wife died in 1909, leaving three children.

Almost from the beginning, the church in Sumatra had a thoroughly Batak flavor. The New Testament had been translated into Batak by 1878. Nommensen sought to preserve the social structure of the village community, and many features of the local customary law were maintained. He introduced a teacher-preacher office to aid in the growth and support of the local churches and their schools and sought missionaries "who take God at his word, who count with God as they count with numbers, and who joining in battle look forward to victory." An indigenous church order was drafted by Nommensen and was in use until 1930.

The Batak Christian community prospered and grew under the benevolent leadership of Nommensen until his death on May 23, 1918. It continued in much the same form until 1940 when the missionaries were interned and the Batak people took over full management of their own church, adopting a church constitution in 1950 and joining the Lutheran World Federation in 1952. The Batak church, which now numbers more than half a million members, presided over by the Ephorus, a bishop of set term, is a living memorial to the vision of Nommensen. In 1952 a monument to him was erected in the Silindung Valley where he had labored; it now includes a bust of the missionary sculpted by an artist from Düsseldorf. In 1954 Nommensen University was founded by the Batak church to serve the educational needs of the area, and in 1961 Christians in Europe and Indonesia celebrated the one hundredth anniversary of the establishment of the church and published a volume of studies in Nommensen's honor. He is commemorated on the *Evangelical Calendar of Names* (1962) and on the calendar in the *Lutheran Book of Worship* (1978). *Evangelical Lutheran Worship* has joined his commemoration to that of Heyer and Ziegenbalg and observes the three missionaries together on November 7.

FOR FURTHER READING

Anderson, Gerald H. *Asian Voices in Christian Theology.* New York: Orbis, 1976. Appendix has the text of the Batak Confession.

Petersen, Lorman M., ed. *"My God Told Me to Stay Here": The Life and Work of Missionary Ludwig Ingwer Nommensen.* Appleton, Wisc.: Privately printed, 2000. Incorporates William B. Nommensen's English translation of John Warneck's *Dr. Ludwig Nommensen: Ein Lebensbild,* 4th ed., 1934.

De Waard, Nellie. *Pioneer in Sumatra.* London: China Inland Mission, 1962.

READING

Nommensen's Covenant Prayer aboard ship to Sumatra

Today, on the 13th day of April, 1862, I renew here in the Indian Ocean the covenant which I made with you, my God and Father, through your Son Jesus Christ. A thousand times I have given you thanks because you have never removed your protective hand from over me because of my faults and sins. More often you have blessed me more than many other people. You have made my ears receptive to the sound of your voice which compels me to give myself entirely over to you for the praise of your Name.

You have chosen, sustained, and taught me from childhood on that I should be a messenger of the Gospel to the heathen. Therefore, I give you in return my life, my time, my body, spirit, and soul as well as all the powers and gifts you have bestowed upon me. If ever I should forsake you, or be led astray by the Devil to forsake your way or commit sin, then torment me day and night. And if I ever should forget your loving-kindness, then strike me with sickness, affliction, and grief until I turn back again and on bended knee implore your grace.

Strengthen my faith in you, increase my love for you and my fellowmen—also for my enemies. Revive my hope to bear with gentleness and patience what I must bear, and thus in humility spend my life with a pure heart and in the fear of God. Help me, Lord, to be faithful both in little things and in big things, that I know you even better just as you have known me that my soul be healed through fellowship with you. Give me your light that I may ever know more clearly what is needful for me and sinners which are not yet freed from the power of Satan.

I herewith renew my covenant to fight against the Devil and his hosts from within and without. I curse every relationship I have ever had with him. Teach me to hate sin. Protect me from my enemies when they become too numerous and too powerful, that they may not deceive me and overcome me. Seal my covenant with you in the heavens just as I have sealed it in my book on this ship. Whether in heaven or in the sea, may your servant and angel, which you have given me, become a fortress around me; all these I present as evidence that I will be completely your possession.

You, the world, and the Devil should know and be convinced that I belong entirely to the Lord Jesus, and that I will protect what belongs to him. O Lord Jesus, you have yourself sealed me to you through your Word and your death on Golgotha. I believe this and say "Amen" to it. I must through my life and death make clear that I have been purchased by you and am your possession. Strengthen me always, receiving approval from you, merciful Father, my Father through Jesus Christ, your beloved Son, and through the Holy Spirit. Amen.

Signed and sealed on April 13, 1862, L. I. Nommensen.

(In 1866 his wife Karolina Margaretha also signed the covenant.)

Lorman E. Petersen, ed. *"My God Told Me to Stay Here": The Life and Work of Missionary Ludwig Ingwer Nommensen* (Appleton, Wisc.: Printed privately, 2000), 57–58.

PROPERS

Almighty God, you planted in your servant Ludwig Nommensen a burning desire to take the gospel of our Lord Jesus Christ to those who had not heard it, and led him to be an apostle to the Batak people of Sumatra: Give to your church that same Spirit and teach us to respect the value of the cultures into which the gospel is brought that your people may rejoice in the diverse richness of your kingdom; through your Son Jesus Christ our Lord, who lives and reigns with you and the Holy Spirit, one God, now and forever.

PHP

Readings: Isaiah 49:1-6
                 Psalm 98
                 Acts 17:22-31
                 Matthew 29:16-20
Hymn of the Day:
                 "Jesus shall reign where'er the sun" (LBW 530, LSB 832, ELW 434, H82 544)
Prayers: For the Batak church
                 For respect for the indigenous customs and traditions in missionary churches
                 For faithfulness to God rather than to human demands
                 For native scholars and teachers
Preface: Epiphany
Color: White

May 24

Nicolaus Copernicus, 1542; Johannes Kepler, 1630; and Leonhard Euler, 1783; Teachers

Copernicus (Mikolaj Kopernik) was born February 19, 1473, at the port city of Torun in eastern Poland, the son of a socially prominent copper merchant. His parents died before he was twelve, and he was entrusted to a maternal uncle. In 1491 he entered the University of Krakow where he became interested in astronomy. He returned to his uncle's home about 1494, and his uncle, the newly elected bishop of Ermland, wanted him to become a canon of Frauenburg Cathedral in Polish Prussia in order that he might have a life of financial security. While Copernicus waited for a vacancy, his uncle sent him to the University of Bologna, where he associated with the German students and spent three and a half years in the study of Greek, mathematics, and Plato. In 1497 he was elected canon. He went to Rome in 1500, returned briefly to his cathedral, and left again for Italy to continue his study at the University of Padua in law and medicine. In 1503 he was granted the degree of Doctor of Canon Law by the University of Ferrara and returned to Poland, acting as his uncle's advisor until the uncle's death in 1512. Copernicus then settled permanently in Frauenburg, making use of his medical knowledge in helping the poor. In 1520 he was made commander of the defenses of Ermland in a war with the Teutonic knights.

Copernicus's interests were wide ranging: mathematics, astronomy, medicine, theology, poetry. His fame as an astronomer increased, but he, like many others of his time, was increasingly dissatisfied with the Ptolemaic geocentric model of the universe. Although as far back as the third century B.C.E. the Greek astronomer Aristarchus of Samos had suggested that the sun was the center of the universe, the geocentric theory had become firmly entrenched in astronomical and theological thought. It had, however, become an unwieldy and enormously complex system of circles upon circles that attempted to account for the observed variations in the movement of the heavens. Copernicus searched for a simpler description, and he renewed interest in the old heliocentric theory. With meager instruments he eventually verified to his own satisfaction the heliocentric system and cautiously announced his theory in a manuscript first circulated in 1530 privately among friends, who urged its publication. After decades of hesitation, Copernicus sent his pupil Georg Joachim Rhäticus with the manuscript to Nuremberg for printing. Rhäticus, appointed professor at Leipzig, went to that city with the manuscript where it was published, with a preface, unknown to Copernicus, by the Lutheran pastor Andreas Osiander emphasizing that the hypothesis of a stationary sun was only a convenient way of simplifying the model of the universe. A copy of the printed book, *De Revolutionibus Orbium Caelestium* ("The Revolution of the Heavenly Bodies"), was brought to Copernicus a few hours before his death May 24, 1543, at Frauenburg.

Copernicus's revolutionary rejection of the prevailing model of the solar system eventually displaced the Earth from the center of the universe. The Earth could no longer be seen as the epitome of creation, and Copernicus's theory implied a much larger universe than had been imagined previously. His writing was on the Index of Prohibited Books from 1616 to 1758.

Copernicus, who was not a notably devout layman, was included on the calendar in the *Lutheran Book of Worship* because of his contribution to the history of ideas that ultimately required Christianity to expand its understanding of the size of the universe and to come to terms with the position of the Earth not at the center but as part of the solar system that is on the fringe of the universe. Copernicus thus taught Christians a new kind of humility before the cosmos.

FOR FURTHER READING

Armitage, Angus. *Copernicus: The Founder of Modern Astronomy.* 1938. London: W. H. Allen, 1957.

———. *Sun, Stand Thou Still.* Toronto: Oxford University Press, 1947.

Bogucka, Maria. *Nicholas Copernicus: The Country and Times.* Trans. Leon Szwajcer. Warsaw: Ossolinski State Publishing House, 1973.

"The Copernican Revolution." *Horizon* 14, no. 1 (Winter 1972): 38–45.

Ferris, Timothy. *Coming of Age in the Milky Way.* New York: William Morrow, 1988.

Kuhn, Thomas S. *The Copernican Revolution.* Cambridge: Harvard University Press, 1957.

North, John. *Astronomy and Cosmology.* New York: Norton, 1995.

MAY

Johannes Kepler, mathematician and astronomer, was born in Weil der Stadt, in Württemberg, Germany, December, 27, 1571. He studied at nearby Tübingen University to prepare for the Lutheran ministry, but there he was introduced to the work of Copernicus and chose to devote his life to the sciences of mathematics and astronomy. His life was a series of forced dislocations caused by territorial struggles between Lutherans and Roman Catholics. He taught at Graz in Austria but was forced to leave during the Counter Reformation and went to Prague as Imperial Mathematician, succeeding the Danish mathematician and astronomer, Tycho Brahe. In 1612 the Lutherans were forced out of Prague, and Kepler moved to Linz. His wife and two sons died; he remarried and two daughters died in infancy. He returned to Württemberg to defend his mother, a noted herbalist and healer, against charges of witchcraft. He died in Regensburg November 15, 1630, and was buried in the church. Within two years, his grave was demolished by the Swedish army during the Thirty Years' War. He is commemorated on the *Evangelical Calendar of Names*.

As a scholar, Kepler was scrupulously honest regarding his data. His most influential work was the seven-volume *Epitome of Copernican Astronomy* (1620), an exhaustive consideration of the heliocentric theory, and his laws of planetary motion. He also took astrology seriously. He remained profoundly Lutheran throughout his life, seeing it as his Christian duty to understand the works of God and to discover the design employed by the Creator in his vast creation, and interspersing his scientific work with prayers and theology. Kepler did not, however, accept the doctrine of the real presence of Christ in the Sacrament because it conflicted with his understanding of spirit and matter, and so he refused to sign the Formula of Concord. He therefore excluded himself from the reception of the Sacrament and was regarded with suspicion by orthodox Lutherans. Nonetheless, he refused to become a Calvinist, just as he refused to become a Catholic to preserve his position when the political climate changed in his several posts.

FOR FURTHER READING

Baumgardt, Carola. *Johannes Kepler: Life and Letters.* New York: Philosophical Library, 1951.

Caspar, Max. *Kepler 1571–1630.* Trans. C. Doris Hellman. London and New York: Abelard-Schuman, 1959; New York: Dover, 1993.

Field, J. V. *Kepler's Geometric Cosmology.* London: Athlone, 1988.

Kepler, Johannes. *The Harmony of the World.* Ed. and trans. E. J. Aiton, A. M. Duncan, and J. V. Field. Philadelphia: American Philosophical Society, 1997.

Koestler, Arthur. *The Watershed: A Biography of Johannes Kepler.* Garden City: Anchor Books, 1960.

Stephenson, Bruce. *Kepler's Physical Astronomy.* Princeton: Princeton University Press, 1994.

————. *The Music of the Heavens: Kepler's Harmonic Astronomy.* Princeton: Princeton University Press, 1997.

Leonhard Euler, one of the most prolific mathematicians in history, was born in Basel April 15, 1710, the son of a Calvinist pastor who himself had an interest in mathematics. Euler, at his father's insistence, pursued the study of theology but then was permitted to turn his attention to mathematics and earned a master's degree at the age of seventeen. It was not a promising profession; there were few jobs for mathematicians in Switzerland at that time.

In 1727 he became an associate of the St. Petersburg Academy of Sciences and in 1730 was appointed to the chair of mathematics. In 1738, through disease, he lost the sight of his right eye.

In 1741 he was invited to Berlin by Frederick the Great. Euler remained there for twenty-five years and kept up a steady stream of publications in geometry, calculus, mechanics, number theory, and astronomy. He was also responsible for numerous administrative duties and served as a consultant to the government.

When Frederick became less cordial, Euler returned to Russia in 1766. A cataract formed in his good eye. Surgery helped only temporarily, and in 1771 he went totally blind. His work was nonetheless not interrupted, for he had a remarkable facility at mental computation. He continued his scholarly studies until the day of his death, September 18, 1783. He was buried in the Lutheran Smolenskoye Cemetery in St. Petersburg but remained a Calvinist throughout his life.

FOR FURTHER READING

Youschkevitch, A. P. "Leonhard Euler." In *Dictionary of Scientific Biography* IV:467–84. New York: Scribner's, 1971.

READING

From John Calvin's *Institutes of the Christian Religion*

Since the perfection of blessedness consists in the knowledge of God, God has been pleased, in order that none might be excluded from the means of obtaining happiness, not only to plant in our minds the seed of religion. . . , but so to display his perfections in the whole structure of the universe and daily place himself in our view, that we cannot open our eyes without being compelled to behold him. His essence, indeed, is incomprehensible, utterly transcending all human thought; but on each of his works his glory is engraved in characters so bright, so distinct, and so illustrious, that no one, however dull and illiterate, can plead ignorance as an excuse. Thus, with perfect truth, the Psalmist exclaims, "You wrap yourself with light as with a cloak" [Ps. 104:2]. It is as if he had said that God for the first time was arrayed in visible attire when, in the creation of the world, he displayed

MAY

those glorious banners on which, wherever we turn, we behold his perfections visibly portrayed. In the same place, the Psalmist aptly compares the stretched-out heavens to God's royal tent, and says, "You lay the beams of your chambers upon the waters above; you make the clouds your chariot; you ride on the wings of the wind" [v. 3], sending forth the winds and lightnings as swift messengers. And because the glory of God's power and wisdom is more refulgent in the vault of the sky, that dome is frequently designated as his palace. Thus, wherever you turn your eyes, there is no portion of the world, however minute, that does not exhibit at least some sparks of beauty; and it is impossible to contemplate the vast and beautiful fabric as it spreads abroad without being overwhelmed by the immense weight of glory [see 2 Cor. 4:17].

John Calvin, *The Institutes of the Christian Religion,* trans. Henry Beveridge (Grand Rapids: Eerdmans, 1957 [1845]), 1:51; rev. PHP.

PROPERS

O Lord our God, creator of stars and planets and worlds beyond our ken: We give you thanks that by the work of your servants Nicolaus Copernicus, Johannes Kepler, and Leonhard Euler, you have enabled us to understand more clearly the pattern of what you have made and hold in being and direct in movement, and to recognize our place within the vastness of your wonderful creation: through Jesus Christ our Lord, who lives and reigns with you and the Holy Spirit, one God, now and forever.

PHP

Readings:	Job 9:2a-10 *or* Isaiah 40:22-26
	Psalm 8
	Philippians 4:8-9
	Matthew 13:44-52
Hymn of the Day:	
	"Eternal Ruler of the ceaseless round" (LBW 373, H82 617)
	or "And have the bright immensities" (LBW 391, H82 459)
Prayers:	For astronomers and watchers of the skies
	For mathematicians and all scientists who explore the beauty of number and order
	For courage to pursue truth
	For humility and awe in the face of mystery
	For a new vision of the beauty of creation
Preface:	Weekdays
Color:	White

On this date the *Book of Common Prayer* commemorates **Jackson Kemper** (1789–1870), the first Episcopal missionary bishop to the United States. His work was centered primarily in the Midwest.

The *Lutheran Service Book,* following Löhe's calendar, on this date commemorates **Esther the Queen**, whose story is told in the Old Testament book that bears her name.

May 25

Bede the Venerable, Priest, Monk of Jarrow, 735

Bede, influential scholar and "the father of English history," was born in 672 or 673 near Durham in northeast England. When he was seven years old, his parents brought him to the new monastery of Wearmouth for his education, and from there he went to the monastery of Jarrow when it was founded *ca.* 681. The two places were considered one monastery. He was ordained deacon at the early age of nineteen (the canonical age was twenty-five) and priest when he was thirty (703).

His life was that of a scholarly monk, remarkably uneventful. He traveled little and devoted himself to study, teaching, and writing, making considerable use of the monastic library. He was the greatest scholar of his time, the most learned man in western Europe. He had a wide-ranging interest in history, grammar, metrics, chronology (he introduced the dating of years from the birth of Christ), and Scripture. His *Ecclesiastical History of the English People,* written in Latin, remains the primary source for the period 597–731 when Anglo-Saxon culture developed and Christianity triumphed. He wrote of himself: "I have spent all my life in this monastery, applying myself entirely to the study of the Scriptures; and, amid the observance of the discipline of the Rule and the daily task of singing in the church, it has always been my delight to learn or to teach or to write."

Bede's traditional title "the Venerable" was applied from the fourth century to people of notable sanctity and learning. In 836 a church council at Aachen referred to Bede as "the Venerable, that is, worthy of honor."

Bede died on the eve of Ascension Day, May 25, 735, while dictating an English translation of St. John's Gospel. In 1020 his remains were transferred to Durham Cathedral; in the turmoil of the Reformation in 1541 his bones were scattered, but the tomb with its inscription remains. For many centuries his feast day was observed on May 27, but on the present Roman Catholic calendar, and the calendar in the *Book of Common Prayer,* the *Lutheran Service Book,* and the Methodist

MAY

For All the Saints, he is remembered on the actual date of his death, May 25. The calendar in the *Lutheran Book of Worship* and in *Evangelical Lutheran Worship*, in an effort not to overwhelm the calendar with too many saints' days, joined Bede's commemoration with that of Columba and Aidan, two other confessors from the British Isles, who with Bede kept alive the light of learning and devotion in the dark ages, and observes the triple commemoration on June 9.

FOR FURTHER READING

Blair, Peter Hunter. *The World of Bede.* New York: St. Martin's, 1971.
Duckett, Eleanor Shipley. *Anglo-Saxon Saints and Scholars.* New York: Macmillan, 1947.
Farmer, David Hugh, ed. *The Age of Bede.* New York: Penguin, 1983.
Roy, James Charles. *Islands of Storm.* Chester Springs: Durfour, 1991.
Thompson, A. Hamilton, ed. *Bede: His Life, Times, and Writings.* Oxford: Clarendon, 1935.
Ward, Benedicta. *The Venerable Bede.* New York: Continuum, 2002.

READING

From a letter on the death of the Venerable Bede by Cuthbert

When it came to the Tuesday before Ascension Day, his breathing became very much worse, and a slight swelling had appeared in his feet; but all the same he taught us the whole of that day, and dictated cheerfully, and among other things said several times: "Learn your lesson quickly now; for I know not how long I may be with you, nor whether after a short time my Maker may not take me from you." But it seemed to us that he knew very well when his end should be. So he spent all that night in thanksgiving, without sleep; and when day broke, which was the Wednesday, he gave instructions for the writing, which we had begun, to be finished without delay. We were at it until nine o'clock; at nine o'clock we went in procession with the relics, as the custom of that day required. One of us stayed with him, and said to him: "There is still one chapter short of that book you were dictating, but I think it will be hard on you to ask any more questions." But he replied: "It is not hard. Take your pen and mend it, and then write fast." And so he did. At three o'clock he said to me: "I have a few treasures in my box, some pepper, and napkins, and some incense. Run quickly and fetch the priests of our monastery, and I will share among them such little presents as God has given me." I did so, in great agitation; and when they came, he spoke to them and to each one singly, urging and begging them to offer masses and prayers regularly on his behalf, and they promised with a will. But they were very sad, and they all wept, especially because he had said that he thought they would not see his face much longer in this world. Yet they rejoiced at one thing that he said: "It is time, if it so please my Maker, that I should be released from the body, and return to Him who formed me out of nothing, when as yet I knew not. I have lived a long time, and the righteous Judge has well provided for me all my life long. The time of my departure is at hand, and my soul longs to see Christ my King in all His beauty."

This he said, and other things, to our great profit, and so spent his last day in gladness until the evening. Then the boy of whom I spoke, whose name was Wilberht, said once again, "There is still one sentence, dear master, that we have not written down." And he said: "Write it." After a little the boy said: "There! Now it is written." And he replied: "Good! It is finished; you have spoken the truth. Hold my head in your hands, for it is a great delight to me to sit over against my holy place in which I used to pray, that as I sit there I may call upon my Father." And so upon the floor of his cell, singing "Glory be to the Father and to the Son and to the Holy Spirit" and the rest, he breathed his last. As well may we believe without hesitation that, inasmuch as he had laboured here always in the praise of God, so his soul was carried by the angels to the joys of Heaven which he longed for. So all who heard or saw the death of our saintly father Bede declared that they had never seen a man end his days in such great holiness and peace; for, as I have said, as long as his soul remained in the body, he chanted the "Gloria Patri" and other songs to the glory of God, and spreading out his hands ceased not to give God thanks.

Bede's Ecclesiastical History of the English People, ed. Bertram Colgrave and R. A. B. Mynors (New York: Oxford University Press, 1961), 581–87.

PROPERS

Heavenly Father, you called your servant Bede, while still a child, to devote his life to your service in the disciplines of religion and scholarship: Grant that as he labored in the Spirit to bring the riches of your truth to his generation, so we, in our various vocations, may strive to make you known in all the world; through Jesus Christ our Lord, who lives and reigns with you and the Holy Spirit, one God, forever and ever.

CMG, adapt. South African *Ministers' Book Liturgy*; LFF

MAY

Readings:	Wisdom 7:15-22
	Psalm 78:1-4 *or* 19:7-11 (12-14)
	Matthew 13:47-52
Hymn of the Day:	
	"A hymn of glory let us sing" (H82 217, 218; LBW 157, LSB 493, ELW 393)
Prayers:	For all those who through the darkness keep alive the light of learning
	For those who persevere in prayer
	For universities, colleges, and schools
	For students and teachers of history
	For biblical scholars and translators
Preface:	All Saints (LBW, ELW), A Saint (1) (BCP)
Color:	White

May 26

Augustine, First Archbishop of Canterbury, Missionary, 605

Gregory the Great, before he became pope, according to the pleasant story preserved by Bede, saw blond, blue-eyed Saxons being sold in the Roman slave market and asked who these people were. When he was told they were Angles, he is said to have replied, "Ah, surely not Angles but angels!" and determined that they should be taught Christianity. In 596 Gregory, now pope, sent Augustine, a Sicilian from Messina and prior of St. Andrew's monastery, which Gregory had founded in his paternal mansion in Rome, together with forty other monks, to reestablish Christianity in England, which had been virtually wiped out by the Anglo-Saxon invasions. While the missionaries were still in France, they heard such alarming reports of the savagery of the heathen English that Augustine returned to Rome to ask permission to discontinue the effort, but the pope encouraged them to press on. They landed at Thanet in Kent in the spring of 597 and were politely received by Ethelbert, King of Kent, whose wife, Bertha, a Frankish princess, was a Christian. Augustine was given permission to preach the gospel and to establish himself at Canterbury, where he was permitted to use the ancient St. Martin's Church, which had been built by Christians in Roman times. Within a year, Ethelbert was baptized along with many of his people, and in 598 Gregory wrote to Eulogius of Alexandria, "While the people of the English, placed in a corner of the world, still remained without faith, worshipping stocks and stones, I resolved . . . that I ought with God's assistance to send to this people a monk from my monastery to preach. . . . He and they who were sent with him are radiant with such great miracles among this people, that they seem to reproduce the powers of the apostles in the signs they display."

Augustine was consecrated the first archbishop of Canterbury at Arles in France. He built the first cathedral of Canterbury on the site of an old Roman basilica and dedicated it to Christ the Savior. His final act was to consecrate two of his monks as bishops of London and Rochester to extend the evangelization of England. His comparatively brief mission was confined to a limited area; his attempts at extending his authority to the existing Christians in Wales and southwest England were unsuccessful. These Britons were suspicious and wary, and their bishops refused to recognize Augustine as their archbishop.

Augustine died May 26, probably in 605, and was buried in his monastic church of St. Peter and St. Paul, later known as St. Augustine's Abbey in Canterbury. He is commemorated in the *Book of Common Prayer* on the date of his death; the Roman calendar commemorates him on the following day, May 27.

FOR FURTHER READING

Deanesly, Margaret. *Augustine of Canterbury.* New York: Nelson, 1964.

READING

From a letter by Gregory the Great to Augustine of Canterbury

Who . . . is capable of describing the great joy of believers when they have learned what the grace of Almighty God and your own cooperation achieved among the Angles? They abandoned the errors of darkness and were bathed with the light of holy faith. With full awareness they trampled on the idols which they had previously adored with savage fear. They are now committed to Almighty God. The guidelines given them for their preaching restrain them from falling into evil ways. In their minds they are submissive to the divine precepts and consequently feel uplifted. They bow down to the ground in prayer lest their minds cling too closely to earthly things. Whose achievement is this? It is the achievement of him who said: "My Father is at work until now, and I am at work as well."

God chose illiterate preachers and sent them into the world in order to show the world that conversion is brought about not by men's wisdom but rather by his own power. So in like manner God worked through weak instruments and wrought great things.

From the English translation of the Office of Readings from The Liturgy of the Hours © 1974 the International Committee on English in the Liturgy, Inc. All rights reserved.

PROPERS

O Lord our God, by your Son Jesus Christ you called your apostles and sent them forth to preach the Gospel to the nations: We bless your holy Name for your servant Augustine, first Archbishop of Canterbury, whose labors in propagating your Church among the English people we commemorate today, and we pray that all whom you call and send may do your will, and bide your time, and see your glory; through Jesus Christ our Lord, who lives and reigns with you and the Holy Spirit, one God, forever and ever.

CMG, combined from Canadian BCP and CSI *Book of Common Worship*; LFF

MAY

Readings:	Psalm 66:1-8 *or* 103:1-4, 13-18
	2 Corinthians 5:17-20a
	Luke 5:1-11
Hymn of the Day:	
	"Christ is the world's true Light" (H82 542)
Prayers:	For the Archbishop of Canterbury
	For the church in England

For the churches of the Anglican Communion
For a willingness to share the faith
For all missionaries

Preface: Apostles
Color: White

May 27

John Calvin, Renewer of the Church, 1564

with John Knox, Reformer, 1572

John Calvin, who possessed one of the most penetrating theological minds that the church has known, gave Reformed doctrine its most systematic formulation. He was a more rigorous and logical thinker than Luther and more aware of the importance of organization both of ideas and institutions.

He was born in Noyon, France, July 10, 1509, the second son of Gérard Cauvin ("Calvin" is a Latinized form), secretary to the bishop. The son was a serious and able student, and at age thirteen or fourteen he was sent to Paris to continue his studies in grammar, rhetoric, and theology. He took particular interest in the church fathers, especially Augustine. He received the M.A. in 1528 at the age of nineteen.

His father, believing that law would be a more lucrative profession (and because of his own excommunication over a dispute concerning the closing of an estate), encouraged his son to change his course of study. He went to the University of Orléans, then to Bourges to study law, and there he became familiar with humanism. Calvin's father died in May 1531, and Calvin left the study of law and turned to literary scholarship at the new Collège de France in Paris, studying both Greek and Hebrew.

Late in 1533 or 1534, he underwent a "sudden conversion," as he called it. He broke with the Roman Church and devoted himself to the cause of the Protestant Reformation. In 1535 he left France for Protestant Basel. Here he began the formulation of new theological ideas and published the first edition of the *Institutes of the Christian Religion* in March 1536. In that year Calvin returned briefly to Paris to settle some family business. In July he left Paris, intending to go to Strasbourg, but he was forced to detour through Geneva where his friend Guillaume Farel (1489–1565) persuaded him to remain and assist in organizing the Reformation there. (The neighboring city of Bern had been Protestant since 1528 and supplied Geneva with Protestant preachers from 1532. Farel was one of these.)

In January 1537 Calvin drew up articles regulating the organization of the church and worship in Geneva under rigidly uniform, theocratic discipline. In 1538 the government of Geneva came under the influence of its neighbor Bern, and Farel and Calvin, refusing to obey the city council's explicit instructions to conform to the Zwinglian religious practices of Bern, were ordered to leave the city. From April 1538 to September 1541, they were at the French congregation in Strasbourg by invitation from Martin Bucer. In 1540 Calvin married Idelette de Bure, the widow of one of his converts. She bore him a son who died shortly after birth; she died in 1549, leaving Calvin to care for her two children by her previous marriage. Calvin agreed to return to Geneva in September 1541 after the town had returned to the rule of the pro-Calvin faction. The new constitution distinguished four ministries in the church—pastors, teachers, elders, and deacons—and made provision for a consistory of elders and pastors to maintain discipline.

Struggle and conflict over doctrinal points led to the beheading of Jacques Gruet for blasphemy (1547) and in October 1553 the burning of Michael Servetus, an anti-trinitarian Spanish physician. Although dispute continued, Calvin's rule was secure. From 1555 onward, he offered refuge in Geneva to Protestant exiles from England. Despite ill health in his last years, he kept up preaching, teaching, and writing. He died at Geneva May 27, 1564.

Calvin is commemorated on the German Lutheran *Evangelical Calendar of Names* (1962), on the calendar in the *Lutheran Book of Worship,* on the Methodist calendar in *For All the Saints,* and the calendar in *Evangelical Lutheran Worship.*

FOR FURTHER READING

Benedict, Philip. *Christ's Churches Purely Reformed: A Social History of Calvinism.* New Haven: Yale University Press, 2002.

Bouwsma, William J. *John Calvin: A Sixteenth Century Portrait.* New York: Oxford University Press, 1987.

Calvin, John. *Calvin's Commentaries.* ed. John Beveridge. (Grand Rapids, Michigan: Baker, 1979) vol. 4, pp. xxxv–xlix.

Cottret, Bernard. *Calvin: A Biography.* Trans. M. Wallace McDonald. Grand Rapids: Eerdmans, 2000.

Gerrish, B. A. *Grace and Gratitude: The Eucharistic Theology of John Calvin.* Minneapolis: Fortress Press, 1993.

Harkness, Georgia E. *John Calvin: The Man and His Ethics.* New York: Abingdon, 1958.

McGrath, Alister E. *A Life of John Calvin: A Study of the Shaping of Western Culture.* Oxford: Blackwell, 1990.

McKee, Ann, ed. *John Calvin. Writings on Pastoral Piety.* New York: Paulist, 2002.

McKim, Donald K., ed. *The Cambridge Companion to John Calvin.* Cambridge: Cambridge University Press, 2004.

Parker, T. H. L. *Calvin: An Introduction to His Thought.* Louisville: Westminster John Knox, 1995.

MAY

Wendel, Francois. *Calvin: Origins and Development of His Religious Thought.* Trans. Philip Mairet. New York: Harper, 1964.

Zachman, Randall C. *John Calvin as Teacher, Pastor, and Theologian.* Grand Rapids: Baker, 2006.

John Knox, the Scottish Reformer, might be remembered with Calvin. Knox was born *ca.* 1513 at Haddington, Scotland. He was ordained in minor orders, but gave up the ministry to become a private tutor. Soon afterward, he embraced the principles of the Reformation, and in 1547 he became preacher at St. Andrew's. He was taken prisoner by the French, released in 1549, and went to England, where he was made chaplain to Edward VI and assisted in the final stages of the revision of the Second Prayer Book (1552). Upon Mary's accession to the throne in 1553, he fled to the continent where he met Calvin in Geneva.

In 1555 the French-born queen regent of Scotland attempted to end the expansion of Protestantism in her realm, and the Protestants recalled Knox for their defense. England and Scotland stood together against France, which had designs on both countries. Knox's preaching and writing met with success, but continuing persecution led him to move to the English Church in Geneva in 1556. Even there, he was in constant conflict with the crown, but in the grim winter of 1559, Knox's resolution kept the British cause alive until their victory the following spring.

Becoming the leader of the Reforming party, Knox turned to the organization of the Scottish Church. In a democratic fashion he gave a large role to the laity in the government of the Church. Deep, personal, and vindictive hatred grew between Knox and Queen Mary until her abdication in 1567. After suffering a paralytic stroke, Knox died November 24, 1572, at Edinburgh.

Fearlessly outspoken in his hatred of Catholicism, he easily made enemies, yet he was occasionally tender, single-minded in his devotion to his religious belief, and wielded an enormous influence. Knox is commemorated on the German *Evangelical Calendar of Names* on November 24.

FOR FURTHER READING

Kyle, Richard G. *The Mind of John Knox.* Lawrence: Coronado, 1984.

MacGregor, Geddes. *The Thundering Scot: A Portrait of John Knox.* Philadelphia: Westminster, 1957.

Reid, W. Stanford. *The Trumpeter of God: A Biography of John Knox.* New York: Scribner's, 1974.

Ridley, Jasper G. *John Knox.* New York: Oxford University Press, 1968.

READING

From John Calvin, Institutes of the Christian Religion

What avails it, in short, to know a God with whom we have nothing to do? The effect of our knowledge rather ought to be, *first*, to teach us reverence and fear; and, *secondly,* to induce us, under its guidance and teaching, to ask every good thing from him, and, when it is received, ascribe it to him. For how can the idea of God enter your mind without instantly giving rise to the thought, that since you are his workmanship, you are bound, by the very law of creation, to submit to his authority, that your life is due to him, that whatever you do ought to have reference to him?

First of all, the devout mind does not devise for itself any kind of God, but looks alone to the one true God; nor does it feign for him any character it pleases, but is contented to have him in the character in which he manifests himself, always guarding, with the utmost diligence, against transgressing his will and wandering with a daring presumption from the right path. Those by whom God is thus known, perceiving how he governs all things, confide in him as their guardian and protector, and cast themselves entirely upon his faithfulness. Perceiving him to be the source of every blessing, if they are in any difficulty or feel any want, they instantly turn to his protection and trust his aid. Persuaded that he is good and merciful, they lean upon him with sure confidence, and doubt not that in the divine mercy a remedy will be provided for every time of need. Acknowledging him as Father and Lord, they consider themselves bound to have respect for his authority in all things, to reverence his majesty, aim at the advancement of his glory, and obey his commands. Regarding him as a just judge, armed with severity to punish crimes, they keep the judgment-seat always in view. Standing in awe of it, they curb themselves and fear to provoke his anger. Nevertheless, they are not terrified by an apprehension of judgment as to wish they could withdraw themselves, even if the means of escape lay before them; rather, they embrace him not the less as the avenger of wickedness than as the rewarder of the righteous; because they perceive that it equally appertains to his glory to store up punishment for the one and eternal life for the other. Besides, it is not the mere fear of punishment that restrains them from sin. Loving and reverencing God as their father, honoring and obeying him as their master, even if there were no hell, they would revolt at the very idea of offending him.

Such is pure and genuine religion, namely, confidence in God coupled with serious fear—fear, which both includes in it willing reverence and brings along with it such legitimate worship as is prescribed in the law. And it ought to be more carefully considered that all people freely do homage to God, but very few truly reverence him. On all hands there is abundant evidence of ostentatious ceremonies, but sincerity of heart is rare.

John Calvin, *Institutes of the Christian Religion,* trans. Henry Beveridge (Grand Rapids: Eerdmans, 1957 [1845]), 1:41–42; rev. PHP.

MAY

PROPERS

God of sovereign majesty and majestic order, you have revealed yourself as the source of every blessing: Teach us, by the clarity and precision of the doctrines of your servant John Calvin, to respect your authority in all things, to aim always at the advancement of your glory, and joyfully submit to your decrees that we may come to know you, the one true God, through your Son, Jesus Christ our Lord; who lives and reigns with you and the Holy Spirit, one God, now and forever.

PHP

Readings:	Jeremiah 1:4-10
	Psalm 8
	Romans 8:28-30
	John 15:1-11
Hymn of the Day:	
	"Before Jehovah's awesome throne" (LBW 531, H82 391)
Prayers:	For a sense of the majesty and sovereignty of God
	For earnestness in God's presence
	For excellence in preaching
	For the Reformed Churches
Preface:	Epiphany
Color:	White

May 29

Juraj Tranovsky, Hymnwriter, 1637

Juraj Tranovsky (or Trzanowski), "the Luther of the Slavs" and the creator of Slovak hymnody, was born April 9, 1592, in Tešin, in Silesia, the son of a blacksmith of Polish descent. His first name also appears as Jiří or, in the non-Slavonic form, George; his family name often appears in the Latinized form Tranoscious. He studied at Guben and Kolberg and in 1607 entered the University of Wittenberg. After about 1612, he traveled through Bohemia and Silesia and taught in the Gymnasium of St. Nicholas in Prague and in 1613 became rector of a school in Holesov in Moravia near the Hungarian border. Two years later he taught in the school and was a leader of a singing society in Medziriečie. There he and Anna Polani were married. Tranovsky was ordained in 1616, but in the following year, with the accession of Ferdinand II of Bohemia, toleration of Lutheranism ended. For a time in 1621, Tranovsky, together with the entire population of the city, fled to Tešin. He was imprisoned in 1624, and in the following year lost three of his children in the plague and famine that carried off two thousand of his neighbors, including half of his congregation.

In 162,5 Tranovsky was called to be pastor in Bilska, Silesia, and in 1627 he became chaplain to Count Kaspar Illehazy. From 1631 until his death at forty-six years of age, Tranovsky was pastor of Svaty Mikulas in Liptov in Slovakia. He died after a long illness May 29, 1637, and was buried in an unmarked grave in his church.

Tranovsky was long a lover of poetry and compiler and author of hymns. Even in his student days, he composed poetry in both Czech and Latin. During the deprivations of the Thirty Years' War, his creative work flourished. In 1620 he issued a translation of the Augsburg Confession that has gone through many editions; in 1930, on the four hundredth anniversary of the Presentation of the Augsburg Confession, a jubilee edition of the Tranovsky translation with historical notes was issued. In 1629 he issued a collection of hymns (*Odarum Sacrarium sive Hymnorum Libri III*), and his famous hymnal *Cithara Sanctorum* ("Lyre [or Harp] of the Saints"), which appeared in 1636, has remained the basis of Slovak Lutheran hymnody to the present day. The *Cithara Sanctorum* and the Kralice Bible translation are the two great monuments of the Reformation among the Slavs.

The *Cithara Sanctorum*, which is often referred to by the compiler's Latinized name as "Tranoscius," is a collection of originally four hundred fourteen hymns and spiritual songs. Some are translations of old Latin hymns or German Reformation chorales, but the majority are adaptations of hymns used by the Hussites or the Czech Brethren. About 150 of them were by Tranovsky himself and some were by his contemporaries. The *Tranoscius* has gone through over a hundred editions and is a proud possession of many Slovak Lutheran households, often being beautifully printed and bound and placed in a position of honor.

In 1935 to 1936 the three hundredth anniversary of the appearance of the *Cithara Sanctorum* was widely celebrated in what was then Czechoslovakia and elsewhere, and the pastor and hymnodist of the Reformation among the Slavs was commemorated. He was added to the Lutheran calendar in the *Lutheran Book of Worship*.

MAY

FOR FURTHER READING

Brock, Peter. *The Slovak National Awakening*. Toronto: University of Toronto Press, 1976.

Skodacek, A. A. *Slovak Lutheran Liturgy Past and Present*. N.p., 1968.

Vajda, Jaroslav. *A History of the Cithara Sanctorus (Tranoscius)*. B.D. Thesis. Concordia Seminary, St. Louis, 1944.

———. "Slovak Hymnody." In *Hymnal Companion to the Lutheran Book of Worship*. 51–57. Ed. Marilyn Stulken. Philadelphia: Fortress Press, 1981.

READING

From Martin Luther, "Preface to Georg Rhau's *Symphoniae Iucundae*"

Next to the Word of God, music deserves the highest praise. She is a mistress and governess of those human emotions—to pass over the animals—which as masters govern men or more often overwhelm them. No greater commendation than this can be found—at least not by us. For whether you wish to comfort the sad, to terrify the happy, to encourage the despairing, to humble the proud, to calm the passionate, or to appease those full of hate—and who would number all these masters of the human heart, namely, the emotions, inclinations, and affections that impel men to evil or good?—what more effective means than music could you find? The Holy Ghost himself honors her as an instrument for his proper work when in his Holy Scriptures he asserts that through her his gifts were instilled in the prophets, namely, the inclination to all virtues, as can be seen in Elisha. On the other hand, she serves to cast out Satan, the instigator of all sins, as is shown in Saul, the king of Israel.

Thus it was not without reason that the fathers and prophets wanted nothing else to be associated as closely with the Word of God as music. Therefore, we have so many hymns and Psalms where message and music join to move the listener's soul, while in other living beings and [sounding] bodies music remains a language without words. After all, the gift of language combined with the gift of song was only given to man to let him know that he should praise God with both word and music, namely, by proclaiming [the Word of God] through music and by providing sweet melodies with words. For even a comparison between different men will show how rich and manifold our glorious Creator proves himself in distributing the gifts of music, how much men differ from each other in voice and manner of speaking so that one amazingly excels the other. No two men can be found with exactly the same voice and manner of speaking, although they often seem to imitate each other, the one as it were being the ape of the other.

But when [musical] learning is added to all this and artistic music which corrects, develops, and refines the natural music, then at last it is possible to taste with wonder (yet not to comprehend) God's absolute and perfect wisdom in his wondrous work of music.

Luther's Works 53, Liturgy and Hymns, ed. Ulrich S. Leupold (Philadelphia: Fortress Press, 1965), 323–24.

PROPERS

Almighty God, beautiful in majesty, majestic in holiness: you have taught your people to praise you in psalms and hymns and spiritual songs: We praise you for your servants to whom you have given skill in the composition of hymns, especially on this day for Juraj Tranovsky; and we pray that by your grace we may find strength in your praise during this present life and finally attain to the perfect harmony of the life to come; through your Son Jesus Christ our Lord, who lives and reigns with you and the Holy Spirit, one God, now and forever.

PHP, after James E. Kiefer

Readings:	2 Chronicles 20:20-21
	Psalm 96
	Ephesians 5:18b-20
	Matthew 13:44-52
Hymn of the Day:	
	"Make songs of joy to Christ, our head" (LBW 150, LSB 484)
Prayers:	For the Slovak churches
	For those who teach congregations to sing
	For faithful pastors
	That song might lift the hearts of the depressed and the despondent
Preface:	All Saints
Color:	White

May 31

The Visitation

An element of the larger event of the incarnation is celebrated today as Mary the mother of Jesus pays a visit to Elizabeth the mother of John during their mutual pregnancies. The day, a little jewel, breathes the spirit of freshness and springtime and fecundity, associating the miracle of childbirth with Mary's visit to the uplands of Judah. Spring becomes a symbol not only of hope but of salvation.

The Feast of the Visitation was first observed by the Franciscans in the thirteenth century. It was added to the Roman calendar by Pope Urban IV in 1389 and was extended to the whole Western Church by the Council of Basel in 1441. In the Eastern Church the festival is unknown, except for a few Uniate churches that have adopted it from the Latin Rite. Although the Visitation is a minor festival and a late addition to the calendar, Lutheran calendars generally retained it because of its scriptural basis. The Church of England, however, dropped it from the calendar, but beginning with the 1662 calendar of the Church of England, all churches in the Anglican Communion, except the Irish and the American, made it a "black letter day," a day listed on the calendar but without official provision of propers for liturgical observance. In the 1979 American *Book of Common Prayer*, the festival is included and propers are provided.

MAY

The Visitation is basically a festival of Christ, celebrating a stage of his incarnation. The homely event of two expectant mothers discussing their hopes and fears, transfigured by the eternal purpose of God in which they humbly accept their part is the occasion of the Song of Mary, the Magnificat.

On earlier Roman Catholic and Lutheran calendars (it was not on the calendar in the *Book of Common Prayer*) the day was observed on July 2, but following the lead of the present Roman calendar, the Lutheran and Episcopal churches have moved the observance to May 31 so that the day would make better chronological sense by coming before the birthday of John the Baptist, June 24. In the Roman Catholic Church, during the Marian year 1954, May 31 was made the feast of the Queenship of Mary to crown the closing of the month of May, the month dedicated to Mary. On the present Roman calendar, that feast has been moved to August 22, the octave of the Assumption.

READING

From "The Life of Our Blessed Lord and Saviour Jesus Christ" by Bishop Jeremy Taylor

When the almighty God meant to stoop so low as to be fixed in our centre, he chose for his mother a holy person and a maid. She received the angel's message with such sublimity of faith that her faith was turned to vision, her hopes into actual possession, and her grace into glory. She who was full of God, bearing God in her virgin womb and the Holy Spirit in her heart, arose with haste and gladness to communicate that joy which was designed for all the world. . . .

Mary found no one so fit as her cousin Elizabeth to share the first emanations of her overjoyed heart, for she was to be the mother of the Baptist, who was sent as forerunner to prepare the way of the Lord her son. It is not easy to imagine what collision of joys was at this blessed meeting; two mothers of two great princes, the one the greatest that was born of woman, and the other his Lord. When these who were made mothers by two miracles came together, they met with joy and mysteriousness. The mother of our Lord went to visit the mother of his servant, and the Holy Ghost made the meeting festival. Never, but in heaven, was there more joy and ecstasy. For these women were hallowed and made big with religion and they met to unite their joy and their eucharist. By this, God would have us know that when the blessings of God descend upon us, they should be published in the communion of the saints, so that our charity and eucharist may increase that of others, and the praises of God be sung aloud, till the sound strike at heaven and join with the alleluias which the morning stars in their orbs pay to their great creator.

Jeremy Taylor, "The Life of Our Blessed Lord and Saviour Jesus Christ," given in Brother Kenneth C.G.A., ed., *From the Fathers to the Churches*, Daily Spiritual Readings mainly from "The Divine Office" (London: Collins, 1983), 689–90.

PROPERS

Almighty God, in choosing the Virgin Mary to be the mother of your Son, you made known your gracious regard for the poor, the lowly, and the despised, and you inspired her to visit Elizabeth and assist her in her need: Grant us grace to receive your word in humility, and so to be made one with your Son, Jesus Christ our Lord, who lives and reigns with you and the Holy Spirit, one God, now and forever.

PHP: Strasbourg 1524, CB, CSB, SBH ✛ RS; see William Bright, *Ancient Collects,* rev. BCP; ELW: August 15.

Readings:	Zephaniah 2:14-18a
	Psalm 113 *or* Isaiah 12:1-6
	Romans 12:9-16
	Luke 1:39-47
Hymn of the Day:	
	"Blest are the pure in heart" (H82 656, SBH 394)
	"Hark, the glad sound! The Savior comes" (LBW 35, LSB 349, ELW 239)
Prayers:	For the poor, the forgotten, the despised
	For grace to acknowledge Christ and to perceive his coming
	For hospitality to visitors and travelers
	For a deepening sense of Emmanuel, God with us
	For God's blessing on homes and family life
	For all expectant mothers
	For a proper devotion among all Christians to Mary, the bearer of God
Preface:	Christmas (LBW/ELW); Epiphany (BCP)
Color:	White

June 1

Justin, Martyr at Rome, *ca.* 165

A perennial necessity for Christianity is to make connection between the claims of the gospel and the needs and interests of the current age, while clearing away misunderstandings, prejudices, and slanders. When in the century *ca.* 120–220 Christianity began to make converts among educated people and also to come into conflict with the state over its right to exist, a number of writers set themselves to the task of making a reasoned defense and recommendation of their faith to outsiders and opponents. These Apologists, as they are known, defenders of the faith, in their effort to gain a fair hearing for Christianity and to dispel popular slanders and misunderstandings, gave some account of Christian belief and practice that has proved invaluable in our understanding of the early years of Christianity.

JUNE

Justin, the most specifically Christian of the Apologists and perhaps the greatest figure between the apostles and Irenaeus, was born of pagan Greek parents at Flavia Neapolis in Samaritan territory (ancient Schechem, modern Nablus) about the year 100. Early in his life he began an intense search for a satisfying philosophy and religious truth. To this end, he studied philosophy at Ephesus. Justin was impressed with the Christian martyrs, and after all his study, an old Christian by the seashore, whom he met by chance, told him of the Old Testament prophets, and Justin became a Christian. He taught Christian philosophy for a time at Ephesus, but soon after 135 he appeared in Rome. There he addressed two famous defenses of Christianity, first to the emperor Antoninus Pius and then to the Roman Senate, precious testimonies to primitive Christian liturgy and belief. He became involved in a bitter debate with the Cynic philosopher Crescens. About 165, perhaps as a result of this controversy, Justin and some of his students, refusing to make a pagan sacrifice, were scourged and beheaded. He had written in his second *Apologia,* "No one believes in Socrates to the point of dying for what he taught . . . . But for the sake of Christ not only philosophers and scholars but even laborers and uneducated people have scorned fame, fear, and death." A Greek account of his martyrdom survives in three forms and seems to rest on a contemporary record.

Many writings have been attributed to him, but only his *Dialogue with Trypho* and the two *Apologies* (defenses) seem authentically his. This son of Palestine as much as any other saw to it that the gospel remained rooted in the religion of the Old Testament. Justin is also an important witness to the emerging New Testament corpus, and he was the first Christian thinker to seek to reconcile the claims of faith and reason. He saw no sharp discontinuity between Platonism and Christianity: Christianity fulfilled the highest aspirations of Platonism, and the pagan thinkers found truth by studying the Hebrew Scriptures, he suggested, as well as by independent revelation.

Justin is commemorated on June 1 in both East and West. He is on the calendar in the *Book of Common Prayer,* the *Lutheran Book of Worship, Evangelical Lutheran Worship,* the *Lutheran Service Book,* and the Methodist *For All the Saints.*

FOR FURTHER READING

Barnard, L. W. *Justin Martyr. His Life and Thought.* Cambridge: Cambridge University Press, 1967.

Von Campenhausen, Hans. *The Fathers of the Greek Church.* Trans. Stanley Goodman. New York: Pantheon, 1959.

Chadwick, Henry. "Justin Martyr's Defense of Christianity." *Bulletin of the John Rylands Library* 47 (1965): 275–97.

Justin Martyr. *The Dialogue with Trypho.* Trans. A. L. Williams. New York: Macmillan, 1931.

READING

From the *Acts of the Martyrdom of Saint Justin and His Companion Saints*

The saints were seized and brought before the prefect of Rome, whose name was Rusticus. As they stood before the judgment seat, Rusticus the prefect said to Justin, "Above all, have faith in the gods and obey the emperors." Justin said, "We cannot be accused or condemned for obeying the commands of our Savior, Jesus Christ."

Rusticus said, "What system of teaching do you profess?" Justin said, "I have tried to learn about every system, but I have accepted the true doctrines of the Christians, though these are not approved by those who are held fast in error."

The prefect Rusticus said, "Are these doctrines approved by you, wretch that you are?" Justin said, "Yes, for I follow them with their correct teaching."

The prefect Rusticus said, "What sort of teaching is that?" Justin said, "Worship the God of the Christians. We hold him to be from the beginning the one creator and maker of the whole creation, of things seen and things unseen. We worship also the Lord Jesus Christ, the Son of God. He was foretold by the prophets as the future herald of salvation for the human race, and the teacher of distinguished disciples. For myself, since I am a human being, I consider that what I say is insignificant with his infinite godhead. I acknowledge the existence of a prophetic power, for the one I have just spoken of as the Son of God was the subject of prophecy. I know that the prophets were inspired from above when they spoke of his coming among men."

Rusticus said, "You are a Christian then?" Justin said, "Yes, I am a Christian."

The prefect said to Justin, "You are called a learned man and think you know what is true teaching. Listen: if you were scourged and beheaded, are you convinced that you would go up to heaven?" Justin said, "I hope that I shall enter God's house if I suffer in that way. For I know that God's favor is stored up until the end of the whole world for all who have lived good lives."

The prefect Rusticus said, "Do you have an idea that you will go up to heaven to receive some suitable rewards?" Justin said, "It is not an idea that I have; it is something I know well and hold to be most certain."

The prefect Rusticus said, "Now let us come to the point at issue, which is necessary and urgent. Gather round then and with one accord offer sacrifice to the gods." Justin said, "No one who is right-thinking stoops from true worship to false worship."

The prefect Rusticus said, "If you do not do as you are commanded you will be tortured without mercy." Justin said, "We hope to suffer torment for the sake of our Lord Jesus Christ, and so be saved. For this will bring us salvation and confidence as we stand before the more terrible and universal judgment-seat of our Lord and Savior."

In the same way the other martyrs also said, "Do what you will. We are Christians; we do not offer sacrifice to idols."

The prefect Rusticus pronounced sentence, saying, "Let those who have refused to sacrifice to the gods and to obey the command of the emperor be scourged and led away to suffer capital punishment according to the ruling of the laws." Glorifying God, the holy martyrs went out to the accustomed place. They were beheaded, and so fulfilled their witness of martyrdom in confessing their faith in their Savior.

Chaps. 1–5. From the English translation of the Office of Readings from the Liturgy of the Hours © 1974, the International Committee on English in the Liturgy, Inc. All rights reserved.

PROPERS

Almighty and everlasting God, through the folly of the cross you taught your martyr Justin the sublime wisdom of Jesus Christ: Grant that all who seek you may be found by you, and, rejecting all falsehood and deception, remain loyal to the faith revealed to us in Jesus Christ our Lord; who lives and reigns with you and the Holy Spirit, one God, now and forever.

PHP, 1952 Roman Missal, RS, LFF

Readings:	Psalm 16:5-11 *or* 116:1-8
	1 Corinthians 1:18-25
	John 12:44-50
Hymn of the Day:	
	"Let us now our voices raise" (H82 237, SBH 546)
	"Thine is the glory" (LBW 145, ELW 376)
Prayers:	For those who search for truth, especially philosophers and theologians
	For those who defend the faith against the doubts of those who cannot believe
	For those who preserve and interpret the liturgical traditions of the church
Preface:	A Saint (3) (BCP); All Saints (LBW); Saints (ELW)
Color:	Red

June 2

Blandina and Her Companions, Martyrs at Lyons, 177

Blandina, a slave, was a leader of the martyrs who suffered at Lyons in the south of France along with their aged bishop, Pothinus. While the governor of the province was absent, mobs began to attack the Christians in Lyons and the neighboring city of Vienne, seeking them out, beating and torturing them, and throwing them into prison. Bishop Pothinus, who was more than ninety years old, died in prison from his beating. Some of the victims were denounced by their own servants. The governor returned, and the emperor Marcus Aurelius confirmed the death penalty for those Christians who refused to renounce their faith. At a pagan festival, the Christians who were Roman citizens were beheaded, and the others, many of whom were natives of the provinces of Asia Minor, were killed by wild beasts in the amphitheater. Against relentless torture and accusations of canni-balism and incest, Blandina, Eusebius reports, would only say, "I am a Christian, and we do nothing vile." Her tormenters declared that they had never seen such endurance. At length she was tied in a net and thrown to a bull, which gored her to death. The bodies of the victims were burned and their remains were cast into the Rhone.

The names of forty-eight martyrs are recorded, many of them Greek. With Blandina and her bishop were her mistress; a fifteen-year-old boy, Ponticus, whom she encouraged to endure bravely; Sanctus, a deacon; the newly baptized Maturus; and Attalus, a "man of repute." The diverse collection of martyrs made a united witness. Eusebius says, "They offered up to the Father a single wreath, but it was woven of diverse colors and flowers of all kinds."

The martyrdom in Lyons and Vienne took place during the reign of Marcus Aurelius, and the persecution was carried out methodically and unscrupulously. Many others have suffered for their faith and have been forgotten, but the martyrs at Lyons are remembered because of the letter written by the survivors of the persecution in Lyons and Vienne to the churches in Asia and Phrygia, preserved in the pages of Eusebius's *Church History*. The letter, one of the most precious documents of Christian antiquity, vividly describes the evil of which ordinary people are capable when incited to mob violence. It is also a moving record of the triumph of steadfast and heroic faith when confronted by such evil.

Blandina is commemorated on the German Lutheran *Evangelical Calendar of Names* (1962); the Martyrs of Lyons are commemorated on the calendar in the 1979 *Book of Common Prayer* and the Methodist calendar in *For All the Saints*. They are not on the general Roman calendar.

READING

From the Letter from the Gallican Churches

About ten were not able to stand the strain of the conflict, a great grief and sorrow unbounded to us. But every day they took more who were up to standard, and that made up the numbers again until they had got all those keen ones through whom the Christian cause in the two congregations had been established. . . .

As for Blandina, through her Christ showed that what to men seems cheap, not much to look at, easy to despise, may be valued as of great glory to God.

JUNE

We all trembled for her. Her mistress was herself one to suffer, but this was her suffering, lest the girl through weakness of her body should not be able to dare the confession. But Blandina was so filled with power that, compared with those who in turns from dawn to dark were giving her every sort of torture, she was the one who seemed free. And they confessed, "We are beaten. . . . There is nothing more we can do to her. We don't know how breath remains in a body so torn and broken." But the blessed woman, like a noble athlete, was refreshed by her confession, relieved and rested, rid of pain, in saying "I am a Christian" and "With us there is nothing vile." For the amphitheater they kept her till last. She had encouraged all others, like a noble mother sending her children before her victorious to the King. She watched all their conflicts, then herself endured them, scourging, the beasts, the iron chair over a fire, being put in a net and tossed by a bull. And so she hastened after them, rejoicing and exulting at her departure, as one, not thrown to the wild animals, but called to a wedding feast.

Eusebius, *Historia Ecclesiae* I, 11-56, trans. John Foster, *Five Minutes a Saint* (London: SCM, 1963), 41–42.

PROPERS

Grant, O Lord, that we who keep the festival of the martyrs Blandina and her companions may be rooted deep in your love, and may endure the sufferings of this life with inflexible courage for the glory that one day shall be ours; through Jesus Christ our Lord, who lives and reigns with you and the Holy Spirit, one God, now and forever.

Hours of Prayer, trans. DvD et al.; see LFF

Readings:	Psalm 126 *or* 34:1-8
	1 Peter 1:3-9
	Mark 8:34-38
Hymn of the Day:	
	"Blessed feasts of blessed martyrs" (H82 238, 239)
Prayers:	For those who suffer discrimination, imprisonment, torture, or death because of their faith
	For the Church and diocese of Lyons
	For our selves that we may not be careless or lukewarm in our Christian life and witness
Preface:	A Saint (3) (BCP)
Color:	Red

June 3

The Martyrs of Uganda, 1886

Scarcely seven years after the arrival of the first Christian missionaries in Uganda, one hundred Christians, Catholic and Protestant, were brutally murdered. Joseph Mkasa Balikuddembe was beheaded after having rebuked King Mwanga of the Baganda for his debauchery and for the murder of the Anglican missionary bishop James Hannington on October 29, 1885 (remembered on that date in the calendar in the *Book of Common Prayer*). Eight months later there was a literal holocaust, a burnt offering, at Namugongo, when on June 3, 1886, thirty-two men and boys from thirteen to thirty years of age, many of them young pages in the court of King Mwanga of Buganda, were burned to death for their refusal to renounce Christianity. Their leader, Charles Lwanga, is remembered by name in the commemoration on the Roman calendar: "Charles Lwanga and companions, martyrs."

In the months that followed, many other Christians died by fire or spear because of their faith. The king's attempt to exterminate Christianity was turned upside down by the example of the martyrs who went to their death singing hymns and praying for their enemies and so inspired many who saw these things to understand that Christianity was truly African and not simply a white religion and to seek instruction in the Christian faith. Led mostly by Africans, the original band of converts multiplied many times and spread far beyond the court.

Charles Lwanga and his companions were canonized by the Roman Catholic Church in 1964. The Martyrs of Uganda were added to the calendar in the 1979 American *Book of Common Prayer*.

FOR FURTHER READING

Faupel, J. F. *African Holocaust: The Story of the Ugandan Martyrs.* New York: P. J. Kenedy, 1962.

Taylor, John V. *The Growth of the Church in Buganda.* London: SCM, 1958.

Thoonen, J. P. *Black Martyrs.* London: Sheed and Ward, 1941.

Tuma, A. D. T., and P. Mutibwa, eds. *A Century of Christianity in Uganda 1877–1977.* Nairobi, 1978.

READING

From an account of the martyrdom by Denis Kamyuka, one of the three survivors

We arrived at the place of execution, a mile and a quarter from the residence of Mukajanga [the chief executioner], and sat down in a group. We kept saying to one another, "Here we are, at Heaven's gates. In the twinkling of an eye, we shall see Jesus." The poor pagans laughed at us, saying, "Hark at their ravings! Don't they fear the flames? Do they think we are preparing a treat for them?"

Then Mukajanga gave each of us a small gourdful of plantain wine (mwenge), it being the custom of the Baganda to give plantain wine to everyone who is about to be put to death. James Buzabaliawo, (probably in memory of his Master's refusal on Calvary) refused to drink.

This final rite completed, Mukajanga dedicated us to his pagan deities and addressed us with a number of mock-farewells. Then he gave the order to tie us up.

We were stretched on reeds held together with fibre thongs, our hands tied firmly behind our backs, and our legs strapped together. The edges of the reed covers were folded over our bodies, and we were rolled in them so as to make movement impossible. Whilst one group of executioners was busy tying us up in this way, others built the pyre from the piles of firewood which had been collected. Then lifting the human faggots they had prepared, they laid them on the pyre. When they came to Sebuta, Werabe and myself, they tied us up perfunctorily, but instead of throwing us on the heap of firewood . . . they placed us to one side.

When all the victims had been laid on the pyre, the executioners brought more wood, which they piled on top of them. While this was being done, I heard the Christians, each reciting the prayers which came to his mind at that supreme moment. . . .

When Mukajanga saw that all was ready, he signaled to his men to station themselves all round the pyre, and then gave the order, "Light it at every point." The flames blazed up like a burning house and, as they rose, I heard coming from the pyre the murmur of the Christians' voices as they died invoking God.

From the moment of our arrest, I never saw one of them show any lack of courage. The pyre was lit towards noon.

J. F. Faupel, *African Holocaust: The Story of the Ugandan Martyrs* (New York: P. J. Kenedy, 1962), 194–95, 196, 197.

PROPERS

O God, you make the blood of the martyrs the seed of the church: Grant that we who remember before you the blessed martyrs of Uganda, who opened in the heart of Africa the new and living way of your Son Jesus Christ, may, like them, persevere unfalteringly in the faith for which they died; through the same Jesus Christ our Lord, who lives and reigns with you and the Holy Spirit, one God, forever and ever.

Heb. 10:20, Phil. 2:8, Heb. 5:8; PHP, RS ✤ LFF

Readings: Psalm 138 *or* 116:10-17
Hebrews 10:32-39
Matthew 24:9-14
Hymn of the Day:
"Hearken to the anthem glorious" (H82 240)
Prayers: For the church in Uganda
For the growth of Christianity in Africa
For all African Christians who suffer persecution for their faith
For the enemies of the cross of Christ and for the persecutors of his disciples
For those who have recently become Christians
Preface: Holy Week (BCP)
Color: Red

June 4

John XXIII, Bishop of Rome, Renewer of the Church, 1963

Angelo Roncalli, the third of thirteen children, was born to a family of farmers November 25, 1881, at Sotto il Monte in northern Italy. At the age of twelve, he entered the diocesan seminary at Bergamo and came under the influence of progressive leaders of the Italian social movement. He then went to seminary in Rome on a scholarship, interrupted his education there to serve for a year as a volunteer in the Italian army, and returned to the seminary to take a doctorate in theology. He was ordained priest August 10, 1904.

He was appointed secretary to the new bishop of Bergamo and with him learned forms of social action and gained an understanding of the problems of the working classes. Meanwhile he taught at the diocesan seminary.

In 1915 he was recalled to the army in World War I and served in the medical and chaplaincy corps. After the war, he was made spiritual director of the seminary. In 1921 the pope called him to Rome and made him director of the Society for the Propagation of the Faith in Italy.

He was consecrated archbishop in 1925 and made apostolic representative to Bulgaria. At Sofia, the capital, he dealt with the problem of Eastern Rite Catholics in a troubled oriental land.

In 1934 he was named apostolic delegate to Turkey and Greece. There he fostered harmony among various national groups in Istanbul in a time of anti-religious fervor under Kemal Ataturk. Archbishop Roncalli introduced the use of the Turkish language in worship and in the official documents of the Church and eventually won the esteem of some high Turkish statesmen. He made a series of conciliatory gestures toward the Orthodox and met with the Ecumenical Patriarch Benjamin in 1939. During World War II, Istanbul was a center of intrigue and espionage, and the

JUNE

archbishop gathered information useful to Rome and helped Jews flee persecution. His work in Greece, which was occupied by the Nazis, was less successful.

In 1944, when he was sixty-four years old, an age when many people are thinking of retirement, Pope Pius XII chose Archbishop Roncalli for the difficult post of nuncio to Paris, where he worked to heal the divisions caused by the war. He traveled widely.

At the age of seventy-two, he was made a cardinal and patriarch of Venice, and he had charge of a large diocese for the first time in his life. He quickly won the affection of his people, visiting parishes, caring for the working classes, establishing new parishes, and developing forms of social action.

In 1958, nearly seventy-seven years old, upon the death of Pius XII, he was elected pope and chose the biblical name of John. He was expected by many to be a caretaker and transitional pope, but he astonished the Church and the world with his energy and reforming spirit. He expanded and internationalized the college of cardinals, called the first diocesan synod of Rome in history, revised the code of canon law, and called the Second Vatican Council to revitalize the Church. This council was the major achievement of his life to renew the life of the Church and its teaching, with the ultimate goal of the unification of Christianity. Moreover, as Bishop of Rome, he was unremitting in the care of his diocese, visiting hospitals, prisons, and schools. When he died June 3, 1963, he had won the widespread affection of Christians and non-Christians alike.

John XXIII was added to the calendar in the *Lutheran Book of Worship* on the date of his death, June 3. To accommodate the commemoration of the Martyrs of Uganda, his commemoration is appropriately moved to the next day, as it is on the 1988 calendar of the Uniting Church in Australia (Methodist, Presbyterian, Congregationalist).

FOR FURTHER READING

Cahill, Thomas. *Pope John XXIII*. New York: Penguin Putnam, 2001.

Elliott, Lawrence. *I Will Be Called John: A Biography of Pope John XXIII*. London: Collins, 1974.

Hebblethwaite, Peter. *Pope John XXIII: Shepherd of the Modern World*. New York: Doubleday, 1985.

John XXIII. *Journal of a Soul*. Trans. Dorothy White. New York: McGraw-Hill, 1965.

Johnson, Paul. *Pope John XXIII*. Boston: Little Brown, 1974.

READING

From *Journal of a Soul* by John XXIII

[1959] Since the Lord chose me, unworthy as I am, for this great service, I feel I have no longer any special ties to this life, no family, no earthly country or nation, nor any particular preferences with regard to studies or projects, even good ones. Now, more than ever, I see myself only as the humble and unworthy "servant of God and servant of the servants of God" (Gregory the Great, *Epistolarum* XIII, 1). The whole world is my family. The sense of belonging to everyone must give character and vigor to my mind, my heart, and my actions.

The welcome immediately accorded to my unworthy person and the affection still shown by all who approach me are always a source of surprise to me. The maxim "Know thyself" suffices for my spiritual serenity and keeps me on the alert. The secret of my success must lie there: in not "searching into things which are above my ability" (Ecclesiasticus 3:23) and in being content to be "meek and humble of heart." Meekness and humbleness of heart give graciousness in receiving, speaking, and dealing with people, and the patience to hear, to pity, to keep silent and to encourage. Above all, one must always be ready for the Lord's surprise moves, for although he treats his loved ones well, he generally likes to test them with all sorts of trials such as bodily infirmities, bitterness of soul, and sometimes opposition so powerful as to transform and wear out the life of the servant of God, the life of the servant of the servants of God, making it a real martyrdom.

John XXIII, *Journal of a Soul,* trans. Dorothy White (New York: McGraw-Hill, 1965), 298–99.

PROPERS

Heavenly Father, shepherd of your people, it is your will to heal division and discord among all who are called by the Name of your Son: We pray that the open and reconciling spirit shown by your servant John XXIII may teach us to listen to our fellow Christians with humility and a willingness to learn, and to speak the truth in love to the healing of our divisions and the renewal of our witness to the world; through Jesus Christ our Lord, who lives and reigns with you and the Holy Spirit, one God, now and forever.

PHP, after James E. Kiefer

Readings:	Ezekiel 34:11-16
	Psalm 84
	1 Peter 5:1-4
	John 21:15-17
Hymn of the Day:	
	"Thee will I love, my strength, my tower" (LBW 502, LSB 694)
	"Sometimes a light surprises" (H82 667, SBH 495)
Prayers:	For the renewal of the church
	For the unity of Christ's church
	For humility and humor
	For the spirit of love and service
	For openness to the surprises of God
Preface:	Apostles
Color:	White

JUNE

June 5

Boniface, Archbishop of Mainz, Missionary to Germany, Martyr, 754

The Apostle of Germany, whose original name was Wynfrith (Wynfrid or Winfred), was born in Crediton in Devonshire, England, sometime between 672 and 675. When his father became seriously ill, the son was sent to the Benedictine school at Exeter and then to the Benedictine monastery at Nursling, between Winchester and Southampton, a place of learning and concern for missionary activity. Wynfrid was ordained there, and he became director of the monastic school and wrote a Latin grammar and several poems.

When he was about forty years old, *ca.* 716, he received permission from his abbot to begin missionary work in Frisia (northwest Germany and the northern Netherlands), a part of the kingdom of the Franks and the scene of widespread rejection of Christianity. Willibrord, the Apostle of Frisia (remembered in the *Book of Common Prayer* on November 7), had prepared the way from his base at Utrecht by establishing relations with the Frankish rulers and gaining papal support for missionary work there. After exploring the possibility of a mission, Wynfrith recognized that the time was not ripe, and within a year he returned to his monastery. His abbot died in 717, and Wynfrith was elected his successor, but in 718 he resigned in order to go to Rome to ask the pope for a missionary assignment. On May 15, 719, Gregory II gave him broad missionary jurisdiction, urged him to consult with Rome whenever difficulties arose, and gave Wynfrith the name of Boniface (Bonifatius), perhaps from *bonum facere* (to do good) or *bonum fatum* (good destiny) or perhaps a Latin approximation of the Old English Wyn-frith, "delight in peace."

The newly commissioned missionary went to Thuringia, preaching to secular leaders and attempting to reform the partly pagan clergy. In 719 he went again to Frisia, after the hostile Duke Radbod had died, to study Willibrord's missionary methods. In 721 he went on his own to Hesse, established a monastery there, and baptized many converts (thousands, his biographer says) on the Day of Pentecost, 722.

The pope, learning of his success, invited Boniface to Rome and November 30, 722, consecrated him bishop for the German frontier without a fixed diocese. He provided him with a collection of rules and letters of recommendation to important persons whose protection was essential to Boniface's success. He returned to the mission field, and one of his first acts, it is said, was to fell the sacred oak tree of Thor at Geisman in Hesse. When he was not harmed for this action, many of the people were converted, and with the wood of the tree, Boniface built a chapel in honor of St. Peter.

Bishop Boniface stayed two years in Hesse and then for ten years (725–735) worked again in Thuringia, where Frankish and Irish missionaries had made a start. Despite struggles with pagan corruption of Christian clergy and ceremonies, Boniface enjoyed a fruitful mission, supported by gifts from the Benedictines in England.

Pope Gregory III elevated Boniface to the rank of archbishop in 732 and asked him to consecrate missionary bishops. In 737 Boniface made his final visit to Rome, spent a year there, and was asked by the pope to organize the German Church. In 738 he returned to Germany as papal legate and established new bishoprics and abbeys. In 744 he established the most famous of his monasteries at Fulda, which became the center of German spiritual and intellectual life. Boniface assisted in reforming the Frankish Church (742–747), and upon the deposition of Gewiliob, the bishop of Mainz, who had killed his father's murderer, Boniface was made archbishop of Mainz, for although he had been archbishop since 742, he had never been assigned a see. For about a year Boniface was successful in one last mission to the Frisians. But at sunrise on June 5, 754, at Dokkum, Boniface, while reading the Gospel to a group of neophytes on Pentecost, a band of pagan Frisians attacked, and all were massacred. At Fulda, along with the remains of Boniface, is preserved a Gospel book that has been slashed in several places and that is purported to have been held by Boniface when he was killed.

Boniface is on the calendar in the *Book of Common Prayer,* the *Lutheran Book of Worship, For All the Saints, Evangelical Lutheran Worship,* and the *Lutheran Service Book.*

FOR FURTHER READING

Anderson, Clinton, S.J. *Anglo-Saxon Saints and Heroes.* New York: Fordham University Press, 1967.

Duckett, Eleanor Shipley. "Boniface of Devon." In *Anglo-Saxon Saints and Scholars.* Chap. 4. New York: Macmillan, 1947.

Emerton, Ephraim. *The Letters of St. Boniface.* New York: Columbia University Press, 1940.

Greenaway, George William. *Saint Boniface.* London: A. & C. Black, 1955.

Kylie, Edward, ed. and trans. *The English Correspondence of St. Boniface.* London, 1911, 1924. Reprinted 1966.

Reuter, Timothy, ed. *The Greatest Englishman: Essays on St. Boniface and the Church at Crediton.* Exeter: Paternoster, 1980.

Sladden, John Cyril. *Boniface of Devon.* Exeter: Paternoster, 1980.

Williamson, James M. *The Life and Times of St. Boniface.* London: Henry Frowde, 1904.

Willibald. *The Life of St. Boniface.* Trans. G. W. Robinson. Cambridge: Harvard University Press, 1916.

JUNE

READING

From the Letters of St. Boniface

In her voyage across the ocean of this world, the Church is like a great ship being pounded by the waves of life's different stresses. Our duty is not to abandon ship but to keep her on her course.

The ancient fathers showed us how we should carry out this duty: Clement, Cornelius, and many others in the city of Rome, Cyprian at Carthage, Athanasius at Alexandria. They all lived under emperors who were pagans; they all steered Christ's ship—or rather his most dear spouse, the Church. This they did by teaching and defending her, by their labors and sufferings, even to the shedding of blood.

I am terrified when I think of all this. "Fear and trembling come upon me and horror" of my sins "overwhelms me." [Psalm 55:5] I would gladly give up the task of guiding the Church which I have accepted if I could find such an action warranted by the example of the fathers or by Holy Scripture.

Since this is the case, and since the truth can be assaulted but never defeated or falsified, with our tired mind let us turn to the words of Solomon, "Trust in the Lord with all your heart and do not rely on your own insight. In all your ways acknowledge him, and he will make straight your paths" [Prov. 3:5-6]. In another place he says, "The name of the Lord is a strong tower; the righteous run into it and are safe." [Prov. 18:10]

Let us stand fast in what is right and prepare our souls for trial. Let us wait upon God's strengthening aid and say to him, "Lord, you have been our dwelling place in all generations." [Ps. 90:1]

Let us trust in him who has placed this burden upon us. What we ourselves cannot bear let us bear with the help of Christ. For he is all-powerful and he tells us, "My yoke is easy, and my burden is light." [Matt. 11:30]

Let us continue the fight on the day of the Lord. "Arrogance and scorn have now become strong; it is a time of ruin and furious anger." If God so wills, let us give our lives "for the covenant of our ancestors" [1 Macc. 2:50], so that we may enter into the eternal inheritance with them

Let us be neither dogs that do not bark nor silent onlookers nor paid servants who run away before the wolf. Instead let us be careful shepherds watching over Christ's flock. Let us preach the whole of God's plan to the powerful and to the humble, to rich and to poor, to men of every rank and age, as far as God gives us strength, in season and out of season. . . .

Letter 78. From the English translation of the Office of Readings from the Liturgy of the Hours © 1974, the International Committee on English in the Liturgy, Inc., rev. PHP.

PROPERS

Almighty God, you called your servant Boniface to bring your Word and Sacraments to the German people, to build up your Church among them, and to seal his ministry by martyrdom: We praise you for his life lived and laid down in your service, and we pray you to bestow on us and on all called to be missionaries an undaunted devotion to your people and to our Redeemer Jesus Christ our Lord; who lives and reigns with you and the Holy Spirit, one God, now and forever.
DvD, JWP, PHP

Readings:	Psalm 115:1-8 *or* 31:1-5
	Acts 20:17-28
	Luke 24:44-53
Hymn of the Day:	
	"Lord of our life and God of our salvation" (LBW 366, LSB 659, ELW 766, H40 395)
	or "Lead us, heavenly Father, lead us" (H82 559, CSB 274)
Prayers:	For the church in Germany and the Netherlands
	For the government and people of Germany and the Netherlands
	For those who teach the faith
	For courage in the face of disappointments
	For missionaries, especially those whose lives are in danger
Preface:	Apostles
Color:	Red

June 6

William Alfred Passavant, Renewer of Society, 1894

William Passavant's family was among the early settlers of western Pennsylvania. He was born October 9, 1821, in Zelienople, which had been named after his mother Zelie, and was a tireless worker in the cause of relieving human suffering. He was a pastor, a mission organizer, a founder of hospitals in Milwaukee, Chicago, Pittsburgh, and Jacksonville, Illinois; of orphanages in Mount Vernon, New York, Philadelphia, and Boston. He was also a founder of Thiel College, Chicago Seminary, and the General Council. He introduced the deaconess movement to America.

He grew up in western Pennsylvania, graduated from Jefferson College (a Presbyterian institution), and from Gettysburg Seminary in 1842. He served a congregation in Baltimore for two years. As pastor of First English Lutheran

JUNE

Church in Pittsburgh, 1844–1855, he gave new life and purpose to a struggling and dispirited congregation. His activity was incessant, and his missionary spirit and farsightedness led him to secure lots in various suburbs and in the surrounding country for mission congregations. Regular services were held in the jail, and the poor and the sick and the neglected were sought out and ministered to. He was an organizer of the Pittsburgh Synod and served as its missionary president.

Passavant in his parish in Baltimore and in his first years in Pittsburgh had been an advocate of organic union with the Cumberland Presbyterian Church and of the "new measures" of the various Protestant denominations, but in 1846 his outlook changed. A visit to a Jewish orphanage in London introduced him to a broader vision of charitable work and evoked his conscious decision to serve God by ministering to God's needy ones. His journey continued on the continent and opened his eyes to a kind of Lutheranism he had not known: conservative, confessional, liturgical. His encounter with great religious and charitable enterprises, especially Fliedner's deaconess community at Kaiserswerth, gave him further encouragement in his philanthropic and missionary interests. He became convinced that ministering love was lacking in American Christianity, whereas it ought to be its chief witness. In 1848 he began a church paper, *The Missionary,* and in 1880 he created *The Workman* to foster appreciation of historical and confessional Lutheran theology and stimulate missionary and philanthropic activity. In 1861 the *Missionary* was merged with *The Lutheran* in Philadelphia, which had been founded in 1856, and the paper became the popular English forum for constructive Lutheran thought and practice.

Mercy Hospital in Pittsburgh had been established by the Roman Catholic Church in 1847. There was no Protestant hospital in the United States, and Passavant in January 1849 equipped a small hospital, the Pittsburgh infirmary, to care for soldiers returning from the Mexican War, received two who had been taken ill, and with the aid of a student ministered to them with his own hands. He chartered the hospital "in order that the suffering and sick might be cared for in a becoming and Christian manner, without distinction of color, creed, or country." He had an enormous confidence in God's providence. He received the patients first and was sure that the Lord would provide by opening hearts to offer "the mite of the poor and the bounty of the rich." In July Pastor Theodor Fliedner (commemorated October 7) came to visit and brought four deaconesses with him to begin the motherhouse in Pittsburgh. In 1850 the first American deaconess, Catherine Louisa Marthens, who had been confirmed by Passavant, was consecrated for the ministry of mercy. She served until her death in 1899. The progress did not, however, fulfill the promise of the beginning. In thirty-five years only sixteen probationers entered the motherhouse. Some were consecrated, but all except three left the service after a period of one to nine years. Two of the Kaiserswerth sisters were married in 1853. Of the four who came first, only one, Elisabeth Hupperts, served until her death, in 1895, after serving sixty years as a deaconess.

At length Passavant recognized that he could not care for his parish and give himself sufficiently to his many-sided activities. Thus, in 1855, he resigned his pastorate in Pittsburgh to give himself entirely to his widespread interests of missions and mercy and publication.

The practical side of Christianity captivated him as a man and as a pastor. Passavant had a remarkable ability in raising money for support of social ministries. He lavishly and compassionately bestowed love and support on the suffering and the needy, whom he was adept at finding. He tirelessly and effectively summoned individual Christians and the Christian church to live the gospel it proclaimed.

In all this, William Passavant was supported and encouraged by his wife, Eliza Walter of Baltimore, whom he married in 1845. A woman of "extraordinary energy, unselfish industry, tenacity of purpose, and administrative gifts," she encouraged him when he doubted his right to sacrifice all in an unknown venture. She gave him her full cooperation, her counsel, prayers, and relieved him almost entirely of the care of a large family. She supported and advised the deaconesses, and served the Pittsburgh Hospital for a long time as matron, when no other could be found.

Passavant died June 3, 1894, and is remembered for his contribution to the growth of Lutheran loyalty and the organization of the benevolence of the Church. His close associate H. W. Roth said of him, "When others dreamed, he dared and did."

FOR FURTHER READING

Gerberding, George H. *The Life and Letters of William A. Passavant, D.D.* Greenville: Young Lutheran Co., 1906.

Mergner, Julie. *The Deaconess and Her Work.* Trans. Harriet R. Spaeth. Philadelphia: General Council Publication House, 1915.

READING

From *The Workman*

The idea of *The Workman* may be set forth in a few words. It is to labor for the reproduction in the Church of the life and works of Christ. The Church must not only be a witnessing Church but also a working Church. If she is not this, her testimony for the truth and her solemn services are in vain. Only when the Church truly believes, is she in a position to teach, to confess, and to live the life of her blessed Lord. Therefore a heartfelt and justifying faith in Christ as the Son of God will be unceasingly set forth as the only factor of a true Christian life. And because of such faith, bringing with it forgiveness of sin and the peace of God, the Church must follow in the footsteps of her Lord, and out of the depths of her grateful love

JUNE

do His works. Having been much forgiven, she will love much. And to do this, she must daily sit at His feet and learn of Him.

We are not satisfied with a mere intellectual and scholarly orthodoxy. We believe that every doctrine pertaining to salvation must become an experience. In the alembic of the inner spirit it must become transmuted into life. It must become transformed into the being and personality of him who is to teach it. Only thus does it really become his own. Only thus does he become a true and living teacher of the truth. The witness that the divine Spirit brings to him in the Word and in a Theology drawn from that Word must become a witness in him. Out of a heart moved and melted by penitence, soothed and saved by faith, fervid and filled with love, he testifies. He is a living witness, a true prophet, an ambassador who teaches and beseeches in Christ's stead, moved and constrained by the love of Christ.

For All the Saints, vol. 4, ed. Frederick J. Schumacher and Dorothy Zelenko (Delhi, N.Y.: American Lutheran Publicity Bureau, 1996), 933–34.

PROPERS

Almighty God, by your Holy Spirit you call us to care for those whom the world would forget, the ill, the orphaned, the homeless, the aged: We pray that by the gifts and graces bestowed upon your servant William Passavant and by the example of his perseverance and service, we may be encouraged to bring the comfort and joy of the gospel to those who have no one to care for them; through your Son Jesus Christ our Lord, who lives and reigns with you and the Holy Spirit, one God, now and forever.
PHP

Readings:	Genesis 22:9-14
	Psalm 10
	John 9:1-4
Hymn of the Day:	
	"Lord, whose love through humble service" (LBW 423, LSB 848, ELW 712, H82 610)
Prayers:	For confidence in God's care and providence
	For social service agencies
	For social workers
	For those in prison
	For children, especially orphans
	For homeless
	For the aged
Preface:	Weekdays
Color:	White

June 7

Sealth (Seattle), Chief of the Duwamish Confederacy, 1866

Noah Sealth (the name is usually transliterated as Seattle) was born *ca.* 1786 in the Puget Sound area of Washington state. When he was six years old, he saw a European for the first time when Captain George Vancouver sailed into town on a ship heavy with guns. Impressed with these and with the commercial products that followed, his fascination with the newcomers grew. He became chief of the Suquamish Tribe and then became chief of the Allied Tribes, the Duwamish Confederacy.

In the 1830s he became a Roman Catholic, and from that time on he lived in such a way that he earned the respect of both Native Americans and whites. Unlike many of his time, he rejected war and chose the path of peace. He began the custom, which survived his death, of holding morning and evening prayer in the tribe. He befriended the area's white settlers, who arrived in the early 1850s. On January 22, 1855, he signed a treaty at Point Elliott in the heart of the modern city that bears his name, Seattle, which ceded to the whites his ancestral land and by which the Duwamish accepted a small reservation north of Seattle. At a ceremony marking the occasion, Governor Isaac Stevens of the newly formed Washington Territory addressed the residents, and Sealth responded with a rich and poignant oration. Dr. Henry A. Smith took notes and later reconstructed the speech. The exact words of Sealth's speech are uncertain, as is the case with the transcription and translation of many great Native American speakers, but beneath what may be the fustian oratorical style of the translator, there lies an undeniable base of graceful and moving poetry that characterized the Indian speeches of the time. In his day Sealth was regarded as extraordinarily eloquent, and on the occasion of this treaty he refused to speak the pidgin English or Chinook preferred by Governor Stevens and used instead his native Duwamish tongue. (In 1971 a statement created by Ted Perry, a screenwriter, was mistaken by some as the words of Sealth and was promulgated as an environmental manifesto. Its several anachronisms mark it as not genuine.)

Sealth died June 7, 1866. Twenty years after his death, in 1886, the *Seattle Sunday Star* printed excepts from the diary of Henry A. Smith, who had taken notes of some of Sealth's speeches. The diary describes the Chief as "the largest Indian I ever saw, and by far the noblest-looking. He stood six feet tall in his moccasins, was broad-shouldered, deep-chested, and finely proportioned. His eyes were large, intelligent and expressive and friendly when in repose, and faithfully mirrored the varying moods of the great soul that looked through them. He was usually solemn, silent, and dignified, but on great occasions moved among assembled multitudes like a Titan among Lilliputians, and his lightest word was law." On the centennial of his birth the city of Seattle, Washington, named for him against his wishes, erected a monument over his grave.

Sealth, spelled Seattle, was included in the calendar of the *Lutheran Book of Worship* and is on the calendar of the Methodist *For All the Saints* and *Evangelical Lutheran Worship.*

FOR FURTHER READING

Bagley, C. B. "Chief Seattle and Angeline." *Washington Historical Quarterly* 22 (October 1931): 243–75.

Carlson, Frank. *Chief Sealth.* M.A. thesis, University of Washington, 1903.

Prosch, T. W. "Seattle and the Indians of Puget Sound." *Washington Historical Quarterly* 2 (July 1908): 303–08.

Starnes, Luke. "The Saga of Seattle" *Golden West Magazine* 4, no. 2 (January 1968).

Uncommon Controversy: A Report Prepared by the American Friends Service Committee. Seattle: University of Washington Press, 1970.

Watt, Roberta Frye. *The Story of Seattle.* Seattle: Lowman and Hanford, 1931.

READING

From Chief Sealth's speech at the ceding of his land

It matters little where we pass the remnant of our days. They will not be many. The Indian's night promises to be dark. Not a single star of hope hovers above the horizon. Sad-voiced winds moan in the distance. Grim fate seems to be on the Red Man's trail, and wherever he goes he will hear the approaching footsteps of his fell destroyer and prepare stolidly to meet his doom, as does the wounded doe that hears the approaching footsteps of the hunter.

A few more moons. A few more winters—and not one of the descendents of the mighty hosts that once moved over this broad land or lived in happy homes, protected by the Great Spirit, will remain to mourn over the graves of a people— once more powerful and hopeful than yours. But why should I mourn the untimely fate of my people? Tribe follows tribe, and nation follows nation, like the waves of the sea. It is the order of nature, and regret is useless. Your time of decay may be distant, but it will surely come, for even the White Man whose God walked and talked with him as friend with friend, cannot be exempt from the common destiny. We may be brothers after all. We will see.

We will ponder your proposition and when we decide we will let you know. But should we accept it, I here and now make this condition that we will not be denied the privilege without molestation of visiting at any time the tombs of our ancestors, friends, and children. Every part of this soil is sacred in the estimation of my people. Every hillside, every valley, every plain and grove, has been hallowed by some sad or happy event in days long vanished. Even the rocks, which seem to be dumb and dead as they swelter in the sun along with the silent shore, thrill with memories of stirring events connected with the lives of my people, and the very dust upon which you now stand responds more lovingly to their footsteps than to yours, because it is rich with the blood of our ancestors, and our bare feet are conscious of the sympathetic touch. Our departed braves, our fond mothers, glad, happy-hearted maidens, and even our little children who lived here and rejoiced here for a brief season, will love these somber solitudes and at eventide they greet the shadowy returning spirits.

And when the last Red Man shall have perished, and the memory of my tribe shall have become a myth among the White Men, these shores will swarm with the invisible dead of my tribe, and when your children's children think themselves alone in the field, the store, the shop, upon the highway, or in the silence of the pathless woods, they will not be alone. In all the earth there is no place dedicated to solitude. At night when the streets of your villages are silent and you think them deserted, they will throng with the returning hosts that once filled them and still love this beautiful land. The White Man will never be alone.

Let them be just and deal kindly with my people, for the dead are not power-less. Dead, did I say? There is no death, only a change of worlds.

From Louis Thomas Jones, *Aboriginal American Oratory* (Los Angeles: Southwest Museum, 1965), 99.

PROPERS

Lord God, Great Spirit, you inspired your noble servant Noah Sealth to renounce war and to walk in the way of peace and gave him dignity in his bearing and elo-quence in his speech: Give us the courage to acknowledge the common destiny of all mortals that we may gladly embrace the life you offer in Jesus Christ our Lord; who lives and reigns with you and the Holy Spirit, one God, now and forever. PHP

Readings:	Micah 6:6-8
	Psalm 19
	1 Corinthians 1:26-31
	Luke 6:20-23
Hymn of the Day:	
	"Jesus, still lead on, till our rest is won" (LBW 341, LSB 718, ELW 624)
Prayers:	For faithfulness in daily prayer
	For hospitality to strangers and newcomers
	For the strengthening of the life and culture of the Native Americans
	For understanding of the traditions of the Americans who came to this land first
Preface:	Baptism (BCP, LBW)
Color:	Of the season

JUNE

June 9

Columba, Abbot of Iona, 597; Aidan, Bishop of Lindisfarne, 651

Two missionaries to Britain who kept alive the light of learning and devotion during the dark ages may be commemorated together today.

Columba (his name is said to have been originally Cremthann; in Irish he is Colum Cille, "Dove of the Church"), was born at Gartan, Donegal, of the royal Niall (O'Neill) dynasty, about 521. He was educated in Irish monasteries by some of the leading teachers of his time and ordained deacon at the monastery of Moville; he studied at Clonard and was ordained priest in 551 at Glasnevin, near Dublin. He established several churches and monasteries in Ireland.

About 563, at the age of forty-two, as a "pilgrim for Christ," he left Ireland with twelve companions and established a community on the island of Hy (later called Iona), off the west coast of Scotland, where, legend has it, his tiny boat had washed ashore. This monastery served as a center for missions to the Irish who had settled in Scotland and also to the Picts (the original inhabitants of Scotland), and the Northumbrians. Columba lived at Iona more than thirty years (Bede says thirty-two), evangelizing the mainland and establishing monasteries in the islands nearby. He often returned to Ireland for synods, establishing Iona as a link between Irish and Pictish Christians.

There is a legend that in 565 he rebuked the Loch Ness monster with the sign of the cross and commanded it to cease its vicious ways after it had killed one man and was about to attack another. The miracle is said to have caused the conversion of Brude, king of the Picts. A powerful personality, a great open-air preacher, an able organizer, and a poet, Columba has been described (Thomas Hodgkin, *Political History of England*) as a kind of sixth-century John Wesley. Bede calls him "a true monk in life no less than in habit," who turned the Picts to the "faith of Christ by his words and example and so received the island of Iona from them to establish a monastery there." Columba died on Sunday, June 9, 597, according to Bede, aged seventy-seven. He was buried on his island, but his remains were moved to Kells in Ireland in 849 for safekeeping in a time of turmoil.

Viking raiders in the eighth and ninth centuries ravaged the island, and it underwent periodic destruction. But throughout the unsettled centuries of invasion and warfare, the reputation of Iona as a holy place flourished, and it became the burial place of Scottish, Irish, and Norwegian kings. The monastery was suppressed at the time of the Reformation. The Norman church, built in the thirteenth century, was abandoned at the time of Cromwell and fell into decay. In 1899 the ruined abbey became the property of the Church of Scotland, and it was gradually rebuilt and opened again for worship in 1912. In 1938 George MacLeod, a Glasgow minister of the Church of Scotland, founded the Iona Community to restore both the church and the spiritual life of the island. The members of the community, ministers and laypeople, are bound together by the common experience of shared work and worship on Iona, by a common intention in their work on the mainland, and by a common discipline of daily prayer and Bible study and thoughtful budgeting of time and money.

Samuel Johnson was deeply impressed by his visit to the island, described in his *Journey to the Western Islands of Scotland* (1775). "We were now treading that illustrious island which was once the luminary of the Caledonian regions, whence savage clans and roving barbarians derived the benefits of knowledge and the blessings of religion. . . . That man is little to be envied . . . whose piety would not grow warmer among the ruins of Iona. . . . Perhaps in the revolutions of the world Iona may be sometime again the instructress of the western regions. . . ."

Evelyn Underhill in her *Collected Papers* (1945) tells of a woman who had spoken to a gardener on Iona of the beauties of the Island. "Yes, mum," he said. "Iona's a thin place." Asked what he meant by that, he explained, "Well, on Iona, mum, there's very little between you and God."

Columba is commemorated on this date in the calendar in the *Book of Common Prayer*. He is not included on the General Roman calendar; he is, however, commemorated on the Roman Catholic calendar in both Ireland and Scotland. Columba and Aidan are remembered together on this date on the calendar in the Methodist book *For All the Saints*; Columba, Aidan, and Bede are commemorated on this date in the *Lutheran Book of Worship* and in *Evangelical Lutheran Worship*.

FOR FURTHER READING

Adomnan of Iona. *Life of St. Columba.* Trans. Richard Sharpe. New York: Penguin, 1995.

Bullough, D. A. "Columba, Adomnan and the Achievement of Iona." *Scottish Historical Review* 43 (1964): iii–130; and 44 (1965): 17–33.

Menzies, Lucy. *St. Columba of Iona.* London: John Dent, 1920; Glasgow: Iona Community, 1975.

Simpson, W. Douglas. *The Historical St. Columba.* Edinburgh: Oliver and Boyd, 1963.

JUNE

READING

From Adomnan's *Life of Columba* (Adomnan or Adamnan
was the ninth abbot of Iona and wrote this account
between 679 and 704.)

The saint entered the church for the vesper office of the Lord's night. As soon as
that was finished, he returned to his lodging, and reclined on his sleeping-place,
where during the night he used to have for a bed, the bare rock; and for pillow,
a stone, which even today stands beside his grave as a kind of epitaph. So while
reclining there, he gave his last commands to the brothers, in the hearing of his at-
tendant alone, and said: "I commend to you, my children, these latest words, that
you shall have among yourselves mutual and unfeigned charity, with peace. If you
follow this course after the examples of the holy fathers, God, who gives strength
to the good, will help you; and I, abiding with them, shall intercede for you. And
not only will the necessities of this life be sufficiently provided by him, but also the
rewards of eternal good things will be bestowed, that are prepared for those who
follow the divine commandments."

We have carried down to this point, briefly told, the last words of the venerable patron, when he was, as it were, crossing over to the heavenly country from
this weary pilgrimage.

After them the saint was silent for a little, as the happy latest hour drew near.
Then, when the beaten bell resounded at midnight, he rose in haste and went to
the church and, running, entered in advance of the others, alone; and bowing his
knees in prayer he sank down beside the altar. In that moment Diormit, the at-
tendant, following later, saw from a distance the whole church filled inside with
angelic light about the saint. As Diormit approached the doorway, that light that
he had seen quickly faded. A few more of the brothers also had seen it, when they
too were a little way off.

So Diormit entering the church cried with a tearful voice, "Where are you,
where are you, father?" And groping in the darkness, since the lamps of the brothers had not yet been brought, he found the saint lying before the altar. Raising him
a little, and sitting down beside him, he placed the holy head upon his lap. Meanwhile the company of monks ran up with lights; and when they saw that their
father was dying they began to lament. And as we have learned from some men
who were present there, the saint, whose soul had not yet departed, opened his
eyes, and looked around on either side, with wonderful joy and gladness of countenance; for he was gazing upon the holy angels that had come to meet him. The
Diormit raised the holy right hand, to bless the saint's company of monks. And
the venerable father himself at the same time moved his hand, as much as he was
able, in order that he might be seen to bless the brothers even by the movement of
his hand, a thing that in the departure of his soul he could not do by voice. And
after the holy benediction thus expressed, he presently breathed out his spirit.

When that had left the tabernacle of the body, his face continued to be ruddy, and in a wonderful degree gladdened by the vision of angels, so much that it seemed like the face not of a dead man, but of a living sleeper. Meanwhile the whole church resounded with sorrowful lamentations.

Adonman's "Life of Columba," by St. Adamnan ed. and trans. by A. O. Anderson and M. Ogilvie. Revised Ed. (1991), 525–31. Reprinted by permission of Oxford University Press.

PROPERS

O God, you called your servant Columba from among the princes of Ireland to be a herald and evangelist of your kingdom to the Scottish people: Grant that your Church, having his faith and courage in remembrance, may so proclaim the splendor of your grace, that all the world may know your Son as their Savior and serve him as their King; who lives and reigns with you and the Holy Spirit, one God, forever and ever.

Church of Ireland, rev. DvD; see LFF

Readings: Psalm 97:1-2, 7-12 *or* 98:1-4
              1 Corinthians 3:11-23
              Luke 10:17-20
Hymn of the Day:
              "Christ is the world's Redeemer" (LSB 539), attributed to St. Columba
              or "The King of love my shepherd is" (H82 645, LBW 456, ELW 502), tune *St. Columba*
Prayers: For the church in Scotland
              For the Iona Community
              For a spirit of gentleness and self-denial and for the gift of joy in our hearts
              For perseverance in prayer
Preface: Apostles
Color: White

Aidan, a monk of Iona, was, like Columba, born in Ireland. He was trained at the monastery of Iona and was invited by St. Oswald (*ca.* 605–642), the Christian king of Northumbria, who himself had lived at Iona and where he was converted and baptized, to revive missionary work in his kingdom and reconvert the lapsed Northumbrians. The first monk who had been sent returned to report that the people were unwilling to hear his message. Aidan replied that perhaps a gentler approach would have been more successful. Aidan was therefore chosen to go; he was consecrated bishop in 635 and established his headquarters on the island of Lindisfarne, off the northeast coast of England in imitation of his home monastery at Iona. From there he made long journeys to the mainland as far south as London, strengthening Christian communities and founding new missionary outposts and teaching the practice of the Celtic Church. The Irish Church from the beginning

JUNE

was organized on a different basis from the Church of Rome. It had a primitive and tribal organization, suited to a rural and rather rude society, was monastic rather than episcopal in administration, and emphasized right living rather than elaborate theology. The Irish monasteries were Christian colonies in a pagan land, "holy experiments" for the practice of Christian living and virtue.

Aidan organized a monastery on Lindisfarne, where English boys were educated and trained to be missionaries among the English. One of these was Chad (see March 2). No wealth was allowed to accumulate; surpluses were applied to the relief of the poor and the manumission of slaves. When Aidan preached, King Oswald himself served as his interpreter, since Aidan was not fluent in English. The death of King Oswald, his friend and patron, was a great loss, but Oswald's successor, Oswin, was no less dear to him. Aidan adhered to the Celtic method of dating Easter, which depended on an eighty-four-year cycle, rather than the Roman nineteen-year cycle.

Aidan was admired for both his asceticism and his gentleness. He died August 31, 651, at Bamborough. The cause of his death is said to have been grief at the murder of King Oswin, who had been a companion in his missionary travels. Aidan was buried on Lindisfarne.

Aidan's traditional feast day is August 31, and he is commemorated on that date on the calendar in the *Book of Common Prayer*. He is not on the General Roman calendar. He is remembered with Columba on this day on the Methodist calendar in *For All the Saints*.

FOR FURTHER READING

Adams, Bruce Wilmot. "St. Aidan of Lindisfarne: Missionary of the Celtic Church," *Lutheran Forum* 39, no. 1 (Easter/Spring 2005): 12–15.

Fryer, Alfred C. *Aidan, the Apostle of the North*. London: Partridge, 1902.

Gougaud, Louis. *Christianity in Celtic Lands*. Trans. Maud Joynt. London: Sheed and Ward, 1932.

READING

From the Venerable Bede, *Ideals of the Priesthood,* section 5

From this island [Iona], then, from the company of these monks, Aidan, having received episcopal rank, was sent to the province of the Angles to instruct it in Christ. Among other teachings of how life ought to be lived, he left his clergy a most wholesome example in his abstinence and chastity. His doctrine was particularly recommended to all by the fact that he himself taught nothing different from the way he lived with his monks. He desired to seek nothing of this world, to love nothing. Everything given him by the kings or the wealthy of this world he was soon glad to give to the poor who came to beg from him. He used to journey about through all the cities and countryside, not on horseback but on foot, unless, greater necessity compelled him to ride. Whenever he saw, as he walked, either rich or poor, turning at once to them, he would summon those not of the faith to the sacrament of receiving faith; or if he saw the faithful, he would strengthen them in that faith itself and would arouse them by word and deed to perform acts of charity and good works.

Early Medieval Theology, vol. 9, The Library of Christian Classics, trans. and ed. George E. Mc-Cracken, 406–07. London: SCM and Philadelphia: Westminster, 1957.

PROPERS

O loving God, you called your servant Aidan from the peace of a cloister to re-establish the Christian mission in northern England, and endowed him with gentleness, simplicity, and strength: Grant that we, following his example, may use what you have given us for the relief of human need, and may persevere in commending the saving Gospel of our Redeemer Jesus Christ; who lives and reigns with you and the Holy Spirit, one God, forever and ever.

CMG, LFF August 31

Readings:	Psalm 97:1-2, 7-12 *or* 85:8-13
	1 Corinthians 9:16-23
	Matthew 19:27-30
Hymn of the Day:	
	"Blest are the pure in heart" (H82 656, SBH 394)
Prayers:	For missionaries in inhospitable places
	For evangelists in areas untouched by the church in cities and towns
	For all lapsed Christians
	For a commitment to simplicity and love for human souls
Preface:	Apostles
Color:	White

June 10

Ephrem of Edessa, Deacon, 373

JUNE

Ephrem (Ephraem), the most celebrated father of the Syrian Church, gained fame as a poet and hymnwriter as well as a theologian. He was born of a Christian family *ca.* 306 in Syria, where Christianity had been established very early and where Antioch was the major center of a flourishing church. He was student of James, bishop of Nisibis, and completed his education at Edessa. He visited Basil at Caesarea and was ordained deacon, and later, when the Persians captured the city of Nisibis and drove out the Christians, he became head of a successful theological school at Edessa. There he championed the faith of the Nicene Creed. He became well known for the sanctity and austerity of his life as well as for his learning. His writings are voluminous and include biblical commentaries, essays on dogma, history and biography, and metrical homilies, as well as hundreds of hymns, many of which have long been an integral part of Syrian Orthodox liturgy. The Syrians therefore called him "the harp of the Holy Spirit." Ephrem died in Edessa in June 373. He is remembered on June 9 on the Roman Catholic calendar and, so as not to displace Columba, on June 10 on the calendar in the *Book of Common Prayer*. His feast day in the East in January 28. He is commemorated on the *Evangelical Calendar of Names* on June 17.

FOR FURTHER READING

Brock, Sebastian. *The Harp of the Spirit.* London, 1983.
———. *The Luminous Eye: The Spiritual World Vision of St. Ephrem.* Rome: Cistercian, 1985.
Ephrem the Syrian. *Hymns on Paradise.* Trans. Sebastian Brock. Crestwood, N.Y.: St. Vladimir's Seminary Press, 1990
McVey, Kathleen E., trans. and ed. *Ephrem the Syrian: Hymns.* New York: Paulist, 1989.
Russell, Paul S. "Saint Ephraem, the Syrian Theologian." *Pro Ecclesia* 7, no. 1 (Winter 1998): 79–90.

READING

From a sermon by Ephrem

Lord, shed upon our darkened souls the brilliant light of your wisdom so that we may be enlightened and serve you with renewed purity. Sunrise marks the beginning of daily toil, but in our souls, Lord, prepare a dwelling for the day that will never end. Grant that we may come to know the risen life and that nothing may distract us from the delights you offer. Through our unremitting zeal for you, Lord, set upon us the sign of your day that is not measured by the sun.

In your Holy Mysteries we daily embrace you and receive you into our bodies; make us worthy to experience the resurrection for which we hope. We have had your treasure hidden within us ever since we received baptismal grace; it grows ever richer at your sacramental table. Teach us to find our joy in your favor. Lord, we have within us your memorial, received at your spiritual table; let us possess it in its full reality when all things shall be made new.

We glimpse the beauty that is laid up for us when we gaze upon the spiritual beauty your immortal will now creates within our mortal selves.

Savior, your crucifixion was the end of your bodily life; teach us to crucify ourselves and to live in the Spirit. May your resurrection, Jesus, bring us authentic spiritual greatness and may your sacraments be the mirror wherein we may know you.

Savior, your divine plan for the world is a mirror for the spiritual world; teach us to walk in that world as spiritual people.

Lord, do not deprive our souls of the spiritual vision of you nor our bodies of your warmth and sweetness. Our mortality corrupts us; let the spiritual waters of your love cleanse the effects of mortality from our hearts. Grant, Lord, that we may hasten to our true city and, like Moses on the mountaintop, glimpse it already from afar.

Sermon 3. From the English translation of the Office of Readings from the Liturgy of the Hours © 1974, International Committee on English in the Liturgy, Inc. rev. PHP.

PROPERS

We pray you, O Lord, pour into our hearts your Holy Spirit, by whose inspiration the deacon Ephrem loved to sing your mysteries with a single-minded devotion to your service; through your Son Jesus Christ our Lord, who lives and reigns with you and the Holy Spirit, one God, now and forever.

1952 Roman Missal, RS, June 9, trans. JWP

Readings:	Proverbs 3:1-7
	Psalm 98:5-10 *or* 33:1-5, 20-21
	Matthew 13:47-52
Hymn of the Day:	
	"From God Christ's deity came forth" (H82 443)
Prayers:	For the ancient churches of the East, particularly the Syrian Orthodox Church
	For all Christians living in Muslim countries
	For theologians and presidents and deans of theological schools
	For church musicians and hymnwriters
Preface:	A Saint (1) (BCP)
Color:	White

June 11

St. Barnabas, Apostle

Barnabas, a Jew from the tribe of Levi, was born on the island of Cyprus (Acts 4:36) about the beginning of the Christian era. He was, therefore, like Paul, a Jew of the Diaspora in contrast to Palestinian Jews like Peter. A man of means, he gave the young church the proceeds from the sale of a piece of land. His name was originally Joseph, but the apostles gave him the surname Barnabas, meaning "son of encouragement" (Acts 4:36), perhaps because of his impressive ability as a preacher. He is mentioned repeatedly in the Acts of the Apostles and several places in Paul's letters, and everything that is known with certainty about him is found in these New Testament passages. Although he was not one of the original Twelve, he was, like St. Paul, called an apostle (Acts 14:14).

The book of Acts lists Barnabas among the early believers in Jerusalem. He is traditionally regarded as one of the seventy disciples commissioned by Jesus (Luke 10:1), and he is commemorated as such by the Eastern Churches. It was Barnabas at Jerusalem who was convinced of the genuineness of Paul's conversion and vouched for him to the community (Acts 9:27). Somewhat later, the church at Jerusalem sent Barnabas to Antioch to the growing group of Gentile Christians there, and he in turn brought Paul from Tarsus to assist him (Acts 11:19-22).

After the church at Antioch reached a flourishing state with its own leaders, the two apostles, after fasting and prayer and the laying-on of hands by the faithful, set off on missionary travels, taking young John Mark with them. They preached the gospel on Cyprus and in Pamphylia, where Mark left them, and they continued in the cities of Asia Minor, preaching to Jews and Gentiles but winning converts chiefly from the latter group. On the island of Cyprus, it seems, Paul took over the leadership, and when they moved on to the mainland the group was known as "Paul and his company."

In the disagreement over the responsibilities of Jewish and Gentile Christians, Barnabas tended to side with his fellow worker Paul, although on one occasion he followed Peter in refraining from eating with Gentiles. Somewhat later, Barnabas and Paul disagreed on whether to take John Mark with them again, and they finally separated from each other, with Barnabas taking Mark to Cyprus with him, while Paul went to Syria and Cilicia with Silas (Acts 15:36-41). Nothing is known of the life of Barnabas after this. As far as the record goes, the rift was final, although in 1 Corinthians 9:6 Paul praises Barnabas as a working apostle. Legend has it that Barnabas was stoned to death in the city of Salamis on Cyprus, probably about the year 60.

Several writings bearing the name of Barnabas have circulated at various times. One of them, the *Epistle of Barnabas*, was widely read in the early church and was held by many to be genuine and worthy of inclusion in the New Testament. Modern scholarship attributes it to the second century, but it is acknowledged to be a valuable early Christian document. Tertullian proposed Barnabas as the author of Hebrews.

St. Barnabas's Day was observed by the Eastern Churches at least as early as the fifth century; they also commemorate St. Bartholomew on the same day, June 11. The observance in the West began in the ninth century, and the Anglican reformers kept his feast day on the Prayer Book calendar as did many Lutheran church orders.

FOR FURTHER READING

Kollmann, Bernd. *Joseph Barnabas: His Life and Legacy.* Trans. Miranda Henry. Collegeville: Liturgical, 2004.

READING

From *Worship* by J.-J. von Allmen

The Church . . . appears as . . . an apostolic or missionary community.

First of all, why does the Church, in and through its cult, emerge as an apostolic community? Because by its worship—to quote the words of K. Barth—"it issues, without pretension, but firmly, from the profanity of the milieu in which it is normally immersed," i.e., by its worship it is differentiated from the world. And this is in two ways. Firstly, it does not yet embrace all men, but only the baptized. From this fact there emerges a special attitude towards those who are not yet members of the Church. Her very existence is, for those who do not yet belong to her, at once a challenge and a promise. Secondly, it does not include all men. But also it is not always gathered together but has a day of its own, a day of worship, Sunday. The fact that one day is singled out for divine worship teaches the Church that it is still in the world, that the hour of the great Sabbath has not yet struck. If the comparison were not too bold, I would say that the Church emerges, week by week, rather as a cetaceous animal, at regular times, comes up for air. But this very intermission, that fact that the cult is not continuous but sporadic, emphasizes the Church's otherness in relation to the world, and thus confronts the Church with the question of its justification for existing in the world and for the world.

And how does the Church, in and through its worship become aware of itself as an apostolic community? . . . [I]t does so precisely through the realization that it is only as yet . . . the firstfruits of the creatures (Jas. 1:18), and not the totality, and that as yet it is gathered together only on the first day of the week (cf. Acts 20:7 etc.) and not every day of the week. In other words, the cult is an epiphany of the Church as a missionary community in the sense that it obliges the Church to send forth, into the world throughout the rest of the week, those whom it has assembled out of the world on the first day.

This gives us an opportunity of introducing a brief aside on the term "Mass" which, from the fourth century, gradually supplanted in the West all other terms denoting the cult and which, among the Lutherans, even survived the Reformation. The origin of the word has given rise to some doubt. It now seems established, in spite of some risky hypotheses, that the term "Mass" comes from the Low Latin *Missa—missio*—i.e. *dismissal*: in other words it is the last note of the cult, the solemn act of dismissal which sends the faithful forth into the world (cf. Luke 24:46-53), which has been used to denote the cult as a whole as though to emphasize the justification of the Christian cult in the world which is not yet the Kingdom. "The cult," affirms A. D. Müller, who insists on the term, "must be understood as the Mass, *missio,* dismissal. In it is kindled the light which is to illuminate the world."

Worship: Its Theology and Practice, by J.J. von Allmen, (1965), 132–33, 51–52, 37, 55–56. Reprinted by permission of Oxford University Press.

PROPERS

Grant, O God, that we may follow the example of your faithful servant Barnabas, who, seeking not his own renown but the well-being of your Church, gave generously of his life and substance for the relief of the poor and the spread of the Gospel; through Jesus Christ our Lord, who lives and reigns with you and the Holy Spirit, one God, forever and ever.

Acts 4:34-37; 1979 BCP; alt. in LBW, ELW

Readings:	Isaiah 42:5-12
	Psalm 112
	Acts 11:19-30; 13:1-3
	Matthew 10:7-16
Hymn of the Day:	
	"Lift high the cross, the love of God proclaim" (LBW 377, LSB 837, ELW 660, H82 473)
Prayers:	For preachers of the gospel
	For reconciliation of those at variance with one another
	For Cyprus and Turkey
Preface:	Apostles
Color:	Red

June 12

Lesser Feasts and Fasts 2003 added on this date the commemoration of **Enmegahbowh**, the first recognized Native American priest in the Episcopal Church. He died in 1902.

The *Lutheran Service Book* lists the **Ecumenical Council at Nicaea**, 325 C.E., for commemoration on this date. The traditional date for the opening of what the Eastern Churches call "the Synod of the 318 Fathers" is May 20; it closed July 25.

June 14

Macrina, Monastic Teacher, 379; Basil the Great, Bishop of Caesarea, 379; Gregory of Nazianzus, Bishop of Constantinople, *ca.* 389; Gregory, Bishop of Nyssa, *ca.* 385

Theologians of the Eastern Church are sometimes commemorated in groups. In the East, "Three Holy Hierarchs" are remembered together on January 30: Basil, Gregory of Nazianzus, and John Chrysostom. In the West, Basil and Gregory of Nazianzus are remembered together on January 2; with John Chrysostom and Athanasius, they are honored as the four Greek Doctors (that is, Teachers) of the Church. In the *Lutheran Book of Worship* and *Evangelical Lutheran Worship,* the three Cappadocian Fathers are commemorated jointly: Basil, Gregory of Nazianzus, and Gregory of Nyssa. It is appropriate to remember Macrina with them. Each of the men is remembered separately on the Episcopal calendar; *Lesser Feasts and Fasts 1997* has added a separate commemoration of Macrina on July 19.

Macrina, the eldest of ten children of a wealthy and aristocratic family, was born at Caesarea *ca.* 327 and is sometimes called "Macrina the Younger" to distinguish her from her paternal grandmother of the same name. Her father Basil, a successful lawyer, betrothed her to a younger member of his profession, but he died before the marriage. Macrina vowed never to marry, preferring instead the closeness of her family. Although she left no writings, by the strength of her character she exercised a deep influence on her family, especially in convincing Basil to leave a promising secular career for the Christian priesthood, and throughout her life giving her brothers theological and moral counsel. She persuaded her widowed mother to renounce their wealthy life and helped her establish a little monastic community on the family's estate on the river Iris in Pontus. Macrina's twin ideals of joyous discipline and hospitality were lived in the monastery and served as model for her brothers Basil, Gregory, Naukratios, and Peter. After the deaths of her mother Emmelia and her brothers Naukratios and Basil, Macrina was the strength of the surviving family.

The chief source of knowledge about her life is her brother Gregory of Nyssa's *Life of Macrina the Younger,* which preserves a vivid account of their meeting at her deathbed. Gregory also testifies to her competence as a theologian, referring to her as his "sister the teacher." She died at Pontus in 379 and was buried with her parents in their family Church of the Forty Martyrs of Sebaste. Her feast day is July 19, and she is remembered on that date on the calendar in the Episcopal *Lesser Feasts and Fasts* and the calendar in the Methodist book *For All the Saints.*

JUNE

FOR FURTHER READING

Clarke, W. K. Lowther, trans. *The Life of Macrina the Younger [Vita Macrinae Ju-nioris]*. London: SPCK, 1916.

Pelikan, Jaroslav. *Christianity and Classical Culture: The Metamorphosis of Natural Theology in the Christian Encounter with Hellenism*. New Haven: Yale University Press, 1994.

READING

From *The Life of Macrina* by Gregory of Nyssa

[Gregory is visiting his dying sister]

As I told my own trouble and all that I had been through, first my exile at the hands of the Emperor Valens on account of the faith, and then the confusion in the Church that summoned me to conflicts and trials, my great sister said, "Will you not cease to be insensible to the divine blessings? Will you not remedy the ingratitude of your soul? Will you not compare your position with that of your parents? And yet, as regards worldly things, we make our boast of being well born and thinking we come of a noble family. Our father was greatly esteemed as a young man for his learning; in fact his fame was established throughout the law courts of the province. Subsequently, though he excelled all others in rhetoric, his reputation did not extend beyond Pontus. But he was satisfied with fame in his own land. But you," she said, "are renowned in cities and peoples and nations. Churches summon you as an ally and director, and you do not see the grace of God in it all? Do you fail to recognize the cause of such great blessings, that it is your parents' prayers that are lifting you up on high, that you have little or no equipment within yourself for such success?"

Thus she spoke, and I longed for the length of the day to be further extended, that she might never cease delighting our ears with sweetness. But the voice of the choir was summoning us to the evening service, and sending me to church, the great one retired once more to God in prayer.

The Life of Macrina, trans. W. K. Lowther Clarke (London: SPCK, 1916).

Basil, known as the Administrator and the Patriarch of Eastern monks, was born *ca.* 329 into a saintly family: his parents and grandparents were all canonized. Basil was trained in rhetoric and the best of classical and Christian culture at Constantinople and Athens. He became a close friend of Gregory of Nazianzus, and they were baptized together *ca.* 358, and Basil yielded to the urging of his sister Macrina and gave up what promised to be a brilliant administrative career for the then unpopular life of asceticism that his family was leading at Annesi in Pontus. His brother Peter and others soon joined him.

After a brief period in Syria and Egypt, Basil settled as a hermit by the River Iris in Caesarea. He joined the clergy there and was ordained *ca.* 365. In the famine of 367–368, he sold his extensive property for the benefit of the starving, raised further money, and organized relief work, forbidding any distinction between Christian and Jew.

Before this time, monks had lived alone as hermits, but Basil established a common life for the service of society, following a simple rule and discouraging extreme asceticism. He is therefore honored as the father of Eastern communal monasticism, and monastic life in the Orthodox Church is still based on principles he laid down.

In the spring of 370, he was elected Bishop of Caesarea, a post that had jurisdiction over the dioceses in nearly all of Asia Minor and Armenia. He was consecrated June 14, and this became his traditional feast day in the West. He struggled against the Arianism of the civil administration and also against the party that denied the divinity of the Holy Spirit. Basil's ascetic training convinced him that only the purified spirit could know the divine incomprehensibility. He is sometimes known as the Doctor (Teacher) of the Holy Spirit, and his treatise *On the Holy Spirit* was a major contribution to the doctrine of the Trinity.

He organized missionary activity in Armenia. He sought to reunite all the Orthodox churches divided by the schism of Antioch. He was a major contributor to the liturgy that bears his name, the Liturgy of St. Basil, still used in the Eastern Church during Lent, Maundy Thursday, the vigils of Easter, Christmas, and the Epiphany, and on Basil's feast day, January 1. He was eloquent, statesmanlike, and of surpassing holiness. He died January 1, 397, and was mourned by the entire city, Jews and pagans as well as Christians. He was immediately eulogized by his brother Gregory of Nyssa and his friend Gregory of Nazianzus, but none of his contemporaries wrote his biography. Basil's feast day in the East is January 1, and on January 30 he is commemorated together with Gregory (Nazianzus) "the Theologian" and John Chrysostom. On the present Roman Catholic calendar, January 1 being the Solemnity of Mary the Mother of God, Basil's feast day is January 2. His commemoration in the *Book of Common Prayer* and the Methodist book *For All the Saints* is June 14, the date of his consecration as bishop (and his feast day on the former Roman Catholic calendar). Basil is commemorated on June 14, together with Gregory of Nyssa and Gregory Nazianzus, on the calendar in the *Lutheran Book of Worship* and *Evangelical Lutheran Worship;* in the *Lutheran Service Book* (2006) the three Cappadocian fathers are remembered on January 10, the date in the Eastern Church of the commemoration of Venerable Gregory of Nyssa.

JUNE

FOR FURTHER READING

Attwater, Donald. *The Golden Book of Eastern Saints.* Milwaukee: Bruce, 1938.

Barrios, George, ed. *The Fathers Speak.* Crestwood: St. Vladimir's Seminary Press, 1987.

Von Campenhausen, Hans. *The Fathers of the Greek Church.* 80–94. Trans. Stanley Godman. New York: Pantheon, 1959.

Clarke, W. K. Lowther, ed. *The Ascetic Works of St. Basil.* London: SPCK, 1925.

Fedwick, P. J., ed. *Basil of Caesarea, Christian Humanist, Ascetic: A Sixteen-Hundredth Anniversary Symposium.* Toronto: Pontifical Institute of Medieval Studies, 1981.

Rousseau, Philip. *Basil of Caesarea.* Berkeley: California University Press, 1994, 1998.

READING

From a letter of St. Basil

Christians should not be envious of others' good reputation, nor rejoice over their faults. Through love for Christ they should be grieved and distressed at their brothers' or sisters' faults and rejoice over their successes. They should not be indifferent to sinners or silent before them. Those who reprove others should do so with all tenderness, in fear of God and with a view to reforming the sinner. The one who is reproved or reprimanded should endure it willingly, recognizing the benefit received in being set right. When a person is being accused, a Christian should not, before that person or others, contradict the accuser. But if the accusation should ever seem unjust, the Christian should arrange a private conversation with the accuser, and either give or receive full information.

All should, according to their ability, entertain kindly feelings for everyone who has a grievance against them. They should not hold past wrongs against a repentant sinner, but should genuinely grant forgiveness. Those who say that they repent of a sin should not only feel remorse for their sin, but should also produce fruits worthy of repentance. And those who have been corrected for their first faults and have been thought worthy of forgiveness, if they sin again, prepare for themselves a judgment of anger worse than the first. And those who, after the first and second admonition, persist in their shortcoming, should be disclosed to the one in authority, if perhaps they may repent when admonished further. If even by this they are not set right, they should be cut off from the rest as a cause for scandal, and should be regarded as heathen and outcasts, for the sake of the safety of those zealous in obedience, according to the saying, "When the impious fall, the righteous tremble." Yet all should mourn for such, as though a member has been cut off from the body.

The sun should never set on one's wrath, lest night intervene and leave an inevitable charge for the day of judgment. Christians should not await an opportunity for personal reform, because the morrow is not secure, since many who have made great plans have not reached the morrow. They should not be deceived by the filling of their belly, for this causes nightmares. They should not busy themselves with excessive work, and thus step beyond the bounds of sufficiency, as the apostle says, "if we have food and clothing, we will be content with these" [1 Tim. 6:8]; because an abundance which goes beyond necessity gives appearance of avarice, and avarice has the condemnation of idolatry. They should not be desirous of money, nor treasure up unnecessary things to no avail. Those who approach God ought to embrace poverty in all things, and be pierced with the fear of God, according to the one who said, "my flesh trembles for fear of you, and I am afraid of your judgments" [Ps. 119:120].

The Lord grant that you may receive all these admonitions with all assurance, and that you may exhibit fruits worthy of the Holy Spirit to the glory of God, with God's approval and the assistance of our Lord Jesus Christ.

Saint Basil, the Letters, trans. PHP, based on the Loeb Classical Library edition, trans. Roy J. Deferrai, vol. 1 (Cambridge: Harvard University Press, 1926), 137–41.

Gregory, called "the Theologian" by the Eastern Church because of his profound influence and eloquence, was born of well-to-do parents at Arianzus near Nazianzus in Cappadocia (present-day Turkey) *ca*. 330. His father was a bishop. (Celibacy had not yet become universal.) Gregory was educated at Caesarea, where he met Basil, and then in Palestine, Alexandria, and Athens. On the way to Athens, he was shipwrecked, and in thanksgiving for his deliverance he dedicated the remainder of his life to God (although a catechumen, he had not yet been baptized). Throughout his career he was torn between his desire to live a life of solitary contemplation and the Church's summons to involvement in its conflicts and controversy. At Athens he again met Basil. After eight years of study, in 367 or 368, he left for Nazianzus. There he was baptized, probably by his father. He taught rhetoric briefly, but soon joined Basil at his monastery on the river Iris. Together they drew up monastic rules, which transformed the solitary anchorites into a disciplined community of prayer and work, edited the sayings of Origen, and enlisted Gregory of Nyssa for the monastery.

Gregory's father, in poor health, brought his son back to Nazianzus for ordination at Christmas in 362. Gregory assisted his father and helped elect Basil to the see of Caesarea.

The Arian emperor Valens in 372 divided the province of Cappadocia in half. To save the new diocese for Orthodox Christianity, Basil compelled Gregory to accept election as bishop of Sasima, the new diocese, described by Gregory as "a detestable little place without water or grass or any mark of civilization," but under threats of violence from the bishop of the new capital city of Tyana he never took possession of it. A rift between Basil and Gregory resulted that was never fully healed.

Gregory continued to assist his father until his father died in 374. Gregory then withdrew to Isauria until 378 and accepted a call to be bishop of the Nicene community in the capital city of Constantinople. The hostility of the Arian majority became violent. At the Council of Constantinople in 381 Gregory resigned the see to prevent further division in the Church and retired to his estate at Arianzus, where he spent the last years of his life writing works that are among the most profound that the Eastern Church has given. He died there in 389.

JUNE

His feast day in the West has traditionally been May 9; in the East it is January 25, and he is also commemorated together with Basil and John Chrysostom on January 30, the Feast of the Three Hierarchs. On the present Roman Catholic calendar, he is remembered with Basil on January 2. On the calendar in the *Book of Common Prayer* and in *For All the Saints*, his feast day is May 9.

FOR FURTHER READING

McGucken, John Anthony. *St. Gregory of Nazianzus: An Intellectual Biography.* Crestwood: St. Vladimir's Seminary Press, 2001.

Ruether, Rosemary Radford. *Gregory of Nazianzus: Rhetor and Philosopher.* Oxford: Oxford University Press, 1969.

Winslow, Donald F. *The Dynamics of Salvation: A Study in Gregory of Nazianzus.* Cambridge: Philadelphia Patristic Foundation, 1979.

READING

From Gregory's second *Theological Oration,* On God

What is this that has happened to me, O friends, and initiates, and fellow lovers of the truth? I was running to lay hold on God, and thus I went up into the Mount, and drew aside the curtain of the cloud, and entered away from matter and material things, and as far as I could I withdrew within myself. And then when I looked up, I scarce saw the back parts of God; although I was sheltered by the rock, the Word that was made flesh for us. And when I looked a little closer, I saw, not the first and unmingled nature, known to itself—to the Trinity, I mean; not that which abides within the first veil, and is hidden by the cherubim; but only that nature, which at last even reaches to us. And that is, as far as I can learn, the majesty, or, as holy David calls it, the glory which is manifested among the creatures, which it has produced and governs. For these are the back parts of God, which he leaves behind him, as tokens of himself, like the shadows and reflection of the sun in the water, which show the sun to our weak eyes, because we cannot look at the sun himself, for by his unmixed light he is too strong for our power of perception. In this way then you shall discourse of God; even were you a Moses and a god to Pharaoh; even were you caught up like Paul to the third heaven, and had heard unspeakable words; even were you raised above them both, and exalted to angelic or archangelic place and dignity. For though a thing be all heavenly, or above heaven, and far higher in nature and nearer to God than we, yet it is farther distant from God, and from the complete comprehension of his nature, than it is lifted above our complex and lowly earthward-sinking composition.

Therefore we must begin again thus: It is difficult to conceive God, but to define him in words is an impossibility. . . . But in my opinion it is impossible to express him, and yet more impossible to conceive him. For that which may be conceived may perhaps be made clear by language, if not fairly well, at any rate imperfectly, to anyone who is not quite deprived of his hearing, or slothful of understanding. But to comprehend the whole of so great a subject as this is quite impossible and impracticable, not merely to the utterly careless and ignorant, but even to those who are highly exalted, and who love God, and in like manner to every created nature; seeing that the darkness of this world and the thick covering of the flesh is an obstacle to the full understanding of the truth.

Christology of the Later Fathers, vol. 3, The Library of Christian Classics, ed. Edward Rochie Hardy and Cyril C. Richardson (Philadelphia: Westminster, 1954), 137–39.

Gregory of Nyssa, "the Philosopher and Mystic," was born at Caesarea *ca.* 335 of a famous Christian family; he was the brother of Macrina and Basil. Gregory was ordained a lector but seems to have abandoned his vocation to follow the profession of his father, a rhetorician. He married, but after the death of his wife, Gregory was persuaded to enter the monastery founded by his family on the river Iris. At Basil's insistence, he was consecrated bishop of Nyssa, a suffragan see of Cappadocia, in 371. He lacked his brother's administrative talent and was falsely accused of negligence in financial matters and deposed by an Arian-dominated synod in 376. After the death of the Arian emperor Valens in 378, Gregory returned to Nyssa. When in 379 Basil died and then several months later Macrina died in Gregory's arms, Gregory, although deeply affected, was freed to develop as a philosopher and theologian and to become a leader in the Church. He took part in the Council of Antioch in 379, and at the Council of Constantinople in 381, he was acknowledged to be a pillar of orthodoxy. When he went to Constantinople, he remarked on the people's zeal for theology was well as the pervasiveness of Arianism: "If you ask someone how many obols a certain thing costs, he replies by dogmatizing on the born and unborn. If you ask the price of bread, they answer you, 'The Father is greater than the Son and the Son is subordinate to him.' If you ask, 'Is my bath ready?' they answer you, 'The Son has been made out of nothing.'"

In his last years Gregory was involved in a bitter controversy over Apollinarianism, the first great Christian heresy, which claimed that Christ lacked perfect manhood. Gregory died after attending the Council of Constantinople in 394.

His is a long and impressive list of writings, refuting heresies and clarifying the corresponding Orthodox position, especially regarding the Holy Trinity. In his exposition of Scripture, he attempted to explain Genesis in light of the philosophical and scientific accounts of the formation of the world. Gregory is the most speculative of the Greek fathers, with a strong interest in philosophy. In him three strands come together: Scripture, philosophy, and mysticism.

His traditional feast day in the West is March 9, and he is commemorated on that date on the calendar in the *Book of Common Prayer* and *For All the Saints*; Gregory of Nyssa is not on the Roman Catholic general calendar. His feast day in the East is January 10.

JUNE

FOR FURTHER READING

Von Campenhausen, Hans. *The Fathers of the Greek Church.* 107–16. Trans. Stanley Godman. New York: Pantheon, 1959.

Daniélou, Jean, comp. *From Glory to Glory: Texts from Gregory of Nyssa's Mystical Writings.* Ed. and trans. Herbert Musurillo. New York: Scribners, 1961; Crestwood: St. Vladimir's Seminary Press, 1979.

Malherbe, Abraham J., and Everett Ferguson, trans. *Gregory of Nyssa: The Life of Moses.* New York: Paulist, 1978.

Meredith, Anthony. *Gregory of Nyssa.* New York: Routledge, 1999.

Messinger, Ernest C. *Evolution and Theology.* New York: Macmillan, 1932.

Pro Ecclesia 2, no. 3 (Summer 1993): 345–63.

READING

From *An Address on Religious Instruction* (Catechetical Oration) by Gregory of Nyssa

God's goodness, wisdom, justice, power, and incorruptible nature are all to be seen in his plan for us. His goodness is evident in his choosing to save one who was lost. His wisdom and justice are to be seen in the way he saved us. His power is clear in this: that he came in the likeness of man and in the lowly form of our nature, inspiring the hope that, like man, he could be overcome by death; and yet, having come, he acted entirely in accordance with his nature. Now it belongs to light to dispel darkness, and to life to destroy death. Seeing, then, we have been led astray from the right path, with the result we were diverted from the life we once had and were involved in death, what is there improbable in what we learn from the gospel revelation? Purity lays hold of those stained with sin, life lays hold of the dead, and guidance is given to those astray, so that the stain may be cleansed, the error corrected, and the dead may return to life.

There is no good reason for those who do not take too narrow a view of things to find anything strange in the fact that God assumed our nature. For when he considers the universe, can anyone be so simple-minded as not to believe that the Divine is present in everything, pervading, embracing, and penetrating it? For all things depend on Him who is, and nothing can exist which does not have its being in Him who is. If then, all things exist in him and he exists in all things, why are they shocked at a scheme of revelation which teaches that God became man, when we believe that even now he is not external to man? For, granted that God is not present in us in the same way as he was in the incarnation, it is at any rate admitted he is equally present in us in both instances. In the one case he is united to us in so far as he sustains existing things. In the other case he united himself with our nature, in order that by its union with the Divine it might become divine, being rescued from death and freed from the tyranny of the adversary. For with *his* return from death, our mortal race begins *its* return to immortal life.

Christology of the Later Fathers, vol. 3, The Library of Christian Classics, ed. Edward Rochie Hardy and Cyril C. Richardson (Philadelphia: Westminster, 1954), 301–02.

PROPERS

Almighty God, you have revealed to your Church the eternal Being of glorious majesty and perfect love as one God in Trinity of Persons: Give us grace that, like your servants Macrina, Basil, Gregory Nazianzus, and Gregory of Nyssa, we may continue steadfast in the confession of this faith, and constant in our worship of you, Father, Son, and Holy Spirit; for you live and reign one God, now and forever.

LFF March 9, May 9, June 14, rev. PHP

Readings:	Isaiah 6:1-8 *or* Wisdom 7:24-28
	Psalm 19:7-11 (12-14) *or* 119:97-104
	Romans 11:33-36
	John 3:1-15 *or* John 5:19-24 *or* 14:23-26
Hymn of the Day:	
	"Come, Holy Ghost, our souls inspire" (LBW 472, 473; H82 503, 504)
Prayers:	For the Eastern Orthodox Churches
	For the relief of the poor
	For zeal for the truth
	For teachers of the Catholic faith
	For pastors who long for time for prayer and contemplation
Preface:	Trinity Sunday
Color:	White

ALSO ON JUNE 14

The Eastern Church on this date commemorates the prophet ***Elisha***. The calendar in the *Lutheran Service Book* (2006), following the calendar of Wilhelm Löhe, also lists Elisha on this date.

June 15

Evelyn Underhill, Teacher, 1941

E velyn Underhill, who by her prolific writing, lectures, retreats, and publications made the life and literary utterances of the mystics of every denomination or none accessible to a wide readership, was born in England in 1875 and educated at King's College, London. She was already well on her way to a promising literary career in London, when in 1907 she married Hubert Stuart Moore, who, like her father, was a lawyer, and underwent an experience of religious conversion. She was drawn to the Roman Catholic Church, but after its condemnation of modernism, she felt unable to join it and turned to the study of the mystics.

The resulting huge volume *Mysticism* (1911), which revealed her immense acquaintance with the Christian mystics and saints, was complemented with translations of some of these classic accounts of the spiritual life, making them available in English. The following decade of her life was devoted to translations and critical editions and introductory essays to devotional writers. She had a remarkable ability to make these men and women come alive again for her century.

From 1911 she was under the influence of Baron Friedrich von Hügel (1852–1925), a Roman Catholic, who became her spiritual director in 1921 and taught her to accept gladly the little things of each day. In 1926 *Concerning the Inner Life* moved beyond quotation from spiritual masters; and to her intimate familiarity with the saints and the thought and writings of the spiritual guides throughout the sweep of Christian history is added a new series of concerns, a new realization of the power of the redemptive sufferings of Christ. There appears a new clarity in her witness to the besieging love of God that draws us to respond and a new appreciation of the worship of the church in its many forms. Her most mature and lasting work is *Worship*, published in 1936.

An honest and earnest inquirer, her religious life moved in stages, including her long interest in Roman Catholicism, but eventually she concluded that Anglicanism was the place for her to be, and she became a communicant in the Church of England. Her own progress in the spiritual life made her a compelling leader of retreats, conducted most of all at the little Anglican retreat house at Pleshy. *The Letters of Evelyn Underhill*, published posthumously in 1943, indicates the extent of her "after care" of those she had led in retreat. "A certain wise Prioress said, 'Most books on religion have thousands of words—we need only one word, GOD—and that surrounded not by many words but by silence'"*

Evelyn Underhill died in London in 1941. She was added to the Episcopal calendar in the 1997 edition of *Lesser Feasts and Fasts* and is included on the Methodist calendar in *For All the Saints*.

FOR FURTHER READING

Armstrong, Christopher J. R. *Evelyn Underhill, 1875–1941: An Introduction to Her Life and Writings*. Grand Rapids: Eerdmans, 1976.

Cropper, Margaret. *Evelyn Underhill*. London: Longmans Greene & Co., 1958.

Greene, Dana. *Evelyn Underhill: Artist of the Infinite Life*. New York: Crossroad, 1990.

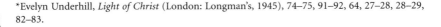

*Evelyn Underhill, *Light of Christ* (London: Longman's, 1945), 74–75, 91–92, 64, 27–28, 28–29, 82–83.

READING

From *Light of Christ* by Evelyn Underhill

You know sometimes how one goes to see a church which one is told has magnificent windows—and seen from outside they all look alike—dull, thick, grubby. We probably say, "Well! It is obvious there is good glass here but we cannot realize it." Then we open the door and go inside—leave the outer world, enter the inner world—and the universal light floods through the windows and bathes us in their colour and beauty and significance, shows us things of which we had never dreamed, a loveliness that lies beyond the fringe of speech. And so in the same way we cannot realize God and all our Lord's lovely meaning as a revelation of God and His eternal Truth and Beauty, from the outside. One constantly hears people commenting on Christianity from outside and missing the point every time. They are on the wrong side of the wall. How important then it is for us to be familiar with the inner vision. It is from within the place of prayer, recollection, worship and love, where the altar is, where the sacrifice is made, where we are all bound together in a life of communion and self-giving to God, that we fully and truly receive the revelation which is made through Christ. Then we see the different acts and stages of His life like a series of windows through which streams into our souls the pure light of God, mediated to us in a way that we can bear: Eternity and Reality given to us in human terms. To re-enter that Cathedral, receive a fresh gift from its inexhaustible beauty, see through those windows more and more of the light of God, that is the secret of meditation. Julian says at the end of her *Revelations* that what she received from her vision of Christ was "Light, Life and Love"; everything was gathered in that; an energy to show us the Truth, quicken us to fresh vitality and fill us with adoring devotion. What a contrast to our stodgy, vague, twilit inner life! We come into the silence to get more Light, Life and Love. We come to contemplate our Christian treasure from inside.

Evelyn Underhill, *The Light of Christ* (London: Longmans, 1945), 74–75, 91–92, 64, 27–28, 28–29, 82–83. Reprinted by permission of Wipf and Stock Publishers.

PROPERS

O God, Origin, Sustainer, and End of all your creatures: Grant that your Church, taught by your servant Evelyn Underhill, guarded evermore by your power, and guided by your Spirit into the light of truth, may continually offer you all glory and thanksgiving and attain with your saints to the blessed hope of everlasting life, which you have promised by our Savior Jesus Christ; who with you and the Holy Spirit, lives and reigns, one God, now and forever.

LFF

JUNE

Readings: Wisdom 7:24-8:1
              Psalm 96:7-13 *or* 37:3-6, 32-33
              John 4:19-24
Hymn of the Day:
              "Hope of the world, thou Christ of great compassion" (H82 472, LBW 493, LSB
              690)
Prayers: For a deeper spiritual life
              For those who conduct retreats and those who make retreats
              For religious writers and artists
Preface: The Dedication of a Church (BCP)
Color: White

June 16

Joseph Butler (1692–1752), Bishop of Durham, contributed to the renewal
of the Church of England in the eighteenth century by defending orthodox
Christianity against the prevailing Deism of the time. He is remembered on this
date on the calendar in the *Book of Common Prayer.*

June 18

Bernard Mizeki, a catechist and martyr in Rhodesia in 1896, is remembered
on this date on the calendar in the *Book of Common Prayer.* He is honored by
the Anglican Churches of Central and South Africa as their primary native martyr
and witness.

June 21

Onesimos Nesib, Translator, Evangelist, 1931

with Frumentius, Apostle of the Abyssinians, ca. 380

Onesimos, born in 1855, was captured by slave traders and taken from his
native Galla homeland in western Ethiopia to Eritrea, where he was bought
and freed by Swedish missionaries. They educated, baptized, and shared with
him their concern for the evangelizing of the Galla (some now prefer the name
Oromo), the largest ethnic group in Ethiopia. He took the Christian name Onesimos (spelled in the Greek way), the runaway slave who carried Paul's letter to
Philemon. Onesimos became an evangelist, translated the entire Bible into Galla,
and, in spite of difficulties, returned to preach the Gospel, in his homeland. He

died at Naqamte, Wollega Province, Ethiopia, according to the Ethiopian calendar on Sunday Sene 25, 1923. The Gregorian date is June 21, 1931. According to the diary of Olle Eriksson, a missionary who conducted the funeral service, Onesimos fell ill just before he reached the present Mekane Yesus Church at Naqamte where he was to preach. He died peacefully in the evening. On his tombstone is an inscription from Jeremiah 22:29, "O Land, O Land, hear the word of the Lord."

FOR FURTHER READING

Dahlberg, Nils. *Onesimos. Fran slav till bibel översättare.* Stockholm, 1932.

Trimingham, John Spencer. *The Christian Church and Missions in Ethiopia, including Eritrea and the Somalilands.* New York: World Dominion, 1950.

With Onesimos, **Frumentius**, the Apostle of the Abyssinians, might also be remembered. He was a fourth-century Syrian who converted Ethiopia to Christianity. His dates are uncertain (*ca.* 300–380). He and Adesius were companions of a Tyrian merchant, Meropius. On their way back from India, they were captured by barbarians. Meropius was executed, but the other two, who were Christians, were taken to the king, whom they later assisted in the government of his country. Frumentius was consecrated bishop for the region of his apostolate by Athanasius, linking the Ethiopian Church and the see of Alexandria. Frumentius's feast day is October 27 in the West, August 1 in the Ethiopian Church, November 30 for the Greeks, and December 18 for the Copts. He is commemorated on the *Evangelical Calendar of Names* on October 26.

READING

From Martin Luther, *Lectures on Galatians,* 1519

Behold, this is what Christ has gained for us, namely, that the name of the Lord (that is, the mercy and truth of God) is preached to us and that whoever believes in this name will be saved. Therefore if your conscience troubles you and you are a sinner and are seeking to become righteous, what will you do? Will you look around to see what works you may do or where you may go? No. On the contrary, see to it that you hear or recall the name of the Lord, that is, that God is righteous, good, and holy; and then cling to this, firmly believing that he is such a One for you. Now you are at once such a one, like him. But you will never see the name of the Lord more clearly than you do in Christ. There you will see how good, pleasant, faithful, righteous, and true God is, since he did not spare his own Son (Rom. 8:32). Through Christ he will draw you to himself.

And so you must not imagine that the Christian's life is a standing still and a state of rest. No, it is a passing over and a progress from vices to virtue, from

JUNE

clarity to clarity, from virtue to virtue. And those who have not been en route you should not consider Christians either. On the contrary, you must regard them as people of inactivity and peace, upon whom the prophet calls down their enemies. . . . Love is not idle, but it continually crucifies the flesh and is unable to rest content at its own level; it expands itself to purge a man throughout his being.

Therefore . . . the servitude of the spirit and freedom from sin, or from the Law, are identical, just as the servitude of sin and of the Law are identical with freedom from righteousness, or from righteousness and the Spirit. A person goes from servitude to servitude, from freedom to freedom, that is, from sin to grace, from fear of punishment to love of righteousness, from the Law to fulfillment of the Law, from the word to reality, from a figure to truth, from a sign to substance, from Moses to Christ, from the flesh to the spirit, from the world to the Father. All this takes place at the same time.

"Lectures on Galatians," in *Luther's Works Vol. 27* © 1964, 1992 Concordia Publishing House. Used with permission.

PROPERS

God of grace and might, we praise you for those who planted the Church in Ethiopia and especially for your servant Onesimos, to whom you gave gifts to make the good news known to the Galla people and to furnish them with the Scriptures in their own tongue. Raise up, we pray, in this and every land, heralds and evangelists of your kingdom, so that the world may know the immeasurable riches of our Savior, Jesus Christ our Lord.

BCP, LBW, rev. PHP

Readings:	Isaiah 62:1-7
	Psalm 48
	Romans 10:11-17
	Luke 24:44-53
Hymn of the Day:	
	"How blest are they who hear God's Word" (LBW 227)
Prayers:	For the church in Ethiopia
	For social justice
	For courage to press on in the Christian pilgrimage
	For deepened understanding of political and social freedom
Preface:	Baptism (BCP, LBW)
Color:	White

June 22

Alban, the First Martyr in Britain, *ca.* 304

Alban was a soldier in the Roman army stationed in Verulamium, a city about twenty miles northeast of London, and now called St. Alban's. He gave shelter to a Christian priest who was being pursued and was converted by him. When soldiers came to his house, Alban dressed in the cloak of the priest and gave himself up, allowing the priest to escape. Alban was tortured and martyred in place of the priest, on the hilltop where the Abbey of St. Alban's now stands. His shrine in the abbey is still a place of pilgrimage.

The first known reference to Alban is in the fifth-century *Life of St. Germanus of Auxerre*, and Gildas, writing *ca.* 540, gives the core of the tradition. The traditional date of Alban's martyrdom is 304 or 305, but the first account of his martyrdom places it in the reign of Septimus Severus (193–211). Alban is the earliest Christian in Britain who is known by name, and he is traditionally honored as the first Christian martyr in the British Isles. An abbot of St. Alban's, desiring to have his house honored, turned to the popular literary handyman John Lydgate (d. *ca.* 1449), a monk of Bury St. Edmonds, who wrote in verse the *Life of Albon and Amphabel*.

Alban is on the calendar in the *Book of Common Prayer* and in *For All the Saints*; he is not on the General Roman calendar.

READING

From Bede's *History of the English Church and People*

When these unbelieving emperors were issuing savage edicts against all Christians, Alban, as yet a pagan, gave shelter to a Christian priest fleeing from his pursuers. And when he observed this man's unbroken activity of prayer and vigil, he was suddenly touched by the grace of God and began to follow the priest's example of faith and devotion. Gradually instructed by his teaching of salvation, Alban renounced the darkness of idolatry, and sincerely accepted Christ. But when the priest had lived in his house some days, word came to the ears of the evil ruler that Christ's confessor whose place of martyrdom had not yet been appointed, lay hidden in Alban's house. Accordingly he gave orders to his soldiers to make a thorough search, and when they arrived at the martyr's house, holy Alban, wearing the priest's long cloak, at once surrendered himself in the place of his guest and teacher, and was led bound before the judge.

The judge ordered Alban to be flogged, but when they saw that no torture would break him or make him renounce the worship of Christ, he ordered his immediate decapitation.

JUNE

Saint Alban suffered on the twenty-second day of June near the city of Verulamium. Here, when the peace of Christian times was restored, a beautiful church
worthy of his martyrdom was built.

Bede, *History of the English Church and People,* trans. with an introduction by Leo Sherley-Price,
Revised by R. E. Latham (Penguin Classics 1955, Revised edition 1968), 45–47. Copyright © Leo
Sherley-Price, 1955, 1968. Reprinted by permission of Penguin Books Ltd.

PROPERS

Almighty God, by whose grace and power your holy martyr Alban triumphed
over suffering and was faithful even to death: Grant us, who now remember him
in thanksgiving, to be so faithful in our witness to you in this world, that we may
receive with him the crown of life; through Jesus Christ our Lord, who lives and
reigns with you and the Holy Spirit, one God, forever and ever.
BCP, LFF

Readings: Psalm 34:1-8 *or* 31:1-5
              1 John 3:13-16
              Matthew 10:34-42
Hymn of the Day:
              "Lo! What a cloud of witnesses" (H82 545)
Prayers: For all Christians in England
              For soldiers and all who serve in military forces
              For courage to profess our faith when it would be easier to deny it
Preface: A Saint (3) (BCP)
Color: Red

June 24

The Nativity of St. John the Baptist

The birthday of John the Baptizer was one of the earliest festivals in the calendar of the church, an exception to the general principle that the church
remembers martyrs on the day of their death. In addition to the celebration of the
birth of Jesus, the church remembers just two other birthdays: that of his mother
(September 8) and that of his forerunner John.

The feast of the Visitation of St. Elisabeth by the Blessed Virgin Mary (see May
31) celebrated the meeting of two related and prospective mothers. This day celebrates the birth of the first of the two infants, John the Baptist. It is the next event
leading to the incarnation, as God is pictured stirring up his strength to visit and
rescue his people. The very name "John" means "God's gracious gift," and so even by

his name, given by the angel, the forerunner points toward the one who is to come.

The day marks the occasion of the song of Zechariah, used daily at Morning Prayer, for it sings of the sunrise that is dawning upon the world. Each clause of this fourfold proclamation carries us one step further back into antiquity, to remind us that behind the continuity of Israel's history, now about to reach its climax in the arrival to the long-awaited Messiah, there lies the divine plan, to which God is faithful in spite of the faithlessness and recalcitrance of his human agents. So also the primal certainties of nature—that day dependably follows night— remind us of an order that follows its course, despite the madness of mortals.

John the Baptist was born into a priestly Jewish family several months before the birth of Jesus. Events of his life and teaching are known from accounts in all four Gospels and in the writings of Flavius Josephus, the first-century Jewish historian. According to the Gospels, the birth of John was predicted miraculously to Zechariah and Elizabeth (see November 5). At his birth the aged father sang the hymn of praise called the Benedictus, the traditional Gospel canticle at the church's Morning Prayer (Lauds or Morning Praise).

John lived "in the desert" where he apparently came into contact with the beliefs and practices of the Jewish sect called the Essenes, or as they called themselves, the Sons of Zadok. Some think that John may have been a novice in this community and that his own teachings represent an adaptation for ordinary Jewish people of the exclusive ethic of the Essenes with its requirements of celibacy, common property, and pacifism. In any case, about the year 29 in the wilderness of Judea, near the Jordan River, John began to preach a call to repentance and a baptismal washing. He gathered a group of disciples; Andrew and probably Peter and John the apostle were among them.

In the course of his preaching, John the Baptist denounced the immoral life of the Herodian rulers, and Herod Antipas, the tetrarch of Galilee, had him arrested and imprisoned, perhaps in the huge fortress of Machaerus, which Herod the Great had built in the wilderness east of the Dead Sea. It was there that Herod Antipas had John beheaded. The story of his death has been told again and again in music and in art as well as in the lessons and devotions of the church.

St. John the Baptist was highly regarded by the early Christians, and the Eastern Churches especially have always accorded him an important place in their prayers and worship. (His right hand, the hand that baptized Jesus, was the only part of John's body that St. Luke could take away from the village where he was buried, according to a curious legend. The hand was given to the royal family of Russia to protect the country from Napoleon's advancing armies. When the Bolshevik revolution broke out, the hand was taken to central Europe.) The Eastern Orthodox Churches observe days of commemoration of the Old Testament prophets, the "Holy Ancestors," of whom John was the last and greatest. In the West, the preparatory proclamation of John is a focus of the Second and Third Sundays in Advent, and he is also honored on the First Sunday after the Epiphany as the baptizer of Jesus. The commemoration of his death by order of King Herod is observed on many calendars on August 29.

Both East and West commemorate the beheading of John on August 29; the Orthodox Churches also remember him as the baptizer on the day after the Epiphany and on September 23 and commemorate his parents on September 5. A Feast of St. Zachariah and St. Elisabeth is kept in Palestine and elsewhere on November 5. At the time of the Reformation, the Feast of the Nativity of St. John the Baptist was retained on Lutheran and Anglican calendars, and a few also retained the day of his martyrdom.

St. John the Baptist is the patron saint of Quebec, and his birthday is celebrated as an important holiday in French Canada.

Midsummer eve and day were times of great revelry throughout Europe. Bonfires were lit, and a wheel, sometimes aflame, was rolled down a hill. Such practices are rooted in ancient sympathetic magic, intended to encourage the sun not to begin its annual loss of strength as the days grow shorter after midsummer. St. Augustine in the fourth century notes John's declaration about himself and Jesus, "He must increase, but I must decrease" (John 3:30) and relates it to this midsummer feast after which the days decrease in length.

FOR FURTHER READING

Bulgakov, Sergius. *The Friend of the Bridegroom: On the Orthodox Veneration of the Forerunner.* Trans. Boris Jakim. Grand Rapids: Eerdmans, 2003.

Kraeling, Carl H. *John the Baptist.* New York: Scribner's, 1951.

Murphy, Catherine M. *John the Baptist: Prophet of Purity for a New Age.* Collegeville: Liturgical, 2003.

Scobie, Charles H. H. *John the Baptist.* Philadelphia: Fortress Press, 1964.

Wink, Walter. *John the Baptist in the Gospel Tradition.* Cambridge: Cambridge University Press, 1968.

READING

From *A Search for God in Time and Memory* by John S. Dunne

The turning points in Jesus' life, according to our hypothesis, were the points where his life intersected with that of John the Baptist. At each of these junctures he went over from an ignorance to a knowledge. The first was in his baptism at the hands of John. That he presented himself for a baptism of repentance suggests that he was uncertain of his standing with God. His uncertainty, however, was changed into assurance as he underwent the baptism and experienced himself as beloved and well-pleasing to God. This left him still uncertain, nevertheless, as to whether the boundless acceptance he was receiving from God was for him alone or whether it was for others too. This uncertainty was removed at the second turning point, the imprisonment of John, when he saw John silenced and felt himself called upon to step into John's place and proclaim the kingdom of God. At this point the uncertainty remained as to how the kingdom would come about, whether it would come through a conversion of Israel to God by his preaching. The third turning point, the execution of John the Baptist, seems to have been the beginning for Jesus of the realization that the kingdom would not come in this way, that instead his preaching would fail, and he himself would be put to death.

John S. Dunne, *A Search for God in Time and Memory* (New York: Macmillan, 1970), 212–13.

PROPERS

God of justice and grace, you raised up blessed John the Baptist to prepare a holy people for Christ the Lord: Give to your Church gladness of spirit, and guide all who believe in you into the way of salvation and peace; through your Son Jesus Christ our Lord, who lives and reigns with you and the Holy Spirit, one God, now and forever.

Leonine sacramentary ✚ 1952 Roman Missal, RS, trans. PHP

> *or*

Lord God, heavenly Father, through your servant John the Baptist you bore witness that Jesus Christ is the Lamb of God who takes away the sin of the world, and that all who believe in him shall inherit eternal life: Enlighten us by your Holy Spirit that we may at all times find comfort and joy in this witness, continue steadfast in the true faith, and at last with all believers attain eternal life; through the same your Son Jesus Christ our Lord, who lives and reigns with you and the Holy Spirit, one God now and forever.

Lüneburg 1564, CSB, SBH

> *or*

Almighty God, by whose providence your servant John the Baptist was wonderfully born, and sent to prepare the way of your Son our Savior by preaching repentance: Make us so to follow his teaching and holy life, that we may truly repent according to his preaching; and, following his example, constantly speak the truth, boldly rebuke vice, and patiently suffer for the truth's sake; through Jesus Christ your Son our Lord, who lives and reigns with you and the Holy Spirit, one God, forever and ever.

1549 BCP

Readings:	*Roman Lectionary*	*LBW/ELW*	*BCP*
	Isaiah 49:1-6	Malachi 3:1-4	Isaiah 40:1-11
	Psalm 139:1-3, 13-15	Psalm 141	Psalm 85 *or* 85:7-13
	Acts 13:22-26	Acts 13:13-26	Acts 13:14b-26
	Luke 1:57-66, 80	Luke 1:57-67 (68-80)	Luke 1:57-80

Hymn of the Day:

"Comfort, comfort, ye my people" (H82 67, LBW 29, LSB 347, ELW 256), written for St. John the Baptist

or "The great forerunner of the morn" (H82 271, 272)

or "The Lord will come and not be slow" (H82 462, LBW 318)

JUNE

Prayers: For justice
             For a zeal for truth
             For renewal of life
             For an earnest expectation of the coming of Christ
             For all who proclaim Christ's presence among us
             For courage to witness when the world condemns us
Preface: Advent
Color: White

June 25

The Presentation of the Augsburg Confession, 1530

Philipp Melanchthon, Renewer of the Church, 1560

Just as all Christians can look to the Day of Pentecost as the birthday of the Christian church, many Lutheran Christians regard June 25 as the anniversary of the formation of what may be properly called the Church of the Augsburg Confession. On that day in 1530 the statement of faith called the Augsburg Confession, sometimes referred to by its Latin title the Augustana (from *Confessio Augustana*) which had been drafted by Philipp Melanchthon and endorsed by Luther, was read aloud to the emperor of the Holy Roman Empire, Charles V, at his Diet (assembly) of Princes at Augsburg. ("Confession" here means "statement of faith" rather than "acknowledgment of guilt.")

Philipp Schwarzerd, better known by the Greek form of his surname, Melanchthon ["black earth"], was born February 16, 1497, at Bretten in Baden. He was a talented child; at the age of twelve he was completely fluent in Latin, and at thirteen he was fluent in Greek. After attending Latin school in Pforzheim, he attended the University of Heidelberg (1509–1512) and then the University of Tübingen (1512–1518), where he received his master's degree in 1516. He was a brilliant student of the classics and soon became known as one of the outstanding young scholars of the humanist movement. In 1518, twenty-one years old, he was called to the new University of Wittenberg as its first professor of Greek. At Luther's urging, Melanchthon undertook the teaching of theology and Scripture in addition to his work on Aristotle and classical studies. He was a popular teacher, lecturing often to hundreds of students, and the combination of Luther and Melanchthon made Wittenberg one of the leading universities in Europe during much of the sixteenth century.

In the fall of 1520, Melanchthon married the daughter of the mayor of Wittenberg; the couple had four children. One child died in infancy; another died at sixteen. Katherine Melanchthon died in 1557. Although his salary was small, both husband and wife were extremely generous to others.

In 1521 Melanchthon published his *Loci Communes,* the first compendium of Lutheran doctrine; the work appeared in an annotated English edition only in 1944. Beginning in 1525, Melanchthon turned his attention to the question of general education. With Luther he reorganized the schools in Magdeburg and Eisleben, and he established the gymnasium (secondary school) in Nuremberg. In 1527 Melanchthon took part in the visitation of schools in Saxony, and in 1528 he made a similar tour through parts of Thuringia. Melanchthon thus played a leading role in the development of elementary and secondary education in Germany, making the study of the classics the basis of Christian education in a system that lasted for centuries. Indeed, he came to be called *Praeceptor Germaniae,* the Teacher of Germany.

He frequently traveled to meetings and disputations, and he was often called upon to draft statements of positions, refutations, and bases for reconciliation between differing groups. The private chaplain to Emperor Charles V, Father Aegidus, said to Melanchthon, "You have a theology which can be understood only by someone who prays a great deal."

Melanchthon, a layman, remained a professor at Wittenberg until his death on April 19, 1560. He is remembered on the Methodist calendar in *For All the Saints* on the date of his death, April 19; in the *Lutheran Service Book* on the date of his birth, February 16. On the calendars in the *Lutheran Book of Worship* and *Evangelical Lutheran Worship,* he is remembered in connection with his greatest achievement, the Augsburg Confession.

In April 1530, Emperor Charles V summoned a diet to settle the religious controversies of his realm and so present a united front in his military ventures against the Turks. Since Luther himself was under papal excommunication and imperial ban, it was Melanchthon who had the duty of being the chief representative of the Lutheran cause. He drafted a confession in early May which he twice revised, sending it each time to Luther for approval. On June 25, at three o'clock in the afternoon, it was presented to the emperor and his diet in Latin and in German by Christian Bayer, the chancellor of Saxony; it was signed by seven German princes and the representatives of two free cities.

Their statement of faith attempts to make clear that the Lutherans were not to be lumped together with other opponents of the Roman Catholic Church, and it emphasizes not the differences from Rome but the agreements with Rome. As the Preface declares,

> We are prepared, in obedience to your Imperial Majesty, our most gracious Lord, to discuss . . . such practical and equitable ways as may restore unity. Thus . . . our differences may be reconciled, and we may be united in one, true religion, even as we are all under one Christ and should confess and contend for Christ . . . [T]hat it may be done according to divine truth we invoke Almighty God in deepest humility and implore him to bestow his grace to this end. Amen.

Luther saw in the presentation of the Confession the fulfillment of Psalm 119:46, which has ever since been carried as the motto in editions of the Augustana: "I will tell of your decrees before kings and will not be ashamed."

The Augsburg Confession spread rapidly among the churches, and within fifteen years almost all of evangelical Germany subscribed to it. After 1535, assent to the doctrines of the Confession was required for the ordination of evangelical pastors at Wittenberg. During the sixteenth century, many copies of the Confession circulated, some with expansions and changes of wording. The best known of these is the so-called *Variata* ("altered") edition of 1540, which contained a number of changes made by Melanchthon in an effort to reconcile the Lutherans and the Calvinists. Almost all Lutheran Church bodies today specify the Unaltered (*Invariata*) Augsburg Confession of 1530 in their official statements of confessional subscription.

From the day of its delivery, translations into other languages were made. Three years after its presentation to the emperor, a Danish translation was published, and in 1536 an English edition. A version in classical Greek was prepared by the reformers and used in discussions with the Orthodox Churches. In some areas of Europe, the Augsburg Confession was among the first documents to be published in a newly established literary language; such was the case with the translation of the Slovenian reformer Primoz Trubar. In later centuries, as Lutheran missionaries on other continents translated the Bible and Luther's *Small Catechism* into local languages and the younger churches came into being, the Augsburg Confession began to appear in languages of Asia and Africa, such as Chinese, Japanese, Hindi, Tamil, Swahili, Zulu, and Malagasy.

The four-hundredth anniversary of the Augsburg Confession was celebrated in 1530 by Lutherans in many countries, and the numerous jubilee editions of the Confession and volumes of historical and theological studies which came out at that time testify to the vitality of this symbol of the Christian faith, which for Lutherans takes its place after the great creeds of Christendom as a "pure exposition of the Word of God." It portrays Lutheranism not as a separate or distinct religious body but as a reforming movement within and for the Catholic Church of the West, recalling the Church to the purity of its best ages and teachers.

It is customary among Lutherans to read a portion of the Augsburg Confession at the services of the Church on this day. The selection should be made according to concerns of the moment locally, nationally, or internationally.

FOR FURTHER READING

Gritsch, Eric W., and Robert W. Jenson. *Lutheranism: The Theological Movement and Its Confessional Writings.* Philadelphia: Fortress Press, 1976.

Kolb, Robert. *Confessing the Faith: Reformers Define the Church, 1530–1580.* St. Louis: Concordia, 1991.

————, and Timothy Wengert, eds. *The Book of Concord: The Confessions of the Evangelical Lutheran Church.* Minneapolis: Fortress Press, 2000.

Lackmann, Max. *The Augsburg Confession and Catholic Unity.* New York: Herder and Herder, 1963.

Manschreck, Clyde L. *Melanchthon, the Quiet Reformer.* New York: Abingdon, 1958.

Pelikan, Jaroslav. *Credo: Historical and Theological Guide to Creeds and Confessions of the Faith in the Christian Tradition.* New Haven: Yale University Press, 2003.

Stupperich, Robert. *Melanchthon.* Trans. Robert H. Fischer. London: Lutterworth, 1967.

Vajta, Vilmos, ed. *Luther and Melanchthon in the History and Theology of the Reformation.* Philadelphia: Fortress Press, 1961.

READING

From Philipp Melanchthon, *Loci Communes Theologicae*

The Lord God Almighty clothed his Son with flesh that he might draw us from contemplating his own majesty to a consideration of the flesh, and especially of our own weakness. Paul writes in 1 Corinthians 1:21 that God wishes to be known in a new way, i.e., through the foolishness of preaching, since in his wisdom he could not be known through wisdom. Therefore, there is no reason why we should labor so much on those exalted topics such as "God," "The Unity of the Trinity of God," "The Mystery of Creation," and "The Manner of the Incarnation." What, I ask you, did the Scholastics accomplish during the many ages they were examining only those points? Have they not, as Paul says, become vain in their disputations (Romans 11:21), always trifling about universals, formalities, connotations, and various other foolish words? Their stupidity could be left unnoticed if those stupid discussions had not in the meantime covered up for us the gospel and the benefits of Christ.

Now, if I wanted to be clever in an unnecessary pursuit, I could easily overthrow all their arguments for the doctrines of the faith. Actually, they seem to argue more accurately for certain heresies than they do for the Catholic doctrines.

But as for the one who is ignorant of the other fundamentals, namely, "The Power of Sin," "The Law," "Grace," I do not see how I can call him a Christian. For from these things Christ is known, since to know Christ means to know his benefits not only as *they* teach, to reflect upon his natures and the modes of his incarnation. For unless you know why Christ put on flesh and was nailed to the cross, what good will it do to you know merely the history about him? Would you say that it is enough for a physician to know the shapes, colors, and contours of plants, and that it makes no difference whether he knows their innate power? Christ was given us as a remedy and, to use the language of Scripture, a saving

JUNE

remedy (Luke 2:30; 3:6; Acts 28:28). It is therefore proper that we know Christ in another way than that which the Scholastics have set forth.

This, then, is Christian knowledge: to know what the law demands, where you may seek power for doing the law and grace to cover sin, how you may strengthen a quaking spirit against the devil, the flesh, and the world, and how you may console an afflicted conscience.

Melanchthon and Bucer, Library of Christian Classics 19, ed. Wilhelm Pauck (Philadelphia: Westminster, 1969), 21–22.

PROPERS

Almighty God, through the preaching of your servants, the blessed Reformers, you have caused the light of the Gospel to shine forth: Grant, we pray, that, knowing its saving power, we may faithfully guard and defend it against all enemies and joyfully proclaim it to the salvation of souls and the glory of your holy Name; through your Son Jesus Christ our Lord, who lives and reigns with you and the Holy Spirit, one God, now and forever.

CSB, SBH Reformation Day

Readings:	Jeremiah 31:31-34
	Psalm 46
	Romans 3:19-28
	John 8:31-36
Hymn of the Day:	
	"O God, O Lord of heaven and earth" (LBW 396, LSB 834)
Prayers:	For the unity of the church
	For the preaching and teaching of pure doctrine
	For a deeper knowledge of Christ and his benefits
	For the power of the gospel to fill the church
Preface:	Apostles
Color:	White

June 26

The calendar in the *Lutheran Service Book* (2006), following Wilhelm Löhe's calendar, lists **Jeremiah** on this date. The Eastern calendar remembers the prophet Jeremiah on May 1.

June 27

Cyril of Alexandria, Bishop, Teacher, 444

Cyril of Alexandria is commemorated on the calendar for his contributions as a theologian rather than for his administrative and pastoral oversight as a bishop or for his personal character, which were less than exemplary. He was born in Alexandria *ca.* 380, the nephew of Theophilus of Alexandria who engineered the deposition of John Chrysostom in which Cyril of Alexandria had a hand. In 412 he succeeded his uncle as bishop, and the young and fiery patriarch was soon exercising his authority with ruthlessness and even violence. He closed the churches of the Novatianist schismatics, expelled the Jews, and quarreled with the imperial prefect, Orestes. The Neo-Platonist philosopher Hypatia, a respected woman of noble character and friend of Orestes, was brutally murdered by a mob; it has not been established that Cyril was directly involved, but the crime was the work of those who looked to him as their leader.

Cyril's contribution to Christianity was his learned and energetic defense of the unity of Christ's person, divine and human, against the teaching of Nestorius. Cyril was head of a rival theological school to that of Antioch where Nestorius had studied. Cyril presided at the general Council of Ephesus in 431 at which the teaching of Nestorius was condemned and the Virgin Mary was given the title *Theotokos* ("birth giver of God"; the Latin version of the title is *mater Dei*, "mother of God"). In the years following the council, Cyril became more moderate and conciliatory, his natural vehemence restrained by the admonition of his spiritual father, Isidore of Pelusium.

He left a great number of writings, mostly scriptural and other expository works and treatises arising out of the Nestorian controversy. His orthodox teaching is cited several times in the Lutheran Confessions. He died in Alexandria in 444 after an episcopate of nearly thirty-two years. He is commemorated on this date in the Roman Catholic calendar, *Evangelical Lutheran Worship,* and the *Lutheran Service Book.* His feast day was formerly February 9. In the East, Cyril is honored as "the seal of the Fathers"; he is remembered on January 18 and also June 9.

READING

From a Letter by St. Cyril of Alexandria, Bishop

I am astonished that anyone could doubt the right of the holy Virgin to be called the Mother of God. If our Lord Jesus Christ is God, and she gave birth to him, surely she must be the Mother of God. Our Lord's disciples may not have used

JUNE

those exact words, but they delivered to us the belief those words enshrine, and this has also been taught us by the holy fathers.

In the third book of his work on the holy and consubstantial Trinity, our father Athanasius, of glorious memory, several times refers to the holy Virgin as "Mother of God." I cannot resist quoting his own words: "As I have often told you, the distinctive mark of holy Scripture is that it was written to make a twofold declaration concerning our Savior; namely, that he is and has always been God, since he is the Word, Radiance, and Wisdom of the Father; and that for our sake in these latter days he took flesh from the Virgin Mary, Mother of God, and became man."

Again further on he says: "There have been many holy people, free from all sin. Jeremiah was sanctified in his mother's womb, and John while still in the womb leaped for joy at the at the voice of Mary, the Mother of God." Athanasius is a man we can trust, one who deserves our complete confidence, for he taught nothing contrary to the sacred books.

The divinely inspired Scriptures affirm that the Word of God was made flesh, that is to say, he was united to a human body endowed with a rational soul. He undertook to help the descendents of Abraham, fashioning a body for himself from a woman and sharing our flesh and blood, to enable us to see in him not only God, but also, by reason of this union, a man like ourselves.

It is held, therefore, that there are in Emmanuel two entities, divinity and humanity. Yet our Lord Jesus Christ is nonetheless one, the one true Son, both God and man; not a deified man on the same footing as those who share the divine nature by grace, but true God who for our sake appeared in human form. We are assured of this by Saint Paul's declaration, "When the fullness of time had come, God sent his Son, born of a woman, born under the law, in order to redeem those who were under the law, so that we might receive adoption as children." [Gal. 4:4]

Letter 1. From the English translation of the Office of Readings from the Liturgy of the Hours by the International Committee on English in the Liturgy, Inc., rev. PHP.

PROPERS

O God, your bishop Cyril courageously taught that Mary was the Mother of God: In your mercy grant that we who cherish this belief may embrace salvation through the incarnation of your Son, Jesus Christ our Lord; who lives and reigns with you and the Holy Spirit, one God, now and forever.

RS, trans. PHP

Readings: 1 Corinthians 2:10-16
              Psalm 119:89-96
              Mark 4:1-9
Hymn of the Day:
              "From east to west, from shore to shore" (LBW 64, LSB 385, H82 77)

Prayers:	For a deeper understanding of the incarnation
	For theologians
	For bishops who must deal with difficult situations
Preface:	Weekdays
Color:	White

June 28

Irenaeus, Bishop of Lyons, *ca.* 202

A disciple of Polycarp of Smyrna (see February 23), Irenaeus was born in Asia Minor perhaps between 130 and 160. Little is known of his life. For reasons that are not known, he migrated to Gaul (perhaps stopping at Rome for study) and there became a presbyter of the church in Lyons during the reign of Marcus Aurelius. Lyons in the second century was an important commercial city, the seat of a garrison and headquarters for three provinces, a gateway between the Mediterranean world and the provinces north of the Alps. Like Rome, Lyons had a large Greek-speaking element in its population, and it was among this group that Christianity was first established.

During the Montanist controversy (the Montanists were an apocalyptic party that expected the immediate outpouring of the Holy Spirit), Irenaeus was sent as an envoy to Rome by the Christians at Lyons. Upon his return, he was elected bishop of that city to succeed Pothinus, who had died in prison during the persecution of 177 (see June 2). Irenaeus perhaps introduced Christianity into parts of eastern Gaul. He strenuously opposed Gnostic dualism in his major writing, *Against Heresies.* In that work he makes the memorable observation, "The glory of God is the human being fully alive; the life of a human being is the vision of God" (Book 4.20.7).

Eusebius says that Irenaeus, as his name implies, was a promoter of peace in the Church and firmly protested Pope Victor's threatened excommunication of the Eastern Churches, which observed Easter on the Jewish date, the fourteenth of Nisan, rather than on the following Sunday.

Nothing is known of the last years of his life. He died perhaps *ca.* 202. In the late sixth century Gregory of Tours refers to Irenaeus as a martyr, but the tradition seems not to be older than that.

Irenaeus is important as a witness to the apostolic tradition (he knew Polycarp and Polycarp knew St. John the Apostle) and as a champion of the inspiration of both the Old and the New Testaments. Most of his works were written to refute the heresies of his time, attacking them with positive ideas as well as negative criticisms, and setting out a clear and comprehensive teaching of the

Christian faith. In contrast to the fashionable theories of his opponents, which deceived many by their use of Christian terminology, Irenaeus emphasized the traditional elements in the Church handed on from the time of the apostles, especially the Bible, the episcopate, and the creeds.

His feast day in the East is August 23. He was added to the calendar in the 1979 *Book of Common Prayer,* the *Lutheran Book of Worship,* and *For All the Saints.*

FOR FURTHER READING

Von Campenhausen, Hans. *The Fathers of the Greek Church.* Trans. Stanley Godman. 21–28. New York: Pantheon, 1959.

Grant, Robert M. *Irenaeus of Lyons.* New York: Routledge, 1996.

Osborn, Eric. *Irenaeus of Lyons.* Cambridge: Cambridge University Press, 2001.

Wingren, Gustav. *Man and the Incarnation: A Study in the Biblical Theology of Irenaeus.* Philadelphia: Muhlenberg, 1959 (1947).

READING

From Irenaeus *Against Heresies*

Having received this preaching and this faith, the Church, although scattered in the whole world, carefully preserves it, as if living in one house. She believes these things everywhere alike, as if she had but one heart and one soul, and preaches them harmoniously, teaches them, and hands them down, as if she had but one mouth. For the languages of the world are different, but the meaning of the Christian tradition is one and the same. Neither do the churches that have been established in Germany believe otherwise, or hand down any other tradition, nor those among the Iberians, nor those among the Celts, nor in Egypt, nor in Libya, nor those established in the middle parts of the world. But as God's creature, the sun, is one and the same in the whole world, so also the preaching of the truth shines everywhere, and illumines all who wish to come to the knowledge of the truth. Neither will those powerful speakers who preside in the churches anything different from these things, for they are not above their teachers, nor will one who is weak in speech diminish the tradition. For since the faith is one and the same, those who can say much about it do not add to it, nor do those who can say little diminish it.

The splendor of God gives life, and therefore those who see God shall live. This is the reason why the intangible, incomprehensible, and invisible God offers himself to be seen, comprehended, and grasped by human beings: that they may have life. It is impossible to live without life, and life comes only from participating in God; participating in God comes through seeing him and enjoying his goodness.

Human beings therefore are to see God and live. Through the vision of God they live for ever and attain to God himself. This was foretold in parables by the prophets: God will be seen by those who have his Spirit and constantly await his coming. Moses said in the Book of Deuteronomy, "Today we have seen that God may speak to someone and the person may still live." [Deut. 5:24]

God holds the universe in being, although his power and greatness cannot be seen or described by any of his creatures. Nonetheless, he is known to them all. Through his Word the whole creation learns that there is one God the Father, who holds all things together and gives them their being. It is written in the Gospel, "It is the only Son, who is close to the Father's heart, who has made him known." [John 1:18] From the beginning, it is the Son of God, who was with the Father from the beginning, who reveals the Father to us. He came to reveal to the human race prophetic visions, the diversity of spiritual gifts and ministries, the glory the Father, all in proper order and harmony, at the appointed time, and for our instruction.

The Word revealed God to human beings and presented them to God. He guarded the invisibility of the Father to prevent human beings from treating God with contempt and to set before them a goal toward which to move. At the same time he revealed God to human beings and made him visible in many ways to prevent them from being totally separated from God and so cease to be.

Now the glory of God is humanity fully alive, for the life of humanity is the vision of God. If the revelation of God through creation gives life to all who live on the earth, much more does the revelation of the Father by the Word give perfect being to those who see God.

From Books I.10.2 and IV.20.5-7, trans. PHP

PROPERS

Almighty God, you upheld your servant Irenaeus with strength to maintain the truth and to bring peace to your Church: Keep us, we pray, steadfast in your true religion, that in constancy and peace we may walk in the way that leads to eternal life; through Jesus Christ our Lord, who lives and reigns with you and the Holy Spirit, one God, now and forever.

RS ✛ LFF

Readings:	Psalm 85:8-13 *or* 145:8-13
	2 Timothy 2:22b-26
	Luke 11:33-36
Hymn of the Day:	
	"Holy Spirit, ever dwelling in the holiest realms of light" (H82 511, LBW 523, LSB 650, ELW 582)
Prayers:	For peace in the world
	For peace in the church
	For a renewed appreciation of the apostolic tradition
	For bishops who guard and defend the apostolic faith
Preface:	Epiphany (BCP) or Christmas
Color:	White

JUNE

June 29

St. Peter and St. Paul, Apostles

The two great apostles whose ministry embraced the whole Jewish and Gentile worlds have been associated in Christian devotion since earliest times. The Feast of Saints Peter and Paul is one of the oldest of the saints' days, having been observed at least since 258, and it was of such importance in the Middle Ages that it marked a turning point in the time after Pentecost, as also did the days of St. Lawrence (August 10) and St. Michael (September 29).

Simon, a son of Jonah, later called Cephas or Peter (Aramaic and Greek for "rock"), was probably born in Bethsaida of Galilee. He was a fisherman, working in partnership with the sons of Zebedee. He was married, and his mother-in-law, whom Jesus cured of a fever, lived with them; later he took his wife on his missionary travels. It is likely that he and his brother Andrew, as well as the apostle John, were among the followers of John the Baptist before they joined Jesus. Peter has a special place among the apostles. He was not only one of the inner circle with James and John, but he was often the speaker for the Twelve as a whole, and his name invariably was put at the head of the lists of the apostles. After the resurrection, Peter was the first of the Twelve to see the risen Lord, and he clearly acted as the leader, taking the initiative in the selection of Matthias, explaining the events of Pentecost to the assembled crowd, performing miracles, and making decisions.

Peter turned increasingly to missionary work, chiefly among the Jews, and the leadership of the church in Jerusalem passed to James the brother of Jesus. Peter was active in Samaria and in the towns of Lydda, Joppa, and Caesarea in Palestine. Of his later missionary travels, little is known in detail, but tradition has connected his name with Antioch, Corinth, and Rome, and his stay, at least in the first of these, is confirmed by the New Testament. Although the Scriptures are silent about the latter part of his life, the weight of tradition (Clement, Ignatius, Dionysus, Irenaeus, Origen, Tertullian, and others) makes it probable that Peter left Antioch about the year 55 and later went to Rome and suffered martyrdom there *ca.* 64.

Saul, later to be known by the Greek form of his name, Paul, the apostle to the Gentiles, was born in the city of Tarsus in Cilicia, a Jew of the tribe of Benjamin. He probably attended a local synagogue school, and he studied with the rabbi Gamaliel in Jerusalem. He learned the trade of the tentmaker, and apparently at times supported himself by it. He was a Roman citizen and was "Hellenized" and cosmopolitan in outlook, but he was also a Pharisee and an ardent defender of the Jewish law and way of life. He persecuted the new and disruptive sect of Christians, and he was present at the stoning of St. Stephen the deacon (see December 26.)

After his conversion, perhaps about the year 34 or 35, he became a vigorous evangelist of the new faith. Because of the wealth of material in his preserved letters and in the Acts of the Apostles, probably more is known about the life of Paul than about the life of any other leader of the church in the apostolic period.

Paul began his missionary work in Syria and continued it in Asia Minor, Cyprus, Greece, and Macedonia. In some places he stayed only a short time; in others much longer. Ephesus was his home for two and a half years. On several occasions in his travels, he visited Jerusalem, and on his final visit there, perhaps about the year 55, he was arrested, tried before Felix the governor on the charge of provoking riots, and kept in prison for two years. He appealed his case to the emperor, and the account in Acts ends with Paul in the capital city of the empire, awaiting his hearing.

According to tradition, Paul made Rome his headquarters, traveled east, possibly to Spain, and was killed in Rome during the persecution under Nero. Paul's traditional symbol is a sword, by which he was beheaded.

From the earliest days it has been believed that Peter and Paul suffered martyrdom on the same day, June 29, in the year 67, although some accounts give the year as 68 or the date as February 22. Traditions assert that Peter was crucified upside down on Vatican Hill (because he said that he was not worthy to die in the same way as his Lord) and that Paul, a Roman citizen, was beheaded near the Via Ostia, south of Rome. St. Peter's Basilica and St. Paul's Outside-the-Walls are said to contain the tombs of the two apostles; their skulls are said to be preserved in the church of St. John Lateran, the cathedral of the city of Rome. The pope's claim to primacy is in large measure based on his being bishop of the city in which Peter and Paul died.

See also under January 18, the Confession of St. Peter, and January 25, the Conversion of St. Paul.

FOR FURTHER READING

Krautheimer, Richard. *Rome: Profile of a City 318-1308*. Princeton: Princeton University Press, 1980.

Lampe, Peter. *From Paul to Valentinus: Christians at Rome in the First Two Centuries*. Trans. Michael G. Steinhauser. Minneapolis: Fortress Press, 2003.

READING

From Irenaeus *Against Heresies*

We learned the plan of of our salvation from no others than from those through whom the Gospel came to us. They first preached the Gospel, and afterwards by the will of God handed it down to us in the Scriptures, to be the foundation and pillar of our faith. For it is not true to say that they preached before they had come

JUNE

to perfect knowledge, as some dare to say, boasting that they are correctors of the apostles. For after our Lord had risen from the dead, and the apostles were clothed with power from on high when the Holy Spirit came upon them, they were filled with all things and had perfect knowledge. They went out to the ends of the earth, preaching the good things that came to us from God, and proclaiming peace from heaven to humanity, all and each of them equally being in possession of the gospel of God. So Matthew among the Hebrews issued a writing of the gospel in their own language, while Peter and Paul were preaching the Gospel at Rome and founding the Church. After their departure, Mark, the disciple and interpreter of Peter, also handed down to us in writing what Peter preached. Then Luke, the follower of Paul, recorded in a book the Gospel as it was preached by him. Finally, John, the disciple of the Lord, who had also reclined against his chest, himself published a Gospel, while he was residing at Ephesus in Asia. All of these handed down to us that there is one God, maker of heaven and earth, proclaimed by the law and the prophets, and one Christ the Son of God.

Book III.1.1-2, trans. PHP, based on Edward Rochie Hardy, *Early Christian Fathers*, vol. 1, Library of Christian Classics (Philadelphia: Westminster, 1953), 370.

PROPERS

Almighty God, whose blessed apostles Peter and Paul glorified you by their martyrdom: Grant that your Church, instructed by their teaching and example, and knit together in unity by your Spirit, may ever stand firm upon the one foundation, which is Jesus Christ our Lord; who lives and reigns with you and the Holy Spirit, one God, now and forever.

Leonine sacramentary, Sarum, RS trans. BCP; LBW; rev. in ELW

Readings:	RC	BCP
	Acts 12:1-11	Ezekiel 34:11-16
	Psalm 34:2-9	Psalm 87
	2 Timothy 4:6-8. 17-18	2 Timothy 4:1-8
	Matthew 16:13-19	John 21:15-19
Hymn of the Day:		
	"God has spoken by his prophets" (LBW 238, LSB 583)	
	or "O where are kings and empires now?" (SBH 154, H40 382)	
	or "Two stalwart trees both rooted in faith and holy love" (H82 273, 274)	
Prayers:	For the church of the West	
	For the nations of the world	
	For the continuation of the apostolic zeal and spirit	
Preface:	Apostles	
Color:	Red	

June 30

Johan Olof Wallin, Archbishop of Uppsala, Hymnwriter, 1839

with Magnus Brostrup Landstad, Hymnwriter, 1880

Johan Olaf Wallin (pronounced Wa-LEEN) was born at Stora Tuna, Dalarne province, October 15, 1779, the son of a noncommissioned officer. Despite poverty and ill health, he graduated from the University of Uppsala in 1799, received the M.A. in 1803, and his doctorate in theology in 1809. He became pastor at Solna in that year and in 1810 married Anna Maria Dimander. In 1812 Wallin was called to Adolf Frederick Church in Stockholm. Four years later, in 1816, he was made Dean of Västerås, in 1824 a bishop, chief royal preacher in 1830, and in 1837, two years before his death, was consecrated Archbishop of Uppsala and Primate of the Church of Sweden.

He was the leading churchman of his day in Sweden, yet his lasting fame rests upon his poetry and his hymns. In 1805 and in 1809, he was awarded the highest prize for poetry by the Swedish Academy. As early as 1807 he began to publish collections of old and new hymns. He led the commission set up in 1811 to edit a new Swedish hymnbook to replace the 1695 book, and when the committee's first draft failed to meet general approval, the entire task of revising and completing the work was given to Wallin. He completed his work November 28, 1816, and after a few minor modifications, the new *Psalmbook* was authorized by King Karl XIV on January 29, 1819. In this book of five hundred hymns, some one hundred thirty were written by Wallin, and nearly two hundred more were revised or translated by him. For more than a century, the Church of Sweden made no change in the 1819 *Svenska Psalm-Boken*. In the 1937 hymnal still a third of the hymns were written or translated by Wallin.

E. E. Ryden (*The Story of Christian Hymnody*, 1959) quotes Wallin on the high standards that ought to apply to the language of hymns: "A new hymn, aside from the spiritual considerations, which must never be compromised in any way, should be so correct, simple, and lyrical in form, and so free from inversions and other imperfections in style, that after the lapse of a hundred years a father may be able to say to his son, 'Read the *Psalmbook*, my boy, and you will learn your mother tongue.'"

Henry Wadsworth Longfellow, who had a great interest in Scandinavian literature, translated a poem by Bishop Esaias Tegner as "The Children of the Lord's Supper" and introduced the name of Wallin to the English-speaking world:

Like as Elias in heaven, when he cast from off him his mantle,
So cast off the soul its garments of earth; and with one voice
Chimed in the congregation, and sang an anthem immortal
Of the sublime Wallin, of David's harp in the North-land
Tuned to the choral of Luther; the song on its mighty pinions
Took every living soul, and lifted it gently to heaven,
And each face did shine like the Holy One's face upon Tabor.

Wallin, a man of brooding melancholy, has been praised as the unsurpassed interpreter of collective feeling in Swedish literature. In 1839 he published an epic poem of melancholic inner restlessness, *The Angel of Death*, which he had begun during a cholera epidemic in Stockholm in 1834 and which he had completed but a few weeks before he died at Uppsala, June 30, 1839.

Magnus Brostrup Landstad, the dominant figure in Norwegian hymnody, is fittingly commemorated on this day also. He was born in 1802 at Maaso, Finnmarken, in the extreme north of Norway, was ordained and served several parishes, finally serving in Oslo. He is best remembered for his collections of folk literature and for his work on the Norwegian hymn commission. He introduced popular language into the hymns he wrote to make them contemporary expressions of faith. He died October 8, 1880.

READING

From *Centuries* by Thomas Traherne

Are not praises the very end for which the world was created? Do they not consist as it were of knowledge, complacency, and thanksgiving? Are they not better than all the fowls and beasts and fishes in the world? What are the cattle upon a thousand hills but carcasses, without creatures that can rejoice in God and enjoy them? It is evident that praises are infinitely more excellent than all creatures because they proceed from men and angels. For as the streams do, they derive an excellency from their fountains, and are the last tribute that can possibly be paid to the Creator. Praises are the breathings of interior love, the marks and symptoms of a happy life, overflowing gratitude, returning benefits, an oblation of the soul, and the heart ascending upon the wings of divine affection to the Throne of God. God is a Spirit and cannot feed on carcasses: but he can be delighted with thanksgivings, and is infinitely pleased with the emanations of our joy, because his works are esteemed and Himself is admired.

What can be more acceptable to love than that it should be prized and magnified? Because therefore God is love, and His measure infinite, He infinitely desires to be admired and beloved, and so our praises enter into the very secret of His Eternal Bosom, and mingle with Him who dwelleth in that light which is inaccessible. What strengths are there even in flattery to please a great affection? Are not your . . . affections melted with delight and pleasure, when your soul is precious in the eye of those you love? When your affection is pleased, your love is prized, and they satisfied? To prize love is the highest service in the whole world that can be done unto it. But there are a thousand causes moving God to esteem our praises, more than we can well apprehend. However, let these inflame you, and move you to praise Him night and day forever.

Thomas Traherne, *Centuries,* intro. John Farrar (New York: Harper, 1960), 155.

PROPERS

Almighty God, beautiful in majesty, majestic in holiness, you bestowed upon your servant Johan Olof Wallin abundant lyrical gifts: We praise you for his enduring work, and we pray that your church may always have in its midst those who by providing and promoting noble hymns may lead your people to know you and to sing your praise; through your Son Christ our Lord, who lives and reigns with you and the Holy Spirit, one God, now and forever.

PHP

Readings:	2 Chronicles 20:20-21
	Psalm 96
	Ephesians 5:18b-20
	Matthew 13:44-52
Hymn of the Day:	
	"We worship you, O God of might" (LBW 432)
Prayers:	For an increased love of congregational singing
	For the bishops and leaders of the church that by their example they may strengthen and renew the church's worship
	For all interpreters of the feelings of their people
Preface:	Epiphany
Color:	White

JUNE

July 1

John Mason Neale, 1866; and Catherine Winkworth, 1878; Hymnwriters

Two translators of hymns may appropriately be remembered together today. Catherine Winkworth made the riches of German hymnody available to English-speaking Christians, and John Mason Neale made available the wealth of the ancient Latin and Greek hymns.

John Mason Neale was born in London on January 24, 1818, the son of a clergyman. His father died in 1823, and the son's education was largely at the hands of his mother. He won a scholarship to Trinity College, Cambridge, where he excelled in study (he was a master of twenty languages), and there in 1838, together with Benjamin Webb (1819–1885), he founded the Cambridge Camden Society, later called the Ecclesiological Society, for the study of ecclesiastical art, architecture, and ritual.

He was ordained a priest in 1842 and was given the living of Crawley, Sussex, but lung disease, from which he had long suffered, prevented him from taking up his duties. He went to Madeira until the summer of 1844. In 1846 he was made warden of Sackville College, East Grinstead, an institution for the poor. It was not considered a position of distinction in the church, for both his predecessor and his successor were laymen. Neale remained at this post for the rest of his short life.

In 1854 with Miss S. A. Gream, the daughter of a nearby rector, Neale founded the Sisterhood of St. Margaret for the care of the sick, with rules based on those of St. Vincent de Paul's Sisters of Charity, who had made a deep impression on many in the Anglican and Lutheran churches of the time (see September 27). Opposition to Neale's churchmanship and to the society was strong and sometimes violent. He was once attacked and mauled at a funeral for a member of the sisterhood. His opponents threatened to burn his house and at another time threatened to stone him. He was Inhibited, prevented from exercising his priestly duties, from 1847 to 1863 by the Bishop of Chichester because of his allegedly Romish leanings. He was denied preferment in his own church, and even his doctorate was from an American institution, Trinity College in Hartford, Connecticut (1860). Nonetheless, his gentleness eventually won the respect even of his ecclesiastical superiors, and the sisterhood that he founded developed into one of the leading communities of the Church of England. It was brought to America in 1873.

Neale was a student of the liturgy and church history. He translated the Eastern liturgies into English, created a monumental mystical commentary on the Psalms, composed children's liturgies, wrote novels and an excellent guidebook to Portugal. His most enduring accomplishment, however, was his translations of the great hymns of the church from Greek and Latin. He had spent his career in an obscure almshouse, but the minimal obligations of this position together with his wife's income (he had married Sarah Norman Webster in 1842), which left him financially independent, gave him leisure for reading, study, and writing, which gained for him a worldwide reputation as a writer of prose and verse, and that reputation has endured. His work stands above all others in translation from the Latin and stands nearly alone in translation from the Greek.

Neale, after five months of suffering, died on the Feast of the Transfiguration, August 6, 1866, and is commemorated on the calendar in the *Book of Common Prayer* and the Methodist calendar in *For All the* Saints on the following day, August 7. For a suggestion concerning the commemoration of the ancient hymn writers whose work was translated by Neale, see the commemoration of Isaac Watts, November 25.

FOR FURTHER READING

Chandler, Michael. *The Life and Work of John Mason Neale.* Leominster: Fowler Wright, 1996.

Litvack, Leon. *John Mason Neale and the Quest for Sobornost.* Oxford: Clarendon, 1995.

Lough, Arthur. *The Influence of John Mason Neale.* London: SPCK, 1962.

———. *John Mason Neale—Priest Extraordinary.* Devon: Newton Abbot, 1975.

Neale, John Mason. *Selections from the Writings of John Mason Neale.* London, 1884.

Catherine Winkworth was born in London on September 13, 1829. Her family soon after moved to Manchester, where she spent most of her life. Her mother died in 1841, and in the spring of 1845, the year in which her father remarried, she went to Dresden to stay for a year with an aunt.

Her *Lyra Germanica* was published in 1855, a second series with the same title appeared in 1858, and this book of translations of German hymns met with extraordinary success. By 1857 it was in its fifth edition. Winkworth had a remarkable ability to preserve the spirit of the great German hymns while rendering them in English, and she has remained the foremost translator of German hymns into English. She is also the translator of *The Life of Pastor Fliedner* (1861) and *The Life of Amelia Sieveking* (1863).

She supported the efforts of her time toward a recognition of women's rights. In 1862 she and her family moved to Clifton, England, where she became secretary of the Clifton Association for Higher Education for Women, a supporter of the Clifton High School for Girls, and a member of the Cheltenham Ladies' College.

Her father died in 1869, and in the same year Catherine and her sister Susanna went to Darmstadt, Germany, as delegates to the German Conference of Women's

Work, presided over by Princess Anne. Catherine Winkworth died suddenly of heart disease at Monnetier, near Geneva, in Savoy, July 1, 1878, at the age of fifty-one. She is buried there. A monument to her memory has been erected in Bristol Cathedral.

While the translations of the ancient Greek and Latin hymns were almost exclusively by male high-churchmen, the translation of the important body of post-Reformation German hymnody was wrought almost entirely by women. In addition to Catherine Winkworth, these translators included Jane Borthwick (1813–1897) and her sister Sarah Borthwick Findlater (1823–1907), both Scottish Presbyterians, and Anglicans Frances Elizabeth Cox (1812–1897), Jane Montgomery Campbell (1817–1878), and Elizabeth Rundle Charles (1828–1896).

FOR FURTHER READING

Bradley, Ian. *Abide with Me: The World of Victorian Hymns.* London: SCM, 1997.
Leaver, Robin A. *Catherine Winkworth: The Influence of Her Translations on English Hymnody.* St. Louis: Concordia, 1978.

READING

From J.-J. von Allmen, Worship

If we love the Kingdom which will both restore and complete the mystery of the first creation, we cannot refuse it—where its self-expression is most appropriate, i.e. in the cult [liturgy] of the Church—some means of expression, even if that means is ambiguous and unsatisfactory. The Church's worship . . . is the most splendid proof of love for the world. Those who do not love the cult, do not know how to love the world.

But to say that the cult is the heart of Christian community is not merely to remind them that the cult is the criterion of the real life to which they are called; it is also to remind them that if the cult ceases the community dies. It is by its worship that the Church lives, it is there that its heart beats. And in fact the life of the Church pulsates like the heart by systole and diastole. As the heart is for the animal body, so the cult is for church life a pump which sends into circulation and draws in again, it claims and it sanctifies. It is from the life of worship—from the Mass—that the Church spreads itself abroad into the world to mingle with it like leaven in the dough, to give it savor like salt, to irradiate it like light, and it is towards the cult—towards the Eucharist—that the Church returns from the world, like a fisherman gathering up his nets or a farmer harvesting his grain. The only parochial activities which have any real justification are those which spring from worship and in their turn nourish it.

Worship: Its Theology and Practice, by J.J. von Allmen, (1965), 132–33, 51–52, 37, 55–56. Reprinted by permission of Oxford University Press.

PROPERS

God our Father, beautiful in majesty, majestic in holiness, by the examples of your servants John Mason Neale and Catherine Winkworth, refine our learning with devotion, enlarge our understanding by sympathetic exploration of cultures and people separated from us by space and time, and foster in us a concern for those who are slighted, ignored, or forgotten; that we may know the inexhaustible riches of your new creation in Jesus Christ our Lord; who lives and reigns with you and the Holy Spirit, one God, now and forever.

PHP

Readings:	2 Chronicles 20:20-21
	Psalm 96 *or* Psalm 106:1-5 *or* 33:1-5, 20-21
	Colossians 3:14-17
	Matthew 13:44-52
Hymn of the Day:	
	"Christ is made the sure foundation" (Neale) (H82 518; alt in LBW 367, LSB 909, ELW 645)
	"If you but trust in God to guide you" (Winkworth) (LBW 453, LSB 750, ELW 769)
Prayers:	For students of the worship of the church
	For those who revise and translate hymns that new ages may sing old songs
	For the gift of gentleness and patience
	For those who work for women's rights
Preface:	Dedication of a Church (BCP)
Color:	White

July 6

Jan Hus, Martyr, 1415

with Jerome of Prague, Martyr, 1416

Jan Hus (his name is sometimes anglicized as John Huss) was born of peasant parents in Husinec in southwest Bohemia (now the Czech Republic) *ca*. 1373. He was educated at the newly founded Charles University in Prague, where he took his master of arts degree in 1396. At the university he continued to use his full name Jan of Husinec, but soon an abbreviated form, Jan Hus, became common among his fellow students. ("Hus" in Czech means "goose," and this led to great amusement.) Two years after receiving his master's degree, the penniless student who had been making a living as a choirboy became a professor of theology. In *ca*. 1400 he was ordained to the priesthood, and in 1402 he served a six-month term as rector of the university, a position he held again in 1409. Also in 1402 he was named preacher in the Chapel of the Holy Innocents of Bethlehem, a large church founded in 1391 in which, by its charter, the preaching was in the Czech language rather than in Latin, and which was the center of the growing national reform movement. It was for Bohemia a time of national awakening and prosperity. In the Church there was schism in the papacy (at the time of the Council of Pisa in 1409 there were three who claimed to be pope) and a time of the erosion of authority caused by general corruption and disillusionment.

John Wyclif (or Wycliffe), "the morning star of the Reformation," was born *ca.* 1330 in Yorkshire, England, and was the first master of Balliol College, Oxford. In 1374 by royal appointment he became rector of Lutterworth, and he held that position until his death December 31, 1384. He encouraged the translation of the Bible into English (if he did not in fact make the translation himself), preached that the Bible is the only sure and certain source of knowledge about God, rejected transubstantiation as an inadequate explanation of the real presence of Christ in the Sacrament, and denied the pope's claims of authority. After Princess Anne of Bohemia, sister of the king, married Richard II of England in 1382, Wyclif's writings became especially influential in Bohemia.

Hus was deeply influenced by Wyclif's writings, although he differed from him on several points, generally in the direction of moderation and conservatism, and in his own sermons and writings, Hus began to include condemnations of church abuses. As his strictures became more severe, the local archbishop and hierarchy turned against him, and after Pope Alexander V in 1409 issued a bull condemning Wyclif's writings, the archbishop excommunicated Hus in 1412 not for heresy but for failing to answer a summons to Rome.

Hus's doctrinal statements were largely on questions of Church discipline and practice rather than on basic theological issues; there he generally followed the orthodox teachings of the Church of his day. He believed in the administration of the Holy Communion in both kinds to the laity, he opposed the secular power of the Church, and he denied that St. Peter was the head of the Church. Later, some of his followers, called "Lollards" (apparently "mumblers"), recognized only two sacraments, Holy Baptism and Holy Communion, and rejected much of the ceremonial of the Roman Church.

Hus had offended the prelates who were guilty of the avaricious life he preached against, and he was summoned to the Council of Constance in Switzerland 1414 with an imperial promise of safe-conduct for his return to Bohemia even if adjudged guilty. When he arrived in November, he was immediately confined for some months in the dungeon of the Dominican monastery. He eventually faced the Council on June 7 and the days following. The panel of judges consisted of his enemies. After refusing to recant articles falsely ascribed to him, Hus on July 6, 1415, was sentenced to death, and on the same day on the outskirts of the city he was burned at the stake, audibly praying the *Kyrie eleison* as he died. In its attempt to stamp out what they perceived as heresy, the Council sent orders to the Archbishop of Canterbury that the bones of John Wyclif were to be removed from their grave and burned.

The University of Prague set aside July 6 for an annual commemoration of this hero of the faith, and the day of Hus's martyrdom is included on the calendar of the Moravian Church. He is also listed on the German Lutheran *Calendar of Names* and on the Methodist calendar in *For All the Saints*.

Jerome of Prague (*ca.* 1370–1416), a disciple of Hus, supported him when other friends did not dare to do so. He intended to come to the Council of Constance but was imprisoned, condemned, and burned at the stake a year after Hus. Jerome is listed on the *Evangelical Calendar of Names* on May 29.

After Hus's death, his followers continued his teaching and repeatedly won victories of arms over the forces sent to subdue them. Hus was the hero of the Bohemian people, who fought against the power of their landlords, the ethnic discrimination of their German rulers, and the corruption and secular power of the Church. Finally, in 1436, a pact was signed by the king, the Hussites, and the Roman Church, which stabilized the situation, allowing the national Church of Bohemia to administer the sacrament in both kinds, not just the bread only—a practice that lasted in Bohemia for centuries.

The followers of Hus and his friend Jerome of Prague continued as the Czech Brethren and eventually as the Moravian Church of the present day. Martin Luther admired the life and teachings of "St. John Hus," as he once called him, and he approved the Moravian Confession of 1535. Several Lutheran churches in North America have been named for Hus; there are also Presbyterian churches named for him, such as the one in New York City which was the center of extensive observances of the five hundredth anniversary of his death in 1915.

FOR FURTHER READING

Holeton, David R. "The Celebration of Jan Hus in the Life of the Churches," *Studia Liturgica* 35 (2005): 32–59.

Spinka, Matthew. *John Hus and the Czech Reform*. Chicago: University of Chicago Press, 1941. Reprinted 1966.

———. *John Hus: A Biography*. Princeton: Princeton University Press, 1968.

———. *John Hus at the Council of Constance*. New York: Columbia University Press, 1965.

READING

From Jan Hus *On Simony*

. . . I have found that ordinary poor priests and poor laymen—even women— defend the truth more zealously than the teachers of the Holy Scriptures, who out of fear run away from the truth and do not have courage to defend it. I myself,

I am sorry to say, had been one of them, for I did not dare to preach the truth plainly and openly. Why are we like that? Solely because some of us are timid, fearing to lose worldly favor and praise, and others of us fear to lose benefices; for we fear to be held in contempt by the people for the sake of the truth, and to suffer bodily pain. We are like . . . those of whom Saint John says in his Gospel that "many, even of the authorities, believed in him. But because of the Pharisees they did not confess it, for fear that they would be put out of the synagogue; for they loved human glory more than the glory that comes from God." [12:42-43] . . . How many there are—princes, masters, priests, and others—who, being afraid of excommunication, do not have courage to confess the truth of Christ, and therefore Christ himself; and how many there are who are afraid to confess the truth lest they lose their wretched goods, or, above all, who, lacking the courage to risk their earthly life, abandon the truth.

Those three fears—of losing human praise and favor, of losing goods, and of losing earthly life—cause the timid to abandon the truth of confessing the Savior Jesus Christ, who promised honor, goods, and life. He promised honor, saying, "Those who shall confess me and my words in this adulterous and sinful generation, the Son of Man will also confess when he comes in the glory of his Father with the holy angels." [See Mark 8:38] The goods he promised under an oath, saying, "Truly, I tell you, there is no one who has left house or brothers or sisters or mother or father or children or fields, for my sake and for the sake of the good news, who will not receive hundredfold." [Mark 10:29-30] And he promises life, saying, "And in the age to come eternal life." [Mark 10:30] And elsewhere he says, "Those who lose their life for my sake, and for the sake of the gospel, will save it." [Mark 8:35] . . . Woe to us, unhappy people, that we do not value everlasting glory more than the temporal, lean, and transient, and that we do not esteem the eternal goods more than the temporal. Concerning this the Savior says, "What will it profit them to gain the whole world, and forfeit their life?" [Mark 8:36] Woe to us because we do not dare to risk this miserable, sorrowful, and painful life, which is ever dying, for the eternal life—glorious, joyous, and free from pain.

Trans. PHP. See *Advocates of Reform: From Wyclif to Erasmus,* vol. 14, The Library of Christian Classics, ed. Matthew Spinka (London: SCM and Philadelphia: Westminster 1953), 263–64.

PROPERS

Most kind God, without you we can do nothing, and unless you draw us we cannot follow you: Give us, we pray, a courageous spirit, a fearless heart, a true faith, a sure hope, and perfect love, that with great patience and joy we may offer our lives to you; for the sake of Jesus Christ our Lord, who lives and reigns with you and the Holy Spirit, one God, now and forever.

From a letter by Jan Hus, June 23, 1415, rev. PHP

Readings: Ezekiel 20:40-42
Psalm 5
Revelation 6:9-11
Matthew 23:34-37

Hymn of the Day:
"Once he came in blessing" (LBW 312, LSB 333, H82 53)
"Jesus Christ, our blessed Savior" (TLH 311, LSB 627) (The Wittenberg Hymnal, 1524, gives the caption, "The Hymn of St. John Hus, improved")

Prayers: For fearless and faithful preachers
For the renewal of the Christian life
For the church in the Czech Republic
For the Moravian Church

Preface: All Saints
Color: Red

JULY

ALSO ON JULY 6

The calendar in the *Lutheran Service Book* (2006), following Wilhelm Löhe, lists *Isaiah* on this date. The Eastern Church commemorates the prophet Isaiah on May 9.

July 11

Benedict of Nursia, Abbot of Monte Cassino, *ca*. 547; Scholastica, Monastic, *ca*. 547

Benedict, the creator of Western monasticism, was born to a distinguished family at Norcia (Nursia) in central Italy *ca*. 480. Little is known of his life apart from what Gregory the Great reports in his *Dialogues* (593–594), especially Book II, which is apparently based on the testimony of eyewitnesses and disciples of Benedict.

He studied in Rome where he was influenced by the Byzantine monastic centers. He was offended by the licentiousness of society and withdrew to become a hermit in a grotto thought to have been near Subiaco, forty miles west of Rome. Disciples soon came to him, among whom were Maurus and Placidus from a senatorial family, and Benedict, turning from solitary life to the communal, created twelve monasteries of twelve monks each. He was apparently not ordained and did not contemplate an order for the clergy.

Local jealousy forced him to leave Subiaco, and he took his community to Monte Cassino, a fortified hill midway between Rome and Naples, where he destroyed a sacred wood and transformed the groves into places of Christian prayer consecrated to John the Baptist and St. Martin. Monte Cassino remained the principal monastery, although another was founded at Terracina. Benedict kept in careful touch with other monastic leaders and composed his famous *Rule,* which is in part an adaptation of an earlier rule, the *Rule of the Master,* an Italian work of the sixth century. Benedict's *Rule* is relatively short and is marked by a spirit of "prudent leniency" compared to other rules from which it is descended and fixes a daily routine of common worship, labor, and rest.

Benedict's sister, perhaps his twin, **Scholastica**, who was born *ca.* 480, was dedicated to God at an early age but probably continued to live in her parents' home. Later she was living not far from Monte Cassino, whether alone or in a community is not known. All the little that is known about her is revealed in the *Dialogues* of Gregory the Great. Brother and sister used to meet once a year in a house near the monastery. She had a notable influence on her brother. Gregory tells how on what was to be the last of these meetings, Scholastica asked her brother not to leave her but to continue talking until morning. Benedict refused, saying, "I cannot stay outside my cell." Scholastica prayed, and there was such a storm that Benedict could not leave. They stayed awake the whole night talking about the spiritual life. Gregory observes about her, "It is not surprising that she was more effective than he; since, as John says, 'God is love,' it was absolutely right that she could do more, because she loved more." Three days later, Scholastica died. Benedict buried her in the tomb that he had prepared for himself and in which he was later to be buried. Gregory comments, "Their minds had always been united in God; their bodies were to share a common grave."

St. Scholastica's feast day on the present Roman Catholic calendar is February 10. Since so little is known of her, it is therefore appropriate to remember her together with her brother.

In *ca.* 577 the Lombards destroyed Monte Cassino. When it was restored a century and a half later, a cult developed around the tomb of Benedict. Eventually, March 21 was observed as the day of his death and July 11 as the feast of the Patronage of St. Benedict. It was on July 11 that his supposed relics were transferred to a monastery at Fleury near Orleans, although Monte Cassino still claimed to have the true remains. The present Roman Catholic, Episcopal, Lutheran, and Methodist calendars commemorate St. Benedict on July 11.

On February 15, 1944, the monastery at Monte Cassino was again destroyed by an Allied attack on what was thought to be a Nazi stronghold. The monastery has since been restored and was reconsecrated by Paul VI in 1964.

FOR FURTHER READING

Butler, E. C. *Benedictine Monachism.* 2d ed. New York: Barnes and Noble, 1961.

Dunn, Marilyn J. *The Emergence of Monasticism: From the Desert Fathers to the Early Middle Ages.* London: Blackwell, 2001.

JULY

Ellis, John. *Cassino: The Hollow Victory: the Battle for Rome, January–June, 1944.* New York: McGraw-Hill, 1984.

Hopgood, David, and David Richardson. *Monte Cassino.* New York: Congdon and Weed, 1984. The destruction of the monastery in 1944.

Knowles, David. *Christian Monasticism.* London: Weidenfeld, 1969.

Lindsay, Thomas F. *St. Benedict: His Life and Work.* London: Burns & Oates, 1959.

Schuster, Idelphonse. *St. Benedict and His Times.* Trans. G. J. Roetttiger. St. Louis: Herder, 1951.

READING

From the *Rule of St. Benedict* (Prologue, 19, 20)

I am to erect a school for beginners in the service of the Lord: which I hope to establish on laws not too difficult or grievous. But if, for reasonable cause, for the retrenchment of vice or preservation of charity, I require some things which may seem too austere, you are not thereupon to be frightened from the ways of salvation. Those ways are always strait and narrow at the beginning. But as we advance in the practices of religion and in faith, the heart insensibly opens and enlarges through the wonderful sweetness of his love, and we run in the way of God's commandments. If then we keep close to our school and the doctrine we learn in it, and persevere in the monastery till death, we shall here share by patience in the passion of Christ and hereafter deserve to be united with him in his kingdom. Amen.

We believe God is everywhere, and his eye beholds the good and wicked wherever they are: so we ought to be particularly assured of his special presence when we assist at the divine office. Therefore we must always remember the advice of the prophet, "To serve God in fear": "to sing wisely": and that "the angels are witnesses of what we sing." Let us then reflect what behavior is proper for appearing in the presence of God and the angels, and so sing our psalms that the mind may echo in harmony with the voice.

If we want to ask a favor of any person in power, we presume not to approach but with humility and respect. How much more ought we to address ourselves to the Lord and God of all things with a humble and entire devotion? We are not to imagine that our prayers shall be heard because we use many words, but because the heart is pure and the spirit penitent. Therefore prayer must be short and pure, unless it be prolonged by a feeling of divine inspiration. Prayer in common ought always to be short. . . .

Western Asceticism, Library of Christian Classics 12, trans. Owen Chadwick (Philadelphia: Westminster, 1958), 291, 293, 309–10.

PROPERS

Almighty and everlasting God, you made your servant Benedict a worthy guide to teach us how to live in your service: Grant that by preferring your love to everything else and following the examples of Benedict and Scholastica, we may ever walk in the way of your commandments; through your Son Jesus Christ our Lord, who lives and reigns with you and the Holy Spirit, one God, now and forever.

RS, trans. PHP

Readings:	Proverbs 2:1-9
	Psalm 1 *or* 34:1-8
	Luke 14:27-33
Hymn of the Day:	
	"Jesus, priceless treasure" (H82 701, LBW 457, 458, LSB 743, ELW 775)
Prayers:	For courage to put Christ before everything else
	For the gift of obedience to God's commandments
	For all who seek purity of life
	For those who live among us as signs of the kingdom of heaven
	For monastic communities everywhere who follow the Rule of St. Benedict
Preface:	A Saint (2) (BCP)
Color:	White

July 12

Nathan Söderblom, Archbishop of Uppsala, 1931

Nathan Söderblom, theologian and ecumenist, was born in Trönö, Sweden, on January 15, 1866, the son of a pietist pastor. He studied at the University of Uppsala and was ordained a priest of the Church of Sweden in 1893. He served as chaplain to the Swedish legation in Paris from 1894 to 1901, and while he was there he studied comparative religion and received his doctorate from the Sorbonne in 1901. From 1901 to 1914 he was professor of the history of religion at Uppsala and also held a lectureship at Leipzig from 1912 to 1914. In 1914, despite the opposition of more conservative elements in the Swedish Church, he was elected Archbishop of Uppsala and Primate of the Church of Sweden. (*Evangelical Lutheran Worship*—which, curiously, never employs the title "archbishop"—is in error in listing Söderblom as "Bishop of Uppsala." There is another person who is the diocesan bishop and is not the primate.)

Söderblom was attracted to the liturgy and piety of the Roman Catholic Church, but at the same time he was influenced by liberal Protestant scholars.

He sought to achieve an "evangelical catholicity" among Christian communions through practical cooperation on social issues. During World War I, he intervened on behalf of prisoners of war and displaced persons. This, together with his advocacy of peace through church unity, earned him the Nobel Prize for peace in 1930.

His interest in Christian unity began during his student years and increased following a visit to the United States in 1890. As a result of his efforts, the Universal Christian Council on Life and Work was formed at a meeting in Stockholm in August 1925. This body, together with the predominately Anglican Conference on Faith and Order, merged in 1948 to form the World Council of Churches.

As archbishop, his remarkable zeal and energy were directed largely toward counteracting the growing alienation from the church of both intellectuals and labor. His concern was for a greater involvement in social and ethical issues as well as for a deepened devotional life. Söderblom died July 12, 1931.

FOR FURTHER READING

Curtis, Charles J. *Söderblom: Ecumenical Pioneer.* Minneapolis: Augsburg, 1971.

Katz, Peter. *Nathan Söderblom: A Prophet of Christian Unity.* London: J. Clarke, 1949.

Rouse, R., and Stephen Neill, eds. *A History of the Ecumenical Movement, 1517–1948.* London: SPCK, 1954.

Sharpe, Eric J. *Nathan Söderblom and the Study of Religion.* Chapel Hill: University of North Carolina Press, 1990.

Sundkler, Bengt G. *Nathan Söderblom: His Life and Work.* Lund: Gleerup, 1968.

READING

From *The Living God* by Nathan Söderblom

God's revelation is not finished—it continues. Here a most essential distinction must be made. Heaven was not shut up after the manifestation of God recorded in the Bible. We see it open over the Bible and in the Bible as nowhere else, and go to it in order to see the Eternal Light shine through the grey mist of existence. God is ever revealing himself. God's continued revelation is history. Of course, I hold that the Church is God's work and God's instrument. The religious value of the Church is sometimes overrated, but often also underrated. God has entrusted the Church with the divine privilege and the tremendous duty of giving to the world in word and deed and sacrament the Grace of God. Our belief in God's continued revelation in history makes us consider, more diligently and more reverently than before, the value of men, means, and institutions, which God has given to the Church in the course of history. But God's revelation is not confined to the Church, although the Church has, in the Scripture and in its experience, the means of interpreting God's continued revelation. The Church ought to open its eyes, more than it does, to see how God is perpetually revealing himself. The Evangelic statement that God has revealed himself once for all in the Bible is true and must be maintained in its true sense about divine action recorded in the Scriptures. But we often fail to learn the lesson of the Bible, that our God is a living, a still living God, who has not become older and less active than in earlier days.

Nathan Söderblom, *The Living God: Basal Forms of Personal Religion,* The Gifford Lectures (London: Oxford, 1933), 378–79.

PROPERS

Almighty God, you planted in your servant Nathan Söderblom an appreciation of both the evangelical and the catholic character of the church, and stirred up in him a fervor for the unity of your church and the welfare of your people: Grant that by the power of your Holy Spirit we may be strengthened to remove the barriers that divide Christian from Christian, and in deeds of kindness and generosity may show forth your love to all the world; through your Son Jesus Christ our Lord, who lives and reigns with you and the Holy Spirit, one God, now and forever.

PHP, after James E. Kiefer

Readings:	Ezekiel 34:11-16
	Psalm 84
	Ephesians 3:14-21
	John 21:15-17
Hymn of the Day:	
	"In Adam we have all been one" (LBW 372, LSB 569)
Prayers:	For the unity of the church
	For the understanding and growth of evangelical catholicity
	For the peace of the world
	For a new respect for the insight of religions other than our own
Preface:	Epiphany
Color:	White

July 13

Johannes Flierl, Missionary to Australia and Papua New Guinea, 1947

Johannes Flierl was born April 16, 1858, to a peasant family in Buchof, Bavaria, and was educated at the mission seminary at Neuendettelsau in Bavaria. In 1878 he was sent to Australia, and for seven years he did mission work among the aborigines in the interior of that continent. On July 12, 1886, he landed at

Finschafen, Papua New Guinea, the capital of the German colony of Kaiser-Wilhelmsland, the first Lutheran missionary on that island. European contact had begun in 1871 when a Russian biologist explored the Rai coast and introduced new foods. German settlers soon arrived and built tobacco, coffee, and cotton plantations. Flierl established a mission near Simbang, but only after fourteen years was he able to baptize his first Jabêm converts. The Roman Catholic Church established missions in 1900 and 1904. For nearly half a century, Flierl worked among the Papuans and was a champion of the rights of the natives against government oppression. Flierl retired to Australia in 1930, moved to Europe in 1937, and died September 30, 1947. In 1957, in memory of his work, the Senior Flierl Seminary was established in Finschafen.

The mission was taken over by the American Lutheran Church during World War II, and in 1956 it organized itself into the Evangelical Lutheran Church of New Guinea and became autonomous as the Evangelical Lutheran Church of Papua New Guinea in 1975. This church, together with the Batak Church in Indonesia, is the largest of all Lutheran mission churches.

On the calendar of the Evangelical Lutheran Church of Papua New Guinea, July 12, the date he landed on the island, is celebrated as the birthday of their church. The day is sometimes also observed in Australia.

FOR FURTHER READING

Herwig Wagner and Hermann Reiner eds. *The Lutheran Church in Papua New Guinea: The First Hundred Years 1886–1986.* Adelaide: Lutheran Publishing House, 1987.

READING

From a charge by George Augustus Selwyn to his Synod, 1847

God has already so abundantly blessed the work of his servants, that not an island remains to the eastward of New Zealand to which the Gospel has not been preached. But there is still a dark expanse, over which the banner of Christ has not yet been advanced. If any motive could justify the wish to live the full period of the patriarchal age, it would be to see Borneo, Celebes, New Guinea, and all the islands of our north, converted to the faith. It may be presumptuous to wish, yet it cannot be wrong to think of such things; for it seems to be an indisputable fact, that however inadequate a Church may be on its own internal wants, it must on no account suspend its Missionary duties; that this is in fact the circulation of its life's blood, which would lose its vital power if it never flowed forth to the extremities, but curdled at the heart. We may hope that a statement of the highest aims, and most comprehensive definition of duty, will be a means of raising the whole tone of our minds; that we shall feel thereby the full weight of the unfulfilled purposes of our ministry; and be humbled, even in the midst of our success, by thinking how far greater is the work which still remains than that which has been done.

H. W. Tucker, *Memoir of the Life and Episcopate of George Augustus Selwyn, D.D.* (London, 1881), 1:237.

PROPERS

God of grace and might, you called Johannes Flierl to your service and stirred in him zeal to make the good news known to the people of Papua New Guinea, and courage to oppose their oppressors: Raise up, we pray, in this and every land heralds and evangelists of your kingdom, so that the world may know the immeasurable riches of our Savior, Jesus Christ our Lord, who lives and reigns with you and the Holy Spirit, one God, now and forever.

BCP, LBW, rev. PHP

Readings:	Isaiah 62:1-7
	Psalm 48
	Romans 10:11-17
	Luke 24:44-53
Hymn of the Day:	
	"All people that on earth do dwell" (LBW 245, LSB 791, ELW 883, H82 377, 378)
Prayers:	For the church in Papua New Guinea
	For missionaries and their families
	For the younger churches
	For patience in doing the work of God
Preface:	Epiphany
Color:	White

July 15

Olga, Princess of Kiev, Confessor, 969; Vladimir, First Christian Ruler of Russia, 1015

Olga and Vladimir are honored together on the calendar in the *Lutheran Book of Worship* as the first-born of the new Christian people of Russia and its borders.

Olga (Helga), the grandmother of Vladimir, was born at Pskov, Russia, *ca.* 890. She married Prince Igor, and after his death in 945 she acted as regent for their son. She has been praised for her courage and her ability as a ruler, instituting salutary reforms of administration and finance, and was an early convert to the Christian faith among the Scandinavian rulers of the province of Kiev who had followed the extensive river systems east from their traditional homes to the land of the Slavs. In 957 Olga visited Constantinople and, according to some accounts, was baptized there, although other accounts indicate that she had been a Christian for some years before her visit to the principal city of the East. In any case, her baptism did not signal the conversion of her country, for the pagans rallied around her son, who resisted her efforts to instruct him in Christianity. Olga died in 969, and her traditional feast day is July 11. "Blessed Princess Olga" is especially honored in the Ukrainian and Russian Churches.

Vladimir was born in 956, the youngest son of Svyatoslav of Kiev and a great grandson of Rurik, the traditional founder of the Rurkid dynasty and of the Russian state. Vladimir was made prince of Novgorod in 970. Two years later, when his father died, a fierce struggle broke out among the three sons. Oled was killed and Vladimir was forced to flee to Scandinavia. He then returned in 980 with Scandinavian support, killed his brother Yaropolk and made himself master of Russia. A successful military leader, he expanded Russian control from southeast Poland to the Volga valley.

By the late tenth century, the influence of neighboring Christian states had become strong, and Vladimir, having consolidated all the eastern Slavs under his dynasty in Kiev, for political as well as for intellectual and spiritual reasons wanted to know which was the true religion. *The Russian Primary Chronicle* describes how he sent out emissaries to various parts of the world in turn. They were not impressed with the Muslim Bulgars, for they had no joy (they also forbade the use of alcohol); the Jewish Khazars lived in exile from their land and Vladimir had taken considerable pains to create his empire and did not want to risk having to leave it; in German Catholicism the worship lacked beauty, the delegation reported; but when they attended the Divine Liturgy in the great Church of Holy Wisdom (*Hagia Sophia*) in Constantinople, they exclaimed, "We did not know whether we were in heaven or on earth! God dwells there among humans. We cannot forget that beauty." In 988 Vladimir sent six thousand soldiers to the Byzantine emperor Basil II, who needed military help, asking the hand of Basil's sister Anna in return. The emperor agreed, provided that Vladimir become a Christian. Vladimir was baptized by bishops from Byzantium that same year, 988. The emperor was then reluctant to fulfill his part of the agreement; Vladimir attacked the Crimea, and Princess Anna became his wife. When the royal couple returned to Kiev, the people followed his example and urging and were baptized. With what has been called "The Baptism of the Ukraine" or "The Baptism of Russia," Christianity was officially introduced and established.

Despite the circumstances surrounding his conversion, Vladimir was wholehearted in his adherence to the new faith. He put away his former wives and mistresses, amended his life, and publicly destroyed idols. He became an ardent promoter of Christianity and built many churches and monasteries, expanded educational and judicial institutions, aided the poor, and supported Greek missionaries. The Christianization Kievan Russia proceeded rapidly, for despite his personal sincerity, Vladimir relied largely on physical compulsion and heavily punished those who refused baptism. The emerging Russian Church was under the jurisdiction of Constantinople, but it remained friendly toward the West.

Vladimir's last years were troubled by the insurrection of his sons and by his former pagan wives, and he died on an expedition against one of them at Berestova, near Kiev, July 15, 1015.

In 1988, celebrations of a thousand years of Christianity were held in Ukraine, Russia, and elsewhere.

Vladimir is not included on the calendar in the *Book of Common Prayer* nor on the General Roman Calendar. "Equal to the Apostles, Prince Vladimir" is, however, highly regarded by the Eastern Church.

FOR FURTHER READING

Attwater, Donald. *The Golden Book of Eastern Saints.* Freeport: Books for Libraries Press, 1971 [1938], 81–83.

Cross, S. H. *Harvard Studies and Notes in Philology and Literature* 12 (1930): 77–309.

———, and O. P. Sherbowitz-Wetzor, ed. and trans. *The Russian Primary Chronicle.* 64–87, 111. Cambridge: Harvard University Press, 1953.

Dvornik, F. *The Slavs: Their Early History and Civilization.* Boston: American Academy of Arts and Sciences, 1956.

De Grunwald, Constantin. *Saints of Russia.* Trans. Roger Capel. 17–30. New York: Macmillan, 1960.

Vernadsky, G. *Kievan Russia.* New Haven: Yale University Press, 1948.

Volkoff, Vladimir. *Vladimir the Russian Viking.* Woodstock: Overlook, 1986.

READING

From *Unseen Warfare*, a classic of Eastern spirituality

So this spiritual warfare of ours must be constant and never ceasing, and should be conducted with alertness and courage in the soul; they can easily be attained, is you seek these gifts from God. So advance into battle without hesitation. Should you be visited by the troubling thought of the hatred and undying malice, which the enemies harbour against you, and of the innumerable hosts of demons, think on the other hand of the infinitely greater power of God and of His love for you, as well as of the incomparably greater hosts of heavenly angels and the prayers of saints. They all fight secretly for us and with us against our enemies, as it is written: "The Lord will have war with Amalek from generation to generation" (Exodus 17:16). How many weak women and small children were incited to fight by the thought of this powerful and ever ready help! And they got the upper hand and gained victory over all the wisdom of the world, all the wiles of the devil and all the malice of hell.

So you must never be afraid, if you are troubled by a flood of thoughts, that the enemy is too strong for you, that his attacks are never-ending, that the war will last for your lifetime, and that you cannot avoid incessant downfalls of all kinds. Know that our enemies, with all their wiles, are in the hands of our divine Commander, our Lord Jesus Christ, for Whose honour and glory you are waging war. Since He Himself leads you into battle, He will certainly not suffer your enemies to use violence against you and overcome you, if you do not cross to their side with your will. He will Himself fight for you and will deliver your enemies into your hands, when He wills and as He wills, as it is written: "The Lord thy God walketh in the midst of thy camp, to deliver thee, and to give up thine enemies before thee" (Deuteronomy 23:14).

If the Lord delays granting you full victory over your enemies and puts it off to the last day of your life, you must know that He does this for your own good; so long as you do not retreat or cease to struggle wholeheartedly. Even if you are wounded in battle do not lay down your arms and turn to flight. Keep only one thing in your mind and intention—to fight with all courage and ardour, since it is unavoidable. No man can escape this warfare, either in life or in death. And he who does not fight to overcome his passions and his enemies will inevitably be taken prisoner, either here or yonder, and be delivered to death.

Unseen Warfare being the Spiritual Combat and Path to Paradise of Lorenzo Scupoli as edited by Nicodemus of the Holy Mountain and revised by Theophan the Recluse, trans. E. Kadloubovsky and G. E. H. Palmer (London: Faber and Faber, 1963), 54–55.

PROPERS

God the All-Merciful, you brought your servant Princess Olga to the church and by the splendor of the Divine Liturgy you revealed to her grandson Vladimir the glories of your heavenly kingdom: Mercifully grant that we who commemorate them this day may be fruitful in good works and attain to the glorious crown of your saints; through your Son, Jesus Christ our Lord, who lives and reigns with you and the Holy Spirit, One God, now and forever.

PHP ✛ LFF, August 25

Readings:	Micah 6:6-8
	Psalm 9:1-10
	1 Corinthians 1:26-31
	Luke 6:20-23
Hymn of the Day:	
	"God the omnipotent!" (LBW 462, H82 569)
Prayers:	For the people and government of Russia and Ukraine
	For the growth in grace of all new converts to Christianity

For Christian families
For the faculty, students, and benefactors of St. Vladimir's Seminary, Crestwood, New York
Preface: A Saint (2) (BCP)
Color: White

July 16

The *Lutheran Service Book*, following Wilhelm Löhe's calendar, commemorates **Ruth**, the Moabite and grandmother of King David, on this date.

July 17

Bartolomé de Las Casas, Missionary to the Indies, 1566

Las Casas, the apostle to the Indies, was the first to expose the oppression of the native peoples of the West Indies and Central America by the Europeans. He was born in Seville, Spain, in August 1474, the son of a merchant. Originally a lawyer, he went to Cuba in 1502 with Governor Nicolas de Ovando, and for this participation in the expedition he was given an *encomienda,* a royal land grant that included the Indians who lived on the land. He soon gave up colonizing to undertake the reform of a system that he had come to see was inhumane. He was ordained priest probably in Rome in 1507 but delayed his first Mass until he could celebrate it on Hispaniola in 1510. In 1514 he experienced a kind of conversion, and in a sermon on August 15, 1514, he announced that he was returning all his Indian serfs to the governor. From 1515 to 1522 he traveled between Spain and America in a continued attempt to win approval for a series of projects that he was convinced would make for peaceful colonization and the Christianization of the Indians in new towns where Spanish and Indians together would create a new civilization in America. His experiment collapsed in 1522.

Frustrated in this attempt, Las Casas took refuge in the religious life and entered the Dominican Order in 1523. After an extended retreat, he resumed his plans for peaceful evangelization in Hispaniola, Nicaragua, and Guatemala. In 1540 he returned to Spain from Santo Domingo and worked for the "New Laws" of 1542–1543, which prohibited slavery and made colonization more humane. The laws were widely ignored.

Las Casas was made Bishop of Chiapas in Guatemala and returned to the Americas in 1544 with forty-four Dominicans to implement the New Laws himself, but his efforts met with only limited success. Having alienated his colleagues with his uncompromising position on behalf of the Indians, he returned to Spain in 1547 and there entered upon the most fruitful period of his life. About 1550 he engaged in a bitter controversy with the theologian Gines Sepulveda of Cordova, who held that war against the Indians was justified because they were plainly inferior to the Spanish and were among the races that Aristotle had declared to be by nature destined to slavery.

For a time, in his defense of the indigenous peoples, Las Casas supported the replacement of Indian slaves with slaves from Africa, believing that they might be better suited to the work. His observation of the condition of the African slaves soon convinced him, however, that all human slavery is wrong and he came to protest the enslavement of Africans as well as Indians. In this remarkable growth in understanding, his being able to change his mind, Las Casas is worthy of emulation.

Las Casas came to be influential at court and composed three major works: *De unico vocationis modo* (1537), on the theory of evangelical conquest; *Historia apologetica*, a detailed description of Indian abilities, which was an introduction to *Historia de Las Indias,* a condemnation of the thirty years of Spanish colonial policy and a prophetic interpretation of the events. In addition, he wrote doctrinal treatises, letters, and pamphlets. His most famous work is his *Brief Report on the Destruction of the Indians* (also known as *Tears of the Indians*), a sensationalist account to Spanish atrocities attributed to their greed for gold. The little book was translated into many languages and was used by the English as a weapon against Spain and the Spanish empire in the New World.

Las Casas died July 17, 1566, in the Dominican convent of Nuestra Señora de Atocha de Madrid. (Older sources give the date as July 31.) In 1976 the Dominican Order introduced in Rome the cause of his beatification. The *Lutheran Book of Worship* and *Evangelical Lutheran Worship* include him on the calendar on July 17, following the German Lutheran *Evangelical Calendar of Names*, which listed him on the older date of July 31. The 1997 Church of England calendar, the *Christian Year,* commemorates "the Apostle to the Indies" on July 20.

Postage stamps commemorating Las Casas have been issued in Mexico, Cuba, and Nicaragua. There is a statue of him in the New York Public Library.

FOR FURTHER READING

Davis, David Brian. *Inhuman Bondage: The Rise and Fall of Slavery in the New World.* New York: Oxford University Press, 2006.

Friede, Juan, and Benjamin Keen, eds. *Bartolomé de Las Casas in History: Toward an Understanding of the Man and His Work*. De Kalb: Northern Illinois University Press, 1976.

Gustavo Gutiérrez. *Las Casas: In Search of the Poor in Jesus Christ.* Maryknoll: Orbis, 1993.

Hanke, Lewis. *All Mankind is One.* De Kalb: Northern Illinois University Press, 1975.

————. *Aristotle and the American Indians.* Chicago: Regnery, 1959.

————. *Bartolomé de Las Casas: An Interpretation of His Life and Writings.* The Hague, 1951.

————. *Bartolomé de Las Casas: Bookman, Scholar, and Propagandist.* Philadelphia: University of Pennsylvania Press, 1952.

————. *Bartolomé de Las Casas: Historian.* Gainesville: University of Florida Press, 1952.

————. *The Spanish Struggle for Justice in the Conquest of America.* Philadelphia: University of Pennsylvania Press, 1950. Reprinted Boston: Little, Brown, 1965.

Helps, Arthur. *The Life of Las Casas.* London, 1868.

De Las Casas, Bartolomé. *In Defense of the Indians.* Ed. Stafford Poole. De Kalb: Northern Illinois University Press, 1973.

————. *A Short Account of the Destruction of the Indies.* New York: Viking Penguin, 1992.

Macnutt, Francis. *Bartholomew de Las Casas.* New York, 1909.

Parrish, Helen Rand, ed. *Bartolome de Las Casas: The Only Way.* Trans. Francis P. Sullivan. New York: Paulist, 1992.

Pfatteicher, Philip H. "The Fulfillment of Baptism." *Liturgy: With All the Saints* 5, no. 2 (Fall 1985): 15–19.

Wagner, Henry Raup and H. R. Parish. *The Life and Writings of Bartolome de Las Casas.* Albuquerque: University of New Mexico Press, 1967.

READING

From Las Casas, *In Defense of the Indians*

What man of sound mind will approve a war against men who are harmless, ignorant, gentle, temperate, unarmed, and destitute of every human defense? For the results of such a war are very surely the loss of the souls of that people who perish without knowing God and without the support of the sacraments, and, for the survivors, hatred and loathing of the Christian religion.

Among our Indians of the western and southern shores . . . there are important kingdoms, large numbers of people who live settled lives in a society, great cities, kings, judges and laws, persons who engage in commerce, buying, selling, lending, and the other contracts of the law of nations. . . . From the fact that the Indians are barbarians it does not necessarily follow that they are incapable of government and have to be ruled by others, except to be taught about the Catholic faith and to be admitted to the holy sacraments. They are not ignorant, inhuman, or bestial. Rather, long before they had heard the word Spaniard they had properly organized states, wisely ordered by excellent laws, religion, and custom.

They cultivated friendship and, bound together in common fellowship, lived in populous cities in which they wisely administered the affairs of both peace and war justly and equitably, truly governed by laws that at very many points surpass ours, and could have won the admiration of the sages of Athens. . . .

Now Christ wanted his gospel to be preached with enticements, gentleness, and all meekness and pagans to be led to the truth not by armed forces but by holy examples, Christian conduct, and the word of God, so that no opportunity would be offered for blaspheming his sacred name or hating the true religion because of the conduct of the preachers. For this is nothing else than making the coming and passion of Christ useless, as long as the truth of the gospel is hated before it is either understood or heard or as long as innumerable human beings are slaughtered in a war waged on the grounds of preaching the gospel and spreading religion.

The Indians are our brothers, and Christ has given his life for them. Why, then, do we persecute them with such inhuman savagery when they do not deserve such treatment? The past, because it cannot be undone, must be attributed to our weakness, provided that was has been taken unjustly is restored.

The Tears of the Indians: being An Historical and true Account of the cruel Massacres and Slaughters of above Twenty Millions of innocent People; Committed by the Spaniards In the Islands of Hispaniola, Cuba, Jamaica, etc. As also in the Continent of Mexico, Peru,& other Places of the West-Indies, To the total destruction of those Countries, trans. John Phillips (London, 1656), 26, 42–43, 350, 362.

PROPERS

Holy and righteous God, your servant Bartolomé de Las Casas defended indigenous people against those who would enslave them and grew to understand the sinfulness of all slavery: Give to all your people growth in knowledge and understanding of you, and give them courage to contend against evil in society, in others, and in ourselves, that together we may grow into the full stature of our Lord Jesus Christ, who lives and reigns with you and the Holy Spirit, one God, now and forever.

PHP

Readings:	Hosea 2:18-23
	Psalm 94:1-14
	Romans 12:9-21
	Luke 6:20-36
Hymn of the Day:	
	"Lord of all nations, grant me grace" (LBW 419, LSB 844, ELW 716)
Prayers:	For the native people of Central and South America
	For those who fight against slavery and oppression
	For increased sensitivity to human rights
	For justice and reconciliation among all peoples
Preface:	Baptism (BCP, LBW)
Color:	White

ALSO ON JULY 17

O n this date the calendar in the *Book of Common Prayer* remembers **William White** (1748–1836), the first Bishop of Pennsylvania and the first Presiding Bishop, who guided the Episcopal Church through its first decades of independent life.

July 20

Elizabeth Cady Stanton, 1902; Amelia Jenks Bloomer, 1894; Sojourner Truth, 1883; Harriet Ross Tubman, 1912; Renewers of Society

T he Episcopal *Lesser Feasts and Fasts (1997)* on this date has introduced the joint commemoration of four liberators and prophets: Elizabeth Cady Stanton (1815–1902), Amelia Jenks Bloomer (1818–1894), Sojourner Truth (1797–8 to 1883), and Harriet Ross Tubman (1820–1912). Two of these notable women are commemorated on the calendar in the Methodist *For All the Saints*: Sojourner Truth on November 26 and Harriet Ross Tubman on March 10; *Evangelical Lutheran Worship* commemorates these two together on March 10.

Elizabeth Cady, the nineteenth century's most prominent advocate of women's legal and social equality, was born in Johnstown, in upstate New York, into a strict Presbyterian family. In 1840 she married the abolitionist Henry Brewster Stanton, with whom she had seven children. Although she is best known for her contribution to the long struggle for women's suffrage, she was also effective in the temperance movement and in winning property rights for married women, equal guardianship of children, and liberalized divorce laws. With four others, she organized the first Woman's Rights Convention at Seneca Falls, New York, July 19–20, 1848. A witty and popular lecturer, she was also a sharp critic of religion in general and of Christianity in particular. Nonetheless, she attended Trinity Episcopal Church in Seneca Falls with her friend Amelia Bloomer. She died in New York City October 26, 1902.

Amelia Jenks Bloomer, the suffrage pioneer and writer, was born in 1818 in Cortland County, New York, to a devout Presbyterian family. In 1842 she married a lawyer, Dexter C. Bloomer, of Seneca Falls and became a member of the Episcopal Church. She had only two years of formal schooling but became the first woman to own, operate, and edit a newspaper for women, *The Lily*, in Seneca Falls. The initial focus was on temperance but under the guidance of Elizabeth Cady Stanton broadened to include women's rights. He name became associated with the comfortable women's clothing she championed, "Bloomers." In 1852 she moved west and died December 30, 1894, in Council Bluffs, Iowa.

Sojourner Truth was born Isabella Baumfree in 1797 in Hurley, Ulster County, New York, one of thirteen children born to slave parents. She spoke only Dutch until she was eleven and afterward spoke English with a Dutch accent. She was forced to marry an older slave, Thomas, with whom she had five children. New York abolished slavery in 1827, and she settled in New York City. In 1843 she had a spiritual experience that caused her to change her name to Sojourner Truth and as a traveling preacher went through Long Island and Connecticut preaching "God's truth and plan for salvation." She was an imposing woman, six feet tall. She eventually added abolition and women's suffrage to her message. She died November 26, 1883, in Battle Creek, Michigan.

Harriet Ross Tubman Davis was born a slave about 1820 in Dorchester County, Maryland. She escaped in 1848 and ran away, leaving her husband, John Tubman, who was not a slave but a free man. During the next ten years she made frequent trips south and helped some three hundred slaves to freedom by means of the clandestine escape route known as the Underground Railway. She served the Union army in the Civil War as a scout, spy, and nurse. Later she married Nelson Davis. She died March 10, 1913, in her home in Auburn, New York, twelve miles from Seneca Falls.

READING

From the address delivered by Elizabeth Cady Stanton at the Seneca Falls Convention, July 19, 1848

"Voices" were the visitors and advisers of Joan of Arc. Do not "voices" come to us daily from the haunts of poverty, sorrow, degradation, and despair, already too long unheeded. Now is the time for the women of this country, if they would save our free institutions, to defend the right, to buckle on the armor that can best resist the keenest weapons of the enemy—contempt and ridicule. The same religious enthusiasm that nerved Joan of Arc to her work nerves us to ours. In every generation God calls some men and women for the utterance of truth, a heroic action, and our work today is the fulfilling of what has long since been foretold by the prophet (Joel 2:28): "And it shall come to pass afterward, that I will pour out my spirit upon all flesh; and your sons and your daughters shall prophesy."

We do not expect our path will be strewn with the flowers of popular applause, but over the thorns of bigotry and prejudice will be our way, and on our banners will beat the dark storm clouds of opposition from those who have entrenched themselves behind the stormy bulwarks of custom and authority, and who have fortified their position by every means, holy and unholy. But we will steadfastly abide the result. Unmoved, we will bear it aloft. Undauntedly we will unfurl it to the gale, for we know that the storm cannot rend from it a shred, that the electric flash will but more clearly show us the glorious words inscribed upon it, "Equality of Rights."

Elizabeth Cady Stanton, "We Now Demand Our Right to Vote," at http://womenshistory.about. com/library/etext/bl_1848_stanton1.htm (accessed November 7, 2007).

PROPERS

Almighty God, who created us in your own image: Grant us grace fearlessly to contend against evil and to make no peace with oppression; and, that we may reverently use our freedom, help us to employ it in the maintenance of justice in our communities and among the nations, to the glory of your holy Name; through Jesus Christ our Lord, who lives and reigns with you and the Holy Spirit, one God, now and forever.

BCP

Readings:	Wisdom 8:24-28
	Psalm 146
	Luke 11:5-10
Hymn of the Day:	
	"Lord of all nations, grant me grace" (LBW 419, LSB 844, ELW 716)
Prayers:	For the oppressed and for those who oppress them
	For those who struggle against repression and injustice
	For the rights of all people
Preface:	Baptism (BCP, LBW)
Color:	White

ALSO ON JULY 20

The Eastern Church on this date commemorates the Glorious Prophet **Elias** (**Elijah**). The calendar in the *Lutheran Service Book* (2006), following Wilhelm Löhe, also lists Elijah on this date.

July 21

The Eastern Church on this date commemorates the prophet **Ezekiel**. The calendar in the *Lutheran Service Book* (2006) also lists Ezekiel on this date.

July 22

St. Mary Magdalene

Mary of Magdala, called "the apostle to the Apostles" by Bernard of Clairvaux, carried the news of the resurrection to the Twelve. Whenever the Gospels list the women who were with Jesus, Mary Magdalene is listed first (John 19:25 is the sole exception), perhaps because she was the first to see the risen Jesus.

Luke 8:2 reports that Jesus had cured her of possession by seven demons. She has often in the West, but not in the East, been identified with the repentant "woman of the city" who anointed Jesus' feet as he sat at table in the Pharisee's home (Luke 7:36-50), and her title on the medieval calendar was "Penitent." There has been no one else with this title. There is, however, no biblical basis for this identification of Mary with the repentant prostitute. Nor is she to be identified with Mary of Bethany (John 12:3), an identification common in the Western church since the sixth century, although it is rejected in the East.

The nature of the relationship between Jesus and Mary Magdalene has for centuries been the object of often wild speculation, beginning with the second or third century Gnostic Gospel of Philip, which describes Mary Magdalene as the one whom Jesus loved "more than the disciples" and whom he would "kiss often." A popular legend, current by the ninth century, equating Mary Magdalene with Mary of Bethany, had her together with Martha and Lazarus travel to the south of France, where relics were shown. Later, still more fantastic legends arose which imagined that Jesus escaped crucifixion and went with Mary Magdalene to the south of France where, it was claimed, their descendents still live.

According to the Gospels, "the holy myrrh-bearer and equal of the Apostles, Mary Magdalene," as her title in the Eastern Church describes her, is the primary witness of the fundamental facts of the Christian proclamation: she saw the death of Jesus, she saw his burial, she saw his first resurrection appearance. Her commemoration on July 22 is observed in both East and West, and especially since the twelfth century, she has been one of the most widely commemorated women in Christendom. Her witness contrasts to that of the apostles, who, at Jesus' crucifixion, "all deserted him and fled" (Matt. 26:56). Mary of Magdala, remarkable for her devotion and courage, was praised by Eaton Stannard Barrett (1786–1820) in her poem *Woman* (Part 1, lines 143–44),

> She, while Apostles shrank, could dangers brave,
> Last at His cross and earliest at His grave.

FOR FURTHER READING

Barker, James T. "The Red-Haired Saint." *Christian Century* 94, no. 12 (April 6, 1977): 328–32.

Brock, Ann Graham. *Mary Magdalene, the First Apostle: The Struggle for Authority.* Cambridge: Harvard University Press, 2003.

Garth, H. M. *Saint Mary Magdalen in Medieval Literature.* Baltimore: Johns Hopkins University Press, 1950.

Haskins, Susan. *Mary Magdalen.* New York: HarperCollins, 1993.

Hearon, Holly E. *The Mary Magdalene Tradition.* Collegeville: Liturgical, 2004.

Malvern, Marjorie M. *Venus in Sackcloth: The Magdalen's Origins and Metamorphoses.* Carbondale and Edwardsville: Southern Illinois University Press, 1975.

Thompson, Mary R. *Mary of Magdala: Apostle and Leader.* New York: Paulist, 1995.

READING

From a sermon on the Gospels by Gregory the Great

When Mary Magdalene came to the tomb and did not find the Lord's body, she thought it had been taken away and so told the disciples. They came and saw the tomb, and they believed what Mary had told them. The text then says, "The disciples returned to their homes," and it adds, "But Mary stood weeping outside the tomb." [John 20:10, 11]

What great love Mary had for Christ; for although the disciples left the tomb, she remained. She was still seeking the one she had not found, and wept as she sought him; burning with the fire of love, she longed for him who she thought had been taken away. And so it happened that the woman who stayed behind to seek Christ was the only one to see him. For perseverance is essential to any good deed, as the voice of Truth tells us, "The one who endures to the end will be saved." [Matt. 10:22]

At first she sought but did not find, but when she persevered she found what she was looking for. When our desires are not satisfied, they grow stronger, and becoming stronger they take hold of their object. Holy desires likewise grow with anticipation, and if they do not grow they are not really desires. Anyone who succeeds in attaining the truth has burned with such a love. As David says, "My soul thirsts for the living God. When shall I come and behold the face of God?" [Ps. 42:2] And so also in the Song of Songs the Church says, "I am faint with love", and again, "My soul is melted with love." [see 2:5; 5:8].

"Woman, why are you weeping? Whom do you seek?" [John 20:13, 15] Jesus asks so that her desire may grow; for when she names him whom she is seeking, her love reaches new intensity.

"Jesus said to her, 'Mary.'" [John 20:16] When he called her "woman" she did not recognize him; so he calls her by name, as though he were saying, "Recognize me as I recognize you; for I do not know you as one among many; I know you as yourself. And so Mary, addressed by name, recognizes who is speaking. She immediately calls him "rabbouni," that is to say, "teacher," because the one whom she sought outwardly was within her impelling her to seek him.

Sermon 25, trans. PHP, based on *A Short Breviary* by the monks of St. John's Abbey and the English translation of the Office of Readings from the Liturgy of the Hours by the International Committee on English in the Liturgy.

PROPERS

Almighty God, whose blessed Son restored Mary Magdalene to health of body and mind and first entrusted to her the joyful news of his resurrection: Mercifully grant that by your grace we may be healed of all our infirmities and know you in the power of his unending life; who lives and reigns with you one God, now and forever.

1736 Paris Missal + 1954 Ambrosian Missal, RS + 1928 English Proposed BCP, BCP, LBW, rev. PHP

Readings:	Judith 9:1, 11-14
	Psalm 42:1-7
	2 Corinthians 5:14-18
	John 20:11-18
Hymn of the Day:	
	"Lift your voice rejoicing, Mary" (H82 190)
	"Christians to the Paschal victim" (LBW 137, LSB 460, ELW 371)
Prayers:	For those in mental darkness
	For grace to perceive signs of new life around us
	For insight to find in each act of worship the presence of the risen Christ
	For love to lay hold of salvation and to share it with others
Preface:	Easter
Color:	White

July 23

Birgitta of Sweden, Renewer of the Church, 1373

Bridget, or as she is called in Swedish, Birgitta, was born about 1303, the daughter of Birger Persson, the "lawman" (chief judge or governor) of the province of Upland in Sweden, one of the most important men in the country.

On several occasions in her childhood, Birgitta had dreams of Christ crucified and of Mary his mother. Her own mother died when Birgitta was twelve, and the next year Birgitta was married to Ulf Gundarsson, the young son of the lawman of West Gothland. The marriage was a happy one, and they had four sons and four daughters, one of whom, Katarina (Catherine), later accompanied her mother to Rome and later was venerated as St. Katherine of Vadstena (died 1381). Although she was beatified in 1489, she was never formally canonized; her feast day is March 22.

About 1335 Birgitta, who by virtue of her father's and her husband's positions moved in the highest circles of the realm, was called to be the principal lady-in-waiting to the newly married queen of Sweden, Blanche of Namur. At the court, Lady Birgitta became known for her remarkable dreams and her strong denunciation of wickedness in court life. Such fearless denunciation was typical of Birgitta's actions throughout her life in dealing with high officials in church and state.

In 1340, after the death of her youngest son, Birgitta made a pilgrimage to the shrine of St. Olav in Nidaros (Trondheim), Norway, thus beginning the extensive pilgrimages of her life. In 1341–1342 Birgitta took her husband with her on a pilgrimage to Santiago de Compostella in Spain, one of the most popular pilgrim centers in the Middle Ages (see July 25). On the return trip Ulf was taken ill, and, although he recovered, his health was broken, and in 1344 he died in the monastery of Alvastra.

After her husband's death, Birgitta began to live a more ascetic life, her visions became stronger and more dominant in her life, and she devoted more of her time and efforts to helping the needy of Sweden and later of Rome. She continued in her criticisms and warnings to kings and popes and tried to make peace between warring rulers. Like St. Catherine of Siena (see April 29), she repeatedly urged the pope to return from Avignon to his diocese of Rome. In 1349, with a number of companions, she went to Rome to observe the holy year of 1350 and to obtain papal approval of the monastic order she wanted to establish. Except for a pilgrimage to Jerusalem, she remained in Rome for the rest of her life.

In 1351 Birgitta founded the Order of the Holy Savior, commonly called the Brigittines, centered on the monastery she started at Vadstena in Sweden in accordance with the instructions she had received in a vision. The order consisted of both monks and nuns, governed by an abbess, and after St. Birgitta's death it spread widely in Europe. The cloister at Vadstena was one of the most important cultural and religious centers in Sweden during the Middle Ages, and at the time of the Reformation when monastic orders were abolished, it was the last to go (1595).

St. Birgitta is best known for her *Revelations*, which are still read throughout Western Christendom. They come down to us in a Latin version and an Old Swedish version, and modern translations and editions exist in a number of languages. The *Revelations* concern chiefly the sufferings of the Savior and judgments on persons and events.

In May 1371 Birgitta felt that God commanded her to make a pilgrimage to the Holy Land, and she set out with three of her children and a number of other companions. The journey was marred by shipwreck and the death of her son Charles. A few months after her return to Rome, she died on July 23, 1373. Her body was temporarily buried in a church there, but a little later was removed to the abbey at Vadstena where it is still enshrined.

St. Birgitta was soon recognized as a patron of Sweden (she was canonized eighteen years after her death through the efforts of her daughter Catherine), and interest in her life and work has continued to the present. The Society of St. Birgitta, founded in 1920, is composed of clergy and laity within the Church of Sweden inspired by her life and *Revelations,* and who seek more frequent celebration of the Eucharist, observance of daily prayer, biblical preaching and teaching in accord with the creeds of the Church. St. Birgitta had been commemorated on October 8, the date of her canonization in 1391, but the date of her death, July 23, her "heavenly birthday," has also been observed in Sweden, and she is remembered on that date on the present Roman General Calendar, on the *Evangelical Calendar of Names,* and on the calendar in the *Lutheran Book of Worship*, the *Lutheran Service Book*, and *Evangelical Lutheran Worship.*

On October 5, 1991, the six hundredth anniversary of her canonization, a historic joint Catholic-Lutheran prayer service was held in St. Peter's Basilica in Rome, led by Pope John Paul II and the Lutheran Archbishops of Sweden and Finland. The king and queen of Sweden attended; Queen Silvia read one of the lessons.

FOR FURTHER READING

Anderson, Ingvar. *A History of Sweden.* Trans. Carolyn Hannay. 54–62. Westport: Greenwood, 1975 [1968]).

Hampton, William R. "Pilgrimage to Vadstena." *Lutheran Forum* 35, no. 4 (Christmas/Winter 2001): 814.

Harris, Marguerite Tjader, ed. *Birgitta of Sweden: Life and Selected Writings.* New York: Paulist, 1990.

Jorgensen, Johannes. *St. Bridget of Sweden.* 2 vols. New York: Longman's Green, 1954.

READING

From the prayers attributed to St. Birgitta

Blessed are you, my Lord Jesus Christ. You foretold your death and at the Last Supper you marvelously consecrated bread which became your precious body. And then you gave it to your apostles out of love as a memorial of your most holy passion. By washing their feet with your holy hands, you gave them a supreme example of your deep humility.

Honor be to you, my Lord Jesus Christ. Fearing your passion and death, your poured forth blood from your innocent body like sweat, and still you accomplished our redemption as you desired and gave us the clearest proof of your love.

Blessed may you be, my Lord Jesus Christ. After you had been led to Caiaphas, you, the judge of all, humbly allowed yourself to be handed over to the judgment of Pilate.

Glory be to you, my Lord Jesus Christ, for the mockery you endured when you stood clothed in purple and wearing a crown of sharp thorns. With utmost endurance you allowed vicious men to spit upon your glorious face, blindfold you and beat your cheek and neck with the cruelest blows.

Praise be to you, my Lord Jesus Christ. For with the greatest patience you allowed yourself like an innocent lamb to be bound to a pillar and mercilessly scourged, and then to be brought, covered with blood, before the judgment seat of Pilate to be gazed upon by all.

Honor be to you, my Lord Jesus Christ. For after your glorious body was covered with blood, you were condemned to death on the cross, you endured the pain of carrying the cross on your sacred shoulders, and you were led with curses to the place where you were to suffer. Then stripped of your garments, you allowed yourself to be nailed to the wood of the cross.

Everlasting honor be to you, Lord Jesus Christ. You allowed your most holy mother to suffer so much, even though she had never sinned nor even consented to the smallest sin. Humbly you looked down upon her with your gentle loving eyes, and to comfort her you entrusted her to the faithful care of your disciple.

Eternal blessing be yours, my Lord Jesus Christ, because in your last agony you held out to all sinners the hope of pardon, when in your mercy you promised the glory of paradise to the penitent thief.

Eternal praise be to you, my Lord Jesus Christ, for the time you endured on the cross the greatest torments and sufferings for us sinners. The sharp pain of your wounds fiercely penetrated even to your blessed soul and cruelly pierced your most sacred heart till finally you sent forth your spirit in peace, bowed your head, and humbly commended yourself into the hands of God your Father, and your whole body remained cold in death.

Blessed may you be, my Lord Jesus Christ. You redeemed our souls with your precious blood and most holy death, and in your mercy you led them from exile back to eternal life.

Blessed may you be, my Lord Jesus Christ. For our salvation you allowed your side and your heart to be pierced with a lance; and from that side water and your precious blood flowed out abundantly for our redemption.

Glory be to you, my Lord Jesus Christ. You allowed your blessed body to be taken down from the cross by your friends and laid in the arms of your most sorrowing mother, and you let her wrap your body in a shroud and bury it in a tomb to be guarded by soldiers.

Unending honor be to you, my Lord Jesus Christ. On the third day you rose from the dead and appeared to those you had chosen. And after forty days you ascended into heaven before the eyes of many witnesses, and there in heaven you gathered together in glory those you love, whom you had freed from hell.

Rejoicing and eternal praise be to you, my Lord Jesus Christ, who sent the Holy Spirit into the hearts of your disciples and increased the boundless love of God in their spirits.

Blessed are you and praiseworthy and glorious for ever, my Lord Jesus. You sit upon your throne in your kingdom of heaven, in the glory of your divinity, living in the most holy body you took from a virgin's flesh. So you will appear on that last day to judge the souls of all the living and the dead; you who live and reign with the Father and the Holy Spirit forever and ever. Amen.

Revelations of St. Brigid 2. From the English translation of the Office of Readings from the Liturgy of the Hours © 1974, the International Committee on English in the Liturgy, Inc. All rights reserved.

PROPERS

Lord our God, you revealed the secrets of heaven to Birgitta of Sweden as she meditated on the suffering and death of your Son: Grant that your people may ever rejoice in the revelation of your glory; through Jesus Christ our Lord, who lives and reigns with you and the Holy Spirit, one God, now and forever.

1952 Roman Missal, RS, rev. PHP

Readings:	Micah 6:6-8
	Psalm 9:1-10
	1 Corinthians 1:26-31
	Luke 6:20-23
Hymn of the Day:	
	"Jesus, refuge of the weary" (LBW 93, LSB 423)
Prayers:	For growth in the spiritual life
	For courage and zeal to oppose corruption and vice
	For the religious orders for women and men in the Lutheran Church and throughout Christianity
	For the Society of St. Birgitta
Preface:	Passion (Holy Week)
Color:	White

July 24

Thomas à Kempis, Priest, 1471

Thomas of Kempis, the author (or at least the compiler) of the treasured devotional book *The Imitation of Christ,* a book that has been described as next to Dante "the most perfect flower of medieval Christianity," was born in 1380 at Kempen (hence his name), near Krefeld, the son of humble parents John and Gertrude Hämerken or Hemmerken. He left home at the age of thirteen to join his elder brother in the Brethren of the Common Life at Deventer in Holland, where he received his education. The brotherhood had been founded by Geert Groote (1340–1384; see April 29) and was approved by Pope Gregory XI in 1376. The order was composed of clergy and laity who cultivated a biblical piety of a practical nature and who supported themselves by copying manuscripts and teaching; their influential spirituality was known as the "New Devotion" (*Devotio moderna*).

In 1399 Thomas entered the monastery of Mount St. Agnes, near Zwolle in the Netherlands, where his brother had become prior. There he made his profession as an Augustinian Canon Regular in 1407 and was ordained priest in 1413 at the age of thirty-three. In 1425 he was elected sub-prior. He acted as master of novices and kept the Chronicle of the monastery. His principal work, *The Imitation of Christ,* was first put in circulation in 1418. Thomas's successor as chronicler of the monastery records that in the spring of 1471, on the feast of St. James (July 25),

> . . . after Compline, our brother Thomas Hämerken, born at Kempen, a town in the diocese of Cologne, departed from this earth. He was in the ninety-second year of his age, the sixty-third of his religious clothing, and the fifty-eighth of his priesthood. . . . He copied out our Bible and various other books, some of which were used by the convent, and others were sold [to raise funds for the monastery]. Further, for the instruction of the young, he wrote various little treatises in a plain and simple style, which in reality were great and important works, both in doctrine and efficacy for good. He had an especial devotion to the Passion of Our Lord, and understood admirably how to comfort those afflicted by interior trials and temptations. Finally, having reached a ripe old age, he was afflicted with dropsy of the limbs, slept in the Lord in the year 1471, and was buried in the east side of the cloister. . . .

The monastery of Mount St. Agnes was nearly obliterated in 1573, but in 1672 the Elector of Cologne searched for Thomas's tomb, discovered and authenticated it, and placed the remains in a casket and put it in the chapel of St. Joseph. Two centuries later, the remains were transferred to the Church of St. Michael in Zwolle where they are preserved to this day.

The 1979 American *Book of Common Prayer* included the commemoration of Thomas, moved forward one day from the actual date of his death, to July 24, as is also done on the *Evangelical Calendar of Names* (1962) and on the Methodist calendar in *For All the Saints.*

FOR FURTHER READING

Kettlewell, S. *Thomas à Kempis and the Brothers of the Common Life.* 2 vols. London: Kegan Paul, Trench, 1882.

READING

From Thomas à Kempis, *The Imitation of Christ*

While in the prison-house of this body, I acknowledge my need of two things—food and light. You have therefore given me in my weakness Your sacred Body to be the refreshment of my soul and body, and You have set Your Word as a lamp to my feet. Without these two, I cannot rightly live; for the Word of God is the light of my soul, and Your Sacrament is the bread of my life. One might describe them as two tables, set on either side of the treasury of holy Church. The one is the table of the holy altar, having on it the holy bread, the precious Body of Christ; the other is that of the divine law, that enshrines the holy doctrine, teaches the true faith, an unerringly guides our steps even within the veil that guards the Holy of Holies.

O Lord Jesus, Light eternal, I thank You for the table of holy teaching that You have given us through Your servants the Prophets, Apostles, and other teachers. O Creator and Redeemer of men, in order to manifest to the whole world the depths of Your love, You have prepared a great Supper, at which You offer us, not the Lamb of the old Law, but Your own most holy Body and Blood to be our food. In this sacred Feast, You give joy to all the faithful, granting them to drink deeply from the Cup of Salvation, which holds all the joys of Heaven, while the holy Angels share the feast with us, but with even deeper delight.

Thomas à Kempis, *The Imitation of Christ*, trans. Leo Sherley-Price (Baltimore: Penguin, 1952), 68–69, 88–89, 83, 206–206, 72. Introduction and Translation copyright 1952 by Leo Sherley-Price. Reprinted by permission of Penguin Books Ltd.

PROPERS

Holy Father, you have nourished and strengthened your Church by the inspired writings of your servant Thomas à Kempis: Grant that we may learn from him to know what is necessary to be known, to love what is to be loved, to praise what highly pleases you, and always to seek to know and follow your will; through Jesus Christ our Lord, who lives and reigns with you and the Holy Spirit, one God, forever and ever.

LFF

Readings: Psalm 34:1-8 *or* 33:1-5, 20-21
               Philippians 4:4-9
               Luke 6:17-23
Hymn of the Day:
               "Strengthen for service, Lord, the hands" (H82 312, SBH 286; rev. in LBW 218 and
                   ELW 497)
Prayers: For the desire to conform our whole life to that of Christ
               For grace and strength to advance in holiness
               For closer attention to the Bible
               For deeper love for the Holy Communion
Preface: A Saint (2) (BCP)
Color: White

July 25

St. James the Elder, Apostle

James the Elder or the Great was born in Galilee and was, like his father Zebedee and his brother John and the apostles Peter and Andrew, a fisherman. He is believed to have been older than his brother, hence his title "the elder," because his name is almost always put before John's in the biblical lists of the apostles. Shortly after calling Andrew and Peter from their fishing to be disciples, Jesus saw the sons of Zebedee in a boat with their father, mending nets. He called them, and they left their father and followed him. James and his brother were called *Boanerges*, "sons of thunder" (Mark 3:17), presumably because of their impetuous spirit and flashing temper (Luke 9:49, 54; Mark 10:37).

Incidents in St. James's life are recorded in all four Gospels and in the book of Acts. As a member with Peter and John of the privileged "inner circle" of the disciples, he witnessed the cure of Peter's mother-in-law (Luke 4:38-39) and the raising of the daughter of Jairus (Mark 5:37), and was with Jesus at the Transfiguration and at his suffering in Gethsemane on the night of his arrest.

James was apparently an active leader in the early church, although there is no reliable information on where he preached or what he did. He was the first of the apostles to die a martyr's death and the only apostle whose death is recorded in the Bible. He was beheaded by Herod Agrippa I (Acts 12:2) just before Passover in 43 or 44, and this date is reflected in the date of his commemoration in the East: the Orthodox Churches remember him on April 30, the Copts on April 12. He is said to have been buried in Jerusalem. The Western date of his commemoration, July 25, seems to derive from the burial of his supposed relics in the great Church of Santiago de Compostella, July 25, 816. According to several sacramentaries of the eighth century, St. James's feast day was celebrated on July 25; his feast has been celebrated in Rome only from the ninth century. The claim of his relics in Santiago de Compostella in Spain made it one of the great pilgrimage centers of the Middle Ages. St. Birgitta of Sweden visited it with her husband in 1341–1342. James's traditional symbol, the scallop shell, became the emblem of those who had made the pilgrimage.

James the Elder is not to be confused with James the Less (the younger), the son of Alphaeus, who is commemorated on May 1, nor with James the Just, the brother of the Lord and leader of the church in Jerusalem, who is commemorated on October 23.

FOR FURTHER READING

Conant, Kenneth John. *The Early Architectural History of the Cathedral of Santiago de Compostella.* Cambridge: Harvard University Press, 1926.
Fletcher, R. A. *Saint James' Catapult: The Life and Times of Diego Gelmirez of Santiago de Compostella.* Oxford: Clarendon, 1984.

READING

From *The Ladder of Perfection* by Walter Hilton

A real pilgrim going to Jerusalem leaves house and land, wife and children; he divests himself of all that he possesses in order to travel light and without encumbrances. Similarly, if you wish to be a spiritual pilgrim you must divest yourself of all that you possess; that is, both of good deeds and bad, and leave them all behind you. Recognize your own property, so that you will not place any confidence in your own work; instead, be always desiring the grace of deeper love, and seeking the spiritual presence of Jesus. If you do this, you will be setting your heart wholly on obtaining the love of Jesus and whatever spiritual vision of Himself that He is willing to grant, for it is to this end alone that you have been created and redeemed; this is your beginning and your end, your joy and your bliss. Therefore, whatever you may possess, and however fruitful your activities, regard them all as worthless without the inward certainty and experience of this love. Keep this intention constantly in mind and hold on to it firmly; it will sustain you among all the perils of your pilgrimage.

You are now on the road, and you know how to proceed. But beware of enemies who will set themselves to obstruct you if they can. Nothing distresses them more than your desire and longing for the love of Jesus, and their whole purpose is to uproot this from your heart, and turn you back again to the love of earthly things. Your chief enemies are the bodily desires and foolish fears which the corruption of human nature stirs up in your heart, and which would stifle your desire for the love of God and take full possession of your heart. These are your deadliest enemies. There are also others, for evil spirits employ all their tricks to deceive you.

But you have one remedy, as I told you before. Whatever they say, do not believe them; keep on your way, and desire nothing but the love of Jesus. Let your answer always be, "I am nothing, I have nothing, I desire nothing but the love of Jesus."

Your enemies may begin by troubling your mind with doubts, hinting that your confessions have been invalid; that some old sin lies unremembered and unconfessed in your heart; that you must give up your desire, go back to the beginning, and make a full confession. But do not believe their lies, for your have received full absolution. Rest assured that you are on the right road, and there is no need for you to ransack your conscience about the past: keep your eye on the road and your mind on Jerusalem. And if they tell you, "You are not worthy to enjoy the love of God, so why hanker after what you cannot have and do not deserve?" carry on and take no notice of them. Reply, "I desire the love of God not because I am worthy, but because I am unworthy; for if I had it, it would make me worthy. And since I was created to this end, although I may never enjoy it, I will still desire it, pray for it, and hope to attain it." If your enemies see that your courage and determination to succeed is growing, they will begin to fear you.

However, so long as you are on the road they will not cease to harass you; at one time they will intimidate and threaten you, at another they will try to flatter you and seduce you, to make you abandon your purpose and turn back. If you persist in this desire for Jesus and continue in your first fervour, you will ruin your health or suffer from delusions and fits, as some do. Or you will beggar yourself, or suffer some injury, and no one will be willing to help you. Or the devil may put such subtle temptations in your way that you cannot resist them. For it is a dangerous course for anyone to forsake the world completely, and give himself entirely to the love of God, seeking nothing but His love, because he will encounter many perils of which he knows nothing. So turn back and forget this desire which you can never fulfill, and behave like other people in this world.

Such are the arguments of your enemies, but do not believe them. Hold firmly to your desire and reply that you desire to have Jesus and to be at Jerusalem.

Walter Hilton, *The Ladder of Perfection*, trans. Leo Sherley-Price, introduction by Clifton Wolters (Penguin Classics, 1957, Reissued 1988), 157, 159–60. Copyright © Leo Sherley-Price, 1955, 1968. Reprinted by permission of Penguin Books Ltd.

PROPERS

O gracious God, we remember before you today your servant and apostle James, first among the Twelve to suffer martyrdom for the Name of Jesus Christ; and we pray that you will pour out upon the leaders of your Church that spirit of self-denying service by which alone they may have true authority among your people; through Jesus Christ our Lord, who lives and reigns with you and the Holy Spirit, one God, now and forever.

1979 BCP; rev. in LBW, ELW

Readings: Jeremiah 45:1-5
             Psalm 7:1-10
             Acts 11:27—12:3
             Matthew 20:20-28
Hymn of the Day:
             "They cast their nets in Galilee" (H82 661, LBW 449)
             "For thy blest saints, a noble throng" (H82 276)
Prayers: For the gift of generosity and self-sacrifice
             For courage and faith gladly to follow Christ
             For the spirit of service
Preface: Apostles
Color: Red

July 26

The Parents of the Blessed Virgin Mary

In the second century an unknown Christian, in an apocryphal gospel known as the *Protoevangelium of James* or *The Nativity of Mary,* supplied a fuller picture of the home of Mary the Mother of Jesus to supplement what the Gospels imply. Echoing the stories of the births of Isaac and of Samuel (whose mother's name, Hannah, is the Hebrew original of the Latin *Anna* and English *Ann* or *Anne*, meaning "grace") and of John the Baptist, the apocryphal gospel says that Anne and her husband Joachim were childless. At last the elderly couple had a daughter, Mary, whom they dedicated to God and who was raised in the Temple, taught by the priests.

The cult of St. Anne (or Ann) goes back to the fifth century when in 550 the emperor Justinian I in Constantinople built the first church dedicated to her. In the East, her feast day is July 25, the Repose of Righteous Anna, mother of Theotokos. Her feast was introduced in the West in the twelfth century and her cult developed as a result of increasing devotion to the Conception of Mary, celebrated December 8. In 1378 Pope Urban VI fixed her feast day on July 26 (July 25 having been assigned to St. James). In 1570 Pope Pius V removed her name from the calendar, but his successor Gregory XIII restored it in 1584. The cult of St. Anne was popular in Germany and in England. When Luther barely escaped a bolt of lightning, so the story goes, he cried out, "St. Anne, help me! I will become a monk." A number of churches in England were dedicated to St. Anne dating from the eighteenth century, not only honoring the mother of Our Lady but also a compliment to Queen Anne, who was a devoted servant and benefactor of the Church of England.

In Canada, devotion to St. Anne, patron of Brittany and of fertile soil, began with the first settlers of New France who began to till the soil of the Beauprè hillside. A chapel, dedicated to her, was built in 1658, and the present basilica of St. Anne de Beauprè (1876) is the fifth church on the site. During the last quarter of the nineteenth century the church became a popular pilgrimage shrine at which miraculous cures were expected.

Joachim has been honored at a more recent date than Anne. His feast day was not authorized until early in the sixteenth century by Julius II; he has had several dates assigned to his commemoration (March 20, August 16). The present Roman Catholic calendar joins his feast with that of Anne on July 26 as "Joachim and Ann, parents of Mary." The *Book of Common Prayer* does the same but, because of questionable accuracy of the second-century apocryphal gospel, does not give the names of Mary's parents and calls this feast simply "The Parents of the Blessed Virgin Mary." In the East, the "Ancestors of God," "the righteous Parents Joachim and Anna," are commemorated on September 9, the day following the Nativity of the Virgin Mary; July 25 commemorates the Repose of Righteous Anna, Mother of Theotokos.

Whatever the accuracy of the legends, Jesus' grandparents represent the line of generations who awaited the Messiah and prepared for his coming by dutifully practicing their faith. Their feast day further roots Jesus in human history.

FOR FURTHER READING

Ashley, Kathleen, and Pamela Scheingorn, eds. *Interpreting Cultural Symbols: Saint Anne in Late Medieval Society.* Athens: University of Georgia Press, 1990.

Nixon, Virginia. *Mary's Mother: Saint Anne in Late Medieval Europe.* University Park: Penn State University Press, 2004.

Ronan, Myles V. *S. Anne: Her Cult and Her Shrines.* London: Sands and Co., 1927.

READING

From a sermon by John of Damascus (*ca.* 655–*ca.* 750),
On the Birth of the Blessed Virgin Mary

Ann was to be the mother of the Virgin Mother of God, and hence nature did not dare to anticipate the flowering of grace. She was barren until grace produced its fruit. For she who was to be born had to be a first-born daughter, since she would be the mother of the first-born of all creation, in whom "all things hold together." [Col. 1:7]

Joachim and Ann, how blessed a couple. All creation is indebted to you through whom the Creator was offered a gift excelling all other gifts: a chaste mother, who alone was worthy of him.

And so rejoice, Ann, "O barren one who did not bear; burst into song and shout, you who have not been in labor." [Isa. 54:1] Rejoice, Joachim, because from your daughter "a child has been born for us, a son given to us; and he is named Wonderful Counselor, mighty God." [Isa. 9:6] For this child is God.

Joachim and Ann, how blessed and spotless a couple. You will be known by the fruit you have borne, as the Lord says, "Your will know them by their fruits." [Matt. 7:16] Your lives were pleasing to God and were worthy of your daughter. For by the chaste and holy life you led together, you have fashioned a jewel of virginity; she who remained a virgin before, during, and after giving birth. She alone for all time would maintain her virginity in mind and soul as well as in body.

Joachim and Ann, how chaste a couple. While safeguarding the chastity prescribed by the law of nature, you achieved with God's help something which transcends nature in giving the world the Virgin Mother of God as your daughter. You lived devout and holy lives in your humanity and gave birth to a daughter nobler than the angels, whose queen she now is. Child of utter beauty and delight, daughter of Adam and mother of God, blessed the loins and blessed the womb from which you come. Blessed the arms that carried you, and blessed your parents' lips, which you were allowed to cover with chaste kisses, ever maintaining your virginity. "Make a joyful noise to the Lord, all the earth. Worship the Lord with gladness; come into his presence with singing." [Psalm 100:1] Lift up your voice with strength; lift it up, do not be afraid. [See Isa. 40:9]

Sermon 6. Trans. PHP, based on *A Short Breviary* by the monks of St, John's Abbey and the English translation of the Office of Readings of the Liturgy of the Hours by the International Committee on English in the Liturgy.

PROPERS

Almighty God, heavenly Father, we remember in thanksgiving this day the parents of the Blessed Virgin Mary; and we pray that we all may be made one in the heavenly family of your Son Jesus Christ our Lord; who lives and reigns with you and the Holy Spirit, one God, forever and ever.

LFF

Readings: Genesis 17:1-8 *or* Sirach 44:1, 10-15
            Psalm 132:11-19 *or* 85:8-13
            Luke 1:26-33 *or* Matthew 13:16-17
Hymn of the Day:
            "Our Father, by whose name all parenthood is known" (LBW 357, LSB 863, ELW
                640, H82 587)
Prayers: For all parents and all homes
            For single parents
            For grandparents that their good examples may influence generations to come
            For grandchildren that they may respect the longer perspective of earlier
                generations
            For homes where love is lacking
            For children who are abused and unloved

For those who care for children and who love them as our Lord commanded

Preface: The Incarnation
Color: White

July 27

The *Book of Common Prayer* commemorates today **William Reed Huntington**, a liturgical scholar, whose reconciling spirit helped preserve the unity of the Episcopal Church in a period of intense conflict, who revived the order of deaconesses, and who proposed the grounds for Church unity that were adopted by the Lambeth Conference in 1888. He died in 1909.

July 28

Johann Sebastian Bach, 1750; Heinrich Schütz, 1672; George Frederick Handel, 1759; Musicians

The joint commemoration of three musicians of the Lutheran tradition was introduced in the *Lutheran Book of Worship*. The Methodist calendar *For All the Saints* commemorates the two who are better known, Bach and Handel, on this date; the *Lutheran Service Book* commemorates Bach alone. The *Evangelical Calendar of Names* commemorates Bach on July 28 and Schütz on November 6.

Johann Sebastian Bach, the most illustrious member of a family of distinguished musicians, was born in Eisenach in Thuringia March 21, 1685. His father and brother were both musicians, and from an early age he learned to play the violin and organ and later served as a choirboy. By the age of eighteen, he already had a considerable reputation as a composer, organist, and violinist. He served for a time as organist in the New Church at Arnstadt from 1703 to 1707 and St. Blasius in Muhlhausen, where he married his cousin, Maria Barbara Bach. In 1708 he accepted an important post as court organist and chamber musician to the Duke of Weimar, and at Weimar he became acknowledged as an outstanding organist and wrote his chief works for the organ. In 1714 he was promoted to concertmaster. In 1717 he went to Cöthen as Kapellmeister (director of music) to Prince Leopold of Anhalt. His wife died in 1720, and the following year he married Anna Magdalena Wülcken, a singer for whom he composed a famous set of keyboard pieces. From 1723 until his death, he was at Leipzig where he was cantor at the famous St. Thomas school and music director of both St. Thomas and St. Nicholas

Churches, as well as the Pauliner-Kirche at the University. It was in these churches that his compositions were first performed.

Bach was a deeply religious, introspective man, who was consciously serving God in his composing and playing of music. Drawing on the treasury of German hymn tunes, he wrote nearly two hundred cantatas, including sets that provide a cantata for each Sunday and holy day of the Lutheran church year. These cantatas have elaborate choir settings for most of the stanzas and a plain four-part setting for the final stanza to be sung by the congregation with the choir. Bach is more widely known for his great works such as the *B Minor Mass* and the *St. Matthew Passion*, which was first performed in St. Thomas Church on Good Friday 1729.

Bach had twenty children by his two wives; nine of the children survived him. Four of them also possessed outstanding musical ability: Wilhelm Friedemann (1710–1784), Carl Philipp Emanuel (1714–1788), Johann Christoph Friedrich (1732–1795), and Johann Christian (1735–1782). Johann Sebastian Bach died at Leipzig, July 28, 1750, one of the greatest figures in all Western music and such an ornament of the Church of the Reformation that Archbishop Nathan Söderblom called him "the fifth evangelist." The body of the great musician was buried without ceremony in St. John's churchyard and only on the one hundredth anniversary of his death was a tablet to his memory placed in the church. Finally, on the two hundredth anniversary, in 1950, Bach's remains were moved to a resting place within St. Thomas's Church, Leipzig.

FOR FURTHER READING

Blume, Friedrich. *Protestant Church Music.* London: Gollancz, 1976.

Boyd, Malcolm. *Bach.* 3rd ed. New York: Oxford University Press, 200.

Geiringer, Karl. *Music of the Bach Family.* Cambridge: Harvard University Press, 1955.

Neumann, Werner. *Bach and His World.* Trans. Stefan de Haan. Rev. ed. London: Thames and Hudson, 1970.

Pelikan, Jaroslav. *Bach among the Theologians.* Philadelphia: Fortress Press, 1986.

Schweitzer, Albert. *J. S. Bach.* Trans. Ernest Newman. London, 1911; reissued 1923.

Spitta, Philipp. *Johann Sebastian Bach.* Trans. C. Bell and J. A. Fuller-Maitland. 3 vols. London, 1884. 2d ed., New York, 1951.

Schwendowius, Barbara, and Wolfgang Dömling, eds. *J. S. Bach: Life, Times, Influence.* New Haven: Yale University Press, 1985.

Stiller, Günther. *Johann Sebastian Bach and Liturgical Life in Leipzig.* Trans. Herbert J. A. Bouman, Daniel F. Poellot, Hilton C. Oswald; ed. Robin Leaver. St. Louis: Concordia, 1984.

Wolff, Christoph. *Johann Sebastian Bach: The Learned Musician.* Oxford: Clarendon, 2000.

JULY

Heinrich Schütz, the greatest German composer before Bach, was born in Köstritz, now Bad Köstritz, Saxony, October 8 (or 14), 1585, one hundred years before Bach. As a boy he sang in the chapel choir of Landgrave Moritz of Hesse-Kassel, who provided him with a wide general education. In 1608 Schütz entered Marburg University to study law, but in the following year Landgrave Moritz sent him to Venice to study music with Giovanni Gabrielli, who had a powerful influence on the young student.

After the death of Gabrielli in 1612, Schütz returned to Germany and went to Leipzig to resume his study of the law. Shortly afterward he became the second organist at the court of Kassel. In 1614 he entered the service of the Elector of Saxony, Johann Georg I, at Dresden and there introduced the Italian style that he had learned in Venice. Schütz returned to Venice in 1628 and perhaps studied with Claudio Monteverdi, then the chief musical figure of the city. In 1629 Schütz completed writing the melodies and simple four-part harmonizations for the metrical Psalm paraphrases of Cornelius Becker; this project, it is said, gave him comfort after the untimely death of his wife, Magdalene. By 1630 Schütz was back in Dresden, but three years later he left the court which was afflicted with the plague and suffering from the disorder of the Thirty Years' War. From 1633 to 1635 Schütz was Kapellmeister at the royal court of Copenhagen. He spent time in Brunswick and Lüneberg and then returned to the elector's court in 1645 when the Dresden chapel was reestablished, and, except for visits to the Danish court, he remained in the elector's service until his death at Dresden November 6, 1672. He was a man of noble character and a veritable father to his chapel. His special achievement was the introduction into German music of the new style of the Italian modalists, typified by Monteverdi, without creating an unsatisfying hybrid; the music of Schütz remains individual and German in feeling. Most of all, his choral settings of biblical texts show unsurpassed mastery.

FOR FURTHER READING

Geier, Martin. *Funeral Sermon for Heinrich Schütz*. Ed. and trans. Rod Laver. St. Louis: Concordia, 1985.

Moser, Hans Joachim. *Heinrich Schütz*. Trans. Carl F. Pfatteicher. St. Louis: Concordia, 1959.

George Frederick Handel (the German form of his name is Georg Friedrich Händel) was born at Halle, February 23, 1685, the son of a surgeon and a pastor's daughter. His father died when Handel was eleven. He was educated at the University of Halle, originally for the law. He became organist at the Reformed cathedral there from 1702 to 1703. He then left the university and went to Hamburg to work on operas from 1703 to 1706. For the next four years he was in Italy. He then went to England and in 1726 became a British subject. He enjoyed court appointments and worked for private patrons, but chiefly he was engaged in the

JULY

production of Italian operas and English oratorios. In 1729, while on a visit to the continent, Bach tried to arrange a meeting with the man whose work he admired, but the two never met.

The opera began to decline in popularity, and Handel turned to the oratorio, a large-scale work developed around a religious theme, written not to be staged but sung by soloists and chorus. In 1741–1742 at Neal's Musick Hall in Dublin his most popular work, *Messiah,* was performed. In his last years, like Bach, Handel had eye trouble. He died in London, April 14, 1759, and was buried in the Poet's Corner of Westminster Abbey on April 20, mourned by a congregation of three thousand. He had involved himself in public affairs by his generous gifts and had sent bequests to his relatives in Germany. His strong sense of charity and concern for others won for him the affection of the English people.

Handel's church music is relatively unimportant. He was primarily a dramatic composer, and even his oratorios were written for the theater, not the church. Nonetheless, they have been memorable proclamations and interpretations of Scripture.

FOR FURTHER READING

Abraham, Gerald E. H. *Handel: A Symposium.* New York: Oxford University Press, 1954.

Burrows, Donald. *Handel and the English Chapel Royal.* New York: Oxford University Press, 2006.

Deutsch, Otto Erich. *Handel: A Documentary Biography.* New York: Norton, 1955.

Hogwood, Christopher. *Handel.* New York: Thames and Hudson, 1985.

Lang, Paul H. *George Frederic Handel.* New York: Norton, 1966.

READING

From *Behold the Spirit* by Alan Watts

Music at its highest, as in Bach or Mozart, is pure play. The preludes and fugues of Bach are simply a complex arrangement of glorious sounds, entirely sufficient in themselves. They need no programme notes to explain a moral or sociological message, or to call our attention to effects imitating natural noises or conveying emotional qualities. The intricate melodies flow on and on, and there never seems any necessity for them to stop. He composed them in tremendous quantities, with the same Godlike extravagance to be found in the unnecessary vastness of nature. Inferior music, however, needs props and commentaries, since it proceeds from human purpose rather than that playfulness of divine perfection which we find not only in Bach and Mozart, but also in the long Alleluias of Gregorian chant, the arabesques of Persian miniatures, the illuminate margins of medieval manuscripts, the wind-swept bamboos of Chinese painting, and the entirely self-satisfying and purposeless figures of the dance as it may sometimes be seen in Russian ballet. Such playfulness is the very nature of the divine Wisdom.

Alan Watts, *Behold the Spirit: A Study in the Necessity of Mystical Religion* (New York: Random House, 1947), 178.

PROPERS

God of glory, whose praise by saints and angels in heaven is unceasing, you have given to your servants Johann Sebastian Bach, Heinrich Schütz, and George Frederick Handel abundant and manifold gifts to proclaim your glory: Be ever present with your servants who seek through music to perfect the praises offered by your people on earth; and grant that they may even now hear the sound of your beauty and at the last rejoice in the perfection of praise in your eternal kingdom; through your Son Jesus Christ our Lord, who lives and reigns with you and the Holy Spirit, one God, now and forever.

BCP, rev. PHP

Readings:	2 Chronicles 20:20-21
	Psalm 106:1-5 *or* 33:1-5, 20-21
	Ephesians 5:15-20
	Luke 19:37-40
Hymn of the Day:	
	"When in our music God is glorified" (LBW 555, LSB 796, ELW 850, 851; H82 420)
Prayers:	For all who make music for the church
	For a renewed appreciation of music as a gift from God
	For God to raise up new musicians for the church and his people
Preface:	All Saints
Color:	White

July 29

Mary, Martha, and Lazarus of Bethany

This little family of Bethany were Jesus' friends who opened their home to him, and it was at their house that he found refreshment, especially before the passion. Their names, on various dates, appear on lists of martyrs from the seventh or eighth centuries.

Mary, a form of Miriam, is portrayed in Luke 10:38-42 and John 11:1–12:8 as a contemplative person with single-minded absorption in the kingdom of God. In

John's account, at dinner six days before the passion, Mary anointed Jesus, perhaps as a sign of his royal dignity, which he took to be a consecration of himself for his approaching sacrifice.

Martha, the name means "lady" or "mistress," has come rather unfairly to represent the unrecollected activist. She was of a practical turn to be sure, but she enjoyed the friendship and esteem of Jesus nonetheless, and it was she who made the confession of faith when Jesus came after the death of Lazarus, "If you had been here, my brother would not have died" (John 11:21-22).

In Luke 10:38 the house where the three siblings lived is called Martha's. In John 12:1-3 the supper at Bethany at which Lazarus was present and at which Martha again served, is held at the house of Simon the leper (Matt. 26:6; Mark 14:3). This has led some to suggest that Mary may have been the widow of Simon.

Lazarus, who was raised from the dead by Jesus, is in the Fourth Gospel a sign of the eternal life possessed by those who believe. This most striking resurrection story, however, is not found in the Synoptic Gospels. Lazarus's high character is evidenced by the love that Mary, Martha, and Jesus all had for him.

Devotion to Lazarus was apparently widespread in the early church. He is commemorated in the Eastern Church on the Saturday before the Sunday of the Passion, called "Lazarus Saturday," which anticipates the resurrection of Jesus on the following Saturday night. According to a curious legend, Lazarus, his sisters, and some friends were put in a leaky boat by their enemies and miraculously made their way to Cyprus where Lazarus was made a bishop. In 890 what were thought to be his relics were taken to Constantinople and a church was built there in his honor. In an eleventh-century legend, Lazarus had been bishop of Marseilles and was martyred under Domitian. (The legend perhaps confuses Lazarus of Bethany with a fifth-century Bishop Lazarus of Aix.)

In the Western church the traditional feast day of Lazarus has been December 17. The Roman General Calendar commemorates Martha alone on July 29 and Mary, together with Mary the wife of Cleopas, and Mary the mother of James ("the three Marys") on May 25. The calendar in the *Book of Common Prayer*, followed by the calendar in *For All the Saints,* has joined the commemoration of Mary with that of Martha on July 29. The calendars in the *Lutheran Book of Worship* (1978) and in *Evangelical Lutheran Worship* (2006) extend the commemoration to include their brother as well; Mary, Martha, and Lazarus are also remembered together in *The Christian Year: Calendar, Lectionary and Collects* (1997) of the Church of England.

FOR FURTHER READING

Constable, Giles. "The Interpretation of Mary and Martha." In *Three Studies in Medieval Religious and Social Thought.* 1–41. Cambridge: Cambridge University Press, 1995.

READING

From *Mixed Pasture* by Evelyn Underhill

St. Theresa said that to give our Lord a perfect service, Mary and Martha must combine. The modern tendency is to turn from that attitude and work of Mary; and even call it—as I have heard it called by busy social Christians—a form of spiritual selfishness. Thousands of devoted men and women today believe that the really good part is to keep busy, and give themselves no time to take what is offered to those who abide quietly with Christ; because there seem such a lot of urgent jobs for Martha to do. The result of this can only be a maiming of their human nature, exhaustion, loss of depth and of vision; and it is seen in the vagueness and ineffectuality of a great deal of the work that is done for God. It means a total surrender of the busy click-click of the life of succession; nowhere, in the end, more deadly than in the religious sphere. I insist on this because I feel, more and more, the danger in which we stand of developing a lopsided Christianity; so concentrated on service, and on this world's obligations, as to forget the needs of constant willed and quiet contact with that other world, wherefrom the sanctions of service and the power in which to do it proceed.

Evelyn Underhill, *Mixed Pasture* (London: Methuen, 1933), 74–75.

PROPERS

O God, heavenly Father, your Son Jesus Christ enjoyed rest and refreshment in the home of Mary and Martha [and Lazarus] of Bethany: Give us the will to love you, open our hearts to hear you, strengthen our hands to serve you in others for his sake [and confirm in us your power even over death through him], who lives and reigns with you and the Holy Spirit, one God, now and forever.

LFF, rev. PHP

Readings:	Psalm 36:5-10 *or* 33:1-5, 20-21
	Romans 12:9-13
	Luke 10:38-42 *or* John 11:19-27
Hymn of the Day:	
	"O Jesus, King most wonderful" (LBW 537, LSB 554)
Prayers:	For those whose work enables others to mediate and pray and study
	For times of quiet contemplation
	For those whose lives are devoted to prayer and contemplation
	For the practice of hospitality among Christians
	For a certain hope of the resurrection
Preface:	All Saints (LBW, ELW) or Epiphany (BCP)
Color:	White

ALSO ON JULY 29

Olaf, King of Norway, Martyr, 1030

Olaf Haraldsson was born in Oplandet in 995, the son of a minor king and his queen Asta. His father died before Olaf was born, and Asta married King Sigurd Syr of Ringerike, a fertile island district near the centers of trade in southern Norway, where Olaf was raised. Many details of his life are known, and these comprise what is probably the earliest Norwegian historical work extant. As soon as fifty years after his death, however, stories of his life were elaborated with moralizing elements.

When Olaf was still young he went on Viking expeditions with his foster father, and then with Thorkel the Tall he fought in Friesland, Holland, and England. The next year, on an expedition to France and Spain, the legend has it that he dreamed of a strange, powerful figure telling him to go back to his family lands, "for you shall be the eternal king of Norway." After his baptism, or more probably his confirmation, in Rouen, France, in 1014, Olaf sailed for Norway in 1015 with the intention of establishing Christianity firmly there, which Olaf Trygvasson (Olaf I) had failed to do, and unifying the nation under his own rule.

Olaf succeeded in rallying many to his cause and after several battles was recognized by all as the king of Norway in 1019. In the years that followed, Olaf, an ardent Christian, sought to uproot the last traces of paganism in Norway and spread Christianity throughout his kingdom, and with the help of Bishop Grimkel and others he had brought with him from England and Normandy, he gave the church a code of laws written in the Norwegian language. He also completely revised the civil laws of the nation, known as the "Laws of St. Olaf," became the basis of all later Norwegian jurisprudence.

King Olaf enforced his laws with strict impartiality, a practice not always welcome to the aristocracy, whose power was diminishing. When the powerful King Knut (Canute), who at that time ruled Denmark and all of Britain, joined forces with the king of Sweden in 1028 to attack King Olaf, many of the Norwegian nobles deserted their king, who was defeated and fled to Russia, taking refuge at the court of his brother-in-law Duke Jaroslav. In 1030 Olaf returned from exile and attempted to regain his kingdom, but on July 29 at the battle of Stiklestad, north of Trondheim, he was slain, and Knut added Norway to his domain.

Soon after the battle, the people began to talk of the dead king as a holy man, and a little over a year later his body was removed from its temporary burial place to the town of Nidaros, later called Trondheim, which Olaf I had founded in 997. The hero-king was recognized by the church and the nation as the patron saint and "eternal king of Norway," and the date of his death became the date of his annual commemoration. From this time on, Christianity was the dominant religion in Norway.

At the beginning of the thirteenth century, the Icelandic historian Snorri Sturlusson wrote in his *Heimskringla* a full biography, the "Saga of Olaf the Saint," and Olaf the king and saint has repeatedly been the subject of literary works, painting, and sculpture ever since. The commemoration of St. Olaf spread to other countries, and churches have been named for him not only in Norway but elsewhere in Scandinavia, in Great Britain, the Baltic countries, and Russia. In the United States, Lutherans of Norwegian origin especially remember him, and there are more than thirty-five churches named for him. St. Olaf College in Northfield, Minnesota, founded by Berndt Julius Muus of Trondheim, and its choir are well known. The presence of St. Olaf on English calendars recalls the time when the Church of Norway had jurisdiction over a large part of the British Isles.

Already in the eleventh century, a church was built over the burial place of St. Olav in Nidaros, and in the twelfth and thirteenth centuries, it was rebuilt as a Gothic cathedral, the most beautiful in northern Europe and long a center of pilgrimage and a place of celebrating his feast day. During the late middle ages this was the seat of the archbishop and was the religious and cultural center of Norway and an important pilgrimage center for all of northern Europe. In the course of the years, the cathedral was severely damaged by fires and other accidents. Its restoration was begun in 1869. The present building of marble and native blue soapstone is perhaps the finest Gothic cathedral in Scandinavia.

FOR FURTHER READING

Sturlusson, Snorri. *Heimskringla: History of the Kings of Norway.* Trans. Lee M. Hollander. Austin: University of Texas Press, 1964; reissued 1991.
Turville-Petre, G. *The Heroic Age of Scandinavia.* New York: Longmans, 1951.

READING

From *Heimskringla: History of the Kings of Norway.*

As he grew up, Olaf Haraldsson was not tall of stature, but of middle height and of stout frame and great strength. His hair was of light chestnut color and his face, broad, of light complexion, and ruddy. His eyes were unusually fine, bright and piercing, so that it inspired terror to look into them when he was furious. Olaf was a man of many accomplishments. He was a good shot, and second to none in hurling spears. He was skilled and had a sure eye for all kinds of handicraft work, whether the things were made for himself or others. He was nicknamed Olaf the Stout. He was bold and ready in speech, mature early in all ways, both in bodily strength and shrewdness; and he endeared himself to all his kinsfolk and acquaintances. He vied with all in games and always wanted to be the first in everything, as was proper, befitting his rank and birth.

It was the habit of the king to rise betimes in the morning, to put on his clothes and wash his hands, then go to church and listen to matins and morning mass, then go to meetings and reconcile people, or else deal with other matters such as seemed needful to him. He gathered at court men of high and low degree, and all who were of keen understanding. He had often recite in his presence the laws of Hakon, the foster son of Aethelstan, had given to the Trondheim district. He changed laws with the advice of the wisest men, taking away or adding as seemed best to him. The Christian code of laws he gave in accordance with the advice of Bishop Grimkel and other priests, laying great stress on abolishing heathendom and ancient practices such as seemed to him contrary to the spirit of Christianity. In the end the farmers agreed to the laws the king gave. As says Sigvat:

> Do thou, leige-lord, lay down
> laws for all the land that
> may prevail among all
> men and stand forever!

King Olaf was well-mannered, of an agreeable disposition, a man of rather few words, open-handed [yet also] eager to have possessions.

[The final battle]

Thorir struck at the king, and then they exchanged some blows; and the king's sword took no effect where Thorir's reindeer skin protected him, yet he received a wound on his hand. . . .

The king said to Bjorn, his marshal, "Strike down the dog on whom steel takes no effect!"

Bjorn turned his battle-axe and hit him with the hammer of it. The blow fell on Thorir's shoulder. It was a mighty one, and Thorir tottered. At the same moment the king turned on Kalf and his kinsmen dealt Olaf, Kalf's kinsman, his deathblow. Then Thorir the Hound thrust with his spear at Bjorn and pierced him in the middle and that was his death.

Then Thorir said, "Thus we beat the bears!" [The Old Norse *Bjorn* means "bear."]

Thorstein Shipbuilder hewed at King Olaf with his battle-axe, and the blow struck his left leg above the knee. Finn Arnason instantly killed Thorstein. Receiving that wound the king leaned against a boulder. He threw down his sword and prayed God to help him. Then Thorir the Hound thrust at him with his spear. It pierced him from below his coat of mail and through the belly. Then Kalf slashed at the king, and the blow struck his neck on the left side. Men disagree as to which Kalf wounded the king. These three wounds caused King Olaf's death. After his fall most of the company which had advanced with him fell also.

On the sand flat where the body of King Olaf had been interred, a fine spring arose, and people obtained relief from their ailments by drinking its water. It was walled in, and its water has been safeguarded ever since. First a chapel was built there and an altar erected where the burial place of the king had been; but now

Christ Church stands on that spot. When Archbishop Eystein built the large minster which stands there now he had its high altar erected on the very spot where
the king's grave had been. And on that spot stood the high altar in the old Christ
Church. It is said that Saint Olaf's Church now stands where the shed in which the
body of King Olaf reposed during the night. The rise up which the holy remains
of the king were borne from the boat is now called Olaf's Slope, and that is now
in the middle of the town.

Men who have kept close account say that the Holy King Olaf was king of
Norway for fifteen years after Earl Svein left the country, but that he assumed the
royal title the winter before. . . . According to Priest Ari the Learned, Holy King
Olaf was thirty-five years old when he fell. He had fought twenty large battles.

Snorri Sturlusson, *Heimskringla: History of the Kings of Norway,* trans. Lee M. Hollander (Austin:
University of Texas Press, 1964), 245–46, 289, 514–15, 530, 533. Used by permission.

PROPERS

God of justice and love, you raised up your servant Olaf to be the eternal king
of Norway, to establish your church in his kingdom, and to revise the laws of the
nation: Grant to all leaders of the earth the will and the courage to administer the
law with strict impartiality, and to fear no one but you, the Judge of all; through
Jesus Christ our Lord, who lives and reigns with you and the Holy Spirit, one God,
now and forever.

PHP

Readings:	Wisdom 3:1-9
	Psalm 21:1-7
	Luke 12:22-31
Hymn of the Day:	
	"Who is this host, arrayed in white" (LBW 314, ELW 425) ("The head that one was crowned with thorns" is sung to the tune *St. Magnus,* who was the son of St. Olaf.)
Prayers:	For the Church and people of Norway
	For the king and government of Norway
	For those who administer justice
Preface:	A Saint (2) (BCP)
Color:	White

July 30

William Wilberforce, Renewer of Society, 1833

William Wilberforce was born into an affluent family in Hull, Yorkshire, in 1759. As a young man he wanted to become a priest but was persuaded that he could serve Christ more effectively as a member of Parliament. This he did for forty-five years, from 1780 to 1825, using his position in the House of Commons to fight for the abolition of the slave trade. His reading of the New Testament convinced him to lead a more disciplined Christian life. He became a devout Evangelical and gave himself unsparingly to the promotion of overseas missions as well as many Christian and humanitarian causes in England. He was an eloquent speaker, and this eloquence, combined with his personal holiness and deep moral conviction, gave power to his earnest beliefs.

Wilberforce died on July 29, 1833, three days after the bill for the Abolition of Slavery in the British Dominions had passed its second reading in the House of Commons. He is buried in Westminster Abbey.

FOR FURTHER READING

Coupland, Reginald. *Wilberforce: A Narrative.* London: Collins, 1945.

Furneaux, Robin. *William Wilberforce.* London: Hamish Hamilton, 1974.

Hague, William. *William Wilberforce: The Life of the Great Anti-Slavery Trade Campaigner.* London: HarperCollins, 2007.

Hochschild, Adam. *Bury the Chains: The British Struggle to Abolish Slavery.* London: Macmillan, 2005.

Warner, Oliver. *William Wilberforce and His Times.* London: B. T. Batsford, 1962.

Wilberforce, Robert I. and Samuel. *The Life of William Wilberforce.* 5 vols. London: John Murray, 1838.

READING

From William Wilberforce, An Appeal to the Inhabitants of the British Empire on behalf of the Negro Slaves in the West Indies

To all the inhabitants of the British Empire, who value the favour of God, or are alive to the interests of honour of their country, to all who have respect for justice or any feelings of humanity. I would solemnly address myself, I call upon them, as they shall hereafter answer, in the great day of account, for the use they shall have made of any power or influence with which Providence may have entrusted them, to employ their best endeavours, by all lawful and constitutional means, to mitigate, and, as soon as it may be safely done, to terminate the Negro Slavery of the British Colonies; a system of the grossest injustice, of the most heathenish irreligion and immorality, of the most unprecedented, and unrelenting cruelty. . . .

Let us not presume too far on the forbearance of the Almighty. Favoured in an equal degree with Christian light, with civil freedom, and with greater measure of national blessings than perhaps any other country upon earth ever before enjoyed, what a return it would be for the goodness of the Almighty, if we were to continue to keep the descendents of the Africans, whom we have ourselves wrongfully planted in the eastern hemisphere, in their present state of unexampled darkness and degradation! . . .

In a country in which the popular voice has a powerful and constitutional influence on the government and legislation, to be silent when there is a question of reforming abuses repugnant in justice and humanity is to share their guilt. Power always implies responsibility; and the possessor of it cannot innocently be neutral, when by his exercise moral good may be promoted, or evil lessened or removed.

William Wilberforce, *An Appeal to the Inhabitants of the British Empire on behalf of the Negro Slaves in the West Indies* (London: 1823), 3, 54–56.

PROPERS

Let your continual mercy, O Lord, kindle in your Church the never-failing gift of love, that, following the example of your servant William Wilberforce, we may have the grace to defend the poor, and maintain the cause of those who have no helper; for the sake of him who gave his life for us, your Son our Savior Jesus Christ, who lives and reigns with you and the Holy Spirit, one God, now and forever.

LFF

Readings:	Psalm 146:4-9 *or* 112:1-9
	Galatians 3:23-29
	Matthew 25:31-40
Hymn of the Day:	
	"Father, all loving, who rulest in majesty" (H82 568)
	"The Son of God, our Christ, the Word" (LBW 434, ELW 584)
Prayers:	For all areas of the world where slavery is still practiced or tolerated
	For all who must sell themselves into slavery through the system of bonded labor
	For all Christians in Congress and Parliament
	For all who are working to set free those who suffer from political or economic oppression
Preface:	A Saint (2) (BCP)
Color:	White

ALSO ON JULY 30

The *Lutheran Service Book* commemorates **Robert Barnes** (1495–1540), an English Lutheran confessor and martyr. He was born in Norfolk, studied at Cambridge University, and became prior of the Augustinian friars there. In 1526 he was brought before the vice-chancellor for what was thought to be a heterodox sermon and imprisoned. In 1528 he escaped to Antwerp and visited Wittenberg, where he met Luther. In 1531 he returned to England and served as an intermediary between the English government and Lutheran Germany. He openly embraced Lutheranism and was martyred on this date in London in 1540.

July 31

Ignatius of Loyola, Priest, Monastic, and Founder of the Society of Jesus, 1556

Iñigo de Recalde de Loyola was born *ca.* 1491 of a noble Basque family. He spent time as a page at the court of Ferdinand and Isabella, where, he later testifies, he led a dissolute life. Having gotten into trouble with the law, he joined the army. In 1521 he was struck in the knee with a cannon ball while fighting the French at Pamplona. During his convalescence (after which he walked with a limp), he read a life of Christ as well as stories about the saints, which made him resolve to devote himself from that time on to the service of Christ. After a year's retreat that influenced his whole life, he went on pilgrimage to Jerusalem, and from 1524 to 1534 he studied in Barcelona and at the University of Paris.

After graduating from Paris, at the age of forty-three, he gathered around him a group of nine companions, among whom was Francis Xavier (see December 3). In 1537 they went to Rome as the Company (or Society) of Jesus and offered their services in any capacity to Pope Paul III. The ten were ordained to the priesthood and undertook various assignments. Three years later the pope formally approved the Society of Jesus, which was organized along military lines with Ignatius as its first Superior General. Its members promised complete obedience to him and to the pope.

Ignatius died July 31, 1556. By the time of his death, the Jesuits, as the order is popularly known, were established throughout Europe and had also become successful missionaries in Asia, Africa, and America. The original group of ten had become one thousand, and the strongest instrument of the Counter-Reformation had been created, with Ignatius's insistence that the Society be an example of charity and moderation. Ignatius was canonized in 1622; his *Spiritual Exercises*, designed to train his followers to conquer their passions and give themselves to

God, has had influence far beyond the Roman Catholic Church. The method he prescribes is to begin with an event in the life of Christ, to imagine the scene in detail as if one were a witness to the event, and then use this experience as a motive for love, gratitude, and dedication to the service of God. Ignatius is on the Roman General Calendar and the calendar in *Uniting in Worship* (1988) of the Uniting Church in Australia (Methodist, Presbyterian, and Congregationalist). He was added to the Episcopal calendar in *Lesser Feasts and Fasts 1997*.

FOR FURTHER READING

Broderick, James. *St. Ignatius Loyola: the Pilgrim Years, 1491–1538*. San Francisco: Ignatius, 1998 (1956).

Lonsdale, David. *Eyes to See, Ears to Hear: An Introduction to Ignatian Spirituality*. London: Darton, Longman and Todd, 1990.

Ignatius of Loyola. *Spiritual Exercises and Selected Works*. Ed. George E. Ganss, et al. Mahwah: Paulist, 1991.

Meissner, William W. *Ignatius Loyola: The Psychology of a Saint*. New Haven: Yale University Press, 1992.

Rahner, Hugo. *Ignatius the Theologian*. San Francisco: Ignatius Press, 1990.

———, and Leonard von Matt. *St. Ignatius of Loyola: A Pictorial Biography*. Chicago: Henry Regnery, 1956.

Ravier, Andre. *Ignatius of Loyola*. San Francisco: Ignatius, 1987.

READING

From the life of Saint Ignatius from his own words by Luis Gonzalez (Louis Consalvo)

Ignatius was passionately fond of reading worldly books of fiction and tales of knight-errantry. When he felt he was getting better from his wound, he asked for some of these books to pass the time. But no book of that sort could be found in the house; instead they gave him a life of Christ and a collection of the lives of the saints written in Spanish.

By constantly reading these books he began to be attracted to what he found narrated there. Sometimes in the midst of his reading he would reflect on what he had read. Yet at other times he would dwell on many of the things which he had been accustomed to dwell on previously. But at this point our Lord came to his assistance, insuring that these thoughts were followed by others which arose from his current reading.

While reading the life of Christ our Lord or the lives of the saints, he would reflect and reason with himself: "What if I should do what Saint Francis or Saint Dominic did?" In this way he let his mind dwell on many thoughts; they lasted a while until other things took their place. Then those vain and worldly images would come into his mind and remain a long time. This sequence of thoughts persisted with him for a long time.

But there was a difference. When Ignatius reflected on worldly thoughts, he felt immense pleasure; but when he gave them up out of weariness, he felt dry and depressed. Yet when he thought of living the rigorous sort of life he knew the saints had lived, he not only experienced pleasure when he actually thought about it, but even after he dismissed these thoughts, he still experienced great joy. Yet he did not pay attention to this, nor did he appreciate it until one day, in a moment of insight, he began to marvel at the difference. Then he understood his experience: thoughts of one kind left him sad, the others full of joy. And this was the first time he applied a process of reasoning to his religious experience. Later on, when he began to formulate his spiritual exercises, he used this experience as an illustration to explain the doctrine he taught his disciples on the discernment of spirits.

Chapter 1. From the English translation of the Office of Readings from the Liturgy of the Hours © 1974 The International Committee on English in the Liturgy, Inc. All rights reserved.

PROPERS

Teach us, good Lord, to serve you as you deserve: To give and not to count the cost; to fight and not to heed the wounds; to toil and not to seek for rest; to labor and not to ask for any reward, save that of knowing that we do your will; through Jesus Christ our Lord.

Attributed to St. Ignatius Loyola

Readings:	Psalm 34:1-8
	1 Corinthians 10:31-11:1
	Luke 9:57-62
Hymn of the Day:	
	"O God, I love thee; not that my poor love" (H82 682, LBW 491)
Prayers:	For the members of the Society of Jesus throughout the world
	For seminaries and theological colleges and all those responsible for the training of clergy
	For closer relationships between the Roman Catholic Church and the Churches of the Reformation
	For a dedication of all our works to the greater glory of God.
Preface:	A Saint (3) (BCP)
Color:	White

August 1

Joseph of Arimathea

Joseph of Arimathea is the disciple of Jesus who is remembered for his brave act of generosity. After the crucifixion he asked Pilate for the body of Jesus and "wrapped it in a clean linen cloth and laid it in his own new tomb." Matthew says that Joseph was a rich man and that it was he who rolled the great stone to the door of the tomb; Mark describes Joseph as "a respected member of the council [the Sanhedrin], who was also himself waiting expectantly for the kingdom of God" and adds the detail that Joseph bought the linen burial cloth; Luke notes that although Joseph was a member of the council "he had not agreed to their plan and action" and makes it explicit that no one had ever been put in the new tomb; John indicates that Joseph was a "secret" disciple of Jesus and associates him with Nicodemus. Nothing further is known of him.

By the fourth century, legends about Joseph were in circulation. In the middle of the thirteenth century appears the story of his being sent by St. Philip from Gaul to be a missionary to Britain. He took with him, the legend says, the chalice used at the Last Supper, the Holy Grail, containing the blood of Jesus shed on the cross. At Glastonbury Joseph struck his staff into the earth and from it grew the Glastonbury Thorn. The thorn was hacked down by a Puritan, but the thorn that grows there to this day came from a shoot of it. Glastonbury was long honored as the holiest place in England.

A still more curious story is that Joseph was a tin merchant, and long before he was sent by Philip to preach the Gospel, he came often to the tin mines of Cornwall. Joseph, the legend says, was an uncle of the Virgin Mary and he brought the young Jesus on one of his voyages. William Blake with delicate questions refers to this legend in his lines that are still sung as a hymn,

> And did those feet in ancient time
> Walk upon England's mountains green?
> And was the Holy Lamb of God
> In England's pleasant pastures seen?
> And did the Countenance Divine
> Shine forth upon our clouded hills?
> And was Jerusalem builded here,
> Among those dark Satanic mills?

These stories, lovely as they are but without any historical foundation, were given wide credence and made Joseph of Arimathea a greatly loved figure in England. He had been commemorated with a memorial collect on March 17 on the old Roman Catholic calendar, and he was included in the calendar in the 1979 *Book of*

Common Prayer and in the *Lutheran Service Book* (2006) on July 31, his feast day in the East, but in *Lesser Feasts and Fasts 1997* his commemoration was moved to August 1 to make room for Ignatius of Loyola.

FOR FURTHER READING

Barber, Richard. *The Holy Grail: Imagination and Belief.* London: Allen Lane/Penguin, 2004.

Robinson, J. Armitage. *Two Glastonbury Legends: King Arthur and St. Joseph of Arimathea.* Cambridge: Cambridge University Press, 1926.

Treharne, R. F. *The Glastonbury Legends: Joseph of Arimathea, the Holy Grail, and King Arthur.* London: Abacus, 1975.

READING

From William Barclay, *The Gospel of Matthew*

According to Jewish law, even a criminal's body might not be left hanging all night, but had to be buried that day. "His body shall not remain all night upon the tree, but thou shalt in any wise bury him that day" (*Deuteronomy* 21:22, 23). This was doubly binding when, as in the case of Jesus the next day was the Sabbath. According to Roman law, the relatives of a criminal might claim his body for burial, but if it was not claimed it was simply left to rot until the scavenger dogs dealt with it. Now none of Jesus' relatives were in a position to claim His body, for they were all Galilaeans, and none of them possessed a tomb in Jerusalem. So the wealthy Joseph of Arimathea stepped in. He went to Pilate and asked that the body of Jesus should be given to him; and he cared for it, and put it into the rock tomb where no man had ever been laid. Joseph must forever be famous as the man who gave Jesus a tomb.

It is often said that Joseph gave to Jesus a tomb after He was dead, but did not support him during His life. Joseph was a member of the Sanhedrin (*Luke* 23:50); and Luke tells us that "he had not consented to the counsel and deed of them" (*Luke* 23:51). Is it possible that that meeting of the Sanhedrin called in the house of Caiaphas in the middle of the night was a meeting selectively called? It hardly seems likely that the whole Sanhedrin could have been there. It may well be that Caiaphas summoned those whom he wished to be present, and packed the meeting with his supporters, and that Joseph never even got a chance to be there.

It is certainly true that in the end Joseph displayed the greatest courage. He came out on the side of a crucified criminal. He braved the possible resentment of Pilate; and he faced the certain hatred and mockery of the Jews. It may well be that Joseph of Arimathea did everything that it was possible for him to do.

William Barclay, *The Gospel of Matthew*, vol. 2 (Philadelphia: Westminster, 1958), 410–11, 412.

PROPERS

Merciful God, whose servant Joseph of Arimathea with reverence and godly fear prepared the body of our Lord and Savior for burial, and laid it in his own tomb: Grant to us, your faithful people, grace and courage to love and serve Jesus with sincere devotion all the days of our life; through Jesus Christ our Lord, who lives and reigns with you and the Holy Spirit, one God, forever and ever.

LFF

Readings: Proverbs 4:10-18
                 Psalm 16:5-11 *or* 112:1-9
                 Luke 23:50-56

Hymn of the Day:
                 "Abide with me, fast falls the eventide" (H82 662, LBW 272, LSB 878, ELW 629)
                 or "Despair not, my heart, in thy sorrow" (SBH 296)

Prayers: For courage to do the right thing
                 For generosity of substance and spirit
                 For those who care for the dead and prepare them for burial
                 For sure and certain hope of the resurrection

Preface: Commemoration of the Dead (BCP) or Burial of the Dead (LBW)
Color: White

FORMERLY ON AUGUST 1

In the Western church the only celebration of an Old Testament saint that has more than local observance is the commemoration of the **Holy Maccabees** on August 1. In *ca.* 168 B.C.E., seven brothers and their mother were put to a horrid death by Antiochus IV Epiphanes for refusing to eat pork. Their story, reported in 2 Maccabees 7 and probably alluded to in Hebrews 11:35, impressed the imagination of the early church, especially St. Gregory Nazianzus and St. Augustine, and the seven, together with their mother, were honored as forerunners of the Christian martyrs. The commemoration was common throughout the church before the fifth century. The observance of the day in the Roman Church was encouraged by their preservation of what were thought to be their bones in the church of St. Peter ad Vincula. In the mid-twentieth century, the bones were determined to be canine and were removed from the church and the commemoration removed from the Western calendar. The day continues to be observed in the East. It also lingers on the calendar in the 1962 Canadian *Book of Common Prayer*.

August 3

O n this date the *Lutheran Service Book* of the Lutheran Church—Missouri Synod has introduced the commemoration of ***Joanna, Mary, and Salome***,

Myrrh-bearers. It is an adaptation of the commemoration in the Orthodox Churches of the myrrh-bearing women Mary Magdalene, Mary Theotokos (the Virgin Mary), Joanna, Salome, Mary the wife of Cleopas, Susanna, Mary of Bethany, and Martha of Bethany. In the Byzantine Rite the commemoration takes place on the Third Sunday of Pascha (Easter). Righteous Joseph of Arimathea and Nicodemus are often included in the commemoration. See Mark 15:42—16:1; John 19:38-42.

August 6

The Transfiguration of Our Lord

This feast commemorates the fleeting glimpse that three disciples experienced of the glory of God, the glory in which he will come at the close of the age. Like the accounts of Jesus' baptism, the visit of the Magi, and Jesus' first miracle at Cana in Galilee, this event on the mountain is an "epiphany," a manifestation of Jesus' true nature. For a moment, the veil that separates the invisible world of splendor from the visible world of familiarity is lifted, and truth and reality are revealed.

The vision of the transfigured Christ, resplendent in glory, is of such significance and richness that it is celebrated twice on the calendar. In the Lutheran Church, the Transfiguration is celebrated on the Last Sunday after the Epiphany as a glimpse and promise of the glory of the resurrection to strengthen the church before it descends into the valley of Lent and Holy Week. The Episcopal Church has the same theme for the Last Sunday after the Epiphany, although it does not use the title *Transfiguration*. The collect in the *Book of Common Prayer* for that Sunday makes the Paschal connection: "O God, who before the passion of your only-begotten Son revealed his glory upon the holy mountain: Grant to us that we, beholding by faith the light of his countenance, may be strengthened to bear our cross, and be changed into his likeness from glory to glory." The Roman Catholic Church uses the image of the Transfiguration on the Second Sunday in Lent each year, reflecting an ancient practice, as a foreshadowing of the resurrection.

In addition to these observances of the vision of Peter, James, and John on the mount that are oriented toward the Paschal mystery, the Feast of the Transfiguration also has its own date, August 6. The feast is held in highest esteem by the Eastern Churches and was celebrated as early as the fifth century in East Syria. In the West, it is found for the first time in the tenth-century Franco-Roman churches and entered widespread Western use only on the eve of the Reformation when, in 1457, Pope Calixtus III added it to the calendar of the entire Western church in gratitude for the victory of Juan Capistrano and John Hunyadi over the Turks at Belgrade on July 22, 1456, the news of which reached Rome on August

6. Because of its recent introduction, the Feast of the Transfiguration was not included on the calendar of the Church of England. The feast, however, continued to be observed in Sweden after the Reformation and was included on the calendar in the *Service Book and Hymnal* of 1958. The American *Book of Common Prayer* of 1892 introduced it to Episcopal use, and from there it has been taken into most modern Anglican calendars. It is also listed on the Methodist calendar in *For All the Saints*.

The experience of the transfigured Christ is a promise of the *parousia*, the return of Christ in all his glory, and encourages Christians on their way through the long stretch of the time after Pentecost, "ordinary time," as they grow in grace and wait for the glorious appearing.

By a horrid irony, it was on August 6, 1945 that the United States dropped on the Japanese city of Hiroshima the first atomic bomb used in warfare. Dropped from a clear sky at 8:15 in the morning from an American propeller-driven B-29 Superfortress, the bomb exploded one minute later, about 1,900 feet above the port city, with "the light of a thousand suns." The entire city was obliterated, human flesh consumed, metal melted; perhaps ninety thousand people were killed. Three days later a second bomb was dropped on Nagasaki with the loss of forty thousand more lives. The blinding light of nuclear destruction and the blinding light of the transfigured Christ are now inseparably joined. Human beings cannot forget the one; Christians dare not forget the other.

FOR FURTHER READING

McGuckin, J. A. *The Transfiguration of Christ in Scripture and Tradition*. Lewiston: Edwin Mellen, 1986.

Ramsey, Arthur Michael. *The Glory of God and the Transfiguration of Christ*. London: Longmans, 1949.

READING

From *Light of Christ* by Evelyn Underhill

Some of us perhaps remember the experience of standing for the first time in Chartres Cathedral; the solemn, coloured majesty that enfolds us and silences us when we come into the place of adoration and sacrifice; and how gradually we become aware of the light that strikes us through those great coloured windows. A Retreat can be such an experience of God's glory. But the absolute Light only dazzles us; in its wholeness it is more than we can bear. It needs breaking-up before our small hearts can deal with it. The windows of Christ's Mysteries split it up into many-coloured loveliness, disclose all its hidden richness and colour, make its beauty more accessible to us; convince us of the reality of beauty and holiness and of the messy unreality of most of our own lives. And within this place we too are bathed in the light transmitted by the windows, a light which is yet the very radiance of Eternity. It fills the place where we are, it drowns us in its solemn beauty and glows in the Figure and acts which we see. The universal light of the Father, the interior radiance of the Holy Spirit, linked together in this vision of the Son, so far above us and yet so divinely near.

Evelyn Underhill, *The Light of Christ* (London: Longmans, 1945), 74–75, 91–92, 64, 27–28, 28–29, 82–83. Reprinted by permission of Wipf and Stock Publishers.

PROPERS

O God, in the transfiguration of your Son you confirmed the mysteries of the faith by the witness of Moses and Elijah, and in the voice that came from the bright cloud you foreshadowed out adoption as your children: Make us with the King heirs of your glory, and bring us to enjoy its fullness; through Jesus Christ our Lord, who lives and reigns with you and the Holy Spirit, one God, now and forever.

Latin, fifteenth century, RS, trans. CB rev.

Readings:	Exodus 34:29-35
	Psalm 99
	2 Peter 1:13-21
	Luke 9:28-36
Hymn of the Day:	
	"O wondrous type, O vision fair" (H82 136, 137; LBW 80, LSB 413, ELW 316)
Prayers:	For an assurance of the glory of Christ, the reigning Sovereign of the cosmos
	For confidence that the church will share Christ's glory
	For continued life in Christ
	For devout attention to the word of Christ
	For an end to war and violence
	For peace
Preface:	Epiphany
Color:	White

August 8

Dominic, Priest and Friar, 1221

D ominic, a contemporary of Francis of Assisi, was born in 1170 to a noble Spanish family in Calaruega, Castile. Even as a young man he applied himself to the pursuit of learning and the practice of self-denying charity.

He was born in a time when great wealth had corrupted the Church, moral laxity prevailed, and many Christians were drifting into the ranks of the Albigensian heresy. The Albigensians asserted that Jesus Christ never existed, except in spirit, thus denying the incarnation, and by teaching that all matter is inherently evil, it denied the goodness of God's creation. To combat this popular movement, Dominic founded an order of missioners; he and his followers obeyed literally Jesus' instructions to his disciples as found in Matthew 10: they became itinerant preachers, begging their bread from place to place. Others tried to stamp out the false teaching by force and fear; the pope launched a bloody crusade against the heretics. Dominic, however, relied solely on the power of truth to prevail and used the weapons of sound learning, fervent preaching, and personal holiness of life.

Pope Honorious III approved the order in 1216. Its official name is the Order of Friars Preachers; its members are commonly called Dominicans or Black Friars because their habit is a black cloak worn over a white tunic. Dominic also founded an order of nuns.

Dominic combined rare organizational ability with a devotion and piety that were an inspiration to many who joined him. He died August 6, 1221, in Bologna, Italy, and by the time of his death the Order of Friars Preachers had spread to all parts of Europe. He was canonized in 1234.

The Dominicans' reputation for learning and scholarship is the fruit of their founder's insistence on a humble devotion to the truth. They contributed significantly to the rise of the universities, and count among their number some of the greatest scholars and teachers of medieval Europe, the best known of whom is Thomas Aquinas.

Dominic was added to the Episcopal calendar in the 1979 *Book of Common Prayer* and was introduced to the Lutheran calendar in the Spanish-language service book *Libro de Liturgia y Cántico* (1998) under the Spanish form of his name, Domingo de Guzman. He is also on the Methodist calendar in *For All the Saints*.

FOR FURTHER READING

Bedouelle, Guy. *In the Image of Saint Dominic.* San Francisco: Ignatius, 1994.
Jarrett, Bede. *Life of St. Dominic (1170–1221).* New ed. London: Blackfriars, 1955.
Koudelka, Vladimir J., ed. *Dominic.* London: Darton, Longman & Todd, 1997.
Tugwell, Simon. *Early Dominicans: Selected Writings.* New York: Paulist, 1982.
Vicaire, M. H. *St. Dominic and His Times.* New York: McGraw-Hill, 1964.

READING

From various writings on the history of the Order of Friars Preachers

Dominic was of such great integrity and was so strongly motivated by divine love, that without a doubt he proved to be a chosen vessel of grace. He was a man of great equanimity, except when carried away with compassion and mercy. Often his face became radiant with inner joy, and the serene composure of his spirit showed outwardly in his kindness and cheerfulness.

Wherever he went he proved himself in word and deed to be a servant of the gospel. During the day no one was more community-minded or pleasant toward his brothers and companions. During the night no one was more persistent in every kind of vigil and prayer. He seldom spoke unless it was with God in prayer, or about God, exhorting his brothers.

Frequently he made a special personal petition that God would fill him with genuine love, effective in caring for and obtaining the salvation of others. For he believed that he would be truly a member of Christ only when he had given himself totally for the salvation of others, just as the Lord Jesus, the Savior of all, had offered himself completely for our salvation. So, for this work, after a long period of careful and provident planning, he founded the Order of Friars Preachers.

In his conversations and letters he often urged the brothers of this Order to study constantly the Old and New Testaments. He always carried with him the Gospel according to Matthew and the epistles of Paul, and studied them so well that he almost knew them by heart.

Two or three times he was chosen bishop, but he always refused, preferring to live with his brothers in poverty.

Trans. PHP, based on *A Short Breviary* by the monks of St. John's Abbey and the English translation of the Office of Reading from the Liturgy of the Hours by the International Committee on English in the Liturgy.

PROPERS

O God of the prophets, you opened the eyes of your servant Dominic to perceive a famine of hearing the word of the Lord, and moved him, and those he drew about him, to satisfy that hunger with sound preaching and fervent devotion: Teach your Church, in this and every age, to find its life in your word and to live always close to its truth; through Jesus Christ our Lord, who lives and reigns with you and the Holy Spirit, one God, forever and ever.

LFF **+** PHP

Readings:	Psalm 96:1-7 *or* 98:1-4
	Romans 10:13-17
	John 7:16-18
Hymn of the Day:	
	"Look from your sphere of endless day" (LBW 402)
Prayers:	For the members of the Dominican Order and for their schools and colleges
	For the educational work of the church
	For all evangelists and missioners
	For patience and tenderness in dealing with those whom we are convinced are mistaken or wrong
Preface:	A Saint (2) (BCP)
Color:	White

August 10

Lawrence, Deacon and Martyr at Rome, 258

Lawrence (or Laurence) was born, perhaps of Spanish parents, in the early part of the third century. While still a young man he came to Rome where Bishop Sixtus (Xystus) II ordained him deacon, and he was made the chief of the seven deacons of Rome, responsible for the distribution of the charities of the Church and the care of its properties.

In 257 the Roman emperor Valerian began a vigorous persecution of the Church, aimed primarily at the clergy and laity of the upper classes. All the properties of the Church were confiscated, and assemblies for worship were forbidden. On August 4, 258, Sixtus II, who had just become the Bishop of Rome the year before, and his deacons were apprehended at the cemetery of Callistus where they were celebrating the liturgy, and all except Lawrence were summarily executed and buried in the same cemetery. The Roman calendar commemorates them on August 7 as "St. Sixtus II, Pope, and Companions, Martyrs." Lawrence, who knew of the location of the Church's treasure, was tortured and then executed three days later, August 10.

The traditions that have come down to us concerning the martyrdom are unreliable, but they are nonetheless amusing. When the prefect of Rome demanded the treasures, Lawrence is said to have gathered together a great number of the blind, the lame, the maimed, lepers, orphans, and widows of Rome, brought then to the prefect's palace, and declared to him, "Here is the treasure of the Church." It is said that the behavior of Lawrence in prison was such as to have led to the conversion and baptism of his jailer Hippolytus and his family. Lawrence was, tradition says, condemned to die slowly and painfully by being roasted on an iron grill. Even there Lawrence's courage and humor were apparent, for he is reported to have said to his executioners at one point in the procedure, "I am done on this side; turn me over." (More probably, Lawrence was beheaded, as was Sixtus, as was customary with Roman citizens.)

St. Lawrence met his death August 10, 258, and his feast is listed in the martyrologies as early as the fourth century. During the reign of the emperor Constantine, a church was built over his tomb in the catacomb on the Via Tiburtina. It was enlarged by Pelagius II (579–590) into the basilica now known as St. Lawrence outside the Walls (San Lorenzo fuori de Mura) and became one of the seven principal churches of Rome and a favorite place for Roman pilgrimages.

The torture and execution of a Roman citizen by Roman authorities made a deep impression on the young Church, which was stunned by such hostility, and his martyrdom was one of the first to be commemorated by the Church.

Lawrence is commemorated universally but especially in the West where hundreds of churches and many cities have him as their patron. In the middle ages, St. Lawrence's Day, the Feast of Saints Peter and Paul (June 29), and the Feast of St. Michael (September 29) became the feasts that divided the time after Pentecost (or after Trinity) into quarters. Lawrence was added to the Episcopal calendar in the 1979 Prayer Book, restored to the Lutheran calendar in the *Lutheran Book of Worship*, and included on the Methodist calendar in *For All the Saints*.

FOR FURTHER READING

Kennedy, V. L. *The Saints of the Canon of the Mass.* Vatican City, 1938.

AUGUST

READING

From a sermon by St. Augustine

The Church at Rome commends to us today the anniversary of the triumph of St. Lawrence. For on this day he trod the furious pagan world underfoot and flung aside its allurements, and so gained victory over Satan's attack on his faith.

As you have often heard, Lawrence was a deacon of the Church at Rome. There he distributed the sacred blood of Christ; there for the sake of Christ's Name he poured out his own blood. Saint John the apostle was clearly teaching us about the mystery of the Lord's Supper when he wrote, Christ "laid down his life for us—and we ought to lay down our lives for one another." [1 John 3:16]. Lawrence understood this, and, understanding, he acted on it. Just as he had partaken of a gift of self at the table of the Lord, so he prepared to offer such a gift of himself. In his life he loved Christ; in his death he followed in his footsteps.

We too must imitate Christ if we truly love him. We shall not be able to render a better return on that love than by modeling our lives on his. "Christ also suffered for you, leaving you an example, so that you should follow in his steps." [1 Peter 2:21] In saying this, the apostle Peter seems to have understood that Christ's passion is of no avail to those who do not follow him. The holy martyrs followed Christ even to shedding their life's blood, even to reproducing the very likeness of his passion. They followed him, but not they alone. It is not true that the bridge collapsed after the martyrs crossed; nor is it true that after they had drunk from it, the fountain of eternal life dried up.

In the Lord's garden are to be found not only the roses of his martyrs. In it there are also the lilies of the virgins, the ivy of wedded couples, and the violets of widows. On no account may any class of people despair, thinking that God has not called them. Christ died for all. What the Scriptures say of him is true: He "desires everyone to be saved and to come to the knowledge of the truth." [1 Tim. 2:4]

Let us understand, then, how a Christian must follow Christ apart from shedding blood for him, and when faith is not called upon to undergo the great test of the martyr's sufferings. The apostle Paul says that Christ our Lord, "Though he was in the form of God, did not regard equality with God as something to be exploited" (how unrivalled his majesty), "but emptied himself, taking the form of a slave, being born in human likeness and being found in human form." [Phil. 2:7] (How deep his humility.)

"Christ humbled himself." Christian, that is what you must make your own. "Christ became obedient." How then can you be proud? Only after his humbling was completed and death itself lay conquered, did Christ ascend into heaven. Let us follow him there, for we hear Paul saying, "If you have been raised with Christ, seek the things that are above, where Christ is, seated at the right hand of God." [Col. 3:1].

Sermon 304. Trans. PHP, based on *A Short Breviary* by the monks of St. John's Abbey and the English translation of the Office of Readings from the Liturgy of the Hours by the International Committee on English in the Liturgy.

PROPERS

Almighty God, you called your deacon Laurence to serve you with deeds of love, and gave him the crown of martyrdom: Grant that we, following his example, may fulfill your commandments by defending and supporting the poor, and by loving you with all our hearts; through Jesus Christ our Lord, who lives and reigns with you and the Holy Spirit, one God, forever and ever.

RS, trans. LFF

Readings: Psalm 112:1-9 *or* 126
              2 Corinthians 9:6-10
              John 12:24-26
Hymn of the Day:
              "How firm a foundation, O saints of the Lord" (H82 636, 637; LBW 507, LSB 728, ELW 796)
Prayers: For those who maintain and care for the property of the church
              For those who serve the poor and needy
              For a recognition of the true treasure of the church
              For courage and good humor to get us through times of frustration, misunderstanding, or persecution
Preface: A Saint (3) (BCP)
Color: Red

August 11

Clare, Abbess at Assisi, 1253

Clare, the founder of the Poor Clares, was born at Assisi *ca.* 1194 to a noble family. In her youth she refused two proposed marriages, but only after she came in contact with St. Francis in her native town did she make up her mind to "leave the world." At the age of eighteen, having heard St. Francis preach a Lenten sermon in her parish church, she left home secretly, and Francis put her in the care of Benedictine nuns at Bastia. Her family tried in vain to convince her to come home; she was joined by her sister and later on by her widowed mother. St. Francis installed them as the nucleus of a community in a house, drawing up a "way of life" for them, and this was the beginning of the order now known as the Poor Clares.

Clare obtained from Innocent III *ca.* 1215 permission for her nuns to live wholly on alms, the "privilege of poverty," without possessing any property whatsoever, either personal or communal. The Poor Clares' mode of life was more difficult than that of any other nuns of the time, and Clare had to fight for the maintenance of this life as designed by St. Francis. She knew the proper limitations, however, and wrote to a nun who had begun a convent in Prague not to overdo her austerities, "for our bodies are not made of brass." Clare, "the most authentic expression of evangelical perfection as understood by St. Francis of Assisi," guided her community for forty years, during many of which she was suffering from serious ill health. Nonetheless she outlived St. Francis by twenty-seven years and after a long illness died at Assisi on August 11, 1253. The Poor Clares are a contemplative order in both the Roman Catholic and the Anglican Churches.

Clare was included on the German Lutheran *Evangelical Calendar of Names* of 1962, the 1979 *Book of Common Prayer,* the Methodist calendar in *For All the Saints,* and the calendar in *Evangelical Lutheran Worship.*

FOR FURTHER READING

Armstrong, Regis. *Clare of Assisi: Early Documents.* St. Bonaventure: Franciscan Institute, 1993.

———— and Ignatius C. Brady. trans. *Francis and Clare: The Complete Works.* Mahwah: Paulist, 1983.

Mueller, Joan. *Clare of Assisi: The Letters to Agnes.* Collegeville: Liturgical, 2003.

Stace, Christopher. *Saint Clare of Assisi: Her Legend and Selected Writings.* London: SPCK, 2001.

Thomas of Celano. *The Life of St. Clare, Virgin.* Trans. Catherine Bolton Magrini. Assisi: Editrice Minerva, 2000.

READING

From a letter from Clare to Agnes of Prague

Happy indeed is she who is granted a place at the divine banquet, for she may cling with her inmost heart to him whose beauty the blessed hosts of heaven for ever adore; to him whose love inspires love, whose contemplation refreshes, whose generosity satisfies, whose gentleness delights, whose memory shines sweetly as the dawn; to him whose fragrance revives the dead, and whose glorious vision will bless all the citizens of that heavenly Jerusalem. For he is the splendor of eternal glory, "the reflection of eternal light and a spotless mirror." [Wis. 7:26]

Queen and bride of Jesus Christ, look into that mirror daily and study well your reflection, that you may adorn yourself, mind and body, with an enveloping garment of every virtue, and thus find yourself attired in flowers and gown befitting the daughter and most chaste bride of the King on high. In this mirror blessed poverty, holy humility, and ineffable love are also reflected. With the grace of God the whole mirror will be your source of contemplation.

Contemplate the birth of this Mirror, his poverty even as he was laid in the manger and wrapped in swaddling clothes. What wondrous humility, what marvelous poverty: the King of angels, the Lord of heaven and earth resting in a manger. Look more deeply into the Mirror and meditate on his humility, or simply on his poverty. Behold the many labors and sufferings he endured to redeem the human race. Then, in the depths of this very Mirror, ponder his unspeakable love which caused him to suffer on the wood of the cross and to endure the most shameful kind of death. The Mirror himself, from his position on the cross, warned passersby to weigh carefully this act, as he said, "All you who pass by, look and see if there is any sorrow like my sorrow." [Lam. 2:12] Let us answer his cries and lamentations with one voice and one spirit, "I will be mindful and remember, and my heart is wrung within me." [see Lam. 1:20] In this way, queen of the King of heaven, your love will burn with an even brighter flame.

Consider also his indescribable delights, his unending riches and honors, and sigh for what is beyond your love and your heart's content as you cry out, "Draw me after you. We will run after your drawn by your fragrant perfume, heavenly Spouse." Let me run and not faint until you lead me into your wine cellar; your left hand rests under my head, your right arm joyfully embraces me, and you kiss me with the sweet kiss of your lips. [see Song 1:4, 6, 2] When you contemplate all this, remember your poor mother and know that I have indelibly written your happy memory into my heart, for you are dearer to me than all the others.

From the English translation of the Office of Readings from the Liturgy of the Hours by the International Committee on English in the Liturgy, rev. PHP.

PROPERS

God of mercy, you instilled in your servant Clare the love of poverty: Grant that, inspired by her devotion, we may follow Christ in singleness of heart and come to the joyful vision of your glory, shown to us in Jesus Christ our Lord: who lives and reigns with you and the Holy Spirit, one God, now and forever.

Franciscan, RS, rev. PHP

Readings:	Song of Solomon 2:10-13
	Psalm 63:1-8 *or* 34:1-8
	Luke 12:32-37
Hymn of the Day:	
	"Jesus, the very thought of thee" (H82 642, SBH 481; alt. in LBW 316, ELW 754)
Prayers:	For all contemplatives
	For joy and simplicity in our own lives
	For increased devotion and love to Christ
Preface:	A Saint (2) (BCP)
Color:	White

AUGUST

August 13

Florence Nightingale, 1910; Clara Maass, 1901; Renewers of Society

The calendars in the *Lutheran Book of Worship* and *Evangelical Lutheran Worship* remember on this date two self-sacrificing nurses.

Florence Nightingale was born May 12, 1820, at Florence, Italy, and was named for the city in which she was born. Her parents were well-to-do, and she grew up in the family's homes in Derbyshire, Hampshire, and London. She received a large measure of her education from her father and became adept at languages.

She found social life unsatisfying, and February 7, 1837, she heard what she described as the voice of God telling her that she had a mission, although it was not yet specified.

Her study had made her an acknowledged expert on public health and hospitals. In 1846 a friend sent her the yearbook of the Kaiserswerth Motherhouse of Deaconesses. Her interest in the institution was aroused, and in 1850 she entered the school for training as a nurse. In 1853 she became the superintendent of the Institution for the Care of Sick Gentlewomen, but she was dissatisfied with the hospital.

The Crimean War broke out in March 1854, and reports of the conditions of the sick and wounded shocked Britain. Women were urged to serve as nurses like the French Sisters of Charity. Miss Nightingale, with thirty-eight nurses she had recruited, left for Turkey and arrived at Scutari, Turkey, November 5, 1854. They found conditions intolerable and the doctors hostile. A huge influx of wounded forced the officials to ask her help, however, and she worked hard and long, late into the night, and the picture was created of the "lady with the lamp." By May 1855 her concern shifted to the welfare of the British army. After sickness and struggle, her position as general superintendent of the Female Nursing Establishment of the Military Hospitals of the Army was confirmed March 16, 1856. Not until the last patient had left Barrack Hospital did Nightingale leave for England, where she had become a national hero. There she worked against considerable opposition for improvement in health and living conditions of the British soldiers. A Royal Commission on the Health of the Army was appointed in May of 1857, and a similar commission for the Army in India was authorized in 1859.

From 1857 Florence Nightingale was an invalid, suffering from chronic brucellosis, but she continued to work untiringly to keep up her enormous correspondence and to give advice from her sickbed to countless visitors. In 1860 she established, with funds subscribed in commemoration of her work in the Crimea, the Nightingale School for Nurses at St. Thomas Hospital. Her concern for the broader conditions of society led her to press for the reform of workhouses. In 1901 she became blind but nonetheless managed to continue her work. In 1907 she was awarded the Order of Merit—the first woman to be so honored. She died August 13, 1910, and in accordance with her wishes, she was buried in her family's grave in the churchyard of East Wellow, Hampshire, where her tombstone reads simply, "F. N. Born 1820. Died 1910."

Florence Nightingale was included on the calendar of the Anglican Church in Canada in 1959, the German Lutheran *Evangelical Calendar of Names* (1962) on August 14, on the calendar in the *Lutheran Book of Worship* (1978), in the Methodist *For All the Saints,* and the Episcopal calendar in *Lesser Feasts and Fasts* (2000) where she is remembered on August 12, August 13 being the commemoration of Jeremy Taylor. There have been repeated attempts to discredit her motivation, character, religion, and significance for nursing, but these attacks have generally not been convincing.

FOR FURTHER READING

Cook, Sir Edward. *The Life of Florence Nightingale.* 2 vols. London: Macmillan, 1913.

Woodham-Smith, Cecil. *Florence Nightingale: 1820–1910.* New York: McGraw-Hill, 1951. Reprinted 1964.

McDonald, Lynn *et al.,* eds. *The Collected Works of Florence Nightingale.* 7 vols. Waterloo: Wilfrid Laurier University, 2002.

McGinley, Phyllis. *Saint Watching*. New York: Viking, 1969.

Palmer, Alan. *The Banner of Battle: The Story of the Crimean War*. New York: St. Martin's, 1987.

Webb, Val. *Florence Nightingale: The Making of a Radical Theologian*. St. Louis: Chalice, 2002.

Clara Louise Maass was born June 28, 1876, in East Orange, New Jersey, the first of nine children of German immigrant parents, Hedwig and Robert Maass. At the age of fifteen, she began working at the Newark Orphans' Asylum and two years later entered the Christina Trefz Training School for Nurses at Newark German Hospital. She completed the two-year program in 1895 at the age of nineteen, one of the first five graduates of the school. At the age of twenty-one, she was named head nurse at Newark German Hospital, but in April 1898 she resigned her post at the hospital to volunteer as a contract nurse for the army during the Spanish-American War (1898–1899). She served in Jacksonville, Florida; Savannah, Georgia; and Santiago, Cuba; caring for large numbers of soldiers with malaria, typhoid fever, and dysentery until her discharge in February 1899. In November of the same year, she again responded to a call for contract nurses and was sent to the Philippines to care for soldiers with smallpox, typhoid, and yellow fever. There she contracted another tropical disease, breakbone, and was sent home.

Yellow fever, one of the scourges of the world, had killed more soldiers in the Spanish-American War than were killed in battle. A United States-Cuba research project in Havana singled out the mosquito as the probable transmitter of yellow fever. At the request of Major William Gorgas, chief sanitation officer of Havana, Clara Maass returned to Cuba in October 1900. A Cuban physician, Dr. Carlos Juan Finlay, had suggested that transmission of yellow fever was not by personal contact but rather through the stegomyia fasciata mosquito. Major Gorgas and Dr. John Guiteras hoped that by inducing a controlled case of the disease from a mosquito bite they could treat the light illness and help patients develop an immunity. Clara Maass was one of twenty people who responded to the call for subjects in experimentation. Her first mosquito bite led to a slight case of yellow fever from which she soon recovered. She agreed to be bitten a second time. This time the case was virulent, and ten days later, August 24, she died at the age of twenty-five. She was the only woman and the only American to give her life in the research which demonstrated that this acute, infectious tropical disease was caused by a virus transmitted by the bite of the yellow fever mosquito. The disease is now preventable.

She was buried in Havana, but the United States Army later moved her body to Fairmount Cemetery in Newark, her grave marked with a simple Army stone.

Leopoldine Guinther, Superintendent of Newark Memorial Hospital (formerly Newark German Hospital), moved by a portrait of Clara Maass, rescued the brave young nurse from obscurity, made her story known, and had the simple Army marker replaced with a pink granite gravestone with a bronze plaque.

In 1952 the name of the Newark German Hospital was changed to the Clara Maass Memorial Hospital. It has since moved to Belleville, New Jersey. Cuba issued a postage stamp honoring her in August 1951, the fiftieth anniversary of her death. In 1976, the centennial of her birth, a United States postage stamp was issued in her honor.

FOR FURTHER READING

Bullough, V. L., O. M. Church, and A. P. Stein, eds. *American Nursing: A Biographical Dictionary.* New York: Garland, 1988.

Cunningham, J. T. *Clara Maass: A Nurse, A Hospital, A Spirit.* Cedar Grove: Rae, 1968.

Guinther, Leopoldine. "A Nurse among the Heroes of the Yellow-Fever Conquest." *American Journal of Nursing* 32, no. 2 (February 1932): 173–76.

Herrmann, E. K. "Clara Louise Maass: Heroine or Martyr of Public Health?" *Public Health Nursing* 2, no. 1 (1985): 51–57.

Knollmueller, R. N. "Historical Perspective: Clara Louise Maass." *Public Health Nursing* 2, no. 3 (1985): 178–79.

Samson, J. "A Nurse Who Gave Her Life So That Others Could Live: Clara Maass." *Imprint* 37, no. 2 (1990): 81–82, 84, 87, et passim.

READING

From *Notes on Nursing* by Florence Nightingale

It seems a commonly received idea among men and even among women themselves that it requires nothing but a disappointment in love, the want of an object, a general disgust, or incapacity for other things, to turn a woman into a good nurse.

This reminds me of the parish where a stupid old man was set to be schoolmaster because he was "past keeping the pigs."

What cruel mistakes are sometimes made by benevolent men and women in matters of business about which they know nothing and think they know a great deal.

The everyday management of a large ward, let alone of a hospital—the knowing what are the laws of life and death for men, and what the laws of health for wards—(and wards are healthy or unhealthy, mainly according to the knowledge or ignorance of the nurse)—are not these matters of sufficient importance and difficulty to require learning by experience and careful inquiry, just as much as any other art? They do not come by inspiration to the lady disappointed in love, nor to the poor workhouse drudge hard up for a livelihood.

And terrible is the injury which has followed to the sick from such wild notions!

In this respect (and why is it so?), in Roman Catholic countries, both writers and workers are, in theory at least, far before ours. They would never think of such a beginning for a good working Superior or Sister of Charity. And many a Superior has refused to admit a *Postulant* who appeared to have no better "vocation" or reasons for offering herself than these.

It is true *we* make no vows. But is a "vow" necessary to convince us that the true spirit for learning any art, most especially the art of charity, aright, is not a disgust to everything or something else? Do we really place the love of our kind (and of nursing, as one branch of it) so low as this?

I would earnestly ask my sisters to keep clear of both the jargons now current everywhere (for they *are* equally jargons); of the jargon, namely, about "rights" of women, which urges women to do all that men do, including the medical and other professions, merely because men do it, and without regard to whether this is the best that women can do; and of the jargon which urges women to do nothing that men do, merely because they are women, and should be "recalled to a sense of their duty as women," and because "this is women's work," and "that is men's," and "these are things which women should not do," which is all assertion, and nothing more. Surely woman should bring the best she has, *whatever* that is, to the work of God's world, without attending to either of these cries. For what are they, both of them, the one *just* as much as the other, but listening to the "what people will say," to opinion, to the "voices from without"? And as a wise man has said, no one has ever done anything great or useful by listening to the voices from without.

You do not want the effect of your good things to be, "How wonderful for a *woman*!" nor would you be deterred from good things by hearing it said, "Yes, but she ought not to have done this, because it is not suitable for a woman." But you want to do the thing that is good, whether it is "suitable for a woman" or not.

It does not make a thing good, that it is remarkable that a woman should have been able to do it. Neither does it make a thing bad, which would have been good had a man done it, that it has been done by a woman.

Oh, leave these jargons, and go your way straight to God's work, in simplicity and singleness of heart.

Florence Nightingale, *Notes on Nursing* (New York: Dover, 1969 [1859, 1860]), 133–36.

PROPERS

God of compassion, courage, and love, you strengthened your servants Florence Nightingale and Clara Maass to give themselves in self-sacrificing service to those in need: Lead us by their examples of courageous service to give hope to the hopeless, love to the unloved, and peace to the dying; through Jesus Christ our Lord, who lives and reigns with you and the Holy Spirit, one God, now and forever.

PHP

Readings: Isaiah 58:6-11 *or* Ezekiel 34:11-16
                 Psalm 73:23-29
                 Matthew 25:31-46
Hymn of the Day:
                 "The Son of God goes forth to war" (LBW 183, LSB 661, H40 549) (Florence
                      Nightingale's favorite hymn, which she loved to quote: "who follows in his
                      train?")
Prayers: For nurses and all in the medical professions
                 For compassion, gentleness, and dedication
                 For courage to pursue new ways of service
                 For invalids that they might continue to find ways of service
Preface: A Saint (1) (BCP)
Color: White

ALSO ON AUGUST 13

Jeremy Taylor, Bishop of Down, Connor, and Dromore, 1667

Jeremy Taylor, a major influence on Anglican piety, was born in 1613 in Cambridge, the son of a barber. He was educated at Gonville and Caius College, of which he was elected a Fellow. He was ordained, and his fame as a preacher, although still a young man, came to the ears of William Laud, the Archbishop of Canterbury, who made him his chaplain. He became Vicar at Uppinham, and when the Civil War broke out, he supported King Charles against Parliament, and became a chaplain in the Royalist army. During the first years of the Commonwealth he lived quietly in Wales, but in 1658 he accepted a teaching post in Ireland. At the Restoration he was appointed Bishop of Down and Connor. To this was later added the small adjacent diocese of Dromore. As bishop, he worked tirelessly to rebuild churches, restore the use of the Prayer Book, and overcome continuing Puritan opposition. He died August 13, 1667, of a fever caught while visiting the sick of his diocese.

Taylor wrote two treatises on the real presence of Christ in the Eucharist, episcopacy, and moral theology. But he is chiefly remembered for his two little books on the Christian life, written while he was in forced retirement in Wales, *Holy Living* and *Holy Dying* (1651). They are characterized by a balanced sobriety and an insistence on a well-ordered piety that stresses temperance and moderation in all things. His continuing influence is through a prayer, "O God, whose days are without end," adapted from *Holy Dying,* which is in the burial office in the *Book of Common Prayer* (pp. 489, 504), in the *Lutheran Book of Worship* (p. 208, no. 282), and the 1958 Lutheran *Service Book and Hymnal* (p. 266). A second prayer by Taylor in the *Book of Common Prayer* is "for a child not yet baptized" (p. 444).

FOR FURTHER READING

Askew, Reginald. *Muskets and Altars: Jeremy Taylor and the Last of the Anglicans.* London: Mowbrays, 1997.

Carroll, Thomas K., ed. *Jeremy Taylor: Selected Works.* Mahwah: Paulist, 1990.

———. *Wisdom and Wasteland: Jeremy Taylor in His Prose and Preaching Today.* Dublin: Four Courts Press, 2001.

Porter, H. Boone. *Jeremy Taylor, Liturgist.* Alcuin Club Collections no. 61. London: SPCK, 1979.

READING

From *Holy Living* by Jeremy Taylor

AUGUST

God is present everywhere by his power. He rolls the orbs of heaven with his hand; he fixes the earth with his foot; he guides all the creatures with his eye, and refreshes them with his influence; he makes the powers of hell shake with his terrors, and binds the devils with his word, and throws them out with his command; and sends the angels on embassies with his decrees; he hardens the joints of infants, and confirms the bones, when they are fashioned beneath secretly in the earth. He it is that assists at the numerous production of fishes; and there is not one hollowness at the bottom of the sea, but he shows himself to be Lord of it by sustaining there the creatures that came to dwell in it; and in the wilderness, the bittern and the stork, the dragon and the satyr, the unicorn and the elk, live upon his provisions, and revere his power, and feel the force of his almightiness.

God is especially present in the hearts of his people, by his Holy Spirit: and indeed the hearts of holy men are temples in the truth of things, and, in type and shadow, they are heaven itself. For God reigns in the hearts of his servants: there is his kingdom. The power of grace hath subdued all his enemies: there is his power. They serve him night and day, and give him thanks and praise: that is his glory. This is the religion and worship of God in the temple. The temple itself is the heart of man; Christ is the High Priest, who from thence sends up the incense of prayers, and joins them to his own intercession, and presents all together to his Father; and the Holy Ghost, by dwelling there, hath also consecrated it into a temple; and God dwells in our heats by faith, and Christ by his Spirit, and the Spirit by his purities, so that we are also cabinets of the mysterious Trinity; and what is this short of heaven itself, but as infancy is short of manhood, and letters of words? The same state of life is, but it is not the same age. It is heaven in a looking glass, dark, but yet true, representing the beauties of the soul, and the graces of God, and the images of his eternal glory, by the reality of a special presence.

Jeremy Taylor, *Holy Living*, rev. and ed. by Thomas Smith (London: Henry G. Bohn, 1851), 20–23.

PROPERS

O God, whose days are without end, and whose mercies cannot be numbered:
Make us, like your servant Jeremy Taylor, deeply aware of the shortness and uncertainty of human life; and let your Holy Spirit lead us in holiness and righteousness all our days; through Jesus Christ our Lord, who lives and reigns with you
and the Holy Spirit, one God, now and forever.

Jeremy Taylor, BCP p. 504, SBH, rev. LFF

Readings:	Psalm 139:1-9 *or* 16:5-11
	Romans 14:7-9, 10b-12
	Matthew 24:42-47
Hymn of the Day:	
	"Awake, my soul, stretch every nerve" (H82 546, SBH 552)
Prayers:	For all bishops that they may be devoted to Christian learning and zealous in guarding the faith
	For all Christians in Ireland and for an increase of trust among them
	For the church in Ireland
	For all who write about the spiritual life
Preface:	A Saint (1) (BCP)
Color:	White

August 14

Maximilian Mary Kolbe, Priest, Martyr, 1941

The Roman Catholic Church has introduced on this date the commemoration
of Maximilian Mary Kolbe, priest and martyr. The commemoration is also
included on the Methodist calendar, the calendar in *Evangelical Lutheran Worship,*
and the 1997 calendar of the Church of England, the *Christian Year.*

Raymond Kolbe was born in 1894 near Lodz, in a part of Poland then under
Russian rule. He joined the Franciscan order in 1907 and took the name Maximilian. Because of his intense love for Mary Immaculate he added the name Mary
when he pronounced his solemn vows in 1914. He studied in Rome, was ordained
in 1919, and for a time taught church history in seminary. He founded an association to spread the Roman Catholic faith and to publish a periodical dealing
largely with a defense of Christianity. He built a friary west of Warsaw that eventually housed 762 Franciscans and founded friaries in Nagasaki and in India. In
1939 Germany invaded Poland. Kolbe's friary sheltered three thousand Poles and
fifteen hundred Jews and continued to publish a newspaper encouraging fidelity
to the Catholic faith.

In May 1941 the friary was closed and Kolbe and four companions were taken to Auschwitz where he surreptitiously carried on his priestly work, hearing confessions and celebrating Mass with bread and wine that were smuggled in. In July a man from Kolbe's bunker escaped. Ten were selected at random from the remaining men, among whom was Sergeant Francis Gajowniczek, a married man with a family. Father Maximilian offered to take the man's place. The commander, who had more use for a young man than for an older one in weak health, accepted the offer. The ten were placed in a large cell and left there to starve. After two weeks, only two were alive and only Kolbe was fully conscious. The two were killed with injections of carbolic acid on August 14, 1941.

READING

From Maximilian Kolbe, *The Knight of the Immaculate*

No one in the world can change Truth. What we can do and should do is to seek truth and to serve it when we have found it. The real conflict in an inner conflict. Beyond armies of occupation and the hecatombs of extermination camps, there are two irreconcilable enemies in the depth of every soul: good and evil, sin and love. And what are the victories on the battlefield if we ourselves are defeated in our innermost personal selves?

Mary Craig, Blessed Maximilian Kolbe—Priest Hero of a Death Camp, at http://www.ewtn.com/library/MARY/KOLBE2.htm (accessed November 16, 2007).

PROPERS

God of grace, you filled your priest and martyr Maximilian Kolbe with zeal for souls and love for his neighbor: through the example of this devoted servant of Mary Immaculate, grant that in our efforts to serve others for your glory we too may become like your Son Jesus Christ, who loved his own in the world, even to the end, and who now lives and reigns with you and the Holy Spirit, one God, now and forever.

RS, alt. PHP

Readings:	Wisdom 3:1-9 *or* 1 John 3:13-18
	Psalm 116:10-17
	John 15:12-16
Hymn of the Day:	
	"Do not despair, O little flock" (LBW 361)
Prayers:	For faithfulness in suffering and persecution
	For those who are imprisoned for the faith
	For kindness to others whatever our situation
Preface:	A Saint (3) (BCP)
Color:	Red

The Episcopal *Lesser Feasts and Fasts 1997* added on this date a commemoration of **Jonathan Myrick Daniels** (1939–1965), an Episcopal seminarian and witness for civil rights who was shot and killed in Haynesville, Alabama, August 20, 1965.

August 15

St. Mary the Virgin, Mother of Our Lord

In the person of the Virgin Mary, the church has seen an image of itself, the representative of the community of the faithful, a model of what each Christian ought to be: prayerful, humble, joyfully submissive to the will and word of God, devoted to her Son and loyal to him even when she did not understand him. The honor paid to her goes back to the earliest days of Christianity, and because she is the mother of the Redeemer she is accounted preeminent among the saints. The words of the song ascribed to her, the Magnificat, as well as her humble acceptance of the will of God bear more than accidental similarity to the Lord's Prayer and the Beatitudes of the Sermon on the Mount (Matt. 5:1-11). More is known about her than about most of the apostles.

Mary the mother of Jesus is mentioned in a number of places in the Gospels and the book of Acts, and a dozen incidents of her life are recorded: her betrothal to Joseph (Matt. 1:18); the annunciation by the angel that she was to bear the Messiah (Luke 1:26-38); her visitation to Elizabeth, the mother of John the Baptist (Luke 1:39-45); the birth of her Son (Matt. 1:24-25; Luke 2:1-7); the visits of the shepherds (Luke 2:8-20) and of the Magi (Matt. 2:1-12); the presentation of the infant Jesus in the Temple in accordance with the Law (Luke 2:22-38); the flight into Egypt (Matt. 2:13-15); the Passover visit to Jerusalem when Jesus was twelve (Luke 2:41-51); the wedding at Cana in Galilee (John 2:1-11); her presence at the crucifixion when her Son commended her to the care of St. John (John 19:25-27); and meeting with the apostles in the upper room after the ascension, waiting for the promised Spirit (Acts 1:14). She is thus pictured as being present at all the important events of her Son's life.

The other books of the New Testament are silent about Mary. St. Paul, not recording her name, says simply that Jesus was "born of a woman" (Gal. 4:4). Little is known about the rest of her life, which traditions say she spent in Jerusalem (the tomb of the Virgin is shown in the Kidron Valley) or Ephesus. The second-century *Protoevangelium of James* identifies her parents as Anne and Joachim (see July 26).

The angel's words in Luke 1:32 imply that Mary was descended from David (or that the early church believed that she was descended from David). She is a model of bold but tender love: she stood at the cross to watch her Son die as an enemy of the state; Jesus' brothers are not reported to have been present. The earliest feasts celebrating her death were observed in Palestine from the fifth century, possibly at Antioch in the fourth century. The date of August 15, ordered by the emperor Maurice (582–603), probably originated with the dedication of a church in her honor. By the sixth century the observance of the date of August 15 was widespread in the East, and the feast day gradually became known as the Feast of the Dormition (*Koimesis*), the "Falling Asleep," or passing from this life, of the Virgin. In the seventh century this feast day was observed in Rome, and from there it spread throughout the West, where by the ninth century it had come to be called the Feast of the Assumption (referring to the reception of Mary's body and soul into heaven in anticipation of the general resurrection of the bodies of all the dead at the last day). The belief, apparently unknown to Ambrose (d. 397) and Epiphanius (d. 403), appears in certain New Testament apocrypha from the latter fourth century and was first formulated in orthodox circles in the West by Gregory of Tours (d. 594). In the East, writings of Germanus, Patriarch of Constantinople, and other seventh-century authors testify to the acceptance of the doctrine. In 1950 Pope Pius XII proclaimed that the teaching of the Assumption was elevated to the status of a dogma in the Roman Catholic Church.

The feast day of the Virgin Mary remained on some Lutheran calendars well beyond the Reformation. The Church Orders of Nassau (1536) and Mark Brandenburg (1540) retained the Assumption; the Schwäbish Hall calendar designated the day as "The Departure of Mary"; Martin Luther in his *Festpostils* (1527) wrote sermons for the Assumption and in his 1523 pamphlet "Concerning the Order of Public Worship" advised that as a sign of continuity and order the festivals of the Nativity of Mary, the Purification, the Annunciation, and the Assumption be observed among Evangelical Catholics. Nonetheless, in reaction to what was perceived as the excessive attention of the Roman Catholic Church, the remembrance of Mary eventually disappeared in Lutheran Churches. The other days on the calendar associated with Mary—the Presentation, the Annunciation, and the Visitation—were retained on Lutheran calendars because they are events in the life of Christ.

The commemoration of Mary was added to the calendar in the *Lutheran Book of Worship* (1978) and the 1979 *Book of Common Prayer*. The drafters of the Lutheran calendar, fearing lingering anti-Catholic sentiment, did not give Mary the title *Saint*, even though the title was applied to all the apostles and the Evangelists and St. Paul, and simply identified her has the "mother of our Lord." The service book published by the Lutheran Church—Missouri Synod, *Lutheran Worship*

(1982), however, called the mother of Jesus "St. Mary." Her title on the Episcopal calendar is "Saint Mary the Virgin, Mother of our Lord Jesus Christ."

Mary's perpetual virginity (virgin before, during, and after the birth of Jesus) is first asserted in the apocryphal book of James, may have been taught by Irenaeus (see June 28) and Clement of Alexandria, and was certainly held by Athanasius (d. 373; see May 2) who used the term "ever virgin." The teaching was accepted by East and West from the fifth century onward and was given additional impetus at the Council of Ephesus (431), which upheld the title *Theotokos* (bearer of God), common from the fourth century.

A feast of the Conception of Mary on December 8 (see the Nativity of Mary, September 8) was known from the seventh century. Her immaculate conception (that Mary, by divine dispensation, was conceived without sin) was a matter of dispute through the Middle Ages. It was denied by Anselm, Bernard, and Thomas Aquinas. The doctrine was defined for the Roman Catholic Church December 8, 1854; it is denied in the East, which observes a Feast of Conception of the Virgin Mary on December 9.

FOR FURTHER READING

Anderson, H. George, J. Francis Stafford, Joseph A. Burgess, eds. *The One Mediator, the Saints, and Mary.* Lutherans and Catholics in Dialogue VIII. Minneapolis: Augsburg, 1992.

Blancy, Alian, Maurice Jourjon, and the Dombes Group. *Mary in the Plan of God and in the Communion of Saints.* Mahwah: Paulist, 2002.

Braaten, Carl E. and Robert W. Jenson, eds. *Mary, Mother of God.* Grand Rapids: Eerdmans, 2004.

Brown, Raymond E., Karl P. Donfried, Joseph A. Fitzmyer, John Reumann, eds. *Mary in the New Testament.* Philadelphia: Fortress Press, 1978.

Duckworth, Penelope. *Mary: the Imagination of Her Heart.* Cambridge: Cowley, 2004.

Gaventa, Beverly Roberts. *Mary: Glimpses of the Mother of Jesus.* Minneapolis: Fortress Press, 1999.

Johnson, Maxwell E. *The Virgin of Guadalupe: Theological Reflections of an Anglo-Lutheran Liturgist.* Lanham: Rowman and Littlefield, 2002.

O'Carroll, Michael ed. *Theotokos: A Theological Encyclopedia of the Blessed Virgin Mary.* Wilmington: Glazier, 1982.

Pelikan, Jaroslav. *Mary Through the Centuries: Her Place in the History of Culture.* New Haven: Yale University Press, 1996.

———, David Flusser, Justin Lang. *Mary: Images of the Mother of Jesus in Jewish and Christian Perspective.* Philadelphia: Fortress Press, 1986.

Shoemaker, Stephen J. *The Ancient Traditions of the Virgin Mary's Dormition and Assumption.* New York: Oxford University Press, 2002.

READING

From "The Magnificat" by Martin Luther

For he who is mighty has done great things for me,
and holy is his name.

The "great things" are nothing less than that she became the Mother of God, in which work so many and such great good things are bestowed on her as pass man's understanding. For on this there follows all honor, all blessedness, and her unique place in the whole of mankind, among which she has no equal, namely, that she had a child by the Father in heaven, and such a Child. She herself is unable to find a name for this work, it is too exceedingly great; all she can do is break out in the fervent cry: "They are great things," impossible to describe or define. Hence men have crowded all her glory into a single word, calling her the Mother of God. [The "single word" is the Greek *Theotokos*, God-bearer, a favorite title for Mary in the Eastern Church.] No one can say anything greater of her or to her, though he had as many tongues as there are leaves on the trees, or grass in the fields, or stars in the sky, or sand by the sea. It needs to be pondered in the heart what it means to be the Mother of God.

Luther's Works, vol. 21, ed. Jaroslav Pelikan (St. Louis: Concordia, 1956), 326.

PROPERS

O God, you have taken to yourself the blessed Virgin Mary, mother of your incarnate Son: Grant that we, who have been redeemed by his blood, may share with her the glory of your eternal kingdom; through Jesus Christ our Lord, who lives and reigns with you and the Holy Spirit, one God, now and forever.

South African BCP, rev. BCP, LBW

Readings:	Isaiah 61:10-11 (LBW 61:7-11)
	Psalm 34 or 34:1-9 (LBW Psalm 45:11-16)
	Galatians 4:4-7
	Luke 1:46-55
Hymn of the Day:	
	"Sing of Mary, pure and lowly" (H82 277; alt. in *Hymnal Supplement 1991*, 756)
	"Ye watchers and ye holy ones" (LBW 175, LSB 670, ELW 424)
	"Blest are the pure in heart" (H82 656, SBH 394)
Prayers:	For the poor and the forgotten
	For a deeper understanding of the mystery of the incarnation
	For the gift of glad obedience to the word of God
	For faithfulness to Christ
Preface:	Christmas/Incarnation
Color:	White

August 16

Stephen, King of Hungary, 1038

Stephen was born at Esztergom *ca.* 969 and was baptized in his fifth year with his father Duke Geza by St. Aalbert of Prague. In 995 he married Gisela, sister of the emperor Henry II and in 997 succeeded to his father's dukedom. Having bestowed order on the country and consolidated his position, he received a royal crown from Pope Sylvester II and in 1001 was crowned the first king of Hungary. The crown sent to Stephen by the pope was carried off to Bohemia in 1270 and disappeared. A substitute crown was made with a distinctive skewed cross. Called mistakenly "the crown of St. Stephen," it was taken to the United States in 1945 at the end of World War II, but it was finally returned to Hungary in 1978, after communist rule ended.

The Byzantine Church had undertaken the evangelization of Hungary, but by the eleventh century was compromised because the Eastern Church had lost its ancient prestige. King Stephen, aware of the political dangers inherent in this situation, chose to adopt the manners and culture of the West and worked energetically for the conversion of his people to Christianity, setting up dioceses after the Roman pattern and establishing monasteries. His methods with recalcitrant pagans, however, were marked by the roughness of the age and place, and at times there was a lively resistance, supported by his political rivals.

Stephen holds an honored place in Hungarian history and seems personally to have a better claim to the title of saint than some other royal and national heroes. His last years were embittered by ill health and the shameless quarrels among his relatives over succession to the crown. Stephen had taken much trouble to train his only son Emeric (Imre) to succeed him, but he died prematurely, killed in a hunting accident in 1031. Stephen died at Buda August 15, 1038, and was buried in the basilica on August 20; in Hungary this date is observed as his feast day. His relics were enshrined in 1083, at the same time as those of his son, who is also revered as a saint. Stephen's feast day on the present Roman calendar is August 16.

FOR FURTHER READING

Kelleher, P. J. *The Holy Crown of Hungary.* Rome: American Academy in Rome, 1951.

Klaniczay, Gabor. *The Uses of Supernatural Power: The Transformation of Popular Religion in Medieval and Early Modern Europe.* Princeton: Princeton University Press, 1990.

Kosztolnyik, Z. J. *Five Eleventh Century Hungarian Kings: Their Politics and Their Relations with Rome.* New York: Eastern European Monographs, 1981.

Molnar, Miklos. *A Concise History of Hungary.* Trans. Anna Magyar. New York: Columbia University Press, 2002.

READING

From Stephen's admonitions to his son

My dearest son, if you desire to honor the royal crown, I advise, I counsel, I urge you above all things to maintain the Catholic and apostolic faith with such diligence and care that you may be an example for all those placed under you by God and that all the clergy may rightly call you a genuine Christian. Failing to do this, you may be sure that you will not be called a Christian or a son of the Church. Indeed, in the royal palace after the faith itself, the Church holds second place, first founded as she was by our head, Christ; then transplanted, firmly constituted and spread through the whole world by his members, the apostles and holy fathers. She is always producing new children, even though in some places she has existed since antiquity.

Dearest son, even now in our kingdom the Church is proclaimed as young and newly planted; and for that reason she needs more prudent and trustworthy guardians lest what the divine mercy, despite our unworthiness, bestowed on us should be destroyed and annihilated through your idleness, indolence or neglect.

My beloved son, delight of my heart, hope of your posterity, I pray, I command, that at every time and in everything, strengthened by your devotion to me, you may show favor not only to relations and kin, or to the most eminent, be they leaders or wealthy or neighbors or fellow-countrymen, but also to foreigners and to all who come to you. By fulfilling your duty in this way you will reach the highest state of happiness. Be merciful to all who are suffering violence, keeping always in your heart the example of the Lord who said, "I desire mercy and not sacrifice." [Hosea 6:6 AV] Be patient with everyone, not only with the powerful, but also with the weak.

Finally be strong lest prosperity lift you up too much or adversity cast you down. Be humble in this life, that God may raise you up in the next. Be truly moderate, punishing no one unduly. Be gentle so that you may never oppose justice. Be honorable so that you may never knowingly bring disgrace upon anyone. Be chaste, avoiding lust like the pangs of death.

All these virtues make up the royal crown, and without them no one is fit to rule here on earth or reach the heavenly kingdom.

Chaps. 1, 2, 10. From the English translation of the Office of Readings from the Liturgy of the Hours by the International Committee on English in the Liturgy, rev. PHP.

AUGUST

PROPERS

Almighty Father, heavenly king, your servant Stephen of Hungary fostered the growth of your Church on earth: Grant that we, following his example, may by our prayer and labors support the growth of your Church in our time and land; through your Son, Jesus Christ our Lord, who lives and reigns with you and the Holy Spirit, one God, now and forever.

1952 Roman Missal, RS rev. PHP

Readings:	Micah 6:6-8
	Psalm 9:1-10
	Romans 8:26-30
	Luke 12:35-40
Hymn of the Day:	
	"O where are kings and empires now" (SBH 154, H40 382)
Prayers:	For Christian kings and queens
	For the increase of virtues in all who have authority in the nations of the world
	For the strengthening of the church everywhere
Preface:	A Saint (2) (BCP)
Color:	White

ALSO ON AUGUST 16

The *Lutheran Service Book*, following Wilhelm Löhe's calendar, commemorates the patriarch *Isaac* on this date. His story is given in Genesis 21ff.

August 17

The *Lutheran Service Book* on this date commemorates *Johann Gerhard* (1582–1637), the Lutheran theologian and ardent controversialist who taught at Jena from 1616 until his death. His massive *Loci Theologici* became a standard compendium of Lutheran theology. His devotional masterpiece, *Meditationes Sacrae*, went through many editions in many languages.

August 18

The *Book of Common Prayer* remembers on this date *William Porcher* [por-SHAY] *DuBose* (1836–1918), "probably the most original and creative thinker that the American Episcopal Church has ever produced," who taught at the University of the South, in Sewanee, Tennessee.

August 20

Bernard, Abbot of Clairvaux, 1153

Bernard, the third of seven children, was born of noble lineage at Fontaines-les-Dijon, a village near Dijon, France, in 1090. He studied at a monastic school. His mother died when he was seventeen, and he was deeply affected. In the year 1111 Bernard withdrew from the world and was soon joined by four of his five brothers and other relatives. At Citeaux, a recently founded Benedictine monastery and motherhouse of the Cistercian Order, they followed the strict rule of the Cistercians with excessive asceticism. After three years Bernard was chosen abbot of a new monastery. With twelve companions he chose the valley near the Aube, called Clara Vallisor Clairvaux. There he was ordained priest. He carefully organized and strengthened the new monastery as a model of strict observance and established sixty-eight other houses. From a debate with the great Benedictine monastery at Cluny grew his friendship with its abbot, Peter the Venerable.

In 1130 the Western Church was fractured when two rival popes were elected, representing two factions in the college of cardinals. Bernard sought tirelessly to secure the recognition of Innocent II and eventually won the recognition of one of his own monks and pupil, Eugenius III, in 1145, and so the schism was healed.

Skilled in controversy and convinced of the correctness of his views, Bernard led the opposition to those he perceived as heretics, notably the popular teacher Abelard. In 1146–1147 he led the preaching of the Second Crusade and was sharply disappointed by its failure.

By modern standards, Bernard was wrong on almost every count. Yet, despite his authoritarianism, Bernard was a man of spiritual attractiveness, powerful eloquence, zealous in defense of the faith. His theology is characterized by a desire to deepen the inner experience of prayer and contemplation, and he enriched the devotion of the church by his mystical writings and by the hymns he either wrote or inspired, such as "Jesus, the very thought of thee," "Light of the anxious heart," "O sacred Head, now wounded." In his zeal he attacked the luxury of the clergy, the persecution of the Jews, and the abuses of the Roman curia. Renowned as a great preacher, he brought to an end the prescholastic era, and he is therefore sometimes called "the last of the Fathers."

Bernard died at his monastery August 20, 1153. He was canonized in 1174, proclaimed a Doctor of the Church in 1830, and given the title "Doctor Melliflu-ous" (mellifluous teacher) in 1953, the eight hundredth anniversary of his death. He was added to the calendar in the 1979 *Book of Common Prayer,* the *Lutheran Book of Worship* (following the *Evangelical Calendar of Names),* and the Methodist *For All the Saints.*

FOR FURTHER READING

Bernard of Clairvaux. *Bernard of Clairvaux: Selected Works.* Trans. G. R. Evans.
 New York: Paulist, 1987.

Bredero, Adrian H. *Bernard of Clairvaux: Between Cult and History.* Edinburgh:
 T&T Clark, 1997.

Daniel-Rops, Henri. *Bernard of Clairvaux.* New York: Hawthorne, 1964.

———. *Bernard of Clairvaux and the Cistercian Spirit.* Trans. Claire Lavoie. Kalamazoo: Cistercian, 1976.

Evans, G. R. *The Mind of St. Bernard of Clairvaux.* Oxford: Clarendon, 1983.

Leclercq, Jean. *The Love of Learning and the Desire for God: A Study of Monastic Culture.* Trans. Catherine Misrah. New York: Fordham University Press, 1961.

Scott-James, Bruno. *Saint Bernard of Clairvaux.* London, 1957.

Williams, W. E. *Saint Bernard of Clairvaux.* Westminster: Newman, 1952.

READING

From *On the Love of God,* VII, by St. Bernard

The cause of our loving God is God, for he is both origin of our love and its final
goal. He is himself the occasion of human love; he also gives the power to love and
brings desire to its consummation. In his essential being he is himself the Lovable
One, and he provides himself as the object of our love. He desires that our love for
him result in our happiness, not that it be empty and void. His love both opens up
the way for our love and is our love's reward. How kindly does he lead us in love's
way, how generously he returns the love we give, how sweet is he to those who wait
for him! He is rich to all who call upon him, for he can give them nothing better than
himself. He gave himself to be our Righteousness, and he keeps himself to be our
great Reward. He sets himself to the refreshment of our souls and spends himself to
free the prisoners. You are good, Lord, to the soul that seeks you. What, then are you
to the soul that finds you? The marvel is, no one can seek you who has not found you
already. You desire us to find so that we may seek so that we may find. We can both
seek you and find you, but we can never anticipate you, for though we say "Early
shall my prayer come before you" (Psalm 88:13), a chilly, loveless thing that prayer
would be, were it not warmed by your own breath and born of your own Spirit.

Trans. PHP, based on a translation by "A Religious of C.S.M.V." (1950), included in the *Late
Medieval Mysticism,* ed. Ray C. Petry, Library of Christian Classics 13, (Philadelphia: Westminster, n.d.), 59–60. The hymn "Jesus, the very thought of thee" derives from this passage.

PROPERS

Almighty God, your servant Bernard of Clairvaux was filled with zeal for your
house and was a radiant light in your Church: Grant that we, like him, may be
filled with your zealous Spirit, and walk always as children of light; through your

Son Jesus Christ our Lord, who lives and reigns with you and the Holy Spirit, one God, now and forever.

Cistercian, RS, rev. PHP

Readings:	Ecclesiasticus 39:1-10
	Psalm 139:1-9 *or* 19:7-11 (12-14)
	John 15:7-11
Hymn of the Day:	
	"Jesus, the very thought of thee" (H82 642, SBH 481; alt in LBW 316, ELW 754)
Prayer:	For a deepened life of prayer
	For grace to contemplate the life of Christ
	For wisdom to discern the paths to truth
	For more vocations to the religious life
	For all who hold positions of responsibility and influence in the church
Preface:	A Saint (1) (BCP)
Color:	White

AUGUST

ALSO ON AUGUST 20

The Eastern Church on this date commemorates the prophet **Samuel**. The calendar in the *Lutheran Service Book* (2006), following Wilhelm Löhe, also lists Samuel on this date.

August 24

St. Bartholomew, Apostle

Prominence, as the Gospel appointed in the *Book of Common Prayer* for St. Bartholomew's Day (Luke 22:24-30) declares, has no correlation with importance in the apostolic mission. Nothing certain is known of Bartholomew, not even his name.

Bartholomew appears in the New Testament simply as one of the twelve apostles listed in the Gospels of Matthew (10:3), Mark (3:18), and Luke (6:14), and again in Acts (1:13). The name is a patronymic representing the Aramaic "son of Tolmai [Ptolmey]" (cf. Simon Bar-jonah in Matthew 16:17). Bar-tholomew may therefore have another, personal name. In the Synoptic lists he is joined with Philip. In the Fourth Gospel, however, Philip is associated with Nathanael (1:45) rather than Bartholomew, and it is sometimes suggested that the apostle's given name was Nathanael. The identification of Nathanael with Bartholomew, dating from the ninth century, is reflected in the Roman Catholic and Lutheran Gospel for the day. (The previous Roman Catholic Gospel was Luke 6:12-19.) Nathanael was from the town of Cana in Galilee where Jesus performed his first miracle. He was invited to discipleship by Philip, who told him that he and Andrew and Peter had found the Messiah in the person of Jesus of Nazareth. At first Nathanael was doubtful, but after a word from Jesus, he followed. Early patristic writers suggest that Nathanael was not one of the Twelve and stands in St. John's Gospel as a representative of Israel coming to God.

The story of his call (John 1:45-51) is all that is recorded in the New Testament of the life of Nathanael, but there are several traditions about the life and labors of Bartholomew. Some sources credit Bartholomew with having written a Gospel, the existence of which was known to Jerome and Bede, but which is now lost. Bartholomew is variously reported to have preached in Asia Minor, Mesopotamia, Persia, and India. In connection with India, Eusebius says that Bartholomew left a copy of the Gospel of Matthew in Hebrew that Pantaenus of Alexandria, a missionary of the second half of the second century, found there in the hands of the local people. Most of these stories agree that St. Bartholomew spent his last years preaching in Armenia and was flayed and beheaded in Albanus (modern Derbend) on the Caspian coast. He is so represented in the white marble statue by Cibo in the Milan Cathedral. In the Sistine Chapel in Michelangelo's fresco of the last judgment, the flayed Bartholomew is portrayed in a prominent place near Christ the Judge. The Armenian Church believes that the apostles Bartholomew and Thaddeus were the first to bring the Gospel to the Armenians, and that Bartholomew spent a number of years there before his death. The Armenian Church commemorates him on two days during the year: once together with St. Thaddeus and again together with another Armenian martyr.

A very different story of Bartholomew's mission appears in the traditions of the Coptic and Ethiopian Churches, which also revere him highly, observing his feast day on August 29. Their accounts tell of his preaching at an oasis in Upper Egypt (there is a special commemoration of the event on November 15), then going among the Berbers where he was rescued from wild beasts by a cannibal, and finally preaching along the coast of North Africa where a local king, Agrippa, had him sewn into a leather bag and dropped into the sea.

Bartholomew's relics are venerated in the tenth-century Church of St. Bartholomew on the island Isola Tiberina in Rome. He is the patron of the city and the cathedral of Frankfurt, which claims to possess his skull.

The collect of the day in the *Book of Common Prayer* and in the *Lutheran Book of Worship* (and formerly in the Roman Missal) derives from the Leonine sacramentary. The prayer may appear as vague as the details of Bartholomew's life, but, in fact, in the concise manner of the collect form, it is quite precise. "What he believed" and "what he taught" is not to imply *sotto voce,* "Whatever that was." Rather, the prayer asks God to preserve the church on the apostolic foundation, believing, teaching, and preaching the word of God.

August 24 has been St. Bartholomew's feast day on calendars of the Western church since the eighth century, but the reason for the date is not known. The Eastern Orthodox Churches commemorate him with St. Barnabas on June 11.

In European history St. Bartholomew's Day is remembered for the massacre of Protestants that took place on this day in Paris in 1572.

FOR FURTHER READING

Browne, D. "Who was Nathanael?" *Expository Times* 38 (1927): 286.

Goodspeed, E. J. *The Twelve: The Story of the Apostles.* New York: Holt, Rinehart, Winston, 1963 [1957].

Scott, R. B. Y. "Who was Nathanael?" *Expository Times* 38 (1927): 93–94.

READING

From *The Living God* by Nathan Söderblom

Great men of genius when serving God consciously and with all their hearts be-long to the saints. The doctrine of saints lost its importance in Evangelic theology when the cult of the saints was abolished in the name of the Gospel. In this matter I agree with the Roman Church and its theology in so far as the saints are Christian men and women who specially reveal the power of God. But divine power ought not to be assigned in a primitive way to extraordinary cases of suggestion. It ought not to be defined as a miracle, but be regarded in accordance with a Christian conception of God.

A place of honor is due to those saints of religion who have put their whole soul into seeing and apprehending God's will in *history*. It is on that purpose that I put "serving" first and then "apprehending." For in God's kingdom and in the realm of the Spirit and of moral truth, man can see nothing, so long as he is standing as a mere spectator; only those who serve God fully and self-sacrificingly can perceive God's will. In other things one usually wants to look ahead and to understand before undertaking anything. But in God's kingdom it is the reverse.

Where God's rule has penetrated man's heart and life, so that the divine love and righteousness become the main factor, we speak of a saint. . . . Here I give only my definition: a saint is he who reveals God's might. Saints are such as show clearly and plainly in their lives and deeds and in their very being that God lives.

Nathan Söderblom, *The Living God*. Basal Forms of Personal Religion, The Gifford Lectures 1931 (London: Oxford, 1933), 367, 386.

PROPERS

Almighty and everlasting God, who gave to your apostle Bartholomew grace truly to believe and to preach your Word: Grant that your Church may love what he

believed and preach what he taught; through your Son Jesus Christ our Lord, who
lives and reigns with you and the Holy Spirit, one God, forever and ever.

Leonine sacramentary, trans. 1549 BCP; LBW; alt. in ELW

Readings:	Deuteronomy 18:15-18 *or* Exodus 19:1-6
	Psalm 91 *or* 12
	1 Corinthians 4:9-15 *or* 12:27-31a
	Luke 22:24-30 *or* John 1:43-51
Hymn of the Day:	
	"You servants of God, your Master proclaim" (H82 535, LBW 252, ELW 825)
Prayers:	For the church in Armenia
	For grace and strength to recognize the Son of God
	For strength and guidance to find ways of serving him
	For the gift of innocence and purity of heart
Preface:	Apostles
Color:	Red

August 25

Louis, King of France, 1270

Louis was born on April 25, 1214, at Poissy, and was crowned Louis IX, King of
France, at Rheims on November 29, 1226, when he was twelve years old. He would
rather have been a monk. His mother, Blanche of Castille, was a devout woman, who
exercised a profound and lasting influence on her son's spiritual development. In
1235 he took over the government of his kingdom from the regency of his mother.
A man of unusual integrity and purity of life, he was sincerely committed to his faith
and to its moral demands. He had a loveable personality, was a kind husband to his
wife, Margaret of Province, a father of eleven children, and at the same time a strict
ascetic. He walked barefoot, but wore soleless shoes so that his private penance would
not be obvious. Like Joan of Arc after him, he detested profane or blasphemous language; he would never use it himself and would not tolerate it in his presence.

Throughout his life, Louis was diligent in attending divine worship, and his
charities, both open and secret, were constant. He took a lively interest in the
theological issues of the day. Louis's involvement in the crusades in the Middle
East and North Africa was typical of the piety of the time. He led a crusade to
the East in 1248 and easily took the port of Damietta in Egypt, but in 1250 the
crusaders were routed at Mansurah and Louis himself was taken prisoner. He
returned to France after an absence of six years. In 1270 Louis again sailed with an
army, mobilized after much difficulty, and eight weeks later he died of dysentery

at Tunis in North Africa on August 25, 1270. He was buried in the basilica of St. Denis near Paris. After his canonization in 1297, his relics were transferred to the Sainte Chapelle, the exquisite Gothic chapel that he had built in 1248 as a shrine for the crown of thorns and other relics of Jesus' passion.

He personified the highest ideals of a medieval Christian ruler. He is on the General Roman Calendar and was added to the Episcopal calendar by the 1979 *Book of Common Prayer.*

FOR FURTHER READING

Le Goff, Jacques. *Saint Louis.* Paris: Gallinard, 1996.
Jordan, William Chester. *Louis IX and the Challenge of the Crusade.* Princeton: Princeton University Press, 1979.
Richard, Jean. *Saint Louis: Crusader King of France.* Trans. Jean Birrell. New York: Columbia University Press, 1992.

READING

From a spiritual testament to his son by Saint Louis

My dearest son, my first instruction is that you should love the Lord your God with all your heart and with all your strength. Without this there is no salvation. Keep yourself, my son, from everything that you know displeases God, that is to say, from every mortal sin. You should permit yourself to be tormented by every kind of martyrdom before you would allow yourself to commit a mortal sin.

If the Lord has permitted you to have some trial, bear it willingly and with gratitude, considering that it has happened for your good and that perhaps you well deserved it. If the Lord bestows upon you any kind of prosperity, thank him humbly and see that you become no worse for it, either through vain pride or anything else, because you ought not to oppose God or offend him in the matter of his gifts.

Listen to the divine office with pleasure and devotion. As long as you are in church, be careful not to let your eyes wander and not to speak empty words, but pray to the Lord devoutly, either aloud or with the interior prayer of the heart.

Be kindhearted to the poor, the unfortunate, and the afflicted. Give them as much help and consolation as you can. Thank God for all the benefits he has bestowed upon you, that you may be worthy to receive greater. Be just to your subjects, swaying neither to right nor left, but holding the line of justice. Always side with the poor rather than with the rich, until you are certain of the truth. See that all your subjects live in justice and peace, but especially those who have ecclesiastical rank and who belong to religious orders.

Be devout and obedient to our mother the Church of Rome and the Supreme Pontiff as your spiritual father. Work to remove all sin from your land, particularly blasphemies and heresies.

Finally, dearest son, I give you every blessing that a loving father can give a son. May the three Persons of the Holy Trinity and all the saints protect you from every evil. And may the Lord give you the grace to do his will so that he may be served and honored through you, that in the next life we may together come to see him, love him and praise him unceasingly. Amen.

From the English translation of the Office of Readings from the Liturgy of the Hours by the International Committee on English in the Liturgy, rev. PHP

PROPERS

O God, you called your servant Louis of France to an earthly throne that he might advance your heavenly kingdom, and gave him zeal for your Church and love for your people: Mercifully grant that we who commemorate him this day may be fruitful in good works, and attain to the glorious crown of your saints; through Jesus Christ our Lord, who lives and reigns with you and the Holy Spirit, one God, forever and ever.

RS, rev. LFF

Readings:	Wisdom 3:1-9
	Psalm 21:1-7 *or* 112:1-9
	Luke 12:22-31
Hymn of the Day:	
	"Jesus, I will ponder now on thy holy passion" (LBW 115, LSB 440, ELW 345)
	or "The head that once was crowned with thorns" (H82 483, LBW 173, LSB 532, ELW 432)
Prayers:	For the church and people of France
	For all Christian rulers and all engaged in the business of government
	For those who administer justice
	For all who have power and authority in political, economic, and social life
Preface:	Baptism (BCP, LBW)
Color:	White

August 27

Monica, Mother of Augustine, 387

The mother of Augustine was born of Christian parents in North Africa, probably at Tagaste in Numidia, about 322. She married a pagan official Patricius, a man of violent temper but who treated her respectfully and whom she converted to Christianity just before he died in 371. After she bore Augustine, Monica seems to have had two other children, a son, Navigius, and a daughter, Perpetua.

She followed her elder son's career with pride and attention and had him enrolled as a catechumen to prepare for baptism. Apprehensive at her son's waywardness, she prayed for his conversion, and in 383 she followed him to Rome and then to Milan where he came under the influence of Bishop Ambrose. She tried to arrange a marriage for her son, but this hope was frustrated although her prayers were answered when her son was baptized and converted to a celibate life.

Following her son's baptism, the two planned to return to North Africa in the fall of 387. But at Ostia, Monica fell sick and, after sharing a beautifully mystical experience with her son, died and was buried there.

In 1162 her bones were removed to an Augustinian monastery near Arras, France, and her cult spread throughout the Western Church. Other relics of her were brought to the Church of St. Agostino (Augustine) in Rome in 1430. A fragment of her actual tombstone has been discovered at Ostia, on which her name was spelled Monnica, and it is spelled thus on the Episcopal calendar in the *Book of Common Prayer.*

The present Roman Catholic calendar and the *Lutheran Service Book* commemorate Monica the day before the feast day of her son, whose life was so interwoven with her own. The calendars in the *Book of Common Prayer,* the *Lutheran Book of Worship, Evangelical Lutheran Worship,* and *For All the Saints* retain the previous date of her commemoration, May 4, making Monica available as a model for Mother's Day in places where that observance is expected.

READING

From St. Augustine's *Confessions*

The day was now approaching when my mother Monica would depart from this life; you knew that day, Lord, though we did not. She and I happened to be standing by ourselves at a window that overlooked the garden in the courtyard of the house. At the time we were in Ostia on the Tiber. We had gone there after a long and wearisome journey to get away from the noisy crowd, and to rest and prepare for our sea voyage. I believe that you, Lord, caused all this to happen in your own mysterious ways. And so the two of us, all alone, were enjoying a very pleasant conversation, "forgetting what lies behind and straining forward to what lies ahead." [Phil. 3:14] We were asking one another in the presence of the Truth—for you are the Truth—what it would be like to share the eternal life enjoyed by the saints, which "eye has not seen, nor ear heard, which has not entered into the human heart." [see 1 Cor. 2:9] We desired with all our hearts to drink from the streams of your heavenly fountain, the fountain of life.

That was the substance of our talk, though not the exact words. But you know, O Lord, that in the course of our conversation that day, the world and its pleasures lost all their attraction for us. My mother said, "Son, as far as I am concerned, nothing in this life now gives me any pleasure. I do not know why I am still here, since I have no further hopes in this world. I did have one reason for wanting to live a little longer: to see you become a Catholic Christian before I died. God has lavished his gifts on me in that respect, for I know that you have even renounced earthly happiness to be his servant. So what am I doing here?

I do not really remember how I answered her. Shortly, within five days or thereabouts, she fell sick with a fever. Then one day during the course of her illness she became unconscious and for a while she was unaware of her surroundings. My brother and I rushed to her side but she regained consciousness quickly. She looked at us as we stood there and asked in a puzzled voice, "Where was I?"

We were overwhelmed with grief, but she held her gaze steadily upon us and spoke further, "Here you shall bury your mother." I remained silent as I held back my tears. However, my brother haltingly expressed his hope that she might not die in a strange country but in her own land, since her end would be happier there. When she heard this, her face was filled with anxiety, and she reproached him with a glance because he had entertained such earthly thoughts. Then she looked at me and spoke, "Look what he is saying." Thereupon she said to both of us, "Bury my body wherever you will; let not care of it cause you any concern. Only one thing I ask you, that you remember me at the altar of the Lord wherever you may be." Once our mother had expressed this desire as best she could, she fell silent as the pain of her illness increased.

Then on the ninth day of her sickness, the fifty-sixth year of her age and the thirty-third of mine, that religious and holy soul was freed from the body.

Augustine, *Confessions* IX:10-11. Text from the English translation of the Office of Readings from the Liturgy of the Hours © 1974, International Committee on English in the Liturgy, Inc. All rights reserved. The last paragraph, added to the text of the Office of Readings, trans. PHP.

PROPERS

God of mercy, comfort of those in sorrow, the tears of St. Monica moved you to convert her son St. Augustine to the faith of Christ: By their examples, help us to turn from our sins and to find your loving forgiveness; through your Son Jesus Christ our Lord, who lives and reigns with you and the Holy Spirit, one God, now and forever.

1952 Roman Missal, RS, alt. PHP

Readings:	1 Samuel 1:10-11, 20 *or* Sirach 26:1-4,16-21
	Psalm 115:12-18 *or* 116:10-17
	Luke 7:11-17 *or* John 16:20-24
Hymn of the Day:	
	"O what their joy and their glory must be" (H82 623, LBW 337, LSB 675)
Prayers:	For mothers that by their prayers and example they may bring up their children in the faith
	For homes where only one parent is Christian

For the spirit of unceasing prayer
For the unity of families in Christ

Preface: Baptism (BCP, LBW)
Color: White

ALSO ON AUGUST 27

The Episcopal *Lesser Feasts and Fasts 1997* commemorates on this date (Monica is commemorated on May 4) **Thomas Gallaudet** with **Henry Winter Syle**. An Episcopal priest, Gallaudet (1822–1902) began ministry to the deaf in the Episcopal Church; Syle (d. 1890) was the first deaf person ordained in the Episcopal Church.

August 28

Augustine, Bishop of Hippo, Teacher, 430

Aurelius Augustinus, generally known as St. Augustine, was born in the town of Tagaste, modern Souk Ahras in Algeria, November 13, 354. His mother Monica was a Christian, and she attempted to raise him as a Christian, but without success. He attended school in Carthage, where he was a serious student but was converted to Manichaeism, a dualistic religion of Persian origin that was popular at the time. He had a son by a concubine, whom he named Adeodatus, "Gift of God."

Sometime after 383 Augustine went to Rome, where he taught rhetoric and continued his studies. In 384 he went to Milan to teach, and there he was drawn by stages to the Catholic faith. First he renounced Manichaeism for a study of Neo-Platonism and then came under the influence of St. Ambrose, the Bishop of Milan. After a great struggle his doubts were dispelled, and Ambrose baptized him at the Easter Vigil in 387. His mother died as she and her son were on their way back to North Africa. There Augustine lived a kind of monastic life for several years with a group of his friends. In 391, on a visit to the city of Hippo Regius (modern Annaba), against his will the Christians there chose him to be their pastor. From that time until his death, Hippo was his residence. He was ordained to the priesthood, four years later was consecrated bishop, and shortly afterwards became the Bishop of Hippo. The city no longer exists, but at the time was second in ecclesiastical importance in Africa. Augustine served as bishop for thirty-five years. He made many time-consuming journeys and yet was able to produce an enormous body of writing.

St. Augustine was one of the great teachers of the church, and Christian thinkers, Catholic and Protestant, acknowledge his importance as a theologian and defender of the Christian faith. Of his many writings the most famous are his autobiographical *Confessions* (*ca.* 400) and *The City of God* (after 412). The *Confessions* tell of his life and conversion; *The City of God* contains his social and political views, occasioned by the collapse of Rome; a defense of Christianity; and a vision of the ideal Christian society. He also wrote a number of more purely theological works, among them attacks on Manichaeism and polemics against various heresies such as Donatism and Pelagianism. Some of his treatises were commentaries on parts of the Scriptures. His books, sermons, and letters have been published in many languages and many editions, and there is a vast literature about him and his work.

He established the monastic rule of St. Augustine, and more than a millennium later, Martin Luther became a monk of the Augustinian Order.

St. Augustine's last years were full of turmoil from the ravages of the Vandal tribes in North Africa. City after city was destroyed, churches were burned, and clergy scattered. During the Vandals' siege of Hippo, St. Augustine was seized with a fever and died on August 28, 430, the date on which he is now commemorated. His body was taken to Sardinia, and in the middle of the eighth century it was moved again to the capital of Lombardy, Pavia, where it now rests in a splendid marble monument (*ca.* 1362) in the Church of San Pietro in Ciel d'Oro, one of the great sculptured shrines of Italy.

FOR FURTHER READING

Augustine. *Augustine of Hippo: Selected Writings.* Trans. Mary T. Clark. Mahwah: Paulist, 1984.

Bonner, Gerald. *St. Augustine of Hippo: Life and Controversies.* Philadelphia: Westminster, 1963.

Brown, Peter R. L. *Augustine of Hippo.* Rev. ed. Berkeley: University of California Press, 2000.

Burnaby, J. *Amor Dei: A Study of the Religion of St. Augustine.* London: Hodder and Stoughton, 1938. Reprinted 1960.

Von Campenhausen, Hans. *The Fathers of the Latin Church.* Trans. Manfred Hoffmann. Stanford: Stanford University Press, 1964.

Harrison, Carol. *Augustine: Christian Truth and Fractured Humanity.* New York: Oxford University Press, 2000.

Lancel, Serge. *St. Augustine.* Trans. Antonia Nevill. London: SCM, 2003.

Van der Meer, F. *Augustine the Bishop.* Trans. B. Battershaw and G. R. Lamb. New York: Sheed and Ward, 1962.

Stump, Eleonore and Norman Kretzmann. *The Cambridge Companion to Augustine.* New York: Cambridge University Press, 2001.

READING

From St. Augustine's *Confessions*

I probed the hidden depth of my soul and drew together and heaped up all my misery in the sight of my heart; there arose a mighty storm, bringing a great deluge of tears. In order that I might freely pour forth those tears, I left Alypius. Solitude was more suitable for weeping, so I moved far enough away that even his presence could not embarrass me. He perceived something of what I was feeling, for I suppose that I had said something and my voice was choked with weeping. I arose, and he remained where we had been sitting, utterly bewildered. I threw myself down under a fig tree, giving full vent to my tears; and the floods of my eyes gushed out the sacrifice that you will not despise. And, not indeed in exactly these words, yet after this manner I spoke to you: "How long, O Lord, how long?" "How long, Lord, will you be angry? Remember not our past sins" [Ps. 6:3; 79:5, 8], for I felt that I was bound fast by them. I sent up these sorrowful words, "How long, how long? Tomorrow and tomorrow? Why not now? Why is there not this moment an end to my wickedness?"

So I was speaking and weeping in the bitter contrition of my heart, when suddenly I heard from a neighboring house a voice, of a boy or girl, I know not, chanting and often repeating, "Take up and read; take up and read." Instantly my countenance changed. I began to think most intently whether children in any kind of play sing such words, for I could not remember ever having heard them. So, stopping the torrent of my tears, I arose, interpreting it to be nothing else but a command from God to open the book and read the first chapter I should find. (I had heard of Antony, who, coming in to church during the reading of the Gospel, received its admonition as if what was being read was spoken to him: "Go, sell your possessions, and give the money to the poor, and you will have treasure in heaven; then come, follow me" [Matt. 19:21]. By such a command he was at once converted to you.) Eagerly then I returned to the place where Alypius was sitting, for when I had left there I had laid down a book of the Apostle's writings. I took it, opened it, and in silence read that passage on which my eyes first fell: "Not in reveling and drunkenness, not in debauchery and licentiousness, not in quarrelling and jealousy. Instead, put on the Lord Jesus Christ, and make no provision for the flesh, to gratify its desires" [Rom. 13:13-14]. I did not desire to read further, nor did I need to. Instantly, at the end of this sentence, a light of serenity flooded my heart and all the darkness of doubt vanished away.

Augustine, *Confessions* VIII, 12. Trans PHP, based on the translation of Edward B. Pusey.

PROPERS

Lord God, the light of the minds that know you, the life of the souls that love you, and the strength of the hearts that serve you: Help us, following the example of your servant Augustine of Hippo, so to know you that we may truly love you, and so to love you that we may fully serve you, whom to serve is perfect freedom; through Jesus Christ our Lord, who lives and reigns with you and the Holy Spirit, one God, now and forever.

Prayer attributed to Augustine; LFF

Readings:	Psalm 87 *or* 84:7-12
	Hebrews 12:22-24, 28-29 *or* 1 John 4:7-16
	Matthew 23:8-12 *or* John 14:6-15
Hymn of the Day:	
	"Jerusalem, my happy home" (H82 620, LBW 331, LSB 673, ELW 628)
Prayers:	For the churches in North Africa
	For those who search for the truth, especially young people who are struggling to find meaning
	For their lives
	For teachers
	For those who defend the faith
	For a deeper love of the Scriptures
Preface:	Baptism (BCP)
Color:	White

ALSO ON AUGUST 28

Moses the Black, Monk and Martyr, *ca.* 400

August 28 is also the feast day of Moses the Black. He was a large and imposing Ethiopian slave of an Egyptian government official who dismissed him for theft and suspected murder. He became the leader of a gang of thieves who roamed the Nile valley spreading terror and violence. They attacked a monastery in the desert of Scete (Skete) near Alexandria, intending to rob it, but they were met by the abbot, whose dedication, contentment, and peace, so impressed Moses that he abandoned his old way of life and joined their community.

Later Moses was ordained to the priesthood, not a common practice among the desert fathers, and founded a monastery of seventy-five monks, the same number as his former band of thieves. He was known for his humility, wisdom, love, and refusal to judge others. About the year 405 the monastery was attacked by a group of marauding Berbers. Moses forbade the monks to defend themselves. Most of them fled, but Moses and seven others remained to welcome the invaders, as he had once been welcomed by an abbot. This time, however, the outcome was different: all eight were killed. Monks still live at the monastery where Abba Moses is buried, Dair al-Baramus in the Wadi Natrun.

St. Moses the Black is honored as an apostle of nonviolence and is regarded as a patron saint of African Americans.

He is not on the General Roman Calendar nor the Episcopal calendar but was included on the calendar in the Methodist book *For All the* Saints as Abba Moses of Scete and on the calendar in *Evangelical Lutheran Worship* (2006). He is remembered on the calendar of the Eastern Church on this date as Venerable Moses the Ethiopian.

READING

From *The Sayings of the Fathers*

A certain brother came to the abbot Moses in Scete seeking a word from him. And the old man said to him, "Go and sit in thy cell, and thy cell shall teach thee all things."

At one time a provincial judge heard of the abbot Moses and set out into Scete to see him: but the old man heard of his coming and got up to flee into the marsh. And the judge with his following met him, and questioned him, saying, "Tell me, old man, where is the cell of the abbot Moses?" And he said, "Why would ye seek him out? The man is a fool and a heretic." So the judge coming to the church said to the clergy, "I had heard of the abbot Moses and came to see him: but lo! We met an old man journeying into Egypt, and asked him where might be the cell of the abbot Moses, and he said, "Why do you seek him? He is a fool and a heretic." The clergy, on hearing this, were perturbed and said, "What was this old man like, who spoke thus to you of the holy man?" And they said, "He was an old man wearing a very ancient garment, tall and black." And they said, "It is the abbot himself: and because he did not wish to be seen by you, he told you these things about himself." And mightily edified, the judge went away.

Once a brother in Scete was found guilty, and the older brethren came in assembly and sent to the abbot Moses, asking him to come: but he would not. Then the priest sent to him, saying: "Come: for the assembly of the brethren awaits thee." And he rose up and came. But taking with him very old basket, he filled it with sand and carried it behind him. And they went out to meet him, asking, "Father, what is this?" And the old man said to them, "My sins are running behind me and I do not see them, and I am come to-day to judge the sins of another man." And they heard him, and said nought to the brother, but forgave him.

Helen Waddell, *The Desert Fathers* (Ann Arbor: University of Michigan Press, 1957 [1936]), 66, 93–94, 96.

PROPERS

Holy and mighty God, you strengthened your monk Moses the Black and crowned him with the glory of martyrdom: In your mercy transform our renegade spirits and grant that by discipline and prayer, our pride may wither within us and that at the last we may attain the heavenly city; where with your Son and the Holy Spirit you live and reign, one God, now and forever.

PHP

August 29

The Beheading of St. John the Baptist

John the Baptist stands at the meeting point of the Old and the New Testaments. As the last of the prophets, he was stern in his denunciation of moral corruption in the society of his day, and he pointed to Jesus, through whom the righteousness of God would be proclaimed not by word alone but by the word made flesh.

His death by order of Herod, whom he fearlessly rebuked for marrying his brother's wife, is the clearest example of his refusal to compromise with evil, even in the highest places in the land. St. Augustine later commented on John's death and Herod's perfidy, "We see how a pledge which was given rashly was criminally kept." As John was the forerunner of Jesus in life so he was Jesus' precursor in death. The commemoration of his beheading (his "Decollation" as the old Latinate title describes it) was retained on many European and some American Lutheran calendars. It is on the General Roman Calendar but not on the Episcopal calendar, although it is included on several Anglican calendars.

FOR FURTHER READING

St. Augustine. *Sermons* 307 and 308. *The Works of Saint Augustine. Sermons III/9 (306–340 A) on the Saints.* 47–54. Trans. Edmund Hill. Ed. John E. Rotelle. Hyde Park: New City, 1994.

Darton. C. C. *St. John the Baptist and the Kingdom of Heaven.* London: Darton, Longman and Todd, 1961.

Scobie, Charles H. *John the Baptist.* Philadelphia: Fortress Press, 1964.

Steinmann, Jean. *St. John the Baptist and the Desert Tradition.* New York: Harper, 1958.

READING

From a sermon by the Venerable Bede

As forerunner of our Lord's birth, preaching, and death, the blessed John showed in his struggle a goodness worthy of the sight of heaven. In the words of Scripture: *Though in the sight of men they were punished, their hope is full of immortality* [Wis. 3:4 RSV]. We rightly commemorate the day of his birth [into heaven] with festive joy, for he made it sacred for us through his own suffering and adorned it with the crimson splendor of his own blood. Rightly do we with joyful hearts revere his memory, for he stamped with the seal of martyrdom the witness he gave on behalf of the Lord.

Without doubt blessed John endured imprisonment and chains and laid down his life as a witness to our Redeemer, whose forerunner he was. His persecutor did not order him to deny Christ, but only that he should keep silent about the truth. Nevertheless, he died for Christ. Christ himself said, "I am the truth"; in shedding his blood for the truth, John surely died for Christ.

By his birth, preaching, and baptizing, he bore witness to the coming birth, preaching, and baptism of Christ, and by his own suffering he showed that Christ would also suffer.

Such was the quality and strength of the one who accepted the end of this present life by shedding his blood after the long imprisonment. He preached the freedom of heavenly peace, yet was thrown into irons by the ungodly; he was locked away in the darkness of prison, though he came bearing witness to the Light of life and deserved to be called a bright and shining lamp by the Light itself, which is Christ. John was baptized in his own blood, he who had been given the privilege of baptizing the Redeemer of the world, of hearing the voice of the Father above him, and of seeing the grace of the Holy Spirit descending upon him. But to endure temporal agonies for the sake of the truth was not a heavy burden for such as John; rather it was easily borne and even desirable, for he knew eternal joy would be his reward.

Since death was ever near at hand through the inescapable necessity of nature, such people considered it a blessing to embrace death and thus gain the reward of eternal life by acknowledging Christ's name. Hence the apostle Paul rightly says, "He graciously granted you the privilege not only of believing in Christ but also of suffering for him as well" [Phil. 1:29]. He tells us why it is a gift of Christ that his chosen ones should suffer for him, "The sufferings of this present time are not worth comparing with the glory that is about to be revealed in us" [Rom. 8:18]

PROPERS

O God, you called John the Baptist to be in birth and death the forerunner of your Son: Grant that as John gave his life in witness to truth and righteousness, so we may fearlessly contend for the right, even unto the end; through your Son Jesus Christ our Lord, who lives and reigns with you and the Holy Spirit, one God, now and forever.

1736 Paris Missal, RS trans. PHP

Readings: Jeremiah 1:17-19
             Psalm 71:1-16
             James 1:1-12
             Mark 6:14-29

AUGUST

Hymn of the Day:
               "From God can nothing move me" (LBW 468, LSB 713)
Prayers: For all who are wrongfully accused
               For courage to obey God's commands in the face of great opposition, to speak the
                   truth, boldly rebuke vice, and patiently suffer for the sake of truth
               For all who are maintaining the Christian faith under intolerant governments
Preface: Advent
Color: Red

August 31

John Bunyan, Teacher, 1688

Bunyan was born in Elstow, near Bedford, England, in the heart of the agricultural midlands, in November 1628. He was the son of a tinker, a maker and mender of metal pots. He had little schooling and learned his father's trade, although his own description in the autobiography of his humble origins may be something of an exaggeration. His mother died in 1644, and shortly afterward, Bunyan's younger sister died. During the Civil War he served in the Parliamentary army, 1644–1646, and married a woman whose name he does not tell us, whose only dowry consisted of two popular Puritan religious books: Arthur Dent's *The Plaine Man's Pathway to Heaven* (1601) and Lewis Bayly's *The Practice of Piety* (1612).

Bunyan endured a time of spiritual torment, and after what he describes as a "dissolute" life turned to the study of the Bible. His wife died in 1656. At last he found peace in a Baptist congregation in Bedford. He became a "mechanic preacher," worked as a tinker, and remarried. He refused to attend Anglican church services.

At the Restoration in 1660, Bunyan was arrested for preaching without a license, and since he refused to desist, spent twelve years in the Bedford jail preaching to his fellow prisoners and studying. Upon his release, he was named pastor of the Bedford Baptist congregation. His first substantial work was a spiritual autobiography, *Grace Abounding to the Chief of Sinners* (1666). It followed a conventional formula for books of its kind, but it was given unusual power through Bunyan's psychological insight and his superb narrative gifts. In 1675 he was again jailed for six months and wrote *The Pilgrim's Progress from This World To That Which Is To Come* (1678, second part 1684), the most successful allegory in the English language. It attained an enormous popularity, and together with the Authorized Version of the Bible was almost the sole reading matter for many centuries in most homes. In 1680 Bunyan wrote *The Life and Death of Mr. Badman,* a series of narrative episodes using the popular fiction of the time; in 1682 he published *The Holy War*, an allegory of salvation, more complicated than *Pilgrim's Progress*, with social and political overtones.

On August 31, 1688, after riding through heavy rain to settle a quarrel between a father and a son, Bunyan contracted a fever (probably pneumonia) and died. He is buried in Bunhill Fields, the Nonconformists' traditional burying ground. Despite his suffering, he was a warm, sympathetic, large-hearted, and loveable man, who by his writing has increased the pleasure and enriched the devotion of countless readers through more than three centuries.

John Bunyan was introduced to the calendar on the German Lutheran *Evangelical Calendar of Names* (1962) and has subsequently been added by the *Lutheran Book of Worship* and the Methodist *For All the Saints*; the Church of England's *Alternative Services Book* and *The Christian Year* (1997) commemorate him on August 30 to avoid conflict with Aidan on August 31 and call him "John Bunyan, spiritual writer."

FOR FURTHER READING

Bunyan, John. *Grace Abounding to the Chief of Sinners.* Ed. W. R. Owens. New York: Viking Penguin, 1987.

———. *The Pilgrim's Progress from This World to That Which Is to Come.* Ed. Roger Sharrock. Baltimore: Penguin, 1965.

Frye, Roland M. *God, Man, and Satan.* Princeton: Princeton University Press, 1960.

Furlong, Monica. *Puritan's Progress: A Study of John Bunyan.* London: Hodder and Stoughton, 1975.

Hill, Christopher. *A Tinker and a Poor Man: John Bunyan and His Church, 1628–1688.* New York: Norton, 1989.

Hofmeyr, Isabel. *The Portable Bunyan: A Transnational History of* The Pilgrim's Progress. Princeton: Princeton University Press, 2004.

Keeble, N. H. *The Literary Culture of Nonconformity in Later Seventeenth Century England.* Athens: University of Georgia Press, 1987.

Lawrence, Anne, *et al.*, eds. *John Bunyan and His England 1628–1688.* N.p.: Hambledon Press, 1990.

Morris, Colin, and Peter Roberts, eds. *Pilgrimage: The English Experience from Becket to Bunyan.* Cambridge: Cambridge University Press, 2002.

Sharrock, Roger. *John Bunyan.* London: Longmans, 1954. Rev. ed. New York: St. Martin's, 1968.

Wakefield, Gordon. *John Bunyan the Christian.* London: Fount/HarperCollins, 1992.

Winslow, Ola E. *John Bunyan.* New York: Macmillan, 1961.

READING

From *Pilgrim's Progress*

Now when he was got up to the top of the Hill, there came two men running against him amain; the name of the one was Timorous, and the name of the other Mistrust. To whom Christian said, "Sirs, what's the matter you run the wrong way?" Timorous answered that they were going to the City of Sion, and had got up that difficult place; "But," said he, "the further we go, the more danger we meet with, wherefore we turned, and are going back again."

"Yes," said Mistrust, "for just before us lie a couple of lions in the way, whether sleeping or waking we know not and we could not think, if we came within reach, but they would presently pull us in pieces."

Christian. Then said Christian, "You make me afraid, but whither shall I fly to be safe? If I go back to mine own country, that is prepared for fire and brimstone, and I shall certainly perish there. If I can get to the Celestial City, I am sure to be in safety there. I must venture: to go back is nothing but death, to go forward is fear of death, and life everlasting beyond it. I will yet go forward." So Mistrust and Timorous ran down the Hill, and Christian went on his way.

Now I saw in my dream, that these two men [Christian and Hopeful] went in at the Gate; and lo, as they entered they were transfigured, and they had raiment put on that shone like gold. There was also that met them, with harps and crowns, and gave them to them, the harp to praise withal, and the crowns in token of honour. Then I heard in my dream, that all the bells in the City rang again for joy; and that it was said unto them, "*Enter ye into the joy of your Lord.*" I also heard the men themselves, that they sang with a loud voice, saying, "*Blessing, honour, glory, and power, be to him that sitteth upon the throne and to the Lamb forever and ever.*"

Now just as the Gates were opened to let in the men, I looked in after them; and behold, the City shone like the sun, the streets also were paved with gold, and in them walked many men with crowns on their heads, palms in their hands, and golden harps to sing praises withal.

There were also of them that had wings, and they answered one another without intermission, saying, *Holy, Holy, Holy, is the Lord.* And after that, they shut up the gates: which when I had seen, I wished myself among them.

John Bunyan, *The Pilgrim's Progress from This World to That Which Is to Come*, ed. Roger Sharrock (Baltimore: Penguin, 1965), 75–76, 203–04.

PROPERS

Lord God, you have called your servants to ventures of which we cannot see the ending, by paths as yet untrodden, through perils unknown: By the witness of your servant John Bunyan, give us faith to go out with good courage, not knowing whither we go, but only that your hand is leading us and your love supporting us;

through Jesus Christ our Lord, who lives and reigns with you and the Holy Spirit, one God, now and forever.

E. Milner-White and G. W. Briggs, *Daily Prayer* (1941); SBH, LBW, ELW, LSB; alt. PHP

Readings:	Genesis 12:1-7
	Psalm 84
	Hebrews 4:1-11
	Luke 9:51-62
Hymn of the Day:	
	"He who would valiant be 'gainst all disaster" (H82 564, 565; LBW 498)
Prayers:	For courage to set out in quest of spiritual truth
	For strength to endure the Christian pilgrimage
	For grace to win heaven at last
	For writers who explore religious truth with narrative skill
Color:	White

September 1

The Episcopal *Lesser Feasts and Fasts 1997* added to the calendar ***David Pendleton Oakerhater***, a deacon and missionary of the Cheyenne, who died August 31, 1931. His commemoration is moved from the date of his death to September 1 because August 31 is the feast day of Aidan.

The *Lutheran Service Book* has introduced on this date the commemoration of ***Joshua***, the successor of Moses.

September 2

Nikolai Frederik Severin Grundtvig, Bishop, Renewer of the Church, 1872

Christianity was brought to Denmark in the ninth century by St. Ansgar (see February 3). The Reformation was introduced between 1520 and 1540. In common with the rest of Lutheranism, Danish Christianity suffered from the dry intellectualism of Lutheran "orthodoxy" in the seventeenth century and experienced a Pietist reaction in the late seventeenth and early eighteenth century. In the nineteenth century two notable figures emerged in Danish theology. Søren Kierkegaard (see November 12) attacked the Established Church because it had sought to accommodate Christian revelation to human desires. N. F. S. Grundtvig led a revival of orthodox Lutheranism that restored the creeds and confessions to a place of honor and attacked the rationalism and state domination of religion.

Grundtvig was born in a parsonage in Udby, Zeeland, September 8, 1783, the youngest of five children of Johan and Catherine Grundtvig. His father was untouched by the rationalism emanating from Germany at that time; he was a man of quiet, orthodox Lutheran piety. His wife came from a long line of talented and capable people, and she taught her own children well.

At nine years of age, Grundtvig left for boarding school at Vejle for six years, after which he enrolled at the gymnasium at Aarhus. In 1800 he entered the University of Copenhagen to study theology and received his degree in three years. At the university, Grundtvig absorbed the spirit of the Enlightenment—its joy, confidence, and optimism. He also discovered ancient mythology, which opened to him new worlds of thought revealed in the ancient Eddas and Icelandic sagas. His interest in poetry was also reawakened, with the conviction that poetry is the appropriate medium to express the spirit.

After receiving his theological degree, Grundtvig lived with his family doing historical study. In 1805 he was appointed tutor in Langeland, where he fell in love with the twenty-six-year-old wife of his employer. In 1808 he left the Langeland estate and returned to Copenhagen to publish *The Mythology of the North*, in which he argued that ancient myth expresses the spirit of humanity in a way that science cannot.

Grundtvig's father became ill and asked his son to assist him in the large Udby parish. His probation sermon, preached before church officials March 17, 1810, was a scathing attack on the prevailing spirit of rationalism in the Danish church. "Why Has the Lord's Word Disappeared from His House?" he asked pointedly. "Holy men of old believed in the message they were called to preach, but the human spirit has now become so proud that it feels itself capable of discovering the truth without the light of the gospel, and so faith has died." Grundtvig was reprimanded by the dean of the theological faculty, and a spiritual crisis followed as he anguished over whether he was awakened and who he was to awaken Denmark. Nevertheless, roused by contemptuous words of an historian of Prussia, he found his vocation, petitioned for ordination, was ordained May 11, 1811, and became a curate to his father, who died in 1813. From 1813 to 1820 he was in Copenhagen writing, unable to receive a call. He made a version of *Beowulf* (1820) that encouraged research in Anglo-Saxon literature. At last, in 1821, he became pastor of Praesto parish in Zeeland. He then moved to Our Savior's Church in Copenhagen (1822–1826), when he resigned following a controversy over his attack upon Henrik N. Clausen. Clausen, Grundtvig said, by rationally explaining human duty in a world governed by God's providence, treated Christianity as a philosophical idea rather than as historical revelation handed down in a living chain of sacramental tradition in baptism and Holy Communion through the generations from the time of the apostles. The Apostles' Creed (which he believed Jesus had taught the apostles during the forty days after his resurrection), the words of institution of baptism and Holy Communion, and the Lord's Prayer are in a sense, the "living word of God" that held the communion of saints together through the ages and opened up the essential meaning of the Bible. Grundtvig lived as a writer from 1826 to 1839. The first of his five volumes of hymns was published in 1837.

Finally, in 1839, he was appointed chaplain to a home for aged women at Vartov, where he remained for the rest of his life. Here he was able to study and make use of his reflections and hymns, surrounded by his friends. His consuming passion for education resulted in the founding of Danish folk high schools, beginning in 1844, raising the educational standards of his people. The movement for popular education spread quickly throughout Denmark and also Sweden, Norway, and Finland. He was active in the movement leading to the introduction of parliamentary government in 1849. In 1861, on the fiftieth anniversary of his ordination, the king gave him the rank and title of bishop, although without a diocese. He died September 2, 1872, aged eighty-nine.

Grundtvig is honored as a scholar and translator, a poet, the creator of Danish hymnody (he composed more than a thousand hymns), a champion of political freedom and liberty in church and state, a supporter of practical education of the people to awaken a love of life. There is a church in Copenhagen dedicated to his memory.

Immigrant Danish Lutherans in America eventually formed two separate bodies, reflecting two parties of the Church of Denmark. One group, the "happy Danes," with the more liberal Grundtvigian outlook, formed what was to become the American Evangelical Lutheran Church, which in 1962 merged with the Lutheran Church in America. The other with a more pietistic view, the "gloomy Danes," formed the United Evangelical Lutheran Church (1896), which merged to form the American Lutheran Church in 1960.

FOR FURTHER READING

Allchin, A. M. *N. F. S. Grundtvig: An Introduction to His Life and Work.* Aarhus: Aarhus University Press, 1997.

Arden, G. Everett. *Four Northern Lights.* Minneapolis: Augsburg, 1964.

Jensen, Niels Lyhne, ed. *A Grundtvig Anthology: Selections from the Writings of N. F. S. Grundtvig (1783–1872).* Trans. Edward Broadbridge and Niels Lyhne Jensen. Cambridge: James Clarke, 1984.

Kjaer, Jens Christian. *History of the Church of Denmark.* Blair: Lutheran Publishing House, 1945.

Knudsen, Johannes. *Danish Rebel: A Study of N. F. Grundtvig.* Philadelphia: Muhlenberg, 1955.

———, ed. *N. F. S. Grundtvig: Selected Writings.* Philadelphia: Fortress Press, 1976.

Koch, Hal. *Grundtvig.* Trans. Llewellyn Jones. Yellow Springs: Antioch, 1952.

SEPTEMBER

Lindhardt, P. G. *Grundtvig: An Introduction.* London: SPCK, 1951.

Nelson, Ernest. *N. F. S. Grundtvig: An American Study.* Rock Island: Augustana Book Concern, 1955.

Plekon, Michael. "N.F.S. Grundtvig: Renewer of the Church." *Lutheran Forum* 17, no. 4 (Advent 1983): 8–11.

Thodberg, Christian, and Anders Pontoppidan Thyssen, eds. *N. F. S. Grundtvig, Tradition and Renewal: Grundtvig's vision of man and people, education and the Church, in relation to world issues today.* Copenhagen: Danish Institute, 1984.

READING

From a sermon by N. F. S. Grundtvig

The Spirit of the Son, our Lord Jesus Christ, which proceeds from the Father . . . reflects the glory of God, so that the church feels the real presence of our Lord Jesus Christ, although the world does not see him. He reveals himself spiritually for all those who hold fast his word with proof as plain as when he revealed himself to his friends after the resurrection and spoke to them about matters that pertain to the kingdom of God. He tells us that he can and will dwell in his church and walk in it as the only-begotten Son from eternity in all the regenerated sons and daughters whom the heavenly Father and the Son embrace, sharing his glory.

Then, and only then, God's kingdom comes to us, not so that one can point to it and say: look here or look there, as one points to the great nations, but in such a way that the whole church lives in it, saying and singing: Now we know that God's kingdom is truly righteousness, peace, and joy in the Holy Spirit. It comes as the Spirit proclaims in deeds and truths what is to come through that which is now worked and created in us. Then we cannot for a moment doubt that what now lives in us, a real and joyful power, though concealed, shall be revealed when he who is our life comes again even as he ascended. Thus it follows that the sufferings of this present time are not worth comparing with the glory that is to be revealed to us, just as surely as this glory has descended and rests upon us.

Therefore, Christian friends, we will not be fearful or despondent in the great transition period from darkness to light, from death to life, and from clarity to clarity, for it holds true throughout the lives of all God's children in this world, and not only during their last days, that they shall not fear evil as they walk through the valley of the shadow of death. We who walked in darkness have seen a great light, and he who is the light of the world is with us. . . .

The Fourth Sunday after Easter, 1855, in *N. F. S.Grundtvig: Selected Writings,* ed. Joahnnes Knudsen (Philadelphia: Fortress Press, 1976), 115–16.

PROPERS

God of grace and eternal Lord of all the years, you have enriched your church with the living faith and the broad learning of your servant Nicolai Frederik Severin

Grundtvig: Awaken in us, who give thanks for his life, such a love of the living tradition of your church and such respect for the wisdom of past ages, that at all times and in all places, in confidence and in joy, we may lift our voices in your praise; through your Son, Jesus Christ our Lord, who lives and reigns with you and the Holy Spirit, one God, now and forever.
PHP

Readings:	Jeremiah 1:4-10
	Psalm 46
	1 Corinthians 3:11-23
	Mark 10:35-45
Hymn of the Day:	
	"O day full of grace" (LBW 161, LSB 503, ELW 627)
Prayers:	For the church and people of Denmark
	For public schools
	For poets who explore and express the human spirit
	For students of theology
	For a deeper regard for the church and its sacraments
Preface:	All Saints
Color:	White

SEPTEMBER

ALSO ON SEPTEMBER 2

The *Lutheran Service Book* has introduced on this date the commemoration of **Hannah**, mother of Samuel. Her story is told in 1 Samuel 1–2.

ALSO ON SEPTEMBER 2 (OR SEPTEMBER 3)

The Martyrs of Papua New Guinea, 1942

When the Japanese invaded New Guinea in 1942, many European missionaries had already been withdrawn; but the Anglican Bishop of New Guinea, Philip N. S. Strong, challenged his clergy to remain and to continue their ministry to their people. Eight missionaries and two Papuan laymen were betrayed to the Japanese invaders and were martyred in August of that year.

In 1948 the Martyrs' Memorial School was opened in Sangara, as a living memorial to their courage and loyalty to Christ. The school has since moved to Agenahambo.

The commemoration of the martyrs of New Guinea was included in the calendar in the 1979 American *Book of Common Prayer*. It originated in the Diocese of New Guinea and is also observed in many dioceses of Australia. The remembrance there also includes the fifteen Lutheran, twenty-four Methodist, and 168 Roman Catholic missionaries who died for their faith in New Guinea, New Britain, and the Solomon Islands during the Second World War.

Those who desire to observe both the commemoration of Grundtvig and also that of the martyrs of Papua New Guinea may appropriately choose to transfer the commemoration of the New Guinea martyrs to the next day, September 3.

READING

From the broadcast to his missionaries by Philip N. S. Strong, Anglican Bishop of New Guinea, January 31, 1942.

As far as I know you are all at your posts, and I am very glad and thankful about this. I have, from the first, felt that we must endeavour to carry on our work in all circumstances, no matter what the cost may ultimately be to any of us individually.

The Church at home, which sent us out, expects this of us. The Universal Church expects it. The tradition and history of missions requires it of us. Missionaries who have been faithful to the uttermost and are now at rest are surely expecting it of us. The people whom we serve expects it of us. Our own consciences expect it of us. We could never hold up our faces again if, for our own safety, we all forsook [Christ] and fled when the shadows of the Passion began to gather round Him in His Spiritual and Mystical Body, the Church in Papua. Our life in the future would be burdened with shame and we could not come back here and face our people again; and we would be conscious always of rejected opportunities. . . .

I cannot foretell the future. I cannot guarantee that all will be well—that we shall all come through unscathed. One thing only I can guarantee is that, if we do not forsake Christ here in Papua in His Body, the Church, He will not forsake us. He will uphold us; He will sustain us; He will strengthen us, and he will guide and keep us through the days that lie ahead. . . . Let us trust and not be afraid.

Faithful Unto Death: The Story of the New Guinea Martyrs, ed. E. C. Rowland (Australian Board of Missions, 1967).

PROPERS

Almighty God, we remember before you this day the blessed martyrs of New Guinea, who, following the example of their Savior, laid down their lives for their friends; and we pray that we, who honor their memory, may imitate their loyalty and faith; through Jesus Christ our Lord, who lives and reigns with you and the Holy Spirit, one God, forever and ever.

John 15:13; CMG, LFF

Readings:	Psalm 116:1-8 *or* 126
	Revelation 7:13-17
	Luke 12:4-12
Hymn of the Day:	
	"Hearken to the anthem glorious" (H82 241)
Prayers:	For peace and reconciliation between the nations of the earth
	For strength for all who are tempted to abandon their good work and flee from danger
	Of thanksgiving for all who faithfully remained at their posts in time of war
Preface:	Holy Week
Color:	Red

September 4

Albert Schweitzer, Missionary to Africa, 1965

The lure of the mysterious "dark continent" of Africa seemed irresistible in the nineteenth century. David Livingstone (1813–1873) as a young man in Scotland was moved by Robert Moffat (1795–1883), a fellow Scot home from Africa, who spoke of the vast untouched regions of central Africa and "the smoke of a thousand villages" where the gospel had never been preached. After study in medical school, Livingstone was ordained a missionary in 1840, landed in South Africa, and pushed northward in search of converts. A consistent opponent of the slave trade, he believed that Christianity, commerce, and European civilization together would bring light to Africa. In 1855 he saw and named Victoria Falls, and returned to Great Britain in the following year to find himself a national hero. In 1858 he organized an expedition to the Zambezi, but disillusionment with his leadership set in, navigating the Zambezi proved impossible, and in April 1862 his wife, the daughter of Robert Moffat, died. Moreover, his eldest son, who had gone to the United States, was killed in the Civil War. In 1864 Livingstone returned to Africa to begin his search for the source of the Nile, an object of great fascination at the time. Reports of his death were circulated by some of his followers who had deserted him, and a newspaper correspondent, Henry Morton Stanley (1841–1904) was sent by the New York *Herald* to find Livingstone. They met November 10, 1871, with Stanley's famous greeting, "Dr. Livingstone, I presume?" Livingstone died May 1, 1873, at Chitambo's Village in what is now Zambia. He was buried in Westminster Abbey April 18, 1874.

Nine months later, January 14, 1875, Albert Schweitzer was born at Kaysersberg, Upper Alsace (now France), the eldest son of a Lutheran pastor. The family soon moved to Günsbach, which became Schweitzer's European home until his death.

He studied philosophy and theology at Strasbourg and also served as organist. In 1899 he received his doctorate in philosophy and was a lecturer in philosophy and preacher at St. Nicholas' Church. He was ordained January 29, 1900, and later that year received his doctorate in theology. He studied organ in Paris under Charles-Marie Widor, who encouraged him to write a study of the life and art of Bach; the book that resulted was published in 1905, the English translation, *J. S. Bach,* in 1911. His *Quest for the Historical Jesus* (1906, English 1910), in which he suggested that the attitudes of Jesus were shaped by his expectation of the immanent end of the world, established Schweitzer as a leading figure in theological studies.

In 1905 Schweitzer announced his intention of becoming a mission doctor. He resigned his university appointments and abandoned a promising career. In 1912 he married Hélène Bresslau, a scholar and a nurse, and in the following year received his doctorate in medicine. On Good Friday 1913 the husband and wife set out for Lambaréné in Gabon Province of French Equatorial Africa, and on the banks of the Ogooue River they built a hospital.

During World War I, Schweitzer, a native of Germany, was interned as an enemy alien and was held as a prisoner in France. While there, he turned his attention to world problems and wrote the two-volume *Philosophy of Civilization* (1923) in which he set forth his "reverence for life" in all its forms, which attitude he believed was essential for the survival of civilization. After his release from the internment camp, he was again preacher at St. Nicholas' Church until April 1921. In 1924 he returned to Africa to rebuild the ruined hospital, which he moved two miles up the river. A leper colony was added. In 1952 Schweitzer won the Nobel Prize for Peace for his work on behalf of the "brotherhood of nations."

Despite his life in Africa, Schweitzer never wholly abandoned his former interests. He continued to write and to lecture throughout Europe, to make recordings, and to edit the works of Bach. In 1958 he broadcast from Oslo three appeals called *Peace or Atomic War?* His autobiography, *Out of My Life and Thought,* was published in 1933.

Schweitzer has been criticized as patriarchal and autocratic, primitive in his medical practice. Nevertheless, he remains the twentieth century's greatest humanitarian, who by adherence to standards that the world found hard to accept, prodded its conscience and inspired generations with his example of sacrifice in response to the Gospel parable of the rich man and Lazarus.

Schweitzer died September 4, 1965, in his ninety-first year and was buried at his hospital beside his wife. He is commemorated on the calendar in the *Lutheran Book of Worship* and on the Methodist calendar in *For All the Saints.*

FOR FURTHER READING

Brabazon, James. *Albert Schweitzer: A Biography.* New York: Putnam, 1975.

Dungan, David L. "Reconsidering Albert Schweitzer." *The Christian Century* 92, no. 32 (October 8, 1975): 874–80.

Marshall, George, and David Poling. *Schweitzer: A Biography.* Baltimore: Johns Hopkins University Press, 2000.

Seaver, George. *Albert Schweitzer: The Man and His Mind.* New York: Harper & Row, 1947.

READING

From *Civilization and Ethics* by Albert Schweitzer

Reverence for life does not allow me to appropriate my own happiness. At moments when I should like to enjoy myself without a care, it brings before me thoughts of the misery I have seen and surmised. It refuses to allow me to banish my uneasiness. Just as the wave has no existence of its own, but is part of the continual movement of the ocean, thus I am destined never to experience my life as self-contained, but always as part of the experience which is going on around me. An uncomfortable doctrine prompts me in whispered words. You are happy, it says. Therefore you are called to give up much. Whatever you have received more than others in health, in talents, in ability, in success, in a pleasant childhood, in harmonious conditions of home life, all this you must not take to yourself as a matter of course. You must pay a price for it. You must render in return an unusually great sacrifice of your life for other life. The voice of the true ethic is dangerous for the happy when they have the courage to listen to it. For them there is no quenching of the irrational fire which glows in it. It challenges them in an attempt to lead them away from the natural road, and to see whether it can make them the adventurers of self-sacrifice, of whom the world has too few.

Albert Schweitzer, *Civilization and Ethics,* Part II of *The Philosophy of Civilization,* trans. C. T. Campion (New York: Macmillan, 1929), 267f.

PROPERS

God of grace and might, you gave to your servant Albert Schweitzer abundant gifts and led him to show by the example of his life the responsibility to care for those whom it seems easy to ignore: Raise up in our day servants whose lives will recall your people to their duty and proclaim the reality of your kingdom of sacrificial love; through your Son Jesus Christ our Lord, who lives and reins with you and the Holy Spirit, one God, now and forever.

LBW, rev. PHP

Readings: Isaiah 58:6-9
                Psalm 146
                Matthew 25:31-40
Hymn of the Day:
                "Hope of the world, thou Christ of great compassion" (LBW 493, LSB 690, H82 472)

Prayers:	For the spirit of selfless and sacrificial love
	For those who relieve suffering
	For strength to share the pain of the world
	For a recognition of the interrelatedness of all life
Preface:	Epiphany
Color:	White

September 4

The Episcopal *Lesser Feasts and Fasts 1997* included the commemoration of **Paul Jones** (1880–1941), Episcopal Bishop of Utah until he was pressured to resign, an open opponent of war and an uncompromising advocate of peace.

The Byzantine calendar on this date commemorates the Holy Prophet **Moses**. The calendar in the *Lutheran Service Book* (2006), following Wilhelm Löhe, also lists Moses on this date.

September 5

Mother Teresa of Calcutta, Renewer of Society, 1997

Small in stature, firm in faith, Mother Teresa took as her mission the demonstration of God's love for the poorest of the poor. Gonxha Agnes Bojaxhiu was born in Skopje, Albania, August 26, 1910. Her father died when she was eight years old, and her religious education was given by her mother and the vibrant Jesuit parish of the Sacred Heart. In September 1928, at the age of eighteen, intent on becoming a missionary, she left home to join the Institute of the Blessed Virgin Mary, known as the Sisters of Loreto, in Ireland. There she received the name Sister Mary Teresa after St. Thérèse of Lisieux. In December she left for India, arriving in Calcutta January 6, 1929, and taught at St. Mary's School for Girls. She made her final profession of vows on May 24, 1937, and from then on was called Mother Teresa and was known for her charity, unselfishness, courage, capacity for hard work, and talent for organization.

On September 10, 1946, on the train from Calcutta to Darjeeling for her annual retreat, she received her "inspiration" and became convinced that it was the desire of Jesus for her to establish a religious community, the Missionaries of Charity, dedicated to the service of the poorest of the poor. After two years of testing and discernment, she received permission to begin, and on August 17,

1948, she dressed for the first time in a white, blue-bordered sari and left the Loreto convent to enter the world of the poor. She went out each day, rosary in hand, to find and serve her Lord in the unwanted, the unloved, the uncared for.

Former students began to join her in the work. In 1950 the new congregation of the Missionaries of Charity was established in Calcutta. The sisters moved into other parts of India; houses were opened in Venezuela, Rome, Tanzania, and eventually on every inhabited continent. She extended the work further by founding the Missionaries of Charity Brothers (1963), the contemplative branch of the sisters (1976), the contemplative brothers (1979), and the Missionaries of Charity Fathers (1984). Mother Teresa was honored in 1979 with the Nobel Prize for Peace. She described herself, "By blood I am Albanian. By citizenship, an Indian. By faith, I am a Catholic nun. As to my calling, I belong to the world. As to my heart, I belong entirely to the Heart of Jesus."

She died September 5, 1997, in Calcutta, was given a state funeral by the government of India and was buried at the motherhouse of the Sisters of Charity. Only after her death did her continuing sense of being separated from God become known. What she called "the darkness" began about the time she began her work with the poor, and through it she participated in the thirst of Jesus, his painful and burning longing for love, and she shared in the interior desolation of the poor.

FOR FURTHER READING

Mother Teresa. *Mother Teresa: Come Be My Light.* Ed. and with commentary by Brian Kolodiejchuk. New York: Doubleday, 2007.

READING

From the Nobel Lecture by Mother Teresa

The poor are very wonderful people. One evening we went out and we picked up four people from the street. And one of them was in a most terrible condition. And I told the sisters, "You take care of the other three. I take [care] of this one who looked worse. So I did for her all that my love can do. I put her in bed, and there was such a beautiful smile on her face. She took hold of my hand, and she said one word only: "Thank you." And she died.

I could not help but examine my conscience before her, and I asked what I would say if I was in her place. And my answer was very simple. I would have tried to draw a little attention to myself, I would have said I am hungry, that I am dying, I am cold, I am in pain, or something, but she gave me much more—she gave me her grateful love. And she died with a smile on her face. As that man whom we picked up from the drain, half eaten with worms, and we brought him to the home. I have, he said, lived like an animal in the street, but I am going to die like an angel, loved and cared for. And it was so wonderful to see that greatness of that man [who] could speak like that, who could die like that with blaming anybody, without cursing anybody, without comparing anything. Like an angel—that is the greatness of our people. And that is why we believe what Jesus had said: I was hungry—I was naked—I was homeless—I was unwanted, unloved, uncared for—and you did it to me.

http://nobelprize.org/nobel_prizes/peace/laureates/1979/teresa-lecture.html (accessed November 28, 2007).

PROPERS

Most holy God, whose great name is love, you raised up Mother Teresa to be a towering example of self-sacrificing love toward the lowest members of society: Stir your people to follow her example and give themselves to the service of those from whom the world turns away and puts out of mind, and so to make real the love of your Son Jesus Christ our Lord; who lives and reigns with you and the holy Spirit, one God, now and forever.
PHP

    or

Lord, make me a channel of thy peace that, where there is hatred, I may bring love; that, where there is wrong, I may bring the spirit of forgiveness; that, where there is discord, I may bring harmony; that, where there is error, I may bring truth; that, where there is doubt, I may bring faith; that, where there is despair, I may bring hope; that, where there are shadows, I may bring light; that, where there is sadness, I may bring joy.

Lord, grant that I may seek rather to comfort than to be comforted, to understand than to be understood; to love than to be loved; for it is by forgetting self that one finds; it is in forgiving that one is forgiven; it is by dying that one awakens to eternal life.

The prayer attributed to St. Francis of Assisi adapted by the Missionaries of Charity

Readings:	Isaiah 58:6-9
	Psalm 82
	Romans 12:1-21
	Matthew 25:31-46
Hymn of the Day:	
	"Where restless crowds are thronging along the city ways" (LBW 430)
Prayers:	For the poor of the world
	For those in need who are ignored or rejected by society
	For those who serve the poor and forgotten
	For a spirit of charity and generosity
Preface:	A Saint (1) (BCP)
Color:	White

September 8

The Nativity of the Blessed Virgin Mary

The Church celebrates just three birthdays on its calendar: the nativity of Christ the Lord, the nativity of his forerunner John the Baptist, and the nativity of his mother. It is not known why September 8 was chosen to commemorate the birth of the Virgin Mary. Scripture reports only that she was a lineal descendent of the royal family of David, and says nothing about the date, place, or circumstances of her birth. Nonetheless, since early times, in Rome at least from the seventh century, the Church has kept this day to remember the birth of her to whom the angelic messenger said, "Blessed are you among women."

The celebration of Mary's birth originated in the East and probably goes back to the dedication of St. Anne's Church in Jerusalem, which was built in the fifth century on the supposed site of the house in which Mary was born. There is a legend that a company of angels was heard in the air proclaiming the day as her birthday. The hymns of Romanos, a deacon in Constantinople around 500, imply that the feast of Mary's birth had been fervently accepted by the people.

The Nativity of Mary, celebrated on this date in East and West, was continued on many Lutheran calendars down into the nineteenth century and occurs in a number of American Lutheran service books and calendars. The feast was omitted in the first Anglican Prayer Book of 1549 but was reinstated in subsequent books, although it has not been included in American Episcopal Prayer Books.

SEPTEMBER

READING

From a discourse by Andrew of Crete (*ca*. 660–732)

The radiant and manifest coming of God to humanity required a joyful prelude to introduce the great gift of salvation to us. This day's festival, the birth of the Mother of God, is the prelude, while the final act is the union of the Word with flesh. Today the Virgin is born, nourished, and formed, and to be fit for her role as Mother of God, who is the divine King of the everlasting ages.

Justly then do we celebrate this mystery because it signifies for us a double grace. We are led toward the truth, and we are led away from our condition of slavery to the letter of the law. How can this be? Darkness yields before the coming of light, and grace exchanges legalism for freedom. But midway between the two stands today's mystery, at the frontier where types and symbols give way to reality, and the old is replaced by the new.

Therefore, let all creation sing and dance and contribute its fullest measure of joy to the celebration of this day. Let saints in heaven and us on earth join in one festival. Let everything, things of earth and things above, rejoice together. Today this created world is raised to the dignity of a holy place for him who made all things. The creature is newly prepared to be a divine dwelling place for the Creator.

Sermon 1. From the English translation of the Office of Readings from the Liturgy of the Hours by the International Committee on English in the Liturgy, abbreviated and rev. PHP.

PROPERS

We pray you, O Lord, pour into our hearts the abundance of your heavenly grace, that as the childbearing of the Blessed Virgin Mary was to us the dawn of salvation, so the devout celebration of her nativity may draw us closer to him who is our peace, Jesus Christ our Lord; who lives and reigns with you and the Holy Spirit, one God, now and forever.

Gregorian sacramentary, RS, trans. PHP, et al.

Readings:	Micah 5:1-4a
	Psalm 12:5-7
	Romans 8:28-30
	Matthew 1:18-23
Hymn of the Day:	
	"Ye who claim the faith of Jesus" (H82 268, 269)
Prayers:	Of thanksgiving for the Virgin Mary, who brought into the world the Son of God
	For all Christian mothers
	For those who continue to prepare for the coming of the kingdom
Preface:	Advent
Color:	White

September 9

Peter Claver, Priest, Missionary to Colombia, 1654

Peter Claver was born at Verdu in Catalonia, Spain, in 1580. From 1596 he studied arts and letters at the University of Barcelona; in 1602 he entered the Society of Jesus. An old hall-porter at the Jesuit college in Majorca, St. Alphonsus Rodriguez, encouraged the young Jesuit to respond to the call to the mission fields of the New World. In 1610 Claver landed at Cartagena in what is now Colombia and came under the influence of Father Alonso de Sandoval, another Jesuit who devoted his life to the local slaves.

After his ordination in 1616, Claver began the work that was to last for thirty-three years, among the black slaves, being, as he put it, "the slave of the blacks for ever." The slave trade inflicted atrocious sufferings on its African victims, whose religious squalor and neglect matched their physical condition. Father Claver was in their service from the moment a slave ship docked at Cartagena; his mission was to relieve them and to redeem them (the number of those he baptized was enormous), and he worked in conditions that were often almost as terrible for him as for them. He did all he could to follow up the slaves in the mines and on the plantations to which they were allotted, and the opposition he encountered came from others as well as slave owners. At least one Spanish lady, Isabel de Urebina, however, never ceased to help and encourage him.

Father Claver spent much time at the city jails, the inmates of which included prisoners of the Inquisition. Claver had "a great esteem" for the Inquisition, but he also had a deep compassion for the people, many of them Portuguese, who had come under its suspicion. He also interested himself in numbers of the English and other foreigners who had been captured off marauding ships. His work in the hospitals gave rise to great admiration among his contemporaries; his care for the sick and diseased, white and black, showed extraordinary control over natural revulsion, although it was often manifested in ways that now seem gratuitous and offensive.

He was stubborn and sometimes difficult, but his defense of the oppressed against the rich and powerful required strength of will. For the last four years of his life, he was half paralyzed and in constant pain, left in a small room, alone and ignored. A servant, ironically a negro, who had been told to look after him, neglected the old man and treated him unkindly. Peter Claver died at Cartagena on September 8, 1654.

He was canonized in 1888 and is remembered on the Roman Catholic calendar in the United States; he was added to the Lutheran calendar in the Spanish-language service book, *Libro de Liturgia y Cántico* (1998) under the Spanish form of his name, Pedro de Claver. He is included in the calendar in *Evangelical Lutheran Worship*.

FOR FURTHER READING

Valtierra, Angel. *Peter Claver, Saint of the Slaves.* Trans. Janet Perry and L. J. Woodward. Westminster: Newman, 1960.

READING

From a letter by Peter Claver

Yesterday, May 30, 1627, on the feast of the Most Holy Trinity, numerous blacks, brought from the rivers of Africa, disembarked from a large ship. Carrying two baskets of oranges, lemons, and sweet biscuits, and I know not what else, we hurried toward them. When we approached their quarters, we thought we were entering another Guinea. We had to force our way through the crowd until we reached the sick. Large numbers of the sick were lying on the wet ground or rather in puddles of mud. To prevent excessive dampness, someone had thought of building up a mound with a mixture of tiles and broken pieces of bricks. This then was their couch, a very uncomfortable one not only for that reason, but especially because they were naked, without any clothing to protect them.

We laid aside our cloaks, therefore, and brought from a warehouse whatever was handy to build a platform. In that way we covered a space to which we at last transferred the sick, by forcing a passage through the bands of slaves. Then we divided the sick into two groups: one group my companion approached with an interpreter, while I addressed the other group. There were two blacks, nearer death than life, already cold, whose pulse could scarcely be detected. With the help of a tile we pulled some live coals together and placed them in the middle near the dying men. Into this fire we tossed aromatics. Of these we had two wallets full, and we used them all up on this occasion. Then, using our own cloaks, for they had nothing of this sort, and to ask the owners for others would have been a waste of words, we provided for them a smoke treatment, by which they seemed to recover warmth and the breath of life. The joy in their eyes as they looked at us was something to see.

From the English translation of the Office of Readings from the Liturgy of the Hours © 1974 the International Committee on English in the Liturgy. All rights reserved.

PROPERS

Merciful and loving God, you offer to all peoples the dignity of sharing your life: By the example of Peter Claver, strengthen us to overcome all racial hatred, and to love one another as brothers and sisters; for the sake of Jesus Christ our Lord, who lives and reigns with you and the Holy Spirit, one God, now and forever.

RS, trans. PHP

Readings:	Isaiah 58:6-11
	Psalm 1
	Matthew 25:31-46
Hymn of the Day:	
	"Rise, shine, you people! Christ the Lord has entered" (LBW 393, LSB 825, ELW 665)
Prayers:	For all who work with the poor and disadvantaged
	For those who do not share in the wealth and prosperity of the world
	For the conversion of those who oppress the poor and weak
Preface:	Baptism (BCP)
Color:	White

ALSO ON SEPTEMBER 9

The Episcopal *Lesser Feasts and Fasts 1997* added to the calendar the commemoration of **Constance**, nun, and her companions, three other sisters and two priests, the Martyrs of Memphis, who died ministering to victims of the Yellow Fever epidemic that ravaged Memphis in August, 1878. (See Clara Maass, August 13.)

September 10

Lesser Feasts and Fasts 1997 added to the calendar **Alexander Crummell** (1819–1898), an African American pioneer priest, missionary to Liberia, and educator.

September 12

The 1979 *Book of Common Prayer* added to its calendar **John Henry Hobart** (1775–1830), Bishop of New York, who expanded and strengthened the Episcopal Church throughout New York state.

September 13

John Chrysostom, Bishop of Constantinople, 407

John, since the sixth century called *Chrysostom*, "golden-mouthed," was born *ca.* 349 in Antioch, one of the largest and most cosmopolitan cities of the world at that time. His father, who died when John was very young, was a well-to-do army general; John's mother, Anthusa, was a Christian.

John studied for a career in the law under the well-known pagan philosopher Libanius, who regarded him as his most brilliant student. He also came under the influence of the biblical scholar Diodorus, however, and at the age of eighteen he turned away from his proposed career and was baptized at Easter *ca.* 368 and ordained a lector in the church. He first thought to become a monk, and for several years he did live an ascetic life as a hermit. He returned to Antioch, however, and served as deacon under the saintly and beloved Bishop Melitius from 381 to 386.

In 386 John was ordained to the priesthood and became an assistant to Melitius's successor, Bishop Flavian of Antioch. John regularly preached in the cathedral, where he became famous for his sermons. He proved himself an excellent expositor of Scripture, able to understand the author's meaning and to make practical application of the message, in opposition to the allegorical interpretation that was then popular. In 387 he preached a dramatic series of sermons, "On the Statues," to the people of Antioch as they awaited the imperial decree of punishment for the rioting in which they had destroyed the statues of the emperor. During the twelve years that he preached in Antioch, his themes included pleas for social justice, opposition to slavery, the equality of women and the sanctity of the home, and insistence on the role of laypeople in worship. His sermons were delivered within the framework of the church year, and some of his sermons on particular festivals or occasions are among the most famous. An Easter sermon of his is still read every year in the Paschal services of the Eastern Orthodox Churches.

In 398 John was unexpectedly selected to be the Bishop of Constantinople, one of the most important posts in the Church, and he was consecrated bishop on February 26 of that year. In Constantinople, John of Antioch won the affection and admiration of many by his simple life, his honesty and charity, and the eloquence of his sermons. These same qualities made him many enemies, too, and it was especially his attempts to reform the clergy of the capital of the empire and his denunciation of corruption in the court that turned powerful people against him. He ousted one deacon for murder, another for adultery.

In 403 the empress Eudoxia, previously his admirer, conspired with Theophilus of Alexandria to have John condemned on false charges and banished from the city. The uproar among the people caused by this Synod of the Oak, reinforced by an accident in the palace (probably Eudoxia had a miscarriage) that the empress and others interpreted as a sign from God, brought him back. But since he was just as uncompromising as before, he was forbidden to enter his cathedral. When some three thousand catechumens gathered at the Baths of Constantine for baptism, soldiers broke up the service and the waters ran red with blood.

John was exiled to the obscure town of Cucusus in Armenia. He went into exile on June 24, 404, but from Cucusus he continued to wield great influence, chiefly through correspondence with friends back in the capital and Church leaders in other parts of the world; over two hundred of these letters are extant. Pope Innocent I supported John and condemned the Synod of the Oak as illegal. The papal envoys to Constantinople were treated rudely, jailed, and then sent back to Rome. The pope broke off communication with all of Chrysostom's chief opponents. Despite support by the people of Constantinople, the pope, and the entire Western Church, the emperor in 407 ordered John moved to a still more isolated location, Pityus. John Chrysostom was forced to march on foot, bare-headed, in severe weather, and he died from the rigors of the journey on September 14, 407, at Comana in Pontus. His last words were his customary thanksgiving, "Glory to God for all things."

St. John Chrysostom was one of the great preachers of Christendom, and he is traditionally regarded as the best preacher in the history of the church. His sermons and other writings, including his best-known book, *On the Dignity of the*

Priesthood, have repeatedly been edited and translated. They are available today in many languages and in various editions.

On January 27, 438, John Chrysostom's body was brought to Constantinople and placed in the Church of the Apostles, as Emperor Theodosius II did penance for his parents' offenses. In 1204 the Venetians plundered the city and sent the remains of Chrysostom to Rome; his grave is still shown in the choir chapel of St. Peter's Basilica. January 27, the date of the transfer of his body to Constantinople, is the date that had been observed in the Western church for Chrysostom's commemoration, because the date of his death, September 14, was already a festival, Holy Cross Day. The calendars in the *Book of Common Prayer* and in the Methodist book *For All the Saints* and in the *Lutheran Service Book* retain January 27 as the date of his commemoration. The present Roman Catholic and Lutheran calendars commemorate him on September 13, the day before his actual death. In the East his chief commemoration takes place on November 13, but the translation of his relics is remembered on January 27 as well.

The principal liturgy of the Eastern Orthodox Churches bears his name, the Liturgy of St. John Chrysostom, although its main features had developed before his lifetime and it probably reached its final form after his death.

FOR FURTHER READING

Baur, P. Chrysostomos. *John Chrysostom and His Time.* Trans. M. Gonzaga. 2 vols. Westminster: Newman, 1960–1961.

Von Campenhausen, Hans. *The Fathers of the Greek Church.* 129–44. Trans. Stanley Godman. New York: Pantheon, 1959.

J. N. D. Kelly. *Golden Mouth: The Story of John Chrysostom, Ascetic, Preacher, Bishop.* Ithaca: Cornell University Press, 1995.

Mayer, Wendy, and Pauline Allen. *John Chrysostom.* New York: Routledge, 1999.

Wilken, Robert L. *John Chrysostom and the Jews: Rhetoric and Reality in the Late Fourth Century.* Berkeley: University of California Press, 1983.

READING

From a sermon by John Chrysostom

The waters have risen and severe storms are upon us, but we do not fear drowning, for we stand firmly upon a rock. Let the sea rage, it cannot break the rock. Let the waves rise, they cannot sink Jesus' boat. Are we to fear death? "To me, living is Christ, and dying is gain." [Phil. 1:21] Are we to fear exile? "The earth is the Lord's and all that is in it." [Ps. 24:1] Are we to fear the confiscation of our goods? "We brought nothing into the world, and we can take nothing out of it." [1 Tim. 6:7] I have only contempt for the world's threats; I find its blessing laughable. I have no fear of poverty, no desire for wealth. I am not afraid of death nor do I desire to live, except for your good. I concentrate therefore on the present situation, and I urge you, my friends, to have confidence.

Do you not hear the Lord saying, "Where two or three are gathered in my name, I am there among them"? [Matt. 18:20] Will he be absent, then, when so many people united in love are gathered together? I have his promise and need not rely on my own strength. I have what he has written as my staff, my security, my peaceful harbor. Let the world be turned upside down. I cling to his promise and read his message; that is my protecting wall and garrison. What message and promise? "I am with you always, to the end of the age." [Matt. 28:20]

If Christ is with me, whom shall I fear? Though the waves and the sea and the anger of princes are roused against me, they are less to me than a spider's web. Indeed, unless you, my brothers, had detained me, I would have left this very day. For I say always, "Lord, your will be done" [Matt. 6:10]; not what this fellow or that would have me do, but what you want me to do. That is my strong tower, my immovable rock, my staff that never gives way. If God wants something, let it be done. If he wants me to stay here, I am grateful. But wherever he wants me to be, there do I thank him.

Yet where I am, there you are too, and where you are, I am. For we are a single body, and the body cannot be separated from the head nor the head from the body. Distance separates us, but love unites us, and death itself cannot divide us. For although my body die, my soul will live and remember my people.

You are my fellow citizens, my fathers, my brothers, my children, my limbs, my body. You are my light, sweeter to me than the visible light. For what can the rays of the sun bestow on me that is comparable to your love? The sun's light is useful in my earthly life, but your love is fashioning a crown for me in the life to come.

The Sermons before His Exile by John Chrysostom, numbers 1-3. From the English translation of the Office of Readings from the Liturgy of the Hours by the International Committee on English in the Liturgy, rev. PHP.

PROPERS

Almighty God, the strength of all who trust in you, you made John Chrysostom renowned for his eloquence and heroic in his sufferings: Grant that we may learn your righteousness from his teaching and gain courage from his patient endurance; through your Son Jesus Christ our Lord, who lives and reigns with you and the Holy Spirit, one God, now and forever.

RS, rev. PHP

Readings: Jeremiah 1:4-10
              Psalm 49:1-8 *or* 34:15-22
              Romans 10:11-17
              Luke 21:12-15

Hymn of the Day:
        "Awake, O Spirit of the watchmen" (H82 540, LBW 382)
        (*St. Chrysostom* is the name of two tunes: SBH 504, H40 460; and SBH 507)
Prayers: For the Patriarch of Constantinople
        For preachers of the gospel
        For strength to endure suffering with Christ
        For those who are persecuted for their bold witness to the Christian faith and life
Preface: A Saint (2) (BCP)
Color: White

September 14

Holy Cross Day

"The message about the cross" (1 Cor. 1:18) is the central affirmation of Christianity, demonstrating both the depth of human sin that made the death of Christ necessary and the infinite value of every human being that caused God to act to redeem the human race. The cross is shorthand, symbolic language for the redemptive passion and death of Christ.

This feast day of the cross is a celebration of the Johannine view of the crucifixion of Christ as the time of his glorification, the moment of death being the moment of his triumph and victory. His degradation on the cross paradoxically corresponds to his exaltation. Against the darkness is lifted the beacon of hope, against the forces of evil and destruction is erected "the sign of the Son of Man" (Matt. 24:30), against death and defeat is raised the sign of life and victory. It is therefore natural that Christian piety and devotion should attach themselves to the instrument on which the world's sin was taken away. Made holy by its use, stained and washed with Christ's blood, the cross on which the Savior of the world died was surrounded with honor and pious legends. It replaced the tree of disobedience in Eden and became the sign of the perfect Man's obedience. As the first tree brought corruption and death, so the second brought life and health. The sign of death is transformed into the sign of life, that where Satan, who by a tree in the garden once overcame the progenitors of the human race, by a tree is overcome by the Second Adam. Moreover, there is an eschatological dimension to the cross as the "sign of the Son of Man," echoed in a versicle and response in the old *Divine Office* and now in the *Liturgy of the Hours* a Responsory in Evening Prayer I of The Triumph of the Cross, "This sign of the cross shall be in the heavens when the Lord shall come to judge."

In the year 355 the emperor Constantine built two basilicas in Jerusalem. One of the churches was on the supposed site of the Holy Sepulchre, and in the course of excavating for this church, the story goes, the cross on which Christ was crucified was discovered. Cyril of Jerusalem, who seems to be reliable, writing in the year 350, says that the cross of Christ was found at Jerusalem during the time of Constantine. According to a less reliable tradition, St. Helena, Constantine's mother (see May 22), was the one who discovered the true cross. Not one but three crosses were found, it is said, and Helena was able to determine which one was Christ's cross by applying the three crosses to a dead man. One cross brought the dead man to life, and this was declared to be the cross of Christ.

The relic of the true cross was preserved in a silver receptacle in the basilica of the Holy Sepulchre after pieces had been taken away by pilgrims and distributed throughout the world. A Spanish pilgrim, Egeria, who made a journey to Jerusalem *ca.* 385–388 and who describes the ceremonies of the church there, tells of the practice of the veneration of the cross on Good Friday and of how the deacons guarded it so that the pilgrims who kissed it would not bite out pieces to carry away.

The Feast of the Exultation of the Holy Cross, first clearly mentioned by Pope Sergius (687–701), commemorated the exposition of the true cross at Jerusalem in 629 by the emperor Heraclius after he had recovered it from the Persians who had captured it when they destroyed the Church of the Holy Sepulchre in 614. This exposition seems actually to have taken place in the spring, but it was celebrated in the fall at the time of the anniversary of the dedication of the church.

There was on May 3 another festival of the cross called "The Invention of the Cross" or "The Finding of the Cross" (from the Latin *invenio*, I find). This celebration seems to have originated in Gaul in the seventh century and was celebrated in Rome by the beginning of the eighth century. It recalled the discovery of the cross by St. Helena. It was always treated as a secondary celebration and was suppressed by the Roman Catholic Church in 1960. The Eastern Churches originally commemorated the finding of the cross together with the consecration of Constantine's two basilicas.

Holy Cross Day became popular in northern Europe and remained on Lutheran calendars long after the Reformation. Holy Cross has been a popular name for Lutheran churches in America and elsewhere. The present Roman Catholic calendar calls September 14 "The Triumph of the Cross," and it is a festival of Christ's passion and cross, giving opportunity for a joyous commemoration of his redeeming death with a festal emphasis not appropriate during Holy Week.

Holy Cross Day, the legends of the discovery and identification of what was believed to be the true cross apart, is an occasion for the Church to consider what Luther called the "theology of the cross," the divinely-chosen was of humility and service, of death as the path to life and salvation.

Moreover, in the past, Holy Cross Day determined the autumnal Ember Days (from the German Quatember, from the Latin *quattour tempore*, related to the turning of the four seasons), the Wednesday, Friday, and Saturday following Holy

Cross Day. These were originally agricultural festivals kept three times during the year, following Pentecost, Holy Cross, and St. Lucy's Day, December 13; the Wednesday, Friday, and Saturday following the First Sunday in Lent were added later. The autumn Ember Days were at the time of the vintage in Rome and were a time for prayer for the fruits of the earth. They became times for ordination and for prayer for the ministry.

Until the time of Constantine (fourth century), the symbol of the cross was rarely used by Christians because of the need for secrecy as well as because of the shame associated with the crucifixion. In the fifth century in Syria, there is evidence that the cross was placed on the altar during Mass, but this use did not appear in the West until much later. During the fifth and sixth centuries, the use of a glorified cross was common, studded with jewels. It was portrayed as splendid and royal, a throne for Christ, triumphant over the shame attached to the cross in the first centuries. The earliest representation of the body of Christ on the cross is found in the fifth century. He was usually shown as alive, clothed in priestly and royal vestments, reigning from the cross as his throne. By the sixth century, processional crosses were employed and were set up at, but not on, the altar.

Devotional attention was drawn to the cross, which was treated as a living thing, a tree of life that corresponded to the tree in the Garden of Eden by which death entered the world, a creature that could be addressed and asked to bear gently the body of him who hung upon it, as in the passiontide hymn by Fortunatus, "Sing, my tongue, the glorious battle," and in the moving Old English poem, "The Dream of the Rood." Always throughout these centuries, the cross was a sign of salvation and victory. The crucifix increased in popularity during the Middle Ages and the figure of Christ was shown in the agony of death. A "passion mysticism" developed, which emphasized the suffering Servant of God and the cost of salvation.

The use of the sign of the cross, the tracing of a cross on the forehead with the thumb or forefinger, was already customary in private devotion in the second century. By the fourth century it had come into wider use in the liturgy together with a signing of the breast in addition to the forehead. In the eighth century a signing of the lips was added.

The making of the sign of the cross with two fingers was introduced in the East in the sixth century to combat the Monophysites, who said that Christ had only one nature; the use of three fingers emphasized belief in the Holy Trinity. The practice passed into the West and was introduced into the Mass in the ninth century.

The large sign of the cross from forehead to breast to shoulders was used in private devotion in the fifth century, in monasteries by the tenth century. In the thirteenth century Innocent III directed that the shoulders be touched from right to left with three fingers (as in the East still); later, about the time of the Reformation, the sign was made with the whole hand and from left to right. The use of the whole hand to make the sign of the cross is characteristic of the West; the use of three fingers is characteristic of the East. In the West the usual accompanying words are "In the Name of the Father, and of the Son, and of the Holy Spirit." In the East there are various formulas, such as "Holy God, holy mighty one, holy immortal one, have mercy on us."

The meaning of the sign of the cross is variously interpreted. It is a recalling of the sign made at baptism, it is a sealing with the sign of Christ, it is an invocation of God's grace, it is an expression of praise of the Holy Trinity. George Herbert in his poem "The Crosse" suggests another meaning: "With but four words, my words, *Thy will be done.*" The four words correspond to the four points of the sign of the cross: forehead, breast, and shoulders.

FOR FURTHER READING

Andreopoulos, Andreas. *The Sign of the Cross: The Gesture, the Mystery, the History.* Brewster: Paraclete, 2006.

Guardini, Romano. *Sacred Signs.* Trans. Grace Branham. St. Louis: Pio Decimo, 1956.

Laliberte, N., and Edward N. West. *The History of the Cross.* New York: Macmillan, 1960.

Liturgy: The Holy Cross. Vol. 1, no. 1. Washington: The Liturgical Conference, 1980.

Regan, Patrick. "Veneration of the Cross." *Worship* 52, no. 1 (January 1958): 2–13.

Van Tongeren, Louis. *Exaltation of the Cross: Toward the Origins of the Feast of the Cross and the Meaning of the Cross in Early Medieval Liturgy.* Liturgia Condenda 11. Louven: Peeters, 2000.

READING

From *Centuries* by Thomas Traherne

The Cross is the abyss of wonders, the centre of desires, the school of virtues, the house of wisdom, the throne of love, the theatre of joys, and the place of sorrows. It is the root of happiness, and the gate of Heaven.

Of all the things in Heaven and Earth it is the most peculiar. It is the most exalted of all objects. It is an Ensign lifted up for all nations, to it shall the Gentiles seek, His rest shall be glorious: the dispersed of Judah shall be gathered to it, from the four corners of the earth. If Love be the weight of the Soul, and its object the centre, all eyes and hearts may convey and turn unto this Object: cleave unto this centre, and by it enter into rest. There we might see all nations assembled with their eyes and hearts upon it. There we may see God's goodness, wisdom and power: yea His mercy and anger displayed. There we may see man's sin and infinite value. His hope and fear, his misery and happiness. There we might see the Rock of Ages, and the Joys of Heaven. There we may see a Man loving all the world, and a God dying for mankind. There we may see all types and ceremonies, figures, and prophecies. And all kingdoms adoring a malefactor: An innocent malefactor, yet the greatest in the world. There we may see the most distant things in Eternity united: all mysteries at once couched together and explained. The only reason why this Glorious Object is so publicly admired by Churches and Kingdoms, and so little thought of by particular men, is because it is truly the most glorious. It is the Root of Comforts and the Fountain of Joys. It is the only supreme and sovereign spectacle in all Worlds. It is a Well of Life beneath in which we may see the face of Heaven above: and the only mirror, wherein all things appear in their proper colours: that is, sprinkled in the blood of our Lord and Saviour.

The Cross of Christ is the Jacob's ladder by which we ascend into the highest heavens. There we see joyful Patriarchs, expecting Saints, Prophets ministering, Apostles publishing, and Doctors teaching, all Nations concentering, and Angels praising. That Cross is a tree set on fire with invisible flame, that illuminateth all the world. The flame is Love: the Love in His bosom who died on it. In the light of which we see how to possess all the things in Heaven and Earth after his similitude. For He that suffered on it was the Son of God as you are: tho' He seemed only a mortal man. He had acquaintance and relations as you have, but He was a lover of Men and Angels. Was He not the Son of God; and Heir of the whole World? To this poor, bleeding, naked Man did all the corn and wine, and oil, and gold and silver in the world minister in an invisible manner, even as He was exposed lying and dying upon the Cross.

Here you learn all patience, meekness, self-denial, courage, prudence, zeal, love, charity, contempt of the world, joy, penitence, contrition, modesty, fidelity, constancy, perseverance, contentation, holiness, and thanksgiving: With whatsoever else is requisite for a Man, a Christian, or a King. This Man bleeding here was tutor to King Charles the Martyr: and Great Master to Saint Paul, the convert who learned of His activity, and zeal unto all nations. Well therefore may we take up with this prospect, and from hence behold all the things in Heaven and Earth. Here we learn to imitate Jesus in His love unto all.

Thomas Traherne, *Centuries,* Intro. by John Farrar (New York: Harper, 1960), 28–30.

PROPERS

Almighty God, whose Son our Savior Jesus Christ was lifted high upon the cross that he might draw the whole world to himself: Mercifully grant that we, who glory in the mystery of our redemption, may have grace to take up our cross and follow him; who lives and reigns with you and the Holy Spirit, one God, in glory everlasting.

1979 BCP, LBW; alt. in ELW

Readings: *BCP*   *RC*

BCP	*RC*
Isaiah 45:21-25	Numbers 21:4-9
Psalm 98 *or* 98:1-4	Psalm 78:1-2, 34-38
Philippians 2:5-11 *or* Galatians 6:14-18	Philippians 2:6-11
John 12:31-36a	John 3:13-17

Hymn of the Day:

"The head that once was crowned with thorns" (H82 483, LBW 173, LSB 532, ELW 432)

Or "We sing the praise of him who died" (H82 471, LBW 344, LSB 429)

Prayers: For the Church of the Holy Sepulchre in Jerusalem and for the Christians of differing traditions worshipping there

For pilgrims to the Holy Land

For grace to choose the way of the cross

For humility

For the knowledge that suffering can be redemptive

For the gift of hope for all who bear the cross

Preface: Passion/Holy Week

Color: Red

September 16

Cyprian, Bishop and Martyr at Carthage, 258

Cyprian was born *ca.* 200 in Carthage, North Africa, where he became a lawyer and a university lecturer. He did not become a Christian until he was about forty-six, and yet, within two years of his baptism, he was elected Bishop of Carthage. At the time, the Church was deeply troubled with schism. Cyprian had a profound knowledge of Scripture, and in his writings he sought to show how the unity of the Church is founded on and preserved by the bishops. In his book *On the Lord's Prayer* he wrote, "We say 'Hallowed be thy Name,' not that we want God to be made holy by our prayers, but because we seek from the Lord that his Name may be made holy in us, . . . so that we who have been made holy in Baptism may persevere in what we have begun to be." Thirteen centuries later, Luther echoed that insight in his Small Catechism in the explanation of the Lord's Prayer.

When the persecution under the emperor Decius erupted in 250, Cyprian hid himself, for which he was much criticized, because he believed that he was still needed to guide and encourage his people in their suffering. During the plague in 252 in Carthage, Cyprian was tireless in comforting the sufferers, but the pagans blamed the Christians for the epidemic. In 258 another round of persecution broke out, instituted by Valerian. Cyprian gladly gave himself up to those who came to arrest him and on September 14, 258, died a martyr's death. An account of what happened was compiled from contemporary documents.

On the morning of the fourteenth of September a great crowd gathered at the Villa Sexti, in accordance with the order of the governor Galerius Maximus. That same day the governor commanded Bishop Cyprian to be brought before him for trial in the court of Sauciolum. After Cyprian was brought in, the governor asked him: "Are you Thascius Cyprian?" And the bishop replied: "Yes, I am." The governor Galerius Maximus said: "Have you posed as the pontiff of a sacrilegious group?" The bishop answered: "I have." The governor said: "Our most venerable emperors have commanded you to perform the religious rites." Bishop Cyprian replied: "I will not do so." Galerius Maximus said: "Follow your orders. In such a just cause there is no need for deliberation."

Then Galerius Maximus, after consulting with his council, reluctantly issued the following judgment: "You have long lived with your sacrilegious convictions, and you have gathered about yourself many others in a vicious conspiracy. You have set yourself up as an enemy of the gods of Rome and of our religious practices. The pious and venerable emperors, the Augusti, Valerian and Gallienus, and Valerian the most noble of Caesars, have been unable to draw you back to the observance of their holy ceremonies. You have been discovered as the author and leader of these heinous crimes, and will consequently be held forth as an example for all who have followed you in your crime. By your blood the law shall be confirmed." Next he read the sentence from a tablet: "It is decided that Thascius Cyprian should die by the sword." Cyprian responded, "Thanks be to God."

After the sentence was passed, a crowd of his fellow Christians said, "We should also be killed with him!" There arose an uproar among the Christians, and a great mob followed after him. Cyprian was then brought out to the grounds of the Villa Sexti, where, taking off his outer cloak and kneeling on the ground, he fell before the Lord in prayer. He removed his dalmatic and gave it to the deacons, and then stood erect while waiting for the executioner. When the executioner arrived, Cyprian told his friends to give the man twenty-five gold pieces. Cloths and napkins were being spread out in front of him by the brethren. Then the blessed Cyprian covered his eyes with his own hands, but when he was unable to tie the ends of the linen himself, the priest Julian and the sub-deacon Julian fastened them for him.

In this way the blessed Cyprian suffered [death], and his body was laid out at a nearby place to satisfy the curiosity of the pagans. During the night Cyprian's body was triumphantly borne away in a procession of Christians who, praying and bearing tapers and torches, carried the body to the cemetery of the governor Macribius Canndidianus which lies on the Mappalian Way near the fish ponds. Not many days later the governor Galerius Maximus died.

The most blessed martyr Cyprian suffered on the fourteenth of September under the Emperors Valerian and Gallienus, in the reign of our true Lord Jesus Christ, to whom belong honor and glory forever. Amen.*

In the two examinations of Cyprian, the considerateness and even deference with which he was treated and how courteous bishop and proconsuls were to one another are remarkable and contrast sharply with the abuse and ranting that so often appear in less authentic accounts of such proceedings.

On the General Roman Calendar, Cyprian is commemorated together with his friend Cornelius, Bishop of Rome and Martyr, on September 16. In the American *Book of Common Prayer,* his feast day is September 13, although on the 1604 Anglican calendar, his feast day is September 26 (because of a long-standing confusion of Cyprian of Carthage with Cyprian a magician of Antioch). Cyprian was

*Letter 60. From the English translation of the Office of Readings from the Liturgy of the Hours © 1974, International Committee on English in the Liturgy, Inc. All rights reserved.

added to the Lutheran calendar in *Evangelical Lutheran Worship* and the *Lutheran Service Book.*

FOR FURTHER READING

Burns, J. Patout, Jr. *Cyprian the Bishop*. New York: Routledge, 2002.

READING

From Cyprian, *On the Unity of the Catholic Church*

This unity we ought to hold and preserve, especially we who preside in the Church as bishops, that we may prove the episcopate itself to be one and undivided. Let no one deceive the brotherhood with falsehood; no one corrupt the faith in the truth by faithless transgression. The episcopate is one; the individual members have each a part, and the parts make up the whole. The Church is a unity; yet by her fruitful increase she is extended far and wide to form a plurality; even as the sun has many rays, but one light; and a tree many boughs but one trunk, whose foundation is the deep seated root; and as when many streams flow down from the one source though a multitude seems to be poured out from the abundance of the copious supply, yet in the source itself unity is preserved. Cut off a ray from the sun's orb; the unity of light refuses division: Break a branch from the tree; the broken member cannot bud: sever the stream from its fount; once severed it is dried up. So also the Church flooded with the light of the Lord, extends her rays over all the globe, yet it is one light which is diffused everywhere and the unity of the body is not broken up. She stretches forth her branches over the whole earth in rich abundance; she spreads far and wide one bounty of her onward flowing streams, yet there is but one head, one source, one mother, abounding in the increase of her fruitfulness. Of her womb we are born, by her milk we are nourished and we are quickened from her breath. . . .

He cannot have God for his Father who has not the Church for his mother.

Henry Bettenson, ed., *Documents of the Christian Church* (New York: Oxford University Press, 1943, 1944), 102–03.

PROPERS

O God, Shepherd of your church, your servant Cyprian strengthened your people by his ministry and by the witness of his suffering: By his example give us courage boldly to confess your Name, to endure suffering for the gospel, and ever work for the unity of your church; through Jesus Christ our Lord, who lives and reigns with you and the Holy Spirit, one God, now and forever.

PHP, after RS

Readings: Psalm 23 *or* 116:10-17
                 1 Peter 5:1-4, 10-11
                 John 10:11-16
Hymn of the Day:
                 "O God, send heralds who will never falter" (LBW 283)
                 or "God has spoken by his prophets" (LBW 258, LSB 583)
Prayers: For Africa and African Christians
                 For the unity of the church
                 For all who work to heal the divisions between Christians
                 For all who are persecuted or exiled because of their faith
                 For the bishops of the church, that they may show solidarity with their clergy and
                    people
Preface: A Saint (3) (BCP)
Color: Red

ALSO ON SEPTEMBER 16

Ninian, Bishop, Missionary to Scotland, *ca.* 430

SEPTEMBER

N inian was a Romanized Briton, born toward the end of the fourth century in southern Scotland. The tradition current in Bede's time was that Ninian trained for the priesthood in Rome and was ordained a bishop there before returning to Scotland to preach the Gospel among the Picts. In 397 he established himself at Whithorn in Galloway, where he built a white stone church. Further details are given in the untrustworthy *Life of Ninian* by Aelred. There is considerable disagreement about Ninian and the extent of his missionary labors. Despite the turbulence of the times, much of his work survived until the arrival of St. Columba and his Irish missionaries at the end of the sixth century. He died *ca.* 430.

Ninian is on the calendar in the *Book of Common Prayer.* He is not included on the General Roman Calendar. Those who wish to commemorate both Cyprian and Ninian may choose to transfer the commemoration of Ninian to September 15.

FOR FURTHER READING

Anderson, Mosa. *St. Ninian: Light of the Celtic North.* London: Faith Press, 1964.

Brooke, Daphne. *Wild Men and Holy Places: St. Ninian, Whithorn, and the Medieval Realm of Galloway.* Edinburgh: Canongate, 1994.

Simpson, W. Douglas. *St. Ninian and the Origins of the Christian Church in Scotland.* Edinburgh: Oliver and Boyd, 1940.

READING

From *The Life of St. Ninian* by Aelred

Meanwhile the most blessed man, being pained that the devil, driven forth from the earth within the ocean, should find rest for himself in a corner of this island in the hearts of the Picts, girded himself as a strong wrestler to cast out his tyranny; taking, moreover, the shield of faith, the helmet of salvation, the breastplate of charity, and the sword of the Spirit, which is the Word of God. Fortified by such arms, and surrounded by the society of his holy brethren as by a heavenly host, he invaded the empire of the strong man armed, with the purpose of rescuing from his power innumerable victims of his captivity: wherefore, attacking the Southern Picts, whom still the Gentile error which clung to them induced to reverence and worship deaf and dumb idols, he taught them the truth of the gospel and the purity of the Christian faith, God working with him, and confirming the word with signs following. To the font of the saving laver run rich and poor, young and old, young men and maidens, mothers with their children, and, renouncing Satan with all his works and pomps, they are joined to the body of the believers by faith, by confession, and by the sacraments. . . . Then the holy bishop began to ordain presbyters, consecrate bishops, distribute other dignities of the ecclesiastical ranks, and divide the whole land into certain parishes. Finally, having confirmed the sons whom he had begotten in Christ in faith and good works, and having set in order all things that referred to the honour of God and the welfare of souls, bidding his brethren farewell, he returned to his own church, where, in great tranquillity of soul, he spent a life perfect in all sanctity and glorious for miracles.

Aelred, *The Life of St. Ninian,* chap. 6, trans. A. P. Forbes, in *Lives of St. Ninian and St. Kentigernn,* The Historians of Scotland, Volume V (Edinburgh, 1874), 14, 15.

PROPERS

O God, by the preaching of your blessed servant and bishop Ninian you caused the light of the Gospel to shine in the land of Britain: Grant, we pray, that having his life and labors in remembrance we may show our thankfulness by following the example of his zeal and patience; through Jesus Christ our Lord, who lives and reigns with you and the Holy Spirit, one God, forever and ever.

LFF

Readings: Isaiah 49:1-6
              Psalm 97:1-2, 7-12 *or* 96:1-7
              Matthew 28:16-20
Hymn of the Day:
              "Come, labor on" (H82 541)

Prayers: For the Church in Scotland
            For all whom God calls to missionary service
Preface: Pentecost
Color: White

September 17

Hildegard, Abbess of Bingen, Renewer of the Church, 1179

Hildegard of Bingen, one of the most remarkable women of the Middle Ages, was born in 1098 in Bemersheim in the lush Rhineland Valley. Very early in her life, beginning in her sixth year, she gained notoriety for her remarkable visions. As the tenth child of a noble family, she was eligible to become a "tithe," and so, according to the custom, when she was eight years old, her parents entrusted her to the care of her father's sister, Jutta, a well-known recluse at the Benedictine monastery at Disibodenberg. In 1136 Hildegard succeeded her as abbess. Under the rule of Hildegard, the convent grew, and in 1150 a new convent was built at Rupertsberg, near Bingen, to which Hildegard brought eighteen sisters. In 1165 she founded another convent at Eibingen.

She lived during a troubled time for the Church, and she, like several other women of the Middle Ages, was a preacher and prophet, traveling throughout Europe, speaking forthrightly to popes and emperors. She spared neither high nor low in her vigorous denunciations of shortcomings, political as well as moral.

Hildegard wrote a number of works, which she dictated to monks who rendered them in Latin. The longest of her works is *Scivias*, an apocalyptic work denouncing in symbolic and allegorical terms wickedness and warning of coming wrath. She wrote expository works on the Gospels and the Rule of St. Benedict; a book of natural science; a medical book on the human body and its ailments, giving evidence of careful observation; a musical morality play, the oldest play by over a century, *The Order of Virtues;* liturgical music; and more than seventy-five songs and lyrics, distinguished for the way she honors nature, full of brilliant imagery and apocalyptic language, preserved with musical notation.

She died in 1179 at the age of eighty-one and was buried at Rupertsberg. When in 1622, during the Thirty Years' War, the convent was destroyed by the Swedes, her remains were moved to Eibingen. From the fifteenth century she is called a saint in the Roman Martyrology. Her feast day, September 17, is observed in several German dioceses. She was added to the Episcopal calendar in *Lesser Feasts and Fasts 1997* and to the Lutheran calendar by the German *Evangelical Calendar of Names* (1962) and *Evangelical Lutheran Worship* (2006).

SEPTEMBER

FOR FURTHER READING

Bent, Ian D. "Hildegard of Bingen." In *The New Grove Dictionary of Music and Musicians*. London: Macmillan, 1980.

Dronke, E. P. M. *Women Writers of the Middle Ages.* Cambridge: Cambridge University Press, 1984.

Flannigan, Sabine. *Hildegard of Bingen, 1098–1179: A Visionary Life.* London: Routledge, 1991.

Fox, Matthew, ed. *Hildegard of Bingen's Book of Divine Works with Letters and Songs.* Santa Fe: Bear, 1987.

Hildegard of Bingen. *Scivias.* Trans. Mother Columba Hart and Jane Bishop. Mahwah: Paulist, 1990.

King-Lenzmeier, Anne. *Hildegard of Bingen: An Integrated Vision.* Collegeville: Liturgical, 2001.

Maddocks, Fiona. *Hildegard of Bingen: The Woman of Her Age.* London: Headline, 2001.

READING

From *The Divine Works of a Simple Man* by Hildegard of Bingen

And I saw as it were in the mystery of God, in the southern sky, a wonderful and beautiful image in the form of a man, whose face was so brilliant and beautiful that I could more easily have looked into the face of the sun. A large ring of golden colour surrounded His head and His face, But in the same ring above the same head another face like that of an older man appeared, whose chin and beard touched the top of His head, and from each side of His neck one wing proceeded, which ascending above the aforesaid ring joined together. But in the top of the arched curve of the right wing, was as it were the head of an eagle, which I perceived had fiery eyes, in which the splendour of the angels appeared as in a mirror. But in the top of the arched curve of the left wing was as it were the face of a man, which shone like the light of the stars. These faces were turned to the east. But from each shoulder of this image one wing was extended to the knees. Also He was clothed in a tunic like the shining of the sun, and in His hand He had a Lamb, like the splendid light of day.

But He trod under His feet a certain monster of a terrible and poisonous shape, and of a black colour, and a certain serpent, which fixed its mouth in the right ear of the same monster, and bending the rest of his body, in turning away his head, he extended his tail on his left side down to his feet. And this image said:

I am the high and fiery power, Who kindled all living sparks, and I breathed out no human things unless I judge them as they are. I placed that encircling wing with My wings above it rightly, that is surrounding them with wisdom. But I burn in the fiery life of the substance of the divinity above the beauty of the fields, and I shine in the waters, and I burn in the sun, and the moon and the stars, and with an aerial and invisible wind, by a certain life which sustains all things, I quicken all things vitally.

For the air lives in greenness and in flowers, waters flow as if they live, the sun also lives in his light, and when the waning moon shall come to the light of the sun, it is kindled as if it were living again; that stars also shine in their light as if they were living. I created also the columns which support all the world: likewise those winds which had wings placed under them, that is to say the gentler winds, which by their gentleness hold back the stronger winds, lest they spread themselves with danger, as the body covers the soul and contains it lest it should expire.

Francesca Maria Steele, *The Life and Visions of St. Hildegarde* (London: Heath, Cranton and Ousely, 1900), 204–05.

PROPERS

God of all times and seasons: Give us grace that we, after the example of your servant Hildegard, may both know and make known the joy and jubilation of being part of your creation, and show forth your glory not only with our lips but in our lives; through Jesus Christ our Savior, who lives and reigns with you and the Holy Spirit, one God, forever and ever.

LFF

Readings:	Sirach 43:1-2, 6-7, 12, 27-28
	Psalm 104:25-34
	John 3:16-21
Hymn of the Day:	
	"How wondrous great, how glorious bright" (H82 369)
	or "From thee all skill and science flow" (SBH 216, H82 566)
Prayers:	For those who have visions of divine things
	For musicians who rejoice in the natural world
	For all in the medical profession
	For courage to speak the truth
Preface:	The Epiphany (BCP)
Color:	White

September 18

Dag Hammarskjöld, Peacemaker, 1961

Dag Hjalmar Agne Carl Hammarskjöld was born July 29, 1905, at Jonkoping, Sweden, the son of the prime minister. He studied law and economics at the universities of Uppsala and Stockholm and taught political economics at

Stockholm (1933–1936). He joined the Swedish civil service in the Ministry of Finance and subsequently became president of the board of the Bank of Sweden. From 1947 he served in the Ministry of Foreign Affairs and was responsible for dealing with problems of trade. In 1951 he was appointed Minister of State with the functions of deputy prime minister.

In that same year he was chosen vice-chairman of the Swedish delegation to the United Nations and was made chairman the following year. On April 10, 1953, following the resignation of Trygve Lie of Norway as Secretary General, Hammarskjöld was elected to a five-year term. During his term, he had to deal with the end of the Korean War, problems in the Middle East, and the crisis over the Suez Canal. In September 1957 he was unanimously elected to a second five-year term.

The Belgian Congo became independent on June 30, 1960, and civil war followed. Hammarskjöld sent a United Nations force to suppress the violence. On a mission to President Moise Tschombe of the province of Katanga to negotiate a cease-fire between the United Nations and Katanga forces, Hammarskjöld was killed in a plane crash September 18, 1961, near Ndola, Rhodesia, now Zambia.

Hammarskjöld surprised and bewildered the world with the posthumous publication of a devotional notebook, *Markings.* Not until the appearance of the book did people see that he was not only a man of diplomacy but a man of deep spiritual life as well. He effected in his life a remarkable combination of the contemplative life with a life of action in the world. He was a Christian, the depths of whose spiritual life were entirely unsuspected until the publication of *Markings.* Not all critics were sympathetic with his internal struggle nor with his sense of vocation; it was apparently embarrassing to some to learn that Hammarskjöld took Christianity seriously. But the book is a compelling record of his spiritual wrestling with the reality of the Christian revelation and its implications for his life. He combined secular work, primarily diplomatic service, with a deep desire for personal spirituality, and from that struggle produced a remarkable devotional book. Working out his faith in the service of humanity, he strove to learn more about the nature and the work of God. As he wrote in *Markings* (p. 122), "In our era, the road to holiness necessarily passes through the world of action."

Hammarskjöld is commemorated on the calendar in the *Lutheran Book of Worship* and *Evangelical Lutheran Worship* and on the Methodist calendar in *For All the Saints.*

FOR FURTHER READING

Aulén, Gustav. *Dag Hammarskjöld's White Book.* Philadelphia: Fortress Press, 1959.

Van Dusen, Henry P. *Dag Hammarskjold: The Statesman and His Faith.* New York: Harper & Row, 1966.

Foote, Wilder, ed. *Dag Hammarskjöld, Servant of Peace: A Selection of His Speeches and Statements.* New York: Harper & Row, 1962.

Stolpe, Sven. *Dag Hammarksjöld: A Spiritual Portrait.* Trans. Naomi Walford. New York: Scribners, 1966.

Urquhart, Brian. *Hammarskjöld.* London: Bodley Head, 1973.

READING

From Dag Hammarskjöld's *Markings*

God does not die on the day when we cease to believe in a personal deity, but we die when our lives cease to be illumined by the steady radiance, renewed daily, of a wonder, the source of which is beyond all reason. [1950]

> —night is drawing nigh—"
> For all that has been—Thanks!
> To all that shall yet be—Yes!
> Not I, but God in me. [1953]

I am the vessel. The draught is God's. And God is the thirsty one.

In the last analysis, what does the word "sacrifice" mean? Or even the word "gift"? He who has nothing can give nothing, The gift is God's—to God.

He who has surrendered himself to it knows that the Way ends on the Cross—even when it is leading through the jubilation of Gennesaret or the triumphal entry into Jerusalem. [April 7, 1953]

Offspring of the past, pregnant with the future, the present moment, nevertheless, always exists in eternity—always in eternity as the point of intersection between time and timelessness of faith, and, therefore, as the moment of freedom from past and future.

> Thou who art over us,
> Thou who art one of us,
> Thou who *art*—
> Also within us,
> May all see Thee—in me also,
> May I prepare the way for Thee,
> May I thank Thee for all that shall fall to my lot,
> May I also not forget the needs of others,
> Keep me in Thy love
> As Thou wouldest that all should be kept in mine.
> May everything in this my being be directed to Thy glory
> And I may never despair,
> For I am under Thy hand,
> And in Thee is all power and goodness.
> Give me a pure heart—that I may see Thee,
> A humble heart—that I may hear Thee,
> A heart of love—that I may serve Thee,
> A heart of faith—that I may abide in Thee. [1954]

SEPTEMBER

Prayer, crystallized in words, assigns a permanent wave length on which the dialogue has to be continued, even when our mind is occupied with other matters. [1955]

Dag Hammarskjöld, *Markings*, trans. Leif Sjoberg and W. H. Auden, 56, 89, 90, 91, 100, 106. Translation copyright © 1964 by Alfred A. Knopf, Inc., and Faber and Faber. Ltd. Reprinted by permission.

PROPERS

Almighty God, kindle, we pray, in every heart the true love of peace, and guide with your wisdom those who take counsel for the nations of the earth, that in tranquility your dominion may increase until the earth is filled with the knowledge of your love; through Jesus Christ our Lord, who lives and reigns with you and the Holy Spirit, one God, now and forever.

1928 Proposed BCP; 1979 BCP

Readings:	Micah 4:1-5
	Psalm 85
	Ephesians 2:13-18
	Matthew 5:1-9
Hymn of the Day:	
	"O God of love, O king of peace" (LBW 414, LSB 751, ELW 749)
Prayers:	For the United Nations
	For all who make peace—in families, cities, nations
	For confidence in God's care
	For grace to learn the meaning and the practice of prayer
Preface:	Baptism (BCP)
Color:	White

ALSO ON SEPTEMBER 18

The *Book of Common Prayer* commemorates on this date **Edward Bouverie Pusey** (1800–1882), professor of Hebrew at Oxford, patristics scholar, noted preacher, and leader of the Oxford Movement in the Church of England.

September 19

Theodore of Tarsus, Archbishop of Canterbury, 690

In 667 the archbishop-elect of Canterbury, Wighard, died in Rome before his consecration. Pope Vitalian took the appointment into his own hands and chose Hadrian [Adrian], an African monk, who was abbot of a monastery near Naples. Hadrian twice declined the offer and suggested for the vacant see Theodore, a Greek monk from Tarsus, St. Paul's native city, in the Roman province of Cilicia, now a part of Turkey. Theodore, now the pope's choice, was not yet a priest at the time and was over sixty years of age. This surprising appointment turned out to be an event of the greatest importance in the history of the Church in England. The pope consecrated Theodore in 668 and sent Hadrian and Benedict Biscop with him to England.

At this time the Church in England was divided by rivalry and strife between those who followed the traditions of the Celtic mission in the north and those who followed the customs of the Roman mission in the south. Archbishop Theodore provided the strong leadership necessary for the reorganization of the Church. His effective visitation of all England brought unity to the two rival traditions. Among other things, he established a school at Canterbury that gained a reputation for excellence in all branches of learning, recognized Chad's worthiness and regularized his episcopal ordination (see March 2), appointed a bishop for Wessex, divided the dioceses of East Anglia, Northumbria, and Mercia, held a synod at Hertford and another at Hatfield, and put out a book of canons.

Hadrian became abbot of the abbey of Saints Peter and Paul (later St. Augustine's), where he organized the monastic school in which many future bishops and abbots were educated in Latin, Greek, Roman law, theology, plainchant, calendar calculation, astronomy, and poetry. The abbot assisted Theodore in his pastoral work, and the flourishing state of the English Church in Theodore's time owed much to Hadrian. He died at Canterbury in 710 and was buried in the church in his monastery. His feast day is January 9. Hadrian is listed among the "Witnesses to the Faith" in the Lutheran African American service book *This Far by Faith* (1999) for commemoration on January 9, his traditional feast day.

Theodore and Hadrian found the Church in England an unorganized missionary body; they left it a fully ordered province of the Western Church. The framework survived the Reformation and is still the basis of the diocesan system of the Church of England.

Theodore died on September 19, 690, at the age of eighty-eight, and was, according to Bede, "the first archbishop whom all England obeyed." His work of unifying the English Church anticipated and set forward the unification of the English tribes into one nation.

FOR FURTHER READING

Reany, William. *St. Theodore of Canterbury.* St. Louis: Herder, 1944.

READING

From *History of the English Church and People* by the Venerable Bede

Theodore arrived in his see on Sunday 27 May in the second year after his consecration, and held it for twenty-one years, three months, and twenty-six days.

Soon after his arrival, he visited every part of the island occupied by the English peoples, and received a ready welcome and hearing everywhere. He was accompanied and assisted throughout his journey by Hadrian [abbot of the monastery of St. Peter and St. Paul in Canterbury], and he taught the Christian way of life and the canonical method of keeping Easter. Theodore was the first archbishop whom the entire Church of the English obeyed, and since, as I have observed, both he and Hadrian were men of learning both in sacred and in secular literature, they attracted a large number of students, into whose minds they poured the waters of wholesome knowledge day by day. In addition to instructing them in the Holy Scriptures, they also taught their pupils poetry, astronomy, and the calculation of the Church calendar. In proof of this, some of their students still alive today are as proficient in Latin and Greek as in their native tongue. Never had there been such happy times as these since the English settled in Britain; for the Christian kings were so strong that they daunted all the barbarous tribes. The people eagerly sought the new-found joys of the kingdom of heaven, and all who wished instruction in the reading of the Scriptures found teachers ready at hand.

Bede, *History of the English Church and People,* trans. with an introduction by Leo Sherley-Price, Revised by R. E. Latham (Penguin Classics 1955, Revised edition 1968), 207, 208. Copyright © Leo Sherley-Price, 1955, 1968. Reprinted by permission of Penguin Books Ltd.

PROPERS

Almighty God, you called your servant Theodore of Tarsus from Rome to the see of Canterbury, and gave him gifts of grace and wisdom to establish unity where there had been division and order where there had been chaos: Create in your Church, by the operation of the Holy Spirit, such godly union and concord that it may proclaim, both by word and example, the Gospel of the Prince of Peace; who lives and reigns with you and the Holy Spirit, one God, forever and ever.

Patrick J. Russell and CMG, LFF

Readings:	Psalm 34:9-14 *or* 112:109
	2 Timothy 2:1-5, 10
	Matthew 24:42-47
Hymn of the Day:	
	"Thy hand, O God, has guided thy flock from age to age" (SBH 159)
Prayers:	For the Archbishop of Canterbury and all archbishops and bishops
	For the Anglican Communion
	For those responsible for the organization and administration of the church
	For the schools of the church
Preface:	A Saint (1) (BCP)
Color:	White

September 20

The *Book of Common Prayer* remembers on this date **John Coleridge Patteson** (1827–1871), Bishop of Melanesia, and his companions, who were killed in 1871 in mistaken retaliation for brutal outrages committed earlier by slave-traders.

September 21

St. Matthew, Apostle, Evangelist

Matthew appears in the Gospels as a tax collector for the Roman government in the city of Capernaum. He was probably born in Galilee of a Jewish family, although the Jews of the day despised tax collectors and generally excluded them from the activities of the Jewish community.

In the Gospels of Mark and Luke, Levi, not Matthew, is called to discipleship, but Matthew always appears in the lists of the twelve apostles. In Mark and Luke, Matthew and Levi do not seem to be regarded as the same person; Origen and others distinguished between Matthew and Levi. It is sometimes suggested, however, that Levi was his original name and that Matthew, which in Hebrew means "gift from God," was given to him after he joined the followers of Jesus. Mark calls him the son of Alphaeus, a man otherwise unknown and apparently not the Alphaeus who was the father of James the Less.

Since the second century the authorship of the first Gospel has been attributed to St. Matthew. The name Levi does not appear in this Gospel, and in the list of the Twelve the name Matthew, who is identified as "the tax collector" ("publican" in older translations), comes after that of Thomas, which it precedes in the other New Testament lists.

Little is known of St. Matthew's life beyond the story of his call, recounted in the Gospel for the Day, when at the word of Jesus he left his desk and devoted himself to the work of discipleship. Tradition suggests that he was the oldest of the apostles. Eusebius says that after the ascension Matthew preached for fifteen years in Judea and then went to foreign nations. Socrates Scholasticus says he labored in Ethiopia; Ambrose sends him to Persia and Isidore to the Macedonians, while others hold that he preached among the Medes and Persians. Clement of Alexandria said that Matthew was a vegetarian. Heracleon says that Matthew died a natural death, but later legend dramatizes his death by fire or sword.

St. Matthew's feast day is observed on November 16 in most Eastern Churches, but it has always been on September 21 in the West. In Year A of the lectionary cycle, when the Gospel readings are primarily from Matthew, St. Matthew's Day is an especially appropriate observance.

SEPTEMBER

In Christian iconography Matthew's symbol is the angel, derived from Ezekiel 1:10.

On St. Matthew's Day in 1522, Luther's German translation of the New Testament was published, and there is a woodcut of the time showing Luther as the Evangelist Matthew working on the Bible.

FOR FURTHER READING

Goodspeed, Edgar J. *Matthew: Apostle, Evangelist.* New York: Winston, 1959.
Hauerwas, Stanley. *Matthew.* Grand Rapids: Brazos, 2007.
Kingsbury, Jack Dean. *Matthew as Story.* Minneapolis: Fortress Press, 1988.
Senior, Donald P. *What Are They Saying about Matthew?* New York: Paulist, 1996.
Stendahl, Krister. *The School of Matthew and Its Use of the Old Testament.* 2d ed.
    Philadelphia: Fortress Press, 1968.
Westerholm, Stephen. *Understanding Matthew: The Early Christian Worldview of the First Gospel.* Grand Rapids: Baker, 2006.

READING

From Martin Luther, *Lectures on Galatians,* 1519

The Lord is my witness that I am not doing this because of my own inclination or pleasure, since I wish for nothing more ardently than to lie hidden in a corner; but since I am altogether obliged to deal publicly with Holy Writ, I want to render as pure a service as I can to my Lord Jesus Christ. For if Divine Scriptures are treated in such a way as to be understood only with regard to the past and not to be applied to our own manner of life, of what benefit will they be? Then they are cold, dead, and not even divine. For you see how fittingly and vividly, yes, how necessarily, this passage [Gal. 5:26] applies to our age. Because others have not dared this or have not understood it—it is not surprising that the teachers of theology have been hated. To me it is certain that the Word of God cannot have been rightly treated without incurring hatred and danger of death, and that if anyone gives offense—especially to the rulers and aristocrats of the people—this is the one sign that it has been treated rightly.

"Lectures on Galatians," in *Luther's Works Vol. 27* © 1964, 1992 Concordia Publishing House. Used with permission.

PROPERS

God of mercy, you chose a tax collector, Matthew, to share the dignity of the apostles: Help us by his example readily to respond to the transforming call of your Son and to follow him, Jesus Christ our Lord; who lives and reigns with you and the Holy Spirit, one God, now and forever.

RS; rev. in LBW, ELW

Readings: Ezekiel 2:8-3:11
                 Psalm 119:33-40
                 Ephesians 2:4-10
                 Matthew 9:9-13
Hymn of the Day:
                 "Your Word, O Lord, like gentle dew" (LBW 232)
Prayers: For renewed appreciation of our Jewish heritage
                 For ethical renewal
                 For openness to the mystery of the glory of Christ
Preface: Apostles
Color: Red

September 22

Justus Falckner, First Lutheran Pastor Ordained in North America, 1723

Rasmus Jensen (see February 20), a priest of the Church of Denmark, was the first Lutheran pastor in North America. The Swedes were the first to establish congregations in the New World. Torkil Reorus, whose Latinized name is frequently reversed to Reorus Torkillus, was the first Lutheran pastor to organize a congregation on the North American continent. He arrived in 1639 at Fort Christina (Wilmington, Delaware). His ministry there was brief; he died September 7, 1643. The congregation he organized was the earliest church of any denomination established in the Philadelphia area. The first Friends' meeting house was erected in 1682 or 1683; First Baptist Church dates from 1688; First Presbyterian Church in 1692; the first Anglican (Episcopal) church in 1695; the first German Reformed congregation in 1727; the first Mennonite congregation 1731; the first Roman Catholic church also 1731; the Moravian church 1732; the Methodist church 1769.

After Torkil Reorus a series of five other priests served the Swedish colony. The most famous of them was Johann Campanius, who in 1646 on Tinicum Island in the Delaware River below Philadelphia erected the first Lutheran church building in North America. Campanius arrived in the New World with Governor John Printz in 1643. Among the twenty-eight articles of instruction from the Swedish crown was the directive:

> 26. Above all things, the governor shall see to it that divine service be zealously performed according to the Unaltered Augsburg Confession, the Council of Uppsala, and the ceremonies of the Swedish Church. . . .

Campanius was in America from 1643 to 1648 and did missionary work among the Delaware Indians, translating Luther's Small Catechism into their language.

The Swedes dealt justly and peacefully with the Indians whom they regarded as the "rightful lords" of the land. Campanius died in Sweden September 17, 1683, at the age of eighty-two.

Justus Falckner, the first Lutheran pastor ordained in the New World, was born November 22, 1672, in Langenreinsdorf, Saxony, and like his two surviving brothers, he was to follow the vocation of his father and grandfathers on both sides for six generations. He studied at the new University of Halle, where thirteen Swedish theological students were also registered, and then at Leipzig. His brother Daniel had come under the influence of a radical group of Pietists who under the leadership of Johannes Kelpius emigrated to Pennsylvania and established a community along the banks of the Wissahickon Creek. These "Wissahickon hermits" wore white habits, joined in daily public worship, tended gardens, developed herbal medicines, provided spiritual direction, cast horoscopes, did book binding, and introduced one of the first pipe organs in America.

Daniel Falckner returned to Germany to consult with August Hermann Francke (see February 6) and then in August 1700 returned with his brother Justus to the community of hermits. By that time there was a severe shortage of Lutheran pastors in the Delaware Valley. The Swedish priest, Andreas Rudman (1668–1708), appointed as suffragan by the archbishop of Uppsala, persuaded Justus Falckner to accept ordination. Together with two other Swedish priests, Rudman ordained Falckner November 24, 1703, in Gloria Dei ("Old Swedes") Church in Philadelphia to serve the Dutch Lutherans in New York. The elaborate ordination service, a testimony to the international character of Lutheranism (a Swede ordaining a German to serve the Dutch), included Swedish vestments and featured an organ, orchestra, and men's choir singing in Latin.

Falckner, sensing a mission wherever Lutherans settled, extended his ministry from Albany, New York, to the Raritan Valley of New Jersey. He married Gerritje Hardick May 26, 1717; they had three children. He wrote a Dutch catechism for adults, *Fundamental Instruction* (1708) and is remembered for his stirring hymn "Rise, O children of salvation" (LBW 182).

Exhausted by the rigors and privations of pioneer life, Falckner died September 21, 1723, in New York City. He was probably buried in the graveyard of his church in Manhattan, now beneath the skyscrapers of Rector Street.

FOR FURTHER READING

Clark, Delber Wallace. *The World of Justus Falckner.* Philadelphia: Muhlenberg, 1946.

Clay, Jehu Curtis. *Annals of the Swedes on the Delaware.* Philadelphia: J. C. Pechin, 1835.

Falckner, Justus. *Fundamental Instruction.* Trans. and ed. Martin Kessler. Delhi: ALPB Books, 2003.

Williams, Kim-Eric. *The Journey of Justus Falckner.* Delhi: ALPB Books, 2003.

READING

From a letter by Justus Falckner to the Superintendent of Schleswig

The Germans, however, I have spoken of not without cause as merely several Evangelical Lutheran Germans, and not the German Evangelical Lutheran Church: those who are destitute of altar and priest forsooth roam about in this desert . . . a deplorable condition indeed. Moreover, there is here a large number of Germans who, however, have partly crawled in among the different sects who use the English tongue. A number are Quakers and Anabaptists; a portion are Free-Thinkers and assimilate with no one. They also allow their children to grow up in the same manner.

In short there are Germans here, and perhaps the majority, who despise God's Word and all outward good order; who blaspheme the Sacraments, and frightfully and publicly give scandal (for the spirit of errors and sects has here erected for itself an asylum. . . .)

Now I recommend to Your Magnificence, as an intelligent German Evangelical theologian . . . on account of the wretched condition of the German Evangelical communities, some establishment of an evangelical church assembly could be made in America, since the Germans are now increasing rapidly. . . .

Both myself and my brother, who is sojourning here, keep ourselves to the Swedish church, although we understand little or nothing of the language. . . Above all one of the Swedish pastors, Magister Rudman, has offered, regardless of the difficulty, to assume the German dialect. For nothing less than the love of God's honor he has offered to go to this trouble now and then to deliver a German address in the Swedish church, until the Germans can have a church of their own, together with the necessary establishment. Accordingly the Germans who still love the evangelical truth, and a proper outward church order, much prefer to attend the Swedish churches here until they can also have their divine worship in their own language as a people. . . . The means are hereby offered in a measure to spread the Gospel truth in these wilds, whereby many of their brethren and fellow-countrymen may be brought from wrong to right, from darkness to light, and from the whirlpool of sectaries to the peace and quiet of the true Church. . . .

From a letter by Justus Falckner to the Superintendent of Schleswig, Heinrich Mühlen, August 1701, trans. Julius Sachse, 1903.

PROPERS

Eternal God, whose praise by the saints in light thunders like the sea, you brought together a diversity of peoples and traditions in the ordination of your servant Justus Falckner: Strengthen, we pray, all servants of your church in their ministry that, supported by the fellowship of the faithful and bold who were victorious in their spiritual warfare, your people may be steadfast in the truth, united in purpose, and comprehensive in their ministry to the world; through your Son Jesus Christ our Lord, who lives and reigns with you and the Holy Spirit, one God, now and forever. PHP

Readings:	Ezekiel 34:11-16
	Psalm 84
	Ephesians 3:14-21
	John 21:15-17
Hymn of the Day:	
	"Rise, O children of salvation" (LBW 182)
Prayers:	For the increase of faithful missionaries and pastors
	For those who have abandoned the practice of the faith
	For a broad vision of the church and its service
Preface:	Apostles and Ordinations (BCP)
Color:	White

ALSO ON SEPTEMBER 22

*L*esser Feasts and Fasts 2003 introduced to the Episcopal calendar on this date a commemoration of **Philander Chase**, Bishop of Ohio, and of Illinois, indefatigable missionary, organizer, and founder of churches in New York State, Louisiana, Ohio, Michigan, and Illinois, who also established Kenyon College and Bexley Hall Seminary. He died September 20, 1852.

The Byzantine calendar on this date commemorates the prophet **Jonah**. The calendar in the *Lutheran Service Book* (2006), following Wilhelm Löhe's calendar (November 12), lists Jonah on this date.

September 25

Sergius of Radonezh, Abbot of Holy Trinity, Moscow, 1392

Sergius, the most popular of all the Russian saints, was born to a once-rich family at Rostov, Russia, May 2, 1314, and was named Bartholomew. The family was driven from their home by civil war and had to make their living by farming at Radonezh, forty miles northeast of Moscow. As a child, Bartholomew avoided lessons in reading and writing until one day a mysterious monk changed his life. He began to read the Bible, books on liturgy, and the Fathers; he visited monasteries. But despite his increasing desire for solitude, Bartholomew remained with his parents until their deaths.

In 1336, with his elder brother, Stephen, he went into the forest that surrounded Radonezh and there built a chapel in honor of the Holy Trinity. His brother left him for a monastery in Moscow, but Bartholomew persevered. A neighboring priest-monk gave him the tonsure and the name Sergius; he was ordained a priest when he was thirty. Stephen returned to the now established and flourishing monastery and was honored as co-founder. By 1354, at the request of the Patriarch of Constantinople, this place of retreat had become a monastic center, the Troitskaya Laura or the Troiste-Sergieva Laura.

In many ways, Sergius's life was like that of Francis of Assisi. He was known for his love of animals and his detachment from worldly goods. He lived an austere life and was accorded honor throughout Russia. The monastery became a center of religious pilgrimage, a principal center of Russian spirituality. Miracles and visions were attributed to Sergius. He went on numerous missions of peace with various Russian princes with the hope of consolidating Russian hegemony under the principality of Moscow against the ravages of the Tartars. In 1378 Sergius refused the office of Patriarch of Moscow. He supported Prince Dmitiri and urged him to repel the attack of the Mongols in 1380 and so to lay the foundations of independence.

Sergius left no writings, but his teachings were spread by his disciples who founded numerous monasteries. He died at his monastery September 25, 1392, and was buried in the monastery church. Pilgrims continue to flock to his grave. In 1920, following the Communist revolution, the monastery was closed and turned into a museum, but it was later returned to the Church, and a theological academy was opened there.

Sergius, whose death is commemorated on this date in the Eastern Church, was added to the Episcopal calendar in the 1979 *Book of Common Prayer* and to the Lutheran calendar in the 1978 *Lutheran Book of Worship*. The Fellowship of St. Alban and St. Sergius is a society that promotes a closer relationship between the Anglican and the Russian Orthodox Churches.

FOR FURTHER READING

Fedotov, G. P., ed. *A Treasury of Russian Spirituality.* New York: Sheed and Ward, 1948.

De Grunwold, Constantin. *Saints of Russia.* Trans. Roger Capel. 67–86. New York: Macmillan, 1960.

Zernov, N. *Saint Sergius, Builder of Russia.* London: SPCK, 1939.

READING

From *The Way of a Pilgrim*

I felt, as it were, hungry for prayer, an urgent need to pour out my soul in prayer, and I had not been quiet nor alone for forty-eight hours. I felt as though there were in my heart a sort of flood struggling to burst out and flow through all my limbs. To hold it back caused me severe, even if comforting, pain in the heart, a pain which needed to be calmed and satisfied in the silence of prayer. And now I saw why those who really practice interior self-acting prayer have fled from the company of men and hidden themselves in unknown places. I saw further why the venerable Isikhi called even the most spiritual and helpful talk mere idle chatter if there were too much of it, just as Ephraim the Syrian says, "Good speech is silver, but silence is pure gold."

[T]he whole salvation of man depends upon prayer, and, therefore, it is primary and necessary, for by it faith is quickened and through it all good works are performed. In a word, with prayer everything goes forward successfully; without it, no act of Christian piety can be done. Thus, the condition that it should be offered unceasingly and always belongs exclusively to prayer. For the other Christian virtues, each of them has its own time. But in the case of prayer, uninterrupted, continuous action is commanded. *Pray without ceasing.* It is right and fitting to pray always, to pray everywhere. True prayer has its conditions. It should be offered with a pure mind and heart, with burning zeal, with close attention, with fear and reverence, and with the deepest humility.

The Way of a Pilgrim and *The Pilgrim Continues His Way,* trans. from the Russian by R. M. French (New York: Seabury, 1965), 98, 189.

PROPERS

O God our Father, we praise you for St. Sergius, a man of prayer, in whom shone forth the radiance of the Holy Spirit, a true warrior of Christ, and a champion of the faith in Russia; and we ask for such gentle and humble leaders, who shall serve your people faithfully because they serve you first; through Jesus Christ our Lord, who lives and reigns with you and the Holy Spirit, one God, forever and ever.

DvD

Readings:	Ecclesiasticus 39:1-9
	Psalm 34:1-8 *or* 33:1-5, 20-21
	Matthew 13:47-52
Hymn of the Day:	
	"Let all mortal flesh keep silence" (H82 324, LBW 198, LSB 621, ELW 490)
Prayers:	For a deeper attachment to the things that abide
	For an increased love of the natural world
	For peace
	For the church in Russia
Preface:	A Saint (2) (BCP) or All Saints (LBW, ELW)
Color:	White

September 26

Lancelot Andrewes, Bishop of Winchester, 1626

Lancelot Andrewes was a learned preacher, patristic scholar, expert in fifteen languages, including Syriac and Chaldee, a translator of much of the Pentateuch and the historical books of the Old Testament in the Authorized King James' Version of the Bible. Born in London in 1555, Andrewes was educated at Cambridge. Ordained in 1580, he became Dean of Westminster in 1601. He twice refused a bishopric but at length was persuaded by King James I to accept the see of Chichester in 1605. He was transferred to Ely in 1609 and to Winchester in 1619. He died September 25, 1626, and is buried in Southwark Cathedral.

He is remembered today for his profound and original devotional manual drawn from the Scripture and ancient liturgies, *Private Prayers [Preces Privatae],* and for his key role in the formation of the English church. He was James I's favorite preacher, and his sermons have been admired for their learning, theological subtlety, and literary power. He ranks with John Donne as one of the two great preachers of the Jacobean age.

SEPTEMBER

FOR FURTHER READING

Andrewes, Lancelot. *The Private Devotions of Lancelot Andrewes [Preces Privatae].* Ed. F. E. Brightman. New York: Meridian, 1961.

Eliot, T. S. *For Lancelot Andrewes: Essays on Style and Order.* Garden City: Doubleday, 1928.

Hewison, P. E., ed. *Lancelot Andrewes: Selected Writings.* Manchester: Carcanet, 1995.

Lossky, Nicolas. *Lancelot Andrewes.* Paris, 1986. English translation, New York: Oxford University Press, 1991.

McCullough, Peter, ed. *Lancelot Andrewes: Selected Sermons and Lectures.* New York: Oxford University Press, 2006.

Mitchell, W. Fraser. *English Pulpit Oratory from Andrewes to Tillotson.* London: SPCK, 1932.

Nicolson, Adam. *God's Secretaries: The Making of the King James Bible.* San Francisco: HarperCollins, 2003.

Norton, David. *A Textual History of the King James Bible.* Cambridge: Cambridge University Press, 2005.

Reidy, Maurice F. *Bishop Lancelot Andrewes, Jacobean Court Preacher.* Chicago: Loyola University Press, 1955.

Welsby, P. A. *Lancelot Andrewes 1555–1626.* London: SPCK, 1958.

READING

From a sermon by Lancelot Andrewes preached on Good
Friday, 1597

[Christ] was pierced with love no less than with grief, and it was that wound of
love made him so constantly endure all the other. Which love we may read in the
palms of his hands, as the Fathers express it out of Isaiah 49:16; for "in the palms
of his hands he hath he graven us," that he might not forget us. And the print of the
nails in them are as capital letters to record his love towards us. For Christ pierced
on the cross is "the very book of love" laid open before us. And again, this love of
his we may read in the cleft of his heart. "The point of the spear serves us instead
of a key", saith Bernard, "letting us through his wounds see his very bowels [the
seat of mercy, the heart], the bowels of tender love and most kind compassion, that
would for us endure to be so entreated. That if the Jews that stood by said truly of
him at Lazarus' grave, "See how he loved him!" when he shed a few tears out of his
eyes; much more truly may we say of him, "See how he loved us!" seeing him shed
both water and blood, and that in great plenty, and that out of his heart.

   Which sight ought to pierce us with love too, no less than before it did with
sorrow. With one, or with both, for both have power to pierce; but specially love,
which except it had entered first and pierced him, no nail or spear could ever have
entered.

Brother Kenneth C.G.A., *From the Fathers to the Churches* (London: Collins, 1983), 178, 179.

PROPERS

O Lord and Father, our King and our God, by your grace the Church was enriched
by the great learning and eloquent preaching of your servant Lancelot Andrewes,
and by his example of biblical and liturgical prayer: Conform our lives, like his, to
the image of Christ, that our hearts may love you, our minds serve you, and our
lips proclaim the greatness of your mercy; through Jesus Christ our Lord, who
lives and reigns with you and the Holy Spirit, one God, now and forever.

CMG, LFF, rev. DvD

Readings:	Psalm 63:1-8 *or* 34:1-8
	1 Timothy 2:1-7a
	Luke 11:1-4
Hymn of the Day:	
	"We sing of God, the mighty source" (H82 386)
Prayers:	For bishops and other clergy that they may always make room in their lives for private prayer
	For all lay people that they may be faithful in prayer
	For those who exert a quiet and saintly influence on the affairs of the church and the world
Preface:	A Saint (1) (BCP)
Color:	White

September 27

Vincent de Paul, Priest, Renewer of Church and Society, 1660

Vincent de Paul was born of peasant stock in Pouy, Gascony, in southwest France, in 1581, and was ordained when he was only twenty years of age. He visited Rome and in 1608 went to Paris. There he came under the influence of the priest and later Cardinal Peter de Berulle, and he decided to devote his life to serving the poor. It is as a friend of the poor that Vincent is chiefly remembered.

He worked among the galley slaves imprisoned in Paris and, it is said, took the place of one of them for a time. He founded communities and confraternities of both men and women dedicated to serving the poor. In 1625, to supervise the formation of priests and to reawaken churchly life among the rural poor, he founded the Congregation of the Mission, called the Vincentians or Lazarists (the Archbishop of Paris had given Vincent the priory of St. Lazare as his headquarters). In 1633 with Louise de Marillac, he founded the Sisters (or Daughters) of Charity, the first congregation of women who were not enclosed in a convent, took no permanent vows, and were entirely devoted to the sick and the poor. To his sisters he said, "Your convent is the sick room, your chapel the parish church, and your cloister the street of the city." He also established retreats for ordinands to rectify the neglect in the preparation of candidates for the priesthood.

There was no human suffering that he did not seek to relieve, and his single-minded goodness and generosity stirred in others a similar generosity. He instructed his missioners that in their work, Protestants were to be treated as brothers and sisters, with love and respect, without condescension or contentiousness. He is highly praised by the Lutheran deaconess Sister Julie Mergner (*The Deaconess and Her Work,* 1915) both for his personal character and for his vision in establishing the Sisters of Charity. Vincent de Paul died September 27, 1660. He was introduced to the Lutheran calendar (on July 20) by Wilhelm Löhe (1868); he is remembered in the German *Evangelical Calendar of Names* (1962) on September 27.

FOR FURTHER READING

Hubbard, Margaret Ann. *Vincent de Paul: Saint of Charity.* New York: Farrar, Straus and Cudahy, 1960.

Laveda, Henri. *The Heroic Life of St. Vincent de Paul.* London: Sheed and Ward, 1932.

Von Matt, Leonard. *St. Vincent de Paul.* Trans. Louis Cognet. Chicago: Regnery, 1960.

De Paul, Vincent, and Louise de Marillac. *Rules, Confessions, and Writings.* Ed. Frances Ryan and John E. Rybolt. New York: Paulist, 1995.

READING

From the letters of Vincent de Paul

Even though the poor are often rough and unrefined, we must not judge them from external appearances nor from the mental gifts they seem to have received. On the contrary, if you consider the poor in the light of faith, then you will observe that they are taking the place of the Son of God who chose to be poor. Although in his passion he almost lost the appearance of a man and was considered a fool by the Gentiles and a stumbling block by the Jews, he showed them that his mission was to preach to the poor: "The Spirit of the Lord has anointed me to bring good news to the poor." [Luke 4:18] We also ought to have this same spirit and imitate Christ's actions, that is, we must take care of the poor, console them, help them, support their cause.

Since Christ willed to be born poor, he chose for himself disciples who were poor. He made himself the servant of the poor and shared their poverty. He went so far as to say that he would consider every deed which either helps or harms the poor as done for or against himself. Since God surely loves the poor, he also loves those who love the poor. For when one person holds another dear, that person also includes in affection anyone who loves or serves the one who is loved. That is why we hope that God will love us for the sake of the poor. So when we visit the poor and needy, we try to be understanding where they are concerned. We sympathize with them so fully that we can echo Paul's words, "I have become all things to all people." [1 Cor. 9:22] Therefore, we must try to be stirred by our neighbors' worries and distress. We must beg God to pour into our hearts sentiments of pity and compassion and to fill them again and again with these dispositions.

It is our duty to prefer the service of the poor to everything else and to offer such service as quickly as possible. If a needy person requires medicine or other help during prayer time, do whatever has to be done with peace of mind. Offer the deed to God as your prayer. Do not become upset or feel guilty because you have interrupted your prayer to serve the poor. God is not neglected if you leave him for such service. One of God's works is merely interrupted so that another can be carried out. So when you leave prayer to serve some person, remember that this very service is performed for God. Charity is certainly greater than any rule. Moreover, all rules must lead to charity. Since she is a noble mistress, we must do whatever she commands. With renewed devotion, then, we must serve the poor, especially outcasts and beggars. They have been given to us as our masters and patrons.

Letter 2546, trans. PHP, based on the 1974 English translation of the Office of Readings from the Liturgy of the Hours by the International Committee on English in the Liturgy.

PROPERS

O God, you bestowed upon your servant Vincent de Paul apostolic power to bring your love to the poor and to foster the devotion of the church's ministry: Grant, we pray, that we may be aflame with the same spirit, and may love those he loved, and live in the way he showed us by his example; through Jesus Christ our Lord, who lives and reigns with you and the Holy Spirit, one God, now and forever.

Proper of the Congregation of the Mission, RS, trans. PHP, after Brother Kenneth, CGA, *A Pocket Calendar of Saints* (Mowbray, 1981), 127.

Readings:	Psalm 112
	1 Corinthians 1:26-31 *or* 2 Corinthians 8:8-9
	Luke 4:16-21
Hymn of the Day:	
	"Lord, whose love through humble service" (H82 610, LBW 423, LSB 848, ELW 712)
	or "The Church of Christ in every age" (LBW 433, ELW 729)
Prayers:	For all who work among the poor and disadvantaged
	For the Sisters of Charity and all deaconesses
	For children who are abused
	For the poor and the unemployed
Preface:	A Saint (1) (BCP)
Color:	White

September 28

Jehu Jones Jr., Pastor, 1852

The story of Jehu Jones, Jr., the first African American to be ordained a Lutheran pastor, represents a melancholy and indeed shameful aspect of Lutheran history. Jones was born in 1786. His father, the proprietor of a large hotel, purchased the freedom of several slaves and belonged to St. John's Church, Charleston, South Carolina, where its pastor, John Bachman, had begun a ministry to black people in 1815. Jones, a tailor, owned a pew in St. John's. In October 1832, Jones, who had felt a call to be a missionary in Liberia but who knew that southern Lutherans would not ordain him, sought an avenue of service in the North. He arrived in New York City bearing letters from Bachman "and other gentlemen in Charleston" testifying to his character and requesting his ordination as a missionary to Africa. In New York, Jones contacted Pastor William D. Strobel, a former member of St. John's, and was ordained by the Ministerium of New York on October 24, 1832. Upon his return to his native South Carolina to prepare for the voyage to Liberia, he was jailed under the Negro Seamen's Act, which forbade any free Negro from reentering South Carolina and directed that free blacks could be jailed or put on the auction block. He was freed on the condition that he would never return to his native state. He left South Carolina without his family and returned to New York. In the spring of 1834, he went to Philadelphia with his wife Elizabeth and nine children and, although he was urged by Philip Mayer, the prominent pastor of St. John's Lutheran Church, to join the Methodist, Presbyterian, or Baptist church, he organized St. Paul's Church in Philadelphia (on Marvine Street, south of Spruce). The Ministerium of Pennsylvania, when the church encountered financial difficulties, took title of the building and failed to assist its pastor. The building, with its cornerstone still in place, is now the property of the Mask and Wig Club of the University of Pennsylvania. The New York Ministerium rejected his appeal for funds. Disillusioned, Jones disappeared from the scene and was heard from no more. He died September 28, 1852, misunderstood and the victim of prejudice, rejection, and abuse. Those African American pastors who have followed him in the ministry of the Lutheran Church, Douglas Strange observes, "have exhibited, by their decision to do so, a greater tolerance and unfeigned forgiveness toward us than that shown to Jehu Jones, Jr."

Daniel Alexander Payne was born of free parents in Charleston February 24, 1811. When he was eighteen he started his own school. A law passed in 1834 forbade people of color to operate their own schools, and he left Charleston, heading north with letters of introduction and recommendation. There he was continually advised to go to Africa. At the urging of Dr. William Strobel, he attended Gettysburg Seminary where Samuel S. Schmucker encouraged him to join the ministry of the African Methodist Episcopal Zion Church. He was ordained to the Lutheran ministry in 1839, but in Philadelphia, where he was in contact with the great A.M.E. preachers and with the continuing advice of Schmucker, Payne joined the A.M.E. Church, became a bishop, president of Wilberforce University, a respected scholar and world-renowned figure in religion and education. He died December 7, 1893. Jones and Payne are both listed among the "Witnesses to the Faith" in the African American Lutheran service book *This Far by Faith* (1999).

Lutheran history in North America had not always been so shameful. The first baptism of a black person by a Lutheran pastor took place in New York on Palm Sunday, April 13, 1669, when Pastor Jacob Fabritius baptized a black man named Emmanuel. Justus Falckner, the first Lutheran and perhaps the first Protestant, ordained in the New World, baptized and married blacks in Albany, New York City, and northern New Jersey. In 1734 Saltzburger Lutherans settled in Georgia, opposed slavery, and purchased black children from slave ships. In 1742 Henry Melchior Muhlenberg saw slaves for the first time and wrote, "I wonder if it will not produce severe judgments if people who pretend to be Christians use their fellow-creatures, who have been redeemed along with themselves, as mere body slaves and do not concern themselves about their souls. This the future will show." In 1752 a black man was baptized at St. Michael's Church in Germantown (Philadelphia) in Muhlenberg's presence.

John Bachman, who was Jones's and Payne's pastor, was born in Rhinebeck, New York, February 14, 1790. He studied in New York and with Philip Frederick Mayer, pastor of St. John's Church in Philadelphia, the same Philip Mayer who bore such racial hostility toward Jehu Jones. He was ordained in 1813 and served as pastor of St. John's Church, Charleston, South Carolina, from 1815 until his death in 1874. Within a year of his arrival, Bachman notified the vestry of St. John's that he intended to begin a ministry to the black community. Two years later he had thirty-seven members, and the work continued to thrive. Bachman, a remarkable man, was also a noted naturalist and collaborator with John James Audubon.

On February 13 the Episcopal calendar commemorates Absalom Jones. He might fittingly be remembered with Jehu Jones.

FOR FURTHER READING

Bachman, Catherine L. *John Bachman, D.D., L.L.D. Ph.D.* Charleston, 1888.

Cobler, Michael Lee. "What Price Inclusion?" *The Mount Airy Parish Practice Notebook* 19 (Summer 1982): 1–16. Philadelphia: Lutheran Theological Seminary.

Johnson, Jeff G. *Black Christians: The Untold Lutheran Story.* St. Louis: Concordia, 1991.

Strange, Douglas C. "The Trials and Tribulations of one Jehu Jones, Jr., the First Ordained Negro Lutheran Clergyman in America." *Una Sancta* 24, no. 2 (Pentecost 1967): 52–55.

READING

From Martin Luther, "A Brief Instruction on What to Look for in the Gospels"

The chief article and foundation of the gospel is that before you take Christ as an example, you accept him as a gift, as a present that God has given you and that is your own.

Now when you have Christ as the foundation and chief blessing of your salvation, then the other part follows: that you take him as your example, giving yourself in service to your neighbor just as you see that Christ has given himself for you. See, there faith and love move forward, God's commandment is fulfilled, and a person is happy and fearless to do and to suffer all things. Therefore make note of this, that Christ as a gift nourishes your faith and makes you a Christian. But Christ as an example exercises your works. These do not make you a Christian. Actually they come forth from you because you have already been made a Christian. As widely as a gift differs from an example, so widely does faith differ from works, for faith possesses nothing of its own, only the deeds and life of Christ.

Works have something of your own in them, yet they should not belong to you but to your neighbor.

So you see that the gospel is really not a book of laws and commandments which requires deeds of us, but a book of divine promises in which God promises, offers, and gives us all his possessions and benefits in Christ. . . .

When you open the book containing the gospels and read or hear how Christ comes here or there, or how someone is brought to him, you should therein perceive the sermon or gospel through which he is coming to you, or that you are being brought to him. For the preaching of the gospel is nothing else than Christ coming to us, or we being brought to him. When you see how he works, however, and how he helps everyone to whom he comes or who is brought to him, then rest assured that faith is accomplishing this in you and that he is offering your soul exactly the same sort of help and favor through the gospel. If you pause here and let him do you good, that is, if your believe that he benefits and helps you, then you really have it. The Christ is yours, presented to you as a gift.

After that it is necessary that you turn this into an example and deal with your neighbor in the very same way, be given also to him as a gift and example.

Martin Luther, "A Brief Instruction on What to Look for in the Gospels," in *Luther's Works,* vol. 35, ed. E. Theodore Bachmann (Philadelphia: Muhlenberg, 1960), 119–20.

PROPERS

Grant, Lord God, to all who have been baptized into the death and resurrection of your Son Jesus Christ, that as we, having in mind the examples of Jehu Jones and Daniel Alexander Payne, have put away the old life of sin, so we may be renewed in the spirit of our minds and live in righteousness and true holiness; through Jesus Christ our Lord, who lives and reigns with you and the Holy Spirit, one God, now and forever.

PHP, based on BCP

Readings:	Jeremiah 17:7-8
	Psalm 16:5-11
	Romans 6:3-11
	Matthew 9:35-38
Hymn of the Day:	
	"Today your mercy calls us" (LBW 304, LSB 915)
	or "Forgive our sins as we forgive" (H82 674, LBW 307, LSB 843, ELW 605)
Prayers:	For the opening of the church to all people
	For a clear understanding of the mission of the church
	For the support and encouragement of those at the margins of society
	For those who work to expand the ministry of the church
Preface:	Lent (1) (BCP)
Color:	Violet

September 29

St. Michael and All Angels

As All Saints' Day (together with All Souls') is a reminder of the size of the one church in heaven and on earth, so this feast of Michael and the angels is a reminder of the breathtaking size of creation, seen and unseen. The feast teaches an understanding that there are aspects of reality beyond what can be grasped with the senses. Angels, like mortals, are children of the infinite imagination of God. They are a higher order of beings, whose service of God is nonetheless joined with ours (see 2 Kings 6:15-17), and the function of the Preface in the Eucharist is to join mortal songs with the perpetual praise offered by the angelic choirs of heaven.

Following Judaism, Christianity (followed in turn by Islam) speaks of an order of heavenly messengers, the angels, created by God to do his bidding and differing from humans by having a fully spiritual nature and no physical body. They are mentioned by Jesus as watching over children (Matt. 18:10) and rejoicing over penitent sinners (Luke 15:10), and there are numerous references to them throughout Scripture. Michael the archangel is mentioned in the books of Daniel (10:13ff; 12:1), Jude (9), and Revelation (12:7-9), as well as in apocryphal literature. Michael is the only angel assigned a liturgical observance before the ninth century. The present Roman Catholic calendar commemorates the three archangels Michael, Gabriel, and Raphael jointly on September 29; previously they had separate feast days. There is also a feast of the Holy Guardian Angels on October 2. At the time of the Reformation, the Lutherans and the Anglicans retained the feast then called the Dedication of St. Michael the Archangel, commemorating the fifth-century dedication of a basilica on the Via Salaria outside Rome, and expanded the celebration to include not only Michael the Archangel but all the angels of God.

The angelic beings were imagined by Pseudo-Dionysus in the sixth century to be arranged in a ninefold division based on Colossians 1:16. In order descending from those nearest the throne of God to those closest to earth, their ranks, grouped in three "hierarchies" of three "choirs" each, are: seraphim, cherubim, thrones; dominations, virtues, powers; principalities, archangels, angels.

The cult of Michael originated in Phrygia, where he was venerated as a healer. Hot springs were dedicated to him in Greece and Asia. Beginning in the fourth century, churches were dedicated to him, and his popularity spread to the West. He is said to have made an appearance on Mt. Garganus on the southeast coast of Italy in the fifth or sixth century during an invasion of the Goths. The apparition was traditionally commemorated on May 5. Michael, whose name is popularly thought to mean "who is like God," is usually shown in art as youthful, strong, clad in armor. As leader of the angelic hosts, he has been regarded as the helper of

Christian armies, guardian of the church, and protector of individual Christians against the devil, especially in the hour of death, the one who accompanies the departed on their journey home and conducts them into the holy light.

St. Michael's Day was especially popular in England and in northern Europe, and a great many churches are dedicated to him. During the middle ages, St. Michael's Day was one of the three holidays that divided the time after Pentecost, the others being Saints Peter and Paul (June 29) and St. Lawrence (August 10). The special calendar function of Michaelmas, as the day is often called in England, has survived in Great Britain and the Commonwealth in marking the fall term at universities and in the courts of law.

FOR FURTHER READING

Davidson, Gustav. *A Dictionary of Angels Including the Fallen Angels.* New York: Free Press, 1967, 1971.

Johnson, Richard F. *Saint Michael the Archangel in Medieval English Legend.* Woodbridge, Suffolk: Boydell and Brewer, 2007.

Macquarrie, John. *Principles of Christian Theology.* 2d ed. New York: Scribner, 1977. 237.

Patrides, C. A. "The Orders of the Angels." In *Promises and Motifs in Renaissance Thought and Literature.* 3–30. Princeton: Princeton University Press, 1982.

Ward, Theodora. *Men and Angels.* New York: Viking, 1970.

Wilson, P. L. *Angels.* New York: Pantheon, 1980.

READING

From a sermon by John Donne

We paint angels with wings, because they bear God's message and proclaim his laws. . . .

They are Creatures that have not so much of a Body as *flesh* is, as *froth* is, as a *vapor* is, as a *sigh* is, and yet with a touch they shall molder a rocke into lesse Atoms, than the sand that it stands upon; and a millstone into smaller flour than it grinds. They are Creatures *made*, and yet not a minute elder than when they were first made, if they were made before all measure of time began; nor, if they were made in the beginning of Time, and now be six thousand years old, have they one wrinckle of Age in their face or one sobbe of weariness in their lungs. They are *primogeniti Dei,* Gods eldest sonnes; they are super-elementary meteors, they hang between the nature of God and the nature of man, and are of middle Condition; And, (if we may offencessly expresse it so) they are *aenigmata Divina,* the Riddles of Heaven, and the perplexities of speculation. But this is but till the Resurrection; then we shall be like them, and know them by that assimilation.

"A Sermon Preached At the Earl of Bridgewaters house in London at the marriage of his daughter, the Lady Mary, to the eldest sonne of the Lord Herbert of Castle-iland, Novemb. 19. 1627," in *The*

Sermons of John Donne, ed. Evelyn M. Simpson and George R. Potter, vol. 8 (Berkeley: University of California Press, 1956), 106.

PROPERS

Everlasting God, you have ordained and constituted in a wonderful order the ministries of angels and mortals: Mercifully grant that, as your holy angels always serve and worship you in heaven, so by your appointment they may help and defend us here on earth; through your Son Jesus Christ our Lord, who lives and reigns with you and the Holy Spirit, one God, forever and ever.

Gregorian sacramentary, RS, BCP, LBW; alt. in ELW

Readings: Daniel 7:9-10,13-14 *or* Genesis 28:10-17
             Psalm 103
             Revelation 12:7-12
             John 1:47-51
Hymn of the Day:
             "Stars of the morning, so gloriously bright" (H40 121, SBH 148, LSB 520)
             or "Christ, the fair glory of the holy angels" (H82 282, 283)
             or "Praise the Lord! O heavens adore him" (LBW 540, ELW 823)
Prayers: For an enlarged sense of God's creation
             For awe before the immensity of creation
             For purity to join the songs of the angels
             For an awareness of the unity of the praise of heaven and earth
Preface: Trinity Sunday (BCP)
Color: White

September 30

Jerome, Translator and Teacher, Priest and Monk of Bethlehem, 420

Eusebius Hieronymus Sophronius, more commonly called Jerome, the Anglicized form of Hieronymus, was born about the year 345 in Stridon, a village near the city of Aquileia in northeast Italy. He came of a moderately well-to-do Christian family. He was educated at home by a tutor until about the age of twelve when he was sent to Rome to study under the famous grammarian Donatus. From the beginning, Jerome was an outstanding student, and he acquired a considerable reputation. His moral life was far from blameless, but he remained close to Christianity, and at the close of his studies at the age of nineteen, he was baptized.

At the age of twenty, Jerome went to Treves, which at the time was the seat of the Imperial Court, and it was there that the religious experience took place which is called his "conversion." In 370 he went to Aquileia where he acquired a circle of friends such a Rufinus, whose names were to recur often in his life. After several years in that city, he decided to go to the East, where a great part of his life was to be spent. In 374 he reached Antioch, then one of the great cities of the world, its bishop the Patriarch "of all the East." There Jerome continued his studies, but before long his earlier desire to become a hermit was rekindled. Also at this time he had a dream in which God told him, "You are a Ciceronian, not a Christian." That is to say, he was too much concerned with the pagan classics. He withdrew into the desert near Antioch and spent four years there. Letters of his are extant telling of the temptations and hardships and also the joys of his solitary life. He had, moreover, taken his books with him, and during this period, he studied Hebrew and wrote several books.

On his return to Antioch, Jerome was ordained to the priesthood against his wishes by Bishop Paulinus, but he never exercised that office. He soon left the city and went to Constantinople where he came to know the saintly bishop Gregory of Nazianzus, and he attended the third Ecumenical Council in 381. The following year he went to Rome and became secretary of the Bishop of Rome, Damasus, at whose request he made a revision of the Latin version of the Gospels in accordance with the Greek text and completed a first revision of the Latin Psalter.

During his stay in Rome, Jerome attacked the luxurious and scandalous life of some of the wealthy Christians and even some of the clergy, and so he forfeited any hope of succeeding Damasus. He also fostered the growing ascetic movement among the upper class women of Rome and began his association with the Lady Paula and her daughters who were to become his staunch friends. Jerome left Rome in 385 for the East, and after being joined by Paula and her companions in Antioch six months later, he visited Palestine and Egypt, thus acquiring experience in all four of the great cities of the empire: Rome, Antioch, Constantinople, and Alexandria.

In 386 Jerome established himself in a monastery near the basilica of the Nativity in Bethlehem with communities nearby that had Paula as their abbess. He himself lived and worked there in a large rock-hewn cell for the rest of his life, and representations of the saint working in his hermit's cell are frequent in sacred paintings. Jerome opened a school for boys in Bethlehem, translated a number of historical, philosophical, and theological works into Latin, and produced several books of his own, including his valuable collection of Christian biographies, *De Viris Illustribus* ("Illustrious Men"). He also wrote many letters and engaged in long and bitter theological controversies, including one with his old friend Rufinus over the teachings of Origen. The great work of his life, however, was his Latin translation of the Bible, which had remained the standard Latin version for sixteen centuries.

Paula died in 404, and the last years of Jerome's life were full of troubles: incursions of refugees from the sack of Rome and a Vandal invasion (410–412), and violence on the part of religious opponents. The monastery itself was burned by marauders in 416. Jerome died September 30, 420, and was buried next to Paula in the Church of the Nativity. His body was later reportedly moved to Rome.

St. Jerome is universally recognized as the most learned man of the age and one of the greatest of biblical scholars. Although he was a violent polemicist and not at his best in theological writings, the wording of his translation of the Bible had a powerful effect on the thinking of later generations.

He was introduced to the Episcopal calendar in the 1979 Prayer Book, to the Lutheran calendar in the *Lutheran Book of Worship,* and to the Methodist calendar in *For All the Saints.*

FOR FURTHER READING

Von Campenhausen, Hans. *The Fathers of the Latin Church.* Trans. Manfred Hoffman. Stanford: Stanford University Press, 1964.
Friedmann, Herbert. *A Bestiary for Saint Jerome: Animal Symbolism in European Religious Art.* Washington, D.C.: Smithsonian Institution Press, 1981.
Kelly, J. N. D. *Jerome.* London: Duckworth, 1976.
Mierow, Charles. *Saint Jerome: The Sage of Bethlehem.* Milwaukee: Bruce, 1959.
Murphy, F. X., ed. *A Monument to Saint Jerome.* New York: Sheed and Ward, 1952.
Rebenich, Stefan. *Jerome.* New York: Routledge, 2002.
Rice, Eugene F., Jr. *Saint Jerome in the Renaissance.* Baltimore: Johns Hopkins University Press, 1985.

SEPTEMBER

READING

From a letter of St. Jerome to Heliodorus, 374 c.e.

My discourse has now sailed clear of the reefs, and from the midst of hollow crags with foaming waves my frail bark has won her way into deep water. Now I may spread my canvas to the wind, and leaving the rocks of controversy astern, like some merry sailor sing a cheerful epilogue. O wilderness, bright with Christ's spring flowers! O solitude, whence come those stones wherewith in the Apocalypse the city of the mighty king is built! O desert, rejoicing in God's familiar presence! What are you doing in the world, brother, you who are more than the universe? How long is the shade of a roof going to confine you? How long shall the smoky prison of these cities shut you in? Believe me, I see something more of light than you behold. How sweet it is to fling off the burden of the flesh, and to fly aloft to the clear radiance of the sky. Are you afraid of poverty? Christ calls the poor blessed. Are you frightened by the thought of toil? No athlete gains his crown without sweat. Are you thinking about food? Faith feels not hunger. Do you dread bruising your limbs worn away with fasting on the bare ground? The Lord lies by your side. Is your rough head bristling with uncombed hair? Your head is Christ. Does the infinite vastness of the desert seem terrible? In spirit you may always stroll in paradise, and when in thought you have ascended there you will no longer be in the desert. Is your skin rough and scurfy without baths? He who has once washed in Christ needs not to wash again. Listen to the apostle's brief reply to all complaints: "The sufferings of this present time are not worthy to be compared with the glory which shall come after them, when it shall be revealed in us." You are a pampered darling indeed, dearest brother, if you wish to rejoice here with this world than to reign with Christ.

The day will come when this corrupt and mortal body shall put on incorruptibility and become immortal. Happy the servant whom the Lord then shall find on the watch. Then at the voice of the trumpet the earth with its peoples shall quake, and you will rejoice. When the Lord comes to give judgment the universe will utter a mournful groan; the tribes of men will beat their breasts; kings once mighty will shiver with naked flanks; Jupiter with all his offspring will then be shown amid real fires; Plato with his disciples will be reveled as but a fool; Aristotle's arguments will not help him. Then you the poor rustic will exult, and say with a smile: "Behold my crucified God, behold the judge. This is he who once was wrapped in swaddling clothes and uttered baby cries in a manger. This is the son of a working man and a woman who served for wages. This is he who, carried in his mother's arms, fled into Egypt, a God from a man. This is he who was clad in a scarlet robe and crowned with thorns. This is he who was called a magician, a man with a devil, a Samaritan. Behold the hands, ye Jews, that you nailed to the cross. Behold the side, ye Romans, that you pierced. See whether this is the same body that you said the disciples carried off secretly in the night?"

O my brother, that it may be yours to say these words and to be present on that day, what labor now can seem hard?

Reprinted by permission of the publishers and Trustees of the Loeb Classical Library from *St. Jerome: Volume II*, Loeb Classical Library® Volume 262, translated by F. A. Wright, pp. 49–53 Cambridge, Mass.: Harvard University Press, copyright © 1933 by the President and Fellows of Harvard College. The Loeb Classical Library® is a registered trademark of the President and Fellows of Harvard College.

PROPERS

O Lord, O God of truth, you gave your servant Jerome delight in the study of Holy Scripture: Grant that your people my find in your word the food of salvation and the fountain of life and ever walk by your light; through him who is the living Word, your Son Jesus Christ our Lord, who lives and reigns with you and the Holy Spirit, one God, now and forever.

PHP, after RS

Readings:	Nehemiah 8:1-3, 5-6, 8-9
	Psalm 19:7-11(12-14) *or* 119:97-104
	2 Timothy 3:14-17
	Luke 24:44-48
Hymn of the Day:	
	"Father of mercies, in your Word what endless glory shines" (LBW 240)
Prayers:	For an increased love of the Scriptures
	For students and scholars of the Bible
	For translators of the Scripture
Preface:	Epiphany
Color:	White

October 1

Remigius, Bishop of Rheims, *ca.* 533

Remigius or Remi, one of the patron saints of France, was added to the Episcopal calendar in the 1979 *Book of Common Prayer*. He was born *ca.* 438 and was elected Bishop of Rheims at the extraordinarily early age of twenty-two. He was a man of great learning and holiness of life. During his long episcopate, he was particularly ardent in his efforts to convert the Franks to Christianity.

Clovis, the king of the Franks, was locked in battle with the German tribe, the Allemani, and called on Christ for help, promising to become a Christian if victory was given to him. Unexpectedly, he won the day, and in fulfillment of his vow, he was baptized at the hand of Remigius on Christmas Day, 436. Three thousand Franks were baptized with their king. Clovis, by becoming Catholic instead of Arian, as were most of the Germanic peoples of the time, changed the religious history of Europe, uniting the Gallo-Roman population and their Christian leaders behind his expanding authority over the Germanic leaders of the West and liberating Gaul from Roman domination.

Remigius died *ca.* 533, perhaps on January 13, the date on which he is commemorated in Rheims. Rheims has always been considered the cradle of the French church, and the kings of France were crowned in the cathedral there. The commemoration of Remigius on October 1 derives from the translation of his relics to a new abbey church by Leo IX in 1049. He was included on the calendar in the *Book of Common Prayer;* he is not on the General Roman Calendar. The German *Evangelical Calendar of Names* includes him on October 12.

OCTOBER

READING

From The History of the Franks by Gregory of Tours

King Clovis told the Queen how he had won a victory by calling on the name of Christ. She then commanded Saint Remigius, Bishop of the town of Rheims, to be summoned secretly and begged him to speak the saving word to the King. The bishop asked Clovis to meet him in private and urged him to believe in the true God, the Maker of heaven and earth, and to forsake his idols, which were without power to help him or anyone else. The king responded, "Holy father, I have willingly listened to you. There remains, however, one difficulty: the people under my command will not agree to forsake their gods, but I will go to them and tell them what you have just told me." He arranged a meeting with his people, but God in his power had preceded him, so that before the king could say a word, all present shouted together, "We will abandon worshipping our mortal gods, and we are ready to follow the immortal God whom Remigius preaches." This was told to the bishop, who was greatly pleased, and he ordered the baptismal pool to be prepared.

King Clovis asked that he might be baptized first by the bishop. Like a new Constantine, he stepped to the baptismal pool, ready to wash away the sores of his old leprosy and in the flowing water to be cleansed of the stains he had borne for so long. As he came to be baptized, the holy man of God spoke to him these significant words: "Bow your head meekly. Worship what you have burnt; burn what you have worshipped."

St. Remigius was a man of immense learning and a great scholar above all else, but he was also renowned for holiness and for the miracles he performed. King Clovis confessed his faith in God Almighty, the three in one. He was baptized in the Name of the Father, and of the Son, and of the Holy Spirit, and marked in holy chrism with the cross of Christ. More than three thousand of his army were baptized at the same time.

St. Gregory of Tours, *The History of the Franks* II, 30–31, trans. PHP, based on the translation by Lewis Thorpe (New York: Penguin Classics, 1974).

PROPERS

O God, who by the teaching of your servant and bishop Remigius you turned the nation of the Franks from vain idolatry to the worship of you, the true and living God, in the fullness of the catholic faith: Grant that we who glory in the name of Christian may show forth our faith in worthy deeds; through Jesus Christ our Lord, who lives and reigns with you and the Holy Spirit, one God, forever and ever.

Trans. *Hours of Prayer* 1928, rev. Paris Missal 1685, 1739, LFF

Readings: Psalm 135:13-21 *or* 103:1-4, 13-18
              1 John 4:1-6
              John 14:3-7
Hymn of the Day:
              "Come, we that love the Lord" (H82 392, SBH 165, LSB 669)
Prayers: For the church in France
              For the people and government of France
              For all who advise and counsel those who are in authority
              For politicians and civic leaders
Preface: A Saint (1) (BCP)
Color: White

October 4

Francis of Assisi, Friar, Renewer of the Church, 1226

Giovanni Bernadone was born in Assisi in Umbria, Italy, in 1182, the son of a wealthy cloth merchant. He was baptized Giovanni (John), but soon after his birth he was called Francesco ("French") because of his father's travels in France and his admiration of the French. Since his day, the name Francis, which was almost unknown before, has become a familiar given name. After a pleasure-seeking youth and work in his father's business, Francis left his comfortable home for a very different life.

His early ambition was to become a knight, and he took part in a border dispute between Assisi and Perugia. He was captured and imprisoned and, stricken with a serious fever, returned home. Back in Assisi he underwent a complete change of heart, became increasingly given to self-examination. Various encounters with beggars and lepers pricked the young man's conscience. One day in the church of St. Damian outside the walls of Assisi, he heard the crucifix over the altar say, "Francis, go and repair my house which is falling into ruin." Characteristically, he took the words literally, sold a bale of goods from his father's warehouse to pay for the repair of the church, and promptly was disinherited and disowned by his father. Francis went away penniless "to wed Lady Poverty."

On the morning of St. Matthias' Day, February 24, 1209, Francis went to the chapel of Portiuncula near Assisi, and as he heard the priest read the words of what was then the Gospel for the Day, Matthew 10:7-13, he accepted them as a divine revelation for himself. As Francis left the church he took off his shoes, staff, and cloak, replaced his belt with a piece of rope over his long peasant's smock, and began his mission. Ten years later, this garb was the uniform of five thousand men.

St. Francis gathered around him a band of men who would follow Jesus' life of poverty, preaching by word and example the Beatitudes of the Sermon on the Mount. This was a new vision of the Christian life, one that combined complete lack of earthly possessions and a rigorous asceticism with a joyful, comradely fellowship, strong sense of humor, and gladness in God's creation. Francis also had a profound respect for the Church and its clergy, although he himself never became a priest but remained a deacon until his death. In 1210 St. Francis and some of his disciples went to Rome and obtained the oral permission of Pope Innocent III for their preaching and way of life, thus beginning the Order of Franciscan Friars. Francis presented poverty, chastity, and obedience in the manner of the Troubadours and of the courtly love that was popular at the time, and he attracted thousands of followers.

The brothers wandered through Italy preaching, filling their simple physical needs by working or begging. As the brotherhood spread, Francis sent his followers to other parts of the world. He himself attempted a mission to Syria but was shipwrecked in Dalmatia. A projected journey to Morocco was thwarted by an illness in Spain. In 1219–1220 he went to the Holy Land where he attempted to convert the Sultan of Egypt and walked among the towns and shrines of the Holy Land amidst the warring armies of the Fifth Crusade.

On his return to Italy, he held a general assembly of the whole order, now grown to vast proportions, to give it a clearer structure and a firmer organization. The assembly met in the chapel of Portiuncula where St. Francis had first been inspired to carry out his mission. Characteristically, he made no provision for food and shelter for the brothers, who had to be provided for by the devotion and generosity of the local people. St. Francis laid down a new rule for the order and retired himself from active administration of it, a task far removed from the simple life he preached and lived.

Francis's biographer, Thomas of Celano, describes how at Christmas 1223 in Greccio, Italy, Francis arranged for a celebration of the Nativity in a cave with hay and live animals and a figure of the Christ child. It was the origin of the Christmas crèche.

In the final years of his life, St. Francis withdrew more to himself and turned to the inner mystical devotion that he had always had but which now became much stronger. In August of 1224 he went to Mount La Verna (Alvernia), which had been given to the Franciscans as a place for solitary devotions, and there on September 14 (Holy Cross Day), as he was praying, he received the print of the nails and wound in his side, which troubled him until his death. The objective reality of these wounds (the *stigmata*) seems well attested, whatever psychological or supernatural origin to which they may be attributed, for St. Francis desired to find perfect joy through experiencing the sufferings of his Lord. During the last years of his life, he was blind and seriously ill.

St. Francis died October 4, 1226, in a little hut near the Portiuncula chapel, attended by a few of his closest followers. His last act was the singing of Psalm 142. In two years' time he was formally recognized as a saint, and it is often said of him that he is "the one saint whom all succeeding generations have agreed in canonizing." His humility, generosity, love of nature (there are stories of his preaching to birds), simple and unaffected devotion to God have combined to make him one of the most cherished of all the saints. Pierre Sabatier (1682–1742), a French Calvinist pastor, did much to revive interest in St. Francis by his research into early Franciscan documents.

The prayer by an unknown author attributed to St. Francis, "Lord, make us instruments of your peace" (BCP, p. 833; LBW, p. 48; ELW, p. 87; H82 593), cannot be traced back before the twentieth century. It has been adapted by the

Missionaries of Charity as the "Daily Prayer of the Co-Workers of Mother Teresa" (see September 5).

St. Francis was added to the Episcopal calendar in the 1979 *Book of Common Prayer,* to the calendar in the *Lutheran Book of Worship,* and to the Methodist calendar in *For All the Saints.*

FOR FURTHER READING

Armstrong, Edward A. *Saint Francis: Nature Mystic.* Berkeley: University of California Press, 1974.

Armstrong, Regis, ed. *Francis and Clare: The Complete Works.* New York: Paulist, 1988.

Chesterton, G. K. *Saint Francis of Assisi.* New York: Doubleday, 1924.

Cunningham, Lawrence S. *Francis of Assisi: Performing the Gospel Life.* Grand Rapids: Eerdmans, 2004.

House, Adrian. *Francis of Assisi.* London: Chatto and Windus, 2001.

Le Goff, Jacques. *Saint Francis of Assisi.* Trans. Christine Rhone. New York: Routledge, 2003.

McCann, Janet, and David Craig, eds. *Francis and Clare in Poetry: An Anthology.* Cincinnati: St. Anthony Messenger Press, 2005.

Mockler, Anthony. *Francis of Assisi: The Wandering Years.* New York: Dutton, 1976.

Smith, John Holland. *Francis of Assisi.* New York: Scribner's, 1974.

Spotto, Donald. *Reluctant Saint: The Life of Francis of Assisi.* New York: Viking Compass, 2002.

READING

From a letter written to all the faithful by St. Francis

How happy and blessed are those who love the Lord and do as the Lord himself said in the gospel, "You shall love the Lord your God with all your heart and all your soul . . . and your neighbor as yourself." [Matt. 22:38-39] Therefore, let us love God and adore him with a pure heart and mind, for this is what he seeks above all when he says, "True worshippers worship the Father in Spirit and truth." [See John 4:23] For all who adore him must do so in the spirit of truth. Let us also pour out to him our praise and prayer saying, "Our Father in heaven," [Matt. 6:9] since we "need to pray always and not lose heart." [See Luke 18:1]

Furthermore, let us produce fruits worthy of repentance. Let us also love our neighbors as ourselves. Let us have charity and humility. Let us give alms because this cleanses the soul from the stains of sin. Mortals lose all the material things they leave behind them in this world, but they carry with them the right to be repaid for their charity and their almsgiving and they will receive the reward and generous repayment from the Lord.

OCTOBER

We should not be wise and prudent according to worldly standards; instead we should be simple, humble, and pure. We should never desire to be above others, but rather we should be servants who are submissive to every human being for God's sake. The Spirit of the Lord will rest on all who live in this way and persevere in it to the end. He will make his dwelling in them. They will be children of the heavenly Father whose works they do. They are the spouses, brothers, and mothers of our Lord Jesus Christ.

Trans. PHP, based on the English translation of the Office of Readings from the Liturgy of the Hours by the International Committee on English in the Liturgy.

PROPERS

Most high, omnipotent, good Lord, your servant Francis of Assisi sought to reflect the image of Christ through a life of poverty and humility: Grant your people grace to imitate his joyful love, renounce gladly the vanities of this world, and delight in your whole creation; through Jesus Christ our Lord, who lives and reigns with you and the Holy Spirit, one God, now and forever.

PHP, after RS and LFF; the address echoes the opening of St. Francis's *Canticle of the Creatures*, which is the basis of the Hymn of the Day

Readings:	Psalm 148:7-14 *or* 121
	Galatians 6:14-18
	Matthew 11:25-30
Hymn of the Day:	
	"All creatures of our God and King" (H82 400, LBW 527, ELW 835)
Prayers:	For dedication to the imitation of Christ
	For humility to identify with poverty and suffering
	For all who seek to live their lives in greater simplicity
	For joy in the faith of Christ
	For all Franciscans
	For a deeper concern for the natural world of which we are a part
	For all birds and animals
Preface:	A Saint (3) (BCP)
Color:	White

October 5

Frederike Fliedner, 1842; Theodor Fliedner, 1864; and Karolina Fliedner, 1892; Renewers of Society

Theodor Fliedner, the founder of the modern institution of deaconesses, was born in Eppstein, Germany, January 21, 1800. He was the fourth of twelve children, and his father, a pastor of limited means, died in 1813. Fliedner attended the gymnasium in Idstein, the universities of Giessen and Göttingen, and a seminary in Herborn. After a brief period as a tutor in a private home at Cologne, he became pastor of the little parish of Kaiserswerth, January 18, 1822.

Pastor Fliedner managed to visit Holland and England in 1823, 1824, and 1832 on tours to collect funds to aid his needy parish, and on these trips he encountered Moravian deaconesses, who were engaged in several kinds of Christian service. The Moravians had revived the institution in 1745 as it had already existed among their predecessors, the Slavic congregations. But these deaconesses were not full time. Inspired by examples he had seen in England, Fliedner conducted a service of worship in the prison at Düsseldorf in 1825, the first Lutheran service of its kind. In the following year, he founded the Rhenish-Westphalian Prison Society. He continued to conduct these services for two years, walking all the way to Düsseldorf every other Sunday, until in 1828 the first regular prison chaplain was appointed. The prison ministry spread in Germany under Fliedner's inspiration, and he himself visited prisons throughout the Rhineland and Westphalia as well as in the Netherlands, England, and Scotland. In 1833 he opened the Magdalen home for released women prisoners, and then in 1835 he opened the first nursery school in Düsseldorf. It developed into a large and influential teacher-training college, recognized by the government in 1848.

Gradually, Fliedner came to believe that the ancient order of deaconesses should be revived to help care for the poor and the sick, take care of children, and do prison work. In the early church, widows were commissioned as deaconesses to care for the sick and needy women, instruct women catechumens, be present at interviews of women with the clergy, assist at the baptism of women, and in other ways to help in the work of the church. The distinction between widows and deaconesses is obscure. The office of deaconess developed in the third and fourth centuries and is described in the *Didascalia* and the *Apostolic Constitutions*. Because a principal role of the deaconess was to assist at the baptism of women, when adult baptism became rare, the office of deaconess declined in importance. The female diaconate had died out almost everywhere by the seventh century, although it is found in some places until the eleventh century. Some of the tasks previously assigned to deaconesses were carried out by nuns or charitable orders of various kinds, and there were some sporadic attempts to revive the institution at the time of the Reformation.

After fruitless attempts to find support for his project, Pastor Fliedner, encouraged by his wife, finally decided to open a hospital and deaconess-training institute himself in tiny, predominately Roman Catholic Kaiserswerth. On October 13, 1836, the institute was opened and Gertrude Reichardt, the daughter of a physician, became the first deaconess. Frederike Fliedner, Fliedner's wife, was the mother superior. Almost immediately, the institute received help from all sides, and already in 1838 Fliedner was able to send out deaconesses to serve in the city hospital at Eberfeld. Frederike Fliedner, "the first of the deaconesses," as her husband called her, with her insight saved him from many mistakes. The order, simplicity, and frugality that she taught and practiced were, especially in the beginning, of incalculable value. Her charity toward all who were in need was balanced by her firmness toward those who would abuse her kindness. Despite her own heavy burden of family and motherhouse, she was able nonetheless to give strength and assistance to others. Of her ten children, seven died during her lifetime. She herself died April 22, 1842, after fourteen years of married life. A year later, in May 1843, Fliedner married Karolina Bertheau, who was born January 26, 1811, in Hamburg, an associate of Amalie Sieveking (see April 1) and the director of a large hospital in Hamburg. She proved herself eminently suited to the position of superior of the deaconess institution. "Mother Fliedner" for forty years carried on her work, nineteen of which were after her husband's death. She is commemorated on the German *Evangelical Calendar of Names* on April 15, the date of her death in 1892.

In 1849 Fliedner resigned his pastorate at Kaiserswerth in order to devote himself full time to the deaconess work. He established contact with people in Strasbourg, Paris, Switzerland, the Netherlands, and North America. In 1849, at the invitation of William Passavant (see June 6), Fliedner personally brought four deaconesses to Pittsburgh to staff the Infirmary Passavant had established, but that effort was finally unsuccessful; a motherhouse was not established in Pittsburgh. He began the extension of the female diaconate to the Middle East with the founding of a motherhouse in Jerusalem in 1851 and a hospital in Constantinople in 1852. Other motherhouses, patterned after Kaiserswerth, spread to Paris, Strasbourg, Dresden, and Berlin. King Frederik William IV of Prussia silenced critics of the movement by appointing deaconesses to serve the hospital in Berlin.

In 1856 Fliedner's health gave way, and he spent the year 1856–1857 in Cairo recovering from a serious lung condition. In spite of his physical weakness, he visited the deaconess establishments at Jerusalem, Smyrna, and Constantinople on his return trip. When he reached Kaiserswerth he was no longer able to travel, but he kept up active direction and promotion of the work from his study. On the twenty-fifth anniversary in 1861, representatives from deaconess motherhouses in many countries came to Kaiserswerth for the celebration.

In September 1864 he was able to consecrate nineteen sisters, and he was preparing for the second general assembly of deaconess motherhouses when suddenly his strength failed. On October 3 he spoke to his children about his life's work and left his blessings on them and all his "spiritual daughters." He died on the morning of October 4, 1864, leaving his second wife and ten surviving children. His last words are reported to have been, "Conqueror of death—victor!" At the time of his death there were thirty motherhouses, with 1,600 deaconesses in more than a hundred locations from Pittsburgh to Jerusalem. The motherhouse at Kaiserswerth had 425 sisters and a hundred outer stations on four continents.

Theodor Fliedner wrote a number of works related either to the tasks of deaconesses or their training. These included, besides numerous reports and pamphlets, such works as a songbook for nursery schools (*Liederbuch für Klein-kinderschulen*), a Christian calendar, and a book of martyrs. His work was carried on at first by a son-in-law and by his widow until her death April 15, 1892, and it has continued to the present day. The Fliedner diaconate has spread to almost all lands where there are Lutheran churches, and by the late twentieth century there were over thirty-five thousand deaconesses serving parishes, schools, hospitals, and prisons. In June 1884, seven sisters were sent to Philadelphia, and there, supported by John D. Lankenau (1817–1901) and Adolph Spaeth (1839–1910), they established the first motherhouse in the Americas and worked at the German Hospital (now Lankenau Hospital), which had opened in 1866.

Fliedner is remembered on the date of his death, October 4, on the calendars in the *Lutheran Book of Worship* and *Evangelical Lutheran Worship*, but because that day is the commemoration of St. Francis of Assisi, it is appropriate to transfer the commemoration of the Fliedners to the following day, October 5.

OCTOBER

FOR FURTHER READING

Crowner, David, and Gerald Christianson, ed. and trans. *The Spirituality of the German Awakening*. New York: Paulist, 2002.

Daniélou, Jean. *The Ministry of Women in the Early Church*. London: Faith Press, 1961.

Martimort, Aime G. *Deaconesses: An Historical Study*. Chicago: Ignatius, 1986.

Mergner, Julie. *The Deaconess and Her Work*. Trans. Harriet R. Spaeth. Philadelphia: General Council Publication House, 1915.

READING

From Sister Julie Mergner, *The Deaconess and Her Work*

A sisterhood is an association of those in the same calling; the members of this association belong together, are assigned to one another, and must live with one another. One stands for all, and all stand for one. "This coming together in a community for laboring with one another under the sign of the cross—for a life-long association in the same hope—a community of labor, interest, and daily life, this is called a motherhouse" (Bezzel). As a member of the community you have no right to go your own way, and, in general, are no longer your own mistress. But you do not owe it to the Lord alone to "walk worthy of the Lord unto all pleasing" (Col. 1:10), but also to your sisterhood. If you do not walk as is seemly, you injure not only yourself, but all who belong to your motherhouse, yea, the whole noble, sacred cause of the female diaconate. Therefore, bear in mind the great responsibility you take upon yourself, in putting on the garb of a sister.

If you wish for a standard of behavior for your life in the community, you need not go far to find it. Our Lord has given it clearly and plainly, "This is my commandment, that ye love one another as I have loved you" (John 15:12).

But mark, love does not consist in sweet sentiments; love is action. "God so loved the world that He gave His Only-begotten Son." Do you believe that He could have sweet sentiments toward a world which He could only abhor, a world which was to Him, the pure, the holy One, a thousand times more offensive and repulsive than the loathsome, ill-smelling wounds of many a sick person are to you, from which you must sometimes turn aside, lest you faint away? But He *did* something for this world, the best that He *could* do; He gave His Only-begotten Son. Think of that, and you will have some idea of what love is. Love is *doing,* doing for others, without raising the question whether they have shown themselves worthy of the love or not.

But, at the same time, do not rack your brain for lofty deeds of heroism to be done for others. Life consists of a thousand trifles. The opportunity for great deeds may never come. Begin with the little ones. Be considerate and friendly. Do not slam doors and carry on loud conversation when your room-mate is trying to sleep after a wearisome night-watch, or has, perhaps, retired earlier than usual because she is not feeling well, and must try to gain strength for the next day's tasks. Do not rise with a great bustle, and begin a teasing conversation when she wishes to sleep and has a right to do so. Think of what you find good and pleasant, in health or sickness, and try to show the same consideration to your fellow-sister. Do not take for granted, however, that all your preferences must also be hers, but consider her tastes and peculiarities. Here you have a few hints which you can supplement for yourself if you are in earnest about practicing love.

Julie Mergner, *The Deaconess and Her Work,* trans. Mrs. Adolph [Harriet K.] Spaeth (Philadelphia: General Council Publication House, 1915), 157–59.

PROPERS

Eternal God of great compassion, we give you thanks that you have raised up your faithful servants Theodor, Frederike, and Karolina Fliedner to revive the ancient order of deaconesses for the work of your church; and we pray that you would grant to all whom you have set apart for the work of serving love such understanding of your gospel, firmness of purpose, diligence in service, and beauty of life in Christ, that they may be a convincing sign of the meaning and power of Christian love; through Jesus Christ our Lord, who lives and reigns with you and the Holy Spirit, one God, now and forever.

PHP, after no. 69 in SBH

Readings: Psalm 82
              Romans 16:1-2
              Luke 22:24-27

Hymn of the Day:
              "We give thee but thine own" (LBW 410, H82 481, LSB 781, ELW 686)
              or "Jesus, Master, Son of God" (CSB 238) for deaconesses
              or "Savior, thee my heart I tender" (SBH 549) for deaconesses
              or "Blessed Fount of heavenly gladness":

> Blessed Fount of heavenly gladness,
> Jesus, thine are all our powers;
> Thee in sickness, want, and sadness
> To behold and serve is ours.
>
> One another's burdens bearing,
> Bringing comfort in distress,
> We Thy work, O Lord, are sharing,
> Who didst come the poor to bless.
>
> Where a child with love is tended,
> Where the hungry are supplied,
> Where the prisoner is befriended,
> Thou art our reward and guide.
>
> Send Thy love with fire from heaven,
> Love that longs to help and bless,
> Be it in the world a leaven
> Unto peace and righteousness.

A hymn by Theodor Fliedner in *The Hymnal and Order of Service,* Authorized by the Evangelical Lutheran Augustana Synod (Rock Island: Augustana Book Concern, 1925), no. 386. Sung to the tune *Stuttgart.*

Prayers: For deaconesses
          For the increase of vocations to the diaconate
          For those in prison
          For the sick and the forgotten
          For the spirit of joyful service
Preface: Epiphany
Color: White

OCTOBER

October 6

William Tyndale, Priest, Translator, Martyr, 1536

William Tyndale, the translator, humanist, and martyr, was born in Monmouthshire on the border of Wales *ca.* 1491. He was educated at Oxford, from which he received his M.A. in 1515, and he was ordained in the same year. He then went to Cambridge, the best Greek school in England, and came under the influence of the New Learning and revolutionary methods of the study of Scripture. He remained there until 1521. He was for a time a tutor in Gloucestershire and there decided to translate the Bible into English to help revive the Church, which he had found in a state of serous decline. He is reported to have said to a clerical opponent of his plan, "If God spare my life, ere many years I will cause the boy that driveth the plough shall know more of Scripture than thou doest." Tyndale approached the Bishop of London, Cuthbert Tunstall, a distinguished scholar, with his plan but was refused patronage. For a time Tyndale was the preacher at St. Dunstan's-in-the-West, but in May 1524 he moved to Germany and never returned to his native country again. He visited Luther in Wittenberg in 1525.

By 1525 he had completed his translation of the New Testament, from the Greek of Erasmus. The printing of the book began in Cologne, but Tyndale and his secretary William Roy were forced to flee after their discovery by John Cochlaus, a heretic-hunter, and the printing was completed in Worms. The book was widely distributed in England, "sought by the people to read and by the bishops to burn" according to one commentator. Of the eighteen thousand copies printed, only two remain. In 1534 Tyndale brought out a revised edition. He also worked on the translation of the Old Testament and published the Pentateuch and Jonah (1530–1536).

In his translation, Tyndale was able to strike a balance between scholarship, simplicity, and grace. The result was the creation of a masterpiece of vigorous English and a style of Scripture that was to serve as the model for all future English versions for nearly four hundred years.

Tyndale was forced to live abroad in poverty and danger. In May 1535, he was arrested, tried, and condemned for heresy. He was imprisoned in the castle of Vilvorde, the state prison of the Low Countries, and there on October 6, 1536, he was strangled at the stake and his body burned.

Ironically, while Tyndale was awaiting execution, the situation in England had changed. His most vigorous opponent, Thomas More, himself became a martyr in 1535. In the same year, Miles Coverdale published the first complete English Bible, made up of Tyndale's New Testament and Pentateuch, with the addition of Coverdale's own translation of the remainder of the Old Testament and

Apocrypha. Although this Bible was printed on the European continent, it was allowed to circulate freely in England. The "Matthew Bible," another edition of the Tyndale-Coverdale translation, was published with the king's special license in 1537, and in 1540 the second edition of the Great Bible (1539) declared on the title page that it was "appointed to the use of churches" and contained a long preface by Archbishop Cranmer encouraging Bible reading by clergy and laity.

Tyndale was included on the calendar in the 1979 Prayer Book, the *Lutheran Book of Worship, Evangelical Lutheran Worship,* and the Methodist *For All the Saints.*

FOR FURTHER READING

Butterworth, Charles C. *The Literary Lineage of the King James Bible.* Philadelphia: University of Pennsylvania Press, 1941.

Daiches, David. *The King James Bible: An Account of Its Development and Sources.* Chicago: University of Chicago Press, 1941.

Daniell, David. *The Bible in English.* New Haven: Yale University Press, 2003.

———. *William Tyndale: A Biography.* New Haven: Yale University Press, 1994.

———, ed. *Tyndale's Old Testament. Being the Pentateuch of 1530, Joshua to 2 Chronicles of 1537, and Jonah.* New Haven: Yale University Press, 1992.

Moynahan, Brian. *God's Bestseller: William Tyndale, Thomas More, and the Writing of the English Bible—A Story of Martyrdom and Betrayal.* New York: St. Martin's, 2003.

Mozley, J. F. *William Tyndale.* London: SPCK, 1937.

Williams, C. H. *William Tyndale.* London: Nelson, 1970.

OCTOBER

READING

From *Foxe's Book of Martyrs*

Tindall, being in Antwerp, had been lodged about one year in the house of Thomas Pointz, an Englishman, who kept an house of English merchants; about which time there came one out of England whose name was Henry Phillips, a comely fellow like as he had been a gentleman, having a servant with him; but for what purpose he was sent thither no man could tell. Tindall divers times was desired forth to dinner and supper among merchants, by means whereof Phillips became acquainted with him, so that within short space Tindall had great confidence in him and brought him to his lodging, and had him once or twice to dinner and supper, and further entered such friendship with him that through his procurement he lay in the same house; to whom he showed his books and other secrets of his study, so little did Tindall mistrust the traitor.

Then said Phillips, "Mr. Tindall, you shall be my guest here this day." "No," said Tindall, "I go forth this day to dinner and you shall go with me and be my guest where you shall be welcome." So when it was dinner-time Tindall went forth with

Phillips, and at the going forth of Pointz's house was a long narrow entry, so that two could not go in a front. Tindall would have put Phillips before him, but Phillips would in no wise, but put Tindall before, for he pretended to show great humanity. So Tindall, a man of no great stature, went before, and Phillips, a tall person, followed behind him, that the officers might see that it was he whom they should take, as the officers afterward told Pointz, and said, when they had laid him in prison, that they pitied his simplicity when they took him. Then they took him and brought him to the Emperor's procuror-general, where he dined. Then came the procuror-general to the house of Pointz, and sent away all that was there of Tindall's, as well as his books as other things; and from there Tindall was had to the castle at Filford, eighteen miles from Antwerp, and there remained till he was put to death.

Thus Pointz for Tindall was sore troubled and long kept in prison; at length, when he saw no other remedy, by night he made his escape and avoided their hands. But Tindall could not escape their hands, but remained in prison still; who being brought unto his answer was offered an advocate and a proctor; for in any criminal cause there it shall be permitted to have counsel, to make answer in the law. But he refused to have any such, saying that he would answer for himself; and so he did.

At last after much reasoning, when no reason would serve, although he deserved no death, he was condemned by virtue of the Emperor's decree made in the Assembly at Ausbrough, and upon the same brought to the place of execution was tied to the stake, and then strangled first by the hangman and afterwards with fire consumed, in the morning, at the town of Filford, *an.* 1536, crying at the stake with fervent zeal and a loud voce, "Lord, open the king of England's eyes."

Such was the power of his doctrine and sincerity of his life that during his imprisonment, which endured a year and a half, it is said that he converted his keeper, his daughter, and other of his household. The rest that were with him in the castle reported of him that if he were not a good Christian man, they could not tell whom to trust. The procuror-general left this testimony of him, that he was *homo doctus, pius,* and *bonus,* a learned, good, and godly man.

John Foxe, *Acts and Monuments of these Latter and Perilous Days . . .* , 1563, in *Foxe's Book of Martyrs* ed. G.A. Williamson (Boston: Little, Brown, 1966), 125, 127.

PROPERS

Almighty God, you planted in the heart of your servant William Tyndale a consuming passion to bring the Scriptures to people in their native tongue, and endowed him with the gift of powerful and graceful expression and with strength to persevere against all obstacles: Reveal to us your saving Word, as we read and study the Scriptures, and hear them calling us to repentance and life; through Jesus Christ our Lord, who lives and reigns with you and the Holy Spirit, one God, forever and ever.

CMG, LFF

Readings: Psalm 1 *or* 15
James 1:21-25
John 12:44-50*
Hymn of the Day:
"Almighty God, your Word is cast" (H82, 588, 589; LBW 234, LSB 577, ELW 516)
Prayers: For the renewal of the church
For the love of the Holy Scriptures
For those who study English prose and who craft language
Of thanksgiving for those who have created the English Bible
Preface: The Epiphany
Color: Red

*On this day, the Gospel of the Day might be read in Tyndale's translation, available in many libraries, to honor his contribution to the church. It might also be printed out for the congregation with all its (to us) odd spellings and constructions to show how language changes and therefore requires periodically new translations.

October 7

Henry Melchior Muhlenberg, Missionary to America, 1787

Henry Melchior Muhlenberg, whom Lutherans call (in the biblical rather than the ecclesiastical meaning of the term) the patriarch of the Lutheran Church in America, was born in Einbeck, in the province of Hannover, Germany, in 1711, the seventh of nine children. He graduated from Göttingen University and studied also at Halle, where he served as schoolmaster.

In the early part of the eighteenth century, the Lutheran communities in the New World were scattered over a wide territory and came from various ethnic origins. They had built a few churches, but they were without any kind of general organization, and there was considerable dissension among them. When the three desolate congregations at Philadelphia, New Hanover (Swamp), and New Providence (Trappe) united in sending a commission to London and Halle asking for a pastor to be sent to take charge, August Hermann Francke, who had made Halle a great center of Pietism, sent Muhlenberg to America in 1742. He went first to London, where he learned from the court chaplain Frederick Ziegenhagen, as he also had from Halle, something of the needs of the New World. Also, while in London, Muhlenberg had a gown made that was different from both the German and the Scandinavian style, and this was to set the pattern for English Lutheran clerical vesture in America.

He arrived in Charleston, South Carolina, on September 23, 1742, visited the Lutherans there and in Georgia, and reached Philadelphia November 25, 1742.

Muhlenberg was possessed of much courage and perseverance, and gradually the German-speaking churches recognized his authority and the Swedish clergy also cooperated with him.

During the forty-five years he labored in America, Muhlenberg, struggling against schismatics and imposters, traveled incessantly, corresponded widely, and set a course for Lutheranism for coming generations. He preached in German, Dutch, and English, doing so, it is reported, with a powerful voice. He established the first Lutheran synod in America, the Ministerium of Pennsylvania, which can be dated from Sunday, August 14, 1748, when the delegates met in Philadelphia. At this synod Muhlenberg submitted a liturgy that was ratified and remained the only authorized American Lutheran liturgy for forty years. It was revived and used in many places as part of the bicentennial observance of the United States in 1976. Ultimately, this form of the historic Lutheran order developed into the common liturgy of North American Lutherans in the *Common Service Book* (1918), *The Lutheran Hymnal* (1941), the *Service Book and Hymnal* (1958), and the *Lutheran Book of Worship* (1978) as Lutherans slowly moved toward the ideal that Muhlenberg had expressed in 1786, just before he died, of "one church, one book."

Muhlenberg's concern with questions of stewardship, pastoral care, and education strengthened the church life of Lutheran congregations and aided greatly in the transition from the state churches of Europe to the free churches of America; his model congregational constitution of 1762 established the basis for local church government.

Muhlenberg and his sons were also leaders in American public life. His first son, John Peter Gabriel (1746–1807), in January 1776 dramatically left his pastorate in Woodstock, Virginia, to serve the cause of the Revolution and become a brigadier general under George Washington. Another son, Frederick Augustus Conrad (1750–1801), also a Lutheran pastor, became a member of the Continental Congress and the first Speaker of the House of Representatives, much to the disappointment of his father. ("He has buried the talent entrusted to him in the political dunghill," he wrote in his diary January 23, 1783.) Henry Ernst Muhlenberg (1753–1815) was a pastor, president of Franklin College, and a prominent botanist. William Augustus Muhlenberg (1796–1877), a great-grandson of Henry Melchior and grandson of Frederick Augustus, was an outstanding priest of the Episcopal Church (see April 8).

Henry Melchior Muhlenberg died at Trappe, Pennsylvania, on October 7, 1787, and was buried there beside the historic church. A Latin inscription on the worn and weathered monument declares confidently, "Who and what he was future ages will know without a stone."

FOR FURTHER READING

Finck, William J. *Lutheran Landmarks and Pioneers in America.* Philadelphia: United Lutheran Publication House, 1913.

Nelson, Clifford E., ed. *The Lutherans in North America* 2d ed., rev. Philadelphia: Fortress Press, 1980.

Pfatteicher, Helen E. *The Ministerium of Pennsylvania: Oldest Lutheran Synod in America Founded in Colony Days.* Philadelphia: Ministerium Press, 1938.

Tappert, T. G. and J. W. Doberstein, trans. *The Journals of Henry Melchior Muhlenberg.* 3 vols. Philadelphia: Muhlenberg, 1942–1958.

Wallace, Paul W. *The Muhlenbergs of Pennsylvania.* Philadelphia: University of Pennsylvania Press, 1950.

READING

From the *Journals* of Henry Melchior Muhlenberg

1763. August 7.

A large crowd gradually assembled from far and wide. I recorded those who desired to commune. After the crowd had gathered in and around the church, I became very much concerned as to how I was going to baptize the children who had been registered for baptism, for there were twenty-two children to baptize and the church was so crowded that there was hardly any room left for me. The twenty-two children were crying so loudly that the noise was wretched. After I had baptized all of them and dismissed them in peace, the mothers hurried out with them into the open air; others crowded in and we went on with the service. With God's help and the co-operating grace of his Spirit I preached on Luke 19:41ff. I found the listeners inside and outside the church to be very attentive, which is usually the case with those who very seldom have an opportunity to hear a sermon. After the sermon the people had to be moved again so that those who had today declared their intention to commune could be inside the church. For these people I held confessional service and delivered an exhortation. About one o'clock in the afternoon we celebrated holy communion with some ninety members. . . .

When we got home in the evening I conducted devotions with the numerous members of the family and some others. I asked each one what impression he had received today, and from the answers I observed that simple people always retain things better when one gives edifying examples to illustrate the explanation of the Word. For example: Satan plays with some souls as children play with birds. They take a long piece of string, tie the end to the bird's leg, and hold the other end in their hand. The bird may flutter as best it can, but when it goes too far it is pulled back. Application: Satan will allow a lot of external things, like going to church, as long as there is no true turning from darkness to light, from the power of Satan to complete freedom in and through the Son of God, etc.

Another example which I cited was likewise easily comprehensible: I was summoned to go to a neighborhood inhabited by English people who had purchased, as servants, many of our poor Germans who had been shipped to this country. Since these Germans had not for several years heard any preaching at all in their own language and had expressed a desire for it, their masters were Christian enough to invite me to preach, first an English sermon in their church and afterwards in German for their servants. I did so to their pleasure. Afterwards when the German service commenced and the Germans sang beautifully and harmoniously, the English people sat back in their pews and the expressions on their faces showed that they were entranced. When the service was over and I had stepped outside the church, the Germans gathered around me and wept aloud, partly for joy at having again heard the Word of God and partly for sorrow that they had so little opportunity to hear it, whereas in Germany they had plenty and did not make good use of it. Some of the masters asked me what was the meaning of their servants' crying. Were they complaining over lack of food and drink or clothing? When I told them the real reason, some of them wept also and expressed the wish that the servants might soon learn the English language and be able to worship at the English services. An old gentleman who was born in Wales came up and said, "The German people can sing like the holy angels, but some of them live like the devil." He said he had been in a place where he had seen the Germans coming out of church with tears in their eyes, but they went right over to the next tavern and dried their tears with material spirits. The application was easy to make: how heinous the sin and great the offense to hold the truth in unrighteousness in the very light of the Gospel!

Henry Melchior Muhlenberg, *Notebook of a Colonial Clergyman,* ed. T. G. Tappert and J. W. Doberstein (Philadelphia: Muhlenberg, 1959), 87–89.

PROPERS

God, our heavenly Father, your servant Henry Melchior Muhlenberg displayed courage and perseverance in the face of opposition and slander, and brought order both in life and in worship to scattered and dispirited congregations: Give to the pastors of your church such strength and faithfulness that the devotion of your people may be enriched, and that unity and cooperation may be advanced, to the glory of your Name; through your Son Jesus Christ our Lord, who lives and reigns with you and the Holy Spirit, one God, now and forever.

PHP

Readings:	Ezekiel 34:11-16
	Psalm 84
	1 Peter 5:1-4
	John 21:15-17
Hymn of the Day:	
	"If God himself be for me I may a host defy" (LBW 454, LSB 724, ELW 788)
Prayers:	For the Lutheran Churches in America
	For harried administrators and leaders in the church

For a spirit of peace and cooperation
For a commitment to orthodoxy and right teaching
For a deepened piety
Preface: Apostles and Ordinations (BCP)
Color: White

October 9

Robert Grosseteste, Bishop of Lincoln, 1253

Robert Grosseteste ("large head"), born in 1175, rose from humble beginnings in Suffolk, England, to become a distinguished scholar in all branches of learning. The foremost mathematician of his day, he was appointed Master of the Oxford School and encouraged Oxford to emphasize the study of the sciences. He translated Aristotle's *Ethics* from the Greek, composed an allegorical poem, *Le Château d'Amour,* and wrote so extensively that the list of his works fills twenty-five closely printed pages. Among his pupils was Roger Bacon, proponent of the scientific method. Grosseteste had a strong influence on John Wycliffe.

He was consecrated Bishop of Lincoln in 1235 and exercised the episcopal office with conscientious efficiency. He opposed royal infringements on Church liberties and protested papal abuses of local prerogatives. Shortly after be became bishop of Lincoln, he issued a set of Constitutions requiring the clergy in his diocese to know and to teach the people in their mother tongue the Decalogue, the Seven Deadly Sins, the Seven Sacraments, and the Creed. He died in 1253.

Grosseteste was included on the calendar in the 1979 *Book of Common Prayer.*

FOR FURTHER READING

Rhodes, Jim. *Poetry Does Theology: Chaucer, Grosseteste, and the Pearl-Poet.* Notre Dame: University of Notre Dame Press, 2001.

READING

He traveled widely to each rural deanery, called together the clergy and laity, preached, confirmed, and dealt with questions of doctrine. "My lord, you are doing something new and exceptional," remarked some of the people during his first visitation. He replied, "Every new thing which implants and promotes and perfects the new man, corrupts and destroys the old. Blessed is the new, and in every way welcome to him who comes to recreate the old man in newness."

Lesser Feasts and Fasts 1997 (New York: Church Publishing, 1998), 386.

OCTOBER

PROPERS

O God, our heavenly Father, who raised up your faithful servant Robert Grosseteste to be a bishop and pastor in your Church and to feed your flock: Give abundantly to all pastors the gifts of your Holy Spirit, that they may minister in your household as true servants of Christ and stewards of your divine mysteries; through Jesus Christ our Lord, who lives and reigns with you and the Holy Spirit, one God, forever and ever.

BCP, Of a Pastor, LFF

Readings:	Psalm 112:1-9 *or* 23
	Acts 20:28-32
	Luke 16:10-15
Hymn of the Day:	
	"Not far beyond the sea" (H82 422)
Prayers:	For strengthening the intellectual gifts of the bishops of the church
	For increased diligence among the bishops
	For students of the sciences
Preface:	A Saint (1) (BCP)
Color:	White

ALSO ON OCTOBER 9

The *Lutheran Service Book,* following Löhe's calendar, commemorates **Abraham** the patriarch on this date. His story is given in Genesis 11:27—25:11.

October 11

Philip, Deacon and Evangelist

Philip the Evangelist, later regarded as a deacon, who is not to be confused with Philip the apostle, was one of the seven Greek-speaking men chosen by the apostles to distribute food and alms to the widows and poor of Jerusalem (Acts 6:1-6).

After the death of Stephen, Philip went to Samaria to preach the gospel (Acts 8:4-13); Simon Magus is said to have been one of his converts. In his travels south to Gaza, he encountered an Ethiopian eunuch, a servant of the Ethiopian queen, reading the passage in Isaiah about the suffering servant. The two traveled together discussing the passage, and the Ethiopian became a believer, asked for baptism, and received the sacrament from Philip (Acts 8:26-40).

Philip traveled as a missionary, preaching in every city from Azotus (Ashdod) northwards to Caesarea, where he and his four daughters, who were known as prophets, established a residence. It was there that he entertained St. Paul (Acts 21:8-9). Philip's activities toward the end of his life are the subject of speculation, but Basil says he was bishop of Tralles in Lydia in Asia Minor.

His feast day in the Eastern Church is October 11, "Apostle Philip (of the Seventy), Deacon," and in the West the date is usually June 6. Some provinces of the Anglican Communion have observed his feast on October 11, and the commemoration was introduced in the Episcopal Church in *Lesser Feasts and Fasts 2000*. Philip the Deacon is also on the calendar in the *Lutheran Service Book* (2006).

READING

From *Concerning the Inner Life* by Evelyn Underhill

A man of prayer is not necessarily a person who says a number of offices, or abounds in detailed intercessions; but he is a child of God, who is and knows himself to be in the deeps of his soul attached to God, and is wholly and entirely guided by the Creative Spirit in his prayer and his work. This is not merely a bit of pious language. It is a description, as real and concrete as I can make it, of the only really apostolic life. Every Christian starts with a chance of it; but only a few develop it. The laity distinguish in a moment the clergy who have it from the clergy who have it not: there is nothing that you can do for God or for the souls of men, which exceeds in the importance the achievement of that spiritual temper and attitude.

Evelyn Underhill, *Concerning the Inner Life* (New York: Dutton, 1926), 14.

PROPERS

Exalted God of all the earth, you prospered the work of Philip the Evangelist, a man of good standing, full of the Spirit and of wisdom: Grant that from the rising of the sun to its setting your Name may be great among the nations and that in every place, sacrifice and a pure offering may be made to your Name; through your Son Jesus Christ our Lord, who lives and reigns with you and the Holy Spirit, one God, now and forever.

PHP: Acts 6:3 ✠ MR, SBH

Readings: Psalm 67
              Isaiah 53:7-11 *or* Acts 8:26-40
              Matthew 28:18-20
Hymn of the Day:
              "Awake, O Spirit of the watchmen" (LBW 382, H82 540)

Prayers:	For those who administer the affairs of the church
	For those who flee persecution
	For missionaries and their families
	For all Christian families and single-parent homes
	For the younger churches
Preface:	A Saint (1) (BCP)
Color:	White

October 13

Elizabeth Fry, Renewer of Society, 1845

Elizabeth Gurney, the English Quaker prison reformer and philanthropist, was born May 21, 1780, the third child of Joseph, a wealthy Quaker manufacturer, and his wife Catherine, of the Barclay banking family. Soon after bearing her twelfth child, Catherine Gurney died; Elizabeth was twelve years old. On February 4, 1798, she heard the American Friend, William Savery, preach, and afterward wrote, "Today I felt there is a God. I loved the man as if he was almost sent from heaven. We had much serious talk and what he said to me was like a refreshing shower on parched earth." After this meeting, contrary to the more worldly practice of her family, she became a "plain Friend," adopting the plain style of clothing favored by the majority of Quakers and devoted her energies to helping those in need.

She married Joseph Fry, also a member of the Society of Friends, in 1800. Between 1800 and 1812 she gave birth to eight children; there were altogether eleven children. Nonetheless, she remained committed to her reforming interests. In March 1811 she was acknowledged as a Quaker minister, a nonprofessional position open to women and men, dependent on inspiration.

Stephen Grillet (1773–1855), a French aristocrat who had fled France and in America had become a Quaker, called her attention to the wretched conditions of women prisoners and their children in Newgate prison, and from 1813 she worked to relieve the suffering. Her first innovation was a school for the children of prisoners. In April 1817 she established the Ladies' Association for the Reformation of Female Prisoners in Newgate that provided materials with which the prisoners could sew, knit, and make goods for sale in order to buy food, clothing, and fresh straw for bedding, and visited the prison daily to read from the Bible and teach the inmates. The essence of Fry's work was her conviction that all persons, male and female, were fellow human beings and that treatment must be based on " the principles of justice and humanity" and instead of contributing to the degradation of inmates, prisons ought to be "schools of industry and virtue."

In pursuit of these reforms, she made several journeys through England, Scotland, and Ireland and between 1838 and 1843 made numerous visits to the European continent, making contact, among others, with Theodor Fliedner. In 1840 she established the Institution for Nursing Sisters, the first attempt to modernize the practice of nursing in Britain.

Elizabeth Fry died October 13, 1845 in Ramsgate. Over a thousand people stood in silence as she was buried October 20 in the Friends' burial ground in Barking.

At the unveiling of a bust of Elizabeth Fry at the Friends' School in Providence, Rhode Island, the Quaker poet John Greenleaf Whittier (1807–1892) read his two-part poem "The Two Elizabeths," who, "in name and spirit one," showed Christ's love: Elizabeth of Thuringia and Elizabeth Fry.

Elizabeth Fry was included on the Evangelical Calendar of Names (1962) and is on the 1997 calendar of the Church of England, *The Christian Year*.

FOR FURTHER READING

Rose, June. *Elizabeth Fry.* London: Macmillan, 1950, 1994.

Van Drenth, A., and F. De Haan. *The Rise of Caring Power: Elizabeth Fry and Josephine Butler in Britain and the Netherlands.* Amsterdam: University of Amsterdam Press, 1999.

READING

From *The Company of the Committed* by Elton Trueblood

OCTOBER

There is no better way, in contemporary thought, of approaching the meaning of commitment than by reference to Marcel's distinction between "believing that" and "believing in." To be committed is to believe *in*. Commitment, which includes belief but far transcends it, is determination of the total self to act upon conviction. Always and everywhere, as Blaise Pascal and many other thinkers have taught us, it includes an element of wager. This is why in great religious literature, including the New Testament, the best light that can be thrown upon commitment is that provided by marriage. For everyone recognizes the degree to which marriage is a bold venture, undertaken without benefit of escape clauses. The essence of all religious marriage vows is their *unconditional* quality. A man takes a woman not, as in a contract, under certain specified conditions, but "for better, for worse; for richer, for poorer; in sickness and in health." Always, the commitment is unconditional and for life. The fact that some persons fail in this regard does not change the meaning of that glorious undertaking.

One way of stating the crucial difference between belief and commitment is to say that when commitment occurs there is attached to belief an "existential index" which changes its entire character. Belief *in* differs from belief *that*, in the way in which the entire self is involved. "If I believe in something," says Marcel, "it means that I place myself at the disposal of something or again that I pledge myself fundamentally, and this pledge affects not only *what I have* but also *what I am.*"

...A Christian is person who confesses that, amidst the manifold and confusing voices heard in the world, there is one Voice which supremely wins his full assent, uniting all his powers, intellectual and emotional, into a single pattern of self-giving. That Voice is Jesus Christ. A Christian not only believes *that* He was; he believes *in Him* with all his heart and strength and mind. Christ appears to the Christian as the one stable point or fulcrum in all the relativities of history. Once the Christian has made this primary commitment he still has perplexities, but he begins to know the joy of being used for a mighty purpose, by which his little life is dignified.

Elton Trueblood, *The Company of the Committed* (New York: Harper & Row, 1961), 22–23.

PROPERS

Lord God, your Son came among us to serve and not to be served, and to give his life as a ransom for the world: Lead us by his love, and by the example of Elizabeth Fry, to serve all those to whom the world offers no comfort and little help; through us give hope to the hopeless, love to the unloved, peace to the troubled, and rest to the weary; through your Son Jesus Christ our Lord, who lives and reigns with you and the Holy Spirit, one God, now and forever.

BCP, rev. LBW; alt. PHP

Readings:	Hosea 2:18-23
	Psalm 94:1-14
	Romans 12:9-21
	Luke 6:20-36
Hymn of the Day:	
	"Lord, save your world" (LBW 420)
Prayers:	For all who work in prisons
	For those who are in prison
	For nurses and all who care for the sick
Preface:	Epiphany
Color:	White

October 14

O n October 15 the *Book of Common Prayer* commemorates **Samuel Isaac Joseph Schereschewsky** (1831–1906), a convert from Judaism to Christianity and Bishop of Shanghai, who despite severe paralysis, completed his translation of the Bible into Wenle. *Lesser Feasts and Fasts 1997,* to make room for the commemoration of Teresa of Avila on October 15, moved the commemoration of Schereschewsky a day earlier, to October 14.

October 15

Teresa of Avila, Renewer of the Church, 1582

Teresa de Cepeda y Ahumada, who with St. John of the Cross restored an awareness of the disciplines and rewards of the contemplative life, was born in Avila, Spain, March 28, 1515, of an old Spanish family. Her mother died when Teresa was fifteen, leaving the father with ten children. Teresa went to a convent school, where she read the letters of Jerome and decided to become a nun. Her father refused permission, and she ran away. On November 2, 1535, she entered the Carmelite monastery of the Incarnation at Avila. The community was large and open, freely associating with the world outside. There Teresa fell seriously ill, worsened, and lapsed into a deep coma. She revived, but her legs were paralyzed for three years. Despite her recovery, she remained rather lax in her spiritual life. She began to experience visions, and at the age of thirty-nine she experienced a vivid sense of God's presence within her. She wrote of such experiences rather matter-of-factly, but finally she was converted to a life of intense devotion that culminated on November 15, 1572, when, while receiving Holy Communion, she experienced "spiritual marriage with Christ" and took the name of Teresa of Jesus.

In 1560 she resolved to reform the monastery that had, she thought, departed from the order's original intention and had become insufficiently austere. In August 1562, in the face of strong opposition in the town and in the older monastery, a new monastery in Avila was dedicated to St. Joseph. A series of lawsuits resulted as the struggle continued. Her nuns were known as the Discalced Carmelites, because they wore sandals rather than shoes. The community was quite small, compared to the large number of sisters in the ordinary Carmelite houses, and Teresa always limited the number to twenty-one. At length, the Discalced Carmelites were given papal approval in 1580, and Teresa was given permission to establish other reformed monasteries. She traveled throughout Spain founding seventeen monasteries. They were small, poor, disciplined, and strictly enclosed. After great difficulties and deprivations, Teresa fell ill and died at Alba, October 4, 1582.

Teresa was a most attractive person, witty, frank, affectionate. She is remembered for her practical achievements and ceaseless activity in reforming the Carmelite Order and also for her mystic contemplation. An activist who nonetheless explored the spiritual life, she was the first to indicate the existence of states of prayer between discursive meditation and the final state of ecstasy, and she gave a careful description of the entire life of prayer from meditation to mystic marriage. Her *Life* is her autobiography to 1562; *The Way of Perfection* for the instruction of her sisters; the *Book of Foundations* tells of her establishment of convents; and *The*

Interior Castle deals with the spiritual life. She is known to many from Bernini's sculpture depicting her ecstatic vision of an angel who came to her with a long golden spear, burning at the tip. She wrote:

> With this he seemed to pierce my heart several times so that it penetrated to my entrails. When he drew it out, I though he was drawing them out with it, and he left me completely afire with a great love for God. The pain was so sharp that it made me utter several moans; and so excessive was the sweetness caused me by this intense pain that one can never wish to lose it, nor will one's soul be content with anything less than God.

Teresa's spiritual insight represents her major contribution to the church, and she is regarded as one of the greatest writers on the life of prayer.

Teresa's traditional feast day is October 15. She was included with John of the Cross on December 14 on the calendar in the *Lutheran Book of Worship*. The Episcopal *Lesser Feasts and Fasts 1997* added her commemoration to the Episcopal calendar, the Methodist *For All the Saints* includes her on the calendar, and the Lutheran Spanish-language service book *Libro de Liturgia y Cántico* (1998) set her commemoration on her traditional feast day, October 15, under her religious name, Teresa de Jesus. *Evangelical Lutheran Worship* commemorates Teresa of Avila on October 15.

FOR FURTHER READING

Chorpenning, Joseph F. *The Divine Romance: Teresa of Avila's Narrative Theology.* Chicago: Loyola University Press, 1991.

Lincoln, Victoria. *Teresa—A Woman: A Biography of Teresa of Avila.* Stony Brook: State University of New York Press, 1994.

Medwick, Cathleen. *Teresa of Avila: The Progress of a Soul.* New York: Knopf, 2000.

Peers, E. Allison. *Mother of Carmel: A Portrait of St. Teresa of Jesus.* New York: Morehouse, 1946.

———, ed. *The Complete Works of St. Teresa.* 3 vols. London: Sheed and Ward, 1946.

———, trans. *Studies of the Spanish Mystics.* 3 vols. London: SPCK, 1951–1960.

Peterson, Robert. *The Art of Ecstasy: Teresa, Bernini, and Crashaw.* New York: Athenaeum, 1970.

Teresa of Avila. *The Interior Castle.* Trans. Kieran Kavanaugh and Ottilo Rodriguez. New York: Paulist, 1979.

———. *The Life of St. Teresa of Avila by Herself.* Trans. M. A. Screech. New York: Penguin, 1988.

Williams, Rowan. *Teresa of Avila.* Harrisburg: Morehouse, 1991.

READING

From the Life of St. Teresa of Avila

Beginners in prayer, we may say, are those who draw the water from the well; this, as I have said, is very hard work, for it will fatigue them to keep their sense recollected, which is extremely difficult because they have been accustomed to a life of distraction. Beginners must accustom themselves to pay no heed to what they see or hear, and they must practice this during hours of prayer; they must go away by themselves and in their solitude think over their past life—and we must all do this, in fact, whether we are at the beginning of the road or near its end. There are differences, however, in the extent to which it must be done, as I shall show later. At first it causes distress, for beginners are not always sure that they have repented of their sins (though clearly they have, since they have determined to serve God so faithfully). Then they have to endeavour to mediate upon the life of Christ, which fatigues their minds. Thus far we can make progress by ourselves—with the help of God, of course, for without that, as is well known, we cannot think a single good thought.

That is what is meant by beginning to draw water from the well—and God grant that there may be water in it! But that, at least, does not depend on us: our task is to draw it and to do what we can to water the flowers. And God is so good that when, for reasons known to His Majesty, perhaps to our great advantage, He is pleased that the well should be dry, we, like good gardeners, do all that in us lies, and He keeps the flowers alive without water and makes the virtues grow. By water here I mean tears—or at least, if there are no tears, tenderness and an interior feeling of devotion.

What then, will a person do here who finds that for many days he experiences nothing but aridity, dislike and distaste, and has no little desire to go and draw water that he would give it up entirely did he not remember that he is pleasing and serving the Lord of the garden; if he were not anxious that all his service should not be lost, to say nothing of the gain which he hopes for from the heard work of continually lowering the bucket into the well and drawing it up without water? It will often happen that, even for that purpose, he is unable to lift his arms—unable, that is, to think a single good thought, for working with the understanding is of course the same as drawing water from the well.

What, then, as I say, will the gardener do here? He will rejoice and take new heart and consider it the greatest of favours to work in the garden of so great an Emperor; and as he knows that he is pleasing Him by doing so (and his purpose must be to please, not himself, but Him), let him render Him great praise for having placed such confidence in him, because He sees that, without receiving any recompense, he is taking such great care of that which He had entrusted to him; let him help Him to bear the Cross and remember how He lived with it all His life long; let him not wish to have his kingdom on earth or ever cease from prayer; and so let him resolve, even if this aridity should persist his whole life long, not to let Christ fall with His Cross.

E. Allison Peers, trans., *The Mystics of Spain* (London: Allen and Unwin, 1951), 81–83. Reproduced by permission of Taylor & Francis, Inc., http://www.taylorandfrancis.co.uk. (Cf. the English carol, "King Jesus hath a garden full of dviers flowers")

PROPERS

O God, by your Holy Spirit you moved Teresa of Avila to manifest to your Church the way of perfection: Grant us, we pray, to be nourished by her excellent teaching, and enkindle within us a keen and unquenchable longing for true holiness; through Jesus Christ, the joy of loving hearts, who with you and the Holy Spirit lives and reigns, one God, forever and ever.

1736 Paris Missal, RS, trans. LFF

Readings:	Psalm 42:1-7 *or* 139:1-9
	1 Corinthians 2:1-10a *or* Romans 8:22-27
	Matthew 5:13-16
Hymn of the Day:	
	"Come down, O Love divine" (H82 516, LBW 508, LSB 501, ELW 804)
Prayers:	For patience in suffering
	For the gift of love that overcomes opposition and persecution
	For intensity of the spiritual life
	For the contemplative orders of the church
	For those who conduct retreats and for retreat houses
	For those who cannot or who will not pray
Preface:	Baptism (BCP, LBW)
Color:	White

October 16

Thomas Cranmer, Archbishop of Canterbury, 1556

with Hugh Latimer and Nicholas Ridley, Bishops, 1555

The 1979 *Book of Common Prayer* commemorates the three English Reformers together on this date; the Methodist calendar in *For All the Saints* commemorates Thomas Cranmer alone. The German *Evangelical Calendar of Names* (1962) commemorates Ridley alone on October 17; *Evangelical Lutheran Worship* commemorates Thomas Cranmer alone on the date of his martyrdom, March 21.

Thomas Cranmer, the principal figure in the Reformation of the English Church, is of importance beyond the Anglican Communion because of the enormous influence of the *Book of Common Prayer* on the language of worship in all English-speaking denominations. He was born in 1489 and at age fourteen entered Jesus College, Cambridge and there studied the Bible and the new doctrines emanating from the Reformation in Germany. His travel brought him to Germany where he became closely associated with the Lutheran Reformers, especially with Andreas Osiander, whose daughter he married.

Cranmer was consecrated Archbishop of Canterbury March 30, 1533. Cranmer was convinced of the king's supremacy in all matters, civil and religious, and this led to many compromises of his reforming ideals. He was burned at the stake under Queen Mary, March 21, 1556.

The 1979 *Book of Common Prayer* in a rubric in the calendar provides for a commemoration of the First Book of Common Prayer. The book came into use on the Day of Pentecost, June 9, 1549, and the rubric therefore declares, "The First Book of Common Prayer, 1549, is appropriately observed on a weekday following the Day of Pentecost." Other churches may find it appropriate to remember the great and influential achievement of this book in connection with its principal author, Thomas Cranmer.

Hugh Latimer was born *ca.* 1490 and graduated from Clare College, Cambridge. He continued the medieval reforming spirit in having little interest in the refinements of theology but was zealous in preaching against corruption in the Church and in the life of clergy and people. He achieved fame as a preacher of pithy and homey sermons. Latimer was made Bishop of Worcester but in 1539 resigned his see in protest against Henry VIII's policies against the progress of the Reformation. With the accession of Queen Mary in 1553, he was imprisoned and on October 16 was burned at the stake in Oxford. His last words to Bishop Ridley, who was burned with him, are famous: "Be of good comfort, Master Ridley, and play the man; we shall this day light such a candle by God's grace in England as (I trust) shall never be put out."

Nicholas Ridley was educated at Pembroke College, Cambridge. A close friend of Thomas Cranmer, he became chaplain to the archbishop in 1537, Master of Pembroke in 1540, and in 1541 chaplain to Henry VIII. Early in the reign of Edward VI, Ridley was made Bishop of Rochester and member of the commission that prepared the first *Book of Common Prayer* (1549). In 1550 he was transferred to the diocese of London, where he implemented the principles of the Reformation. He contributed significantly to the second Prayer Book of 1552. In 1554 with Cranmer and Latimer, he took part in the Oxford disputations against a group of Roman Catholic theologians. His refusal to recant his Protestant theology, together with his opposition to the accession of Queen Mary, led to his arrest, imprisonment in the Tower of London, and execution with Hugh Latimer October 16, 1555.

OCTOBER

FOR FURTHER READING

Griffiths, David N. *The Bibliography of the Book of Common Prayer, 1549–1999.* London: British Library, 2003.

Hefling, Charles, and Cynthia Shattuck, eds. *The Oxford Guide to the Book of Common Prayer.* New York: Oxford University Press, 2006.

Jacobs, Henry E. *The Lutheran Movement in England during the Reigns of Henry VII and Edward VI and Its Literary Monuments.* Rev. ed. Philadelphia: Frederick, 1892.

MacCulloch, Diarmaid. *Thomas Cranmer.* New Haven: Yale University Press, 1996.

Pearce, Edward G. *The Study of the Lutheran Church in Britain Through Four Centuries of History.* London: Evangelical Lutheran Church of England, 1969.

Targoff, Ramie. *Common Prayer: The Language of Public Devotion in Early Modern England.* Chicago: University of Chicago Press, 2001.

READING

From the Preface to the First Book of Common Prayer by Archbishop Cranmer, 1549

[H]ere you have an order for prayer, and for the reading of the holy scripture, much agreeable to the mind and purpose of the old fathers, and a great deal more profitable and commodious, than which of late was used. It is more profitable, because here are left out many things, whereof some be untrue, some uncertain, some vain and superstitious: and nothing is ordained to be read, but the very pure word of God, the holy scriptures, or that which is evidently grounded upon the same; and that in such a language and order as is most easy and plain for the understanding both of the readers and hearers. It is also more commodious, both for the shortness thereof, and for the plainness of the order, and for that the rules be few and easy. Furthermore by this order, the curates shall need none other books for their public service but this book and the Bible . . .

And whereas heretofore there hath been great diversity in saying and singing in churches within this realm; some following Salisbury use, some Hereford use, and some the use of Bangor, some of York, some of Lincoln; now from henceforth all the whole realm shall have but one use.

http://justus.anglican.org/resources/bcp/1549/frontmatter_1549.htm#Preface

PROPERS

Keep us, O Lord, constant in faith and zealous in witness, that, like your servants, Hugh Latimer, Nicholas Ridley, and Thomas Cranmer, we may live in your fear, die in your favor, and rest in your peace; for the sake of Jesus Christ your Son our Lord, who lives and reigns with you and the Holy Spirit, one God, now and forever.
LFF

or

Almighty and everliving God, whose servant Thomas Cranmer permanently enriched the devotion of your church, carefully rendering its prayer in stately and beautiful language, and with Hugh Latimer and Nicholas Ridley sealed their reforming work with their martyrdom: Teach us to treasure the rich resources of the English language and to worship you with understanding and with reverence in the blest communion of your saints; through your Son Jesus Christ our Lord, who lives and reigns with you and the Holy Spirit, one God, now and forever.

PHP based on DvD and JWP

Readings:	Psalm 96:1-9
	1 Corinthians 3:9-14
	John 15:20—16:1
Hymn of the Day:	
	"For thy dear saints, O Lord" (H82 279, LBW 176, ELW 427)
Prayers:	For liturgical scholars
	For all who order and lead our worship
	For the continuing renewal of the church
	For the reconciliation of Protestant and Catholic Christians throughout the world
	For the understanding of those whose religious beliefs differ from our own
Preface:	A Saint (1) (BCP)
Color:	White

October 17

Ignatius, Bishop of Antioch, Martyr, *ca.* 115

Ignatius is known primarily through seven letters of thanks he wrote to all the churches who had received him on his journey to Rome as a prisoner condemned to die during the reign of Trajan (98–117). The letters are of great value and interest for the light they shed on Christian belief and practice less than a century after Christ's ascension. They express his eucharistic concept of martyrdom, as a culmination of the liturgical sacrifice of love and obedience, and reveal a passion for unity and the proper ordering of the church and its worship. "Flee from schism as the source of mischief," he wrote. "You should all follow the bishop as Jesus Christ did the Father. Follow, too, the presbytery as you would the apostles; and respect the deacons as you would God's law." In these letters, the phrase "the Catholic Church" is found for the first time.

Ignatius was apparently born in Syria *ca.* 35 and was a convert from paganism. He calls himself Theophoros, the God-bearer; a misinterpretation of the title as meaning "God-borne" led to his identification in pious legend with the child that Jesus held in his arms at Capernaum (Mark 9:36). Ignatius appears to have been the second (or third) bishop of Antioch in Syria; according to some, he succeeded St. Peter there. Nothing is known of his life apart from his journey to martyrdom from Antioch to Rome under a guard of ten soldiers, whom he called his "leopards, who only get worse the better you treat them." He expressed his fierce concentration on his mission and his eagerness to become a martyr with extraordinary intensity. "What a thrill I shall have from the beasts that are waiting for me. I hope that they will make short work of me. I shall coax them to devour me at once. . . . If they are reluctant, I shall make them do it. Forgive me: I know what is good for me. Now I am beginning to be a disciple. May nothing, seen or unseen, begrudge me making my way to Jesus Christ. Come fire, cross, fighting with wild beasts, wrenching of bones, mangling of limbs, crushing of my entire body, cruel tortures of the devil—only let me get to Jesus Christ."

Ignatius was received en route with great honor at Smyrna by Polycarp, who attests to his martyrdom at Rome, and by representatives of neighboring Christian communities. While Ignatius was at Smyrna, he wrote to the churches at Ephesus, Magnesia, Tralles, and Rome. He was then taken to Troas, and from there he wrote to the churches of Philadelphia and Smyrna and to Polycarp. He was taken through Macedonia and Illyria to Dyrrachium and then by ship to Italy, where he was executed, doubtless in the Coliseum. Polycarp, writing to the Philippians, says that Ignatius, Zosimus, and Rufus "are now in their deserved place with the Lord, in whose suffering they also shared." Ignatius's relics are preserved in the Church of San Clemente in Rome.

Ignatius's feast day in the old Roman calendar was February 1; in the Eastern Church it is December 20. The present Roman Catholic calendar, followed by the calendar in the *Book of Common Prayer,* the *Lutheran Book of Worship, Evangelical Lutheran Worship,* the *Lutheran Service Book,* and the Methodist *For All the Saints,* commemorates Ignatius on October 17, the date of his commemoration in the Church of Antioch, which was observed there as early as the fourth century.

FOR FURTHER READING

Corwin, V. *Ignatius and Christianity in Antioch.* New Haven: Yale University Press, 1960.
Richardson, Cyril C. *The Christianity of Ignatius of Antioch.* New York: Columbia University Press, 1935.

READING

From a letter to the Romans by St. Ignatius

May I have the good fortune to meet my destiny without interference. I fear that your generosity may stand in my way. You can easily do what you want, but it is difficult for me to get to God unless you let me alone. . . . I shall never again have such an opportunity to get to God, nor, if you keep quiet, can you do a nobler deed. . . .While there is an altar at hand, let me be a sacrifice to God. You can then form a choir and sing praise to the Father in Jesus Christ that God gave the bishop of Syria, whom he had called from the rising of the sun, the privilege of reaching its setting. It is a welcome thing for my life to set on the world and for me to be on my way to God, so that I may rise into his presence.

I am writing to all the churches to let it be known that I am voluntarily dying for God, if only you do not interfere. I plead with you: show me no untimely kindness. Let me be food for the wild beasts, for that us how I can get to God. I am God's wheat and shall be ground by the teeth of wild beasts so that I may become Christ's pure bread. I would rather that you fawn over the beasts so that they may be my tomb and that no scrap of my body remain. Then, when I have fallen asleep, I shall be a burden to no one. Then, when the world sees my body no more, I shall be a true disciple of Jesus Christ. Pray to Christ for me that the animals will be the means of making me a sacrificial victim for God. . . .

Even now as a prisoner I am learning to forego my own desires. All the way from Syria to Rome, by land and sea, by night and day, I am chained to ten leopards (I mean the detachment of soldiers) who only get worse the better I treat them. By their injustices I am becoming a better disciple, "but I am not thereby acquitted" [1 Cor. 4:4]. What a thrill I shall have from the beasts that are waiting for me. I hope that they will make short work of me. I shall coax them to devour me at once and not, as sometimes happens, shrink back through fear. If they are reluctant, I shall make them do it. Forgive me: I know what is good for me. I am beginning to be a disciple. May nothing, seen or unseen, begrudge me making my way to Jesus Christ. Come, fire, cross, fighting with wild beasts, wrenching of bones, mangling of limbs, crushing of my entire body, cruel tortures of the devil—only let me get to Jesus Christ.

No earthly pleasures, no kingdoms of this world can benefit me in any way. I prefer death in Christ Jesus to power over the farthest limits of the earth. The one who died for us is the one for whom I look. The one who rose for us is the one whom I desire. The time for my birth is close at hand. Share my feelings, my brothers. Do not stand in the way of my birth to true life; do not wish me stillborn. My desire is to belong to God. Do not, then, hand me back to the world. Do not try to tempt me with material things. Let me attain pure light, for only on my arrival there can I be fully human. Let me imitate the passion of my God.

Ignatius, *Letter to the Romans* 1:2–2:2; 4:1-2; 5:1–6:3, trans. PHP.

PROPERS

Almighty God, we praise your Name for your bishop and martyr Ignatius of Antioch, who offered himself as grain to be ground by the teeth of wild beasts that he might present to you the pure bread of sacrifice: Accept, we pray, the willing tribute of our lives and give us a share in the pure and spotless offering of your Son Jesus Christ; who lives and reigns with you and the Holy Spirit, one God, forever and ever.

LFF

Readings: Psalm 116:1-8 *or* 31:1-5
              Romans 8:35-39 *or* Philippians 3:17-4:1
              John 12:23-26
Hymn of the Day:
              "With high delight let us unite" (LBW 140, LSB 483, ELW 368)
              or "Rise again, ye lion-hearted" (TLH 470)
              or "King of the martyrs' noble band" (H82 236)
Prayers: For courage to face death unafraid
              For willingness gladly to give all for Christ
              For the church in Syria and throughout the Near East
              For bishops, especially those who face persecution for their faith
              For the unity of the church
Preface: A Saint (3) (BCP)
Color: Red

October 18

St. Luke, Evangelist

Luke was a Gentile, probably a Greek, and is believed to have come from Antioch in Syria or perhaps Philippi. Not much is known of his life except that he was a physician (Col. 4:14) and that he was a disciple of St. Paul and a worker with him. Luke has traditionally been regarded as one of the seventy disciples commissioned by Jesus (a tradition reflected in the Roman Catholic Gospel, Luke 10:1-9), although in his Gospel (1:2) Luke says that he was not an eyewitness of what he writes. A later tradition that he was a painter and painted a portrait of the Virgin Mary seems not to be reliable. Luke accompanied Paul on some of his journeys and may have been left in charge of the church in Philippi between visits by the apostle. He is generally believed to have been with Paul during his last two imprisonments. "Lucius of Cyrene" (Acts 13:1) and "Lucius my fellow countryman" (Rom. 16:21) may refer to Luke. According to early traditions, Luke wrote his Gospel in Greece and preached the faith there and in Bithynia, an important province in northwestern Asia Minor. St. Luke is said to have died at the age of eighty-four, never having married. Some manuscripts give the place of his death as Boetia, and some give Egypt or Bithynia or Achaia. Emperor Constantinus II had the supposed relics of St. Luke transferred from Thebes in Boetia to Constantinople with those of St. Andrew and placed in the Church of the Holy Apostles there on March 3, 357. The observance of the feast date of St. Luke is probably quite old in the East; it appears on Western calendars only in the eighth century. The date of his commemoration is universally October 18, and this may perhaps be based on the actual date of his death.

The traditional symbol of St. Luke in Christian iconography is the ox, derived from Ezekiel 1:10.

St. Luke's Day is a traditional time to emphasize the church's ministry of healing by showing concern for hospitals and nursing homes, for physicians and nurses, and for conducting healing services. It is also an important day to observe in Year C of the lectionary cycle, when the Gospel readings for that year are drawn largely from the third Gospel. It is an especially appropriate time to consider the nature, characteristics, and spirit of the Gospel according to St. Luke and of its sequel, the Acts of the Apostles.

FOR FURTHER READING

Cadbury, Henry. *The Making of Luke-Acts.* 2d ed. London: SPCK, 1958.
———. "The Style and Literary Method of Luke," *Harvard Theological Studies* 6, 1919–1920.
Danker, Frederick W. *Luke.* Proclamation Commentaries. Philadelphia: Fortress Press, 1976.
Fitzmyer, Joseph A. *The Gospel according to Luke.* 2 vols. Garden City: Doubleday, 1981.
———. *Luke the Theologian.* New York: Paulist, 1989.
Green-Armytage, A. H. N. *A Portrait of St. Luke.* Chicago: Regnery, 1955.
Von Harnack, Adolf. *Luke the Physician.* 1907.

READING

From *God in Action* by Karl Barth

The "work of an evangelist" does not consist in proclaiming "ideals." It does not consist in criticizing man, his failures, his weaknesses, or his arrogance. It does not consist in the Kierkegaardian critique of the "religious man." It does not consist in *commanding* men to love God and each other, nor in preaching a social hope. It does not consist in giving a description of the evolution of this or that point in dogmatics, even if it is the best dogmatics.

The "work of an evangelist"—while he may make use of every possible material—is in what his name indicates. It consists in proclaiming the Evangel. The proclamation of the gospel is the proclamation of Jesus Christ. If Jesus Christ is the content, if it is "grace, nothing but grace, and the whole of grace," then there is no need of a supporting practical effect of some deed, because it itself is, and does, the one true deed. The church waits upon this deed, and the world awaits the

OCTOBER

action of this deed from the church. We must learn again to do this work sincerely and thoroughly.

Karl Barth, "The Ministry of the Word of God," in *God in Action* (New York: Round Table Press, 1936), 80–81.

PROPERS

God of healing compassion, you chose Luke the evangelist to reveal by preaching and writing the mystery of your love for the poor: Unite in heart and spirit all who glory in your Name and let all nations come to see your salvation; through your Son Jesus Christ our Lord. . . .

1970 RS, trans. PHP

> *or*

Almighty God, you inspired your servant Luke the physician to set forth in the Gospel the love and healing power of your Son: Graciously continue in your Church this love and power to heal, to the praise and glory of your Name through Jesus Christ our Lord, who lives and reigns with you in the unity of the Holy Spirit, one God, forever and ever.

1549 BCP, rev. 1979 BCP; alt. in LBW, ELW

Readings:	Isaiah 43:8-13 *or* Sirach 38:1-4, 6-10, 12-14
	Psalm 147
	2 Timothy 4:5-13
	Luke 1:1-4 *or* 4:14-21
Hymn of the Day:	
	"Thine arm, O Lord, in days of old was strong to heal and save" (H82 567; LBW 431, LSB 846)
	or "What thanks and praise to thee we owe" (H82 285)
Prayers:	For the gift of the Spirit
	For compassion
	For the poor and the outcast
	For all in the healing professions
	For hospitals and nursing homes
Preface:	All Saints
Color:	Red

October 19

The calendar in the *Book of Common Prayer* commemorates on this day **Henry Martyn**, priest and missionary to India and Persia, whose life and death strongly affected the Church of England in the nineteenth century, inspiring many to offer themselves in the cause of Christian missions, and who died in 1812 at the age of thirty-one.

October 23

St. James of Jerusalem, Brother of Our Lord Jesus Christ, Martyr, *ca.* 62

In the lists in Matthew 13:55 and Mark 6:3, James is listed first among the brothers of Jesus, who formed a distinct class, separate from the apostles: James, Joses or Joseph, Simon, Judas. St. Paul in Galatians 1:19 says that he met James the Lord's brother at Jerusalem on his first visit there.

From at least the second century, there has been some uncertainty about these "brothers of the Lord" mentioned in the New Testament (Mark 6:3; John 7:3; Acts 1:14; 1 Cor. 9:5). Helvidius, who claimed the support of Tertullian, said that Jesus was Mary's first child and that the brothers and sisters mentioned in the Gospels were children of Mary and Joseph, born after Jesus. Epiphanius in the second century challenged this position and suggested that the "brothers" were sons of Joseph by a former marriage. This remains the view of the Eastern Church. Their attempt to control Jesus (Mark 3:31; John 7:3-4) may indicate that they were older than Jesus. Moreover, it is argued, Jesus on the cross would not have had to commend Mary to John's care if the "brothers" had been her children.

Jerome in the fourth century, responding to Helvidius, says that James is the same person as the apostle James the Less (Mark 3:18; 15:40) and that the mother of James and Joses was Mary of Clopas, the younger sister of the Virgin Mary. Jesus and James, therefore, were not brothers but cousins. (The word translated "brother" can sometimes mean "cousin.") Why two sisters would both have the name Mary is not explained. Jerome's view has prevailed in the West for centuries, but it is rejected by nearly all modern New Testament scholars, partly because there is no evidence in the Gospels that James was a disciple during the ministry of Jesus until he became a witness of the resurrection.

James, having seen the risen Jesus (1 Cor. 15:7), is recognized early as a leader in Jerusalem. Although he was not one of the Twelve, he was regarded as an apostle (Gal. 1:19), perhaps as a replacement for James the Son of Zebedee, since James of Jerusalem is not mentioned until after the death of James the Apostle.

James' special vocation was to the Jews (Gal. 2:9). He is traditionally regarded as the first bishop of Jerusalem, the "bishop of bishops." Jewish Christianity exalted him above Peter and Paul since his ministry was in the principal city of the Holy Land. He remained the most respected and authoritative leader in Jerusalem for most of the first Christian generation, no doubt because of his eyewitness testimony to the risen Jesus. James was, according to the secular accounts, put to death by priestly authorities in the mid-sixties. Josephus (*ca.* 94) says that James "with certain others" was stoned to death in 62 at the instigation of the high priest

Annas. Hegesippus says that at Passover "James the Just" claimed that Jesus was the son of Man and was thrown from the Temple and stoned and beaten to death before the siege of 66 C.E.

The Eastern Churches commemorate James the brother of the Lord on this date, and it has also been adopted by several Anglican calendars, including the 1979 American *Book of Common Prayer,* and by the 1978 *Lutheran Book of Worship, Evangelical Lutheran Worship,* and the *Lutheran Service Book.* James of Jerusalem is not on the General Roman Calendar.

FOR FURTHER READING

Bernheim, Pierre-Antoine. *James, Brother of Jesus.* Trans. John Bowden. London: SCM, 1997.

Chilton, Bruce, and Jacob Neusner, eds. *The Brother of Jesus: James the Just and His Mission.* Louisville: Westminster John Knox, 2001.

Hartin, Patrick J. *James of Jerusalem.* Collegeville: Liturgical, 2004

Johnson, Luke Timothy. *Brother of Jesus, Friend of God: Studies in James.* Grand Rapids: Eerdmans, 2004.

———. *The Letter of James.* Anchor Bible. Garden City: Doubleday, 1995. Mackowski, Richard M. *Jerusalem: The City of Jesus.* Grand Rapids: Eerdmans, 1980.

Painter, John. *Just James: The Brother of Jesus in History and Tradition.* 2d ed. Columbia: University of South Carolina Press, 2004.

Reich, Ronny. *Jerusalem as Jesus Knew It.* Atlanta: SBL, 2004.

READING

From *The Imitation of Christ* by Thomas à Kempis

There are two wings that raise a man above earthly things—simplicity and purity. Simplicity must inspire his purpose and purity his affection. Simplicity reaches out after God; purity discovers and enjoys Him. No good deed will prove an obstacle to you if you are inwardly free from uncontrolled desires. And if you are free from uncontrolled desires, and seek nothing but the Will of God and the good of your neighbor, you will enjoy this inner freedom. If your heart be right, then every created thing will be for you a mirror of life and a book of holy teaching. For there is nothing created so small and mean that it does not reflect the goodness of God.

Were you inwardly good and pure, you would see and understand all things clearly and without difficulty. A pure heart penetrates both heaven and hell. As each man is in himself so does he judge outward things. If there is any joy to be had in this world, the pure in heart most surely possess it; and if there is trouble and distress anywhere, the evil conscience most readily experiences it. Just as iron, when plunged into fire, loses its rust and becomes bright and glowing, so the man who turns himself wholly to God loses his sloth and becomes transformed into a new creature.

Thomas à Kempis, *The Imitation of Christ*, trans. Leo Sherley-Price (Baltimore: Penguin, 1952), 68–69, 88–89, 83, 206–206, 72. Introduction and Translation copyright 1952 by Leo Sherley-Price. Reprinted by permission of Penguin Books Ltd.

PROPERS

Grant, O God, that following the example of your servant James the Just, brother of our Lord, your Church may give itself continually to prayer and to the reconciliation of all who are at variance and enmity; through Jesus Christ our Lord, who lives and reigns with you and the Holy Spirit, one God, now and forever.
BCP

Readings:	Acts 15:12-22a
	Psalm 1
	1 Corinthians 15:1-11
	Matthew 13:54-58
Hymn of the Day:	
	"Rise, O children of salvation" (LBW 182)
Prayers:	For the church in Jerusalem
	For the peace of Jerusalem and the Holy Land
	For bishops and others in authority
	For a just and righteous life
Preface:	All Saints
Color:	Red

OCTOBER

October 26

Philipp Nicolai, 1608; Johann Heermann, 1647; Paul Gerhardt, 1676; Hymnwriters

Three of the greatest Lutheran hymnwriters are commemorated together on this date.

Philipp Nicolai was born August 10, 1556, in Mengeringhausen, Waldeck, Germany, the son of a pastor. He studied theology at the universities of Erfurt and Wittenberg (1575–1579). In 1583 he became pastor in Herdecke near Dortmund where his father had introduced the Reformation. The town council was Roman Catholic, and, when the Spanish invaded and the Roman Mass was reintroduced,

Nicolai was forced to flee. He seems to have served secretly as a pastor in Cologne in 1586, holding services in members' homes. (Gerhardt did the same in Berlin.) At the end of 1586, he was appointed *diaconus* at Niederwildungen, and in 1587 became pastor there. In November 1588 he was the pastor at Altwildungen, court preacher to the Countess Margaretha of Waldeck, and tutor to her son. In 1594 he at last received his D.D. degree from Wittenberg. The degree had been delayed because of controversy with the Crypto-Calvinists.

In October 1596 Nicolai became pastor in Unna in Westphalia. It was a time of distress: between July 1597 and January 1598, the plague took thirteen hundred of his parishioners, sometimes thirty in a day, three hundred in July and 170 in one week in August. The parsonage overlooked the graveyard and Nicolai could not avoid the constant presence of death. He wrote a series of meditations to comfort his people, *Mirror of Joy* (the preface was dated August 10, 1598, his forty-third birthday), and to this book, published in 1599, he appended two chorales. One was *Wachet auf*, "Wake, awake, for night is flying," with the title "Of the voice at midnight, and the wise virgins who meet the heavenly Bridegroom. Mt. 25," which was to become known as "the king of chorales." The other was *Wie schön leuchtet der Morgenstern*, "How brightly beams the morning star," which bore the title "A spiritual bridal song of the believing soul concerning Jesus Christ, her heavenly Bridegroom, founded on the 45th Psalm of the prophet David." This, "the queen of chorales," written in the space of a few hours, immediately established itself as a favorite in Germany and came to be regarded as an almost indispensable part of the wedding service. Nicolai's fame as a hymnwriter rests entirely upon these two hymns.

In December 1598, the Spanish army again invaded, and Nicolai was forced to flee once more. He returned in April of the following year. In 1601 he was made pastor of St. Katherine's Church in Hamburg, where he endeared himself to the people with his pastoral concern and won their respect as a courageous and powerful preacher. He was called a "second Chrysostom." In 1596-1597 he wrote a two-volume biblical-theological apocalyptic work on the kingdom of Christ. He was also the author of polemical writings against the Crypto-Calvinists and the Reformed in his impassioned defense of Lutheran orthodoxy. Nonetheless, he was personally gentle and irenic, with a mystical inclination.

Following an ordination at St. Katherine's on October 22, 1608, he returned home ill. His illness grew worse, and Philipp Nicolai died on October 26. He is remembered on the *Evangelical Calendar of Names* on October 25.

FOR FURTHER READING

Piepkorn, Arthur Carl. "Philipp Nicolai (1556–1608)." *Concordia Theological Monthly* 30, no. 7 (July-August 1968): 432–61.

Johann Heermann was born at Raudten, Silesia, October 11, 1585, his parents' only surviving child. His father was a furrier. The son suffered a severe illness as a child, and his mother vowed that if he recovered, he would be educated for the ministry.

After serving as a tutor, he was appointed deacon at Köben, a village near Raudten. Within six months he was elevated to the pastorate of the parish in 1611. An affliction of the throat in 1634 forced him to stop preaching. For four years his preaching was done by assistants, and in 1638 Heermann retired to Lissa and died there on what was then called Septuagesima Sunday (the third Sunday before Lent), February 17, 1647. He is remembered on the *Evangelical Calendar of Names* on the date of his death.

Heermann had suffered not only from poor health but also from the deprivations of the Thirty Years' War. Köben was devastated by fire in 1616, plundered four times between 1629 and 1634, and suffered pestilence in 1631. Heermann was driven from his home and forced to flee again and again, sometimes narrowly escaping death. From this unending affliction, Heermann was able to write hymns of confident faith that have been sung and loved by succeeding generations. As a hymnwriter of the seventeenth century, he ranks second only to Gerhardt. His hymns, John Julian observes, mark a transition from the objective hymns of the Reformation to the more subjective type and are characterized by a depth of feeling and tenderness that is unsurpassed.

FOR FURTHER READING

Dodson, Geran F. "Johann Heermann: Silesian Hymn writer." *The Hymn: A Journal of Congregational Song* 20, no. 2 (April 1969): 58–64.

Teuscher, Gerhart. "A Devout Heart and Spirit: Johann Heermann." *The Hymn: A Journal of Congregational Song* 37, no. 4 (October 1986): 16–20.

Paul Gerhardt, without much doubt the greatest Lutheran hymnwriter, was born March 12, 1607, at Gräfenhaynichen, near Wittenberg. His father, the mayor of the town, died while his son was still young. Gerhardt studied theology at the University of Wittenberg from 1628 to 1642. The Thirty Years' War was raging, and it was a time of suffering and desolation. Gerhardt went to Berlin as a tutor in the home of Andreas Barthold and in 1655 married Barthold's daughter, Anna Maria. His contact with Johann Crüger, the cantor at St. Nicholas' Church in Berlin, stimulated his poetic gifts, and eighteen of his hymns appeared in the third edition of Crüger's *Praxis pietatis melica.*

When he was forty years old, Gerhardt obtained appointment as Probst (chief pastor) at Mittenwalde in Brandenburg, near Berlin, and was ordained November

OCTOBER

8, 1651. He became the third assistant at St. Nicholas' Church in Berlin in 1657, and there he gained fame as a preacher. In doctrinal debates with the Reformed, he maintained the Lutheran position. He refused to sign a pledge not to bring doctrinal discussion into sermons and was deposed by Frederick William of Brandenburg-Prussia in 1666. Although he was restored to his position in the following year, he refused to return and remained without a parish for some years. During this time of trial, his wife and a son died (three of their children had died earlier), and his misery increased. In May 1669 he was appointed archdeacon of Lübben. He lived there with a sister-in-law and his sole surviving son in a somewhat unsympathetic parish. He died May 27, 1676; he is commemorated on the German *Evangelical Calendar of Names*.

Amid affliction and the calamities of the Thirty Years' War and its aftermath, Gerhardt wrote some 133 hymns of faith and confidence. He was, moreover, able to translate orthodox doctrines in such a way that people could experience them with emotional warmth. In the church at Lübben there is a life-sized portrait of Gerhardt with the inscription beneath it, *Theologus in cribro Satanae versatus*, "A Divine [i.e., Theologian] sifted in Satan's sieve" (cf. Luke 22:31).

FOR FURTHER READING

Hess, Deborah L. "The Hymns of Paul Gerhardt." *The Hymn: A Journal of Congregational Song* 45, no. 3 (July 1994): 19–22.

Hewett, Theodore Brown. *Paul Gerhardt as a Hymn Writer and His Influence on English Hymnody*. New Haven: Yale University Press, 1919. Reprinted, abridged, St. Louis: Concordia, 1976.

READING

From Luther's Preface to the Wittenberg Hymnal

That it is good and God-pleasing to sing hymns is, I think, known to every Christian; for everyone is aware not only of the example of the prophets and kings in the Old Testament who praised God with song and sound, with poetry and psaltery, but also of the common and ancient custom of the Christian church to sing Psalms. St. Paul himself instituted this in 1 Corinthians 14 [:15] and exhorted the Colossians [3:16] to sing spiritual songs and Psalms heartily unto the Lord so that God's Word and Christian teaching might be instilled and implanted in many ways.

Therefore I, too, in order to make a start and to give an incentive to those who can do better, have with the help of others compiled several hymns, so that the holy gospel which now by the grace of God has risen anew may be noised and spread abroad.

Like Moses in his song [Exod. 15:2], we may now boast that Christ is our praise and song and say with St. Paul, 1 Corinthians 2 [:2], that we should know nothing to sing or say, save Jesus Christ our Savior.

...Nor am I of the opinion that the gospel should destroy and blight all the arts, as some of the pseudo-religious claim. But I would like to see all the arts, especially music, used in the service of Him who gave them and made them.

Martin Luther, "Preface to the Wittenberg Hymnal," in *Luther's Works,* vol. 52 (Philadelphia: Fortress Press, 1965), 315–16.

PROPERS

O God, our faithful God, whose boundless love no thought can reach nor tongue declare, by the poetry of your servants Philipp Nicolai, Johann Heermann, and Paul Gerhardt you have enabled your people to learn theology while delighting in hymns of richness, depth, and beauty: Grant that by their compositions our reluctance to hear your word may be overcome, our journey through this world lightened, and our joy crowned with music; and by the grand songs of former days guide us safely home; through Jesus Christ our Lord, who lives and reigns with you and the Holy Spirit, one God, now and forever.

PHP

Readings:	2 Chronicles 20:20-21
	Psalm 96
	Colossians 3:12-17
	Matthew 13:44-52
Hymn of the Day:	
	"O Morning Star, how fair and bright" (Nicolai) (LBW 76, LSB 395, ELW 308; H82 496, 497)
	or "O God, my faithful God" (Heermann) (LBW 504, LSB 696, ELW 806)
	or "Evening and morning" (Gerhardt) (LBW 465, LSB 726, ELW 761)
	or "Commit thou all that grieves thee" (H82 669)
Prayers:	For grace to sing in distress and in joy
	For preachers of the gospel
	For confidence and faith
	For a gentle spirit
Preface:	All Saints
Color:	White

OCTOBER

ALSO ON OCTOBER 26

Alfred the Great, King of the West Saxons, 899

The 1979 *Book of Common Prayer* has added King Alfred to the calendar. He was born in 849, the youngest of five sons of King Aethelwulf, and following the death of his father and the brief reigns of his brothers, he became King of Wessex in 871. At that time, the pagan Danes had gained control of large parts of England and were harrying the eastern coast, burning churches and monasteries, and killing the people. In those dark days Alfred never despaired, and, after many setbacks, he was able to drive the Danes out of Wessex, thereby saving his kingdom and his subjects from destruction. He was generous to the defeated enemy and persuaded them to accept baptism.

In his last years Alfred sought to repair the damage wrought by the Danish invasions to culture and learning, especially among the parish clergy. He founded a palace school that was unrivaled in northern Europe; and with the help of scholars from Wales and the European continent, he supervised the translation into English of important theological and historical books. He administered justice with insight and fairness, protected the poor, encouraged art, crafts, and learning, and tried in all he did to rule as a model Christian king. Because of all this, he alone of all English sovereigns is called "the Great." He wrote, "He seems to me a very foolish man, and very wretched, who will not increase his understanding while he is in this world, and ever wish and long to reach that endless life where all shall be made clear."

Alfred died on October 26, 899, and was buried in the Old Minster in his capital city of Winchester.

FOR FURTHER READING

Frantzen, Allen J. *King Alfred.* Boston: Twayne, 1986.

Horspool, David. *King Alfred: Burnt Cakes and Other Legends.* Cambridge: Harvard University Press, 2006.

Keynes, Simon, and Michael Lapidge, trans. *Alfred the Great.* New York: Viking Penguin, 1984.

Smith, A. P. *King Alfred the Great.* New York: Oxford University Press, 1995.

Stenton, F. M. *Anglo-Saxon England.* 3d ed. New York: Oxford University Press, 1971.

READING

From *The Life of King Alfred* by Asser

He was also in the habit of hearing daily the divine office, the mass, and certain prayers and psalms, and of observing both the day and the night hours, and of visiting churches at night-time, as we have said, in order to pray without his followers knowing. Moreover, he showed zeal for almsgiving, and generosity both to his countrymen and to strangers from all nations, and very great and matchless kindness and pleasantness towards all. . . . Also he was accustomed to listen to the Holy Scripture recited by native clergy, but also, if by chance someone had come from elsewhere, to listen with equal earnestness and attention to the prayers along with foreigners. He also loved his bishops and all the ecclesiastical order, his earldormen and his nobles, his officials and all members of his household, with a wonderful affection. And he himself never ceased among other occupations, day and night, to train their sons, who were being brought up in the royal household, in all good behaviour, and to educate them in letters, loving them no less than his own sons. Yet, as if he had no comfort in all these things and as if he suffered no other disquiet from within or without, he complained in anxious sadness by day and night to God and to all who were bound to him in close affection, and lamented with repeated sighs, that Almighty God had not made him skilled in divine wisdom and the liberal arts; emulating in this the pious and most illustrious and rich Solomon, king of the Hebrews, who, despising all present glory and riches, sought first wisdom from God, and found both, wisdom and present glory, as it is written: "Seek therefore first the kingdom of God and his justice, and all these things shall be granted unto you." But God, who always sees into the inmost thoughts, and prompts our designs and all good desires, and also most amply ordains that good desires may be obtained, and who never prompts anyone to desire well without also ordaining what each man well and justly desires to have, stirred up by the king's mind from within, not without; as it is written: "I will hear what the Lord God will speak to me."

Asser, "Life of King Alfred," chap. 76, trans. Dorothy Whitelock, in *English Historical Documents c. 500–1402*, ed. D. C. Douglas, *English Historical Documents* vol. 1 (London: Eyre and Spottiswoode, 1955), 293, 294.

PROPERS

O Sovereign Lord, you brought your servant Alfred to a troubled throne that he might establish peace in a ravaged land and revive learning and the arts among the people: Awaken in us also a keen desire to increase our understanding while we are in this world, and an eager longing to reach that endless life where all will be made clear; through Jesus Christ our Lord, who lives and reigns with you and the Holy Spirit, one God, forever and ever.

Alfred, CMG, LFF

OCTOBER

Readings: Wisdom 6:1-3, 9-12, 24-25
                 Psalm 21:1-7 *or* 112:1-9
                 Luke 6:43-49
Hymn of the Day:
                 "God moves in a mysterious way his wonders to perform" (H82 677, LBW 483, LSB
                     765)
Prayers: For all who are in positions of authority in government, the law, industry, and
                     commerce
                 For universities, colleges, and schools
                 For the Sovereign and Royal Family of Great Britain and for all the people
Preface: Baptism (BCP, LBW)
Color: White

October 28

St. Simon and St. Jude, Apostles

Apart from their inclusion in the apostolic lists of the Twelve (Matt. 10:2-4; Mark 3:16-19; Luke 6:13-16; Acts 1:13) nothing more is known from Scripture about the two apostles Simon and Jude. As with many of the apostolic band, their names are recorded, but details of their work as foundation stones of the church are not provided. The focus is on the power of God and on Christ the chief cornerstone.

Simon, sometimes called "the less" to distinguish him from Simon Peter, is called "the Canaanaean" by Matthew and Mark and is called "the Zealot" by Luke (6:15; Acts 1:13). The Greek word translated "the Canaanean" is probably a transcription of the Aramaic, meaning "zealous," which would explain Luke's term *zealot*, although the word could imply that Simon had been a member of the Zealot party, the fanatical opponents of Roman rule in Palestine. He is variously reported to have labored in Egypt, Cyrene, and Mauritania. Nothing further is known of him.

Jude, called "Judas not Iscariot" in John 14:22, is referred to in Luke 6:16 as "Judas of James." The phrase is taken by modern translations to mean "son of James," but older translations such as the Authorized (King James) Version understand it to be "brother of James," and so it has generally been so understood in the West. Jude is thought to have been the brother of James, the brother of the Lord (see October 23) and the author of the epistle of Jude. He is generally understood to be the same person as Thaddaeus or Lebbaeus of Matthew 10:3 and Mark 3:18—names, like Jude, perhaps given to Judas to avoid confusing him with the Judas who betrayed Jesus. (Thomas Hardy aptly named one of his characters Jude the Obscure.)

The apocryphal *Passion of Simon and Jude* says that St. Jude preached for ten years in Mesopotamia and that he and Simon labored together in Persia and were martyred there on the same day. In the West, the two are always coupled on the calendar. The Armenian Church regards St. Thaddaeus and St. Bartholomew as the first to preach the gospel among the Armenians and have a joint day of commemoration for them. In the Eastern Orthodox Churches, the two apostles have separate feast days: St. Simon on May 10 and St. Jude, called "the brother of the Lord," on June 19.

Legendary accounts of St. Jude's miraculous healing of the King of Edessa and the conflicts between the two apostles and Zoroastrian magicians in Persia have been handed down with all sorts of embellishments. Since the eighteenth century, the Roman Catholic Church has come to regard St. Jude as the saint to turn to for help "in desperate cases," perhaps because, as namesake of the traitor, St. Jude had little cult developed around him and therefore might be the saint most likely to welcome the prayers of the truly desperate.

FOR FURTHER READING

Bauckham, Richard J. *Jude and the Relatives of Jesus in the Early Church.* Edinburgh: T&T Clark, 1990.

Filson, Floyd V. "The Brothers of the Lord." In *Interpreter's Dictionary of the Bible.* 1:470–72. Nashville and New York: Abingdon, 1962.

READING

OCTOBER

From Luther's *Lectures on Galatians,* 1535

Serving another person through love seems to reason to mean performing unimportant works such as the following: teaching the erring; comforting the afflicted; encouraging the weak; helping the neighbor in whatever way one can; bearing with his rude manners and impoliteness; putting up with annoyances, labors, and the ingratitude and contempt of men in both church and state; being patient in the home with a cranky wife and an unmanageable family, and the like. But believe me, these works are so outstanding and brilliant that the whole world cannot comprehend their usefulness and worth; indeed, it cannot estimate the value of even one tiny good work, because it does not measure works or anything else on the basis of the Word of God but on the basis of a reason that is wicked, blind, and foolish.

Therefore men are completely mistaken when they imagine that they really understand the commandment to love. They have it written in their hearts, of course, because by nature they judge that one should do to others what one wants done to oneself (Matthew 7:12). But it does not follow that they understand this. For if they did, they would demonstrate it in their actions and would prefer love to all other works.

PROPERS

O God, we thank you for the glorious company of the apostles, and especially on this day for Simon and Jude; and we pray that, as they were faithful and zealous in their mission, so we may with ardent devotion make known the love and mercy of our Lord and Savior Jesus Christ, who lives and reigns with you and the Holy Spirit, one God, forever and ever.

1979 BCP, LBW, ELW

Readings:	Deuteronomy 32:1-4 *or* Jeremiah 26:1-16
	Psalm 119:89-96
	Ephesians 2:13-22 *or* 1 John 4:1-6
	John 15:17-27 *or* John 14:21-27
Hymn of the Day:	
	"Awake, my soul, stretch every nerve" (H82 546, SBH 552)
	or "Father eternal, Ruler of creation" (H82 573, LBW 413)
Prayers:	For the obscure and the forgotten and the unknown in the work of the church
	For the gift of holiness, which is the creation and gift of God
	For faithful continuation of the apostles' preaching the Gospel to all the world
Preface:	Apostles
Color:	Red

October 29

On this date the *Book of Common Prayer* commemorates **James Hannington** (1847–1885), Bishop of Equatorial Africa, and his companions, who were martyred in 1885 in Uganda. (See the martyrs of Uganda, June 3.)

October 31

Reformation Day

Each of the liturgical churches has a day celebrating its central and formative event or experience. Eastern Orthodoxy has a celebration of the Triumph of Orthodoxy, the first Sunday in Lent, commemorating the settling in 843 of the controversy over the legitimacy of the use of icons in the Church. The Roman Catholic Church has the feast of the Chair of Peter (February 22), emphasizing the founding of the Church upon Peter the prince of the apostles. The Anglican Church commemorates the publication of the first Book of Common Prayer in 1549 as the principal liturgical and theological source for the Anglican

Communion; a rubric in the present Prayer Book reads, "The First Book of Common Prayer, 1549, is appropriately observed on a weekday following the Day of Pentecost." Reformation Day is the distinctive festival of the Lutheran Church.

The Festival of the Reformation is to be understood and observed not as a triumphalist celebration as though all error was purged from the church forever in 1517. Rather, it is a day of humble recollection of the revolutionary and cleansing word of God, which is continually reforming and renewing God's church. It is a day that reminds God's people of the provisional nature of all that is less than God, and of the sovereignty of God alone, who is always free to tear up and destroy in order to build and plant anew. Reform and renewal is not a once-for-all event, nor even an occasional eruption, but rather a continuing condition of the church.

Only six of the several hundred church orders of the sixteenth century made provision for the celebration of the Reformation. The date of the celebration varied: in Pomerania it was celebrated on Luther's birthday, November 10; sometimes it was Trinity Sunday (as Pentecost commemorated the birthday of the church so the following Sunday commemorated the rebirth of the church); sometimes it was the Sunday following the Presentation of the Augsburg Confession, June 25. The observances soon died out.

A new anti-Roman spirit was created by the Thirty Years' War in which Roman Catholic princes attempted to eradicate northern European Protestantism. In 1667, John George II, the Elector of Saxony, ordered a Reformation festival to be celebrated on October 31, the anniversary of Luther's posting of his Ninety-five Theses on the door of the Castle Church in Wittenberg, questioning abuses in the sale of indulgences. The observance of the festival spread and was often moved to the nearest Sunday, whether before or after the date. In the latter twentieth century, as the old anti-Catholic fervor was cooling and a new appreciation of the necessity of the unity of the church was arising, the day became known and was observed in many places as Reformation/Reconciliation Day or Sunday.

A more irenic date for the commemoration of the Reformation is June 25, the Presentation of the Augsburg Confession, which makes clearer the Lutheran understanding of itself not as a separate denomination but as a reforming movement within the Catholic Church of the West.

The Church of England's *Church Year* commemorates Martin Luther on October 31.

FOR FURTHER READING

Asmussen, Hans, et al. *The Unfinished Reformation.* Trans. Robert J. Olsen. Notre Dame: Fides, 1961.

Bergendoff, Conrad. *The Church of the Lutheran Reformation.* St. Louis: Concordia, 1967.

OCTOBER

Bodensieck, Julius, ed. *The Encyclopedia of the Lutheran Church.* 3 vols. Philadelphia: Fortress Press, 1965.

Elert, Werner. *The Structure of Lutheranism.* Trans. Walter A. Hansen. St. Louis:
Concordia, 1962.

Gritsch, Eric W. *Fortress Introduction to Lutheranism.* Minneapolis: Fortress Press,
1994.

MacCulloch, Diarmaid. *The Reformation: Europe's House Divided, 1490–1700.*
New York: Viking, 2003.

Pauck, Wilhelm. *The Heritage of the Reformation.* Glencoe: Free Press, 1961.

Rogers, Nicholas. *Halloween: From Pagan Ritual to Party Night.* New York: Oxford
University Press, 2003.

Rupp, Gordon. *The Righteousness of God.* London: Hodder and Stoughton, 1953.

READING

From C. S. Lewis, *English Literature in the Sixteenth Century*

In reality Tyndale is trying to express an obstinate facet which meets us long before we venture into the realm of theology; the fact that morality or duty (what
he calls 'the Law') never yet made a man happy in himself or dear to others. It is
shocking, but it is undeniable. We do not wish to either to be, or to live among
people who are clean or honest or kind as a matter of duty: we want to be, and to
associate with, people who like being clean and honest and kind. The mere suspicion that what seemed an act of spontaneous friendliness or generosity was really
done as a duty subtly poisons it. In philosophical language, the ethical category is
self-destructive; morality is healthy only when it is trying to abolish itself. In theological language, no man can be saved by works. The whole purpose of the 'gospel',
for Tyndale, is to deliver us from morality. Thus, paradoxically, the 'puritan' of
modern imagination—the cold, gloomy heart, doing as duty what happier and
richer souls do without thinking of it—is precisely the enemy which historical
Protestantism arose and smote. What really matters is not to obey moral rules but
to be a creature of a certain kind.

C. S. Lewis, *English Literature in the Sixteenth Century Excluding Drama* (Oxford: Clarendon,
1954), 187.

PROPERS

Almighty God, gracious Lord, pour out your Holy Spirit upon your faithful people. Keep them steadfast in your Word, protect and comfort them in all temptations, defend them against all their enemies, and bestow on the Church your saving peace; through your Son Jesus Christ our Lord, who lives and reigns with you
and the Holy Spirit, one God, now and forever.

Saxony 1539, trans. CB, rev. in LBW, ELW

Readings:	Jeremiah 31:31-34
	Psalm 46
	Romans 3:19-28
	John 8:31-36
Hymn of the Day:	
	"I trust, O Christ, in you alone" (LBW 395)
Prayers:	For a renewed sense of the free grace of God
	For the living word of God to burn brightly throughout the church
	For a bold, daring, and lively faith
	For the unity of the church
	For increased love of one another
Preface:	Weekdays or Sundays after Pentecost
Color:	Red

November 1

All Saints' Day

This great festival recalls to the mind the size and the solidarity of the church: a vast communion that spreads beyond all bounds of race and language and human condition, beyond even time and space, across the barrier of death. In each faithful person the Christian proclamation has concrete realization, for this is the Christian gospel: to call people to believe that they, in company with multitudes of others, might become holy. When the church praises the saints, it praises God himself, who has triumphed through them. Those who are still in the church on earth are supported and encouraged by the fellowship of a throng of witnesses, who fought their way with effort and pain, and who now in the company of the redeemed are watching and supporting the church on earth in its present struggle.

The origins of All Saints' Day are uncertain. Ephrem of Edessa (see June 10) composed a hymn *ca.* 359 which suggests that a commemoration of all the martyrs was held on the Friday after Easter, suggesting a parallel with Good Friday but informed by the resurrection: Christ died on Friday, so those who follow him in death imitate his passion but do so in the light of the resurrection.

From a sermon by John Chrysostom, it appears that the Church at Antioch commemorated all the martyrs on the Sunday after Pentecost, and Maximus of Turin preached on all the martyrs also on the Sunday after Pentecost. This is still the day of the commemoration of all the saints in the Eastern Churches, and it has logic to it. The birthday of the church, Pentecost, has its parallel in the birthday of the saints, their martyrdom. In the old maxim, the blood of the martyrs is (or waters) the seed of the church. By the seventh century the feast had been extended to include nonmartyrs as well. The *Comes* of Würzburg calls the day "The Sunday of the Birthday of the Saints." Holiness, we are thus reminded, is the work of the Holy Spirit.

On May 13, 609 or 610, Boniface IV dedicated the Roman Pantheon to Mary and all the martyrs. The anniversary of this dedication was kept with great rejoicing, but whether it was because of the martyrs or because of the anniversary of the dedication is unclear. There was a pagan festival to placate the gods (Lemuria) on May 9, 11, and 13; and the Christian celebration on May 13 was probably in part to offset the popular pagan festival.

Gregory II dedicated an oratory in St. Peter's Basilica to all the saints, but the date is unknown (some say it was November 1) and the chapel is a small one and its principal dedication was to the Virgin Mary.

In England at this time, November 1 is listed as the day of all the saints. Perhaps Egbert of York, who had been ordained a deacon in Rome in 732, carried the celebration of November 1 to England. Or the celebration of the day may have originated in Gaul or in Ireland. The Irish often assigned the first day of the month to important feasts, and the oldest Irish martyrology lists November 1 as the feast of all English and Irish saints, April 20 as the day of all the saints of Europe, and December 23 as the day of all the saints of Africa. Moreover, in Celtic lands the mists and frosts of late autumn suggested the visitation and the presence of spirits and made the beginning of November a natural time to remember the departed.

According to John Beleth (died *ca.* 1165), Gregory IV in 835 transferred the feast from May 13 to November 1 after the harvest so that there would be sufficient food in Rome for the pilgrims. In the twelfth century, the date of May 13 for All Saints disappears from the liturgical books.

The 1928 Proposed Book of Common Prayer for the Church of England assigned to the octave of All Saints, November 8, to the "Saints, Martyrs, and Doctors of the Church of England" (on the 1997 calendar, "The Saints and Martyrs of England"); it was broadened on some calendars as a festival of the Saints and Martyrs of the Anglican Communion. The American *Draft Proposed Book of Common Prayer* (1976) listed November 8 as the commemoration of the "Holy Men and Women of the Old Testament," but the commemoration was not carried into the 1977 *Proposed Book of Common Prayer.*

Luther chose the eve of All Saints' Day, October 31, to post his Ninety-Five Theses in Wittenberg because he wanted the crowds who would come to church on the following day to see them. As the anniversary of the posting of the theses came to be observed as Reformation Day, the ancient and universal celebration of all the saints came to be overshadowed in Lutheran churches, although All Saints' Day remained on Lutheran calendars.

READING

From *Centuries* by Thomas Traherne (1637–1674)

To delight in the Saints of God is the way to Heaven. One would think it exceeding easy and reasonable to esteem those whom Jesus purchased with His precious blood, And if we do so how can we choose but inherit all things. All the Saints of all Ages, and all Kingdoms are His inheritance, His treasure, His jewels. Shall they not be yours since they are His whom you love so infinitely? . . .

   With all their eyes behold our Saviour, with all their hearts adore Him, with all their tongues and affection praise Him. See how in all closets, and in all temples; in all cities and in all fields; in all nations and in all generations, they are lifting up their hands and eyes unto His cross; and delight in all their adorations. This will enlarge your Soul and make you dwell in all kingdoms and ages: strengthen your faith and enrich your affections: fill you with their joys and make you a lively partaker in communion with them. Men do mightily wrong themselves when they refuse to be present in all ages: and neglect to see the beauty in all kingdoms, and despise the resentments of every soul, and busy themselves only with pots and cups and things at home, or shops and trades and things in the street: but do not live to God manifesting Himself in all the world, nor care to see (and be present with Him in) all the glory of His Eternal Kingdom. By seeing the Saints of all Ages we are present with them: by being present with them become too great for our own age, and near to our Saviour.

Thomas Traherne, *Centuries* (New York: Harper & Bros., 1960), 41, 43–44.

PROPERS

Almighty God, you have knit together your elect in one communion and fellowship in the mystical body of your Son Christ our Lord: Give us grace to follow your blessed saints in all virtuous and godly living, that we may come to those ineffable joys that you have prepared for those who truly love you; through Jesus Christ our Lord, who with you and the Holy Spirit lives and reigns, one God, in glory everlasting.

1549, 1662 BCP; rev. in LBW, ELW

NOVEMBER

Readings:	Sirach 44:1-10, 13-14 *or* Isaiah 26:1-4, 8-9, 12-13, 19-21
	Psalm 149
	Revelation 7:2-4, 9-17
	Matthew 5:1-12
Hymn of the Day:	
	"For all the saints, who from their labors rest" (H82 287, LBW 174, LSB 677, ELW 422)
Prayers:	For those who waited for the fulfullment of God's promise
	For the apostles and heralds of the kingdom

For those who kept the faith through ages of darkness
For missionaries who brought the gospel to our land
For all who recall the church to love and sacrifice
For all who lead the nations to justice and peace

Preface: All Saints
Color: White

At the service on All Saints' Day, it may be instructive to gather whatever statues there may be in the church together with other representations of individual saints and set them along the chancel walls, suggesting the cloud of witnesses that surrounds and supports the church on earth.

November 2

Commemoration of the Faithful Departed

In the New Testament, the word *saints* is used to describe the entire membership of the Christian church, living and dead. The Episcopal collect for All Saints' Day uses the word *elect* in the same sense; the Lutheran adaptation of that prayer says "your people," intending to mean the same thing. As the church grew in numbers and became part of the society in which it lived, so that it was no longer the church against the world, the word *saint* came to have a more limited meaning and was applied to those within the Christian community who were conspicuous signs of the gospel whose courageous witness and sanctity were remembered with gratitude by later generations. So there were saints, and there were the rest of us.

It is appropriate the day after the celebration of the festival of All Saints, to remember those who, while no less members of the body of the redeemed in Christ, are unknown to the wider fellowship of the faithful. They are still members of the mystical Body of Christ and still held in love by the living; death does not break the communion. Remembering the departed fulfills the natural instincts of human hearts and binds together the whole family of Christ on earth and in paradise.

The practice of commemorating those who have gone before us is an ancient one. Judas Maccabeus thus prayed for some who had died in battle in the expectation of a resurrection (2 Macc. 12:44). Inscriptions in the catacombs and the testimony of the early Fathers show that it was also common practice in the first age of the church.

From the early ninth century onward, monasteries began to commemorate their dead and their departed benefactors. The practice was formalized in 998 by Odilio, Abbot of the great monastery of Cluny as a celebration of masses in memory of all who rest in Christ, to be observed on the day following All Saints' Day. It soon became known popularly as All Souls' Day.

In the Eastern Church, Saturday was a special day of remembrance of the dead, especially the Saturdays before Lent and before Pentecost. Lutheran and Anglican calendars since the Reformation have, from time to time, preserved or restored to the calendar on November 2 what is called the Commemoration of the Faithful Departed. German Lutheran practice was often to remember on the Last Sunday after Trinity, the last Sunday of the church year, members of the parish who died during the year past. A rediscovery of All Saints' Day or Sunday encouraged many to make such remembrance at the All Saints festival.

READING

From Dom Gregory Dix, *The Shape of the Liturgy*

To those who know a little of christian history probably the most moving of all the reflections it brings is not the thought of the great events and the well-remembered saints, but of those innumerable millions of entirely obscure faithful men and women, every one with his or her individual hopes and fears and joys and sorrows and loves—and sins and temptations and prayers—once every whit as vivid and alive as mine are now. They have left no slightest trace in this world, not even a name, but have passed to God utterly forgotten by men. Yet each of them once believed and prayed as I believe and pray, and found it hard and grew slack and sinned and repented and fell again. Each of them worshipped at the eucharist, and found their thoughts wandering and tried again, and felt heavy and unresponsive and yet knew—just as really and pathetically as I do these things. There is a little ill-spelled ill-carved rustic epitaph of the fourth century from Asia Minor:—'Here sleeps the blessed Chione, who has found Jerusalem for she prayed much.' Not another word is known of Chione, some peasant woman who lived in that vanished world of christian Anatolia. But how lovely if all that should survive after sixteen centuries were that one had prayed much, so that the neighbors who saw all one's life were sure one must have found Jerusalem! What did the Sunday eucharist in her village church every week for a life-time mean to the blessed Chione—and to the millions like her then, and every year since? The sheer stupendous *quantity* of the love of God which this ever repeated action has drawn from the obscure christian multitudes through the centuries is in itself an overwhelming thought.

Gregory Dix, *The Shape of the Liturgy* (London: A. C. Black, 1945), 744–45.

PROPERS

Almighty God, with whom still live the spirits of those who die in the Lord, and with whom the souls of the faithful, after they are delivered from the burden of the flesh, are in joy and felicity: We give you heartfelt thanks for the good examples of all your servants who, having finished their course in faith, now find rest and refreshment; and we pray that we, with all who have departed in the true faith of your holy Name, may have perfect fulfillment and bliss, both in body and soul, in your eternal and everlasting glory; through Jesus Christ our Lord, who lives and reigns with you and the Holy Spirit, one God, now and forever.

Medieval, 1549 BCP; CSB, SBH; rev. in LBW

Readings:	Wisdom 3:1-9 *or* Isaiah 25:6-9
	Psalm 130 *or* 116:10-17
	1 Thessalonians 4:13-18 *or* 1 Corinthians 15:50-58
	John 6:51-58 *or* John 5:24-27
Hymn of the Day:	
	"O what their joy and their glory must be" (H82 623, LBW 337, LSB 675)
	or "O Lord of life, whe'er they be safe in thine own eternity" (SBH 600)
	or "Christ the victorious" (H82 358)
Prayers:	For all the faithful departed
	For those whose faith is known only to God
	For those who died without faith and without hope
	For suicides
	For those who mourn
	In thanksgiving for the lives of all faithful Christians
Preface:	Commemoration of the Dead (BCP)
Color:	White

November 3

Martin de Porres, Renewer of Society, 1639

Martin de Porres was born in 1579 in Lima, Peru, the illegitimate son of a Spanish knight, Don Juan de Porres, and a Panamanian woman of Indian or Negro descent, Ana Velazquez. (He described himself as "a mulatto dog.") Raised by his mother, he was trained as a barber-surgeon and learned elements of herbal healing from his mother. He became a Dominican at the age of fifteen and spent his life at the friary at Lima caring for the sick and the poor who thronged the friary gate, especially Negro slaves. He also took care of abandoned cats and dogs and had a great concern for all animals, including vermin, about which amusing tales are told. He also had an aptitude for more delicate matters, solving marriage problems, raising dowries, serving as consultant in many areas for persons of consequence in Lima. He died in 1639, and, although he was credited with supernatural powers while he lived, and although all Lima acclaimed his sanctity when he died, he was not canonized until 1962 as a patron of racial justice and harmony.

Martin de Porres is included in the list of "Witnesses to the Faith" in the African American Lutheran service book *This Far by Faith* (1999) and the calendar in *Evangelical Lutheran Worship*.

FOR FURTHER READING

Cavallini, Giuliana. *St. Martin de Porres.* New York: Herder, 1963.

READING

From a homily at the canonization of Saint Martin de Porres by Pope John XXIII

The example of Martin's life is ample evidence that we can strive for holiness and salvation as Christ Jesus has shown us: first, by loving God "with all your heart, and with all your soul, and with all your mind" and second by loving "your neighbor as yourself." [Matt. 22:38-39]

When Martin had come to realize that Christ Jesus suffered for us and "that he himself bore our sins in his body on the tree" [1 Peter 1:21, 24], he would meditate with remarkable ardor and affection about Christ on the cross. Whenever he would contemplate Christ's terrible torture he could not restrain his tears. He had an extraordinary love for the great sacrament of the Eucharist and often spent long hours in prayer before the blessed sacrament. He sought to receive the nourishment of the Sacrament as often as he could.

Saint Martin, always obedient and inspired by his divine Teacher, dealt with his brothers with that profound love which comes from pure faith and humility. He loved people because he honestly looked on them as God's children and as his own brothers and sisters. Such was his humility that he loved them even more than himself and considered them to be better and more righteous than he was.

He did not blame others for their shortcomings. Persuaded that he deserved more severe punishment for his sins than others did, he would overlook their worst offenses. He was tireless in his efforts to reform the criminal; he would sit up with the sick to bring them comfort; he would provide food, clothing, and medicine for the poor. He did all he could to care for poor farmhands, blacks, and mulattoes who were looked down upon as slaves, the dregs of society in their time. Common people responded by calling him "Martin the charitable."

The virtuous example and even the conversation of this saintly man exerted a powerful influence in drawing many to religion. It is remarkable how even today his influence can still raise our hearts to heaven. Unfortunately, not all of us understand these spiritual values as well as we should, nor do we give them a proper place in our lives. Many of us, in fact, strongly attracted by sin, may look upon these values as of little importance, even something of a nuisance, or we ignore them altogether. It is deeply rewarding for those striving for salvation to follow in Christ's footsteps and to obey God's commandments. If only everyone could learn this lesson from the example that Martin gave us.

From the English translation of the Office of Readings from the Liturgy of the Hours by the International Committee on English in the Liturgy, rev. PHP.

NOVEMBER

PROPERS

God of love, you led your servant Martin de Porres by a life of humility to eternal glory: In your mercy, grant that we may follow his example and have a place with him in the kingdom of heaven; through your Son Jesus Christ our Lord, who lives and reigns with you and the Holy Spirit, one God, now and forever.

RS, rev. PHP

Readings: Micah 6:6-8
               Psalm 9:1-10
               1 Corinthians 1:26-31
               Luke 6:20-23
Hymn of the Day:
               "O God, empower us to stem the hatreds that divide" (LBW 422)
Prayers: For racial justice and reconciliation
               For a deepened commitment to serve those in need
               For those who care for the sick and the poor
               For all who practice the arts of healing
Preface: A Saint (1) (BCP)
Color: White

November 3 (or November 4)

Richard Hooker, Priest, 1600

Richard Hooker, the first and one of the greatest Anglican theologians, was born in 1554 near Exeter and was educated at Corpus Christi College, Oxford. After his ordination he held a living in Buckinghamshire and served in several country parishes.

It was a time when the Church of England was being attacked from two sides. Because it had abolished papal supremacy and revised the liturgy, Roman Catholics considered that it had ceased to be part of the Catholic and Apostolic Church. The Puritans, on the other had, argued that because many of the traditions from the days of the early Church had been retained, it was not faithful to the Bible. Hooker, in his *Laws of Ecclesiastical Polity* (1593) provided a basis for the Anglican approach to Christian truth. The book, written in great charity and unequalled beauty of style, is a masterly defense of the Anglican *via media*, the Middle Way between Roman Catholicism and the Puritans, with a threefold basis: Scripture, tradition, and reason. Against the Puritans, who accepted only Scripture as a guide for organizing the church and its worship, Hooker argues that the law of nature, known by human reason, affords principles that justify the existing organization of the English Church. Transforming controversy into philosophy, his defense of ecclesiastical practices rested on Scripture and on a philosophy of nature and our place in it, our relation to God and to other human beings. This world view is set forth in what is perhaps the finest piece of prose of the Elizabethan age, calm and stately, a genuine literary masterpiece.

Hooker died in 1600. His commemoration was added to the calendar in the 1979 *Book of Common Prayer* and was included on the Methodist calendar in *For All the Saints*. Those who desire to commemorate Martin de Porres may choose to transfer the commemoration of Richard Hooker to the next day, November 4.

READING

From Richard Hooker, *Laws of Ecclesiastical Polity* I, 3, 16

Now if Nature should intermit her course and leave altogether, though it were but for a while, the observation of her own laws; if those principal and mother elements of the world, whereof all things in this lower world are made, should lose the qualities which now they have; if the frame of that heavenly arch erected over our heads should loosen and dissolve itself; if celestial spheres should forget their wonted motions and by irregular volubility turn themselves any way as it might happen; if the prince of the lights of heaven which now as a giant doth run his unwearied course, should as it were through a languishing faintness begin to stand and to rest himself; if the moon should wander from her beaten way, the times and the seasons of the year blend themselves by disordered and confused mixture, the winds breathe out their last gasp, the clouds yield no rain, the earth be defeated of heavenly influence, the fruits of the earth pine away as children at the withered breasts of their mother no longer able to yield them relief, what would become of man himself, whom these things now do all serve? See we not plainly that obedience of creatures unto the law of Nature is the stay of the whole world? . . .

Thus we see how even one and the self same thing is under divers considerations conveyed through many laws, and that to measure by any one kind of law all the actions of men were to confound the admirable order, wherein God hath disposed all laws, each as in nature, so in degree distinct from other. Wherefore that here we may briefly end, of law there can be no lesse acknowledged, then that her seat is the bosom of God, her voice the harmony of the world, all things in heaven and earth do her homage, the very least as feeling her care, and the greatest not exempted from her power, but angels and men and creatures of what condition soever, though each indifferent sort and manner, yet all with uniform consent, admiring her as the mother of their peace and joy.

NOVEMBER

PROPERS

O God of truth and peace, you raised up your servant Richard Hooker in a day of bitter controversy to defend with sound reasoning and great charity the catholic and reformed religion: Grant that we may maintain that middle way, not as a compromise for the sake of peace, but as a comprehension for the sake of truth; through Jesus Christ our Lord, who lives and reigns with you and the Holy Spirit, one God, forever and ever.

CMG, LFF

Readings: Psalm 37:3-6, 32-33 *or* 19:7-11(12-14)
                1 Corinthians 2:6-10, 13-16
                John 17:18-23
Hymn of the Day:
                "All my hope on God is founded" (H82 665, ELW 757)
Prayers: For all theologians
                For those who explain the faith
                For the peace and unity of the church of God
Preface: Baptism (BCP, LBW)
Color: White

November 5

Elizabeth and Zechariah, Parents of St. John the Baptist

A feast of Zechariah and his wife Elizabeth is kept in Palestine and elsewhere on November 5 and other dates. It is curious that this devout couple have not been included on the major calendars of the Western church. Their feast day in the East ("Prophet Zechariah and Righteous Elizabeth") is September 5; this is also the date for their commemoration in the *Lutheran Service Book* (2006). Observing their commemoration closer to the beginning of Advent perhaps makes the November date more suitable for the Western church.

Their essential story is provided by St. Luke (1:5-67; 3:2). Zechariah (the Greek form of his name is Zacharias) was a righteous priest of the division of Abijah (cf. 1 Chron. 24:7-19); Elizabeth, who bore the name of Aaron's wife (Exod. 6:23), was also of priestly descent. It was, therefore, in the eyes of Israel, an ideal marriage, pure priestly lineage and faultless characters in whom the highest form of piety was embodied. Since there were so many of the priestly line, not all could actually perform their priestly duty in the Temple, so the honor was bestowed by lot. The high privilege came to Zechariah to burn incense in the Temple, and while he was performing this service, symbolic of offering prayer, an angel appeared to him and announced that his old prayer for a son would at last be answered. The son was to be called John and would be filled with the Holy Spirit to prepare his people for God's rule.

Zechariah and Elizabeth were both aged, and Elizabeth, like Sarah and Hannah of earlier days, was barren; so the birth of a son seemed impossible. Zechariah cautiously asked for a sign that this would in fact be so. The God-given sign was for him to be mute and apparently also deaf because of his hesitancy to believe, until the promise was fulfilled. When he emerged from the Temple unable to speak and bless the worshipers, they understood that he had seen a vision.

When it came time for the promised child to be circumcised and named, Zechariah contradicted the expectation of the family and friends and, still unable to speak, wrote his acceptance of the angel's announcement nine months earlier, "His name is John." Zechariah's ability to speak was immediately restored and he blessed God with the song that has become the church's morning song, *Benedictus Dominus Deus*, "Blessed be the Lord God of Israel," a prophecy of the fulfillment of the Messianic hope. In some ancient manuscripts of the New Testament, the song ascribed to the Virgin Mary, the *Magnificat*, recalling the song of Hannah (1 Sam. 2:1-10), is assigned to Elizabeth, and in some ways it seems a more appropriate song for her. Elizabeth is described as a "relative" of Mary the mother of Jesus (1:36), but the precise relationship is not defined. It may perhaps suggest that Mary, too, was of priestly lineage.

According to later tradition, Zechariah was murdered in the Temple by order of King Herod.

READING

From a meditation by Frank S. Mead

Over in Herod's temple moved a priest well stricken in years; Zacharias took his turn at altar duties, reading faithfully his Scriptures, firm in the old faith that some day the Deliverer would come.

Honor and glory burst upon him in old age. Selected by lot one day to carry the fire from the outer altar of burnt offering to the golden altar of incense in the inner Holy Place (one in a lifetime, that happened!), he heard an angel speak: ". . . thy wife Elizabeth shall bear thee a son, and thou shalt call his name John . . . and he shall . . . make ready for the Lord a people prepared for him. . . ."

Abraham had laughed at such a greeting. Zacharias did not laugh; he was bewildered. He and Elizabeth were so old. . . . How. . . . For only that Zacharias was struck speechless, dumb.

But speech, nay song, broke from his lips again the day he took the child to be circumcised. Understanding now, Zacharias sang the "Benedictus," that epic of sacred harmony which we sing across Christendom today.

What a gamut of emotions, of puzzlement, despair, and joy, for the last days of an old man! . . .

Elizabeth, wife of Zacharias, was a masterpiece of the handiwork of God. She was righteous. She was blameless. She was sad. All life long she had wanted a child. (What woman does not?) When the babe foretold by Gabriel moved at last in her womb, her spirit touched the pinnacles of heaven. It was true, then! This *was* to be John, the Preparer, a Nazirite like Samson, Samuel, filled with the Holy Spirit even from his mother's womb.

One day a cousin, Mary, came to visit her. Mary was young. She too had talked with Gabriel; she too would have a child. Then Elizabeth "lifted up her voice with a loud cry." The mother of the Lord had come to her own house! There they sat, youth and age, together . . . Mary, mother of Jesus, Elizabeth, mother of John . . . talking in whispers . . . smiling, weeping, brooding, anticipating . . . Mary . . . and Elizabeth.

All too soon their happiness took wings. They and their unborn babies were to suffer much. Elizabeth, likely, was dead before her John died in Herod's prison. But Mary was to climb Calvary with her Jesus and the thieves.

Frank S. Mead, *Who's Who in the Bible* (New York: Harper & Bros., 1934), 186–87.

PROPERS

Almighty and everlasting God, by whose grace Elizabeth and Zechariah, parents of the forerunner of your Son Christ our Lord, were righteous before you and walked blameless in all your commandments: Grant, we pray, that, after their example, we may so faithfully serve you in this life that at the last we may receive the crown of righteousness which you, the righteous judge, will give to all those who truly love you; through the same, Jesus Christ our Lord, who lives and reigns with you and the Holy Spirit, one God, now and forever.

Henry Robert Percival (1854–1903) and Edward C. McCoy (d. 1967)

Readings:	2 John 6-11
	Psalm: Benedictus
	Luke 1:5-25
Hymn of the Day:	
	"Rejoice, rejoice, believers" (H82 68, LBW 25, LSB 515, ELW 244)
Prayers:	For all parents
	For those who cannot become parents
	For priests that they may be faithful in the duties
	For those who bear the scorn and reproach of the world
Preface:	Advent
Color:	White

November 6

William Temple, Archbishop of Canterbury, 1944

The second son of Frederick Temple, Archbishop of Canterbury (1897–1902), William Temple, philosopher, theologian, social teacher, educational reformer, and leader in the ecumenical movement, was born October 15, 1881. Growing up at the heart of the Church of England, he had a love for it that was deep and lifelong. One of his biographers has identified him, with Richard Hooker (see November 3), Joseph Butler (see June 16), and Frederick Denison Maurice (see April 1), as one of the four great doctors (teachers) of the post-Reformation Anglican Communion.

He had a brilliant mind, he was trained in classics and philosophy at Oxford. At the age of twenty-nine he became headmaster of Repton School, and then in quick succession rector of St. James' Church, Piccadilly, Bishop of Manchester, and Archbishop of York. While still a layman, although he had never experienced poverty of any kind, he formed lasting interest in education and social justice. This passion rested upon a profound belief in the Incarnation, which, he wrote, made Christianity "the most materialistic of all religions" and made sacred the person of every man and woman.

In 1917 he resigned from St. James' to devote himself to the "Life and Liberty Movement" for reform in the Church of England. In 1923 he became a member of the Archbishop's commission, which in 1938 produced the report on *Doctrine in the Church of England*. As Archbishop of York he became increasingly prominent in national life through his lively concern with social, economic, and international questions, while remaining independent of political and religious parties. In 1940 he convened the Malvern Conference to reflect on social reconstruction that would be needed in Britain once the Second World War (1939–1945) was over. He supported the Faith and Order and the Life and Work movements as well as the ecumenical movement generally.

He was a prolific writer on theological, ecumenical, and social topics, and his two-volume *Readings in St. John's Gospel*, written in the early days of the war, became a spiritual classic.

His brief tenure as Archbishop of Canterbury (April 23, 1942—October 26, 1944; half as long as his father's brief tenure) was overshadowed by war and ill health. He was added to the Episcopal calendar in *Lesser Feasts and Fasts 2003*.

NOVEMBER

FOR FURTHER READING

Kent, J. *William Temple: Church, State and Society in Britain, 1880–1950.* Cambridge: Cambridge University Press, 1992.

Suggate, A. M. *William Temple and Christian Social Ethics Today.* Edinburgh: T&T Clark, 1987.

READING

From *Personal Religion and the Life of Fellowship* by William Temple

It daily becomes more apparent that God's respect for the freedom of our affections, thoughts, and purposes is complete. It is part of that respect for our freedom that He never forces upon us His own gifts. He offers them, but unless we actively accept them, they remain ineffective as far as we are concerned. "Behold, I stand at the door and knock"—that is always the relation of God our Redeemer to our souls. He has paid the whole price; he has suffered the atoning Death; yet still He waits till we open the door of our hearts to let in His love which will call our love out. He never breaks down that door. He stands and knocks. And this is true not only of His first demand for admission to the mansion of the soul; it is true also of every room within that mansion. There are many of us who have opened the front door to Him, but have only let Him into the corridors and staircases; all the rooms where we work or amuse ourselves are still closed against Him. There are still greater multitudes who have welcomed Him to some rooms, and hope that He will not ask what goes on behind the doors of others. But sooner or later He asks; and if we do not at once take him to see, He leaves the room where we were so comfortable with Him, and stands knocking at the closed door. And then we can never again have the joy of His presence in the first room until we open the door at which He is now knocking. We can only have Him with us in the room that we choose for Him, if we really make Him free of all the house.

William Temple, *Personal Religion and the Life of Fellowship* (London: Longman's, Green, 1926), 79.

PROPERS

O God of light and love, you illumined your Church through the witness of your servant William Temple: Inspire us, we pray, by his teaching and example, that we may rejoice with courage, confidence, and faith in the Word made flesh, and may be led to establish that city which has justice for its foundation and love for its law; through Jesus Christ, the light of the world, who lives and reigns with you and the Holy Spirit, one God, now and forever.

LFF

Readings:	Psalm 119:97-104
	Ephesians 3:7-12
	John 1:9-18
Hymn of the Day:	
	"The Church's one foundation is Jesus Christ her Lord" (H82 525, LBW 369, LSB 644, ELW 654)
Prayers:	For teachers of the faith of the church
	For an increased passion for social justice
	For broadened horizons of responsibility
	For the unity of the church
Preface:	Epiphany
Color:	White

November 7

Willibrord, Archbishop of Utrecht, Missionary to Frisia, 739

Willibrord was born in 658 and received his education at Ripon Abbey and in Ireland where he was ordained priest in 688. He was influenced by the missionary enthusiasm of a Northumbrian monk named Egbert and decided to devote his life to the task of evangelizing northwestern Europe. He set out in 690 and, after some early reverses, settled at Utrecht in what is now the Netherlands, under the patronage of the Frankish ruler, Pepin II. Willibrord was consecrated by Pope Sergius I in 695 as the first bishop of the new see of Utrecht. From this center he laid the foundations of the Church in the Netherlands and worked tirelessly, preaching, teaching, and establishing churches and schools. The success of his work was exaggerated by later writers, but he laid a solid foundation for others to build on. In his old age Willibrord retired to a monastery he had founded at Echternach, in what is now Luxembourg. He died there November 7, 739.

Willibrord was included on the German *Evangelical Calendar of Names* (1962) and the calendar in the 1979 *Book of Common Prayer*; he is not on the General Roman Calendar nor on the American Lutheran calendar. The Society of St. Willibrord fosters links between the Anglican churches and the Old Catholic Church in Holland, with whom the Anglicans are in full communion.

FOR FURTHER READING

Grieve, A. J. *Willibrord, Missionary in the Netherlands*. London: SPG, 1923.

NOVEMBER

READING

From *Life of St. Willibrord* by Alcuin

Pepin, King of the Franks, was delighted at Willibrord's return and begged him to persevere in his divinely appointed task of preaching the Word of God and to root out idolatrous practices and sow the good seed in one place after another. This the devoted preacher strove to carry out with characteristic energy. He traversed every part of the country, exhorting the people in cities, villages and forts where he had previously preached the Gospel to remain loyal to the faith and to their good resolutions. And as the number of the faithful increased day by day and a considerable multitude of believers came to the knowledge of God's Word. Many began in their zeal for the faith to make over to the man of God their hereditary properties. These he accepted. Shortly afterwards he ordered churches to be built there, and he appointed priests and deacons to serve them, so that the new converts should have places where they could assemble on feast days and listen to wholesome instruction and where they could learn the principles of the Christian religion from those servants of God who had baptised them. This the man of God, favored by divine grace, made increasing progress from day to day. . . .

St. Willibrord was officially appointed to preach to the Frisian people, and his episcopal see was fixed at the fortress of Utrecht. He allowed no error or past ignorance to pass unnoticed and lost no time in shedding upon them the light of the Gospel, so that soon among that people the statement of the properly was fulfilled: "In that place where it was said unto them, Ye are not my people, it shall be said unto them, Ye are the sons of the living God."

Alcuin, *Life of St. Willibrord,* chaps. 12 and 13, trans. C. H. Talbot, *The Anglo-Saxon Missionaries in Germany* (New York: Sheed and Ward, 1954), 11, 12.

PROPERS

O Lord our God, you call whom you will and send them where you choose: We thank you for sending your servant Willibrord to be an apostle to the Low Countries, to turn them from the worship of idols to serve you, the living God; and we entreat you to preserve us from the temptation to exchange the perfect freedom of your service for servitude to false gods and to idols of our own devising; through Jesus Christ our Lord, who lives and reigns with you and the Holy Spirit, one God, forever and ever.

CMG, LFF

Readings: Psalm 96:1-7 *or* 98:1-4
               Acts 1:1-9
               Luke 10:1-9
Hymn of the Day:
               "O Zion, tune thy voice" (H82 543)

Prayers:	For Christians in the Netherlands
	For the government and people of the Netherlands
	For missionaries and their families
Preface:	Apostles
Color:	White

November 8

John Christian Frederick Heyer, Missionary to India, 1873

J. C. F. Heyer, the first missionary sent out by American Lutherans, was born in Helmstedt, Germany, on July 10, 1793, to a master furrier and his wife. When he was thirteen, troops of Napoleon were quartered in the city, and his parents, out of concern over the turmoil of the time, sent their son, after his confirmation in 1807, to stay with an uncle in America who cared for him, gave him employment, and encouraged him in his studies. Heyer was active in Zion Church, Philadelphia, and at the age of seventeen decided to enter the ministry. He preached his first sermon, while still a layman, on Trinity Sunday, 1813. He studied theology under two pastors in Philadelphia and returned to Germany in 1814 to continue his education at the University of Göttingen. Upon his return to America in 1817, he became a licensed home missionary, preaching the gospel in Pennsylvania and the neighboring states as far west as Missouri. In 1819 he married, and in 1820 he was ordained by the Ministerium of Pennsylvania.

For a period of more than twenty years, Pastor Heyer traveled extensively not only as a preacher but also as a worker in Christian education, being particularly active in the establishing of Sunday schools in Lutheran parishes and in the work of Gettysburg College and Seminary. In 1839 his wife, Mary Webb Gash, who had borne six children, died.

Aged forty-eight, with two dozen years of pastoral experience in six congregations, Heyer began a new phase of his life. He acquired the fundamentals of Sanskrit and a rudimentary knowledge of medicine and was commissioned a foreign missionary on October 5, 1841, at Saint Paulus' Church, Philadelphia. Leaving his children (the youngest was thirteen), he sailed from Boston for India, visited the mission fields of Lutherans in Tinnevelly, Tranquebar, and Madras, and on July 31, 1842, began the mission work in Guntur, near Madras in southeast India, in the Telegu-speaking region of Andhra, which was to be his life's work. Despite slow initial progress, during the next fifteen years, he established the mission stations at Guntur, Gurzal, and Rajamundry, which became the basis of the large Lutheran Church in that area today. On a furlough from 1846 to1848, he established a church in Baltimore and received his M.D. degree from the University of Maryland (later Johns Hopkins University).

In 1857 he returned to America, visiting countries of the Middle East and Germany. Other missionaries had come to carry on the work, and his health for the second time was nearly ruined from his strenuous life in the extreme climate of Andhra. Once back in the United States, however, his health revived and the indefatigable planter of churches spent twelve years of active evangelism and re-organization of parishes and schools in Minnesota and the neighboring states, culminating in the formation of the Synod of Minnesota in 1860 and his service as its president for eight years.

In August 1869 Father Heyer, as he was now affectionately called by Indians and Americans (the title was common in those days for older Lutheran pastors), dramatically volunteered to return to Andhra where the mission work was in a period of crisis. He stayed there two years, and by his selfless devotion and ascetic life, he infused new spirit in the mission.

Father Heyer returned to Philadelphia and served as chaplain and house-father at the new Lutheran Seminary. He died during the night of November 7–8, 1873 in his eighty-first year and was buried in Friedensburg, Somerset County, Pennsylvania, beside his wife. He is remembered as a pastor, teacher, missionary, and leader in the church.

FOR FURTHER READING

Bachmann, E. Theodore. *They Called Him Father: The Life Story of John Christian Frederick Heyer.* Philadelphia: Muhlenberg, 1942.
Lambert, W. A. *The Life of Rev. J. C. F. Heyer, M.D.* Philadelphia, 1903.

READING

From *They Called Him Father: The Life Story of John Christian Frederick Heyer*

Heyer and Schmidt made their unexpected appearance in Reading [Pennsylvania] on Trinity Sunday, May 23, 1869. At Trinity Church, where the Ministerium had just opened its annual meeting, they caused a stir. Two days later things reached a dramatic climax with an evening celebration of the anniversary of the Ministerium's Missionary Society. Heyer was the last of four speakers. He referred to the vastness of the work in India, to the difficulties lying in the way of real accomplishment, of his own experience in India; to the insignificance of the church's small missioning force among 140,000,000 people. He pleaded for more missionaries; for men who would be capable and well trained. They were needed—and needed now!

With white locks curled at the ends and reaching almost to his shoulders, and with agile movements and rapid speech, he captivated everyone's interest. Among those present was Dr. Henry E. Jacobs, who has perpetuated the story of Heyer's vigorous appeal. Standing on the low platform of the old colonial chancel, the missionary held forth before a hushed audience. "I appeal to you," he exclaimed, "the Ministerium of Pennsylvania, to intervene and prevent the transfer of the Rajahmundry station to the Church Missionary Society of the Anglicans. You, as the Ministerium under whose auspices I was sent out to India in 1842, should again assume the responsibility of supporting some foreign missionaries. It is *not* too late. If this venerable body consents, I shall plead with the General Synod's Board to rescind its decision to abandon Rajahmundry; and I shall communicate with the Church Missionary Society in England to reconsider the grounds on which it would be accepting this station. More than that, Brethren. Although I am nearly seventy-seven now, I am willing to go to India myself and reorganize that work!"

A murmur of surprise ran through the spell-bound convention. Heyer went on, "Twelve thousand miles lie between us and our objective. But let not distance alarm us. If there is someone else who would be more capable of restoring order in our Rajahmundry station, may he be sent forth by this Ministerium. But if not, then, Brethren, I repeat, *I* am ready to go."

Someone jumped to his feet and asked, "Will Father Heyer tell us how soon that will be?"

Stooping to the floor, Heyer picked up his ever-present valise. Holding it so all could see, he replied, "I am ready *now*!" . . .

The last Sunday before his departure he visited in Allentown where his friend Brobst, who was keenly interested in missions, engaged him to preach in three different churches. Brobst did so only after asking Heyer, "How often can you preach on a single Sunday?" Heyer promptly retorted, "Five times, if I must. I don't get tired."

On August 31 he sailed from New York, bound for India at the age of seventy-seven!

E. Theodore Bachmann, *They Called Him Father: The Life Story of John Christian Frederick Heyer* (Philadelphia: Muhlenberg, 1942), 303–04, 306.

PROPERS

Almighty and everlasting God, you blessed your servant John Christian Frederick Heyer with a passion for the Gospel, inexhaustible energy, and a keen awareness of the need of the world for your saving word: Ever give to your church such clear-minded and dauntless servants who rejoice to spend themselves in your service, that your people may be fed with living food and know the inexhaustible riches of our Savior Jesus Christ; who lives and reigns with you and the Holy Spirit, one God, now and forever.

PHP

Readings: Isaiah 62:1-7
                Psalm 48
                Romans 10:11-17
                Luke 24:44-53
Hymn of the Day:
                "O God, send heralds who will never falter" (LBW 283)
Prayers: For the church in India
                For colleges and seminaries
                For the schools of the church
                For the younger churches
                For evangelists and those who establish new congregations
                For zeal in the Lord's service
Preface: All Saints
Color: White

ALSO ON NOVEMBER 8

The *Lutheran Service Book* has introduced on this date the commemoration of **Johannes von Staupitz** (*ca.* 1468–1524), Luther's Father Confessor. Staupitz was vicar of the Augustinian order at the University of Wittenberg and Luther's superior. He showed sympathetic understanding and enormous patience with Luther in his spiritual struggle to find a gracious God. Staupitz died December 28, 1524.

November 9

The *Lutheran Service Book* has introduced on this date the commemoration of the birth of **Martin Chemnitz** (1522–1586), a Lutheran theologian and pastor in Brunswick from 1554 until his death. He was a principal influence in the consolidation of Lutheran theology and practice in the generation following Luther's death, making wide use of patristic evidence. When he had his portrait painted, he chose to be shown holding a rosary. Chemnitz died in Braunschweig April 8, 1586.

November 10

Leo the Great, Bishop of Rome, 461

Leo was pope at a turbulent moment in the Church's history. The Catholic faith was attacked by all kinds of heresies, many of them centered around the nature of the person of Christ. How was Jesus Christ God and man? Leo had the wisdom and knowledge to understand the importance of a right faith in Christ. He earned his title "the Great" by his energy with which he extended and consolidated the influence of the diocese of Rome, imposing his jurisdiction on Africa, Spain, and Gaul, and by his famous *Tome* or letter he sent to Flavian, Patriarch of Constantinople June 13, 449, stating the two-nature Christology with all the clarity for which Latin is renowned. His definition was confirmed at the Council of Chalcedon in 451.

Leo was personally responsible for the safety of Rome in the face of two attacks by the barbarians. By his intervention in 452, Attila the Hun turned away from ravaging Italy, and three years later, in 455, Leo managed to persuade the Vandals to restrain their forces from destroying Rome. Leo also reformed the regulations for entry into the priesthood, and added to the Canon of the Mass words which emphasized the Christian doctrine that matter is not evil but made by God. In this he struck at those heretics who saw all matter as evil.

Clear and forceful, although not profound in doctrine, Leo reveals a remarkable grasp of liturgical principles. The sacramentary that bears his name, the Leonine Sacramentary, the earliest surviving book of Mass prayers according to the Roman rite, exists in an early seventh-century manuscript drawing on Roman material of the fifth or sixth centuries. Its attribution to Leo is arbitrary, but some of the prayers may well be his own compositions in his characteristically clear and forceful language.

For twenty-two years, Leo proved a wide and fearless leader of the Church and a man of great personal sanctity and theological ability. Leo the Great was the first pope to be buried at St. Peter's.

His feast day in the East is February 18. He is on the *Evangelical Calendar of Names* (1962) and was added to the Episcopal calendar in the 1979 *Book of Common Prayer* and to the Methodist calendar in *For All the Saints*.

FOR FURTHER READING

Jalland, T. G. *Life and Times of St. Leo the Great*. 1941.

READING

From the sermons of Leo the Great

Although the universal Church of God is constituted of distinct orders of members, still, in spite of the many parts of its holy body, the Church subsists as an integral whole, just as the Apostle says, "All of you are one in Christ Jesus." [Gal. 3:28] Nor is anyone separated from the office of another in such a way that a lower group has no connection with the head. In the unity of faith and baptism, our community is therefore undivided. There is a common dignity as the apostle Peter says in these words, "Like living stones, let yourselves be built into a spiritual house, to be a holy priesthood, to offer spiritual sacrifices acceptable to God through Jesus Christ." [1 Peter 2:5] And again, " You are a chosen race, a royal priesthood, a holy nation, God's own people." [1 Peter 2:9]

For all who are born anew in Christ are made kings by the sign of the cross; they are consecrated priests by the oil of the Holy Spirit, so that beyond the special service of our ministry as priests, all spiritual and mature Christians know that they are a royal race and are sharers in the office of the priesthood. For what is more king-like than to find yourself ruler over your body after having surrendered your soul to God? And what is more priestly than to promise the Lord a pure conscience and to offer him in love unblemished victims on the altar of one's heart?

From Sermon 4. Trans. PHP.

PROPERS

O Lord our God, you strengthened your servant Leo of Rome through turbulent times: Let your perpetual mercy ever accompany your Church; that while it is placed among the storms of this world, it may both be refreshed with present gladness, and behold the brightness of eternal bliss; through Jesus Christ our Lord, who lives and reigns with you and the Holy Spirit, one God, now and forever.

Leonine sacramentary, trans. William Bright, *Ancient Collects;* PHP

Readings: Psalm 77:11-15 *or* 23
               2 Timothy 1:6-14
               Matthew 5:13-19
Hymn of the Day:
               "A mighty fortress is our God" (H82 688; LBW 228, 229, LSB 656, 657, ELW 503-
               505)
Prayers: For all Christian leaders, particularly those under pressure
               For all who, in difficult times, are upholding Christian standards
               For all theologians and teachers of theology
               For a deeper knowledge of Jesus Christ the Son of God
Preface: Epiphany (BCP)
Color: White

November 11

Martin, Bishop of Tours, 397

Martin was born about the year 316 in the town of Sabaria in the Roman province of Pannonia, present-day Hungary, of a pagan family. His father was a Roman legionary. He spent his boyhood in Pavia in Lombardy where he came under Christian influence, and at the age of ten he decided on his own to become a catechumen. When he was fifteen, being the son of a soldier, he was drafted to serve in the army. He was apparently a good soldier and popular with his comrades.

One winter night when he was stationed in Amiens, Martin, according to a popular legend, saw a poor old beggar at the city gate shivering in the cold, and, having nothing else to give him, he drew his sword, cut his own cavalryman's cloak in two, and gave half to the man to wrap himself in. The next night Martin dreamed of Christ in heaven wearing his half-cloak and saying, "Martin, still a catechumen, has covered me with his cloak."

The young soldier, however, found it increasingly difficult to combine his own ideal of a Christian life with the duties of military service. Eventually, he decided to be baptized and asked to leave the army, since he was no longer willing to kill. Like many of his modern counterparts, this fourth-century "conscientious objector" had difficulty proving that he was not a coward, but finally he was released, now about twenty years old.

After meeting with Bishop Hilary of Poitiers, the great scholar, hymnwriter, and defender of Orthodoxy against Arianism (see January 13), Martin decided to join him. First, however, he returned to Pannonia to convert his family and friends. On his way back to Hilary, he learned that the bishop had been sent into exile by the Arians, and instead of going on to Gaul, he stayed a while in Milan and then went to an island where he lived a hermit's life until Hilary was restored to his see.

Martin spent the next ten years in a hut outside the city of Poitiers. Here he was joined by others until the settlement became in effect a monastery and a center of charitable work and missionary activity. It may be considered the first French monastery. People from the surrounding countryside came to St. Martin for help, and in 371, when the see of Tours became vacant, they got him to the city by a ruse and then insisted that he become their bishop. He finally agreed, but he led a most unusual bishop's life.

Bishop Martin lived in a cave in the cliffs of Marmoutier, two miles from the city. His office space for the work of the diocese was a hut nearby. The new bishop's way of life was quite different from that of his fellow bishops in other cities, but he succeeded in establishing Christianity in rural areas of Gaul; previously it had been limited mostly to the cities. He traveled all over his vast diocese carrying the gospel to peasants and tribespeople, fighting paganism, and setting up centers of Christian life and faith. He was courageous in his dealings with the pagans, and he did not hesitate to speak forcefully to emperors on behalf of the people, but basically he was a gentle and peace-loving man. During the Priscillianist controversies in Spain and Gaul (Priscillian, charged with practicing magic, was executed by Emperor Maxmillian in 386, the first instance of capital punishment for heresy in the history of the Church), Martin strongly opposed the sentence and raised important questions concerning the relations between Church and state.

NOVEMBER

Martin died November 8, 397, in a distant outpost of his diocese, and the date of his commemoration recalls the day of his burial at Tours. He was added to the calendar in the 1979 *Book of Common Prayer,* the *Lutheran Book of Worship,* and the Methodist *For All the Saints.*

Martin was one of the founders of the Celtic Church, which spread the gospel to the British Isles and a great part of what is now France, Germany, and the Low Countries. He is regarded as the patron saint of France, and there are many churches named for him in Britain. During the Middle Ages, he was one of the most popular saints on the calendar, and his tomb at Tours was for several centuries an important center of pilgrimage. After the Reformation, many Lutherans continued to observe St. Martin's Day, in part because Luther was born on November 10 and was baptized the next day and given the name of the saint on whose feast day he was baptized. In the United States there are about fifty Lutheran churches named for St. Martin. He was one of the greatest figures in the Western church, and his life, summed up in his motto *Non recuso laborem*—"I do not turn back from work"—has been an important inspiration to missionaries and Christian workers since his day.

FOR FURTHER READING

Donaldson, Christopher. *Martin of Tours: Parish Priest, Mystic and Exorcist.* London: Routledge and Kegan Paul, 1980.

Foley, L. *St. Martin of Tours: The Greatest Saint of France.* New York: Morehouse, 1931.

Stancliffe, Clare. *St. Martin and His Hagiographer: History and Miracle in Sulpicius Severus.* New York: Oxford University Press, 1983.

READING

From a letter of Sulpicius Severus

Martin knew long in advance the time of his death and he told his brethren that it was near. Meanwhile, he found himself obliged to make a visitation of the parish of Candes, for the clergy there were quarreling, and he wished to reconcile them. Although he knew that his days were few, he did not refuse to undertake the journey for such a purpose, for he believed that he would bring his virtuous life to a good end if by his efforts peace was restored in the Church.

He spent some time in Candes, or rather in its church, where he stayed. Peace was restored, and he was planning to return to his monastery when suddenly his strength began to fail. He summoned his brethren and told them he was dying. All who heard this were overcome with grief. In their sorrow they cried to him with one voice: "Father, how can you abandon us? Who will care for us when you are gone? Savage wolves will attack your flock, and who will save us from their jaws when our shepherd has been struck down? We know you yearn to be with Christ, but your reward is certain and will not be any less for being delayed. You will do better to show pity for us, rather than forsake us."

Thereupon he broke into tears, for he was a man in whom the compassion of our Lord was continually revealed. Turning to our Lord, he made this reply to their pleas, "Lord, if your people still need me, I am ready to do the task. Your will be done."

Here was a man words cannot describe. Death could not defeat him nor toil dismay him. He was quite without a preference of his own; he neither feared to die nor refused to live. With eyes and hands raised to heaven he remained absorbed in prayer. When some priests who had gathered at his bedside suggested that he should give his poor body some relief by lying on his other side. He answered, "Allow me, brothers, to keep looking toward heaven rather than at the earth, so that my spirit may continue straight ahead on my journey to the Lord." As he spoke these words, he saw the devil standing near. "Why do you stand there, you blood-thirsty brute?" he cried. "Murderer, you will not have me for your prey. Abraham is welcoming me into his embrace."

With these words, he gave up his spirit to heaven. Filled with joy, he left this life poor and humble and entered heaven rich in God's favor.

Letter 3. From the English translation of the Office of Readings from the Liturgy of the Hours by the International Committee on English in the Liturgy, rev. PHP.

PROPERS

Lord God of hosts, you clothed your servant Martin the soldier with the spirit of sacrifice, and set him as a bishop in your Church to be a defender of the catholic faith: Give us grace to follow in his holy steps, that at the last we may be found clothed with righteousness in the dwellings of peace; through Jesus Christ our Lord, who lives and reigns with you and the Holy Spirit, one God, forever and ever.

LFF

NOVEMBER

Readings:	Isaiah 58:6-12
	Psalm 15 *or* 34:15-22
	Matthew 25:34-40
Hymn of the Day:	
	"Jesus, thy boundless love to me" (LBW 336, LSB 683)
Prayers:	For the spirit of generosity to the poor
	For the hungry and the homeless
	For those who courageously make their witness for peace
	For strength to support those under attack for their faith
	For all who serve in military forces
	For the church in France
Preface:	A Saint (2) (BCP)
Color:	White

November 12

Søren Aabye Kierkegaard, Theologian, 1855

Søren Aaabye Kierkegaard, the father of modern existentialism, was born in Copenhagen on May 5, 1813, the seventh and last child of an elderly couple. His father, Michael Pederson Kierkegaard, was a farm laborer who led a desperately unhappy life of grinding poverty. As a young man, full of rage at his lot and God's apparent indifference to it, Michael stood on a hill, shook his fists at the sky and cursed God. Not long afterward, by continued remarkably good fortune, he prospered in business and ended his life a rich man, though he carried a great burden of guilt. His wife and five of their children died within two years (the eldest and the youngest survived), and the desolate father became deeply melancholy.

As a theological student, Kierkegaard learned of his father's secret guilt, and this knowledge, "the great earthquake," convinced Søren that God's curse hung over the family. He became estranged from his father and for a time led a life of dissipation. Later he experienced a religious conversion and became reconciled with his father, who died in 1838 and left his sons a considerable fortune. Kierkegaard, a brilliant student, took his degree in theology but never sought ordination.

In 1849 be became engaged to seventeen-year-old Regine Olsen. After great emotional distress, convinced that he could not ask the girl to share his unhappiness, he broke the engagement. In the years immediately following this harrowing experience, he published, not under his own name, a number of significant books: *Either-Or* (1843), *Fear and Trembling* (1843), *The Concept of Dread* (1844), *Philosophical Fragments* (1844), *Concluding Unscientific Postscript* (1846). These writings often assume the character of works of the imagination, employing fictional characters and dramatic narratives. His productivity slackened as he became engaged in a bitter feud with a radical Danish satirical paper, *The Corsair*. His subjection to ridicule in cartoons in that publication led to a feeling of martyrdom and the publication in 1849 of *Sickness Unto Death*.

In 1854 the eulogy of the Primate of Denmark by his successor set off Kierkegaard's last and most violent battle, a conflict with the Danish Church in which he attacked the sterility of "official Christianity." In the midst of this conflict, lonely, with hardly a single follower, Kierkegaard collapsed on the street October 2, 1855, and died at Frederikshospital in Copenhagen on November 11, 1855 at the age of forty-two. His sickness was vaguely diagnosed as a disease of the spine marrow. He was buried November 18 from the Cathedral Church of Our Lady, the largest church in the city, with only two priests present: his brother Paul and the dean of the cathedral. He was buried in the family plot in an unmarked grave.

Kierkegaard's highly personal philosophy was opposed to the objective certainty of truth when led the church of his time to an unjustified security, deprived, Kierkegaard thought, of personal choice, risk, will. The state church, or as Grundtvig preferred to call it, the National Church, institutionalized and killed the essential spirit of Christianity, Kierkegaard charged, and obscured the necessarily "troubled truth." Kierkegaard's notion of truth was revolutionary. In his view, truth was not something to be observed by a detached thinker but rather something to be experienced by a participant in the risks of life and faith. A "poet of faith," he realized that truth could come in other ways than through the intellect, and his writings often exhibit remarkable literary qualities as they require readers to search their hearts and to know themselves. His principal writings are among the most singular inventions in the entire philosophical canon: playful, paradoxical, and teasingly pseudonymous.

He is commemorated on the calendar in the *Lutheran Book of Worship* and *Evangelical Lutheran Worship* and on the Methodist calendar in *For All the Saints*.

FOR FURTHER READING

Garff, Joakim. *Søren Kierkegaard: A Biography.* Trans. Bruce H. Kirmmse. Princeton: Princeton University Press, 2005.

Gouwens, David J. *Kierkegaard as Religious Thinker.* Cambridge: Cambridge University Press, 1996.

Hannay, Alastair. *Kierkegaard: A Biography.* Cambridge: Cambridge University Press, 2001.

Kirmmse, Bruce H. *Kierkegaard in Golden Age Denmark.* Bloomington: Indiana University Press, 1990.

———. *Encounters with Kierkegaard.* Princeton: Princeton University Press, 1996.

Law, David R. *Kierkegaard As a Negative Theologian.* Oxford: Clarendon, 1994.

Oden, Thomas C., ed. *The Humor of Kierkegaard.* Princeton: Princeton University Press, 2004.

NOVEMBER

READING

From *The Sickness unto Death* by Søren Kierkegaard

There is so much said now about people being offended at Christianity because it so dark and gloomy, offended at it because it is so severe, etc. It is now high time to explain that the real reason why man is offended at Christianity is because it is too high, because its goal is not man's goal, because it would make of a man something so extraordinary that he is unable to get it into his head. A perfectly simple psychological investigation of what offense is will explain this, and at the same time it will show how infinitely silly their behavior has been who defended Christianity by taking away the offense. . . , for if it is not present, if it is not an eternally essential constituent of Christianity, it is nonsense, humanly speaking, for Christ, instead of taking it away, to be distressed about it and to give warning against it.

If I were to imagine to myself a day-laborer and the mightiest emperor that ever lived, and were to imagine that this mighty Emperor took a notion to send for the poor man, who had never dreamed . . . that the Emperor knew of his existence, and who therefore would think himself indescribably fortunate if merely he was permitted once to see the Emperor, and would recount it to his children and children's children as the most important event of his life—but suppose the Emperor sent for him and informed him that he wished to have him for his son-in-law . . . what then? Then the laborer, humanly, would become somewhat or very much puzzled, shamefaced, and embarrassed, and it would seem to him, quite humanly (and this is the human element in it), something exceedingly strange, something quite mad, the last thing in the world about which he would say a word to anybody else, since he himself in his own mind was not far from explaining it by supposing (as his neighbors would be busily doing as soon as possible) that the Emperor wanted to make a fool of him, so that the poor man would be the laughing-stock of the whole town. . . .

And now for Christianity! Christianity teaches that this particular individual, and so every individual, whatever in other respects this individual may be, man, woman, serving-maid, minister of state, merchant, barber, student, etc.—this individual exists *before God*—this individual who perhaps would be vain for having once in his life talked with the King, this man who is not a little proud of living on intimate terms with that person or the other, this man exists before God, can talk with God any moment he will, sure to be heard by Him; in short, this man is invited to live on the most intimate terms with God! Furthermore, for this man's sake God came into the world, let himself be born, suffers and dies; and this suffering God almost begs and entreats this man to accept the help which is offered to him! Verily, if there is anything that would make a man lose his understanding, it is surely this! Whosoever has not the humble courage to dare to believe it, must be offended at it.

Søren Kierkegaard, *Fear and Trembling* and *The Sickness unto Death,* trans. Walter Lowrie (Princeton: Princeton University Press, 1941, 1954), 214–16.

PROPERS

Father in heaven, you awaken conscience in our breast and keep us vigilant that we may work out our salvation with fear and trembling: When the law in its seriousness fills us with dread and the thunder booms from Sinai, grant that we may also hear a gentle voice murmuring to us that we are your children; through your Son, Jesus Christ our Lord, who lives and reigns with you and the Holy Spirit, one God, now and forever.

Adapted by PHP from a prayer of Kierkegaard

Readings: Proverbs 3:1-7
Psalm 119:89-104
1 Corinthians 2:6-10, 13-16
John 17:18-23
Hymn of the Day:
"Through the night of doubt and sorrow" (LBW 355, ELW 327; see H82 527)
(by the Danish hymn writer Bernhardt Severin Ingemann)
Prayers: For grace to search our souls and to know ourselves
For courage to reject false security in the search for truth
For courage to risk all for the sake of Christ
For all tormented souls
Preface: Baptism (BCP, LBW)
Color: White

ALSO ON NOVEMBER 12

The calendar in the *Book of Common Prayer* remembers on this date **Charles Simeon** (1759–1836), priest and influential leader of the Evangelical Revival in the Church of England and active in the Missionary Movement.

November 14

The *Book of Common Prayer* in its calendar commemorates today the consecration of **Samuel Seabury** (1729–1796), the first American Episcopal Bishop, in 1784 in Aberdeen, Scotland, by the Bishop and the Bishop Coadjutor of Aberdeen and the Bishop of Ross and Caithness.

The Byzantine calendar on this date commemorates the **Emperor Justinian** and his wife **Theodora**. The calendar in the *Lutheran Service Book* (2006) lists the Emperor Justinian on this date as Christian Ruler and Confessor of Christ. Justinian I (*ca.* 483–565), Roman Emperor from 527, was the most energetic of the early Byzantine emperors. He made it his aim to restore the political and religious unity of the empire in East and West. A great builder, he erected many basilicas in Constantinople (Hagia Sophia among them), Ravenna, and elsewhere. He established a new legal code and championed orthodoxy.

FOR FURTHER READING

Rosen, William. *Justinian's Flea: Plague, Empire, and the Birth of Europe.* London: Cape, 2007.

November 16

Margaret, Queen of Scotland, 1093

Margaret was born of a German mother *ca.* 1045, in Hungary, where her father was exiled. She was the granddaughter of the English king, Edmund Ironside, and in 1057 she was brought to England and brought up at the court of Edward the Confessor. In 1067, after the Battle of Hastings, the family fled from England to seek safety overseas. They were shipwrecked off the coast of Scotland where King Malcolm III welcomed them and soon after fell in love with Margaret and married her. Although it had been Margaret's intention to become a nun, her marriage was a happy one, and eight children were born to it.

The Church in Scotland still clung to the old Celtic ways, but Margaret worked tirelessly to reform it and to introduce a greater conformity to the larger life of the Western church. With her husband she founded several churches, notably that of the Holy Trinity at Dumfermline. Queen Margaret had an enormous influence for good over her husband, and her piety and concern for the sick and the poor were famous throughout the Christian world.

She died in Edinburgh Castle on November 16, 1093, after learning of the death in battle of both her husband and her eldest son, and was buried in Dumfermline Abbey. She is commemorated on the General Roman Calendar, on the calendar in the *Book of Common Prayer,* and on the calendar in the Methodist book *For All the Saints.*

FOR FURTHER READING

Menzies, Lucy. *St. Margaret, Queen of Scotland.* London: J. M. Dent, 1925.

READING

From "The Life of St. Margaret, Queen of Scotland" by Turgot, Bishop of St. Andrews

We need not wonder that Queen Margaret governed herself and her household wisely when we know that she herself acted always under the wisest of governors, the guidance of the Holy Scriptures. . . .

I speak first about her prayerfulness. In church no one was so silent and composed as she, no one so wrapt in prayer. While she was in the house of God she would never speak of worldly matters or do anything which showed traces of earth; she was there simply to pray, and in praying, to pour forth her tears. Then only her body was here below; her spirit was near God, for in the purity of her prayer she sought nothing but God and the things which are God's. As for her fasting, I will say only this, that the strictness of her abstinence brought upon her a very severe infirmity. To these two excellent gifts of prayer and abstinence she added the gift of mercy. Who could be more gentle than she toward those in need? Not only would she have given to the poor all that she possessed, but, if she could have done so, she would have given her very self away. She was poorer than any of her paupers; for they, even when they had nothing, wished to have something; while her whole care was to strip herself of what she had. She was near to God, for in the purity of her prayer she sought nothing but God.

Trans. PHP, based on Brother Kenneth, CGA, *Everyman's Book of Saints following the ASB* (London and Oxford: Mowbray, 1981), 780–81.

PROPERS

O God, you gave your servant Margaret of Scotland a special love for the poor: Give to us, we pray, that same love, that we may be living signs of your goodness and at the last attain the glorious crown of your saints; through your Son Jesus Christ our Lord, who lives and reigns with you and the Holy Spirit, one God, now and forever.

1952 Roman Missal, rev. PHP

Readings:	Proverbs 31:10-11, 20, 26, 28
	Psalm 146:4-9 *or* 112:1-9
	Matthew 13:44-52
Hymn of the Day:	
	"Come, labor on" (H82 541)
Prayers:	For Scotland, its church and people
	For the ministry of women in the church
	For families with many children
	For all parents that they may teach their children to grow in the faith
Preface:	Baptism (BCP, LBW)
Color:	White

NOVEMBER

November 17

Elizabeth of Thuringia, Princess of Hungary, 1231

Elizabeth, the daughter of King Andrew of Hungary, was born in the summer of 1207 at Saros Patak, Hungary. In order to seal a political alliance, she was betrothed at the age of one to Ludwig, the young son of the Landgrave of Thuringia, and when she was four she was taken to the castle of the Wartburg near Eisenach to be raised with her future husband. Elizabeth was a serious child, generous to those who had less than she had, and a devout Christian. Some of the people at the Thuringian court disapproved of her as the future duchess, but Ludwig was very fond of her.

In 1216 Ludwig succeeded his father as Landgrave, and in 1221 when he was twenty-one and Elizabeth was fourteen, the marriage took place. In the course of the next few years they had three children, a boy and two girls, and the marriage was a happy one. Elizabeth in her new position was even more generous to the poor. On one occasion in 1225, when there was a severe local famine, she gave away most of her own fortune and supply of grain to the poor of the area. She was criticized for doing this, but her husband upon his return gave his approval to her action.

Elizabeth founded two hospitals during this period, one at the foot of the steep rock on which the Wartburg was located. She regularly tended the patients in these hospitals herself and gave money for the care of children, especially orphans. In helping the poor, she and her husband also tried to find suitable jobs for those who had no way of earning a living. In 1221, when the Franciscans entered Thuringia, Elizabeth put herself under the spiritual direction of Brother Rodeger, who guided her in the spirit of Francis of Assisi. Her kindness extended to all kinds of unfortunate people, and there is a well-known story of her lodging a leper in the house. The Landgrave was startled and repelled to find him in their bed, but he almost immediately realized that in helping the leper, his wife was serving the crucified Lord.

On September 11, 1227, Ludwig died of the plague while on a journey to join a crusade. During that winter, Elizabeth left the castle—some accounts say that her brother-in-law expelled her—and she went to live in Eisenach. She was rejected by the townspeople and suffered great hardship until she received the protection of her uncle the Bishop of Bamberg. On Good Friday 1228, she formally renounced her worldly cares, adopted coarse garments for clothing, and devoted herself as a follower of St. Francis. After the care of her children was assured, she built a small house near Marburg and with it a hospice for the sick, the aged, and the poor, and devoted her life to their care.

In her last years St. Elizabeth lived a life of unnatural austerity and isolation from her friends, partly out of obedience to her confessor, Conrad of Marburg, who seems to have been almost sadistic in his treatment of her. Her health broke, and on November 17, 1231, she died, at the age of twenty-four. Four years later the Church began annual commemoration of her. Her feast day was November 19, since November 17 already had several saints assigned to it, and November 18 was the commemoration of the dedication of the basilicas of St. Peter and St. Paul. The present Roman calendar has moved her commemoration to the day of her death, November 17, as does the Lutheran calendar. The calendar in the *Book of Common Prayer*, however, because November 17 is the commemoration of Hugh of Lincoln and November 18 the commemoration of Hilda of Whitby, retains the older date, November 19.

She is known as both St. Elizabeth of Thuringia and St. Elizabeth of Hungary. Since her time countless hospitals have been named for her in Europe, America, and other parts of the world.

The Wartburg, in which Elizabeth lived for most of her brief life, is the same castle in which, some three hundred years later, Luther completed his translation of the New Testament into German. The town of Eisenach where Elizabeth took her vows was Luther's childhood home and the birthplace of Johann Sebastian Bach. Marburg, where St. Elizabeth is buried in the beautiful Gothic church that bears her name, is also the site of the first Protestant University, founded by Philip of Hesse, her descendant.

Elizabeth is included on the calendar in the 1979 Prayer Book and in the *Lutheran Book of Worship, Evangelical Lutheran Worship,* and, on November 19, the *Lutheran Service Book.*

FOR FURTHER READING

Canton, William. *The Story of Saint Elizabeth of Hungary.* London: Herbert and Daniel, 1912.

Ancelet-Hustache, J. *St. Elizabeth de Hongrie.* Paris, 1947. English trans. P. J. Oligny and V. O'Donnell. *Gold Tried by Fire.* Chicago: Franciscan Herald Press, 1963.

Seeholtz, Anne G. *Saint Elizabeth, Her Brother's Keeper.* New York: Philosophical Library, 1948.

READING

From *Light of Christ* by Evelyn Underhill

But there is the essence of the spiritual life. Profound submission to the mysterious Will of God declared in circumstance. And being what we are and the world what it is, that means for most of us Gethsemane and the Cross and the darkness of the Cross. Lots of the saints have been through that. We don't begin to understand the Passion till we see what it was in their lives. For union with Christ means accepting the dread fact of human nature, that only those willing to accept suffering up to the limit are capable of giving love up to the limit; and that this is the kind of love which is the raw material of the redeeming life. Only those who place themselves in the hands of God without reserve and without fear are going to be used by Him to save. We want a lot of practice before we can manage this. It will not come out of an easy-going religion.

To look at the Crucifix—"the supreme symbol of our august religion"—and then to look at our own hearts; to test the Cross by the quality of our love—if we do that honestly and unflinchingly we don't need any other self-examination than

NOVEMBER

that, any other judgment or purgation. The lash, the crown of thorns, the mockery, the stripping, the nails—life has equivalents of all these for us and God asks a love for Himself and His children which can accept and survive all that in the particular way in which it is offered to us. It is no use to talk in a large vague way about the love of God; *here* is its point of insertion into the world of men.

Evelyn Underhill, *The Light of Christ* (London: Longmans, 1945), 74–75, 91–92, 64, 27–28, 28–29, 82–83. Reprinted by permission of Wipf and Stock Publishers.

PROPERS

Almighty God, by your grace your servant Elizabeth of Hungary recognized and honored Jesus in the poor of this world: Grant that we, following her example, may with love and gladness serve those in any need or trouble, in the name and for the sake of Jesus Christ; who lives and reigns with you and the Holy Spirit, one God, forever and ever.

RS trans. LFF

Readings:	Tobit 12:6b-9 *or* Isaiah 58:6-11
	Psalm 146:4-9 *or* 112:1-9
	Matthew 25:31-40 *or* Luke 12:32-34
Hymn of the Day:	
	"O God of mercy, God of light" (LBW 425, LSB 852, ELW 714)
Prayers:	For the poor
	For the sick and suffering
	For the unemployed
	For the spirit of self-sacrificing service
	For those who embrace austerity for the love of Christ
Preface:	A Saint (2) (BCP)
Color:	White

ALSO ON NOVEMBER 17

Hugh, Bishop of Lincoln, 1200

Hugh was born at Avalon in France, *ca.* 1135 to a noble Burgundian family. He was raised by monks and was eventually admitted to the Carthusian monastery of the Grande Chartreuse, founded in 1054 in the French Alps. There, in an austere order, Hugh was noted for his austerity. Through the nomination of King Henry II of England, he became prior of a Carthusian monastery at Whitham in Somerset, and later, in 1186, again at the king's insistence, became Bishop of Lincoln, the largest diocese in England.

He was the friend of kings and courtiers, yet he never failed to rebuke them when necessary. He was also the champion of the poor, the oppressed, and outcasts, diligently performed his duties in his large diocese, loved his people, took infinite pains in filling vacant benefices, and was frequent in his saying of Mass. In Lincoln and again in Northampton, he stood up alone to rioting mobs incensed against the Jews. He was a model of piety, courage, and holiness.

Hugh died in London in 1200 and is buried in Lincoln Cathedral, of which he laid the foundation. His funeral was attended by kings, archbishops, bishops, and abbots.

He was included on the calendar in the 1979 *Book of Common Prayer*; he is not on the General Roman Calendar.

READING

From "Carthusians" by Ernest Dowson (1867–1900)

It was not theirs with Dominic to preach God's holy wrath,
They were too stern to bear sweet Francis' gentle sway;
Theirs was a higher calling and a steeper path,
To dwell alone with Christ, to meditate and pray.

A cloistered company, they are companionless,
None knoweth here the secret of his brother's heart:
They are but come together for more loneliness,
Whose bond is solitude and silence all their part.

O beatific life! Who is there shall gainsay,
Your great refusal's victory, your little loss,
Deserting vanity for the more perfect way,
The sweeter service of the most dolorous Cross.

Ye shall prevail at last! Surely ye shall prevail!
Your silence and austerity shall win at last:
Desire and mirth, the world's ephemeral lights shall fail,
The sweet star of your queen is never overcast.

We fling up flowers and laugh, we laugh across the wine;
With wine we dull our souls and careful strains of art;
Our cups are polished skulls round which the roses twine:
None dares look at Death who leers and lurks apart.

Move on, white company, whom that has not sufficed!
Our viols cease, our wine is death, our roses fail:
Pray for our heedlessness, O dwellers with the Christ!
Though the world fall apart, surely ye shall prevail.

Ernest Dowson, "Carthusians," ll. 13–36, in *Poetry of the Victorian Period*, ed. George Benjamin Woods and Jerome Hamilton Buckley, rev. ed. (New York: Scott, Foresman, 1955), 834.

NOVEMBER

PROPERS

O holy God, you endowed your servant and bishop Hugh of Lincoln with wise and cheerful boldness, and taught him to commend the discipline of holy life to kings and princes: Grant that we also, rejoicing in the Good News of your mercy, and fearing nothing but the loss of you, may be bold to speak the truth in love, in the Name of Jesus Christ our Redeemer; who lives and reigns with you and the Holy Spirit, one God, forever and ever.

Eric Milner-White, *An Anglican Calendar* rev. LFF

Readings:	Psalm 112:1-9 *or* 15
	Titus 2:7-8, 11-14
	Matthew 24:42-47
Hymn of the Day:	
	"Now the silence, now the peace" (H82 333, LBW 205, LSB 910, ELW 460)
Prayers:	For the diocese of Lincoln, its bishop, cathedral, clergy, and people
	For the right relation between church and state
	For courage to protect the persecuted
	For all Carthusian monks and nuns
Preface:	A Saint (2) (BCP)
Color:	White

November 18

Hilda, Abbess of Whitby, 680

Hilda (Hild), a Northumbrian princess, the grandniece of King Edwin, was born in 614, and after being instructed by Paulinus, one of the companions of Augustine of Canterbury, she was baptized at York when she was thirteen. She lived at the King's court for twenty years, chaste and respected, and then entered the monastic life. Her life, Bede observes, was thus to fall into two equal parts: thirty-three in secular life and thirty-three in the monastic life. In 649 Aidan made her abbess of a convent at Hartlepool. Some years later at Whitby, she founded a "double house," a monastery for both men and women, of which she was the abbess. This monastery soon became famous as a school known for its learning and for its religious life. Among the members of this house was Caedmon, the first English poet (see November 25). It was here that the Synod of Whitby was held in 664, convened to settle questions dividing the followers of the Celtic traditions and the followers of the Roman practices. The Synod resulted in the union of Roman and Celtic missions in England. Hilda favored the Celtic usages, but she obediently followed the contrary decisions of the Synod.

She was devout in her rule of the monastery, and her reputation for wisdom was such that many people, including kings, princes, and officers of state, visited Whitby and sought her advice. The Venerable Bede has high praise for Abbess Hilda. She insisted on the study of Holy Scripture and on proper preparation for the priesthood. The influence of her example of peace and charity extended beyond the walls of the monastery, and "all who knew her called her Mother, such were her wonderful godliness and grace."

She had a lingering disease during the last six years of her life and died on November 17, 680. Her feast day has been November 17, but the calendar in the *Book of Common Prayer* has moved it to November 18. She is commemorated on that date also on the Methodist calendar in *For All the Saints*. Hilda is not on the General Roman Calendar.

READING

From *History of the English Church and People* by the Venerable Bede

Christ's servant, Abbess Hilda, whom all her acquaintances called Mother because of her wonderful devotion and grace, was not only an example of holy life to members of her own community; for she also brought about the amendment and salvation of many living at a distance, who heard the inspiring story of her industry and goodness.

When Hilda had ruled the monastery for many years, it pleased the Author of our salvation to try her holy soul by a long sickness, in order that, as with the Apostle, her strength might be "made perfect in weakness." She was attacked by a burning fever that racked her continually for six years; but during all this time she never ceased to give thanks to her Maker or to instruct the flock committed to her, both privately and publicly. For her own example taught them all to serve God obediently when in health, and to render thanks to him faithfully when in trouble or bodily weakness. In the seventh year of her illness the pain passed into her innermost parts, and her last day came. About cockcrow she received the Viaticum of the Holy Communion, and when she had summoned all the handmaids of Christ in the monastery, she urged them to maintain the gospel peace among themselves and with others. And while she was still speaking, she joyfully welcomed death, or rather, in the words of our Lord, passed from death to life.

Bede, *History of the English Church and People,* trans. with an introduction by Leo Sherley-Price, Revised by R. E. Latham (Penguin Classics 1955, Revised edition 1968), 248–49. Copyright © Leo Sherley-Price, 1955, 1968. Reprinted by permission of Penguin Books Ltd.

PROPERS

O God of peace, by whose grace the abbess Hilda was endowed with gifts of justice, prudence, and strength to rule as a wise mother over the nuns and monks of her household, and to become a trusted and reconciling friend to leaders of the Church: Give us the grace to recognize and accept the varied gifts you bestow on men and women, that our common life may be enriched and your gracious will be done; through Jesus Christ our Lord, who lives and reigns with you and the Holy Spirit, one God, now and forever.

CMG, LFF

Readings:	Psalm 122 *or* 33:1-5, 20-21
	Ephesians 4:1-6
	Matthew 19:27-29
Hymn of the Day:	
	"Lo! What a cloud of witnesses" (H82 545)
Prayers:	For religious orders, both of men and women
	For all Christians in colleges and schools
	For true cooperation between women and men
	For all who encourage and support scholarship and learning
Preface:	A Saint (1) (BCP)
Color:	White

November 19

Mechtild of Magdeburg, 1282, Mechtild of Hackeborn, 1298, Gertrude the Great, 1302; Renewers of the Church

Three German mystics and spiritual writers are commemorated together. *Mechtild* (sometimes Anglicized as Matilda) *of Magdeburg,* who was born *ca.* 1207, was descended from a noble family in Saxony. She left her home about 1230 and became a Beguine, a member of a lay sisterhood that lived a semireligious communal life without vows and whose aims were primarily philanthropic, and led a life of prayer and penance. She undertook a rigorous regimen of austerity, and at the same time, like several of the other great women mystics of the time, spoke out against the religious laxity and materialism of the contemporary Church. During the years *ca.* 1250–1259, at the command of her confessor, she wrote down her visions under the title *The Flowing Light of the Godhead.* Later, in 1270, she entered the Cistercian foundation of Helfta near Eisleben in Thuringia (Luther's birthplace) and there added another chapter to her book. Her work, written in a forceful and poetic style, deeply influenced German medieval mysticism and is among the most forceful and poetic examples of women's writing to have survived from the Middle Ages. Among her visions was a revelation of the

Sacred Heart. She died in 1281. Her feast day is November 19. She is commemorated on February 26 by the *Evangelical Calendar of Names* (1962). Her commemoration (November 19) is listed on the 1997 calendar, *The Christian Year,* of the Church of England.

FOR FURTHER READING

Clark, Susan L., ed. *Mechtild von Magdeburg, Flowing Light of the Divinity.* Trans. Christiane Mesch Galvani, New York: Garland, 1990.

Mechtild of Magdeburg. *The Flowing Light of the Godhead.* Trans. Frank Tobin. New York: Paulist, 1998.

Mechtild of Hackeborn, with whom Mechtild of Magdeburg is sometimes confused, was born *ca.* 1241. She was mistress in charge of the school at the monastery of Helfta when her sister, Gertrude, Baroness Hackeborn (not to be confused with Gertrude the Great), was the princess abbess there. She thus was the teacher of the child who was to become Gertrude the Great, who wrote of her mistress, "There has never before been anyone like her in our monastery, and I fear there never will be again." Gertrude and another nun wrote an account of Mechtild's spiritual teaching and experiences, *The Book of Special Grace,* which was made public after her death. She was known for her poetic singing as a "nightingale of Christ"; her revelations were written down by her abbess as the *Book of Special Grace.* Mechtild of Hackeborn died at Helfta in 1298. Her traditional feast day is November 19.

Gertrude of Helfta, called the Great, was born at Eisleben in Thuringia in 1256 and at the age of five was entrusted to the Cistercian foundation at Helfta, where she received her education and spent the rest of her life. In her childhood she became fluent in Latin, as did all the sisters at Helfta, was educated in the liberal arts, and was widely read in literature and the sciences. At the age of twenty-five, she began to have mystical visions of Christ, which continued throughout her life, and from that time she lost interest in secular studies and gave all her attention to the Bible, the liturgy, and the writings of the Fathers, especially Augustine, Bernard of Clairvaux, Hugh and Richard of St. Victor (all favorites of Martin Luther two centuries later). Her *Legatus Divinae Pietatis,* of which only the second book was written by herself, is one of the finest literary products of Christian mysticism.

Most of her mystic experiences took place during the liturgical services of the Church, which were the spring of her spirituality. Gertrude was one of the first exponents of devotion to the Sacred Heart, which she believed was revealed to her in several visions, described in her book with great beauty and simplicity. She also wrote a collection of prayers.

Gertrude the Great died November 17, 1302; her feast day on the present Roman calendar is November 16.

NOVEMBER

FOR FURTHER READING

Winkworth, Margaret, trans. *Gertrude of Helfta: The Herald of Divine Love*. New York: Paulist, 1993.

READING

From *The Flowing Light of the Godhead* by Mechtild of Magdeburg

An unworthy creature thought simply about the nobility of God. Then God showed him in his senses and the eyes of his soul, a Fire which burned ceaselessly in the heights above all things. It had burned without beginning and would burn without end. This Fire is the everlasting God Who has retained in Himself Eternal Life from which all things proceed. The sparks which have blown away from the Fire are the holy angels. The beams of the Fire are the saints of God for their lives cast many lovely lights on Christianity. The coals of the Fire still glow; they are the just who here burn in heavenly love and enlighten by their good example: as they were chilled by sin they now warm themselves at the glowing coals. The crackling sparks which are reduced to ashes and come to nothing are the bodies of the blessed, who in the grave will await their heavenly reward. The Lord of the Fire is still to come, Jesus Christ to whom the Father entrusted the first Redemption and the last judgment. On the Last Day He shall make a glorious chalice for the heavenly Father out of the sparks of the Fire; from this chalice the Father will on the day of His Eternal Marriage drink all the holiness which, with His Beloved Son, He has poured into our souls and our human senses.

> Yea! I shall drink from thee
> And Thou shalt drink from me
> All the good God has preserved in us.
> Blessed is he who is so firmly established here
> That he may never spill out
> What God has poured into him.

The smoke of the Fire is made of all earthly things which man uses with wrongful delight. However beautiful to our eyes, however pleasing to our hearts, they yet carry in them much hidden bitterness. For they disappear as smoke and blind the eyes of the highest, till the tears run.

The comfort of the Fire is the joy our souls receive inwardly from God, with such holy warmth from the Divine Fire, that we too burn with it and are so sustained by virtues that we are not extinguished. The bitterness of the Fire is the word God shall speak on the Last Day, *Depart from Me ye cursed into everlasting fire!* [Matt. 25:41] The radiance of the Fire is the glowing aspect of the Divine countenance of the Holy Trinity, which shall so illumine our souls and bodies that we may then see and recognize the marvelous blessedness we cannot ever name here.

These things have come out of the Fire and flow into it again according to God's ordinance in everlasting praise.

> Wouldst thou know my meaning?
> Lie down in the Fire
> See and taste the Flowing
> Godhead through thy being;
> Feel the Holy Spirit
> Moving and compelling
> Thee within the Flowing
> Fire and Light of God.

From *The Revelations of Mechthild of Magdeburg, or The Flowing Light of the Godhead*, trans. Lucy Menzies (London: Longman, Green, 1953), 28–31.

PROPERS

Eternal God of fire and mercy, you filled the hearts of your servants Mechtild of Magdeburg, Mechtild of Hackeborn, and Gertrude the Great with visions of your love and splendor: Bring your light, we pray, into the darkness of our hearts that we may know the joy of your presence and the power of your grace; through your Son Jesus Christ our Lord, who lives and reigns with you and the Holy Spirit, one God, now and forever.

PHP, after RS

Readings:	Jeremiah 1:4-10
	Psalm 46
	1 Corinthians 3:11-23
	Mark 10:35-45
Hymn of the Day:	
	"My God, how wonderful thou art" (H82 643, LBW 524, ELW 863)
Prayers:	For grace to contemplate the mystery of God
	For the purification and the renewal of the church
	For courage to confront wrongdoing and sin
Preface:	A Saint (1) (BCP)
Color:	White

NOVEMBER

November 20

Edmund, King of East Anglia, Martyr, 870

The Episcopal *Lesser Feasts and Fasts 1997*, following other Anglican calendars, commemorates on this date Edmund, who at the age of fifteen became King of the East Angles. During his reign, Danish attacks on the East Coast of England became increasingly frequent. In 869 the twenty-eight-year-old King Edmund led his troops in battle against the raiders and was defeated in battle. The Danes offered peace on the two conditions that Edmund give them half his treasure and that he become a vassal prince. Edmund was willing to comply with the first, but he refused to become a vassal unless his overlord became a Christian. The Danish chieftain ordered him to be scourged and then tied to a tree as a living target for his archers, and finally had him beheaded on November 20, 870. Edmund was almost immediately venerated as a martyr and his body was enshrined at Bury St. Edmunds (St. Edmund's Borough) where a great Benedictine abbey was founded by the Danish King Knut (Canute) in 1020.

Before the promotion of St. George as protector of the Third Crusade and of the Order of the Garter (1348), St. Edmund was regarded as the patron of England.

READING

From *The Passion of St. Edmund* by Abbo of Fleury

Then the holy King Edmund was taken in his palace, as a member of Christ, his weapons thrown aside, and was pinioned and tightly bound with chains, and in his innocence was made to stand before the impious general, like Christ before the governor Pilate, and eager to follow in the footsteps of Him who was sacrificed as a victim for us. And so in chains he was mocked in many ways, and at length, after being savagely beaten, he was brought to a tree in the neighborhood, tied to it, and for a long while tortured with terrible lashes. But his constancy was unbroken, while without ceasing he called on Christ with broken voice. This roused the fury of his enemies, who, as if practising at a target, pierced his whole body with arrow-spikes, augmenting the severity of his torment by frequent discharge of their weapons, and inflicting wound upon wound, while one javelin made room for another. And thus, all haggled over by the sharp points of their darts, and scarce able to draw breath, he actually bristled with them, like a prickly hedgehog or a thistle fretted with spines, resembling in his agony the illustrious martyr Sebastian. But when it was made apparent to the villainous Inguar that not even by these means could the king be made to yield to the agents of his cruelty, but that he continued to call upon the name of Christ, the Dane commanded the executioner to cut off his head forthwith. . . .

Then, as he stood in all meekness, like a ram chosen out of the whole flock, and desirous of hastening buy a happy exchange this life for eternity, absorbed as he was in the mercies of God, he was refreshed by the vision of the light within, for the satisfaction of which he earnestly yearned in his hour of agony. Thus, while the words of prayer were still on his lips, the executioner, sword in hand, deprived the king of life, striking off his head with a single blow. And so, on the 20 November as an offering to God of the sweetest savour, Edmund, after he had been tried

in the fire of suffering, rose with the palm of victory and the crown of righteousness, to enter as king and martyr the assembly of the court of heaven.

Abbo of Fleury, *The Passion of St. Edmund,* chaps. 9 and 10, trans. Lord Francis Hervey, *Corolla Sancti Eadmundi, The Garland of St Edmund King and Martyr* (London: John Murray, 1907), 32–37.

PROPERS

O God of ineffable mercy, you gave grace and fortitude to blessed Edmund the king to triumph over the enemy of his people by nobly dying for your Name: Bestow on us your servants the shield of faith with which we can withstand the assaults of our ancient enemy; through Jesus Christ our Lord, who lives and reigns with you and the Holy Spirit, one God, now and forever.

LFF

Readings:	Psalm 21:1-7 *or* 126
	1 Peter 3:14-18
	Matthew 10:16-22
Hymn of the Day:	
	"Christ is the world's true light" (H82 542)
Prayers:	For all Christian rulers that they may be faithful to the church's teaching
	For all who suffer for the Christian faith
	For the church in England
Preface:	Baptism (BCP, LBW)
Color:	Red

November 22

Clive Staples Lewis, Apologist and Spiritual Writer, 1963

C. S. Lewis was born in Belfast, Northern Ireland, November 29, 1898, his father a prominent barrister and his mother a mathematician. He spent miserable years at a number of boarding schools until he entered University College,
Oxford in 1917. He was Tutor and Fellow of Magdalen College, Oxford, from 1925
to 1954, when he was appointed Professor of Medieval and Renaissance Literature
at Cambridge. His principal works of literary criticism are *The Allegory of Love*
(1936), *A Preface to Paradise Lost* (1942), and *English Literature in the Sixteenth
Century Excluding Drama*, volume three of the Oxford History of English Literature (1954).

Lewis was raised as an Anglican but rejected Christianity during his adolescent years. (His mother had died when he was ten.) His journey from atheism led him to theism in a conversion experience in 1929 and from there to faith in Jesus Christ, sealed on September 22, 1931, when, with his brother Warren, he received Holy Communion for the first time since boyhood. He described his gradual conversion in a book, *Surprised by Joy,* written in 1948 but not published until 1955. His conversion led to an outpouring of Christian apologetics in popular theology, among which are *The Problem of Pain* (1940), *The Screwtape Letters* (1942), *Mere Christianity* (1943), *Miracles* (1947), *Reflections on the* Psalms (1958), *Letters to Malcolm: Chiefly on Prayer* (1964); the seven-part *Chronicles of Narnia* for children; science-fiction novels; and correspondence on spiritual matters with friends and strangers alike. His deep scholarship, clarity, and rapier wit made him perhaps the most effective and persuasive Christian apologist of the twentieth century.

In 1956 he married Joy Davidman Gresham, a recent convert from Judaism to Christianity. Her death four years later led him to a transforming encounter with the Mystery of which he had written so eloquently before and which he explored in *A Grief Observed* (1961), a classic expression of sorrow and Christian hope. Lewis died at his home in Oxford on November 22, 1963. The inscription on his grave, a quotation from *King Lear,* reads, "Men must endure their going hence." He was added to the calendar in *Lesser Feasts and Fasts 2003.*

FOR FURTHER READING

Green, Roger Lancelyn, and Walter Hooper. *C. S. Lewis: A Biography.* London: Collins, 1974.

Hooper, Walter. *C. S. Lewis: A Companion and Guide.* New York: HarperCollins, 1997.

Sayer, George. *Jack: C. S. Lewis and His Times.* New York: Harper & Row, 1988.

Wilson, A. N. *C. S. Lewis: A Biography.* New York: Norton, 1990.

READING

From *Surprised by Joy* by C. S. Lewis

You must picture me alone in that room in Magdalen, night after night, feeling, whenever my mind lifted even for a second from my work, the steady, unrelenting approach of Him whom I so earnestly desired not to meet. That which I greatly feared had at last come upon me. In the Trinity Term of 1929 I gave in, and admitted that God was God, and knelt and prayed: perhaps, that night, the most dejected and reluctant convert in all England. I did not then see what is now the most shining and obvious thing; the Divine humility which will accept a convert even on such terms. The Prodigal Son at least walked home on his own feet. But who can duly adore that Love which will open the high gates to a prodigal who is brought in kicking, struggling, resentful, and darting his eyes in every direction for a chance of escape? The words *compelle intrare*, compel them to come in [Luke 14:23], have been so abused by wicked men that we shudder at them; but, properly understood, they plumb the depth of the Divine mercy. The hardness of God is kinder than the softness of men, and His compulsion is our liberation.

C. S. Lewis, *Surprised by Joy* (New York: Harcourt, Brace, 1955), 228–29.

PROPERS

O God of searing truth and surpassing beauty, we give you thanks for Clive Staples Lewis, whose sanctified imagination lights fires of faith in young and old alike. Surprise us also with your joy and draw us into that new and abundant life which is ours in Christ Jesus, who lives and reigns with you and the Holy Spirit, one God, now and forever.

LFF

Readings:	Psalm 139:1-9
	1 Peter 1:3-9
	John 16:7-15
Hymn of the Day:	
	"Come, thou fount of every blessing" (H82 686, LBW 499, LSB 686, ELW 807)
Prayers:	For colleges and universities
	For all who are searching for meaning and truth
	For those who make the faith of the church clear and compelling
	For converts to Christianity
Preface:	A Saint (3) (BCP)
Color:	White

November 23

Clement, Bishop of Rome, ca. 100

The biographical details of Clement's life are meager. He is perhaps the Clement referred to in Philippians 4:3. He was probably the fourth bishop of Rome, the third after Peter, who is said to have ordained him. In later centuries he became the subject of numerous legends. He was, it is said, banished to the Crimea during the reign of Trajan and forced to work in the mines. Nonetheless, his missionary efforts there met with success. On another occasion he was tied to an anchor, which has now become his emblem, and thrown into the Black Sea. His tomb, the legends continue, was built by angels and was shown once a year to the faithful of that region by a miraculous ebbing of the tide.

Despite the lack of any certain knowledge of Clement's life, he is of considerable importance as an apostolic father. His fame rests on a letter sent by the Church at Rome to the Church at Corinth about the year 96. The letter, with the exception of the New Testament writings, is the earliest Christian document extant, and was written to oppose the factious spirit that had divided the Corinthian Church when some dissatisfied younger members deposed the bishop-presbyters and deacons. First Clement, as the letter is known, is a pastoral letter of advice and warning, written anonymously but is the work, all agree, of Clement. It gives a valuable picture of early Roman Christianity. It was well received in Corinth and was in fact so honored there that it was read in the Corinthian Church along with the Scripture *ca.* 170. Several manuscripts of the New Testament include it among the books of the New Testament.

The document called Second Clement is not a letter but a sermon, and while its authorship is not certain, all agree that it is not by Clement of Rome,

Clement was included on the calendar in the 1979 *Book of Common Prayer*, the *Lutheran Book of Worship, Evangelical Lutheran Worship*, the *Lutheran Service Book*, and the Methodist book *For All the Saints.*

FOR FURTHER READING

Jaeger, Werner W. *Early Christianity and Greek Paideia*. Cambridge: Harvard University Press, 1961.

READING

From the First Letter of Clement

Let us fix our eyes on the Father and Creator of the universe and cling to his magnificent and excellent gifts of peace and kindness to us. Let us see him in our minds and look with the eyes of our souls on his patient purpose. Let us consider how free he is from anger toward his whole creation.

The heavens move at his direction and peacefully obey him. Day and night observe the course he has appointed them, without getting in each other's way. The sun and moon and the choirs of stars roll on harmoniously in their appointed courses at his command, and with never a deviation. By his will and without dissention or altering anything he has decreed the earth becomes fruitful at the proper seasons and brings forth abundant food for men and beasts and every living thing upon it. The unsearchable, abysmal depths and the indescribable regions of the underworld are subject to the same decrees. The basin of the boundless sea is by his arrangement conducted to hold the heaped up waters, so that the sea does not flow beyond the barriers surrounding it, but does just as he bids it. For he said, "Thus far shall you come, and your waves shall break within you." The ocean which men cannot pass, and the worlds beyond it, are governed by the same decrees of the Master. The seasons, spring, summer, autumn, and winter, peacefully give way to each other. The winds from their different points perform their service at the proper time and without hindrance. Perennial springs, created for enjoyment and health, never fail to offer their life-giving breasts to men. The tiniest creatures come together in harmony and peace. All these things the great Creator and Master of the universe ordained to exist in peace and harmony. Thus, he showered his benefits on them all, but most abundantly on us who have taken refuge in his compassion through our Lord Jesus Christ, to whom be glory and majesty forever and ever. Amen.

Early Christian Fathers, vol. I, Library of Christian Classics, trans. and ed. Cyril C. Richardson (Philadelphia: Westminster, 1953), 53–54.

PROPERS

O Lord, in every age you write names in your Book of Life and lead the meek of the earth to be followers of the Lamb of God: Raise up for us teachers like your servant Clement, the disciple of your first Apostles, who by their writings may instruct the Church without thought of self, and open to us the healing fountains of repentance, peace, and love; through Jesus Christ our Lord, who lives and reigns with you and the Holy Spirit, one God, forever and ever.

John Wordsworth in Dearmer, Frere, and Taylor, eds., *The English Liturgy,* 1903, rev. JWP.

Readings:	Psalm 78:3-7 *or* 85:8-13
	2 Timothy 2:1-7
	Luke 6:37-45
Hymn of the Day:	
	"Nature with open volume stands" (H82 434, LBW 119)
	"The day you gave us, Lord, has ended" (LBW 274, LSB 886, ELW 569) (sung to the tune *St. Clement*)
Prayers:	For the Roman Catholic Church and the Bishop of Rome
	For peace in the church
	For the stilling of passions
	For the impatient
	For respect for the natural world
Preface:	A Saint (2) (BCP)
Color:	White

NOVEMBER

November 24

Miguel Agustin Pro, Priest, Martyr, 1927

The Spanish-language Lutheran service book, *Libro de Liturgia y Cántico* (1998), introduced to the calendar the commemoration of Miguel Agustin Pro. He was born January 13, 1891, at Zacatecas, Mexico, the son of a mining engineer. He grew up in a devout home but was also known in childhood for his high spirits and cheerfulness. Born to privilege, he had an affinity for the working classes and for the poor. He became a Jesuit novice at the age of twenty, was exiled during the Mexican revolution, and was ordained in Belgium in 1925. He returned to Mexico in the following year. It was a difficult time. Churches were closed, priests were in hiding, and persecution of the Church was the national policy. Father Miguel used disguises to conduct an underground ministry, bringing pastoral care and the sacraments to the faithful.

In 1927 he was falsely accused of a bombing attempt, Pro was betrayed to the police, and, without trial, was sentenced to death. As he faced the firing squad, he forgave his executioners, refused to be blindfolded, shouted, "Long live Christ the King!" and died. The government prohibited a public funeral, but the faithful lined the streets as his body passed. He was beatified by Pope John Paul II in 1988.

Libro de Liturgia y Cántico and *Evangelical Lutheran Worship* assign his commemoration to the date of his death, November 23.

READING

From a prayer by Miguel Agustin Pro

I believe, O Lord, but strengthen my faith. . . . Heart of Jesus, I love thee, but increase my love. Heart of Jesus, I trust in you, but give greater vigor to my confidence. Heart of Jesus, I give my heart to you, but so enclose it in you that it may never be separated from you. Heart of Jesus, I am all yours, but take care of my promise so that I may be able to put it into practice, even to the complete sacrifice of my life.
http://www.catholic-forum.com/saints/saintm16.htm (accessed December 3, 2007)

PROPERS

God, the sovereign Lord of heaven and earth, you rule your realm with love and with justice: By the example of your servant Miguel Agustin Pro, so strengthen our witness to you that with confidence and without fear we may cry out against injustice, and with our whole life proclaim your love for those whom the world considers of little value; for the sake of Jesus Christ our Lord, who lives and reigns with you and the Holy Spirit, one God, now and forever.
PHP

Readings: Ezekiel 20:40-42
                Psalm 5
                Revelation 6:9-11
                Mark 8:34-38
Hymn of the Day:
                "Lord, save your world" (LBW 420)

Prayers:	For those who work to relieve the suffering of the poor
	For those whom the rulers of the world ignore and dismiss
	For the renewal of society
	For the gift of love of God and of humanity
Preface:	A Saint (3) (BCP)
Color:	Red

November 25

Isaac Watts, Hymnwriter, 1748

English hymnody may be said to have begun with Caedmon, the first singer of Christian songs in England. He was a herdsman who entered the monastery at Whitby at an advanced age. According to the Venerable Bede, one night Caedmon was inspired in a dream to compose a hymn of the creation, and after entering the monastery, he made other paraphrases of biblical narratives. Others in later centuries continued the tradition: George Herbert (d. 1633; see March 1), Samuel Crossman (d. 1683), Richard Baxter (d. 1691), Thomas Ken (d. 1711; see March 21), Joseph Addison (d. 1719). But it is Isaac Watts who is regarded as the creator of the English hymn.

Watts was the eldest of nine children of a Nonconformist minister, who had been twice imprisoned for his dissenting ideas. He was born at Southampton July 17, 1674. He showed great promise as a student (at the age of seven he amused his parents with rhymes), and several friends in the town offered him an education at a university leading to ordination in the Church of England. Refusing the offer, Watts entered the Nonconformist Academy at Stoke Newington in 1690. He left when he was twenty and spent the next two years at home, writing. He was dissatisfied with the poor quality of the versified psalms then in use and began to try to do better. Most of his *Hymns and Spiritual Songs* seem to have been written during this period. He served as a tutor to the son of an eminent Puritan at Stoke Newington and engaged in intense study.

When he was twenty-four, Watts began preaching. He was ordained in 1702 and became pastor of an independent congregation in Mark Lane, of which many distinguished Independents were members, including Cromwell's granddaughter. Watts's health began to fail soon after, and he was forced to spend the last thirty-six years of his life in the house of Sir Thomas Abney, preaching and teaching only occasionally.

He nonetheless earned considerable theological and philosophical fame. His *Logic* was long a textbook at Oxford; *The World to Come* (1745) was a favorite devotional work; *Improvement of the Mind* (1741) and *Speculations on the Human Nature of the Logos* increased his fame. A book of poems and hymns, *Horae Lyricae,* was published 1706–1709, and his *Hymns and Spiritual Songs,* although written earlier, was published 1707–1709, the first hymnbook in English. His versified *Psalms of David* "in the language of the New Testament and applied to the Christian state and worship" was printed in 1719. His sermons appeared in 1721–1724. His *Divine Songs Attempted in Easy Language for Children* was popular enough to be satirized more than a century later in *Alice in Wonderland.* Other works by Watts, his Catechisms and his *Scriptural History,* were used as texts in religious education. In 1721 he published *The Art of Reading and Writing English.* In 1728 he was awarded the D.D. degree by Edinburgh University.

At last, after years of suffering, Watts died November 25, 1748, and was buried in the Puritan burial ground at Bunhill Fields not far from the grave of John Bunyan. Watts had never married. He has been called the Melanchthon of his day because of his learning, gentleness, and devotion. There is a monument to him in Westminster Abbey.

Watts was introduced to the calendar in the *Lutheran Book of Worship* and is on the calendar in the Methodist book *For All the Saints,* the *Christian Year* (1997), and *Evangelical Lutheran Worship.*

FOR FURTHER READING

Benson, Louis Fitzgerald. *The English Hymn.* New York: G. H. Doran, 1915. Reprinted Richmond: John Knox, 1962.

Davis, Arthur P. *Isaac Watts: His Life and Works.* New York: Dryden, 1943.

Escott, Harry. *Isaac Watts: Hymnographer.* London: Independent Press, 1962.

Hope, Norman Victor. *Isaac Watts and His Contribution to English Hymnody.* Papers of the Hymn Society of America XIII. Springfield, 1947.

Manning, Bernard L. *The Hymns of Wesley and Watts.* London: Epworth, 1942.

Routley, Eric. "The Eucharistic Hymns of Isaac Watts." *Worship* 48, no. 9 (November 1974): 526–35.

Watson, J. R. *The English Hymn: A Critical and Historical Study.* Oxford: Clarendon, 1997.

READING

From *Voices and Instruments in Christian Worship* by Joseph Gelineau

If the word holds such a predominant position in Christian worship, does it not render music superfluous? And is it not best to strip words of special sacredness from all melodic ornament so that their message may come through with more certainty? If anyone were to draw that conclusion he would show that he is laboring under a serious misconception of the nature of human language. Also, he would have overlooked several important meanings which pertain to the mystery of song. . . .

The word which is merely spoken is a somewhat incomplete form of human language. It suffices for ordinary utilitarian communications. But as soon as the world becomes charged with emotion, as soon as it is filled with power, as soon as it tends to identify itself with the content of its message—when, in fine, it has to signify the sacredness of actions being performed—than it calls for number and melos, that is, for a musical form. . . . The complete word, the fully developed word, has the nature of song.

Joseph Gelineau, *Voices and Instruments in Christian Worship,* trans. Clifford Howell, S.J. (Collegeville, Minn.: Liturgical, 1964), 44.

PROPERS

O God, whom saints and angels delight to worship in heaven with hymns and spiritual songs of praise: Give us the wings of faith to behold the joyful glory of your saints, and to be so strengthened by the vigorous poetry of your servant Isaac Watts that we may faithfully walk in the path you have set before us, and at last, through your grace, possess the land of pure delight opened to us by your Son Jesus Christ our Lord; who lives and reigns with you and the Holy Spirit, one God, now and forever.

PHP

Readings:	2 Chronicles 20:20-21
	Psalm 96
	Ephesians 5:18b-20
	Matthew 26:26-30
Hymn of the Day:	
	"O God, our help in ages past" (H82 680, LBW 320, LSB 733, ELW 632)
Prayers:	For the spirit of joy in worship
	For those who help the church to sing
	For theological perception on the part of hymnwriters
	For those who teach children to sing
	For those in frail health
Preface:	Epiphany
Color:	White

NOVEMBER

ALSO ON NOVEMBER 25

The Episcopal *Lesser Feasts and Fasts 1997* added to the calendar the commemoration of *James Otis Sargent Huntington* (1854–1935), priest and monk, who was the founder of the Order of the Holy Cross and a leader in the social witness of the church.

November 28

L*esser Feasts and Fasts 1997* added to the Episcopal calendar on this date the commemoration of ***Kamehameha*** (1835–1864) and ***Emma*** (d. 1885), King and Queen of Hawaii, who established the Anglican Church in their realm.

November 29

T he *Lutheran Service Book* has introduced on this date a commemoration of ***Noah***. His story is told in Genesis 6–9.

November 30

St. Andrew, Apostle

V ocation and acceptance, God's summons and an individual's obedient response are the themes of this feast day. Andrew, whose name means "manly," was the brother of Peter, and was born in Bethsaida, a village in Galilee. He was the first apostle to follow Christ (John 1:35-40), his title in the Eastern Church is "the First-Called," and his name regularly appears near the head of the lists of the apostles. In Matthew and in Luke, his name appears second, after Peter, but in Mark and Acts he is listed after Peter, James, and John as the fourth in the list, in company with Philip. Perhaps his greatest work was to bring his brother Simon Peter to Jesus (John 1:40-42); a different, perhaps chronologically, later, account of the call of Andrew and Peter is given in Matthew 4:18-22. Details from both accounts are reflected in the prayer of the day.

After Pentecost, Andrew is said by Eusebius to have preached in Scythia, by Jerome and Theodoret in Greece; by Nicephorus in Asia Minor and Thrace. The Muratorian fragment (late second century) connects him with the writing of St. John's Gospel. A late and rather unreliable tradition says that he was martyred on November 30, *ca.* 70 at Patras in Achaia, Greece. The tradition that he was crucified on an X-shaped cross was popular in the fifteenth century; the earliest examples are from the tenth century. He was martyred, legend has it, for defying the proconsul Aegeas, who ordered Andrew to stop preaching and to sacrifice to the gods.

St. Andrew's body is said to have been taken, together with that of St. Luke, to the Church of the Holy Apostles in Constantinople on 357 and later removed to the cathedral in Amalfi, Italy. The church at Constantinople claimed St. Andrew as its first bishop. The churches in Greece and Russia in particular hold Andrew in high honor. Also, quite early, certain of his relics were taken to St. Andrew's Church in Fife, and he became a patron saint of Scotland; the X-shaped cross of St. Andrew in the Union Jack represents Scotland.

The feast of St. Andrew was observed as early as the fourth century by the Eastern Church and by the sixth century in Rome and elsewhere. It is a national holiday in Scotland.

St. Andrew's Day determines the beginning of the church year, since the First Sunday in Advent is "the Sunday nearest to St. Andrew's Day whether before or after." In many liturgical books, therefore, the list of saints, the sanctoral calendar begins with Andrew.

St. Andrew's eve, as the beginning of the church's year, was long a traditional time for young girls to expect to see in dreams their future husbands, a custom reflected as recently as Goethe's *Faust,* 1831(Part 1, ll. 878 -79). John Keats's "The Eve of St. Agnes" is another version of the same legend.

FOR FURTHER READING

Dvornik, F. *The Idea of Apostolicity in Byzantium and the Legend of the Apostle Andrew.* Cambridge: Harvard University Press, 1958.

Peterson, Peter M. *Andrew, Brother of Simon Peter: His History and His Legends.* Leiden: Brill, 1958.

READING

From *The Quest of the Historical Jesus* by Albert Schweitzer

He was not a teacher, not a casuist; He was an imperious ruler. It was because He was so in His inmost being that He could think of Himself as the Son of Man. That was only the temporally conditioned expression of the fact that He was an authoritative ruler. The names in which men expressed their recognition of Him as such, Messiah, Son of Man, Son of God, have become for us historical parables. We can find no designation which expresses what He is for us.

He comes to us as One unknown, without a name, as of old, by the lakeside, He came to those men who knew Him not. He speaks to us the same word: "Follow thou me!" and sets us to the tasks which He has to fulfill for our time. He commands. And to those who obey Him, whether they be wise or simple, He will reveal Himself in the toils, the conflicts, the sufferings, which they shall pass through in His fellowship, and, as an ineffable mystery, they shall learn in their own experience Who He is.

Albert Schweitzer, *The Quest of the Historical Jesus,* trans. W. Montgomery (New York: Macmillan, 1968), 403.

NOVEMBER

PROPERS

Almighty God, who gave such grace to your apostle Andrew that he readily obeyed the call of your Son Jesus Christ, and brought his brother with him: Give us, who are called by your holy Word, grace to follow him without delay, and to bring those near to us into his gracious presence; who lives and reigns with you and the Holy Spirit, one God, now and forever.

1552 BCP, rev. 1979 BCP; rev. in ELW

Readings:	Deuteronomy 30:11-14 *or* Ezekiel 3:16-21
	Psalm 19 *or* 19:1-6
	Romans 10:8b-18
	Matthew 4:18-22 *or* John 1:35-42
Hymn of the Day:	
	"Jesus calls us; o'er the tumult" (H82 549, 550; LBW 494, ELW 696)
Prayers:	For obedience to God's command
	For a sense of mission
	For those on spiritual pilgrimage
	For the church in Scotland
	For the church in Greece
	For those who minister to their own families
Preface:	Apostles
Color:	Red

December 1

Nicholas Ferrar, Deacon, 1637

Nicholas Ferrar was born in 1593 in London and was educated at Clare Hall, Cambridge, of which he was made a fellow. After Cambridge and five years' travel on the European continent, he became a member of parliament and a trustee of the Virginia Company and had what promised to be a brilliant career ahead of him. In 1625 he gave everything up and settled at the manor house at Little Gidding, in Huntingdonshire, and was ordained a deacon in the following year. At Little Gidding, he founded an Anglican religious community, which, in addition to himself, included his brother and brother-in-law and their families, and which existed from 1626 to 1646. They restored the derelict church near the manor house, became responsible for services there, taught many of the local children, and looked after the health and well-being of the people in the neighborhood. A regular round of prayer according to the Book of Common Prayer was observed, along with the daily praying of the entire Psalter. The members of the community became widely known for fasting, private prayer and meditation, and for writing stories and books illustrating themes of Christian faith and life. The community was visited by George Herbert and Richard Crashaw, and more than once King Charles visited the community and is said to have paid his last visit in secret after his defeat at Naseby in the English Civil War.

Ferrar died in 1637. Ten years later, at the height of the English Civil War, the Puritans broke up the community, contemptuously calling it a "protestant nunnery," and destroyed most of his manuscripts. The chapel was rebuilt in the nineteenth century.

The Little Gidding community was the only example of religious life in the Church of England between the suppression of the monasteries at the Reformation in the sixteenth century and the large-scale revival of religious orders during the Oxford Movement in the nineteenth century. The community at Little Gidding provided the title for the last of T. S. Eliot's *Four Quartets,* one of the great religious poems of the twentieth century. Nicholas Ferrar was added to the calendar in the 1979 *Book of Common Prayer* and is included in the Methodist *For All the Saints.*

FOR FURTHER READING

Carter, T. T., ed. *Nicholas Ferrar: His Household and His Friends.* 1892.
Maycock, A. L. *Nicholas Ferrar of Little Gidding.* London: SPCK, 1963
Skipton, H. P. K. *The Life and Times of Nicholas Ferrar.* London: Mowbray, 1907.

READING

From *The Life of Mr. George Herbert* by Izaac Walton (1593–1683)

Mr. Ferrer [sic] had, by the death of his father, or an elder brother, or both, an estate left him that enabled him to purchase land to the value of four or five hundred pounds a year; the greatest part of which land was at Little Gidden [sic], four or six miles from Huntingdon, and about eighteen from Cambridge; which place he chose for the privacy of it, and for the hall, which had the parish church or chapel belonging and adjoining near to it. . . .

He and his family, which were like a little college, and about thirty in number, did most of them keep Lent and all Ember-weeks strictly, both in fasting and using all those mortifications and prayers that the Church hath appointed to be then used: and he and they did the like constantly on Fridays, and on the Vigils and Eves to be fasted before the Saints' days: and this frugality and abstinence turned to the relief of the poor: but this was but a part of his charity; none but God and he knew the rest.

DECEMBER

This family, which I have said to be in number about thirty, were a part of them his kindred, and the rest chosen to be of a temper fit to be moulded into a devout life; and all of them were for their dispositions serviceable, and quiet, and humble, and free from scandal. Having thus fitted himself for his family, he did, about the year 1630, betake himself to a constant and methodical service of God; and it was in this manner:—He, being accompanied with most of his family, did himself use to read the common prayers—for he was a deacon—every day, at the appointed hours of ten and four, in the parish church, which was very near his house, and which he had both repaired and adorned; for it was fallen into a great ruin, by reason of a depopulation of the village before Mr. Ferrer bought the manor. And he did also constantly read the matins every morning at the hour of six, either in the church, or in an oratory, which was within his own house. And many of the family did there continue with him after the prayers were ended, and there they spent some hours in singing hymns, or anthems, sometimes in the church, and often to an organ in the oratory. And there they sometimes betook themselves to meditate, or to pray privately, or to read a part of the New Testament to themselves, or to continue their praying or reading of the psalms; and in case the psalms were not always read in the day, then Mr. Ferrer and others of the congregation did at night, at the ringing of a watch-bell, repair to the church or oratory, and there betake themselves to prayer and lauding God, and reading the psalms that had not been read in the day: and when these, or any part of the congregation grew weary or faint, the watch-bell was rung, sometimes before and sometimes after midnight, and then another part of the family rose, and maintained the watch, sometimes by praying, or singing lauds to God, or reading the psalms; and when, after some hours, they also grew weary or faint, then they rung the watch-bell and were also relieved by some of the former, or by a new part of the society, which continued their devotions—as hath been mentioned—until morning. And it is to be noted, that in this continued serving of God, the psalter or the whole book of psalms, was in every four and twenty hours sung or read over, from the first to the last verse: and this was done as constantly as the sun runs his circle every day about the world, and then begins again the same instant that it ended.

Thus did Mr. Ferrar and his happy family serve God day and Night; thus did they always behave themselves as in his presence. And they did always eat and drink by the strictest rules of temperance; eat and drink so as to be ready to rise at midnight, or at the call of the watch-bell, and perform their devotions to God. And it is fit to tell the reader that many of the clergy, that were more inclined to practical piety and devotion than to doubtful and needless disputations, did often come to Gidden Hall, and make themselves a part of that happy society, and stay a week or more, and then join with Mr. Ferrer and the family in these devotions, and assist and ease him or them in their watch by night. And these various devotions had never less than two of the domestic family in the night; and the watch was always kept in the church or oratory, unless in extreme cold winter nights, and then it was maintained in a parlour, which had a fire in it; and the parlour was fitted for that purpose. And this course of piety, and great liberality to his poor neighbors, Mr. Ferrer maintained until his death.

Izaac Walton, *The Life of Mr. George Herbert*, paragraphs 81–84, in *Seventeenth-Century Prose and Poetry*, ed. Alexander M. Witherspoon and Frank J. Warnke, 2d ed. (New York: Harcourt Brace Jovanovich, 1982), 285–86.

PROPERS

Grant, we pray you, Almighty God, that we, remembering your deacon Nicholas Ferrar and his household, and their detachment from the ambitions of this world, may be weaned from all that may hinder us from union with you; through Jesus Christ our Lord, who lives and reigns with you and the Holy Spirit, one God, forever and ever.

Oxford Centenary Supplementary Missal, 1933, rev. DvD and PHP

Readings:	Psalm 15 *or* 112:1-9
	Galatians 6:7-10
	Matthew 13:47-52
Hymn of the Day:	
	"Teach me, my God and king" (H82 592)
Prayers:	For religious communities and for all experiments in shared Christian living
	For our families that they may reflect something of the peace, order, and love that marked Little Gidding
	For a wider use of the daily prayer of the church
Preface:	A Saint (1) (BCP)
Color:	White

December 2

The *Book of Common Prayer* includes on its calendar on this date the commemoration of **Channing Moore Williams** (1829–1910), missionary bishop to China and Japan.

DECEMBER

December 3

Francis Xavier, Missionary to Asia, 1552

with Robert Morrison, 1834; Karl Gützlaff, 1851; James Hudson Taylor, 1905; Missionaries to China

Francis Xavier (in Spanish, Francisco do Yasu y Javier), the Apostle of India and Japan and one of the greatest missionaries in the history of the church, was born in the castle of Xavier near Sanguesa, Navarre, Spain, on April 7, 1506. He studied in his native country, went to Paris in 1525, and there met Ignatius Loyola (see July 31) and Pierre Favre. These three friends, together with three others, on August 15, 1534, bound themselves to the service of God with a vow at Montmartre. Francis received his M.A. in 1530 and served as regent at Beauvais College (1530–1534). For the next two years he studied theology. He and Ignatius were ordained June 24, 1537.

They left Paris for Venice on November 15, 1537, expecting to sail from there to Palestine. Their plans did not work out, and Francis spent the fall and winter in Bologna, Italy. In April 1538, he went to Rome and participated in a conference that led to the formation of the Society of Jesus.

He was called to Lisbon in 1540, and in the following year King John III of Portugal appointed him nuncio to the East, and Francis sailed for India. After a difficult three-month voyage, he landed in Goa on May 6, 1542, and immediately set about learning the language and writing a catechism. For the next seven years, he labored in Goa, among the Paravas in the extreme south of India, in Sri Lanka, in the Malay Peninsula, and the Molucca Islands, visiting his headquarters from time to time. The sufferings of the native peoples, both from one another and from the Portuguese made, he said, "a permanent bruise on my soul." In September 1542 he visited the coast opposite Sri Lanka (Ceylon), where the fishing people had been baptized as a condition for receiving help from the king of Portugal against northern robbers but for whom little had in fact been done. He met with huge success there. He wrote on January 15, 1543, that he was so exhausted administering baptism that he could hardly lift his arms. There was also, however, local hostility, and the new Christians were attacked, some were killed, and others were carried off to slavery.

In August 1543 Francis went to Molucca, the easternmost Portuguese port, in what is now Indonesia, for further work, and there he met a Japanese man who interested him in Japan. On August 15, 1549, he landed at Kagoshima in southern Japan. The first European to live in the area, he learned the language and wrote a catechism. Unaccustomed to winter, he suffered greatly from the cold. A year later Francis went to the center of Japan and the then capital of the empire, Kyoto. It was a time of civil strife, and Francis failed in his attempt to see the Mikado. He came to recognize what he described as the noble quality of the Japanese people, their intelligence, and the excellence of their civilization.

Francis returned to Molucca, and at the end of 1551, he was appointed provincial of the Province of India of the Society of Jesus. At length, he turned his attention to China, a country at that time closed to foreigners. He sailed to the island of Chang-Chuen (Sancian) near the mouth of the Canton River on the China coast in August 1552 and waited there while arranging a means of entering China. He was seized with a fever in November, weakened, and, alone except for a young Chinese Christian who had accompanied him from Goa, he died on December 3, 1552. He was forty-six. He was buried there temporarily; later his remains were taken to Goa where they have been enshrined ever since. It was popularly said of him that he made 700, 000 converts.

Francis is on the General Roman Calendar and on the calendar in the *Lutheran Book of Worship* and *Evangelical Lutheran Worship;* he is not on the calendar of the Episcopal Church.

FOR FURTHER READING

Broderick, J. *Saint Francis Xavier (1506–1552).* London: Burns, Oates, & Washbourne, 1952.

Coleridge, H. J. *The Life and Letters of St. Francis Xavier.* 2 vols. London, 1866.

Jaffrey, Madhur "The Last Chance, Probably, to View a Saint's Remains," *Smithsonian* 6, no. 2 (May 1975): 42–49. With photographs.

Moffett, Samuel H. *A History of Christianity in Asia.* San Francisco: HarperSanFrancisco, 1992–.

Robertson, Edith A. *Francis Xavier: Knight Errant of the Cross.* London: SCM, 1930.

Schurhammer, Georg. *Francis Xavier: His Life, His Times (1506–1552).* Trans. M. Joseph Costelloe. 4 vols. Rome: Jesuit Historical Institute, 1976–1982.

On this day three Protestant missionaries to China might also be remembered. **Robert Morrison** (1782–1834) was the first Protestant missionary to the people of China. A Congregationalist minister, he reached Canton in 1807. Through twenty-seven years of extreme hardship, he engaged largely in Bible translation and literary activity. His translations were imperfect, but nonetheless they began the work of putting the Bible into the language of China.

Karl Gützlaff (1803–1851) was the first Lutheran missionary to China, a country then closed to outsiders. He met Morrison and worked with him. Known sometimes as "the father of the German Branch of the China Inland Mission," he aroused European interest in the work in China, and through him, Hudson Taylor received his missionary call.

James Hudson Taylor (1832–1905), a man of intense dedication, landed at Shanghai in 1854 and founded the China Inland Mission to work in the interior of the country. It was an interdenominational effort that was remarkable in that it

DECEMBER

accepted men and women as missionaries without formal college training. Taylor sought identification with the Chinese; he adopted native dress, and he sought the growth of indigenous churches. Hudson Taylor is commemorated on the *Evangelical Calendar of Names* on June 3.

Channing Moore Williams (see December 2) might also be included in a broadened commemoration.

FOR FURTHER READING

Barnett, Suzanne Wilson, and John King Fairbank, eds. *Christianity in China: Early Protestant Missionary Writings.* Cambridge: Harvard University Press, 1985.

Latourette, Kenneth Scott. *A History of Christian Missions in China.* London: SPCK, 1929.

READING

From a letter by Francis Xavier to Ignatius Loyola

Many, many people in these regions are not becoming Christians simply because there is nobody to make them Christians. Again and again I have thought of going round the universities of Europe, especially Paris, and everywhere crying out like a madman to those with more learning than love, "What a tragedy: how many multitudes of souls are being shut out of heaven and falling into hell through your fault."

I wish they would work as hard at this as they do at their books, and so settle their account with God for the learning and the talents entrusted to them.

This would certainly stir most of them to meditate on spiritual realities, to listen actively to what God is saying to them. They would forget their own desire, their human affairs, and give themselves over entirely to God's will and his choice. They would cry out with all their heart, "Lord, I am here. What do you want me to do? Send me anywhere you like—even to India!

Letter 4. From the English translation of the Office of Readings from the Liturgy of the Hours by the International Committee on English in the Liturgy, rev. PHP.

PROPERS

O God, eternal Father, through the preaching and holy life of your servant Francis Xavier, you brought many nations to yourself: Give his zeal for the faith, we pray, to all who believe in you, that your Church may rejoice in continued growth throughout the world; Jesus Christ our Lord, who lives and reigns with you and the Holy Spirit, one God, now and forever.

1970 RS, rev. PHP

Readings:	Psalm 48
	1 Corinthians 9:16-19, 22-23
	Mark 16:15-20
Hymn of the Day:	
	"Hail to the Lord's anointed, great David's greater Son" (H82 616; LBW 87, LSB 398, ELW 311)
	See also "O God, I love thee, not that my poor love" (LBW 491, H82 682)
Prayers:	For the church in Japan and China
	For the church in the East Indies
	For the church in India and Sri Lanka
	For the missionary work of the church
	For all new Christians and for the younger churches
	For courage to share the lot of the poor and to overcome racial hatred and discrimination
Preface:	Epiphany
Color:	White

December 4

John of Damascus, Priest, *ca.* 760

John of Damascus, sometimes called John Damascene, theologian and hymn-writer, was born about 675, grew up in wealth and luxury, and at an early age succeeded his father as an official in the court of the Caliph of Damascus, Abdul Malek. John is said to have been educated by a Greek monk from Calabria whom the Muslims had taken prisoner. He became a monk *ca.* 715 at the famous monastery of Mar Saba, a still-extant hermit colony founded in 484 by St. Sabas (439–532) in the mountain wilderness between Jerusalem and the Dead Sea, and there devoted himself to an ascetic life and to the study of the Fathers. In 725 he was ordained a priest.

About this time a violent controversy concerning the veneration of icons erupted. The Byzantine emperor Leo III forbade the veneration of sacred images, icons, and ordered their destruction. John wrote three treatises in defense of icons, entitled *Against Those Who Attack the Divine Images.* He effectively defended the doctrine of the Real Presence of Christ in the Eucharist, and the veneration of the Virgin Mary. He also wrote a great synthesis of theology called *The Fount of Knowledge,* of which the last part, *On the Orthodox Faith,* is best known. His work is highly regarded in the Eastern Church, and he is considered the last of its Fathers.

He is best known to many as the author of the Easter hymns, "the Golden Canon" or "the Queen of Canons," "The day of resurrection, earth tell it out abroad", and an Ode written for the Sunday of St. Thomas (the Second Sunday of Easter), "Come, ye faithful, raise the strain of triumphant gladness."

John of Damascus died near Jerusalem *ca.* 760. His feast day in East and West is December 4. He is commemorated on the General Roman Calendar and on the calendar in the 1979 *Book of Common Prayer, Evangelical Lutheran Worship,* and the *Lutheran Service Book.*

FOR FURTHER READING

Louth, Andrew. *St. John Damascene: Tradition and Originality in Byzantine Theology.* New York: Oxford University Press, 2003.

READING

From *The First Oration against Those Who Attack the Divine Images* by John of Damascus

In former times, God, who is without form or body, could never be depicted. But now when God is seen in the flesh conversing with men, I make an image of the God whom I see, I do not worship matter; I worship the Creator of matter who became matter for my sake, who willed to take his abode in matter; who worked out my salvation through matter. Never will I cease honoring the matter which wrought my salvation! .... Because of this I salute all remaining matter with reverence, because God has filled it with his grace and power. Through it my salvation has come to me. Was not the thrice-happy and thrice-blessed wood of the cross matter? Was not the holy and exalted mountain of Calvary matter? What of the life-bearing rock, the holy and life-giving tomb, the fountain of our resurrection, was it not matter? Is not the ink of the most holy Gospel-book matter? From it we receive the Bread of Life! .... And over and above all these things, is not the Body and Blood of our Lord matter? Either do away with the honor and veneration these things deserve, or accept the tradition of the Church and the veneration of images. Reverence God and his friends; follow the inspiration of the Holy Spirit. Do not despise matter, for it is not despicable. God has made nothing despicable.

St. John of Damascus, "On the Holy Images," I, 16, trans. David Anderson, in *St. John of Damascus On the Divine Images* (Crestwood: St. Vladimir's Seminary Press, 1980), 23, 24.

PROPERS

Confirm our minds, O Lord, in the mysteries of the true faith, set forth with power by your servant John of Damascus; that we, with him, confessing Jesus to be true God and true Man, and singing the praises of the risen Lord, may, by the power of the resurrection, attain to eternal joy; through Jesus Christ our Lord, who lives and reigns with you and the Holy Spirit, one God, now and forever.

LFF

Readings: Psalm 118:14-21 *or* 16:5-11
                 1 Corinthians 15:12-20 *or* 2 Timothy 1:13-14; 2:1-3
                 John 5:24-27
Hymn of the Day:
                 "Thou hallowed, chosen morn of praise" (H82 198)
Prayers: For artists who adorn churches and who write icons
                 For a proper appreciation of art and outward beauty as a gift from God
                 For the church in Syria
                 For those who teach the church through hymns and song
Preface: Easter
Color: White

December 5

Clement of Alexandria, Priest, *ca.* 210

with Marcus Aurelius Clemens Prudentius, ca. 410; Synesius of Cyrene, ca. 413; Coelius Sedulius, ca. 450; Venantius Honorius Clementianus Fortunatus, ca. 609; Theodulph, 821; Joseph the Hymnographer, 886; Hymnwriters

Clement (Titus Flavius Clemens), a cultured Greek philosopher, who was born about 155, after seeking truth in many schools, settled in Alexandria in Egypt, which was then the chief center of scholarship. He became the head of the catechetical school there and held this post until about 202, when, at an outbreak of persecution under the emperor Severus, he fled the city. The exact date and place of his death are unknown.

His career is a landmark in the history of the church, for he was the first Christian to make a systematic attempt to bring the treasures of pagan culture into the service of the church. For many years he was a defender of the Christian faith to both pagans and Christians, and his learning and allegorical exegesis of the Bible helped to commend Christianity to the intellectual circles of Alexandria. Clement's extant works are *An Exhortation to the Greeks* and *Instruction in Christian Living.* Origen, the deepest thinker and greatest biblical scholar of the early church, was his pupil.

Appended to a prose work by Clement, variously called *The Instructor, The Pedagogue,* or *The Tutor,* instructing converts who were struggling to remake their lives in a Christian pattern, is what is often said to be the earliest Christian hymn. It begins, "Bridle of colts untamed." Henry Martin Dexter made a popular adaptation in 1846, softening the original vigor to "Shepherd of tender youth" (SBH

DECEMBER

179). F. Bland Tucker made a paraphrase, "Master of eager youth" (H40 362), now abbreviated in the *Hymnal 1982* (no. 478). Howard Chandler Robbins turned a prose section of Clement's writing into a hymn for Holy Saturday, "Sunset to sunrise changes now" (H82 163).

Clement is included on the calendar in the 1979 *Book of Common Prayer* and on the Methodist calendar in *For All the Saints*; he is not on the General Roman Calendar.

FOR FURTHER READING

Osborn, Eric. *Clement of Alexandria.* Cambridge: Cambridge University Press, 2006.

With Clement, it is useful to remember also other early hymnwriters whose work helped to establish the tradition of hymn singing in the church and whose work continues to appear in modern hymnals. Other than their hymns, little is known in detail about most of them.

Marcus Aurelius Clemens Prudentius (348–410?), a Spanish lawyer, active in the imperial court at Rome, at age fifty-seven dedicated the remainder of his life to the service of God. His Christmas hymn is his best known, "Of the Father's love begotten" (*Corde natus ex parentis*) [H82 82, LBW 42, ELW 295, LSB 384]. He is also remembered for the Epiphany hymn "Earth has many a noble city" (*O sola magnarium urbium*) [H82 127, SBH 51; LBW 81] and a hymn for the Holy Innocents, "Sweet flowers of the martyr band" (*Salvete, flores martyrum*) [TLH 273].

Synesius of Cyrene (*ca.* 370–*ca.* 413), Bishop of Ptolemais, friend of Augustine and student of the celebrated Neo-Platonist, Hypatia, went to Constantinople to warn against the imminent invasion of Rome and North Africa by the Goths. Edward Gibbon says succinctly, "The court of Arcadius indulged the zeal, applauded the eloquence, and neglected the advice of Synesius." The Greek hymn "Lord Jesus, think on me" [H82 641, LBW 309, ELW 599, LSB 610] is derived from a poem attached to a collection of his works.

Coelius Sedulius (d. *ca.* 450), priest and poet, is remembered for the Christmas hymn, "From east to west, from shore to shore" (*A solis ortus cardine*) [H82 77, LBW 64, LSB 385] and its second part, an Epiphany hymn, "When Christ's appearing was made known" (*Hostis Herodes impie*) [H82 131, 132; LBW 85].

Venantius Honorius Clementianus Fortunatus (540?–609?) was born in northern Italy and settled in Poitiers where he had gone on a pilgrimage of thanksgiving for the miraculous restoration of his eyesight. After serving as chaplain to the convent established by Queen St. Rhadegunda, he became bishop of Poitiers about 600. He is remembered for the Passion hymns "The royal banners forward go" (*Vexilla regis prodeunt*) [H82 162; LBW 124, 125; LSB 455] and "Sing, my tongue, the glorious battle" (*Pange, lingua, gloriosi proelium*) [H82 165, 166; LBW 118; ELW 355, 356; LSB 454], written to welcome a fragment of the true cross to Rhadegunda's convent of St. Croix, and for the Easter hymns "Hail thee, festival day" [H82 175, 216, 225; ELW 394; LSB 489] and "Welcome, happy morning" (*Salve, festa dies*) [H82 179, LBW 153]. Fortunatus's feast day is December 14.

Theodulph, Bishop of Orleans (*ca.* 760–821), born in Spain, was a poet in the court of Charlemagne and a pioneer in education. His one surviving hymn, "All glory, laud, and honor" (*Gloria laus et honor*) [H82 154, 155; LBW 108, ELW 344, LSB 442], which has found a permanent place in the liturgy of the palms on the Sunday of the Passion, was written while Theodulph was in prison at Angiers on a charge of conspiring against Charlemagne's successor, Louis the Pious.

Joseph the Hymnographer (ca. 810–886), a Sicilian, one of the most voluminous of Greek hymnwriters, was a monk of the famed monastery, the Studium, in Istanbul. His hymn on the holy angels, "Stars of the morning, so gloriously bright" [SBH 148, LSB 520] is still useful on September 29; his hymn on the martyrs, "Let us now our voices raise" [H82 237, SBH 546] also survives.

See also Hilary (January 13), Ephrem (June 10), and Ambrose (December 7).

FOR FURTHER READING

Bregman, Jay. *Synesius of Cyrene*. Berkeley: University of California Press, 1982.
Slavitt, David R., trans. *The Hymns of Prudentius*. Baltimore: Johns Hopkins University Press, 1996.

READING

From *The Exhortation* by Clement of Alexandria, inviting the Greeks to listen to and live by the New Song

The maidens strike up their lyres, the angels praise, the prophets speak. The sound of music issues forth; they run and pursue the jubilant choir; those who are called make haste, eagerly desiring to receive the Father.

Come also, O aged Tiresias, leaving Thebes, and throwing away your divinations and your Bacchic frenzy—allow yourself to be led to the truth! I give you the staff [of the cross] on which to lean. Make haste, Tiresias; believe, and you shall see. Christ, by whom the blind have recovered their sight, will shed on you a light brighter than the sun; night will flee from you; the fire will be afraid; death will be gone; and you, Tiresias, who never set eyes on Thebes shall see the heavens. O true and sacred mysteries! O perfect light! My way is lighted with torches, and I see the heavens and my God; I become holy while I am initiated. The Lord is the priest and seals while illuminating those who are initiated, and presents to the Father those who believe, to be kept safe for ever.

So let us haste, let us run, my fellow humans, who are God-loving and God-like images of the Word. Let us haste; let us run; let us take his yoke; let us receive, to conduct us to immortality, the good charioteer of men. Let us love Christ.

Clement of Alexandria, *Protreptikos,* chap. 12, trans. *Ante-Nicene Fathers,* vol. 2, (Grand Rapids: Eerdmans, 1973), 205–06, rev. PHP.

PROPERS

O Lord, the Savior and Guardian of those who fear you, turn away from your Church the deceitful allurements of this world's wisdom; that under the teaching of your Spirit, we, like your servant Clement, may find pleasure in the prophetic oracles and the apostolic instructions, lest the vanity of falsehoods deceive those whom the truth illuminates; through Jesus Christ our Lord, who lives and reigns with you and the Holy Spirit, one God, now and forever.

Gelasian sacramentary, trans. William Bright AC, rev. PHP

Readings:	Psalm 34:9-14 *or* 103:1-4, 13-18
	Colossians 1:11-20
	John 6:57-63
Hymn of the Day:	
	"Jesus, our mighty Lord" (H82 478, SBH 179, LSB 864)
Prayers:	For all theologians, particularly those who are forging links between Christianity and contemporary culture
	For grace to recognize that God is the source and giver of all beauty, truth, and goodness
	For the Coptic Church of Egypt
Preface:	Baptism (BCP, LBW)
Color:	White

December 6

Nicholas, Bishop of Myra, *ca.* 342

Although Nicholas has become one of the most popular saints of the Christian calendar, nearly nothing in known about his life. He was a bishop in Myra, a Mediterranean seaport on the southwest coast of Asia Minor, what is now Turkey, during the fourth century. Beyond those bare facts, nothing else is certain.

In the absence of facts, legends abound. Nicholas as an infant, it is said, refused to nurse on the ancient fast days of Wednesday and Friday. He aided the poor and once saved three daughters of a poor man from a life of prostitution by throwing a bag of gold through the window of their home for three successive nights for their dowries; he is therefore the patron of virgins, and the three bags are said to have inspired the traditional pawnbroker's sign. He miraculously reconstituted two or three boys whom an innkeeper had murdered, cut into small pieces, and put in a brine tub to sell as pickled pork. He saved three unjustly condemned men from death. He aided sailors who were in distress off the coast of his diocese, and once on a voyage to the Holy Land showed courage on board ship during a storm, thus becoming the patron of sailors. He attended the Council of Nicaea and gave the heretic Arius a resounding box on the ear.

Nicholas is the patron of Russia and of Greece; the guardian of virgins and poor maidens; the protector of children, travelers, sailors, and merchants, as well as guardian against thieves and violence. He is the patron of many towns and cities including Bari, Venice, Freiburg, and Galway.

On his feast day this enormously popular saint was impersonated by a man with a white beard, in the vestments of a bishop, who was kind to children. In Germany on this day, St. Nicholas makes his rounds arrayed as a bishop and distributes candies and nuts to good children, accompanied by his servant Knecht Ruprecht, who spanks the bad ones. In Holland, even after the Reformation, Sinter Klaas in bishop's vestments and on a white horse visited children on the eve of his feast day. This popular figure was brought to New Amsterdam (New York) by the Dutch and combined with the English Father Christmas. His activities were moved from his feast day to December 25, his bishop's vesture was replaced by secular clothing, but he retained his cheerful colors, the name Santa Claus, and the traditional association with gift giving. With the added features of the Nordic "Christmas Man," he was given a home and factory at the North Pole and a sleigh and reindeer. (In northern Europe, Thor was the god of peasants and common people, who is represented as an old man, jovial, friendly, stout, with a long white beard, whose element is fire and whose color therefore is red. He fought with the giants of ice and snow and so became a Yule god.)

In 580 the emperor Justinian dedicated a church to Nicholas in Constantinople. Since then, there have perhaps been more churches and chapels dedicated to St. Nicholas than to any other saint.

The remains of St. Nicholas are said to be in the crypt of the basilica of San Nicola in Bari, Italy. In 1087 three ships sailed from the seaport of Bari to Myra on an expedition to bring the bones of Nicholas to their town. They returned to Bari on May 9, 1097, with his relics that were temporarily housed in a church dedicated to San Giovanni a Mare, until a basilica could be built in honor of St. Nicholas. The relics were transferred to their present resting place in 1089 by Pope Urban II, and May 9 has been a day of celebration in honor of St. Nicholas in Bari since that time. The three ships that brought St. Nicholas to Bari play a role in several Christmas carols, the best known of which is "I saw three ships come sailing by on Christmas Day in the morning."

DECEMBER

Nicholas is included on the calendar in the 1979 *Book of Common Prayer,* the *Lutheran Book of Worship, Evangelical Lutheran Worship,* the *Lutheran Service Book,* and the Methodist *For All the Saints.*

FOR FURTHER READING

Crozier, Eric. *The Life and Legends of Saint Nicholas, Patron Saint of Children.* London: Duckworth, 1949.

Jones, Charles W. *Saint Nicholas of Myra, Bari, and Manhattan: Biography of a Legend.* Chicago: University of Chicago Press, 1978.

READING

From *Conversations and Letters on The Practice of the Presence of God* by Brother Lawrence

He told me . . . that God always gave us light in our doubts when we had no other design than to please Him, and to act for His love.

That our sanctification did not depend upon *changing* our works, but in doing that for God's sake which commonly we do for our own. That it was lamentable to see how many people mistook the means for the end, addicting themselves to certain works, which they performed very imperfectly, by reason of their human or selfish regards.

That the most excellent method he had found of going to God was that of *doing our common business* without any view of pleasing men, and (as far as we are capable) *purely for the love of God.*

That it was a great delusion to think that the times of prayer ought to differ from other times; that we are as strictly obliged to adhere to God by action in the time of action as by prayer in the season of prayer.

That his view of prayer was nothing else but a sense of the Presence of God, his soul being at that time insensible to everything but Divine Love; and that when the appointed times of prayer were past, he found no difference, because he still continued with God, praising and blessing Him with all his might, so that he passed his life in continual joy; yet hoped that God would give him somewhat to suffer when he should have grown stronger.

That we ought not to be weary of doing little things for the love of God, who regards not the greatness of the work, but the love with which it is performed.

Brother Lawrence (Nicholas Herman), Fourth Conversation, November 25, 1667, in *Conversations and Letters on the Practice of the Presence of God,* (Cincinnati: Forward Movement, 1941), 15–16.

PROPERS

Almighty God, in your love you gave your servant Nicholas of Myra a perpetual name for deeds of kindness both on land and sea: Grant, we pray, that your

Church may never cease to work for the happiness of children, the safety of sailors, the relief of the poor, and the help of those tossed by tempests of doubt or grief; through Jesus Christ our Lord, who lives and reigns with you and the Holy Spirit, one God, forever and ever.

Eric Milner-White, *An Anglican Calendar,* 1941, rev. LFF

Readings:	Isaiah 10:33—11:9
	Psalm 78:3-7 *or* 145:8-13
	1 John 4:7-14
	Mark 10:13-16
Hymn of the Day:	
	"Comfort, comfort, ye my people" (H82 67, LBW 29, LSB 347, ELW 256)
Prayers:	For the spirit of generosity
	For children, especially those who have no one to care for them
	For mariners and travelers
	For the church in Greece
Preface:	A Saint (1) (BCP)
Color:	White

December 7

Ambrose, Bishop of Milan, 397

Ambrose was the first Latin Church leader to be born, raised, and educated not as a pagan but as a Christian. He was born about 339 in the city of Treves (Trier) in what is now France, where his father was Prefect of Gaul, the governor of a large part of Europe. Ambrose studied the classics and the law at Rome, and before he was thirty-three, he was named governor of Liguria and Aemilia, with headquarters in Milan, which was at that time the seat of the imperial court. When the Arian bishop of Milan died, Ambrose settled the violence that broke out between the Arians and the Catholics. Both sides unanimously insisted that he become their bishop, even though at that time he had not yet been baptized. (It was a custom of the time to delay baptism until late in life so that one might be cleansed close to the time of death.) Ambrose finally bowed to pressure from Church and state authorities and rapidly was baptized, ordained priest, and consecrated bishop; some say it was all done on the same day, December 7, 373 or 374.

He gave a portion of his family wealth to the poor and set an example of strict asceticism. Although the Roman Empire was in decline, Ambrose, by his preaching, writing, organizing, and administration, made Milan one of the most centers of learning and Christian activity, in some ways surpassing even Rome itself. He was a powerful preacher, and his sermons affected many, most notably Augustine of Hippo, whom he baptized in Milan at the Easter Vigil, 387.

The empress Justina, mother of Valentinian, jealous of the growing importance of Ambrose, organized a coalition against the bishop and at the beginning of Lent in 385, demanded that one basilica in Milan be given to the Arians. Ambrose refused, and a riot broke out in the city. Just before Easter, Justina demanded the bishop's own cathedral. On Palm Sunday, there were a series of clashes between the imperial troops and Ambrose's congregations. On Maundy Thursday the court abandoned its attempt to seize and hold a church. The struggle, however, continued. An edict against the Catholics was promulgated in June 386, and Ambrose was summoned to appear before the emperor. He refused and took refuge in his basilica, which was surrounded by imperial troops. Inside, Ambrose and his people spent the time singing psalms and hymns of their bishop's own composition. At length, the court was forced to rescind the edict.

Ambrose was a zealous defender of orthodoxy and one of the most important Latin authors of his day. At the request of the emperor Gratian he wrote *On the Christian Faith*. He is also the author of a work of pastoral care, *On the Duties of the Clergy*. One comes closest to the saintly bishop, perhaps, through his hymns. He was one of the first to write metrical Latin hymns, and many of them are still sung in Christian churches. St. Augustine, addressing God, says,

> The tears flowed when I heard your hymns and canticles, for the sweet singing of your church moved me deeply. The music surged in my ears, truth seeped into my heart, and my feelings of devotion overflowed, so that the tears streamed down. But they were tears of gladness. (*Confessions*, IX, 6-7)

Ambrose is the only Church Father of whom we possess a portrait, idealized to be sure, but an authentic portrait nonetheless. It is a mosaic with his name that adorns a chapel in the basilica dedicated to his brother Satyrus, made at the beginning of the fifth century, shortly after his death.

Ambrose died at Milan on Easter Eve, April 4, 397. Some Anglican calendars have commemorated him on that day, but the traditional date for his remembrance in the Roman Catholic and Eastern Churches, followed by the Episcopal and Lutheran Churches and the calendar in *For All the Saints*, is the date of his baptism-ordination-consecration. It is a more convenient date, since April 4 usually falls near Easter, which requires its observance to be delayed.

FOR FURTHER READING

Von Campenhausen, Hans. *The Fathers of the Latin Church.* Trans. Manfred Hoffman. Stanford: Stanford University Press, 1964.

Dudden, F. H. *The Life and Times of St. Ambrose.* 2 vols. Oxford: Oxford University Press, 1935.

Greenslade, S. L., ed. *Early Latin Theology.* Philadelphia: Westminster, 1956.

McLynn, Neil B. *Ambrose of Milan: Church and Court in a Christian Capital.* Berkeley: University of California Press, 1994.

Paredi, A. *Ambrose.* Trans. J. Costello. Notre Dame: University of Notre Dame Press, 1963.

READING

From St. Augustine's *Confessions*

In Milan I found your devoted servant the bishop Ambrose, who was known throughout the world as a man whom there were few to equal in goodness. At that time his gifted tongue never tired of dispensing the richness of your corn [i.e., wheat], the joy of your oil, and the sober intoxication of your wine. Unknown to me, it was you who led me to him, so that I might knowingly be led by him to you. This man of God received me like a father and, as bishop, told me how glad he was that I had come. My heart warmed to him, not at first as a teacher of the truth, which I had quite despaired of finding in your Church, but simply as a man who showed me kindness. I listened attentively when he preached to the people, though not with the proper intention; for my purpose was to judge for myself whether the reports of his powers as a speaker were accurate, or whether eloquence flowed from him more, or less, readily than I had been told. So while I paid the closest attention to the words he used, I was quite uninterested in the subject-matter and was even contemptuous of it. I was delighted with his charming delivery, but although he was a more learned speaker than Faustus, he had not the same soothing and gratifying manner. I am speaking only of his style for, as to content, there could be no comparison between the two. Faustus had lost his way among the fallacies of Manicheism, while Ambrose most surely taught the doctrine of salvation. But *your mercy is unknown to sinners* such as I was then, though step by step, unwittingly, I was coming closer to it.

For although I did not trouble to take what Ambrose said to heart, but only to listen to the manner in which he said it—this being the only paltry interest that remained to me now that I had lost hope that man could find the path that led to you—nevertheless his meaning, which I tried to ignore, found its way into my mind together with his words, which I admired so much.

Augustine, *Confessions,* trans. R.S. Pine-Coffin (Penguin Classics, 1961), 6–7, 107–08, 231–32. Copyright © Pine-Coffin. Reprinted by permission of Penguin Books Ltd.

PROPERS

O God, you enabled your servant Ambrose to humble the pride of princes, to win the learned, and to teach the simple: Grant that we in our turn may walk humbly before you and resist iniquity in high places, glad to sing your praises before the

DECEMBER

whole assembly of your people; through Jesus Christ our Lord, who lives and reigns with you and the Holy Spirit, one God, now and forever.

Horace Finn Tucker, *Light for Lesser Days*, 1909, rev. JWP, PHP

Readings:	Ecclesiasticus 2:7-11, 16-18
	Psalm 27:5-11 *or* 33:1-5, 20-21
	Luke 12:35-37, 42-44
Hymn of the Day:	
	"O Splendor of God's glory bright" (H82 5, LBW 271, LSB 874, ELW 559)
Prayers:	For lawyers and government officials
	For preachers of the word of God and for hymnwriters
	For a joyful confidence in God's care
	For the church in Milan and in northern Italy
	For all leaders of the church that they may show by their lives the love of God for the world
Preface:	A Saint (1) (BCP)
Color:	White

December 11

Lars Olsen Skrefsrud, Missionary to India, 1910

Lars Olsen Skrefsrud, the Apostle of the Santals, was born in Lysgaard, Norway, February 4, 1840. He grew up in poverty and received little formal education. After studying at the parish school and being confirmed, he was apprenticed to a coppersmith in the town of Skrefsrud and mastered that trade.

He was repeatedly frustrated in his ambitions: he could not afford the education to become a pastor, his poems were rejected by the local publisher, and his companions ridiculed his desire to be a drummer in the army. Increasingly, he turned to alcohol for comfort, following in the footsteps of his father, who was generally a sturdy, hard-working farmer and carpenter, but who was given to bouts of drinking. The son, under the influence of his companions, robbed a bank, and, when he was apprehended, refused to name his accomplices, was found guilty and sentenced to four years in prison.

In jail the nineteen-year-old began to read religious books, became an exemplary prisoner, and was assigned to the infirmary where he tended the sick. One day, after a talk with a visiting pastor, he began to study in earnest to become a pastor. Although his family and his former friends rejected him, one girl, Anna Onsum, visited him in prison and had faith in him. When he was released from prison in 1861, penniless, he worked his way to the Gossner Missionary Society in Berlin where he told of his past and of his desire to become a missionary. He was accepted and began a life of single-minded devotion to his goal. He worked, studied, fasted, prayed, attended church services daily, and lived on little more than bread, cheese, and water.

In the fall of 1863, Skrefsrud left for India. He had to work to pay his passage and slept on the deck of the ship and lived with a mixed crew of Europeans, Africans, and Indians, whose languages and ways of life he began to learn. In 1864 the young missionary reached Calcutta, and in the following year a Danish co-worker, Father Børresen, his wife, and Anna Onsum joined him. He and Anna were married, and the group of four went off on their own, without help from European sources, joining the Baptist E. C. Johnson to preach the gospel among the Santals, an oppressed tribe in northern India who had never seen a Christian missionary.

Skrefsrud, as the leader, worked day and night studying the Santali language and learning the ways of the people. Soon he could preach in the language, and in a little over a year, the first converts were baptized. The work spread from "Ebenezer," the first mission station they built, until at Skrefsrud's death there were nearly twenty thousand baptized Santal Christians. Skrefsrud wrote a grammar and a dictionary of Santali, translated the Gospels and Luther's Small Catechism, and compiled textbooks and hymnals. He defended the Santals against their traditional oppressors and pled their cause with the British government. He taught them agriculture, irrigation, carpentry, and other useful arts. His aim was an indigenous Santal church; he said, "We came to the Santals to bring them Christianity and not to take away their nationality." He was a social reformer as well as a missionary and helped to raise their standard of living.

There were hardships and severe blows: no support from home, opposition from local groups, the death of his wife, and his own serious illness. But in 1873, on a trip back to Europe to take the ailing Mrs. Børresen home, Skrefsrud was received with acclaim in Germany, Great Britain, and Scandinavia. The Church of Norway at last ordained the successful missionary, and he returned with renewed zeal to his work in Santalistan.

In his sixty-ninth year, Skrefsrud had a stroke, but he recovered sufficiently to write with his left hand and kept busy with correspondence, translations, and writing. On December 11, 1910, he died and was buried in the cemetery of Ebenezer, beside his wife, Father Børresen, and other missionaries and Santal Christians.

The Santal Church, begun through the work of Skrefsrud and his associates, is now a flourishing member of the Federation of Evangelical Lutheran Churches in India. In the town of Skrefsrud, in Norway, his parents' home is kept as a memorial to this modern saint, and a nearby museum houses articles related to his life and work.

DECEMBER

The German *Evangelical Calendar of Names* (1962) introduced Skrefsrud to the calendar, followed by the *Lutheran Book of Worship* (1978).

FOR FURTHER READING

Hodne, O. *L.O. Skrefsrud: Missionary and Social Reformer among the Santals of Santal Parganas.* Oslo, 1966.

READING

From St. Augustine's *Confessions*

I have learnt to love you late, Beauty at once so ancient and so new! I have learnt to love you late! You were within me, and I was in the world outside myself. I searched for you outside myself and, disfigured as I was, I fell upon lovely things of your creation. You were with me, but I was not with you. The beautiful things of the world kept me from you and yet, if they had not been in you, they would have no being at all. You called me; you cried aloud to me; you broke my barrier of deafness. You shone upon me; your radiance enveloped me; you put my blindness to flight. You shed your fragrance about me; I drew breath and now I gasp for your sweet odour. I tasted you, and now I hunger and thirst for you. You touched me, and I am inflamed with love of your peace.

Augustine, *Confessions*, trans. R.S. Pine-Coffin (Penguin Classics, 1961), 6–7, 107–08, 231–32. Copyright © Pine-Coffin. Reprinted by permission of Penguin Books Ltd.

PROPERS

Merciful God, you look with compassion on all who by their addictions are in bondage, and you call them to recovery and to purpose: We thank you for releasing your servant Lars Olsen Skrefsrud from his captivity and for leading him to the Santal people to preach the gospel of peace and to build their church; and we pray that you would strengthen us by his example to work for the salvation of all whom the world or the church overlooks or ignores, that your Name may be glorified throughout the earth; through Jesus Christ our Lord, who lives and reigns with you and the Holy Spirit, one God, now and forever.

PHP

Readings:	Isaiah 52:7-10
	Psalm 96
	Acts 1:1-9
	Luke 10:1-9
Hymn of the Day:	
	"Your kingdom come! O Father, hear our prayer" (LBW 376)

Prayers: For those in prison and those who minister to them
              For alcoholics
              For those near despair
              For missionaries in remote places
              For the Santal Church
Preface: Lent (1) (BCP)
Color: White

December 13

Lucy, Martyr at Syracuse, *ca.* 304

Lucy (or Lucia) lived at the end of the third century in Sicily and died as a martyr at Syracuse in Sicily, probably in Diocletian's persecution. Her memory was venerated at an early date, and, as her cult spread, her name was introduced into the Roman Canon of the Mass.

Her life, it is said, was one of purity and gentleness, and she was loved by the poor. Legends about her abound. When her mother was cured of a disease, one story reports, Lucy in gratitude to God gave all her bridal possessions to the Christian poor. Her disappointed suitor then reported her as a Christian to the prefect Paschasius, who condemned her to be arrested and to be taken to a brothel. When she would not cooperate in the activity of the place, they built a fire around her to frighten her into submission. She was finally killed by being stabbed in the neck, probably in the year 304 at Syracuse. Her body was taken to Venice; another supposed body of hers was taken to Corfinium in the eighth century and to Metz in 970.

Lucy is remembered with great affection by the people of Sicily and southern Italy. She is regarded as the patron saint of the laboring poor and, because her name means "light," as a protector against diseases of the eye. Lucy is included on the General Roman Calendar, the calendar in *Evangelical Lutheran Worship* and (as Lucia) the *Lutheran Service Book,* but she is not on the Episcopal calendar. Her feast day in the East is July 6.

In medieval Europe, before the Gregorian reform of the calendar, St. Lucy's day was the shortest day of the year, and the day was celebrated, especially in Scandinavia, as the turning point from the long nights. Swedish communities, including many in America, still have special festivities on this day, "Lussida'n." In private homes one of the young girls of the household, dressed in white and wearing a crown of lighted candles, awakens the family in the morning and offers them coffee and cakes from a tray. For the rest of the day she is called "Lussi" instead of her own name.

DECEMBER

READING

From the book *On Virginity* by Ambrose of Milan

You are one of God's people, a virgin among virgins; you light up our grace of body with your splendor of soul. More than others you can be compared to the Church. When you are in your room, then, at night, think always on Christ, and at every moment wait for his coming.

This is how Christ would have you live, this is what he chose you to be. When to door is opened, he enters, as he who cannot deceive has promised to come in. Embrace him, the one you have sought; turn to him, and be enlightened; hold him fast, ask him not to go in haste, beg him not to leave you. The Word of God moves swiftly; it is not won by the lukewarm and the negligent cannot lay hold of it. Let your soul be attentive to his Word; follow carefully the path God tells you to take, for he is swift in his passing.

What does his bride say? "I sought him, but found him not; I called him, but he gave no answer." [Song 3:1] Do not imagine that, although you have called him, asked him, opened the door to him, you displeased him and that is the reason he has gone so quickly. No, he often allows us to be tested. When the crowds press him to stay, what does he say in the Gospel? "I must proclaim the goodness of the kingdom of God to the other cities also; for I was sent for that purpose." [Luke 4:43] But even if it seems to you that he has left you, go out and seek him once more.

Who but holy Church is to teach you how to hold Christ fast? Indeed, she has already taught you, if you only understood her words in Scripture, "Scarcely had I passed them, when I found him whom my soul loves. I held him and would not let him go." [Song 3:4]

How do we hold him fast? Not by restraining chains or knotted ropes but by bonds of love, by the affections of the spirit, by the longing of the soul.

If you also, like the bride, wish to hold him fast, seek him and do not fear suffering, for it is often easier to find him in the midst of torments of the body, and even in the hand of persecutors.

His bride says, "How short a time it was after I left them." [see Song 3:4] In a little space, after a brief moment, when you have escaped from the hands of your persecutors without yielding to the powers of this world, Christ will come to you, for he will not allow you to be tested for long.

Whoever seeks Christ in this way, and finds him, can say, "I held him, and would not let him go until I brought him into my mother's house, and into the chamber of her that conceived me." [Song 3:4] What is this "house," this "chamber," but the deep and secret places of your heart?

Maintain this house, sweep out its secret recesses until it becomes spotless and rises as a spiritual temple for a holy priesthood, firmly secured by Christ, the cornerstone, and the Holy Spirit shall dwell in it.

Whoever seeks Christ in this way, whoever prays to Christ in this way, is not abandoned by him; on the contrary, Christ comes again and again to visit such a person, for he is with us until the end of the world.

Chapters 12, 13. From the English translation of the Office of Readings from the Liturgy of the Hours by the International Committee on English in the Liturgy, rev. PHP.

PROPERS

God of love and source of all life, we pray that as we celebrate the entrance of your servant Lucy into eternal glory, you may so strengthen our witness to you in this world that we may at last share her blessedness in your kingdom of everlasting light; through your Son Jesus Christ our Lord, who lives and reigns with you and the Holy Spirit, one God, now and forever.

Gelasian sacramentary, RS, rev. PHP

Readings:	Song of Solomon 8:6-7
	Psalm 45
	Romans 8:31b-39
	John 3:17-21
Hymn of the Day:	
	"O very God of very God" (H82 672, CSB 11)
Prayers:	For those who walk in darkness
	For all who treat diseases of the eye
	For those who struggle to resist temptation of the world and its ways
Preface:	A Saint (1) (BCP) or Epiphany (LBW/ELW)
Color:	White

December 14

John of the Cross, Renewer of the Church, 1591

Juan de Yepes y Álvarez was born at Fontiveros in Spain on the feast day of John the Baptist, June 24, 1542, the third son of a disowned silk merchant, who was probably Jewish and who died shortly after his son was born. The son was placed in an institution for the poor. He displayed a remarkable incapacity for manual work and was returned by all to whom he was apprenticed. At seventeen he worked in a hospital in Medina to support himself in the Jesuit College in which he had enrolled.

He was a small man, less than five feet tall, who led a life of extraordinary struggle. Yet he was one whose ambition was only to spend his life in prayer and

DECEMBER

meditation. In 1563 he entered the Order of the Blessed Virgin (Carmelites) and took the name Fray Juan de San Matias. He studied theology at the University of Salamanca (1564–1567). He was ordained in 1567, and at Medina, where he went to sing his first mass, he met Teresa of Avila (see October 15), who had begun a reform of the Carmelite Order to restore the austere and predominately contemplative primitive rule and who wanted to extend the austerity to monks of the order as well. The followers of this reform wore sandals instead of shoes and so were known as "Discalced" (barefoot) Carmelites. Juan promised to adopt this way of life and, in token of his promise, changed his name to Juan de la Cruz, John of the Cross.

John was appointed sub-prior and master of novices at Duruelo and then rector of the house of studies at Alcala. In 1571 Teresa got John appointed confessor to the Convent of the Incarnation, where she was a sister.

Jealousies within the order led to a suspension of the reform. On December 2, 1577, the Carmelites seized John, took him to Toledo, and demanded that he renounce the reform. He refused and was imprisoned for nine months in a six-foot by ten-foot, nearly dark cell. After frequent flogging and a diet of bread, water, and salt fish, he managed to escape—miraculously, some say—in August 1578 and made his way to a Discalced monastery in southern Spain.

He spent his next years in administration of various sorts, writing, and guiding the laity in the spiritual life. He was able to complete the poems and commentaries on them that he had begun in the darkness of the prison. He is, many claim, the greatest Spanish poet. Notable are *The Ascent of Mt. Carmel—the Dark Night,* a treatise on how to reach perfection; *The Spiritual Canticle,* a commentary on the poem dealing with love between the soul and Christ; and *The Living Flame of Love,* a song of a transformed soul.

In 1591 controversy again emerged over the control of the reform, and John was banished to a "desert house" in Andalusia in southern Spain. There he was seized with a fever and went to Ubeda for medical attention because he thought that he was not known there. The prior of the monastery complained of the added expense of an additional monk. John died during the night of December 13–14, 1591, with the words of the Psalm of Compline on his lips, "Into your hands, O Lord, I commend my spirit." The local populace immediately acclaimed him a saint, and before he could be buried, his body had been mutilated by relic-hunters.

St. John of the Cross is known as a supreme lyric poet and as a mystical spiritual writer. Salvador Dali's painting of the crucifixion as seen from above the cross is based on a drawing John of the Cross made of a vision he had.

He is commemorated on the Roman Catholic General Calendar, and the calendars in the *Lutheran Book of Worship, Evangelical Lutheran Worship,* and in the Methodist *For All the Saints.*

FOR FURTHER READING

Brennan, Gerald. *St. John of the Cross: His Life and Poetry*, with a translation of the poetry by Lynda Nicholson. Cambridge: Cambridge University Press, 1973.

Dicken, Eric W. T. *The Crucible of Love: A Study of the Mysticism of St. Theresa of Jesus and St. John of the Cross.* New York: Sheed and Ward, 1963.

Kavanaugh, Kieran. *John of the Cross: Doctor of Light and Love.* New York: Crossroad, 2000.

————, ed. *John of the Cross: Selected Writings.* New York: Paulist, 1987.

Peters, E. A. *Spirit of Flame: A Study of St. John of the Cross.* New York: Morehouse, 1944.

————. *Handbook to the Life and Times of Saint Teresa and St. John of the Cross.* Westminster: Newman, 1954.

Thompson, Colin. *St. John of the Cross: Songs in the Night.* London: SPCK, 2003.

READING

From a spiritual canticle by St. John of the Cross

Though holy teachers have uncovered many mysteries and wonders, and devout souls have understood them in this earthly condition of ours, yet the greater part still remains to be unfolded by them, and even to be understood by them.

We must then penetrate more deeply into Christ, who, like a rich mine has many pockets containing treasures: however deep we dig we can never finish finding them all. Indeed, in every pocket new seams of fresh riches are discovered on all sides.

That is why the apostle Paul said that in Christ "are hidden all the treasures of the wisdom and knowledge" of God. [Col. 2:3] The soul cannot reach these treasures and lay hold of them unless it first crosses into and enters the thicket of interior and exterior suffering, and unless it first receives from God very many blessings in the intellect and in the senses, and has undergone long spiritual training.

All these are lesser things, but they dispose the soul for the lofty sanctuary of the knowledge of the mysteries of Christ, the highest wisdom attainable in this life.

Would that mortals might come at last to see that it is quite impossible to reach the thicket of the riches and wisdom of God except by first entering the thicket of much suffering, in such a way that the soul finds there its consolation and desire. The soul that longs for divine wisdom chooses first, and in truth, to enter the thicket of the cross.

Saint Paul therefore urges the Ephesians not to lose heart in the midst of tribulations, but to be "rooted and grounded in love" so that they "may have the power to comprehend, with all the saints, what is the breadth and length and height and depth and to know the love of Christ that surpasses knowledge, so that you may be filled with all the fullness of God." [Eph. 3:13, 17-19]

The gate to these riches of God's wisdom is the cross. Because it is a narrow gate, while many seek the joy to which the cross leads, few desire the cross itself.

Strophes 36-37. From the English translation of the Office of Readings from the Liturgy of the Hours by the International Committee on English in the Liturgy, rev. PHP.

PROPERS

Almighty God, you taught John of the Cross to find you in trials and hardships, to adore you in the darkness, and to tell of your love in his poems: Grant that, when all is dark, we may wait patiently for the light, and in the silence listen for your voice, and in all things trust your promises in Jesus Christ our Lord; who lives and reigns with you and the Holy Spirit, one God, now and forever.

L. W. Copwie and J. S. Gummer, *The Christian Calendar* (London: Weidenfeld & Nicolson, 1974), 238.

Readings:	Jeremiah 1:4-10
	Psalm 46
	1 Corinthians 2:1-10a
	Mark 10:35-45
Hymn of the Day:	
	"Come down, O Love divine" (LBW 508, LSB 501, ELW 804, H82 516)
Prayers:	For the love of the cross of Christ
	For patience in suffering
	For all on whom the cross of suffering is laid
	For strength and faith to endure the darkness
	For all who find prayer difficult or faith impossible
Preface:	A Saint (2) (BCP)
Color:	White

December 16

On this date the Spanish-language Lutheran service book *Libro de Liturgia y Cántico* notes the beginning of **Las Posadas** ("the inns"), a Mexican custom of visiting a succession of houses for the nine days before Christmas in memory of the Holy Family's search for room in an inn. Each night a party is held at a home in the neighborhood. At dusk, the guests gather outside, and a small child dressed as an angel leads children carrying the figures of Mary and Joseph, followed by boys and girls and the adults, all carrying candles. At the house, half of the number enter and half remain outside begging shelter. The door is opened, and the secular celebration begins.

December 17

O Sapientia

Church calendars often list this date as *O Sapientia*, the first of the seven great "O" Antiphons used with the Magnificat at Vespers on the final seven days before Christmas eve. These gems of liturgical composition address Christ by a succession of biblical titles (O Wisdom; O Adonai; O Root of Jesse; O Key of David; O Rising Dawn; O King of the nations; O Emmanuel) and implore his advent. The initial letter of the Latin form of each of these titles, in reverse order, spells "ERO CRAS" ("I will be there tomorrow"), understood as the reply of Christ to his waiting and praying church. Such wordplay was popular in the Middle Ages.

The antiphon for December 17 is "O Wisdom [*O Sapientia*], proceeding out of the mouth of the Most High, pervading and permeating all creation, mightily ordering all things: Come and teach us the way of understanding." It is woven from Sirach [Ecclesiasticus] 24:3; Wisdom 8:1; and Isaiah 40:14. The O Antiphons are widely known through John Mason Neale's popular Advent hymn, "O come, O come, Emmanuel." On the Sarum calendar in England, *O Sapientia* was assigned to December 16 and an eighth antiphon, "O virgin of virgins," was sung on December 23.

ALSO ON DECEMBER 17

The Byzantine calendar on this date commemorates the **Prophet Daniel and the Three Youths.** The calendar in the *Lutheran Service Book* (2006) also lists Daniel the Prophet and the Three Young Men on this date. See Daniel 1:3-7ff.

December 19

The *Lutheran Service Book* on the date commemorates **Adam and Eve.** Wilhelm Löhe's calendar remembered our first parents the day before Christmas, December 24.

DECEMBER

December 20

Katharina von Bora Luther, 1552

O n this date both *Evangelical Lutheran Worship* (2006) and the *Lutheran Service Book* (2006), following the German *Evangelical Calendar of Names* (1962), have introduced a commemoration of the woman who became known as Martin Luther's wife.

Katharina von Bora was born to an impoverished noble family January 29, 1499, probably in the village of Lippendorf, three miles south of Leipzig. He first education was at a Benedictine school at Brehna near Halle. Her mother died, and in 1505 her father remarried. In 1508 or 1509 she was sent to the Cistercian convent Marienthron at Nimbschen near Grimma. Most of the novitiates at this foundation were of noble extraction. Katharina's maternal aunt, Margarete von Haubitz, was the abbess, and a paternal aunt, Magdalene von Bora, was a nun there. On October 8, 1505, the sixteen-year-old Katharina von Bora made her final vows to live according to the precepts of Bernard of Clairvaux.

Nimbschen was close to the border of Saxony, and the abandonment of cloisters in Saxony was certain to have its effect in neighboring lands as Luther's teaching penetrated even convent walls. On Easter Day in 1523, twelve nuns from Marienthron managed to escape from the convent. They arrived in Wittenberg the next day. Some returned to their families, some found shelter with friends, some married. Katharina at age twenty-four was proud and particular in her choice of a husband. Jerome Baumgärtner, a student at Wittenberg, despite Luther's intercession on Katharina's behalf, lost interest in their developing relationship. The former nun had no interest in Luther's choice for her, Kaspar Glatz, and told Nicholas von Amsdorf that only he or Luther would be acceptable. Martin and Katharina were engaged and married on the same day, June 23, 1525, in the Black Cloister amid a small circle of friends. He was forty-two; she was twenty-six. On June 27 a public service and declaration that they had been married was held in the Town Church, and a celebration for a larger assembly followed.

Marriage brought many changes to Luther's manner of life. In a famous remark he declared, "One wakes up in the morning and finds a pair of pigtails on the pillow which were not there before." He seems not even to have had a pillow before his marriage. "Before I was married, the bed was not made for a whole year and became foul with sweat. But I worked so hard and was so very weary that I tumbled in without noticing."

With a firm and efficient hand Katharina von Bora Luther managed the enormous household in Wittenberg with its many residents and guests. She ran not only the kitchen but also the brewery and the stables of the Black Cloister, where in 1542 there were five cows, nine calves, four goats, thirteen pigs, and several horses. There was a fish pond with pike, perch, carp, and trout. There were gardens in the town and fields outside the gates and also the farm at Zulsdorf, Katharina's favorite property.

Following Martin Luther's death, February 18, 1546, during the disruption of the Smalkaldic War, Katharina fled to Dessau in 1547 and then to Magdeburg. She returned to Wittenberg to find her properties ruined. Plague broke out in Wittenberg in 1552. The University moved to Torgau. In the fall of that year, Katharina also went to Torgau. During the trip the horses were frightened, she fell or leaped from the carriage, and was seriously injured. She died December 20, 1552, in Torgau, and because of the unsettled conditions in Wittenberg, was buried in the Marienkirche in Torgau.

There were six children born to Martin and Katharina; four were living at their mother's death. John, called Hans (born 1526), studied law and became a court advisor. Martin (born 1531) studied theology but never had a regular call. Paul (born 1533) became a prominent physician, had six children, and through his son John Ernst the male line continued until 1759. Margarete (born 1534) married into a noble Prussian family; she died at age thirty-six; her descendents continue to the present.

FOR FURTHER READING

Bainton, Roland. *Women of the Reformation in Germany and Italy.* Minneapolis: Augsburg, 1971.

Markwald, Rudolf K., and Marilynn Morris Markwald. *Katharina von Bora: A Reformation Life.* St. Louis: Concordia, 2002.

Stein, Armin. *Katharine von Bora, Luther's Wife: A Picture from Life.* Philadelphia: G.W. Frederick, 1890; Philadelphia: General Council Publication Board, 1917.

READING

From *Luther and His Times* by E. G. Schwiebert

Although Luther was perfectly honest in admitting that he was not motivated by love in marrying Katharine, it was not long before he grew very fond of her. A year later he already wrote to a friend:

> Kathie sends greetings, and thanks you for thinking her worthy of such a letter. She is well, by the grace of God, and is in all things more . . . obliging than I had dared to hope,—thanks be to God!—so that I would not exchange my poverty for the wealth of Croesus.

Kathie was no doubt just the type of wife Luther needed. She was a conscientious mother, an efficient housekeeper, a wise manager of the farms, gardens, cattle, and other livestock, for which Luther had so little time. After 1540 he occasionally called her the "boss of Zulsdorf," for sometimes she made lengthy visits to the farm which Luther had purchased when her brother was about to lose it through foreclosure.

DECEMBER

Kathie's management must have added considerably to Luther's income, making it easier to provide for his family and some dozen nieces, nephews, aunts, and needy relatives, and also freed Luther from many family details and responsibilities. Luther, who had little time from his labors to help rear obedient, God-fearing children, often thanked God for such a "pious and true wife on whom the husband's heart can rely."

From E. G. Schwiebert, *Luther and His Times: The Reformation from a New Perspective* (St. Louis: Concordia, 1950), 593.

PROPERS

God of steadfast love, you joined your servants Katharina von Bora and Martin Luther in holy marriage and established in their life together a model of the Christian home: Brighten our lives with the wonder of love, bring into order the chaos of our manifold responsibilities, and enrich us with your life, that we may learn the joy of serving others and at last inherit the gladness of your unending kingdom; through your Son Jesus Christ our Lord, who lives and reigns with you and the Holy Spirit, one God, now and forever.

PHP

Readings:	Colossians 3:12-17
	Psalm 67
	John 15:9-12
Hymn of the Day:	
	"Our Father, by whose name all parenthood is known" (LBW 357, H82 587, LSB 863, ELW 640)
Prayers:	For wives and husbands
	For the strengthening of Christian homes
	For all whose duties are many and burdensome
	For faithfulness to Christ to the end
Preface:	Marriage (LBW or BCP)
Color:	White

December 21

St. Thomas, Apostle

Not the "doubter" (for he did believe) but one with a restless, unsatisfied, probing mind who was not easily taken in: such is the apostle who is commemorated this day. He was a man who earnestly sought the truth and who found it in Jesus and who proclaimed his long-sought faith in the ringing declaration of recognition that is the climax of the Fourth Gospel, "My Lord and my God!"

Practically all the information about "Thomas called Didymus" is found in the Fourth Gospel. "Thomas" seems not to be a personal name but an epithet meaning "twin"; *Didymus* is the Greek and *Teoma* (Thomas) is the Aramaic for "twin." There is a tradition that he was the twin of Jesus, at least in appearance. He is portrayed in the Gospel as something of a plodding literalist who is nonetheless an earnest searcher for truth. After Jesus' resurrection Thomas doubted and sought convincing proof that Jesus was in fact alive. His resulting confession of faith went beyond what he saw with his eyes and what he touched with his hands to a statement of the belief of Johannine Christians: "My Lord and my God."

Later legend associates St. Thomas with Bartholomew, Matthew, Simon, and Jude, the five "Apostles of the East," and tells of his evangelization of the lands between the Caspian Sea and the Persian Gulf and of his missionary travels in India. The third-century *Acts of Thomas* says he entered India as a carpenter, preached the gospel, performed miracles, and died a martyr at Mylapore near Madras. One of the greatest of the early basilicas (fourth century) was the Church of St. Thomas in Edessa, Syria, and his body is said to have been buried there, but the stories of his work in India claim that he was buried at St. Thomas Mount near Madras. The *Acts of Thomas* contains not only the earliest accounts of his work in India but the beautiful Syriac poem called the *Hymn of the Soul* as well.

It is possible, although modern scholars think it unlikely, that St. Thomas reached India. There is a body of Christians, the "Christians of St. Thomas," along the Malabar coast in southern India who claim spiritual descent from Thomas and who were in India at least a thousand years before the arrival of European missionaries in the sixteenth century.

Eastern Churches have commemorated St. Thomas since the sixth century, and the Roman observance dates from the ninth century. His feast day in the East is October 6; the Roman Catholic Church has on its present calendar moved the feast out of Advent to July 3, the date of his commemoration in the Syrian Church. *Evangelical Lutheran Worship* accepts that change, but other Lutheran and Episcopal calendars retain the traditional Western date.

In art, St. Thomas is usually shown holding a carpenter's square and rule.

FOR FURTHER READING

Farquahr, J. N. "The Apostle Thomas in North India." *Bulletin of the John Rylands Library* 10 (1926): 80–111; 11 (1927): 20–50.

Medlycott, G. E. *India and the Apostle Thomas.* 1905.

Most, Glenn W. *Doubting Thomas.* Cambridge: Harvard University Press, 2005.

Pick, B., trans. *The Acts of Thomas.* Chicago, 1909.

Turner, H. E. W., and H. Montefiore. *Thomas and the Evangelists.* London: Allenson, 1962.

Wilson, R. McL. *Studies in the Gospel of Thomas.* London: Mowbray, 1960.

DECEMBER

READING

From a sermon by Kaj Munk for the First Sunday after Easter

And now, this Gospel is for you, my Christian friend, who struggles with doubt and faith, with anxiety and denial. This is the Gospel that does not come to catechize you and force upon you certain dogmas, or to condemn you, but comes only to listen to the heartbeat of your soul. If it leans toward Jesus no matter what happens it has chosen Him and wants to belong to Him, then the Gospel says to you: Be faithful, continue in the faith.

It is great to have assurance of faith, but perhaps you do not belong to those who can always take this for granted. However, the Master is also able to use the Thomas type. Such people have a place in His group of disciples. And let me tell you that when the time is at hand, Jesus himself will come and bring an end to your uncertainty and your timid spirit. You will understand that it is not what you fail to understand that matters. Christ has had disciples who did not understand the Virgin Birth and the Resurrection of the body and the Sacraments. Do not just stare blindly at them. Let not the devil fool you into thinking that unless you understand these things, you cannot be a disciple of Christ.

Abstain from empty and morbid speculation about whether you believe or not. This will get you no place but downwards. But be faithful to your inner soul, which once and for all has made its choice. Practice Christianity and at the proper time, even though the doors be ever so tightly closed, Christ himself will appear before you and show you the hands that were pierced for your sin; and you will bow down in prayer, crying to Him in repentance and joy, "My Lord and my God!"

And after you have first addressed Him with so great a name, other things will no longer seen unintelligible. Perhaps it will then come to pass that the things you could not accept before will become dearest to you and your common sense.

But our Gospel for today goes much farther. It embraces those who do not even suspect that it is for them. There are those who deny Christianity because of the worldliness of the Christians, and because of the weakness and sin of the Church. These people, as far as they themselves can tell, deny Christ; but He dwells in their humility of heart and in their search for truth. They may experience the same "Thomas week" of despair. It pains them that what is genuinely good is trodden down with an iron heel, and that the struggle for justice seems hopeless. Yet they are faithful, and they prevail. To them it should be said that at the end of the week Christ will appear before them just as He really is, the guest of their hearts and the final conqueror of death and all its works and all its ways; and each one will greet Him saying, "My Lord, and my God!"

Kaj Munk, *By the Rivers of Babylon: Fifteen Sermons*, trans. J.M. Jensen (Blair: Lutheran Publishing House, 1945), 23–25.

PROPERS

Almighty and everliving God, you strengthened your apostle Thomas with firm and certain faith in your Son's resurrection: Keep us, through all our days, steadfast in that same faith in Jesus Christ, our Lord and our God, who lives and reigns with you and the Holy Spirit, one God, now and forever.

PHP, after BCP and TLH

Readings:	Habakkuk 2:1-4
	Psalm 126 *or* 117
	Hebrews 10:35-11:1 *or* Ephesians 2:19-22
	John 20:24-29
Hymn of the Day:	
	"Lo! He comes with clouds descending" (H82 57, 58; LBW 27, LSB 336; abridged in ELW 435)
	or "How oft, O Lord, thy face hath shone" (H82 242)
Prayers:	For a healthy skepticism
	For a renewal of the Easter faith
	For grace to receive Christ
Preface:	Apostles
Color:	Red

December 23

Thorlak, Bishop of Skalholt, 1193

Thorlak (Thorlakur in Icelandic) Thorhallsson was born in Fljotslith, Iceland in 1133. He was ordained a deacon when he was fifteen (some say thirteen) and a priest when he was twenty (some say eighteen). He went to study in France at Paris and in England at Lincoln, and there he acquired ideas of ecclesiastical discipline that were as yet not enforced in Iceland. Upon his return he surprised his friends by refusing, after some hesitation, to marry a rich widow. Unlike most of the Icelandic clergy, he chose to live apart from others, engaged in a life of prayer, study, and pastoral ministry. In 1168 he received a bequest of land from a farmer at Thykkvibaer and there, having become a Canon Regular of St. Augustine, established a monastery and became its abbot, soon gaining a reputation for his sanctity. In 1178 he was consecrated bishop of Skalholt, and in the face of much opposition he set about a thorough reformation, in which he had the support of his metropolitan in Norway, St. Eystein, Archbishop of Nidaros (1158–1188), with whom Thorlak collaborated in endeavoring to enforce clerical celibacy and drawing up a code of law for both clergy and laity. Perhaps Thorlak's major achievement was to persuade

Iceland's chieftain church-proprietors to cede ownership of buildings and endowments, while still retaining a patron's responsibility for upkeep and maintenance.

Thorlak died in 1193 and was declared a saint by the Althing (Parliament) in 1198. (The popes did not reserve the process of canonization to themselves until 1234.) In 1994 Pope John Paul II, in an Apostolic Letter, acknowledged Thorlak's patronage of Iceland. His feast day is December 23, but he is also remembered in Iceland on a second feast day, July 20, "Thorlak's Mass in summer," when, after he was declared a saint in 1198, his remains were exhumed and enshrined.

He is the subject of an Icelandic saga, *Thorlakssaga*.

Two other Icelandic bishops were locally revered as saints: Jon Ogmundsson (d. 1121) and Gudmundur Arason (d. 1237).

FOR FURTHER READING

Hunter, L. S., ed. *Scandinavian Churches: A Picture of the Development and the Life of the Churches of Denmark, Finland, Iceland, Norway, and Sweden.* London: Faber & Faber, 1965.

Vesteinsson, Orri. *The Christianization of Iceland: Priests, Power, and Social Change 1000–1300.* Oxford: Oxford University Press, 2001.

Vidalin, Jon. *Whom Wind and Waves Obey: Selected Sermons of Jon Vidalin.* Trans. and intro. Michael Fell. New York: Peter Lang, 1998.

READING

From "Death's Uncertain Hour and Christ's Victory" by Hallgrimur Petursson (1614–1674)

> For all, without exception,
> Our fate it is to die.
> Perish the vain deception,
> That I shall be passed by.
> My nature I inherit
> From Adam's fallen strain,
> And by my deeds I merit
> To turn to dust again.
>
> I did not earn possession
> Of this my life on earth.
> My soul, by God's concession,
> Was lent to me at birth.
> God makes his own decision
> When to reclaim his loan,
> And sends death on the mission
> To bring Him back His own.
>
> This messenger so awful
> No mortal can evade.
> His claim is right and lawful,

Surrender must be made.
The summons, without warning,
Will no delay admit,
So, be it night or morning,
I must at once submit.

Our great Redeemer, Jesus,
Now sits on heaven's throne.
With watchful eye He sees us,
And cares for all His own.
Victor o'er Death, by dying,
Himself upon the tree,
For ever justifying
A sinner such as me.

Dying, He crushed Death's power
And broke his poisoned sting.
Now in our latest hour
To Christ's dear cross we cling.
Our frame, like dress discarded,
Surrenders to decay;
Our soul, by angels guarded,
To heaven wings its way.

He ever is before me,
To Him my heart I give.
Whatever may come o'er me,
In Him I move and live.
He is my consolation;
He is my very life.
I rest in His salvation,
And fear not Death's sharp strife.

He gives me strength for living,
In death His help is nigh.
Though weakness cause misgiving,
I do not fear to die.
O, Death, my Lord has spoken,
For me His blood was spilt,
And now thy yoke is broken,
Be welcome, when thou wilt!

Hallgrimur Petursson, *Hymns of the Passion,* trans. Arthur Charles Gook,
stanzas 7-13 (Reykjavik: Hallgrims Church, 1978). This hymn, in whole or
in part, is sung at every funeral in Iceland to this day.

PROPERS

God of ordered strength and holiness, you raised up your priest and bishop Thorlak to deepen discipline in the church in Iceland and to strengthen the morality
of its clergy: Grant that, following his example, your people may give themselves
gladly to live under your rule and commit themselves without reserve to doing
your will in lives of prayer and service to those in need, to the honor of your

DECEMBER

Name; through your Son Jesus Christ our Lord, who lives and reigns with you and the Holy Spirit, one God, now and forever.

PHP

Readings:	Ezekiel 34:11-16
	Psalm 84
	1 Peter 5:1-4
	John 21:15-17
Hymn of the Day:	
	"How marvelous God's greatness" (LBW 515, ELW 830)
Prayers:	For the church and people of Iceland
	For the Church of St. Peter in Skalholt
	For a deepened appreciation of the virtue of discipline and obedience
	For the cathedral, bishop, and people of the Diocese of Nidaros (Trondheim)
Preface:	A Saint (3) (BCP)
Color:	White

December 25

The Nativity of Our Lord

By the year 336 the birthday of Christ was being celebrated on December 25 in the liturgy of the city of Rome. The origin of the festival is a subject of considerable debate. According to the older "history of religions hypothesis," the celebration of December 25 was introduced to replace the pagan festival of the Unconquered Sun, *Natale Solis Invicti*, which the Roman emperor Aurelian, to unite and strengthen his empire, had established throughout the empire in 274 in honor of the Syrian sun-god of Emesa and which he ordered to be kept on December 25, a celebration of the winter solstice. The Church of Rome, according to this hypothesis, remembering biblical passages such as Malachi 4:2, which speaks of the "sun of righteousness," and John 8:12, in which Jesus refers to himself as "the Light of the world," introduced into its worship the celebration of the birthday of the true Sun, which knows no setting. Such Christ-as-sun symbolism was deeply embedded in Christian consciousness.

During the twentieth century, another explanation developed, the "calculation hypothesis." From the third century Christians had attempted to calculate the date of Jesus' birth. Human life, it was thought, ought to begin and end on the same date to form a complete and perfect cycle. Because Jesus, above all others, lived a perfect life, the day of his death must also be the date of his conception. According to a variety of calculations, March 25 was widely held to be the date of Jesus' crucifixion, and therefore it ought also to be the date of his conception.

His birth, exactly nine months later, took place on December 25. (The Eastern Churches, which fixed the date of the conception and crucifixion on April 6, kept the Nativity festival exactly nine months later, January 6.)

Whatever its actual origin, the festival of the nativity of the Lord spread rapidly, in large measure because it focused attention not simply on the work but most of all on the person of the God-man, and the celebration of his incarnation would express liturgically the Catholic faith defined at Nicaea, that Jesus Christ had two natures, divine and human, but was one person.

In the fourth century there was one mass celebrated by the pope on Christmas day, at nine o'clock in the morning. In the fifth century a midnight mass in the Basilica of St. Maria Maggiore (St. Mary Major) was added, and in the sixth century a third mass was introduced in the Church of St. Anastasia, December 25 being her feast day. Since then, in the Roman tradition Christmas is celebrated with three masses: the midnight mass of the angels' announcement of the birth of the Savior, the dawn mass of the shepherds meeting the child in the manger, and the mass during the day, the mass of the faithful, proclaiming the theological meaning of the feast, the mystery of the incarnation, set out in the prologue to St. John's Gospel (1:1-18).

Caesar Baronius (1538–1607), in his revision of the Roman Martyrology of 1586, composed a solemn proclamation of Christmas for use on the Vigil of Christmas, read in chapters and monasteries and more recently read or sung in parish churches. This introduction to the feast, following the chronology accepted at the time it was composed, treats the Nativity of Jesus Christ as the greatest event in the history of the world since creation, eloquently placing the birth of Christ in relation to a variety of significant historical events, from creation to the exodus to the founding of Rome, to declare that this event took place in human history and that it really happened.

> The twenty-fifth day of December.
> In the five thousand one hundred ninety-ninth year of the creation of the world,
> > from the time when God in the beginning created the heaven and the earth;
> the two thousand nine hundred fifty-seventh year after the flood;
> the two thousand fifteenth year from the birth of Abraham;
> the one thousand five hundred tenth year from Moses and the going forth of the
> > people of Israel from of Egypt;
> the one thousand thirty-second year from the anointing of David the king;
> in the sixty-fifth week according to the prophecy of Daniel;
> in the one hundred ninety-fourth Olympiad;
> the seven hundred fifty-second year from the foundation of the city of Rome;
> the forty-second year of the reign of Octavian Augustus;
> the whole world being at peace,
> in the sixth age of the world,
> Jesus Christ, the eternal God and the Son of the eternal Father,
> > desiring to sanctify the world by his most merciful coming,
> > being conceived by the Holy Spirit,
> > and nine months having passed since his conception,
> > [*here the voice is raised and all kneel*]

was born in Bethlehem of Judea of the Virgin Mary, made man.
The Nativity of our Lord Jesus Christ according to the flesh.

It is a most impressive proclamation, and may serve as a reading at Morning Prayer or as an introduction to the celebration of the Eucharist of Christmas Day.

More than a birthday celebration, more than the celebration of the beginning of a new age, Christmas is nothing less than the proclamation of the *Parousia*. The point of the birthday remembrance is to reinforce the church's confidence that he who came once to his waiting people will, with equal certainty, come again in glory to his expectant church.

Pre-Christian symbols have easily been incorporated into the Christmas celebration. Evergreen trees and holly tell of life that endured the cold and darkness of winter. Lights and fires were common to encourage the rebirth of the sun. The custom of decorating trees originated perhaps in Strasbourg at the beginning of the seventeenth century, and German-born Prince Albert brought the custom to England. In 1843 the first commercial Christmas greeting cards were produced in London. There was a persistent belief that on Christmas Eve all the cattle knelt in their stalls. "Now they are all on their knees," an elder in Thomas Hardy's poem "The Oxen" declares on "Christmas Eve and twelve of the clock."

In America the celebration of Christmas was largely a nineteenth-century creation. Puritan influence suppressed the observance of Christmas in New England and elsewhere. In 1847 no New England college had a Christmas holiday. Early in the nineteenth century a master at Boston Latin School on Christmas Day asked his class whether any students knew what day it was; no one knew. Not until 1836 did the first state, Alabama, declare Christmas a holiday; during the Civil War, thirteen states made Christmas an official holiday.

Washington Irving's *Knickerbocker History of New York* (1809) remade St. Nicholas into jolly old St. Nick. In 1822 Clement Clark Moore borrowed the idea for his "An Account of a Visit from St. Nicholas" (" 'Twas the night before Christmas"). Charles Dickens's *A Christmas Carol* gave the holiday a moral anchor. Thomas Nast's illustrations created stories that locate Santa Claus's workshop at the North Pole where he and the elves make toys, and picture him dressed him in fur-trimmed suit. In 1957 Ascension Lutheran Church in Danville, Virginia, introduced the decoration of the Christmas tree in the church with symbols of Christ, which they called "Chrismons" (from "Christ" and "monograms"). The practice spread widely in Lutheran churches in America.

The name Christmas, from Christ-Mass, can be traced to the twelfth century.

FOR FURTHER READING

Coffin, Tristram P. *The Book of Christmas Folklore.* New York: Seabury, 1973.
Kelly, Joseph F. *The Origins of Christmas.* Collegeville: Liturgical, 2004.
Studwell, William E. *Christmas Carols: A Reference Guide.* New York: Garland, 1984.
See also under The Epiphany, January 6.

READING

From a Christmas sermon by Martin Luther

In my sin, my death, I must take leave of all created things. No, sun, moon, stars, all creatures, physicians, emperors, kings, wise men and potentates cannot help me. When I die I shall see nothing but black darkness, and yet that light, "To you is born this day the Savior" [Luke 2:11], remains in my eyes and fills all heaven and earth. The Savior will help me when all have forsaken me. And when the heavens and the stars and all creatures stare at me with horrible mien, I see nothing in heaven and earth but this child. So great should that light which declares that he is my Savior become in my eyes that I can say: Mary, you did not bear this child for yourself alone. The child is not yours; you did not bring him forth for yourself, but for me, even though you are his mother, even though you held him in your arms and wrapped him in swaddling clothes and picked him up and laid him down. But I have a greater honor than your honor as his mother. For your honor pertains to your motherhood of the body of the child, but my honor is this, that you have my treasure, so that I know none, neither men nor angels, who can help me except this child whom you, O Mary, hold in your arms. If a man could put out of his mind all that he is and has except this child, and if for him everything—money, goods, power, or honor—fades into darkness and he despises everything on earth compared with this child, so that heaven with its stars and earth with all its power and all its treasures becomes as nothing to him, that man would have the true gain and fruit of this message of the angel. And for us the time must come when suddenly all will be darkness and we shall know nothing but this message of the angel: "I bring you good news of great joy; for to you is born this day the Savior."

Martin Luther, "Sermon on the Afternoon of Christmas Day, 1530," *Luther's Works,* vol. 51, ed. John W. Doberstein (Philadelphia: Fortress Press, 1959), 214.

PROPERS

Mass at Midnight
O God, you have caused this holy night to shine with the brightness of the true Light: Grant that we, who have known the mystery of that Light on earth, may also enjoy him perfectly in heaven; where with you and the Holy Spirit he lives and reigns, one God, in glory everlasting.

Gelasian, Gregorian sacramentaries; RS, BCP, LBW, ELW

Mass at Dawn
Almighty God, you have poured upon us the new light of your incarnate Word: Grant that this light, enkindled in our hearts, may shine forth in our lives; through Jesus Christ our Lord, who lives and reigns with you, in the unity of the Holy Spirit, one God, now and forever.

Gregorian sacramentary, RS; trans. BCP Christmas 1; LBW, ELW Christmas 2

DECEMBER

or

Almighty God, you have made yourself known in your Son, Jesus, redeemer of the world. We pray that his birth as a human child will set us free from the old slavery of our sin; through Jesus Christ our Lord, who lives and reigns with you and the Holy Spirit, one God, now and forever.

Gelasian sacramentary, LBW

or

O God, you make us glad by the yearly festival of the birth of your only Son Jesus Christ: Grant that we, who joyfully receive him as our Redeemer, may with sure confidence behold him when he comes to be our Judge; who lives and reigns with you and the Holy Spirit, one God, now and forever.

Gelasian, Gregorian sacramentaries, BCP; RS Vigil of Christmas

Mass During the Day

Almighty God, who wonderfully created, and yet more wonderfully restored, the dignity of human nature: Grant that we may share the divine life of him who humbled himself to share our humanity, your Son Jesus Christ; who lives and reigns with you and the Holy Spirit, one God, now and forever.

Leonine sacramentary, RS; BCP Christmas 2; LBW, ELW Christmas 1

or

Almighty God, you have given your only-begotten Son to take our nature upon him, and to be born [this day] of a pure virgin: Grant that we, who have been born again and made your children by adoption and grace, may daily be renewed by your Holy Spirit; through our Lord Jesus Christ, to whom with you and the same Spirit be honor and glory, now and forever.

1549, 1662 BCP; rev. ELW

Mass at Midnight Readings:
Isaiah 9:2-4, (5), 6-7
Psalm 96 *or* 96:1-4, 11-12
Titus 2:11-14
Luke 2:1-14 (15-20)

Mass at Dawn Readings:
Isaiah 62:6-7, 10-12
Psalm 97 *or* 97:1-4, 11-12
Titus 3:4-7
Luke 2:(1-14) 15-20

Mass During the Day Readings:
Isaiah 52:7-10
Psalm 98:1-6 (RC) or Psalm 97 (LBW) or Psalm 98 *or* 98:1-6 (BCP)
Hebrews 1:1-6 (9-12)
John 1:1-14 (15-18)

Hymn of the Day:
        "Of the Father's love begotten" (H82 82, LBW 42, LSB 384, ELW 295)
Prayers: For the light of Christ's glory to shine through us
        For grace to adore the mystery of the incarnation
        For the poor and the despised, first to hear the announcement of Jesus' birth
        For those to whom the coming of God in human flesh means nothing
        For peace in the Holy Land where Christ was born
Preface: Christmas/Incarnation
Color: White

December 26

St. Stephen, Deacon, Martyr

Christmas is the yearly expectation of redemption and the proclamation of the consummation. Three feast days came to be closely associated with Christmas: St. Stephen, St. John, and Holy Innocents. The ancient association of these martyrs' days reinforces the eschatological understanding of the celebration of Christmas. The birth of Jesus is more than a commemoration of his birthday. His birth into this world prefigures the birth into the next world of his martyrs, who follow in his train. The birth of Christ is a judgment on the persecution and rejection of God and his word, and means joy for those who remain faithful and steadfast even in the face of great persecution. These are days of judgment as well as joy.

On what in Germany is called "second Christmas Day," the church celebrates another birth, the birth into heaven of Stephen, the first Christian martyr. His feast day is yet another way of declaring the church's confidence that the out-come of the Christian struggle is certain. It is a further testimony to the kingdom made ready for God's people, prepared now for those who would "take it by force" (Matt. 11:12).

Stephen, who, Luke reports, was "full of grace and power and did great wonders among the people," was the first of the band of martyrs to follow Christ through death into life and is therefore sometimes called "Proto-martyr." His devotion to the faith, his love for his persecutors, and his dramatic death by stoning that is reported in detail in Acts 6–7 make this deacon and martyr a much-revered figure among the saints.

The feast of St. Stephen was established very early in the history of the church, and it is possible that the date of his commemoration recalls the actual day of his death. In the Eastern Church, December 26 is the feast of the God-bearer, Mary the Theotokos, and St. Stephen is remembered on December 27. In the Western church, St. Stephen's Day is the first of a succession of three festivals immediately following Christmas—St. Stephen, St. John, the Holy Innocents—that associate the three "heavenly birthdays" with the birthday of Christ: as he was born into this world from heaven, so they were born from this world into heaven.

In Lutheran churches under German influence, December 26 has been celebrated as the Second Christmas Day, replacing St. Stephen's Day (see Bach's *Christmas Oratorio*). In Finland it is the custom to ride a horse or horse-drawn vehicle on St. Stephen's Day; this observance is probably connected with the Scandinavian legend of Stephen as the stable boy of King Herod.

FOR FURTHER READING

Simon, Marcel. *St. Stephen and the Hellenists in the Primitive Church.* London: Longmans, 1958.
Scharlemann, M. H. "Stephen: A Singular Saint." *Analecta Biblica* 34. Rome, 1958.

READING

From a sermon for St. Stephen's Day by Kaj Munk

The Christ Child is the world's Savior and Prince of Peace because He is the world's greatest war Lord. Apparently there is the most glaring contrast between the Christmas gospel and that for St. Stephen's Day—between the Christ Child and the first Christian martyr, But in reality there is the closest connection.

The pagan Christmas with eating and drinking and parties and family joy may well be contained in the Christian celebration, but it can never take the place of it. Jesus Himself took an interest in family life, and He attended parties; but He was, nevertheless, ever on the way to the cross. Let us sing Ingemann songs and eat goose and play with our children about the glittering Christmas tree; but we must never forget that the coming of Christ to earth means dauntless struggle against evil. And if we kneel by the manger in other than sentimental moods, we shall become aware that one hand of the little Child is open and kindly, the other clenched in blood. . . .

We wish one another Merry Christmas. And we mean: may your Christmas goose be delicious—or your meatballs, if that is the best you can afford this year; may you have fuel to keep your house warm; may you have friends and loved ones about you; may your tree glitter its wonted beauty and the hymns sound with their old power. And may there, through it all, be one song in your heart: "My Jesus, I want to be where Thou alone wilt have me." Yes, but there are so many doubts and questions that spoil my Christmas joy.

Well, but who promised your joy? It may be better that you have a poor Christmas. Don't be like a spoiled child and think of God as a great Santa Claus who has in His bag some sort of electromagnet with which to give your brain cells such a shot that everything becomes gloriously clear to you, and that you can be happy, in harmony with yourself and the world. My friend, perhaps your doctor can do that for you with a stimulant that will send the blood to the brain and clarify your mind so that you can see things in bright perspective. This has nothing to do with real joy. True Christmas joy, no matter how much or how little of it you may comprehend, means that you have Christ, and that your go where He wants you to go.

Kaj Munk, *Four Sermons,* trans. J. M. Jensen (Blair, Neb.: Lutheran Publication House, 1944), 20–22.

PROPERS

We give you thanks, O Lord of glory, for the example of the first martyr Stephen, who looked up to heaven and prayed for his persecutors to your Son Jesus Christ, who stands at your right hand; where he lives and reigns with you and the Holy Spirit, one God, in glory everlasting.

Gregorian sacramentary, RS, BCP, LBW, ELW

Readings: Jeremiah 26:1-9, 12-15 *or* 2 Chronicles 24:17-22
              Psalm 31
              Acts 6:8-7:2a, 51-60
              Matthew 10:17-22 *or* Matthew 23:34-39
Hymn of the Day:
              "Let us now our voices raise" (H82 237, SBH 546) (sung in SBH to *Tempus adest floridum,* familiar as the melody of "Good King Wenceslaus looked out on the Feast of Stephen")
              or "The Son of God goes forth to war" (LBW 183, LSB 661, H40 549)
              or "When Stephen, full of power and grace" (H82 243)
Prayers: For courage to explore the mysteries of both birth and death
              For our enemies
              For the enemies of the nation
              For the gift of love
              For courageously effective preachers
Preface: Christmas/Incarnation
Color: Red

December 27

St. John, Apostle, Evangelist

There has been a tendency in the church to connect the great New Testament saints with the Nativity, joining the day of the Lord's birth to the saints' heavenly birthdays. It has seemed natural, as the church thinks of the incarnation, which displayed God's light and love to the world, to commemorate at this time the apostle through whom that light was seen to shine and who tenderly and lovingly wrote about that love of which he was a witness. It is natural, moreover, for John, who unfolded the great mystery of the incarnation, to stand beside the crib, and for him who saw the new heaven and the new earth (Revelation 21) to be commemorated as the church is confirmed in its hope of the consummation.

John the son of Zebedee was one of the inner circle of the Twelve, along with his brother James and Peter. John was a fisherman, and he is often assumed to be the "disciple whom Jesus loved" (the "beloved disciple" in older translations) of the Fourth Gospel.

St. John is traditionally regarded as the author of the Fourth Gospel and the three epistles that bear his name and also the book of Revelation, the Apocalypse. Especially in connection with Revelation, he is called St. John "the Divine," that is, the Theologian. After a period of exile on the island of Patmos, where tradition says he wrote Revelation, St. John is said to have lived at Ephesus, where he died about the year 100 at an advanced age. Irenaeus, at the end of the second century, liked to recall how Polycarp in his old age had talked about the apostle whom he had known while growing up in Ephesus. In extreme old age, Jerome reports, he would be carried into the church to say to the congregation, "My little children, love one another." It is an instructive contrast to his youth when he and his brother were nicknamed *Boanerges*, "sons of thunder," because of their impetuous and hotheaded nature.

John is believed to be the only one of the twelve Apostles who did not die a martyr's death; thus the three feast days following Christmas Day are woven together to cover the various possibilities of following Christ into death and heavenly birth: Stephen was a martyr in will and deed; John was a martyr in will but not in deed; the Holy Innocents were martyrs in deed but not in will, being too young to make a conscious choice.

In the fourth century a church was dedicated to St. John at Constantinople, and it is possible that the date of his feast is based on the date of that dedication. Some Eastern calendars have December 27 as a day of commemoration of St. John and St. James, the brother of the Lord, but the Western Church, ever since it accepted the feast, has appointed it for St. John alone. In the East, May 8 is the feast day of St. John the Apostle and Theologian.

An interesting custom on St. John's day in northern Europe and England during the Middle Ages was the blessing and drinking of wine, called the "love of St. John." According to legend, John once drank poisoned wine and was unharmed; hence his symbol of a chalice with a serpent in it. This blessed wine was then used ceremonially throughout the year, especially by the bride and groom after weddings. St. John had encouraged his disciples to love one another, and it is his Gospel that tells of Jesus' changing water into wine at the wedding at Cana in Galilee.

FOR FURTHER READING

Brown, Raymond E. *The Gospel according to John.* 2 vols. Anchor Bible. Garden
City: Doubleday, 1966, 1970.

———. *The Epistles of John.* Anchor Bible. Garden City, N.Y.: Doubleday, 1982.

Culpepper, R. Alan. *John the Son of Zebedee: The Life of a Legend.* Minneapolis:
Fortress Press, 2000.

Nunn, H. P. V. *The Son of Zebedee and the Fourth Gospel.* New York: Macmillan,
1927.

Sanders, J. N. "Who was the Disciple Whom Jesus Loved?" In *Studies in the Fourth
Gospel,* ed. F. L. Cross, 72–82. London: Mowbray, 1957.

READING

From *Revelations of Divine Love* by Julian of Norwich

It was at this time that our Lord showed me spiritually how intimately he loves
us. I saw that he is everything that we know to be good and helpful. In his love
he clothes us, enfolds and embraces us; that tender love completely surrounds us,
never to leave us. As I saw it he is everything that is good.

And he showed me more, a little thing, the size of a hazel-nut, on the palm of
may hand, round like a ball. I looked at it thoughtfully and wondered, "What is
this?" And the answer came, "It is all that is made." I marveled that it continued to
exist and did not suddenly disintegrate; it was so small. And again my mind supplied the answer, "It exists, both now and forever, because God loves it." In short,
everything owes its existence to the love of God.

Julian of Norwich, *Revelations of Divine Love,* trans. Clifton Wolters (Baltimore: Penguin, 1966),
67–68.

PROPERS

Shed upon your Church, O Lord, the brightness of your light, that we, being illumined by the teaching of your apostle and evangelist John, may so walk in the
light of your truth, that at length we may attain to the fullness of eternal life;
through Jesus Christ our Lord, who lives and reigns with you and the Holy Spirit,
one God, forever and ever.

Leonine, Gelasian sacramentaries, RS, BCP, LBW, ELW

DECEMBER

Readings: *RC*: Psalm 97:1-2, 5-6, 11-12
                    1 John 1:1-4
                    John 20:2-8
               BCP: Exodus 33:18-23
                    Psalm 92 *or* 92:1-4, 11-14

                    1 John 1:1-9
                    John 21:19b-24
          LBW, ELW: Genesis 1:1-5, 26-3
                    Psalm 116:10-17 (12-19)
                    1 John 1:1—2:2
                    John 21:20-25
          LSB: Revelation 1:1-6
                    1 John 1:1—2:2
                    John 21:20-25
Hymn of the Day:
          "Praise God for John, Evangelist" (H82 245)
          or "O Word of God incarnate" (LBW 231, LSB 523, ELW 514, H82 632)
Prayers: For the work of the new creation in us
              For the spirit of awe and reverence in the presence of God
              For a glimpse of the glory of God in Jesus Christ
              For increased knowledge of the Incarnation
Preface: Christmas/Incarnation or Apostles
Color: White

December 28

The Holy Innocents, Martyrs

The commemoration of the Holy Innocents was introduced to the calendar early in the life of the church, yet there remains uneasiness about its observance as is seen in the frequent revision of the collects appointed for the day.

If the church were interested in a strict chronological reliving of the life of Jesus, this day would be kept after the Epiphany, as is sometimes suggested. The church's interest, however, is in proclaiming the gospel of a kingdom that has begun but which is to be completed in the future. The day of the slaughter of the Innocents fits with the previous two days to make a little trilogy that emphasizes the scope of Christian martyrdom: Stephen was a martyr in will and in deed, John a martyr in will but not in deed, the Innocents martyrs in deed but not in will.

The Holy Innocents were the children of Bethlehem, numbered fourteen thousand on Eastern calendars, who were slaughtered by order of King Herod in his attempt to eliminate the infant Jesus. There is no record of this event outside Matthew's Gospel, but it is not impossible, given Herod's character. He drowned his sixteen-year-old brother-in-law, the high priest; killed his uncle, aunt, and mother-in-law, with several members of his brother-in-law's family; his own two sons; and some three hundred officials he accused of siding with his sons.

Although the Holy Children, as they are called in the Eastern Church, were not believers and were unaware of the reason for their fate, they were nonetheless killed for the sake of Christ, and in a sense, in place of him, and the church by the beginning of the third century recognized them as martyrs. Their feast dates from the fourth century in North Africa; it was universal by the sixth century. It has been suggested that in early times the festival commemorated all newly baptized infants, tying baptism not only to Easter and Pentecost but to Christmas as well.

The fifth-century Latin hymn by Prudentius, *Salvete flores martyrium* ("Sweet flowerets of the martyr band," TLH 273), is the traditional office hymn celebrating the children, the buds of martyrs killed by the frost of persecution as soon as they appeared. The image derives from a sermon by Augustine.

In the medieval Church, until the reforms of the later twentieth century, the three days after Christmas were differentiated by the use of three liturgical colors: St. Stephen's Day was red for his martyrdom, St. John's Day was white because he was not executed for the faith, and Holy Innocents' Day was violet for mourning and repentance.

The day is an appropriate time to remember children and to hold Christmas parties for them. On this day one might also choose to remember, as the Episcopal Collect and Lutheran Prayer of the Day suggests, the innocents of all ages killed in the slaughters of history, such as:

- Sand Creek, Colorado (November 29, 1864), a slaughter of 450 unarmed Cheyenne men, women, and children;
- Wounded Knee, South Dakota (December 29, 1890), a slaughter of nearly three hundred Sioux men, women, and children;
- the massacre by the Turks of the Armenians, who lived in the Turkish part of Armenia (April 24, 1915);
- Guernica (April 26, 1937), destruction of a Spanish town by German and Italian aircraft in the first mass bombing of an urban community;
- Latvia (June 13-14, 1941), over fourteen thousand Latvians deported by the Nazis to slave labor camps;
- Lidice (June 10, 1942), obliteration of a village by the Nazis in reprisal for the death of Reinhard Heydrich;
- Oradour (June 10, 1944), obliteration of a French town and all but ten of its inhabitants by the Nazis;
- Dachau, Auschwitz, and the extermination camps (1939–1945), where six million Jews and others deemed undesirable by the Nazis were killed (see Yom Hashoah, pp. 203 above);
- Dresden (February 13, 1945), the jewel of European Renaissance and baroque architecture, fire-bombed by the British and Americans;
- Hiroshima (August 6, 1945) and Nagasaki (August 9, 1945), the first and second atomic bombs used in warfare destroyed two Japanese cities and their people;
- the martyrs behind the Iron Curtain;

DECEMBER

- massacres on the territory of the former Yugoslavia, in Rowanda, Darfur, and the Sudan;
- infants and children abused by their elders.

READING

From an essay by Elie Wiesel

I admit it sadly: I feel threatened. For the first time in many years I feel that I am in danger. For the first time in my adult life I am afraid that the nightmare may start all over again, or that it has never ended, that since 1945 we have lived in parenthesis. Now they are closed.

Could the Holocaust happen again? Over the years I have often put the question to my young students. And they, consistently, have answered yes, while I said no. I saw it as a unique event that would remain unique. I believed that if mankind had learned anything from it, it was that hate and murder reach beyond the direct participants; he who begins by killing others, in the end, will kill his own. Without Auschwitz, Hiroshima would not have been possible. The murder of one people inevitably leads to that of mankind.

In my naïveté I thought, especially in the immediate postwar period, Jews would never again be singled out, handed over to the executioner. That anti-Semitism had received its deathblow long ago, under the fiery skies of Poland. I was somehow convinced that—paradoxically—man would be shielded, protected by the awesome mystery of the Event.

I was wrong. What happened once, could happen again. Perhaps I am exaggerating. Perhaps I am oversensitive. But then I belong to a traumatized generation. We have learned to take threats more seriously than promises.

... I have chosen until now to place the Holocaust on a mystical or ontological level, one that defies language and transcends imagination. I have quarreled with friends who built entire theories and doctrines on an event which, in my view, is not to be used or approached casually. If I speak of it now, it is only because of my realization that Jewish survival is being called into question.

Hence the fear in me. All of a sudden, I am too much reminded of past experiences. The enemy growing more and more powerful, more and more popular. The aggressiveness of the blackmailers, the permissiveness of some leaders and the total submissiveness of others. The overt threats. The complacency and indifference of bystanders. I feel as my father must have felt when he was my age.

Not that I foresee the possibility of Jews being massacred in the cities of America or in the forests of Europe. Death-factories will not be built again. But there is a certain climate, a certain mood in the making. As far as the Jewish people are concerned, the world has remained unchanged: as indifferent to our fate as to its own.

And so I look at my young students and tremble for their future; I see myself at their age surrounded by ruins. What am I to tell them?

I would like to be able to tell them that in spite of endless disillusionments one must maintain faith in man and in mankind; that one must never lose heart. I would like to tell them that, notwithstanding the official discourses and policies, our people does have friends and allies and reasons to advocate hope. But I have never lied to them, I am not going to begin now. And yet. . . .

Despair is no solution, I know that. What is the solution? Hitler had one. And he tried it while a civilized world kept silent.

I remember. And I am afraid.

Elie Wiesel, "Ominous Signs and Unspeakable Thoughts," *The New York Times*, December 28, 1974. © 1974 by The New York Times Company. Reprinted by permission.

PROPERS

O God, the Holy Innocents this day bore witness to you not by speaking words but by dying in place of your infant Son: Grant, we pray, that the faith we profess with our lips we may proclaim with our lives; thorough your Son Jesus Christ our Lord, who lives and reigns with you and the Holy Spirit, one God, now and forever.

1952 Roman Missal, RS trans. DvD

    or

We remember today, O God, the slaughter of the holy innocents of Bethlehem by order of King Herod. Receive, we pray, into the arms of your mercy all innocent victims, and by your great might frustrate the designs of evil tyrants and establish your rule of justice, love, and peace; through Jesus Christ our Lord, who lives and reigns with you in the unity of the Holy Spirit, one God, forever and ever.

1979 BCP, LBW, ELW

Readings:	Jeremiah 31:15-17
	Psalm 124
	1 John 1:5-2:2 *or* Revelation 21:1-7
	Matthew 2:13-18
Hymn of the Day:	
	"Sweet flowerets of the martyr band" (TLH 273)
	or "Your little ones, dear Lord, are we" (LBW 52, ELW 286)
	or "In Bethlehem a new-born boy" (H82 246)
Prayers:	For children
	For sensitivity to the suffering of others
	For courage to resist oppression and to share the lot of the oppressed
	For repentance for brutality and repression, especially that committed in the name of the Holy Child Jesus
Preface:	Christmas/Incarnation
Color:	Red or Violet

DECEMBER

December 29

Thomas Becket, Archbishop of Canterbury, Martyr, 1170

The son of a London sheriff of Norman descent, Thomas Becket was born in 1118, studied in Paris, and then became a member of the household of Theobald, Archbishop of Canterbury, who sent him abroad to study canon law and in 1154 ordained him a deacon and made him his archdeacon. He became the intimate friend of King Henry II and was soon made chancellor of England. In that position he was able to indulge his taste for extravagant magnificence, living sumptuously. When the king decided that Becket should become the archbishop, he refused, saying, "Should God permit me to be archbishop I should lose your majesty's favor." Henry, however, would not be put off, and so Thomas, not yet a priest, was ordained and consecrated archbishop in 1162.

From that time he changed from being, as he described himself, "a patron of play actors and a follower of hounds to being a shepherd of souls," and he devoted himself to the welfare of the Church, living a careful and restrained life in keeping with his new responsibilities. He quarreled with the king over the right of clergy to be tried in the Church courts. This was only one instance of the more general argument concerning the jurisdiction of the church and state in spiritual matters. The fight was as bitter as the former friendship had been close, and Becket was forced to leave England for France where he lived a strictly monastic life in the Abbey of Pontigny. Upon his return six years later, the quarrel broke out afresh. Henry, in Normandy, is said to have said in a fit of rage, "Who will rid me of this turbulent priest?" Four knights, taking Henry's exasperated words as an order, crossed the channel, seized Thomas in his cathedral in Canterbury, and murdered him in front of the altar in a side-chapel, on December 29, 1170. His last words were, "For the Name of Jesus and in defense of the Church I am willing to die."

The people of England were shocked by the murder of their archbishop, and miracles were reported at his tomb. In 1173 the pope canonized him and the next year Henry did penance at his tomb, being whipped by monks from the abbey. In 1220 Becket's shrine was moved to the choir of the cathedral, and it remained a great center of pilgrimage until it was destroyed by Henry VIII.

The dramatic story of Thomas Becket, imperious, obstinate, and ambitious, yet also possessing more exalted qualities, has attracted dramatists from Alfred, Lord Tennyson's *Becket* through T. S. Eliot's *Murder in the Cathedral* to Jean Anouilh's *Becket*. He is included in the *Evangelical Calendar of Names* (1962) and was added to the Episcopal calendar in *Lesser Feasts and Fasts 1997*.

FOR FURTHER READING

Barlow, Frank. *Thomas Becket.* Berkeley: University of California Press, 1986.

Butler, John. *The Quest for Becket's Bones: The Mystery of the Relics of St. Thomas Becket of Canterbury.* New Haven: Yale University Press, 1995.

Greenaway, George, trans. and ed. *The Life and Death of Thomas Becket.* New York: Folio Society, 1967.

Knowles, M. D. *Archbishop Thomas Becket: A Character Study.* London: British Academy, 1949.

Magnusson, Erik. *Thomas Saga. Erkibyskups: A Life of Archbishop Thomas Becket in Icelandic with English translation, Notes, and Glossary.* 2 vols. London: Longman, 1875, 1883.

READING

From an account of the martyrdom of Thomas Becket by Edward Grim, an eyewitness

Then they laid sacrilegious hands on him, pulling and dragging him that they might kill him outside the Church, or carry him away prisoner, as they afterwards confessed. . . . Then the unconquered martyr seeing the hour at hand which should put an end to this miserable life and give him straightaway the crown of immortality promised by the Lord, inclined his neck as one who prays and joining his hands he lifted them up, and commended his cause and that of the Church to God, to St. Mary, and to the blessed martyr St. Denys. Scarce had he said these words than the wicked knight fearing lest he should be rescued by the people and escape alive, leapt upon him suddenly and wounded this lamb who was sacrificed to God on the head, cutting off the top of the crown which the sacred unction of the chrism had dedicated to God; and by this same blow he wounded the arm of him who tells this. For he, when the others, both monks and clerks, fled, stuck close to the sainted archbishop and held him in his arms till the one he interposed was almost severed. . . . Then he received a second blow on the head but still stood firm. At the third blow, he fell on his knees and elbows, offering himself a living victim, and saying in a low voice, "For the Name of Jesus and the protection of the Church I am ready to embrace death."

Then the third knight inflicted a terrible wound as he lay, by which the sword was broken against the pavement, and the crown which was large was separated from the head. . . . The fourth knight prevented any from interfering so that the others might freely perpetrate the murder. As to the fifth, no knight but that clerk who had entered with the knights, that a fifth blow might not be wanting to the martyr who was in other things like Christ, he put his foot on the neck of the holy priest and precious martyr, and, horrible to say, scattered his brains and blood over the pavement, calling out to the others, "Let us away, knights, he will rise no more."

The Life of Thomas Becket, trans. in *Materials for the History of Archbishop Becket* vol. 2, 430ff. Cited in W. H. Hutton, *St. Thomas of Canterbury,* English History by Contemporary Writers (London: David Nutt, 1899), 242–45.

PROPERS

Almighty God, you granted your martyr Thomas the grace to give his life for the cause of justice: Guide the shepherds of your people, strengthen the defenders of your church, and make us all, for the sake of Christ, willing to renounce our life in this world so that we may find the unending life of heaven; through your Son Jesus Christ our Lord, who lives and reigns with you and the Holy Spirit, one God, now and forever.

PHP: Proper of England, RS ✠ LFF

Readings:	2 Esdras 2:42-48
	Psalm 126
	Matthew 10:16-22
Hymn of the Day:	
	"Give us the wings of faith" (H82 253, SBH 594)
Prayers:	For all bishops and clergy who are confronted by hostile governments
	For Christians living in unjust and totalitarian societies
	For the see of Canterbury and its cathedral
	For all pilgrims and visitors to Canterbury
Preface:	Of a Saint (3) (BCP)
Color:	Red

ALSO ON DECEMBER 29

The *Lutheran Service Book,* following Wilhelm Löhe's calendar (December 30), commemorates **David**, the King of Israel, on this date.

December 31

On the medieval and on the present General Roman Catholic Calendar, this is the feast day of **St. Sylvester, Bishop of Rome**, who died in 335. Little is known of his life, even though he was bishop at a formative time in the development of the Church. Later legend says that he baptized Constantine and established the Church of St. John Lateran as the cathedral of Rome on territory given him by the emperor. His day remained on Lutheran calendars well after the Reformation and, as the conclusion of the civil year, the day became a *Todtenfest,* the time to remember members of the parish who had died during the past year. In other parts of the Lutheran Church, for instance, the Prussian Agenda of 1806, the departed were remembered on the last Sunday after Trinity, the end of the ecclesiastical year.

Appendix 1

Chronological List of Commemorations

BEFORE CHRIST

Abraham, Adam and Eve, Daniel and the Three Young Men, David, Elijah, Elisha, Esther, Ezekiel, Hannah, Isaac, Isaiah, Jacob (Israel), Jeremiah, Job, Jonah, Joseph (patriarch), Joshua, Moses, Noah, Ruth, Samuel, Sarah

FIRST CENTURY

Andrew, [Anne], Apollos, Aquila, Barnabas, Bartholomew, Cornelius the Centurion, Dorcas, Elizabeth, Holy Innocents, James the Elder, James the Less, James of Jerusalem, [Joachim], Joanna, John Apostle and Evangelist, John the Baptist, Joseph, Joseph of Arimathea, Jude, Lazarus, Luke, Lydia, Mark, Martha, Mary the Virgin, Mary of Bethany, Mary Magdalene, Mary the myrrh-bearer, Matthew, Matthias, Michael, Onesimus, Parents of Mary, Paul, Peter, Philip the Apostle, Philip the Evangelist, Phoebe, Priscilla, Salome the myrrh-bearer, Silas, Simon, Stephen, Thomas, Timothy, Titus, Zechariah

SECOND CENTURY

Blandina and companions at Lyons, Clement, Ignatius, Justin, Polycarp

THIRD CENTURY

Clement of Alexandria, Cyprian of Carthage, Fabian, Irenaeus, Lawrence, Perpetua and companions, Valentine

FOURTH CENTURY

Agnes, Alban, Ambrose, Antony, Athanasius, Basil, Constantine, Cyril of Jerusalem, Ephrem, Gregory the Illuminator, Gregory Nazianzus, Gregory of Nyssa, Helen(a), Hilary, Lucy, Macrina, Martin, Monica, Nicholas, Pachomius, Sylvester, Vincent

FIFTH CENTURY

Augustine of Hippo, Coelius Sedulius, Cyril of Alexandria, Jerome, John Chrysostom, Leo the Great, Moses the Black, Ninian, Patrick, Prudentius, Synesius

SIXTH CENTURY

Benedict, Brigid (Bride), Columba, David, Justinian, Remigius, Scholastica

SEVENTH CENTURY

Aidan, Augustine of Canterbury, Chad, Cuthbert, Fortunatus, Gregory the Great, Hilda, Theodore of Tarsus,

EIGHTH CENTURY

Bede, Boniface, John of Damascus, Willibrord

NINTH CENTURY

Alcuin, Alfred the Great, Ansgar, Cyril, Edmund, Joseph the Hymnographer, Methodius, Theodulf

TENTH CENTURY

Dunstan, Olga

ELEVENTH CENTURY

Alphege, Margaret of Scotland, Olaf, Stephen of Hungary, Vladimir, Wulfstan

TWELFTH CENTURY

Aelred, Anselm, Becket, Bernard of Clairvaux, Erik, Henry of Finland, Hildegard, Thorlak

THIRTEENTH CENTURY

Clare, Dominic, Elizabeth of Thuringia, Francis of Assisi, Grosseteste, Hugh, Louis, Mechtild of Hackeborn, Mechtild of Magdeburg, Richard, Thomas Aquinas

FOURTEENTH CENTURY

Birgitta, Catherine of Siena, Eckhardt, Gertrude the Great, Groote, Ruysbroek, Sergius, Suso, Tauler

FIFTEENTH CENTURY

Julian of Norwich, Hus, Thomas a Kempis

SIXTEENTH CENTURY

Agricola, Benedict the African, Bugenhagen, Calvin, Copernicus, Cranach, Cranmer, Dürer, Francis Xavier, Frederick the Wise, Grünewald, Ignatius Loyola, John of the Cross, Juusten, Knox, Latimer, Las Casas, K. Luther, M. Luther, Melanchthon, Michelangelo, Miki and martyrs of Japan, Laurentius Petri, Olavus Petri, Ridley, Ruotsalainen, Teresa of Avila, Tyndale, Walter

SEVENTEENTH CENTURY

Andrewes, Barclay, Bray, Bunyan, Claver, Donne, Eliot, Ferrar, Fox, Francis de Sales, Gerhard, Gerhardt, Heermann, Herbert, Hooker, Jensen, Kepler, Laud, Louise de Marillac, Martin de Porres, Nicolai, Penn, Schütz, Taylor, Tranovsky, Vincent de Paul

EIGHTEENTH CENTURY

Bach, Bray, Butler, Edwards, Egede, Euler, Falckner, Handel, Ken, Law, H. M. Muhlenberg, Schwartz, Seabury, Spener, Watts, Charles Wesley, John Wesley, Woolman, Ziegenbalg, Zinzendorf

NINETEENTH CENTURY

Bloomer, Breck, Brooks, Chase, Constance and companions, Crummell, De Koven, F. Fliedner, K. Fliedner, T. Fliedner, Fry, Grundtvig, Gützlaff, Hannington, Hauge, Heyer, Hobart, A. Jones, J. Jones, Kamehameha and Emma, Keble, Kemper, Kierkegaard, Krauth, Löhe, Martyn, Maurice, Mizeki, Morrison, W. A. Muhlenberg, Neale, Passavant, Patteson, Payne, Pusey, Sealth [Seattle], Selwyn, Sieveking, Simeon, Syle, Sojourner Truth, Uganda martyrs, Wallin, White, Wilberforce, Winkworth, Wyneken

TWENTIETH CENTURY

Berggrav, Brent, Bonhoeffer, Daniels, DuBose, Emery, Enmegahbowh, Fedde, Flierl, E. H. F. Francis, Gallaudet, Hammarskjöld, Hannington and companions, Huntington, John XXIII, P. Jones, Kagawa, King, Kolbe, Lewis, Luwum, Maass, Munk, Nightingale, Nommensen, Oakerhater, Onesimos, Papua New Guinea Martyrs ,Pro, Romero, Schereschewsky, Schweitzer, Skrefsrud, Söderblom, Stanton, H. Taylor, Temple, Teresa, Tubman, Williams, Underhill

Appendix 2

Geographical Distribution of Commemorations

AFRICA

Central Africa: Livingstone
Eastern Equatorial Africa: Hannington
Egypt: Athanasius, Antony, Clement of Alexandria, Cyril of Alexandria, Moses the Black, Pachomius
Ethiopia: Onesimos
Gabon: Schweitzer
North Africa: Augustine, Cyprian, Monica, Perpetua
Rhodesia: Mizeki
Uganda: Luwum, Martyrs of Uganda

THE AMERICAS

Colombia: Peter Claver
El Salvador: Romero
Indies: Las Casas, E. H. F. Francis
Mexico: Pro
North America: Bloomer, Breck, Brooks, Chase, Constance, Crummell, Daniels, De Koven, DuBose, Edwards, Eliot, Emery, Enmegabowh, Falckner, Fedde, Gallaudet, Hobart, Huntington, Jensen, A. Jones, J. Jones, P. Jones, Kemper, King, Krauth, Maass, H. M. Muhlenberg, W. A. Muhlenberg, Oakerhater, Passavant, Seabury, Sealth, Stanton, Syle, Truth, Tubman, White
Peru: Martin de Porres

ASIA

China: Florence Tim-Oi, Schereschewsky
India: Heyer, Martyn, Skrefsrud, Mother Teresa, Ziegenbalg
Japan: Martyrs of Japan, Francis Xavier, Kagawa, Williams
Sumatra: Nommensen

BRITISH ISLES

England: Aelred, Aidan, Alban, Alfred, Alphege, Andrewes, Anselm, Augustine of Canterbury, Becket, Bede, Bray, Bunyan, Butler, Chad, Cranmer, Cuthbert, Donne, Dunstan, Edmund, Ferrar, Fox, Fry, Grosseteste, Handel, Herbert, Hilda, Hooker, Hugh, Julian, Keble, Ken, Latimer, Laud, Law, Lewis, Maurice, Neale, Nightingale, Pusey, Richard, Ridley, Simeon, Taylor, Temple, Theodore, Tyndale, Underhill, Watts, C. Wesley, J. Wesley, Wilberforce, Winkworth, Wulfstan
Ireland: Brigid, Patrick, Ninian
Scotland: Columba, Knox, Margaret
Wales: David

EUROPE

Czech Republic/Slovakia: Cyril, Hus, Methodius, Tranovsky
Denmark: Ansgar, Grundtvig, Kierkegaard, Munk
Finland: Agricola, Henry
France: Alcuin, Bernard, Blandina, Calvin, Hilary, Irenaeus, Louis, Martin, Remigius, Vincent de Paul
Germany: Bach, Bonhöffer, Boniface, Cranach, Dürer, F. Fliedner, K. Fliedner, T. Fliedner, Gerhardt, Gertrude, Grünewald, Heermann, Hildegard, Kepler, Löhe, K. Luther, M. Luther, Melanchthon, Mechtild of Hackeborn, Mechtild of Magdeburg, Nicolai, Schütz, Sieveking, Spener
Hungary: Elizabeth, Stephen
Iceland: Thorlak
Italy: Agnes, Ambrose, Benedict of Nursia, Benedict the Black, Catherine of Siena, Clare, Clement, Fabian, Francis, Gregory, John XXIII, Justin, Lawrence, Leo, Lucy, Michelangelo, Scholastica, Thomas Aquinas
Moravia: Zinzendorf
Netherlands/Low Countries: Groote, Thomas á Kempis, Willibrord
Norway: Berggrav, Hauge, Olaf
Poland: Copernicus
Russia: Euler, Olga, Sergius, Vladimir
Spain: Dominic, Ignatius Loyola, John of the Cross, Teresa, Vincent
Sweden: Birgitta, Erik, Hammarskjöld, L. Petri, O. Petri, Söderblom, Wallin
Switzerland: Francis de Sales

NEAR EAST

Armenia: Gregory
Palestine: Biblical saints, Helen, Jerome, Cyril of Jerusalem
Syria: Ephrem, Ignatius of Antioch, John Damascene
Turkey: Basil, Chrysostom, Gregory Nazianzus, Gregory of Nyssa, Macrina, Nicholas, Polycarp

THE PACIFIC

Hawaii: Emma and Kamehameha
Melanesia: Patteson
New Zealand: Selwyn
Papua New Guinea: Flierl, Martyrs of New Guinea
Philippines: Brent

Appendix 3

Wilhelm Löhe's Calendar of Names

Martyrologium zur Erklärung der herkömlichen Kalendarnamen. Nürnberg, 1868

JANUARY

1	JESUS. The Circumcision and the Name Day of the Lord
2	Abel and Seth, Genesis 4:1-2, 8, 25
3	Enoch, Genesis 5:18-24
4	Abednigo. Daniel 1:1-7; Titus, disciple of St. Paul, Bishop of Crete
5	Simeon, prophet, Luke 2:25-36
6	*Epiphany of the Lord*, Matthew 2:1ff
7	Lucian, priest of Antioch, Martyr, 312
8	Severin, Apostle of Noricum (Austria), 482
9	Julian the Hospitaler, Martyr 313, and his wife Basilissa
10	Paul of Thebes, first hermit, 430
11	Hyginus, Bishop of Rome, Martyr, 139–142
12	Arcadius, Martyr in Mauretania, third century
13	Hilary, Bishop of Poitiers, 368
14	Felix of Nola, Priest and Confessor, 256
15	Maurus, Abbot of Glanfeuil, 584
16	Marcellus, Bishop of Rome, Martyr, 310
17	Antony the Great, Abbot in Thebes, 356
18	Prisca, Virgin, Martyr at Rome, 275
19	Sarah, 2000 B.C.
20	Fabian, Bishop of Rome, Martyr, 250; Sebastian, Centurion, Martyr at Rome, *ca.* 288
21	Agnes, Virgin, Martyr at Rome, 304
22	Vincent, Deacon at Saragossa, Martyr, 304
23	Emerentiana, Virgin, Martyr at Rome, 304
24	Timothy, Disciple of St. Paul, Bishop of Ephesus, Martyr, 97
25	*Conversion of St. Paul*, Acts 6–9
26	Polycarp, Bishop of Smyrna, Martyr, 166; Paula, Matron at Rome, 404
27	John Chrysostom, Patriarch of Constantinople, Martyr, 407
28	Charles the Great, 814
29	Valerius, Bishop of Trier, Disciple of Peter; Francis de Sales, Bishop of Geneva, 1622
30	Aldegundus, Virgin, Abbess of Maubeuge, 680
31	Vigilius, Bishop of Trient, Martyr, 410

FEBRUARY

1	Brigid, Virgin, Abbess in Ireland, sixth century
2	*Purification of Mary*
3	Blaise, Bishop of Sebastea, Martyr, 316; Ansgar, Bishop of Bremen, 865
4	Rhabanus Maurus, Archbishop of Mainz, 856
5	Agatha, Virgin of Catania, Martyr, 251

6	Dorothy, Virgin, Martyr in Caesarea in Cappadocia, 287
7	Richard, King, Father of Walburgis, 720
8	Solomon, King of Israel 1000 B.C.
9	Apollonia, Virgin in Alexandria, Martyr, 249
10	Scholastica, Sister of Benedict of Nursia, Virgin, Abbess,543
11	Euphrosyne, Virgin, 470
12	Eulalia of Barcelona, Virgin, Martyr, 290; Eulalia of Meridia, Virgin, Martyr
13	Agabus, Prophet, Acts 11:28, 21:10ff.; Polyeuctus, Centurion, Martyr, 250
14	Cyril and Methodius, Apostles to the Slavs, ninth century
15	Faustinus and Jovita, Martyrs at Bresca, 121
16	Onesimus, Disciple of St. Paul, Martyr at Rome, 95
17	Flavian, Patriarch of Constantinople, Martyr, 449
18	Simeon, Bishop of Jerusalem, Martyr, 107; Martin Luther, Doctor of the Church, Confessor, 1546
19	Sabinus, Priest, Martyr, 296
20	Tyrannion, Bishop of Tyre, Martyr, 310
21	Pipin of Landen, Steward, 640
22	Peter's Chair in Antioch of Syria, 33
23	Serenus the Gardener, Martyr at Sirmium, 307
24	*Matthias,* Apostle
25	Victoria and Genossen, Martyrs, 284
26	Nestor, Bishop of Sida in Pamphylia, Martyr, 250
27	Gelasinus, Actor, Martyr, 297
28	Sabinus, Priest, Martyr, 296

MARCH

1	Swidbert, Apostle to Frisia, 713
2	Simplicius, Bishop of Rome, 483
3	Cunegund, Empress, 1040
4	Lucius, Bishop of Rome, Martyr, 252
5	Eusebius of Eremond, Abbot of Bethlehem, fifth century
6	Fridolin, Abbot of St. Hilaire, 538
7	Perpetua and Felicity, Martyrs at Carthage, 203; Thomas Aquinas, 1275
8	Philemon the Flute-player, Martyr, 311
9	The Forty Soldiers, Martyrs at Sebastea, Armenia, 320
10	Cajus and Alexander, Martyrs at Apamea in Phrygia, 279
11	Eulogius, Priest at Córdova, Martyr, 859
12	Gregory the Great, Bishop of Rome, 604
13	Euphrasia, Virgin in Egypt, 410
14	Matilda, Queen and Wife of Henry I, 968
15	Longinus, Centurion who pierced the side of the Lord, Martyr
16	Heribert, Archbishop of Cologne, 1022
17	Gertrude, Virgin, Abbess of Nivelles in Brabant, 659
18	Alexander, Bishop of Jerusalem, Martyr, 251
19	Joseph, Foster-father of Jesus
20	Archippus, Companion of St. Paul, Colossians 4:17
21	Benedict of Nursia, Abbot of Monte Cassino, 543
22	Nicholas of Flüe, Hermit, 1487
23	Victorian, Proconsul of Carthage, Martyr, 484

24	Gabriel, Archangel
25	*Annunciation to Mary;* Dismas, the thief on the right side [of Jesus]
26	Ludger, Bishop of Münster, 809
27	Rupert, Archbishop of Bavaria, 550
28	Malchus and Genossen, Martyrs, 260
29	Eustaslus, Abbot, Archbishop of Bavaria, 628
30	Guido, Abbot of Pomposa, 1046
31	Amos, Prophet, 838–759 B.C.

APRIL

1	Hugo, Bishop of Grenoble, 1132
2	Theodosia, Virgin of Tyre, Martyr at Caesarea in Palestine, 308
3	Agape, Chionia, and Irene, Virgins, Martyrs at Thessalonika, 304
4	Ambrose, Bishop of Milan
5	The Martyrs of Easter Day slaughtered in the church by King Genserich, 459
6	Celestine, Bishop of Rome, 432
7	Hegesippus, Church Historian, 180 in Jerusalem
8	Dionysus, Bishop of Corinth, 170
9	Mary, wife of Cleopas, Sister of the Mother of God, John 19:25
10	Daniel, Prophet, 606–536 B.C.
11	Antipas, the Faithful Witness at Pergamum, Revelation 2:13
12	Julius, Bishop of Rome, 352; Sabas the Goth, Martyr, 372
13	Hermenegild, Prince, Martyr, 586
14	Tiburtius and Valerian, Martyrs at Rome, 229
15	Anastasia and Basilissa, Martyrs at Rome under Nero, 66
16	Aaron, High Priest, Brother of Moses
17	Anicetus, Bishop of Rome, Martyr, 173
18	Victor, Bishop of Augsburg, eighth century
19	Timon, one of the Seven Deacons of Jerusalem, Acts 6:5
20	Suplicius and Servilianua, Martyrs at Rome, 117
21	Anselm of Canterbury, Archbishop, 1109
22	Soter and Caius, Bishops, Martyrs at Rome, 177, 296
23	George, Martyr, *ca.* 303; Adalbert, Bishop of Prague, Martyr, 997
24	Egbert, Priest, 729
25	*Mark,* Evangelist
26	Cletus, Bishop of Rome, 89
27	Anastasius, Bishop of Rome, 401
28	Vitalis of Ravenna, Martyr, 62
29	Tychicus of Asia, Disciple of St. Paul, Acts 20:4
30	Eutropius, Bishop of Saintes, Martyr, middle of the third century

MAY

1	*Philip and James,* Apostles; Walburgia, Virgin, Abbess, 779
2	Athanasius, Patriarch of Alexandria, 373
3	Finding of the Cross, 329
4	Monica, Widow, Mother of St. Augustine, 387
5	Gotthard, Bishop of Hildesheim, 1039
6	John before the Latin Gate, 95

7   Flavia Domitilla, Virgin, Martyr at Rome under Trajan, 100
8   Victor the Moor, Martyr in Milan, 303
9   Hermas, Romans 16:14; Gregory Nazianzus, Patriarch of Constantinople, 389
10 Comgall, Abbot of Bangor, 601
11 Gangolf, Martyr in Burgundy, 760
12 Pancratius [Pancras], Martyr at Rome, 304
13 Servatius, Bishop of Tongern, 384
14 Pachomius, Abbot of Upper Thebes, 348
15 Rupert, Confessor in Mainz, ninth century; Dympna, Virgin, Martyr in Gheel in Brabant, seventh century
16 Peregrin, Bishop of Auxerre, Martyr, *ca.* 304
17 Possidius, Bishop of Calama in Numidia. 430
18 Theodot, Schenkwirth, and their Companions, Martyrs, 303
19 Pudentiana, Virgin at Rome, first century
20 Ivo, Bishop of Chartres, 1115
21 Hospitus, Hermit, 681
22 Helena, Empress, 328
23 Desiderius, Bishop of Vienne, Martyr, 608 or 612; Desiderius, Bishop of Langres, Martyr, 262 or 411
24 Esther, Queen; Menaen, Prophet, Acts 13:1; Vincent of Lerins, 450; Johanna, Luke 8:3, 24:10
25 Urban, Bishop of Rome, Martyr, 231
26 Quadratius, Bishop of Athens, Disciple of the Apostles, Apologist, 126
27 Bede the Venerable, Priest, died 26 May 735
28 Germenus, Bishop of Paris, 576
29 Cyrillus, Boy, Martyr, 250 or 260
30 Felix, Bishop of Rome, Martyr, 274
31 Petronella, Disciple of the Apostles

JUNE

1   Justin, Martyr, 167; Pamphilus, Martyr, 309
2   Blandina, Virgin, Martyr at Lyons, 177
3   Caclius, Priest at Carthage, 211
4   Quirinius, Bishop of Syscia, Martyr, 304
5   Boniface, Archbishop of Mainz, Martyr, 755
6   Philip the Deacon, Acts 6
7   Paul, Patriarch of Constantinople, Martyr, 350; Deocar, Abbot of Herrieden, 850
8   William, Archbishop of York, 1154
9   Primus and Felicianus, Martyrs at Rome, 286
10 Landerich, Bishop of Paris, 650
11 Barnabas, Apostle, Martyr, 70
12 Onuphrius, Hermit in Thebes, 404; Basilides and Genossen, Martyrs at Rome, 303
13 Tobias, 722 B.C.
14 Elisha, Prophet, 840 B.C.
15 Vitus, Modestius, and Crescentia, Martyrs at Luciana, fourth century
16 Julitta, Quirinius [Cyricus], Martyrs, 304
17 Ramuold, Abbot of Regensburg, 1001

AUGUST

1	St. Peter's Chains
2	Stephen, Bishop of Rome, Martyr, 257
3	Nicodemus, John 3; Gamaliel, Acts 5:34; Lydia, Acts 16:14
4	Dominic, Founder of Monastic Order, 1221
5	Nonna, Mother of St. Gregory Nazianzen, fourth century; Oswald, King, Martyr, 642
6	*Transfiguration of Christ*
7	Afra, Martyr at Augsburg, 304
8	Cyriacus, Largus, and Smaragdus, Martyrs, 303
9	Romanus, Martyr at Rome, 258
10	Lawrence, Archdeacon, Martyr at Rome, 258
11	Tiburtius, Martyr at Rome, 286
12	Clare of Assisi, Abbess, 1253
13	Cassian, Martyr, 362
14	Athanasia, Widow, Abbess, 861
15	*Departure of Mary*
16	Isaac, Patriarch; Rochus [Roch, Rock] of Montpellier, Confessor, end of fourth century
17	Liberatus and Gefärten, Martyrs, 483
18	Agapitus, Martyr, 273
19	Sebald, Hermit of Nürnberg in eighth or eleventh century
20	Bernard of Clairvaux, 1153
21	Bonosus and Maxmillian, Soldiers, Martyrs, 363
22	Symphorian of Autun, Martyr, *ca.* 178
23	Zacchaeus, Luke 19; Zacchaeus IV, Bishop of Jerusalem
24	*Bartholomew,* Apostle; the Martyrs of Utica, 385
25	Louis, King of France, 1270
26	Samuel, Prophet, 1096 B.C.
27	Caesarius, Bishop of Arles, 542
28	Aurelius Augustine, Bishop of Hippo, 430
29	Beheading of John the Baptist
30	Rebecca; Felix, Priest, and Adauctus, Martyrs at Rome under Diocletian
31	Isabella, Virgin, 1270

SEPTEMBER

1	Aegidius, Abbot, *ca.* 715; Aegidius, Monk, 1203
2	Stephen, King of Hungary, 1038
3	Phoebe, Deaconess at Cenchrea, *ca.* 58, Romans 16:1
4	Moses, Prophet, 1500 B.C.
5	Marinus, Deacon, end of the fourth century
6	Onesiphorus, 2 Timothy 1:16; Magnus, Apostle to Algäu, 665
7	Regina, Virgin, Martyr in Burgundy, 251
8	Nativity of Mary; Corbinian, Bishop, Apostle in Bavaria, 730
9	Gorgonius, Dorothy, and Peter, Martyrs at Rome, 204
10	Pulcheria, Empress, 453
11	Paphnutius, Bishop of Thebes, 335
12	Guido [Guy]of Anderlecht, 1012
13	Amatus, Bishop of Stettin in Wallis, 690

14   Exaltation of the Cross, 629

15   Nicetas, Martyr, 372

16   Euphemia, Virgin, Martyr at Chalcedon, 307; Cyrpian, Bishop of Carthage, Martyr, 258

17   Hildegard, Virgin, Abess of St. Ruppert in Bingen, 1179

18   Richerdius, Empress, 873

19   Januarius, Bishop of Brevent, Martyr, 305

20   Fausta, Virgin, Martyr, and Evilasius, Martyr at Cyzicum, 305–311

21   *Matthew,* Apostle

22   Emmeran, Bishop, Apostle in Bavaria, Martyr, 652

23   Thekla [Thecla], Disciple of St. Paul, Virgin, Martyr, first century

24   Gerhard [Gerard], Bishop, Martyr in Hungary, 1046

25   Cleopas, Luke 24:18

26   Cyprian the Magician and Justine, Virgin, Martyrs at Antioch, 304

27   Cosmas and Damian, Physicians, Martyrs, *ca.* 303

28   Lioba, Virgin, Abbess, 779; Eustochium, Virgin, 419

29   *Michael,* Archangel

30   Jerome, Priest, 419

OCTOBER

1   Remigius, Bishop of Rheims, Apostle to the Franks, 533

2   Leodegar [Leger], Bishop of Autun, Martyr, 678

3   Jairus, Matthew 9:18

4   Francis of Assisi, Founder of Monastic Order, 1226

5   Placid of Subiaco, Abbot of Monte Cassino, Martyr, 546

6   Fides, Virgin at Agen and Her Companions, Martyrs, *ca.* 287

7   Justina, Virgin, Martyr at Padua, 304

8   Pelagia, Penitent at Antioch, fifth century

9   Dionysus the Areopagite, Martyr, Acts 17:34

10   Gideon, Judges 6–8; Gereon of Cologne, Martyr, 259

11   Burkhard, Bishop of Würtzburg, 754

12   Maxmillian, Bishop, Martyr, 284

13   Colomann, Martyr in Austria, 1012

14   Calixtus [Callistus], Bishop, Martyr, 222

15   Teresa [of Avila], Virgin, 1582

16   Gallus [Gall], Abbot of St. Gall, *ca.* 646

17   Hedwig, Duchess of Poland, 1243

18   *Luke,* Physician, Evangelist. Colossians 4:14

19   Ptolemaeus and Lucas, Martyrs at Rome, 166

20   Wendelin, Abbott, 1015

21   Ursula and Her Companions, Virgins, Martyrs, 453

22   Cordula, Virgin, Martyr, 453

23   Severin, Bishop of Cologne, 403; Severin, Bishop of Bordeaux, 404

24   *Raphael,* Archangel

25   Chrysanthus and Daria, Martyrs at Rome, 257

26   Amandus, Bishop of Strassburg, 354; Amandus, Bishop of Bordeaux, 431

27   Frumentius and Aedesius, Apostles to Ethiopia, fourth century

28   *Simon and Jude,* Apostles

29   Narcissus, Bishop of Gerone in Spain, Martyr, 307; Narcissus, Bishop of Jerusalem, 295

| 30 | Marcellus, Centurion, Martyr in Spain, 298 |
| 31 | Wolfgang, Bishop of Brandenburg, 994 |

NOVEMBER

1	*All Saints*
2	All Souls; Victorin, Bishop, Martyr, 304
3	Pirminus, Apostle of the Upper Rhine, 754
4	Vitalis and Agricola, Martyrs at Bologna, 304
5	Berthilla, Abbess of Chelles, 692
6	Leonhard [Leonard], Hermit, Confessor, 559
7	Willibrord, Apostle to Frisia, 738
8	The Four Crowned Ones, Martyrs at Rome, 304
9	Theodorus [Theodore] Tiro, Martyr, 306
10	Florentia, Martyr, 354
11	Matrin, Bishop of Tours, 400
12	Jonah, Prophet, 838–797 B.C.
13	Briccius [Brice], Bishop of Tours, 444
14	Livin, Bishop of Scotland, Martyr, 659; Livin, Presbyter, eighth century
15	Desiderius, Bishop of Cahors, 654; Albertus Magnus, Bishop, 1280
16	Othmar, Abbot of St. Gall, 759
17	Dionysus, Bishop of Alexandria, 265
18	Gregory the Wonderworker, Bishop, 270
19	Elizabeth, Landgravine of Thuringia, 1231
20	Pontianus, Bishop of Rome, Martyr, 235
21	Columbanus, Abbot of Bobbio, 615
22	Cecelia, Virgin, Martyr at the beginning of the third century
23	Clement, Bishop of Rome, Martyr, 100
24	Chrysogonus, Martyr, 303
25	Katherine, Virgin, Martyr, 306
26	Conrad, Bishop of Constance, 976
27	Virgilius, Bishop of Salzburg, 780
28	Günther, Bishop of Regensburg, 938
29	Saturninus, Bishop of Toulouse, Martyr, 250
30	*Andrew,* Apostle

DECEMBER

1	Elegius, Bishop, 659
2	Bibiana [Viviana], Virgin, Martyr at Rome, 363
3	Sola, Abbot of Solenhofen, 760
4	Barbara, Virgin, Martyr, 235
5	Crispina, Martyr in Africa, 304
6	Nicholas, Bishop of Myra, 352
7	Aganthon, Soldier, Martyr, 250
8	Apollos, Assistant to St. Paul
9	Joachim, Father of the Virgin Mary; Gorgonia, Widow, 369
10	Melchiades [Miltiades], Bishop of Rome, 314
11	Damasus, Bishop of Rome, 384
12	Epimachus and Alexander, Martyrs, 250
13	Lucy, Virgin, Martyr at Syracuse, 304; Odelie [Odilia], Virgin, Abbess, 720

14   Spiridon, Bishop of Cyprus, 348
15   Ignatius, Bishop of Antioch, Martyr, 116
16   Adelhild, Empress, 999
17   Olympias, Widow, Deaconess, 410
18   Wunnibald [Winebald], Abbot of Hildesheim, 760
19   Abraham, Patriarch. 2000 B.C.
20   Ammon, Zenon, and others, Confessors, 250
21   *Thomas,* Apostle
22   Ischyrron, Martyr in Egypt, 253
23   Servulus, Beggar at Rome, 590
24   Adam and Eve
25   Nativity of JESUS
26   Stephen, Protomartyr
27   John, Apostle, A.D. 100
28   Holy Innocents' Day
29   Jonathan, Friend of David
30   David, King of Israel, 1050 B.C.
31   Sylvester, Bishop of Rome, 335

Appendix 4

Evangelical Calendar of Names, 1962, 1965

JANUARY

1	Name Day of the Lord: New Year
2	Basil, 379. Bishop and Father of Monks
3	Wilhelm Löhe, 1872. Renewer of the Lutheran Church
4	Gordius, *ca.* 306. Martyr in Cappadocia
5	Fritz von Bodelschwingh, 1946. Exemplar of Charity
6	Feofan, 1894. Russian Monk and Pastor of Souls
7	The Epiphany
8	Walther Paucker, 1919. Baltic Martyr
9	Martyrs of the Sacred Writings, 303/304.
10	Jacob Andreae, 1590. Unifier of Lutheranism
11	Severin, Apostle of Noricum, 482. Confessor
12	Johann Laski, 1580 (from 8th). Reformer in East Frisia and Poland
13	Carpus and Papylus, *ca.* 165. Martyrs in Pergamon
14	Ernst the Confessor, 1546. Defender of the Reformation
15	Remigius of Rhiems, 533 (from 13th). Bishop
16	George Fox, 1691. Founder of the Quakers
17	Traugott Hahn, 1919. Baltic Martyr
18	Hilary of Poitiers, *ca.* 367. Bishop and Confessor
19	George Spalatin, 1545. Preacher and Reformer in Saxony
20	Antony, 356. Father of Monks
21	Ludwig Steil, 1945 (from 17th). Martyr in the Church Struggle (*Kirchenkampf*)
22	Johan Michael Hahn, 1819 (from 20th). Lay Witness
23	Sebastian, 288. Martyr in Rome
24	Matthias Claudius, 1815. Writer
25	Vincent, 304. Martyr in Spain
26	Menno Simons, 1561. Father of the Mennonites
27	Timothy, *ca.* 97. Disciple of the Apostles
28	Erich Sack, 1943. Martyr in the Church Struggle
29	Conversion of the Apostle Paul
30	Heinrich Seuse, 1366. Friend of God in the Upper Rhine
31	Johann Matthäus Meyfart, 1642. Hymn Writer
32	Paavo Ruotsalainen, 1852. Awakener of Finland
33	Charlemagne, 814. Emperor, Promoter of Christianity
34	Thephil Wurm, 1953 (from 28th). Bishop and Confessor in Würtemberg
35	Xavier Marnitz, 1919. Baltic Martyr
	Charles Spurgeon, 1892. Preacher

FEBRUARY

1	Ignatius, *ca.* 110. Bishop and Martyr
2	Klaus Harms, 1855. Renewer of the Reformation Faith
3	Presentation of the Lord (Candlemas)
4	Burkhard of Würzburg, 753. Missionary
5	Ansgar, 865. Apostle of the North

6	Matthias Desubas, 1746 (from 2nd). Martyr, Preacher in France
7	Hrabanus Maurus, 856. Bishop and Teacher
8	Philipp Jakob Spener, 1705. Father of Pietism
9	Amandus, 679. Missionary along the Maas and Schelde Rivers
10	Adolf Stöcker, 1909. Evangelical Statesman
11	Georg Wagner, 1527. Martyr in Austria
12	John Hooper, 1555. Bishop, Martyr in England
13	Friedrich Christoph Öttinger, 1782. Swabian Theologian
14	Hugo of St. Victor, 1141. Teacher of the Church
15	Benjamin Schmolk, 1737. Hymn Writer
16	Valentin Ernst Löscher, 1749. Devout Lutheran Leader
17	Friedrich Schliermacher, 1834. Theologian
18	Christian Frederick Schwartz, 1798. Missionary to India
19	Bruno of Querfurt, 1009. Apostle of Prussia, Martyr
20	Johannes Daniel Falk, 1826. Father to Orphans
21	Georg Maus, 1945. Martyr in the Church Struggle [*Kirchenkampf*]
22	Wilhelm Schmidt, 1924. Layman, Inventor
23	Johann Heermann, 1647. Hymn Writer
24	Martin Luther, 1546
25	Peter Brullius, 1545. Martyr in the Netherlands
26	Friedrich Weissler, 1945 (from 19th). Martyr in the Church Struggle
27	Lars Levi Laestadius, 1861. Spiritual Leader of the Lapps
28	Bartholomäus Ziegenbalg, 1719 (from 23rd). Missionary to India
29	Polycarp, 155. Bishop and Martyr
30	**Matthias the Apostle**
31	Walburga, 779 (from 25th). Abbess in France
32	Johann Christoph Blumhardt, 1880. Prophetic Christian Witness
33	Mechtild of Magdeburg, *ca.* 1285. Abbess and Mystic
34	Patrick Hamilton, 1528 (from 29th). Martyr in England
35	Martin Butzer, 15512. Reformer in Strassburg, Hessen, England
36	Suitbert, 713. Missionary to Lower Rhine

MARCH

1	Martin Moller, 1606 (from 2nd). Hymn Writer and Devotional Writer
2	John Wesley, 1791. Preacher of Revival in England
3	Cunegunde, 1033. Queen of Henry II
4	Johann Friedrich the Stouthearted, 1554. Defender of the Reformation
5	Hermann Friedrich Kohlbrügge, 1875. Publisher
6	Chrodegang of Metz, 766. Bishop
7	Perpetua and Felicity, 202/203. Martyrs in Carthage
8	Thomas Aquinas, 1274 (from 7th). Teacher of the Church
9	Pusei, 344. Persian Martyr
10	The Forty Soldiers of Sebaste, 320. Martyrs in Armenia
11	Pionius, 250 (from 12th). Martyr in Asia Minor
12	Gregory the Great, 604. Bishop of Rome, Promoter of Church Music
13	Georg of Ghese, 1559. Martyr in Italy
14	Mathilde, 968. Queen of Henry I
15	Friedrich Gottlieb Klopstock, 1803. Librettist of *The Messiah*
16	Kaspar Olevianus, 1587. Theologian (Heidelberg Catechism)

17	Heribert of Cologne, 1021. Bishop
18	Patrick of Ireland, 461. Bishop and Confessor
19	Cyril of Jerusalem, 386. Bishop and Teacher of the Church
20	Marie Schlieps, 1919. Baltic Martyr
21	Michael Weisse, 1534. Hymn Writer, Leader of the Bohemian Brethren
22	Albrecht of Prussia, 1568. Reformer of Prussia
23	Benedict of Nursia, 547. Founder of Religious Order, Pastor of Souls
24	Nicholas of Flüe, 1487. Hermit and Spiritual Advisor of the Swiss Confederation
25	August Schreiber, 1903. Missionary to Sumatra
26	Wolfgang of Anhalt, 1566. Father of His People
27	Veit Dietrich, 1549 (from 25th). Preacher in Nuremberg
28	**The Annunciation to Mary**
29	Liudger, 809 (from 26th). Missionary in Westphalia
30	Ernst the Upright, 1675. Father of Saxony-Gotha
31	Karl Schlau, 1919. Baltic Martyr
32	Meister Eckhart, 1327. Mystic
33	Rupert, 718 (from 27th). Missionary Bishop in Bavaria
34	Hans Nielsen Hauge, 1824. Reviver of Norway
35	Johannes Evangelista Gossner, 1858. Preacher of Revival, Patron of the Mission
36	Akazius of Melitene, 260. Confessor of the Eastern Church

APRIL

1	Amalie Sieveking, 1859. Social Worker in Hamburg
2	Friederich von Bodelschwingh, 1910. Exemplar of Charity
3	Gerhard Tersteegen, 1769. Hymn Writer
4	Ambrose of Milan, 397. Church Father
5	Christian Scriver, 1693. Hymn Writer, Devotional Writer
6	Pandita Ramabei, 1922. Indian Missionary
7	Cyril and Methodius, 869/885. Apostles to the Slavs
8	Notker the Stammerer, 912. Monk and Hymn Writer
9	Albrecht Dürer, 1528 (from 6th). Master Painter
10	Johann Hinrich Wichern, 1881. Father of the Inner Mission
11	Martin Chemnitz, 1586. Reformer, Theologian
12	Dietrich Bonhöffer, 1945. Martyr in the Church Struggle, Theologian
13	Thomas von Westen, 1727 (from 9th). Apostle to the Lapps
14	Matthäus Apelles von Löwenstein, 1648. Hymn Writer
15	Peter Waldo, *ca.* 1217. Herald of the Gospel
16	Konrad Hubert, 1577. Hymn Writer
17	Justin, Martyr, *ca.* 165
18	Karolina Fliedner, 1892. Mother of Deaconesses in the Rhineland
19	Sundar Singh, 1939. Indian Evangelist
20	Louis of Berquin, 1529. Martyr in France
21	Max Joseph Metzgar, 1944. Martyr
22	Apollonius, *ca.* 180. Martyr in Egypt
23	Luther at Worms, 1521
24	Philipp Melanchthon, 1560. Co-shaper of the Reformation
25	Johannes Bugenhagen, 1558. Reformer in Northern Germany and Denmark
26	Anselm of Canterbury, 1109. Teacher of the Church

27	Adalbert of Prague, 997 (from 23rd). Missionary in Prussia, Martyr
28	George, *ca.* 303. Martyr in Dalmatia
29	Friedrich Justus Perels, 1945. Martyr in the Church Struggle
30	Johann Walther, 1570. Cantor, Associate of Luther
31	Toyohiko Kagawa, 1960. (from 23rd). Social Reformer in Japan
32	**Mark the Evangelist**
33	Philipp Friedrich Hiller, 1769 (from 24th). Hymn Writer
34	Tertullian, after 220. Teacher of the Church
35	Origen, *ca.* 254. Teacher of the Church
36	Johannes Gramann, 1541 (from 29th). Hymn Writer
37	Catherine of Siena, 1380. Preacher of Repentance
38	David Livingstone, 1873 (from May 1). Missionary in Africa

MAY

1	**Philip and James the Less, Apostles**
2	Athanasius, 373. Teacher of the Church
3	Nikolaus Herman, 1561. Hymn Writer
4	Michael Schirmer, 1673. Hymn Writer
5	Godehard, 1038. Bishop and Reformer of the Church
6	Frederick the Wise, 1525 (from the 5th). Defender of the Reformation
7	Otto the Great, 973. Emperor, Defender of the Church
8	Gregory Nazianzus, *ca.* 390. Teacher of the Church
9	Nicolaus, Count von Zinzendorf, 1760. Founder of the Moravian Brethren, Hymn Writer
10	Johan Hüglin, 1527, Martyr in Meersburg
11	Johann Arnd, 1621. Lutheran Devotional Book Publisher
12	Pancratius, 304. Martyr in Rome
13	Hans Ernst von Kottwitz, 1843. Layman
14	Nikolaus von Amsdorf, 1565. Evangelical Bishop of Naumburg
15	Pachomius, 346 (from 14th). Father of Monks in Egypt
16	The Five Martyrs of Lyons, 1553
17	Valerius Herberger, 1627 (from 18th). Hymn Writer
18	Christian Heinrich Zeller, 1860. Christian Educator in Basel
19	Alcuin, 804. Abbot and Teacher of the Franks
20	Samuel Hebich, 1868 (from 21st). Pioneer of the Mission in India and Ethiopia
21	Constantine the Great, 337 (from 22nd). First Christian Emperor
22	Marion von Klot, 1919. Baltic Martyr
23	Girolamo Savanarola, 1498. Preacher of Repentance in Florence
24	Ludwig Nommensen, 1918. Missionary to Sumatra, Founder of the Batak Church
25	Nikolaus Selnecker, 1592. Theologian, Hymn Writer
26	Augustine of Canterbury, 604 (from 26th). Apostle to the Anglo-Saxons
27	Bede the Venerable, 735. Teacher of the Church
28	John Calvin, 1564. Reformer in Geneva
29	Paul Gerhardt, 1676. Hymn Writer
30	Karl Mez, 1877. Layman
31	Jerome of Prague, 1416 (from 30th). Bohemian Martyr
32	Gottfried Arnold, 1714. Theologian and Hymn Writer
33	Joachim Neander, 1680. Hymn Writer

JUNE

1	Johann Friedrich Flattich, 1797. Swabian Pastor of Souls
2	Friederich Oberlin, 1826. Pastor and Exemplar of Charity in Alsace
3	Blandina, 177. Martyr in Lyons
4	Hudson Taylor, 1905. Founder of the China Mission
5	Morandus, 1115 (from 3rd). Missionary, Apostle of Sundgaus
6	Winfried/Boniface, 754. Missionary in Germany
7	Norbert of Xanten, 1134. Bishop and Founder of a Religious Order
8	Heinrich Schröder, 1883. Martyr of the Mission
9	Ludwig Ihmels, 1933. Theologian, Bishop in Saxony
10	August Hermann Francke, 1727. Father of Pietism
11	Hermann Bezzel, 1917 (from 8th). Bavarian Theologian and Church Leader
12	Friedrich August Tholuck, 1877. Theologian and Father to Students at Halle
13	Barnabas, ca. 70. Disciple of the Apostles
14	Isaak Le Febre, 1702 (from 13th). Confessor in France
15	Anton Court, 1760. A Voice Crying in the Wilderness in France
16	Gottschalk, 1066. Christian Leader, Martyr
17	Georg Israel, 1588. Preacher in the Church of the Brethren in Poland
18	Johannes Tauler, 1361. Mystic
19	Ephraim of Syria, 373. Teacher of the Church, Hymn Writer
20	Albert Knapp, 1864. Hymn Writer
21	August Hermann Werner, 1882. Christian Social Reformer
22	Ludwig Richter, 1884. Master Painter
23	Johann Georg Hamann, 1788 (from 21st). Christian thinker
24	Eve von Teile-Winkler, 1930. Exemplar of Charity
25	Paulinus of Nola, 431. Mon, Bishop, Exemplar of Charity
26	Arguila von Gumbach, 1568. Confessor in Bavaria
27	**John the Baptist**
28	**Augsburg Confession, 1530**
29	Prosper of Aquitaine, ca. 463. Theologian, Student of Augustine
30	Vigilius, 400. Bishop and Martyr in Trent
31	Johann Valentin Andreae, 1564. Church Leader in Württemberg
32	Irenaeus, ca. 202. Teacher of the Church
33	**Peter and Paul, Apostles**
34	Otto of Bamberg, 1139. Bishop, Apostle of Pomerania

JULY

1	Heinrich Voes and Jan van Esch, 1523. Martyrs in the Netherlands
2	**Visitation of Mary**
3	Georg Daniel Teutsch, 1893. Bishop in Siebenbürgen
4	Aonio Paleario, 1570. Martyr in Northern Italy
5	Ulrich of Augsburg, 973. Bishop
6	Johann Andreas Rothe, 1758 (from 6th). Hymn Writer
7	John Hus, 1415. Martyr, Witness to the Gospel
8	Tilman Riemenschneider, 1531. Master Sculptor
9	Kilian, 689. Missionary along the Main, Martyr
10	Georg Neumark, 1681 (from 8th). Hymn Writer
11	William of Orange, 1584. Christian Statesman
12	Renata of Ferrara, 1575 (from 12th). Reform-minded Princess

13	Nathan Söderblom, 1931. Witness to Christian Unity. Swedish Archbishop
14	Henry II, 1024. Emperor, Defender of the Church
15	Karoline Utriainen, 1929
16	John Bonaventure, 1274. Teacher of the Church
17	Anne Askew, 1546. Martyr in England
18	Martyrs of Sicily, 180, in North Africa
19	Paul Schneider, 1939. Martyr in the Church Struggle
20	Johann Marteilhe, *ca.* 1740. Confessor in Galeeren
21	Margaret, *ca.* 507. Martyr in Asia Minor
22	John Eliot, 1690. Missionary to the American Indians
23	Moritz Bräuninger, 1860. Missionary and Martyr in North America
24	Birgitta of Sweden, 1373. Visionary and Preacher of Repentance
25	Thomas a Kempis, 1471 (from 25th). Devotional Writer
26	**James the Elder, Apostle**
27	Johann Heinrich Volkening, 1877. Preacher of Revival
28	Christopher, *ca.* 250. Martyr in Samos
29	Louise Scheppler, 1837 (from 25th). Oberlin's co-worker in Alsace
30	Angelus Merula, 1557 (from 26th). Martyr in the Netherlands
31	Gustav Knak, 1878. Preacher of Revival
32	Johann Sebastian Bach, 1750
33	St. Olaf, 1030. Preparer of the Way for Christianity in Norway
34	William Penn, 1718. Father of the Quakers
35	August Vilmar, 1868. Hessian Theologian
36	Bartolome de Las Casas, 1566. Father of the Indians

AUGUST

1	Gustav Werner, 1887 (from 2nd). Exemplar of Charity in Württemberg
2	Christoph Blumhardt, 1919. Prophetic Witness to Christ
3	Joshua Stegmann, 1632. Hymn Writer
4	Martyrs under Nero, 64
5	Franz Härter, 1874. Father of Deaconesses in Strassburg
6	The Evangelical Saltzburgers (from 5th), 1751
7	Afra, 304. Martyr in Augsburg
8	Jean Valliere, 1523. Martyr in France
9	Adam Reusner, 1575. Hymn Writer
10	Laurence, 258. Martyr in Rome
11	Destruction of Jerusalem, 70
12	Clare of Assisi, 1253. Founder of Religious Order
13	Paul Speratus, 1551. Theologian and Hymn Writer
14	Radegundis, 587. French Princess, Exemplar of Charity
15	Paul Richter, 1942. Martyr in the Church Struggle
16	Georg Balthasar, 1629. Martyr
17	Florence Nightingale, 1910 (from 13th). Exemplar of Charity in England
18	Johann the Steadfast, 1532 (from 16th). Defender of the Reformation
19	Leonhard Kaiser, 1527. Martyr in Passau
20	Johann Gerhard, 1637. Lutheran Theologian
21	Lambert, 705 (from 17th). Bishop, Confessor in Brabant
22	Blaise Pascal, 1662. Christian Thinker
23	Bernard of Clairvaux, 1153. Preacher of the Love of God

24	Geert Groote, 1384 (from 20th). Preacher in the Netherlands
25	Symphorian, 178. Martyr in Burgundy
26	Gaspard de Coligny, 1572 (from 24th). Martyr in France
27	**Bartholomew the Apostle**
28	Gregor of Utrecht, 775. Missionary to Frisia
29	Wulfila, 383. Apostle and Bishop of Goten
30	Werner Sylten, 1942. Martyr in the Church Struggle
31	Caesarius of Arles, 542. Bishop and Exemplar of Charity
32	Augustine, 430. Church Father
33	Martin Boos, 1825. Preacher of Revival in the Rhineland
34	Matthias Gothard Nithart "Grünewald," 1528 (from 31st)
35	John Bunyan, 1688. English Preacher of Revival
36	Ludwig Zimmermann, 1906. Baltic Martyr

SEPTEMBER

1	Sixt Karl Kapff. Prelate and Pastor of Souls in Württemberg
2	Nicolai Frederick S. Grundtvig, 1872. Reformer of the National Church in Denmark
3	Oliver Cromwell, 1658. Christian National Leader
4	Giovanni Mollio, 1553 (from 5th). Martyr in Italy
5	Katharina Zell, 1562. Mother of the Church in Strassburg
6	Matthias Weibel, 1525. Martyr in Swabia
7	Lazarus Spengler, 1534. City Clerk and Defender of the Reformation in Nuremberg
8	Martin Kähler, 1912. Theologian
9	Korbinian, 725. Missionary in Bavaria
10	Luigi Pasquali, 1560. Martyr in Spain
11	Leonhard Lechner, 1606 (from 9th). Church Musician
12	Johannes Brenz, 1570. Reformer in Württemberg
13	Matthäus Ulicky, 1627. Martyr in Bohemia
14	Cyprian, 258 (from 14th). Church Father and Martyr
15	John Chrysostom, 407. Church Father and Preacher
16	Jan van Woerden, 1525. Martyr in the Netherlands
17	Kaspar Tauber, 1524 (from 17th). Martyr in Vienna
18	Hildegard of Bingen, 1179. Princess and Founder of Religious Order
19	Heinrich Bullinger, 1575. Reformer, Theologian in Zurich
20	Gottlieb August Spangenberg, 1792. Moravian Bishop
21	Thomas John Barnado, 1905. Father to Foundlings in London
22	Heinrich Rappard, 1909 (from 21st). Traveling Missionary
23	**Matthew the Apostle and Evangelist**
24	The German New Testament, 1552
25	Mauritius, *ca.* 286. Martyr in Egypt
26	Johann Peter Hebel, 1826. Popular Writer and Prelate in Baden
27	Maria de Bohorques, 1559 (from 24th). Martyr in Spain
28	Hermann the Lame, 1054. Monk and Teacher at St. Gall
29	Paul Rabaut, 1794. Confessor in France
30	Herrezuelo and Leonore de Cisnere, 1559/1568. Martyrs in Spain
31	Vincent de Paul, 1660. Exemplar of Charity in Southern France
32	Lioba, 782. Confessor in the Tauber Valley

33	Adolf Clarenbach, 1529. Martyr in Cologne
34	**Michael the Archangel**
35	Jerome, 420. Church Father

OCTOBER

1	Peter Herbert, 1571. Hymn Writer of the Bohemian Brethren
2	Pietro Carnesecchi, 1567 (from 3rd). Martyr in Italy.
3	Francis of Assisi, 1226. Founder of Religious Order, Witness of the Poverty of Christ
4	Rembrandt, 1669. Master Painter
5	Theodor Fliedner, 1864 (from 4th). Father of Deaconesses in the Rhineland
6	William Tyndale, 1536. Martyr in England
7	Pierre Leclere, 1546. Martyr in France
8	Henry Melchior Muhlenberg, 1787. Father of American Lutheranism
9	Johann Matthesius, 1565. Preacher
10	Justus Jonas, 1555. Luther's Assistant
11	Bruno of Cologne, 965 (from 11th). Bishop
12	Ulrich Zwingli, 1531. Swiss Reformer
13	Elizabeth Fry, 1845 (from 13th). Prison Reformer in England
14	Theodor Beza, 1605. Follower of Calvin
15	James the Notary, *ca.* 430. Martyr in Persia
16	Hedwig of Silesia, 1243. Mother of the Country
17	Gallius, 645. Missionary in Bodensee
18	Lukas Cranach, 1553. Evangelical Painter
19	Nicholas Ridley, 1555 (from 16th). Martyr in England
20	**Luke the Evangelist**
21	Ludwig Schneller, 1896. Father to Orphans in Palestine
22	Monica, 387 (day unknown). Mother of Augustine
23	Karl Sagebrock and Ewald Ovir, 1896. Missionaries and Martyrs
24	Elias Schrenk, 1913. Preacher of Revival
25	Jeremias Gotthilf, 1854 (from 21st). Pastor and Poet
26	Johannes Zwick, 1542. Hymn Writer
27	Starez Leonid, 1841. Russian Monk and Pastor of Souls
28	Philipp Nicolai, 1608 (from 26th). Hymn Writer
29	Frumentius, *ca.* 380. Missionary and Apostle to Ethiopia
30	Olavus and Laurentius Petri, 1552/1574. Swedish Reformers
31	**Simon and Jude, Apostles**
32	Marcellus and Cassius, 298. Martyrs in North Africa
33	Henri Dunant, 1910 (from 30th). Founder of the Red Cross
34	Gottschalk, 868. Monk and Theologian
35	Jakob Sturm, 1553. Mayor of Strassburg
36	31 **Commemoration of the Reformation**, 1517

NOVEMBER

1	**Commemoration of the Saints**
2	Erhard Schnepf, 1558. Reformer in Württemberg
3	Johann Albrecht Bengel, 1752. Swabish Theologian
4	Priman, 753. Missionary in Southwest Germany

5	Claude Brousson, 1698. Martyr in France
6	Hans Egede, 1758. Missionary to Greenland
7	Gustavus Adolphus, 1632. Christian Ruler
8	Heinrich Schütz, 1672. Church Musician
9	Willibrord, 739. Missionary to Frisia
10	Willehad, 789. Bishop of Bremen
11	Emil Frommel, 1896. Preacher
12	Leo the Great, 461. Bishop of Rome
13	Karl Friedrich Stellbrink, 1943. Martyr
14	Martin, 397. Bishop of Tours
15	Christian Gottlieb Barth, 1862. Mission-Preacher
16	Ludwig Harms, 1865 (from 14th). Founder of Hermannsburg Mission
17	Gottfried Wilhelm Leibnitz, 1716. Christian Thinker
18	Albertus Magnus, 1280. Teacher of the Church
19	Johannes Kepler, 1630. Natural Scientist
20	Amos Comenius, 1670 (from 15th). Bishop of the Bohemian Brethren, Educator
21	Jacob Böhme, 1624. Christian Thinker
22	David Zeisberger, 1808. Missionary to India
23	Ludwig Hofacker, 1828. Preacher of Revival
24	Elizabeth of Thuringia, 1251. Christian Princess, Exemplar of Charity
25	Berward of Hildesheim, 1022. Bishop
26	Cecelia, *ca.* 230. Martyr in Rome
27	Columban, 615 (from 23rd). Irish Missionary
28	Clement of Rome, *ca.* 100. Bishop
29	Johannes Okolampad, 1531. Reformer in Basel
30	John Knox, 1572. Scottish Reformer
31	Catherine, *ca.* 307. Martyr in Egypt
32	Conrad, 971. Bishop of Constance
33	Vigilious of Salzburg, 784. Bishop
34	Margaretha Blarer, 1541 (from 27th). Mother of the Church in Constance
35	Saturnius, after 250. Martyr in Rome
36	**Andrew the Apostle**
37	Alexander Roussel, 1728. Martyr in France

DECEMBER

1	Eligius, 660. Bishop of the Franks, Exemplar of Charity
2	Jan van Ruysbroek, 1381. Pastor of Souls in the Netherlands
3	Ämilie Juliane of Schwarzburg-Rudolstandt, 1706. Hymn Writer
4	Barbara, 306. Martyr in Asia Minor
5	Aloys Henhöfer, 1862. Preacher of Revival in Baden
6	Nicholas, *ca.* 350. Bishop in Asia Minor, Exemplar of Charity
7	Ambrose Blarer, 1564. Reformer in Constance
8	Martyrs of the Gates of the Criminal Court, 1724
9	Martin Rinckart, 1649. Hymn Writer
10	Richard Baxter, 1691 (from 8th). Confessor in England
11	Heinrich Zütphen, 1524. Martyr in Ditmarschen
12	Lars Olsen Skrefsrud, 1910. Missionary in India
13	Vicelin, 1154. Missionary, Apostle of Holstein

14	Odelia, *ca.* 720. Abbess in Alsace
15	Christian Fürchtegott Gellert, 1769. Hymn Writer
16	Berthold of Regensburg, 1272. Preacher
17	John Oldcastle, 1417. Martyr in England
18	Gerhard Uhlhorn, 1901. Theologian, Abbot of Loccum
19	Adelheid, 999. Queen of Otto I
20	Abbot Sturm of Fulda, 779. Helper of Boniface
21	Wunibald and Willibald, 761/787. Missionaries to the Franks
22	Paul Blau, 1944. Leader of the Evangelical Church in Poland
23	Katherine von Bora, 1552. Luther's Wife
24	**Thomas the Apostle**
25	Dwight Lyman Moody, 1899. American Preacher of Revival
26	Anne Dubourg, 1559. Martyr in France
27	Mathilde Wrede, 1928. Prison Reformer in Sweden
28	**Nativity of the Lord**
29	**Stephen, First Martyr**
30	**John the Apostle and Evangelist**
31	**The Holy Innocents**
32	Reinhard Hedinger, 1704. Württemberg Preacher
33	Martin Schalling, 1608. Hymn Writer
34	Thomas Becket, 1170 (from 29th). Martyr in England
35	John Wyclif, 1384. Herald of the Gospel

Appendix 5

The Christian Year (1997) of the Church of England

JANUARY

1	THE NAMING AND CIRCUMCISION OF JESUS
2	Basil the Great and Gregory of Nazianzus, Bishops, Teachers of the Faith, 379 and 389
2	*Seraphim, Monk of Sarov, Spiritual Guide, 1833*
2	*Vedanayagam Samuel Azariah, Bishop in South India, Evangelist, 1945*
6	**The Epiphany**
10	*William Laud, Archbishop of Canterbury, 1645*
11	*Mary Slessor, Missionary in West Africa, 1915*
12	Aelred of Hexham, Abbot of Rievaulx, 1167
12	*Benedict Biscop, Abbot of Wearmouth, Scholar, 689*
13	Hilary, Bishop of Poitiers, Teacher of the Faith, 367
13	*Kentigern (Mungo), Missionary Bishop in Strathclyde and Cumbria, 603*
13	*George Fox, Founder of the Society of Friends (the Quakers), 1691*
17	Antony of Egypt, Hermit, Abbot, 356
17	*Charles Gore, Bishop, Founder of the Community of the Resurrection, 1932*
18–25	Week of Prayer for Christian Unity
19	Wulfstan, Bishop of Worcester, 1095
20	*Richard Rolle of Hampole, Spiritual Writer, 1349*
21	Agnes, Child Martyr at Rome, 304
22	*Vincent of Saragossa, Deacon, first Martyr of Spain, 304*
24	Francis de Sales, Bishop of Geneva, Teacher of the Faith, 1622
25	THE CONVERSION OF PAUL
26	Timothy and Titus, Companions of Paul
28	Thomas Aquinas, Priest, Philosopher, Teacher of the Faith, 1274
30	Charles, King and Martyr, 1649
31	*John Bosco, Founder of the Salesian Teaching Order, 1888*

FEBRUARY

1	*Brigid, Abbess of Kildare, c. 525*
2	THE PRESENTATION OF CHRIST IN THE TEMPLE (CANDLEMAS)
3	Anskar, Archbishop of Hamburg, Missionary in Denmark and Sweden, 865
4	Gilbert of Sempringham, Founder of the Gilbertine Order, 1189
6	*The Martyrs of Japan, 1597*
10	*Scholastica, sister of Benedict, Abbess of Plombariola, c. 543*
14	Cyril and Methodius, Missionaries to the Slavs, 869 and 885
14	*Valentine, Martyr at Rome, c. 269*
15	*Sigfrid, Bishop, Apostle of Sweden, 1045*
15	*Thomas Bray, Priest, Founder of the SPCK and the SPG, 1730*
17	Janani Luwum, Archbishop of Uganda, Martyr, 1977
23	Polycarp, Bishop of Smyrna, Martyr, c. 155
27	George Herbert, Priest, Poet, 1633

MARCH

1	David, Bishop of Menevia, Patron of Wales, c. 601
2	Chad, Bishop of Lichfield, Missionary, 672 [or with Cedd on 26 October]
7	Perpetua, Felicity, and their Companions, Martyrs at Carthage, 203
8	Edward King, Bishop of Lincoln, 1910
8	*Felix, Bishop, Apostle to the East Angles, 647*
8	*Geoffrey Studdert Kennedy, Priest, Poet, 1929*
17	Patrick, Bishop, Missionary, Patron of Ireland, c. 460
18	*Cyril, Bishop of Jerusalem, Teacher of the Faith, 386*
19	JOSEPH OF NAZARETH
20	Cuthbert, Bishop of Lindisfarne, Missionary, 687 [or 4 September]
21	Thomas Cranmer, Archbishop of Canterbury, Reformation Martyr, 1556
24	*Walter Hilton of Thurgarton, Augustinian Canon, Mystic, 1396*
24	*Oscar Romero, Archbishop of San Salvador, Martyr, 1980*
25	THE ANNUNCIATION OF OUR LORD TO THE BLESSED VIRGIN MARY
26	*Harriet Monsell, Founder of the Community of St. John the Baptist, 1883*
31	*John Donne, Priest, Poet, 1631*

APRIL

1	*Frederick Denison Maurice, Priest, Teacher of the Faith, 1872*
9	*Dietrich Bonhoeffer, Lutheran Pastor, Martyr, 1945*
10	William Law, Priest, Spiritual Writer, 1761
10	*William of Ockham, Friar, Philosopher, Teacher of the Faith, 1347*
11	*George Augustus Selwyn, first Bishop of New Zealand, 1878*
16	*Isabella Gilmore, Deaconess, 1923*
19	Alphege, Archbishop of Canterbury, Martyr, 1012
21	Anselm, Abbot of Le Bec, Archbishop of Canterbury, Teacher of the Faith, 1109
23	GEORGE, MARTYR, PATRON OF ENGLAND, c. 304
24	*Mellitus, Bishop of London, first Bishop at St. Paul's, 624*
25	MARK THE EVANGELIST
27	*Christina Rossetti, Poet, 1894*
28	*Peter Chanel, Missionary in the South Pacific, Martyr, 1841*
29	Catherine of Siena, Teacher of the Faith, 1380
30	*Pandita Mary Ramabai, Translator of the Scriptures, 1922*

MAY

1	PHILIP AND JAMES, APOSTLES
2	Athanasius, Bishop of Alexandria, Teacher of the Faith, 373
4	English Saints and Martyrs of the Reformation Era
8	Julian of Norwich, Spiritual Writer, c. 1417
14	MATTHIAS THE APOSTLE [may be celebrated instead on 24 February]
16	*Catherine Chisholm, Social Reformer, 1877*
19	Dunstan, Archbishop of Canterbury, Restorer of Monastic Life, 988
20	Alcuin of York, Deacon, Abbot of Tours, 804
21	*Helena, Protector of the Holy Places, 330*
24	John and Charles Wesley, Evangelists, Hymn Writers, 1791 and 1788
25	The Venerable Bede, Monk at Jarrow, Scholar, Historian, 735
25	*Aldhelm, Bishop of Sherborne, 709*

26	Augustine, first Archbishop of Canterbury, 605
26	*John Calvin, Reformer, 1564*
26	*Philip Neri, Founder of the Oratorians, Spiritual Guide, 1595*
28	*Lanfranc, Prior of Le Bec, Archbishop of Canterbury, Scholar, 1089*
30	Josephine Butler, Social Reformer, 1906
30	*Joan of Arc, Visionary, 1431*
30	*Apolo Kivebulaya, Priest, Evangelist in Central Africa, 1933*
31	THE VISIT OF THE BLESSED VIRGIN MARY TO ELIZABETH [or 2 July]

JUNE

1	Justin, Martyr at Rome, c. 165
3	*The Martyrs of Uganda, 1885–7 and 1977*
4	*Petroc, Abbot of Padstow, 6th century*
5	Boniface (Wynfrith) of Crediton, Bishop, Apostle of Germany, Martyr, 754
6	*Ini Kopuria, Founder of the Melanesian Brotherhood, 1945*
8	Thomas Ken, Bishop of Bath and Wells, Nonjuror, Hymn Writer, 1711
9	Columba, Abbot of Iona, Missionary, 597
9	*Ephrem of Syria, Deacon, Hymn Writer, Teacher of the Faith, 373*
11	BARNABAS THE APOSTLE
14	*Richard Baxter, Puritan Divine, 1691*
15	*Evelyn Underhill, Spiritual Writer, 1941*
16	Richard, Bishop of Chichester, 1253
16	*Joseph Butler, Bishop of Durham, Philosopher, 1752*
17	*Samuel and Henrietta Barnett, Social Reformers, 1913 and 1936*
18	*Bernard Mizeki, Apostle of the MaShona, Martyr, 1896*
19	*Sundar Singh of India, Sadhu (holy man), Evangelist, Teacher of the Faith, 1929*
22	Alban, first Martyr of Britain, c. 250
23	Ethelreda, Abbess of Ely, c. 678
24	THE BIRTH OF JOHN THE BAPTIST
27	*Cyril, Bishop of Alexandria, Teacher of the Faith, 444*
28	Irenaeus, Bishop of Lyons, Teacher of the Faith, c. 200
29	PETER AND PAUL, APOSTLES [Peter the Apostle may be celebrated alone, without Paul]

JULY

1	*Henry, John, and Henry Venn the younger, Priests, Evangelical Divines, 1797, 1813, and 1873*
3	THOMAS THE APOSTLE [or 21 December]
6	*Thomas More, Scholar, and John Fisher, Bishop of Rochester, Reformation Martyrs, 1535*
11	Benedict of Nursia, Abbot of Monte Cassino, Father of Western Monasticism, c. 550
14	John Keble, Priest, Tractarian, Poet, 1866
15	Swithun, Bishop of Winchester, c. 862
15	*Bonaventure, Friar, Bishop, Teacher of the Faith, 1274*
16	*Osmund, Bishop of Salisbury, 1099*
18	*Elizabeth Ferard, first Deaconess of he Church of England, Founder of the Community of St. Andrew, 1883*

19	Gregory, Bishop of Nyssa, and his sister, Macrina, Deaconess, Teachers of the Faith, c. 394 and c. 379
20	*Margaret of Antioch, Martyr, 4th century*
20	*Bartolomé de Las Casas, Apostle to the Indies, 1566*
22	MARY MAGDALENE
23	*Bridget of Sweden, Abbess of Vadstena, 1373*
25	JAMES THE APOSTLE
26	Anne and Joachim, Parents of the Blessed Virgin Mary
27	*Brooke Foss Wescott, Bishop of Durham, Teacher of the Faith, 1901*
29	Mary, Martha, and Lazarus, Companions of our Lord
30	William Wilberforce, Social Reformer, 1833
31	*Ignatius Loyola, Founder of the Society of Jesus, 1556*

AUGUST

4	*Jean-Baptiste Vianney, Cure d'Ars, Spiritual Guide, 1859*
5	Oswald, King of Northumbria, Martyr, 642
6	THE TRANSFIGURATION OF OUR LORD
7	*John Mason Neale, Priest, Hymn Writer, 1866*
8	Dominic, Priest, Founder of the Order of Preachers, 1221
9	Mary Sumner, Founder of the Mothers' Union, 1921
10	Laurence, Deacon at Rome, Martyr, 258
11	Clare of Assisi, Founder of the Minoresses (Poor Clares), 1253
11	*John Henry Newman, Priest, Tractarian, 1890*
13	Jeremy Taylor, Bishop of Down and Connor, Teacher of the Faith, 1667
13	*Florence Nightingale, Nurse, Social Reformer, 1910*
13	*Octavia Hill, Social Reformer, 1912*
14	*Maximilian Kolbe, Friar, Martyr, 1941*
15	THE BLESSED VIRGIN MARY [or 8 September]
20	Bernard, Abbot of Clairvaux, Teacher of the Faith, 1153
20	*William and Catherine Booth, Founders of the Salvation Army, 1912 and 1890*
24	BARTHOLOMEW THE APOSTLE
27	Monica, Mother of Augustine of Hippo, 387
28	Augustine, Bishop of Hippo, Teacher of the Faith, 430
29	The Beheading of John the Baptist
30	John Bunyan, Spiritual Writer, 1688
31	Aidan, Bishop of Lindisfarne, Missionary, 651

SEPTEMBER

1	*Giles of Provence, Hermit, c. 710*
2	*The Martyrs of Papua New Guinea, 1901 and 1942*
3	Gregory the Great, Bishop of Rome, Teacher of the Faith, 604
4	*Birinus, Bishop of Dorchester (Oxon), Apostle of Wessex, 650*
6	*Allen Gardiner, Missionary, Founder of the South American Mission Society, 1851*
8	The Birth of the Blessed Virgin Mary
9	*Charles Fuge Lowder, Priest, 1880*
13	John Chrysostom, Bishop of Constantinople, Teacher of the Faith, 407
14	HOLY CROSS DAY
15	Cyprian, Bishop of Carthage, Martyr, 258

16	Ninian, Bishop of Galloway, Apostle to the Picts, c. 432
16	*Edward Bouverie Pusey, Priest, Tractarian, 1882*
17	Hildegard, Abbess of Bingen, Visionary, 1179
19	*Theodore of Tarsus, Archbishop of Canterbury, 690*
20	John Coleridge Patteson, First Bishop of Melanesia, and his Companions, Martyrs, 1871
21	MATTHEW, APOSTLE AND EVANGELIST
25	Lancelot Andrewes, Bishop of Winchester, Spiritual Writer, 1626
25	*Sergei of Radonezh, Russian Monastic Reformer, Teacher of the Faith, 1392*
26	*Wilson Carlile, Founder of the Church Army, 1942*
27	Vincent de Paul, Founder of the Congregation of the Mission (Lazarists), 1660
29	MICHAEL AND ALL ANGELS
30	*Jerome, Translator of the Scriptures, Teacher of the Faith, 420*

OCTOBER

1	*Remigius, Bishop of Rheims, Apostle to the Franks, 533*
1	*Anthony Ashley Cooper, Earl of Shaftsbury, Social Reformer, 1885*
4	Francis of Assisi, Friar, Deacon, Founder of the Friars Minor, 1226
6	William Tyndale, Translator of the Scriptures, Reformation Martyr, 1536
9	*Denys, Bishop of Paris, and his Companions, Martyrs, c. 250*
9	*Robert Grosseteste, Bishop of Lincoln, Philosopher, Scientist, 1253*
10	Paulinus, Bishop of York, Missionary, 644
10	*Thomas Traherne, Poet, Spiritual Writer, 1674*
11	*Ethelburga, Abbess of Barking, 675*
11	*James the Deacon, companion of Paulinus, 7th century*
12	Wilfrid of Ripon, Bishop, Missionary, 709
12	Elizabeth Fry, Prison Reformer, 1845
12	*Edith Cavell, Nurse, 1915*
13	Edward the Confessor, King of England, 1066
15	Teresa of Avila, Teacher of the Faith, 1582
16	*Nicholas Ridley, Bishop of London, and Hugh Latimer, Bishop of Worcester, Reformation Martyrs, 1555*
17	Ignatius, Bishop of Antioch, Martyr, c. 107
18	LUKE THE EVANGELIST
19	Henry Martyn, Translator of the Scriptures, Missionary in India and Persia, 1812
25	*Crispin and Crispinian, Martyrs at Rome, c. 287*
26	Alfred the Great, King of the West Saxons, Scholar, 899
26	*Cedd, Abbot of Lastingham, Bishop of the East Saxons, 664*
28	SIMON AND JUDE, APOSTLES
29	James Hannington, Bishop of Eastern Equatorial Africa, Martyr in Uganda, 1885
31	*Martin Luther, Reformer, 1546*

NOVEMBER

1	ALL SAINTS' DAY
2	Commemoration of the Faithful Departed (All Souls' Day)
3	Richard Hooker, Priest, Anglican Apologist, Teacher of the Faith, 1600

3	*Martin of Porres, Friar, 1639*
6	*Leonard, Hermit, 6th century*
6	*William Temple, Archbishop of Canterbury, Teacher of the Faith, 1944*
7	Willibrord of York, Bishop, Apostle of Frisia, 739
8	The Saints and Martyrs of England
9	*Margery Kempe, Mystic, c. 1440*
10	Leo the Great, Bishop of Rome, Teacher of the Faith, 461
11	Martin, Bishop of Tours, c. 397
13	Charles Simeon, Priest, Evangelical Divine, 1836
14	*Samuel Seabury, first Anglican Bishop in North America, 1796*
16	Margaret, Queen of Scotland, Philanthropist, Reformer of the Church, 1093
16	*Edmund Rich of Abingdon, Archbishop of Canterbury, 1240*
17	Hugh, Bishop of Lincoln, 1200
18	Elizabeth of Hungary, Princess of Thuringia, Philanthropist, 1231
19	Hilda, Abbess of Whitby, 680
19	*Mechtild, Béguine of Magdeburg, Mystic, 1280*
20	Edmund, King of the East Angles, Martyr, 870
20	*Priscilla Lydia Sellon, a Restorer of the Religious Life in the Church of England, 1876*
22	*Cecilia, Martyr at Rome, c. 230*
23	Clement, Bishop of Rome, Martyr, c. 100
25	*Catherine of Alexandria, Martyr, 4th century*
25	*Isaac Watts, Hymn Writer, 1748*
29	Day of Intercession and Thanksgiving for the Missionary Work of the Church
30	ANDREW THE APOSTLE

DECEMBER

1	*Charles de Foucauld, Hermit in the Sahara, 1916*
3	*Francis Xavier, Missionary, Apostle to the Indies, 1552*
4	*John of Damascus, Monk, Teacher of the Faith, c. 749*
4	*Nicholas Ferrar, Deacon, Founder of the Little Gidding Community, 1637*
6	Nicholas, Bishop of Myra, c. 326
7	Ambrose, Bishop of Milan, Teacher of the Faith, 397
8	The Conception of the Blessed Virgin Mary
13	Lucy, Martyr at Syracuse, 304
13	*Samuel Johnson, Moralist, 1784*
14	John of the Cross, Poet, Teacher of the Faith, 1591
17	O Sapientia
17	*Eglantyne Jebb, Social Reformer, Founder of "Save the Children," 1928*
24	Christmas Eve
25	**Christmas Day**
26	STEPHEN, DEACON, FIRST MARTYR
27	JOHN, APOSTLE AND EVANGELIST
28	THE HOLY INNOCENTS
29	Thomas Becket, Archbishop of Canterbury, Martyr, 1170 [or 7 July]
31	John Wycliffe, Reformer, 1384

Bibliography

* indicates major resources

Adels, Jill Haak. *The Wisdom of the Saints: An Anthology.* New York: Oxford University Press, 1987.

Anderson, Gerald, ed. *Biographical Dictionary of Christian Missions.* Grand Rapids: Eerdmans, 1998.

*Attwater, Donald. *Penguin Dictionary of Saints.* Baltimore: Penguin, 1965. *Comprehensive, but dated since it was published before the adoption of the present Roman Calendar.*

Bainton, Roland H. *Women of the Reformation in Germany and Italy.* Minneapolis: Augsburg, 1971.

* Blackburn, Bonnie, and Leofranc Holford-Strevens, eds. *The Oxford Companion to the Year.* Oxford: Clarendon Press, 2000.

Bodensiek, Julius, ed. *Encyclopedia of the Lutheran Church.* 3 vols. Philadelphia: Fortress Press, 1965.

The Book of Saints: A Dictionary of Servants of God Canonised by the Catholic Church compiled by the monks of St. Augustine's Abbey, Ramsgate, England. New York: Macmillan, 1947; Harrisburg, Pa.: Morehouse, 1998.

Brown, Peter. *The Cult of the Saints: Its Rise and Function in Latin Christianity.* Chicago: University of Chicago Press, 1981.

Burghardt, Walter J. *Saints and Sanctity.* New York: Prentice-Hall, 1965.

* Burn, Paul, ed. *Butler's Lives of the Saints.* New Full Edition. 12 vols. Collegeville, Minn.: Liturgical, 1995–.

Chavchavadze, Marina, ed. *Man's Concern with Holiness.* London: Hodder and Stoughton, 1970.

Cohen, Hennig, and Tristram Coffin. *The Folklore of American Holidays.* Detroit: Gale, 1986.

Cox, Patricia. *Biography in Late Antiquity: A Quest for the Holy Man.* Berkeley: University of California Press, 1983.

Cressy, David. *Bonfires and Bells: National Memory and the Protestant Calendar in Elizabethan and Stuart England.* London: Weidenfeld and Nicolson, 1990.

Crook, John. *The Architectural Setting of the Cult of the Saints in the Early Christian West.* Oxford: Clarendon, 2000.

*Cross, F. L., and E. A. Livingstone, eds. *The Oxford Dictionary of the Christian Church.* 3d ed. New York: Oxford University Press, 1997.

Cunningham, Lawrence S. *The Catholic Heritage.* New York: Crossroad, 1983.

Deen, Edith. *Great Women of the Christian Faith.* New York: Harper & Row, 1959.

Delaney, John J. *Dictionary of Saints.* New York: Doubleday, 1980.

———. *Saints For All Seasons.* Garden City, N.Y.: Doubleday, 1978.

Deschusses, J., ed. *Le Sacramentaire Gregorien.* Fribourg, 1971. Gregorian sacramentary; late eighth-century manuscript.

*Farmer, D. H., ed. *The Oxford Dictionary of Saints.* London: Oxford University Press, 1978.

Flannery, Austin et. al. *The Saints in Season. A Companion to the Lectionary.* Collegeville, Minn.: Liturgical, 1977.

Foley, Leonard, ed. *Saint of the Day. A Life and Lesson for Each of the 173 Saints of the New Missal.* 2 vols. Cincinnati: St. Anthony Messenger Press, 1974.

Fox, Adam, and Gareth and Georgina Keene, eds. *Sacred and Secular.* Grand Rapids: Eerdmans, 1976.

Freemantle, Anne. *Saints Alive!* Garden City, NY: Doubleday, 1978.

*Guthrie, Clifton F., ed. *For All the Saints. A Calendar of Commemorations for United Methodists.* Akron: Order of St. Luke, 1995.

Hackel, Serge, ed. *The Byzantine Saint.* London: The Fellowship of St. Alban and St. Sergius, 1982.

Hawley, John Stratton. *Saints and Virtues.* Berkeley: University of California Press, 1987.

Ivanov, Sergey A. *Holy Fools in Byzantium and Beyond.* Trans. Simon Franklin. New York: Oxford University Press, 2007.

Kalberer, Augustine. *Lives of Saints.* Chicago: Franciscan Herald Press, 1976.

Kiekheffer, Richard. *Unquiet Souls: 14th Century Saints and Their Religious Milieu.* Chicago: University of Chicago Press, 1984.

Kiekheffer, Richard, and George Bond, eds. *Sainthood: Its Manifestation in World Religions.* Berkeley: University of California Press, 1988.

Kolb, Robert. *For All the Saints: Changing Perceptions of Martyrdom and Sainthood in the Lutheran Reformation.* St. Louis: Concordia, 1987.

McClendon, James William, Jr. *Biography as Theology: How Life Stories Can Remake Today's Theology.* Nashville: Abingdon, 1975.

McGinley, Phyllis. *Saint-Watching.* New York: Viking, 1969.

McGrath, Michael O'Neill. *Patrons and Protectors: Occupations.* Chicago: Liturgy Training Publications, 2001. *Delightful illustrations and essays.*

Martindale, Cyril Charles. *What Are Saints? Fifteen Chapters in Sanctity.* London: Sheed and Ward, 1932.

Meehan, Brenda. *Holy Women of Russia: The Lives of Five Orthodox Women Offer Spiritual Guidance for Today.* New York: HarperCollins, 1993; Crestwood, N.Y.: St. Vladimir's Press, 1997.

Mohlberg, L. C., ed. *Liber sacramentorum Romanae Aeclesiae Ordinis Anni Circuli.* Rome: Herder, 1968. Gelasian sacramentary, eighth-century manuscript.

———, ed. *Sacramentum Veronese.* Rome: Herder, 1956. Leonine or Verona sacramentary; manuscript *ca.* 600, fifth- and sixth-century material.

The New Catholic Encyclopedia. 15 vols. New York: McGraw-Hill, 1967.

Payne, Robert. *Fathers of the Western Church.* New York: Viking, 1951.

———. *The Holy Fire: Fathers of the Eastern Church.* New York: Harper, 1957.

Perham, Michael. *The Communion of Saints.* London: SPCK, 1982.

Pryce, Mark. *Literary Companion to the Festivals.* Minneapolis: Fortress Press, 2003.

Rollason, David. *Saints and Relics in Anglo-Saxon England.* Oxford: Blackwell, 1990.

Schulz, Frieder, *et al.*, eds. *Evangelical Calendar of Names [Evangelischer Namen Kalender].* Approved by the German Lutheran Liturgical Conference 1962. Given in *Allgemeines Evangelisches Gebetbuch* (Hamburg: Furche-Verlag, 1965), 493–505.

Vauchez, Andre. *Sainthood in the Later Middle Ages.* Trans. Jean Birrell. Cambridge: Cambridge University Press, 1998.

*de Voragine, Jacobus. *The Golden Legend: Readings on the Saints.* Trans. William Granger Ryan. 2 vols. Princeton: Princeton University Press, 1994.

*Walsh, Michael. *A New Dictionary of Saints East and West.* Collegeville: Liturgical, 2007.

Ward, Benedicta. *Harlots of the Desert: A Study of Repentance in Early Monastic Sources.* Kalamazoo: Cistercian, 1987.

———. *Miracles and the Medieval Mind: Theory, Record, and Event 100–1215.* Philadelphia: University of Pennsylvania Press, 1982.

Wescott, Glenway. *A Calender of Saints for Unbelievers.* Hauppage, N.Y.: Leete's Island Books, 1976.

Wilson, Stephen, ed. *Saints and Their Cults: Studies in Religious Sociology, Folklore, and History.* Cambridge: Cambridge University Press, 1984.

Woodward, Kenneth L. *Making Saints: Inside the Vatican: Who Become Saints, Who Do Not, and Why.* New York: Simon & Schuster, 1991.

Wright, Elliott. *Holy Company: Christian Heroes and Heroines.* New York: Macmillan, 1981.

Wyschogrod, Edith. *Saints and Postmodernism: Revisioning Moral Philosophy.* Chicago: Chicago University Press, 1990.

672

Index of Readings

Clare of Assisi. Letter to Agnes of Prague. August 11
Claver, Peter. Letter. September 9
Clement. First Letter of Clement. November 23
Clement of Alexandria. *Exhortation.* December 5
Cranmer, Thomas. Preface to the Book of Common Prayer (1549). October 16
Cullmann, Oscar. *Peter: Disciple, Apostle, Martyr.* January 18
Cuthbert. Letter on the Death of the Venerable Bede. May 25
Cuyler, Theodore L. *Recollections of a Long Life.* April 8
Cyprian of Carthage. Letter about the Death of Fabian. January 20
———. *On the Unity of the Catholic Church.* September 16
Cyril of Alexandria. Letter. June 27
Cyril of Jerusalem. *Catechetical Lectures.* March 18

Davies, J. Gordon. *Holy Week: A Short History.* May 22
De Paul, Vincent. Letter. September 27
Deinzer, J. *W. Löhe's Leben.* January 2
Dix, Gregory. *The Shape of the Liturgy.* November 2
Donne, John. *Devotions Upon Emergent Occasions.* March 31
———. Sermon (1627). September 29
Dowson, Ernest. "Carthusians." November 17
Dunne, John S. *A Search for God in Time and Memory.* June 24

Edwards, Jonathan. *Personal Narrative.* March 22
Ephrem of Edessa. Sermon. June 10

Faithful Unto Death: The Story of the New Guinea Martyrs. September 2
Falckner, Justus. Letter to the Superintendent of Schleswig. September 22
Ferris, Theodore P. Sermon. February 4
Fox, George. *Journal.* January 16
Foxe, John. *Booke of Martyrs.* October 6
Francis of Assisi. A Letter Written to All the Faithful. October 4
Francis de Sales. *Introduction to the Devout Life.* January 24
Francis Xavier. Letter to Ignatius Loyola. December 3

Gallican Churches. Letter. June 2
Gelineau, Joseph. *Voices and Instruments in Christian Worship.* November 25
Gonzalez, Luis. The Life of St. Ignatius. July 31
Gregory the Great. Letter to Augustine of Canterbury. May 26
———. A Sermon on Ezekiel. March 12
———. A Sermon on the Gospels. July 22
Gregory of Nazianzus. *Theological Orations.* June 14
Gregory of Nyssa. *An Address on Religious Instruction.* June 14
———. *Life of Macrina.* June 14
Gregory of Tours. *The History of the Franks.* October 1
Grim, Edward. *Account of the Martyrdom of Thomas Becket.* December 29
Grundtvig, N. F. S. Sermon. September 2
Guardini, Romano. *The Saints in Daily Christian Life.* May 1

Hallgrimur Petursson. "Death's Uncertain Hour." December 23
Hammarskjöld, Dag. *Markings.* September 18

Index of Hymns

Index of Names and Days

Wallin, Johan Olof   June 30
Walter [Walther], Johann   April 24
Walther, Carl Ferdinand Wilhelm   May 7
Watts, Isaac   November 25
Week of Prayer for Christian Unity
    January 18–25
Wesley, Charles   March 2
Wesley, John   March 2
White, William   July 17
Wilberforce, William   July 30
Williams, Channing Moore   December 2
Willibrord   November 7
Winkworth, Catherine   July 1
Woolman, John   January 16

Wulfstan   January 19
Wyclif (Wycliffe), John   July 6
Wyneken, Friedrich Conrad Dietrich
    May 4

Xavier, Francis   December 3

Yom Hashoah   April/May

Zechariah (Zacharias)   November 5
Ziegenbalg, Bartholomäus   February 26
Zinzendorf, Nicolaus Ludwig,
    Count   May 9